THE ECONOMICS OF
NATURAL RESOURCE USE

THE ECONOMICS OF NATURAL RESOURCE USE

John M. Hartwick
Queen's University

Nancy D. Olewiler
Queen's University

HARPER & ROW, PUBLISHERS, New York
Cambridge, Philadelphia, San Francisco,
London, Mexico City, São Paulo, Sydney

1817

Nature's resources are not so much an inheritance from our parents, as a loan from our children.

We dedicate this book to our parents and children.

Sponsoring Editor: John Greenman
Project Editor: Mary G. Ward
Cover Design: John Hite
Text Art: Artset Ltd.
Production: Debra Forrest
Compositor: Progressive Typographers
Printer and Binder: R. R. Donnelley & Sons Company

THE ECONOMICS OF NATURAL RESOURCE USE

Library of Congress Cataloging in Publication Data

Hartwick, John M.
    The economics of natural resource use.

    Includes bibliographies.
    1. Natural resources.   2. Environmental policy.
I. Olewiler, Nancy D.   II. Title.
HC59.H3558 1986   333.7'13   85-14076
ISBN 0-06-042695-0

85 86 87 88 9 8 7 6 5 4 3 2 1

CONTENTS

7   Issues in the Economics of Energy   **183**

8   The Economics of the Fishery: An Introduction   **243**

9   Regulation of the Fishery   **292**

PREFACE

This is a textbook on the economics of using natural resources, a subject that has been intensively refined and developed since the 1960s. The 1960s brought, among other things, the "greening" of industrial countries, particularly the United States. Great concern was focused on pollution, environmental degradation generally, and urban growth. Recycling of paper, bottles, and cans became popular causes, and natural resource scarcity received great attention. Many academic economists immersed themselves in the analysis of environmental problems, urban growth and sprawl, and the use of nonrenewable resources such as oil and iron ore and renewable resources such as forests and fish. This text is a distillation of the work done in these areas by economists in the 1970s and early 1980s.

Since much of this material evolved recently, there were often no established lines of exposition or explanatory diagrams to draw upon, so we have had to innovate. The content of this book has been used in two quite different one-semester courses at Queen's University and has been extensively commented on by independent reviewers. Students who have been exposed to intermediate microeconomics will be well prepared to learn easily from our book. Knowledge of finding maximums and minimums with elementary calculus is the only mathematics relevant to our central analytical sections; complex derivations and more advanced mathematics are in optional appendixes related to particular chapters. Descriptive and institutional material is often highlighted in boxes.

Course Uses of This Book

This book can be used in a variety of courses. Chapters 1–4 and 8–13 formed our one-semester course in the economics of natural resource use at Queen's. For courses in energy economics, Chapters 1, 3–7, and 12–14 would be central. For courses in environmental economics, Chapters 1, 2, 8–9, and 11–13 would be central. If the book were being used as part of the material for a course focusing on policy development and institutional background, then Chapters 1–3, 7–9, and 11–14 would furnish the basics of analysis and issues. The questions at the end of each chapter include issues of policy development.

Acknowledgements

John Hartwick's Ph.D. thesis from Johns Hopkins dealt with regional economics, and his research in the economics of resource use got started during a year (1974–75) of postdoctoral work at MIT in which instruction from and contact with Robert M. Solow proved invaluable. Nancy Olewiler's Ph.D. thesis from the University of British Columbia dealt with externalities, including matters of the environment. We are constantly reminded of our debts to our teachers and our thanks go out to them. Many friends responded quickly to our queries, particularly for specialized bits of information and sometimes for opinion on our material. We thank them. We appreciate the many useful comments provided by the following reviewers of various drafts of the manuscript:

Lee G. Anderson, University of Delaware
Scott Atkinson, University of Wyoming
Peter Berck, University of California, Berkeley
Maureen L. Cropper, University of Maryland
John H. Cumberland, University of Maryland
Nancy T. Gallini, University of Toronto
Terry Heaps, Simon Fraser University
Tracy R. Lewis, University of British Columbia
Edward R. Morey, University of Colorado
Lloyd Orr, Indiana University
Robert S. Pindyck, Massachusetts Institute of Technology
R. Bruce Rettig, Oregon State University
William Schworm, University of British Columbia
Tom Velk, McGill University.

Juanita Hamilton typed and word-processed the manuscript with speed and skill. Our thanks to her and to Queen's University for providing the conditions for letting us write this book.

John M. Hartwick
Nancy D. Olewiler

chapter **1**

Approaching the Study of Natural Resource Economics

INTRODUCTION

Global natural resource use has been an area of concern for economists since the simultaneous births of modern economics and industrial society in the eighteenth century. Malthus was concerned with land and food constraints choking off population growth and the well-being of individuals. Conservationists and the contemporary neo-Malthusians such as Barry Commoner, the ecologist, and Dennis Meadows, the systems analyst, have addressed the same issues from not dissimilar perspectives. Today newspapers and public affairs television programs remind us regularly of impending oil exhaustion, fish stock declines, the increase of carbon dioxide in the atmosphere, the destruction of forests, the land constraints on world food production, and the rapidly growing populations and cities of the Third World.

Many of these issues form a backdrop to the discussion and analysis in this text. But we do not tackle these issues in sequence here; rather, we present a framework for analyzing and discussing them. Economics provides a means for dissecting certain social issues — for systematically analyzing the components of issues and how they are interconnected. For example, to try to understand the issue of oil depletion, we first need to know what determines the rate at which oil is pumped from the ground and whether exploration for new supplies is occurring. Before we delve into the economics of natural resource use, we present some basic concepts in this chapter.

What are *natural resources?* To an economist, they are factors of production — inputs which combined with labor, capital, and materials produce goods and services. We can think of a natural resource as a unique factor input, but most natural resources have characteristics that make them very similar to capital. First of all, to be used for consumption or in production processes, most natural resources have to be

1

extracted or harvested. Copper must be mined before it can be used to mint coins or produce wire. Forests and fish must be harvested and transformed into lumber and filets. So like capital, most resources must be "produced" using other factor inputs such as labor. Second, like capital, natural resources yield productive services *over time*. A fish stock, forest, or mine is typically able to supply resources for long periods of time.

Time is a crucial component of the analysis of natural resource use. Time helps distinguish between different types of resources. A *renewable* natural resource is one that can supply productive inputs to an economic system indefinitely. A *nonrenewable* natural resource is one with a finite stock or supply which, once used up, is gone. We have organized the text into sections on renewable and nonrenewable resources so that we can examine in detail the important economic decisions associated with their use.

But in a sense, all natural resources are renewable. They are distinguished by the length of time it takes a particular resource to be reproduced. Solar energy is an extreme case: The daily flow of solar radiation to the earth will be roughly constant and continue for billions of years. Shrimp can reproduce by the billions each year. Oil deposits take billions of years to be produced by geological processes. For practical purposes, we separate natural resources into those that are renewable — fish, forests, solar energy, and environmental resources such as water and the atmosphere; and those that are nonrenewable — minerals, oil, and gas. There is, however, a caution in this distinction. Most renewable resources can be depleted or exhausted — that is, they can become nonrenewable. A fish population can be harvested to extinction. Forests can be cut and the soil remaining eroded to such an extent that no new trees will survive. Groundwater can be depleted by extensive irrigation of agricultural crops. Clean air and water can be destroyed by pollution. The link between renewable and nonrenewable resources is thus very close.

Economics is the analysis of how to allocate scarce resources among competing uses. How this is done depends not only on the endowments of factor inputs — natural resources in our case — but also on the state of technology of turning inputs into outputs and on the objectives of individuals and society as a whole. Economics has an extensive set of theoretical and empirical techniques which are used to analyze the actions of individuals, once these objectives are given.

We assume that individuals act in their own self-interest — consumers maximize utility, and firms maximize the present value of profits — and then evaluate the outcomes of this maximizing behavior. But economics cannot operate in a social vacuum. We must also specify criteria by which individuals or groups of individuals (including government) evaluate the allocations of resources achieved. Economists typically argue that social interests are maximized when resources and products are allocated to their most valuable uses. However, the value placed on alternative uses is not independent of the institutions and circumstances of each country.

The nature and distribution of property rights, wealth, and income all affect the values placed on alternative uses of natural resources. How are income and wealth distributed? What are the property rights to particular resources? Are they held by individuals who can exclude others from using the resource, or are they held in common, with everyone having free access? Although our focus is on the *allocative efficiency* of natural resource use, we will note distributive effects throughout the text, and especially their role in influencing government policy toward natural resources. Property rights are an important theme which we introduce in this chapter. We also look at the role of government and how to evaluate changes in economic efficiency under different market equilibria and types of government policy.

This may all sound like familiar material. Why do we study natural resources separately, and not as just another example in, say, production theory, capital theory, or public finance? We offer three reasons. First, a large set of policy issues of our day concern natural resources[1] per se. An understanding of the economic principles behind resource use is an invaluable aid to informed discussions of these practical problems. Second, natural resources have unique features not found in other economic topics. One of these is nonrenewability; another is the problem of common property. Third, natural resource economics emphasizes economic *dynamics* and decision-making in an *intertemporal* setting. Certainly, all economic problems can be examined in a dynamic setting, but in many cases a very good approximation of the problem examined can be obtained with a *static* analysis. With natural resources, dynamics is essential. Static models typically fail to capture all the important trade-offs in resource use that occur over time. We will make use of static models to introduce important concepts and show how analyzing the problem using dynamic techniques alters our conclusions.

In the chapters that follow, we will look at nonrenewable and renewable resources individually. We examine how in theory these resources can be extracted or harvested and whether the profit-maximizing decisions of firms yield an efficient equilibrium. If not, we examine government policies designed to promote a more efficient outcome. We then look at a variety of practical issues associated with natural resource use. We believe strongly that theory and practice belong together. Theoretical material is presented first to provide a basis for analyzing particular real world problems. We give examples of practical problems in "boxes" and case studies throughout the text. In these studies we make use of scientific information about natural resources — biological information about forests and fish, geological information about minerals, ecological studies on the environment and interactions among living things. Thus, while our approach to natural resource use is that of economics, we also use the work of allied disciplines. Dajoz (1977), for example, indicates the approach of an ecologist to the analysis of animal, plant, and fish life.

DECISION-MAKING OVER TIME

Natural resource use involves decision-making over time. How much gold should be extracted from a mine this year, how much next year, and so on as long as the reserves of gold in the mine exist? Should salmon be harvested intensively this year, or not at all? The supply curve of a natural resource is always shifting due to depletion of nonrenewable resources and biological or physical changes in renewable resources. This is very different from, say, a shoe factory, in which demand and supply schedules can stay fixed year after year. Working with familiar supply and demand curves is not adequate, because the changes in natural resource supply over time must be part of the analysis. We make use of pairs of demand and supply diagrams — one diagram for period t and another for the next period, $t + 1$. *Intertemporal analysis* involves precisely relating the set of schedules in one period to the set in the other period.

Interest Rate

The interest rate is the crucial link between periods. Let us consider an example.

Should I sell my land in the country? I have an offer of $100,000 now (period t). If I sell and put the proceeds in the bank at 10 percent interest, next year I will have (period $t + 1$) $100,000 plus the interest $10,000 or $110,000.

Suppose I do not sell this year but sell next year (period $t + 1$), for a price of $112,000. This would mean that selling in period t and banking the money is a poorer strategy than selling in period $t + 1$. (Of course, if I will only get $104,000 if I sell in period $t + 1$, it is best to sell early (in period t) and put the proceeds in the bank.)

Owners of mineral deposits make these calculations every day. Substitute "another ton of ore" for "land in the country" in our example, and you have a mine exploitation decision! The interest rate is the Hamlet in this little drama. It is always central to the unraveling of the action.

Recall the basics of interest rate arithmetic—*compounding* and its opposite, *discounting* or getting *present value*. We review these concepts now.

Compounding

Compounding is essentially letting the principal (say V) grow while interest is calculated on the interest earned period by period. After one year, V becomes the original value plus interest on the original value:

$$V(1) = V + Vr = (1 + r)V$$

After two years, V becomes the original value V plus interest for one year on V plus interest on interest on V plus V's interest for the second year:

$$= V + rV + rrV + rV = (1 + r)^2 V.$$

After 12 years, V becomes $V(12) = (1 + r)^{12}V$. And so on for any number of years. We plot $V(t)$ against t in Figure 1.1. The points in Figure 1.1 each represent V compounded over a specific number of years or periods. The series represents the phenomenon of *exponential growth* (sometimes referred to as *geometric growth*). It is V that is growing here.

The *rate of growth* is the change in $V(t)$ divided by the value of $V(t)$. For example, between years 11 and 12, the rate of growth is

$$\frac{V(12) - V(11)}{V(11)} = r$$

Thus, at a constant interest rate, V grows at the rate r.

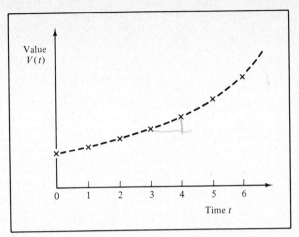

Figure 1.1 We illustrate the value of V(0) growing "by compound interest" or exponentially (or geometrically) at rate r.

Discounting or Getting Present Value

This is the "opposite" or "inverse" of compounding. The *present value* of V dollars delivered five years from now is

$$\frac{V}{(1 + r)^5}$$

rather than V multiplied by $(1 + r)^5$ as in compounding. We say that V is discounted back to the present (period 0). Discounting permits us to compare what are essentially apples and walnuts — values at two different points in the future. We discount both values to the present, and then they are perfectly comparable.

Very frequently we are interested in a stream of values into the future. Suppose your trust fund manager says he will have $800 per year available for you for the next five years. To assess the value of this stream, convert each item to the same period (say the present) and sum them up:

$$PV = 800 + \frac{800}{(1 + r)} + \frac{800}{(1 + r)^2} + \frac{800}{(1 + r)^3} + \frac{800}{(1 + r)^4}$$

This is the discounted present value of a sum of future values.

With a mine, profits often get smaller in the future as the ore thins out, so the stream of future values of concern to the owner would decline. With forests and fish, it has been traditional to arrange production to get a steady harvest into the future, and thus a constant stream is often seen in such problems. (We will see this in Chapters 8 and 11.)

We can summarize in Figure 1.2. Let a stream of future payments be the points with xs. Each value can be discounted to the present, yielding a stream of os. The sum of the o values is the discounted present value of the stream of future values. What does the present value stream of os look like for the xs in Figure 1.1? It will be a horizontal schedule, with each term equal to V at time period 0.

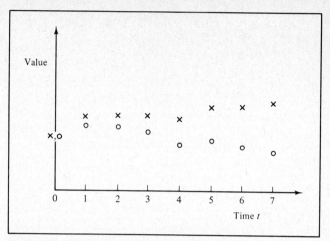

Figure 1.2   The schedule of xs when discounted to period 0 become the schedule of os. The sum of the zero values over time is the discounted present value of the stream.

How long does it take my $100 to double in the bank at 8 percent interest? This is an example of compounding: $100 becomes $108 after one year, $108 × 1.08 after two years, etc. We want

$$\$200 = \$100(1.08)^T$$

where T is the unknown. We find on a calculator that for $T = 9$, $(1.08)^T = 1.99900$, so that *nine years of compounding at 8 percent will double our money.* (It turns out that if we divide 70 by the interest rate, we get a good approximation of the years it takes to double our money. We look more closely at this "trick" in Chapter 6.)

What is $100 a year forever worth as a lump sum today if the interest rate remains at 8 percent per year? This is an example of discounting each future payment and summing up the discounted values to get the sum of discounted present values. That is, we want

$$Z = \$100 + \frac{\$100}{1.08} + \frac{\$100}{(1.08)^2} + \frac{\$100}{(1.08)^3} + \cdots + \frac{\$100}{(1.08)^4} + \cdots$$
$$= \$100 + \$92.59 + \$85.73 + \$79.38 + \cdots +$$
$$= \$1250, \text{ or}$$
$$Z = \frac{\$100}{r}$$

A note paying $100 per year forever at an 8 percent interest rate is worth about $1,250 in a lump sum today. (Sometimes one hears about a million dollar prize being paid out at $100,000 per year for 10 years. Clearly the present discounted value of this stream of $100,000 payments is much less than a one million dollar cash allotment today. For example the tenth payment is worth $100,000 \div (1 + r)^9$ which at $r = .08$ comes, in present value, to $50,024.90.) The interest rate used by individuals to discount streams of payments that occur in the future is called the personal rate of discount or personal *rate of time preference*.

The benefits from building a dam. In deciding the value or benefits from a public work like a dam, which lasts for many decades into the future, assessors evaluate the dollar value of electricity generated year by year and the dollar value of new irrigation made available and arrive at a figure of V dollars of net benefits *per year*. To get the sum of benefits, these yearly figures must be added up. But of course a million dollars of benefits in 1990 is different from a million dollars of benefits in 1995. So the net yearly benefits are discounted at some interest or discount rate r.

The computation of a present value is straightforward; which discount rate is the correct one is the problem. Low values of r in discounting make the sum of present values large and high values of r make the sum of present values small. (Recall the example of receiving $100 forever. If r is 8 percent, then $100 forever is worth $1,250 in present value, whereas if r is 4 percent, it is worth $2,500 in present value.) Hence, individuals much in favor of a dam costing, say, $500 million will favor a low discount rate when assessing the desirability of doing the project and those opposed will favor higher discount rates. There is considerable debate of what is the appropriate discount rate to use when evaluating projects financed by governments. Some economists advocate using an average of *market interest rates*—those rates that private firms would face in borrowing funds for large capital investment projects. Others argue that there should be a *social discount rate*—an interest rate that reflects the government's cost of borrowing (often less than that of the private sector) adjusted for risk and distortions in the economy such as income and commodity taxation. While we will speak of *the* discount rate, it is important to recognize that no single rate is agreed to by all policy analysts.

Techniques of Analysis

The definitions of compounding and discounting and the four examples are reference points. We use these basic concepts frequently in the analysis of different resources throughout the text. But the material that follows does not suddenly get more complex; our approach is to present the economic concepts of natural resource use employing simple mathematical techniques. No analysis has been left out simply because it involves advanced economics or mathematics. Instead, we have put in material originally presented with advanced math and developed it with elementary college math used in many undergraduate economics programs.

For example, finding a program, sequence, or time path of outputs from a mine is a dynamic maximization problem usually analyzed with advanced mathematics. We analyze such problems with elementary maximization techniques, taking first derivatives. We do this consistently and present a diagrammatic exposition as well. Burying basic and exciting economic ideas under a mountain of mathematics is frequently unnecessary and can be a waste of time for the reader. Clearly, for good exposition of fairly intricate ideas in economics, we need a balance between mathematics and prose. Our approach has been to use graphic techniques and only differentiation in the text. We find maximums and minimums and analyze equilibria. We generally use discrete periods of time, and present concepts using smoothly flowing continuous time only when the discrete model is explained fully. This permits us to stick to simple mathematics. (Longer derivations and more complicated optimization problems that may interest some readers are found in appendixes to chapters at the back of the book.)

PROPERTY RIGHTS AND NATURAL RESOURCE USE

A *property right* is a bundle of characteristics that convey certain powers to the owner of the right. There are many different characteristics a property right can possess. To illustrate, let us consider a deed to a piece of land. The deed is a property right which typically gives the holder the power to use the land and to appropriate returns from the land. So, for example, crops can be grown and sold, and the proceeds go to the owner. An apartment building can be constructed and rented, with the rents paid to the owner of the land. The owner can also prevent others from using the land without permission. Thus, the deed is *exclusive* and *enforceable.* The owner of the land may be able to subdivide the property and sell or give others a portion. If so, the property right is both *divisible* and *transferable.*

Rights may also be constrained by restrictions imposed by governments or private individuals. An example of a government constraint is local zoning ordinances that prohibit certain uses of land. One cannot build a metal smelter in the midst of a residential community. Private constraints can be included in the deed, such as restrictive covenants that prevent construction of 10-foot fences in suburban neighborhoods. Other private restrictions may follow from custom — one keeps the grass cut so neighbors won't complain.

The duration of the right is also an important distinguishing feature. For example, *freehold* title to land is an exclusive, enforceable, transferable, and generally divisible right that holds forever. A *leasehold* is also exclusive and enforceable and can be transferable and divisible, but it is of limited duration.

We cannot cover all the different types of property rights that apply to natural resources in detail, but we do want to make one very important distinction between types of rights and see what this implies about the economic analysis of natural resource use. The *exclusivity* of a right is an important distinguishing characteristic. A *private* property right gives the holder the power to the exclusive use of a natural resource. The holder does not have to share the natural resource with any others. A *common* property right is nonexclusive; anyone is free to use the natural resource. Another term used to describe common property is *open access.* No one can prevent another from using the natural resource and appropriating a share of the returns from the resource. Private and common property rights may also differ in other characteristics, but it is on exclusivity that we focus.

The presence or absence of exclusivity has an impact on many economic issues and on the role of government. With private property rights, markets for the production and exchange of natural resources typically exist. It is possible to obtain efficient allocations of resources without government intervention. Natural resources that tend to be parceled out with private property rights are mines (both fuel and nonfuel minerals), private recreational sites, agricultural and some forested land. We empha-

See Bishop & Ciracy-Wantrup

size in Chapters 2 through 6, and in Chapter 11, how an efficient allocation of resources is obtained for land use, mineral extraction, and forest operations through the maximizing behavior of firms. The emphasis is on the operation of markets, because in many cases these private markets function well. We do, of course, examine cases where private markets do not function efficiently. In Chapter 4 we examine different market structures, and in Chapter 5, the effect of uncertainty on nonrenewable resource extraction. But in general, our focus is on the behavior of individual decision-makers who have the exclusive power to use the natural resource.

By contrast, resources characterized by common property rights *cannot* achieve an efficient allocation of resources without some form of government intervention and/or the creation of a private property right. Markets for the production and exchange of these natural resources either do not exist or operate inefficiently. Natural resources held in common include many fisheries and environmental resources such as air and water.[2] We will show in Chapter 8 for fisheries and Chapter 12 for environmental resources that the equilibria obtained when individuals pursue their own self-interests are inefficient. We will thus devote considerable attention, especially in Chapters 9 and 13, to government attempts to promote efficiency in these sectors.

But why are land, forests, and minerals generally exploited under private property rights, while fisheries, air, and water are characterized by common property rights? We cannot give definite answers, but following the work of Scott (1984) and others he cites, we examine some of the characteristics of the different natural resources and the emergence of property rights for these resources over time.

Private property rights for land and minerals have existed for hundreds of years and were created both by actions of governments (e.g., enclosure acts for land) and by actions of private individuals through litigation and the establishment of common law precedent. These rights tend to be either freehold or leasehold. Mineral rights are typically distinct from surface rights to land. In many countries, including Canada, the government (federal and provincial) reserves the mineral rights when land is sold to individuals. If you own property in Canada, in most cases you do not own the right to explore for oil or gold or to extract a mineral if it bubbles to the surface or your child strikes a vein of gold while digging in the sandbox. Those wishing to explore for and develop mineral deposits must first obtain the right to do so from the government. The right is then typically a lease which gives the individual (or firm) exclusive power to search for and then extract gold, nickel, oil, gas, or whatever over the life of the mine. Perhaps the reasons why land and minerals developed exclusive rights was their ease in delineation. These resources are generally immobile.[3] Some have also argued that private property rights will be established when the resource in question is highly valued, thus making exclusive ownership of sufficient benefit to overcome the costs of establishing and enforcing property rights.

Ownership arrangements related to water use have concerned legal scholars for centuries. Two polar cases are: (a) when my use does not interfere with your use, as when I swim in a river through my farm; and (b) when my use interferes with your use, as when I divert large amounts of water upstream from your land. We have some comments on these matters and on water use in the southwestern United States in Chapter 2.

A mixed case is that of forestry. Trees are immobile and of value, so one would think exclusive rights to forests would exist. Yet rights to harvest crops of trees over long periods of time typically do not exist independently. Rights for land and minerals are formal—deeds and agreements are drawn up; in forestry, the arrangements are more casual. Forests automatically accompany freehold title to land. Other forests are held on public land. But when rights to the trees (independent from land) are granted by either the government or private landowners, they have tended to be restricted to the harvest of a particular "crop" of trees, not to successive crops of trees. There is no reason in principle why "tree" rights—rights to practice forestry operations over time—could not be granted. It is not obvious why the severance of tree rights has been slow to occur.[4]

Fisheries and environmental resources, by contrast, have remained as common property for long periods of time. Both the legal system and government have in general failed to produce private property rights for these resources until quite recently. Indeed, governments have even promoted common property. The Magna Carta, for example, abolished the English crown's authority to grant exclusive rights to fish in tidal waters and replaced it with a public right—that is, open access to the fisheries. Why did this happen? There are a number of explanations, none totally convincing. Perhaps the simplest reason why private property rights have not emerged is that unlike minerals and land, it may be technologically or physically very difficult to achieve exclusion.

Consider an ocean fishery such as tuna. Tuna can migrate over large distances. How is one to lay claim to a particular fish or population of tuna? Other common property resources such as air are consumed jointly by a large number of people. Dividing the resource up or obtaining payment for the use of these resources may be quite difficult. Another explanation is that it is optimal not to establish private property rights. Some argue that the costs—known as *transaction costs* of establishing and enforcing private property rights—are higher than the *benefits* (the value of an exclusive right). In particular cases this may be so, but as a general proposition it is dubious.

Whatever the explanation for the persistence of common property rights, it now appears that some changes are underway. In recent years, establishment of some private rights for common property resources has occurred through both legal and government actions. One explanation is that the value (both market and nonmarket) of these resources has now become so great that it pays to design more exclusive rights. Technological change may also play a role. For example, the development in the last century of barb wire allowed ranchers to fence their land much more cheaply than was possible with wood fencing. This greatly reduced the cost of keeping others' cattle off one's land. It reduced the cost of exclusion. Many common resources are in danger of being exhausted. If action is not taken, some fish species will become extinct, and air and water will be severely damaged. Many fisheries are now regulated by governments in ways that reduce open access. Environmental resources have been regulated with antipollution legislation and more recently by the establishment of rights to pollute (or to clean air and water). But the process is by no means complete. In Chapters 8 through 10 and 12 and 13, we will see the inefficiencies arising from common property resources and the attempts by governments and individuals to alleviate these problems.

WELFARE ECONOMICS AND THE ROLE OF GOVERNMENT

In the previous section, we noted that government intervention is necessary if an economy is to achieve an efficient allocation of resources when resources are characterized by common property rights. This is quite clearly not the only role for government in modern economies. Even if there were a full set of private property rights, certain *market imperfections* or *market failures* would still exist and income might not be distributed equitably. Nonrenewable resources get used up too quickly; urban activity "eats up" agricultural land; trees are not harvested quickly enough. These are called market failures because the free interaction of individuals in the economy leads to inefficient outcomes. Some essential ingredient necessary for the efficient allocation of resources is missing.

Nonrenewable resources may be mined too quickly if, for example, firms discount the future at a higher interest rate than does society. Trees may be harvested too slowly if exclusively biological considerations guide the harvester. Other examples of market failure include market structures that are imperfectly competitive (e.g., monopoly), failure of markets to exist for events occurring in the future, and of course the common property market failures that can lead to extinction of fish stocks, air and water pollution, and depletion of water supplies. We examine many of these market failures throughout the text and summarize them in Chapter 14.

To contrast and evaluate the difference between *socially optimal allocations of resources* and those achieved by private actions, we draw on a large body of work called *welfare economics*. Welfare economics, simply put, is the study of the level and distribution of individuals' and groups' well-being in the economy. Different allocations of resources are compared to see under which outcome society will be the best off. People may value alternative allocations differently. Some people may gain under a particular allocation while others lose. Therefore, some means of comparison, taking into account differences in individuals' preferences, income, and so on, has to be devised.

The technique used by economists is the creation of a *social welfare function*— a hypothetical relationship that weighs each individual's well-being or utility in some fashion, then "adds up" the utilities to obtain an aggregate function that is used to compare alternative equilibria. The eighteenth-century philosopher Jeremy Bentham expressed the view that such weights should be equal for all individuals. Hence we speak of a Benthamite social welfare function, and characterize it as being egalitarian. Another way to look at this function is to assume that politicians are responsible for determining the appropriate distribution of income. Economists can then proceed by assuming income has been redistributed such that the marginal utility of one dollar of income is the same for all individuals. The social welfare function can then "add up" individuals without assigning particular welfare weights. We will assume distributional matters are resolved in this manner, but we recognize that problems of income distribution remain in practice. As economists, we have no claim to being better at resolving these issues than other analysts.

A social welfare function and its use can be illustrated easily using concepts familiar from introductory economics—production possibility frontiers and indifference curves. In Figure 1.3 we have drawn a production possibility frontier *(PPF)* that shows the maximum output obtainable of two goods—cars and clean air—

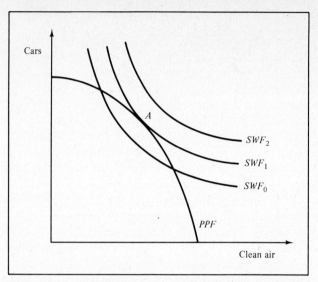

Figure 1.3 An optimal allocation of cars and clean air is reached where society's well-being is maximized. This occurs at *A* where a social welfare function *(SWF)* is tangent to the production possibility frontier *(PPF)* for the two goods.

from the economy's endowment of productive resources. Any combination of cars and clean air lying on or within the boundary of the *PPF* is obtainable. A set of social indifference curves represents society's valuation of the two goods. To achieve a socially or *Pareto* optimal allocation of resources, the highest social indifference curve tangent to the *PPF* should be chosen, as shown at point *A*. The socially optimal allocation is one in which it is not possible to reallocate resources and improve welfare of any one person without making at least one other person worse off. If we assume politicians are handling distribution of incomes, this condition implies that no allocation will lead to a higher net gain in welfare. This is a very simple representation. For a full social optimum, one must assume that consumers maximize utility, firms maximize profits, a full set of property rights exists, and all markets are efficient.

Producer surplus and *consumer surplus* are dollar measures of people's utility and firms' profits, which are used often as an approximation of social welfare. We follow this approach, which permits us to indicate optimal arrangements of resource use and to value different equilibria. Let us look first at the consumer and the valuation of different equilibria, given our assumption that income distribution matters have been resolved.

Suppose we want to know how much "better off" a consumer would be if the price of gasoline fell from 30 cents per liter to 20 cents per liter. What measure would reflect the change in the consumer's well-being or utility? We can use the theory of demand to obtain an answer. Figure 1.4(a) illustrates the situation facing an individual with a fixed income, who spends her income on one good, gasoline, and a market basket of other goods denoted *Y*. Assume the price of these other goods equals 1. Then the *Y* axis reflects the person's income. Given gas prices which are initially set at 30 cents per liter and her income, the woman can consume any combination of gas

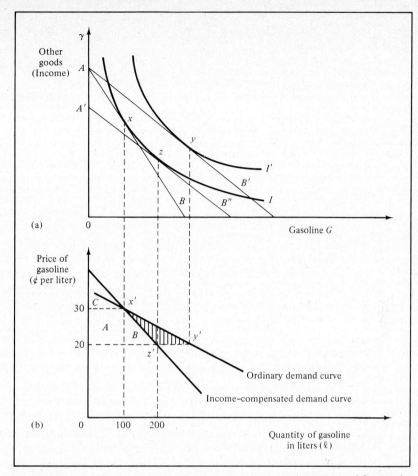

Figure 1.4 The compensating variation and consumer surplus generated from a decrease in the price of one good. When the price of gasoline falls from 30 to 20 cents per liter,
a consumer benefits. Part (a) illustrates the increase in the quantity of gas consumed
holding constant the price of other goods. Point z shows the increase in gasoline consumption holding utility constant on *I*. The initial equilibrium is *x*, the final equilibrium is *y*. In (b), the
income-compensated demand curve links points *x'* and *z'*, while the ordinary demand curve
links points *x'* and *y'*. Compensating variation is the area under the income-compensated
demand curve above the price charged for the good. When the price of gasoline falls from
30¢/*l* to 20¢/*l*, the compensating variation is areas *A* + *B*. Consumer surplus for the price
change is measured under the ordinary demand curve and equals areas *A* + *B* plus the
shaded area.

(G) and other goods as shown by the budget constraint *AB*. Her utility-maximizing
choice is where *AB* is tangent to her highest indifference curve between other goods
and gas. In this case, the solution is point *x* on indifference curve *I*. Demand curves
can be derived from this utility maximization representation, as shown in Figure
1.4(b). At 30 cents per liter, the person will buy, say, 100 liters of gas *given* the price of
other goods and her income. This is shown as point *x'* in panel b. Now let the price of
gas fall to 20 cents per liter, while all other prices are unchanged. The individual's
budget constraint now shifts to *AB'*, allowing her to consume more of the other goods

and gas at point y because her real income has risen and she can reach a higher indifference curve.

But we really want to know how much more gas this person would consume given a change in the price of gas without any change in her level of utility. Suppose her income is reduced just enough to keep her on indifference curve I facing the new set of relative prices. This amount of income is called a *compensating variation*. The person's budget constraint then shifts to $A'B''$ and her utility-maximizing equilibrium is at z. Compensating variation measured in terms of other goods is then the vertical distance AA'. We can also measure compensating variation in terms of an *income-compensated* demand curve. The compensated demand curve shows combinations of prices and income that keep the individual at her initial utility level. The point z' in Figure 1.4(b) shows how much gas would be purchased — 200 liters. This demand curve for gas is then derived holding the price of other goods and utility constant at I for different prices of gas. Note, and we'll return to this, the ordinary demand curve would link points x' and y' and thus lies above the income-compensated demand curve for price decreases (and below it for price increases).

Given the income-compensated demand curve, we can now measure the individual's compensating variation from the change in gas prices from 30 to 20 cents per liter.[5] Think about what has been gained. The consumer was willing to pay 30 cents per liter for 100 liters. That is, we can read off the demand curve what someone is willing to pay for any quantity of the good. But this consumer no longer has to pay 30 cents, so she has saved or benefited by 10 cents per liter of gas consumed for the first 100 liters, or \$10. This is the rectangle A or $(P_0 - P_1)100$. But in addition, the consumer is getting between 100 and 199 liters of gas for 20 cents per liter as well, but would be willing to pay more than 20 cents for these liters. So the consumer also "receives" as a benefit area B. If the demand curve is linear, we can measure area B, a triangle, by the formula $1/2$(base times height). In this case, the base is $(200 - 100 = 100)$, the height is $(P_0 - P_1 = .1)$, so area B is $1/2(100 \times .1) = \$5$. The total gain to the consumer is the area $A + B$, the amount \$15. This is the compensating variation for a price change from P_0 to P_1.

Generally we approximate welfare changes by evaluating areas under the observed (or non-income compensated) demand curve. The measure of welfare change under the ordinary demand curve is called *consumer surplus*. The gain in consumer surplus that results from the decrease in gasoline prices from 30 to 20 cents is the area bounded by $30x'y'20$. So far, we have assumed there exists an income-compensated or Hicksian demand curve for each individual. But can we ever observe such a demand curve? We have an important conflict between theory and applied work here. The theoretical demand curve derived from utility maximization is not the same as the demand curve typically derived from statistical methods. The ordinary demand curve is typically an *aggregate* demand curve — it shows total demand by all consumers (or groups of consumers) for the good at various prices. There is no way to tell how much *each* consumer gains or loses from price changes unless each individual has identical preferences — an unlikely event. In addition, the measured demand curve is not an income-compensated curve, but one that allows utility to vary with the price change. It is a demand curve similar to the one through points x' and y' in Figure 1.4(b).

The observed demand curve includes both income and substitution effects. If estimates of consumer surplus are made from the ordinary demand curve, they will not be a precise measure of consumers' willingness to pay for the good unless the income elasticity of all consumers is 1 (a 1 percent change in income leads to a 1 percent change in consumption of all goods). This is an unlikely situation. But there are practical means of dealing with the problem—situations where using consumer surplus measured from ordinary demand curves will not lead to large errors in estimating willingness to pay.[6]

Producer's surplus is a less controversial measure of welfare changes to the firm in theory, but again can be difficult to estimate in practice. Consider the following example and Figure 1.5, which shows the cost curves of a competitive firm. If the firm is in a long-run equilibrium, price must equal marginal cost at the minimum of the average total cost curve. The producer earns zero economic profits at this point (A on Figure 1.5). But note that the price P exceeds marginal cost (MC) for all units of output less than q_0. The price P reflects the marginal cost of producing the last unit of output sold—the unit for which zero economic profits are made. All previous units of output—the *inframarginal* units—are sold at a price greater than the average variable costs (AVC) of production. At P, there is thus a payment made to the firm above the *opportunity cost* of producing all output to the left of q_0. This opportunity cost is the amount of wages, interest payments, and so on that it would take to produce these units. This payment above opportunity cost is *producer surplus*. More explicitly, producer surplus is the shaded area shown in Figure 1.5 which is bounded

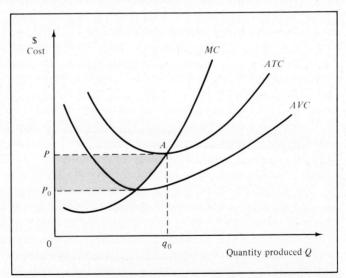

Figure 1.5   The producer surplus for the firm is the area below the market price of the good produced and above the marginal cost of producing all the inframarginal units of the good. At price P, q_0 will be produced, as P represents the marginal cost of supplying the last unit of production at q_0. For all output less than q_0, marginal cost is less than price P. The producer surplus measures the excess return accruing to these units of output above their marginal cost of production, where marginal cost exceeds average variable cost.

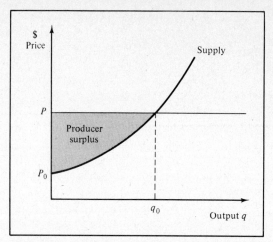

Figure 1.6 Producer surplus is illustrated for the competitive firm's supply curve. Given an equilibrium price of
P, producer surplus is the area below P and above the
supply curve, where supply is the marginal cost of production (above average variable cost).

by the long-run equilibrium price of the good P, output produced, q_0, and the price
where $AVC = MC$, price P_0.

Recall from basic microeconomic theory that the firm's supply curve will be
given by its marginal costs of production lying above AVC. This means that another
way to look at producer surplus is with the supply curve of the competitive firm (or
marginal cost curve of the monopolist). This is shown in Figure 1.6. Given the
equilibrium price P (a competitive firm facing a perfectly elastic demand curve at P),
producer surplus is the shaded area lying above the supply curve up to P. Again,
producer surplus reflects the fact that inframarginal units of the good, output less
than q_0, could have been produced at a price less than P. These units thus earn for the
firm a surplus or rent equal to the difference between the price actually received and
the marginal cost of producing those units. Measurement of a firm's producer surplus
requires information about the firm's marginal cost curve. In practice, it may be hard
to obtain the data to estimate such a curve statistically. Industry supply curves are
easier to quantify, but they will obscure the gains and losses of individual firms.

Now that we have defined and seen how to measure producer and consumer
surplus, we return to the notion of a social welfare function and ask what is the
optimal allocation of resources. In the chapters that follow, we assume that the social
optimum or social welfare maximum is that equilibrium price and output level that
maximizes the sum of consumer plus producer surplus. This is one traditional social
welfare function. Its shortcomings have been extensively studied. (See, for example,
Boadway and Bruce, 1984.) We show what this condition means for a single perfectly
competitive market at a point in time in Figure 1.7. What price and output level
would maximize consumer plus producer surplus? Where supply equals demand in a
competitive market, consumer plus producer surplus is maximized. We can see this
as follows.

At the equilibrium price $P*$ and output $Q*$, consumer surplus is the area $P*ae$, while producer surplus is the area $P*ed$. Our argument is that no other price and output combination can yield a larger sum of producer plus consumer surplus. Consider, say, a price P less than $P*$ (where P could be the result of a government-imposed price ceiling on gasoline). At P, the equilibrium quantity produced and consumed is Q and there is excess demand for gasoline. Consumer plus producer surplus would be the shaded areas. Consumer surplus is area $Pabc$, while producer surplus is area Pcd. Consumers thus gain at the expense of producers, but the total surplus is less than under $P*$ and $Q*$.

Or, consider a price such as P' (due, say, to a price floor set for gasoline). By construction, the equilibrium output consumed is still Q, but there is now an excess supply of gasoline. The sum of producer plus consumer surplus is again the shaded area and thus less than the maximum total. But notice now that producers have gained at the expense of consumers. Consumer surplus has shrunk to area $P'ab$, while producer surplus has grown to $P'bcd$ compared to the previous case. We see that the net loss from a price of P or P' and output Q is the area bce. This is also known as a *deadweight loss*—an efficiency loss for an equilibrium other than that which maximizes welfare. Thus we see that only where supply equals demand and the competitive market clears do we have a social welfare optimum that maximizes the sum of producer plus consumer surplus. We will see different versions of this basic concept in the text. In particular, in Chapter 3 we see how to obtain a social welfare maximum

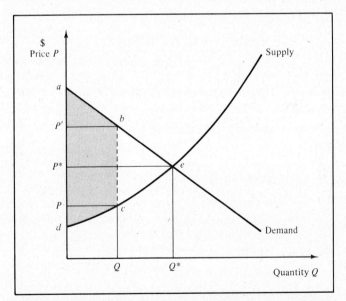

Figure 1.7 Social welfare is at an optimum where the sum of the consumer surplus plus producer surplus is maximized. For a competitive market, this will occur where supply equals demand and yields the equilibrium price $P*$ and output $Q*$. For $P*$ and $Q*$, consumer surplus is the area $P*ae$, while producer surplus is the area $P*ed$. Any other price and output combination such as P and Q or P' and Q will lead to a smaller total surplus.

in an intertemporal setting. But the basic concepts are the same as those developed here. (Other central material of microeconomics is introduced as topics using the concepts as they arise—isoquants in Chapter 2, oligopoly theory in Chapter 4, expected utility in Chapter 5, and elasticities of substitution in Chapter 6.)

There are heroic assumptions to be swallowed in applying the central ideas in welfare economics. Ultimately, a social consensus is required. It is to the political process that we must finally turn for the emergence of the social welfare function. This political welfare function will in general be quite different from our social welfare function. Consideration of political issues takes us into the area of voting, vote trading, dissembling in voting, and so on, an area economists have analyzed at great length and depth. (See, for example, Chapter 16 of Hirshleifer, 1984, for an introduction.) Our approach in the book is that "the government" is a separate agent acting in the social interest when activity by individuals fails to bring about a social optimum. In Chapter 14 we discuss some limitations of this approach, but it permits us to abstract from the details of the political process as it relates to resource allocation in general and natural resource use in particular.

Two alternative approaches for analyzing the development of policies in the area of natural resource use include the historical and the comparative. In the historical approach, we analyze the evolution of a sector over time and try to arrive at policies that could improve the current situation. In the comparative approach, we analyze what is being done in other countries and try to design policies that would improve the situation in our own country. Although we do consider much institutional detail, we make little use of the historical or comparative approaches. Ours is

Table 1.1   U.S. EMPLOYMENT

Timber-based industries: employment (1,000)			
	1970	**1975**	**1981**
Lumber & wood products	554	615	556
Logging camps & contractors	(NA)	74	65
Sawmills & planing mills	196	202	182
Millwork, plywood, structural members	(NA)	166	518

Fisheries: employment, fishing craft, and establishments (1,000)			
	1970	**1975**	**1980**
Persons employed	227	260	296
Fishermen	140	168	193
Shore workers	87	92	103
Craft used	88	103	103
Vessels 5 net tons & over	14	16	9
Fishery shore establishments	3.7	3.6	3.6

Mineral industries: employment (1,000)			
	1970	**1975**	**1981**
All mining	623	752	1132
Metal mining	93	94	104
Coal mining	145	213	222
Oil & gas extraction	270	329	686
Nonmetallic minerals except fuels	115	117	119

Source: U.S. Department of Commerce, Bureau of the Census, *Statistical Abstract of the United States, 1982–83,* Table 1243, 1256, and 1282.

**Table 1.2   CANADA: EMPLOYMENT IN RESOURCE
SECTORS (THOUSANDS)**

	1976	1977	1978
Fishing, hunting, trapping	20	21	23
Forestry and logging	52	54	58
Mining and quarrying	54	53	56

Source: Canada Yearbook 1980–1981, (Ottawa, Ministry of
Supply and Services, 1981), Table 7.5.

basically a welfare economics approach. The merit of this approach to policy design is that it is based on a set of concepts which have been analyzed and refined over many decades. If a policy seems wrong, we can dissect it into its components: who gains, who loses, by how much, at what prices, and over what period of time. There are natural efficiency criteria for better, best, and an improvement. It may not be easy to apply, since requirements for data are often severe, but it is a consistent and extensively analyzed approach turning ultimately on the notion of improving the welfare of individuals in society.

RESOURCES IN THE ECONOMIES OF THE UNITED STATES, CANADA, AND OTHER NATIONS

The importance of the natural resource sectors to the U.S. and Canadian economies can be assessed in part by examining the sizes of the sectors measured in terms of employees. In the United States in 1980–1981, fishing had about 300,000 workers, forestry and wood processing about 1,400,000, and mining, including oil and gas extraction, about 1,100,000. In Canada in 1978, forestry and mining each had about 57,000 workers, whereas fishing had 23,000 workers (see Tables 1.1 and 1.2). A fishing power such as Iceland had 7.1 percent of its wage income originating in agriculture, hunting, forestry and fishing in 1979, down from 10.8 percent in 1970. (OECD *Labour Force Statistics* 1969–1980, pp. 266–267.)

Consider the significance of natural resource sectors as proportions of gross national product for a group of countries for which data are available (United States data were not disaggregated in this compendium.) Norway's 16.5 percent for mining in Table 1.3 reflects the recent oil discoveries in the North Sea. These figures reflect value added in the respective sectors, or primary factors such as labor, capital, and land used in these sectors. A gross measure would reflect the direct and indirect uses of outputs from these primary sectors as intermediate goods in other sectors of the

**Table 1.3   GROSS NATIONAL PRODUCT BY KIND OF ECONOMIC ACTIVITY
AT CURRENT PRICES, 1981, IN PERCENTAGES**

	Norway	Canada	Sweden	Greece
Agriculture	4.7%	3.4%	2.0%	17.2%
Forestry	0.8	0.6	1.5	0.3
Fishing	0.8	0.2	nil	0.4
Mining	16.5	5.3	0.4	1.6

Source: OECD, *National Accounts,* Detailed Tables, Vol. II, 1964–1981.

economy. In Chapter 6 we report on these gross measures for some key minerals in the United States and the United Kingdom.

SUMMARY

1. The economics approach to analyzing natural resource use draws on models in biology, ecology, geology, and geography. The efficiency of an allocation deals with the issue of whether more output (tons of coal, tons of cod, etc.) can be obtained by reorganizing the input into production. Welfare effects involve how much better off consumers are when more outputs can be produced.
2. Welfare improvement involves assessing how much each consumer is better off and how much the aggregate of consumers is better off. A rough and well analyzed measure of "better off" is the increase in producer and consumer surplus.
3. Natural resource use often involves time paths of outputs and inputs in an essential way. Mineral extraction changes the supply schedule period by period. The intertemporal nature of these problems lead us to use discounting, compounding, and present value calculations very frequently. These adjustments are made to terms in different periods because the utility of a dollar today is higher than that of a dollar at a future period. (The reason is that with a dollar today, one can save it and have that dollar in the future, but not vice versa.)
4. Property rights crucially affect the types of outcomes and the efficiency of allocations in natural resource use. For example, common property arrangements are less efficient than private ownership arrangements.
5. The amount of economic activity in the natural resource sectors varies among countries and regions within countries.

DISCUSSION QUESTIONS

1. Suppose you are considering buying a gold deposit. It will cost $1 million per year to construct a mine so that gold can be extracted. The construction period lasts three years. In the fourth year, production starts. Each year the mine operates, it will yield a net return (total revenue minus total cost) of $500,000. What will you pay for the gold deposit if:
    a. Interest rates are 10 percent and gold can be extracted for 10 years?
    b. Interest rates are 5 percent and gold can be extracted for 6 years?
2. What are the important characteristics of a property right? Distinguish between a private property right and a common property right.
3. a. Explain the concepts of consumer surplus and producer surplus.
    b. Suppose the demand for nickel is given by $Q^D = 1.2 - .6P$, while the supply of nickel is given by $Q^S = .3P$. Compute consumer and producer surplus.
    c. For the problem in (b), suppose the government restricts the price to 1. Compute consumer and producer surplus in this new situation.
4. A new bridge is built and a person now makes 35 trips per month to the center of town rather than his former 25 trips per month. The time cost of the trip plus wear and tear on the person's auto declines from $4.75 before the bridge to $3.75 per trip after the bridge. Evaluate the benefit in dollars per month of the bridge to this person. (*Hint:* You might

want to sketch the person's demand curve for trips to decide on how to calculate the dollar benefits.)

5. We indicated in the chapter that a stream of income of $100 per year forever into the future is worth in present value today $100/.08 = $1,250$ when the interest rate is 8 percent per year. What will be the value of this stream if the interest rate were 16 percent per year? 10 percent per year? Suppose the interest rate jumped to 12 percent after 10 years and remained there forever. Would this raise or lower the present value of the income stream?

6. If you inherited an apartment building and were trying to decide whether to sell it and buy some federal government bonds now or keep the building for a few years and then sell it, how would you arrive at your final course of action?

NOTES

1. The final section of this chapter presents some factual information on the importance of natural resources to various countries including the United States.

2. In developing countries, forests and agricultural land may be common property resources.

3. Oil and gas pools can flow underground when pressure differentials exist; we examine the problems that result in Chapter 4.

4. There are examples where firms have been given (or sold) rights to manage forest land, as Scott (1984) notes. But these rights are far more idiosyncratic and ad hoc than the standardized rights developed for oil and gas deposits. The holder has the right to harvest trees and to construct roads, ports, etc., to facilitate the harvest. But the rights are nontransferable and frequently have had limited durations, which are less than the time it takes to grow a tree to a harvestable age.

5. The point of going through the derivation of the income-compensated demand curve is that it is the demand curve required in theory to measure welfare gains or losses. Technically, consumer surplus can be derived from this curve. See Boadway and Bruce (1984) or Just et al. (1982) for more details on the theory behind the derivation of welfare measures.

6. See Just et al. (1982), Chapter 6, for details. In Figure 1.4(b) one can see the "error" of using consumer surplus from the ordinary aggregate demand curve to measure compensating variation. For the price change shown there, the error will be the lightly shaded area. For further discussion on consumer surplus, see Willig (1976) and Morey (1984).

chapter 2

Land Use and Land Value

INTRODUCTION

In this chapter, we examine land—the natural resource that was an important concern in the early decades of modern economics beginning in the late eighteenth century. In a sense, the study of land economics was the beginning of the economics of natural resources. Land is clearly an important input factor into many economic activities—agriculture and forestry; residential, commercial, and industrial uses; and mineral exploration. Land ownership was also for many centuries the key to personal wealth and social power. Our focus is on the economic principles surrounding the efficient use of land as a natural resource, the determination of the value of land, and how different types of ownership of land affects land use and value.

The models examined in this chapter are all static. Land use and land values are determined at a point in time. In subsequent chapters we focus on the valuation and use of natural resources over time—that is, in a dynamic setting. The dynamic models are typically more complex than the static models, which is why we begin with the simpler and fundamental concepts of this chapter. The principles established in this chapter will apply to all natural resources we subsequently study.

Land is fairly complicated to analyze because it is heterogeneous both in terms of intrinsic fertility (physical properties) and also in terms of its relative accessibility—its location relative to the point where the products obtained from the land are demanded. We examine homogeneous land first, then land of diverse fertility. In each case, our primary concern is to show how land is used efficiently and how the value of land is determined. As we will see, we can distinguish many natural resources by differences in their ownership arrangements. The different property rights will also have implications for the need for government policy. We also examine the relationship between land values and location. Land and all natural resources are heterogeneous not just because of differences in their physical characteristics, but because they differ in their location from markets using the resource. A piece of land used to grow carrots or a copper deposit located far from the markets where outputs are consumed will in general have a lower value than an identical piece of land or copper deposit located close to the market. We uncover some general principles about the relationship between land use, land value, and location.

First, we define the return to or price of a unit of land. This value is called *rent,* and it is a residual or surplus paid to land after payments to other factors of production used to work the land are netted out. The rent for a particular piece of land can vary depending on how the land is used. For example, an acre of land used to grow carrots may yield a rental value of $1,000, whereas that same acre used to "grow" apartment buildings may have a rental value of $10,000.

To determine the most efficient use of land, a basic condition is that the rent generated from the use of the land should be a maximum. Thus, when deciding whether to use the acre for carrots or apartments, the conditions say grow apartments. This condition of rent maximization can be formulated in terms of a rule which states that when there are two or more uses for a particular piece of land, the piece of land should be allocated among the uses until the *price or rent of a marginal unit of land is equal for each use.* If we have 100 acres of land and two uses—carrots versus apartments—we would construct apartments on each acre of land until the rental value of the land used for apartments (if it declines as the number of acres used increases) equals $100, the value of an acre used to grow carrots.

We discuss in detail in this chapter how these calculations are made when all plots of land are homogeneous or when the quality of each plot differs. The special case of mixing activities on plots of land (multiple use) is discussed, as are different market structures and the degree to which land and other factor inputs can be substituted for one another in the production of some good. We examine cases where land and labor must be used in fixed proportions (no substitution possibilities), versus a case where the two inputs can be used in variable proportions (substitution is possible). Finally, we see how land values change when land becomes more accessible because transportation costs decrease.

THE CONCEPT OF ECONOMIC RENT

Rent is a surplus—the difference between the price of a good produced using a natural resource and the unit costs of turning that natural resource into the good. The unit costs include the value of the labor, capital, materials, and energy inputs used to convert the natural resource into a product. What remains after these factor inputs are netted out is the value of the natural resource itself—the land, or as we will see later, minerals, fish, forests, and environmental resources such as air and water. This is the definition of *rent per unit* (per acre or per hectare).

The rent per unit can be an average value—the difference between the price of the good and the average costs of the inputs used to produce the good, or it can be a marginal value—the difference between the price of the last unit of the good sold and the costs of the last units of inputs used to produce that marginal unit. In many cases, average and marginal rents will coincide because we make simplifying assumptions that the price of the good is constant and that factor inputs (other than the natural resource itself) are available in perfectly elastic supply at a given factor price.

In what follows, we are typically concerned with the rent on the margin, although in empirical measurements of land and other resource rent, it is often difficult to obtain marginal measures. Average calculations must be made. We will also talk about *aggregate rent*—the value of the entire parcel of land. One must therefore be careful as to which concept is being used. We emphasize rent because it is an important concept in understanding the efficient and optimal use of a natural resource.

Rent on Homogeneous Land

In England as well as in other countries, up to the Industrial Revolution, land represented economic and political power. Explaining the nature of that economic power was high on the agenda of classical British economics, starting with Adam Smith in 1776. How is the ownership of land related to the high income of landlords? More narrowly, what is the relationship between the *value of land* and the *price* fetched by agricultural products grown on that land? How is the size of the labor force on the land related to the income of the landlord and the price of products grown on the land? These questions received much attention among economists in Britain in the first half of the nineteenth century.

The pivotal idea in the classical literature on rent and land use is the way the value of the product grown on land "spills back" into an income to the landowner. The threads were difficult to untangle. For example, there was serious and longstanding debate over whether the "high" price of land (land rent for the moment) made wheat expensive, or whether the "high" price of wheat made the value of land "high." Sorting these matters out took considerable time. Let's see what the arguments were. Consider first the case of *homogeneous* land.

Suppose a landlord owns 150 acres and employs 10 people on the land. The people use basic implements and seed to cultivate wheat. Assume that the costs of these tools and seed are zero for simplicity. The landowner can then harvest, say, 1,800 bushels of wheat at the end of the season (see Figure 2.1). On the vertical axis, we show output per worker; on the horizontal axis, the number of workers. Each point on the graph then gives us the average product *(AP)* of labor. If the landlord employed 11 workers instead, 1,900 bushels could be produced at the season's end. Employing another worker yields more output, but will cost the landlord more in payments to his work force. Notice that although total output rises when one more worker is employed, the *AP* of that additional worker declines. Land rent on the 150 acres is then the value of crops harvested less the cost of inputs—namely, the work force here.

If a worker is paid 100 bushels a year, then the cost of labor with 10 workers is 1,000 bushels leaving 800 bushels as land rent to the landowner. With 11 workers, the cost is 1,100 bushels for the year, leaving total rent on the 150 acres again at 800 bushels. *The average product of labor* declines from 180 to 173 bushels. The *marginal product* of the eleventh worker is the change in total product resulting from the employment of that worker divided by the change in the amount of input, one

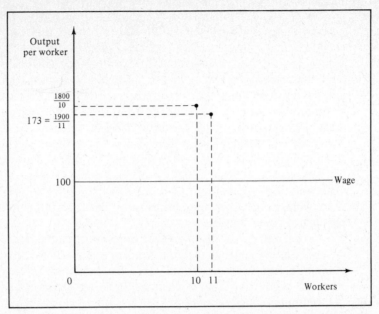

Figure 2.1 Average product per worker for two different amounts of labor on a fixed plot of land. Output per worker exceeds the wage per worker, which results in a residual income or rent left for the landowner.

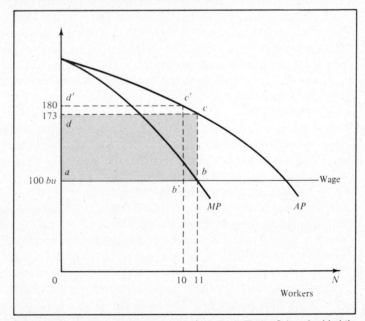

Figure 2.2 In this illustration we have "filled in" Figure 2.1 and added the marginal product schedule. Total rent (total product less total wages) is a maximum when the marginal product of a worker equals his wage "cost" to the landowner. (Total product is *AP* times quantity of labor, or the area under the marginal product schedule *MP* up to the current amount of labor used in production.)

worker. We have then $(1,900 - 1,800)/(11 - 10) = 100$ bushels as the marginal product of the eleventh worker. This is 73 bushels less than the worker's average product. The 100-bushel marginal product here equals the "cost" of the worker to the landowner, the annual wage of 100 bushels.

We complete the schedules of Figure 2.1 in Figure 2.2. The condition for the landowner to maximize his total rent on his 150 acres is to maximize total wheat produced net of payments to workers by choosing the optimal number of workers. That is, the landowner will maximize total rent, which equals total product minus $(100 \, bu \times N)$, where N is the number of workers. Total product has two representations in Figure 2.2: First, it is output per worker, AP, times the total number of workers; second, it is the area under the MP curve up to the total workers employed. The condition for total rent to be a maximum is that the marginal product of one more worker equals the wage payment or $MP_N = 100$, where MP_N is the marginal product of the last added worker.

Total rent is a surplus, residual, or profit accruing to the landowner. It can also be viewed as the return to the input land, as a factor of production used to grow wheat along with the other inputs. Total rent is the shaded area $abcd$ in Figure 2.2; where the marginal product of labor equals the "price" of labor, this rent is maximized. The maximum rent $abcd$ exceeds the rent that would be obtained if only 10 workers were employed (the rectangle $ab'c'd'$).

Observe that if a government levied a tax of, say, 10 bushels per acre, then the landowner would still maximize total rent, but now net of 150 acres $\times$ 10 bushels $=$ 1,500 bushels tax payment at the outset. That is, the landowner would maximize rents by choosing the number of workers N, where the total product from the land minus the total cost of the workers is the greatest — or equivalently, where the marginal product of labor equals the marginal cost of labor. Total product minus $(100 \, bu \times N) - 1,500 \, bu$ is the landlord's profit. Maximization yields the same optimal amount of employment N^* and the same output $Q(N^*)$ would be produced.

The tax simply reduces the rents received by the landowner by 10 bushels per acre regardless of how many bushels are produced. The landowner can do no better than to continue to produce where the marginal product and marginal cost of labor are equal. Thus a land tax is *neutral* in the sense that factor use and output remain unchanged before and after the tax.

A rise in the annual wage of 100 bushels to 110 bushels would lower rent to the landlord and lower the output and number of workers employed. A reduction in wages would raise employment, rent, and wheat production. The *share* of rent relative to total wages depends on the shape of the marginal product schedule and where the points of comparison are in the schedule. Of great political interest in nineteenth-century England was whether landlords or workers were increasing their respective share of total output as time passed. As with many such issues, it depends on certain elasticities. Here the concern is with the elasticity around the point on the marginal product of labor schedule where the equilibrium is. (The *elasticity* of the marginal product curve is the percentage change in the marginal product divided by percentage change in N, the labor force. If labor increases by 10 percent and the marginal product of labor falls by 10 percent, the aggregate income to labor will be unchanged, but aggregate rent might rise or fall as labor increases.

In this reasonably general situation, note that we have been dealing with an aggregate income flow — rent as income to the landlord. There is no obvious way to translate this aggregate into rent per acre of land. We will pursue this point below and develop a somewhat different notion — rent per acre like a price per acre of land.

Plots of Differing Quality

Suppose there are two separate plots, A and B, each consisting of 150 acres. Plot A is very fertile; plot B is less so. The higher quality of plot A is reflected in its marginal product of labor (MP_A), which exceeds the marginal product of labor for plot B (MP_B). Does this difference in quality mean that only plot A will be farmed? Let's see. The rent-maximizing allocation of labor to land requires the product of the marginal worker on each plot to be the same and equal to the "cost" of the marginal worker. Making all the calculations in terms of bushels and proceeding with a constant wage of 100 bushels per year, we illustrate the equilibrium in Figure 2.3.

The horizontal axis shows the total amount of labor available to the two plots. As we move from zero to the right on this axis, labor used on plot A increases. Plot B has its horizontal axis reversed — more labor on B means moving from right to left. N_A and N_B are the rent-maximizing levels of labor on the respective plots. Given a constant wage, more workers will be employed on each plot as long as their marginal product exceeds the wage rate. An equilibrium is reached on each plot where the marginal product equals the wage rate.

Notice that workers are used on both plots of land, but relatively more are employed on plot A — the most fertile site. Total rent on plot A is the area abc in Figure 2.3 and on plot B the total rent is the area bed. If ed is relatively small, it means

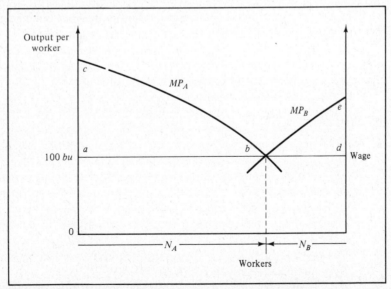

Figure 2.3 Efficient labor use on two plots of land. The sum of rent on the two plots is a maximum when labor is allocated to each plot until the respective marginal products of labor are (a) equal to each other and (b) equal to the wage rate for workers.

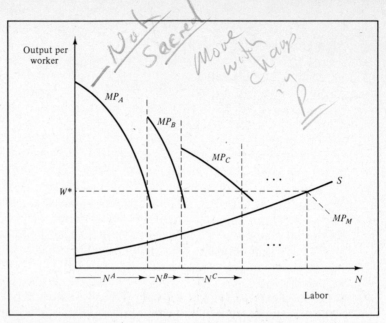

Figure 2.4 There are *m* plots of differing fertility and a rising supply curve for labor. More fertile (higher marginal product of labor) plots are brought into use first. The wage rate is determined by the intersection of the supply of labor and the marginal product of labor on the least productive plot. Total land rent will be the sum of areas under the marginal product schedules, less wage "costs."

that the initial "dose" of labor used on plot *B* barely covers its cost. Land of marginal quality or *marginal land* has the property that its net product ($MP - MC$) is approximately zero. Productivity is essentially a technical datum depending on the skill level of the workers and the fertility of the soil, assuming other inputs are held constant.

In what sense does the rent on marginal land determine the rent on more productive plots of land? Suppose the supply of labor is positively related to the wage offered. The higher the wage, the greater the amount of labor supplied. Then, with many plots of land, the most productive plots with the highest initial rent and marginal productivity would be brought into cultivation first, the less productive plots later, and so on. Plots would continue to be brought on stream until the (rising) prevailing wage was equal to the *initial* marginal product on the marginal land. We illustrate the equilibrium in Figure 2.4. In Figure 2.4, *S* is the schedule for the supply of labor in the economy. The marginal product of labor curves for plots *A*, *B*, and *C* are shown as MP_A, MP_B, and MP_C. We start each new plot at a different vertical axis shown by the dashed lines. These plots are all brought into production with the amount of labor used per plot indicated by N^A, N^B, N^C. The marginal plot is indicated as the MP_M for marginal. There may indeed be other plots of land available, but they are of such low quality that their marginal product of labor curves fail to intersect the supply of labor schedule.

The wage rate w^* is determined where the MP_M intersects the supply of labor schedule. The quality of the marginal plot of land *determines the wage rate* and the *aggregate rent on the intramarginal plots.* The rent on the intramarginal plots such as

A, B, and *C* in Figure 2.4 has been labeled *differential* or *Ricardian rent.* It is differential rent because it is rent above what is being earned on the marginal plot—the difference between the rent on any plot *i* and the rent on the marginal plot. Notice in Figure 2.4 that there is no rent on the marginal plot *(M);* the total returns to the plot are paid to labor. All land of higher quality than plot *M* yields a positive rent. However, if the last plot under cultivation were plot *C,* it would receive a rent.

Whether rent accrues to the plot or not depends on its *net product*—the difference between the marginal product of the factor inputs and their marginal cost. Plot *M* has a net product of zero, while plot *C* has a positive net product. It is Ricardian rent (named for David Ricardo, the nineteenth-century English economist) because it is attributed to differences in intrinsic quality of the land. If there were no quality decline, there would be no marginal plot, or all plots would be the same.

A well-known nineteenth century tenet was that the supply of labor is infinitely elastic at the *subsistence wage.* This principle was used as a basis of the Malthusian doctrine which held that population growth would outstrip the growth of the food supply. In terms of Figure 2.4, the supply schedule would be flat at a wage w^*, the subsistence wage. In this situation of a perfectly elastic labor supply curve, the quality of the marginal land still interacts with the cost of labor to determine the rent on the intramarginal plots. The rent on the intramarginal plots is still differential rent and Ricardian rent in the same sense that such rents were defined for the case of a rising supply curve of labor.

As an empirical matter, observers were unsure when population growth would push wages to subsistence and bring the genuinely marginal plots into production. In fact, the doctrine was slowly abandoned as industrialization and technical progress continually short-circuited the supposed decline in wages. New demands for labor arose, offsetting the effect of population growth in forcing down wages. The Malthusian vision was revived in the late 1960s in Jay Forrester's *World Dynamics* and in a report of the Club of Rome, *Limits to Growth* (see Chapter 6). Population is anticipated to press hard on the world's natural resource base generally. To people of the nineteenth century, available land represented the world's relevant natural resource base. Relatively small demands were being imposed on stocks of oil and minerals until the twentieth century.

BOX 2.1
Land Use in the United States

Of the 2.2 billion acres (890,308,000 hectares) in the United States, 17 percent is tilled for farming, 30 percent is in grass and pasture, 32 percent is wooded. Only 1.5 percent is used for cities, and 70 percent of the population lives in those cities and outlying areas, occupying 2 percent of the land. The market value of the land in 1980 was estimated at $1,500 billion. There is on average 10 acres per person.

The federal government is the dominant owner with 96 percent of Alaska, 86 percent of Nevada, 45 percent of California, 33 percent of New Mexico, down to .6 percent of Maine. There are also thousands of laws and statutes at the federal, state, and local levels regulating privately owned land. For example, in the 1960s the Department of Agriculture was paying farmers to keep 50 million acres of farmland idle. Remarkably, it is estimated that 95 percent of all private land is owned by just 3 percent of the population. This in large part reflects the

Table 1 TOTAL U.S. POPULATION, NUMBER OF FARMS, AND USE IN FARMS, 1800 TO 1975

Year	Population (millions) Total	Farm	Number of farms (thousands)	Land in farms (million acres) Total	Cropland	Pasture
1800	5.8			(69)	(21)	
1810	7.2			(86)	(26)	
1820	9.6			(115)	(34)	
1830	12.9			(155)	(46)	
1840	17.1			(205)	(61)	
1850	23.2		1449	294	(88)	
1860	31.4		2044	407	(122)	
1870	39.8		2660	408	(123)	
1880	50.2	22.0	4009	536	(161)	
1890	62.9	24.8	4565	623	166	
1900	76.0	29.9	5740	841	283	
1910	92.0	32.1	6366	881	311	
1920	105.7	32.0	6454	959	349	
1925	115.8	31.2	6372	924	505	218
1930	122.8	30.5	6295	990	522	270
1935	127.2	32.2	6812	1054	514	311
1940	131.7	30.5	6102	1065	531	394
1945	139.9	24.4	5859	1142	451	481
1950	150.7	23.0	5388	1162	478	417
1955	165.3	19.1	4654	1202	460	460
1960	179.3	15.6	3962	1177	448	466
1965	194.3	12.4	3356	1140	434	490
1970	203.2	9.7	2954	1103	459	389
1975	213.6	8.9	2314	1107	467	

Source: M. Clawson, "Forests in the Long Sweep of American History," Science, 204 (June 15, 1979), pp. 1168–1174. Copyright 1979 by the AAAS.

Table 2 LAND IN FORESTS IN THE UNITED STATES, 1630 TO 1977

Year	Land in commercial forest (million acres) Total	Land in noncommercial forest (million acres) Total	Standing sawtimber volume (million acres) Total
1630	850	100	
"Original"	828		7625
"Original"	850		5200
1800			
1895			2300
1900 to 1908			
1902			2000
1905			1970
1907	580		
1908			2500
1909			2826
1920	464	150	2215
1930	495	120	1668
1938	462	168	1764
1944	461	163	1601
1952	495	163	2412
1962	508		2430
1970	500	254	2421
1977	488	252	2569

Source: M. Clawson, "Forests in the Long Sweep of American History," *Science,* 204 (June 15, 1979), pp. 1168–1174. Copyright 1979 by the AAAS.

fact that a small fraction of the population lives outside the urban areas, but also reflects the fact that many farms are very large and many are owned by large corporations. Fifty percent of farms as firms disappeared between 1960 and 1980 in the United States while total acres in farming remained unchanged. Consolidation was under way. Del Monte operates 11 farms in the United States and owns 96,400 acres, and Tenneco owns 86,000 acres of farmland. Then other corporations have large holdings of land: Exxon, 40 million acres. Though use patterns have stabilized in the aggregate, according to Marion Clawson, regulations and the distribution of ownership may continue to change markedly.

Source: Peter Meyer. "Land: The Vast Estate—The American Dream," *The American Annual 1980,* Grolier, pp. 51–58.

Institutional Arrangements: The Role of Market Structure and Property Rights in the Determination of Rent

How much land is used productively and at what price is a function of the ownership arrangements and property rights in society. In our single-plot illustration, we had a single owner who varied the employment of labor until the rent or surplus from land was at a maximum. Suppose the landowner operated in a competitive market — where there were many such plots of land. How would the equilibrium obtained by the landowner compare to that of a government-managed property? If the land were controlled by a government planner charged with maximizing public welfare, we assume the planner would maximize the consumer and producer surplus[1] in the market for the wheat grown on each plot of land. We can look at one plot in this competitive market and extend the result to all the other plots. The planner would choose a labor force N, such that the welfare function in equation (2.1) was at a maximum

$$W = B(q(N)) - p100N \qquad (2.1)$$

where W = aggregate consumer plus producer surplus
   $B(q)$ = the area under the demand curve for wheat at each quantity of wheat produced
   p = the equilibrium "price" of wheat, 100 bushels is the annual payment in wheat per worker

The function $q(N)$ shows how much output is obtainable with different numbers of workers; it is a simple production function. Maximizing W by choice of N results in $MP_N = 100$, where MP_N is again the marginal product of a worker.[2] This condition for hiring labor is the same as the one we observed for the case of a single private landowner. This implies an important principle: *Privately organized production on land yields the socially efficient outcome.*

Suppose that there is no unique owner of a parcel of land, nor any government planner to allocate labor. If anyone is free to use the land however he or she sees fit, we have what has come to be known as a *common property* or *open access* arrangement. In this case each worker is concerned only with whatever he or she can "take" from the land. Since there is no landowner trying to maximize rent from the land, the landowner's "take" is available to be shared among the workers. Is each worker better off in this common property arrangement? As long as there is open access to the land, the worker is no better off under common property than under private property arrangements. Any surplus income to a worker above his or her market wage induces "outside workers" to come in to work the land and receive the going share of product. *If such entry by outside workers is unrestricted and product is shared equally among all workers who enter and work the plot, the return per worker will be driven down to the market wage of 100 bushels per year.* Aggregate employment will increase, but the return per worker will not. A new equilibrium emerges in which the average product of each worker equals the wage attainable in other sectors of the economy. This is a common-property, open-access equilibrium (see Figure 2.5).

In Figure 2.5, the equilibrium under a common-property free-entry regime occurs with labor at N_{CP}. Average product per worker equals the wage, and there is no surplus to go to the worker or to a landlord. Corresponding to N_{CP}, will be a total output of wheat $q(N_{CP})$ greater than that occurring with a single owner or under government management. The private property equilibrium utilizes N_{SO} workers and yields a rent abc to the landlord. Total output of wheat under private property is

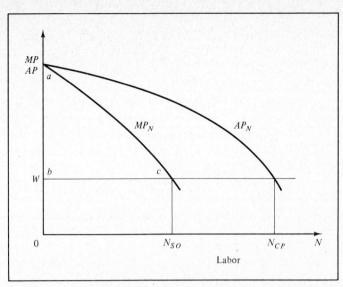

Figure 2.5 A private landowning equilibrium has N_{SO} workers on the plot of land and total rent or income to the landlord of area *abc*. A common property system in which the working laborers use the land in common has N_{CP} workers on the plot in equilibrium and no income left for a landowner. Rent is said to be dissipated under common property.

$q(N_{SO})$, which is less than $q(N_{CP})$. The common property solution leads to excessive use of labor and produces too much output compared to the efficient solution of the single owner, which we saw was socially optimal. Alternatively, for a given amount of labor, aggregate output on the land is not as large as it could be in the absence of a common property approach.

Example. Suppose we have a plot of land. The production function relating labor to output is given by $q = 12N - 2N^2$ per day. Suppose the wage rate is $8 per worker per day. Equating average product per person to the wage yields the common property solution. We find that $8 = 12 - 2N$ or $N = 2$. With 2 workers, total output will be 16, and output per worker equal to 8.

If the marginal product of labor is equated to the wage rate, the private property solution is obtained. We find that $8 = 12 - 4N$ and $N = 1$. Total output is now 10 bushels, resulting in output per worker in the economy of 10 bushels as well. This illustrates the efficiency of the private property allocation of workers, which equalizes marginal products. The equity or fairness of distributing the total product among the workers is a separate issue.

Common property with free entry of "owners" involves excessive use of variable inputs and excessive output. Moreover, the workers are no better off; they receive the same wage although more may be employed. This latter statement is not true if the *supply schedule for labor is rising,* as it was in Figure 2.4. When more labor is used, workers receive a higher wage. Because the common property equilibrium results in higher levels of employment than under private property (as shown in

BOX 2.2
The Enclosure Movement and the Allocation of
Workers on Land

Cohen and Weitzman contend that the equalization of average product per worker on land is a good description of English agriculture before the enclosure of commonly held lands or before the mid-fifteenth century. In the pre-enclosure era, many agricultural workers moved about in an effort to improve their position. Tradition was the force regulating the allocation of resources. For the landlord, land was a means of obtaining loyalty, esteem, military aid, and power, rather than merely a source of income. In short the medieval landlord was not an income or land rent maximizer. However, an exogenous rise in a capitalistic ethic occurred, transforming these landlords into income maximizers, and this resulted in (a) the enclosure of the commons and (b) the allocation of workers to land so that the marginal product of each worker on different plots of land was equal (the land rent maximizing condition.) This enclosure movement took place mostly from the mid-fifteenth to the mid-eighteenth centuries. Adam Smith's *The Wealth of Nations,* heralding a new industrial capitalistic era, was published in 1776. Cohen and Weitzman emphasize that the principles governing the allocation of labor before and after the enclosure movement define general tendencies, and much variation should be expected: "It is not the amount of variance that is important for our purposes so much as the central principle around which variation is occurring" (p. 317).

Their approach leads to the following predictions in the transformation to the private ownership of the commons: (1) Peasants are displaced from the newly enclosed land, (2) the standard of living of the working population declines, (3) aggregate rents rise and the surplus increases, (4) less labor-intensive techniques are used on the newly enclosed land, (5) the population of other villages rises, (6) new lands are brought into cultivation, (7) national income is higher, (8) agricultural output is produced more efficiently, (9) the terms of trade move in favor of agriculture against industry, and (10) there is a net flow of labor out of agriculture. They cite evidence to support their view that indeed these predictions from their model were realized in England. They dispute the contention of some historians that a substantial exogenous increase in population took place over this three-hundred-year period of the enclosure movement. They suggest that the casual evidence of increased number of vagrants and paupers fits well with their theory and is a dubious clue supporting the view of an increase in population. Data are not available to settle these debates definitely. The Cohen-Weitzman analysis is labelled Marxian because the initiator of change was the rise of the "capitalist mentality," a point emphasized by Marx.

Source: J. S. Cohen and M. L. Weitzman. "A Marxian Model of Enclosures," *Journal of Development Economics,* 1 (1975) pp. 287–236.

Figure 2.5), each worker is better off under common property. From an income distribution perspective, the common property solution is advantageous to workers in certain situations, and this advantage could motivate them to reorganize the institutional setting of wheat production. The reverse is also true. If one person can claim the land and hire workers, that person can earn rent. This may lead to a substantial reduction in the labor force. We return to these issues in Chapter 8 in our discussion of the fishery, a natural resource often characterized by open access.

LOCATION AND LAND VALUE
The Price of an Acre of Land

We derive schedules of prices for pieces of land in different locations—schedules called *bid-rent curves*. The land is heterogeneous, since different pieces are in different locations and thus have different values.

Suppose that in adding workers to land on a large farm, some must be active farther from a central place where the output is processed than others. Some product will be used up in payment to get the output to the processing place. Diminishing productivity can now take two forms simultaneously. On a fixed parcel of land, more workers will eventually lead to diminishing marginal product per worker (for a given amount of capital). By adding land farther from the central processing point, output per acre and per worker can fall as higher transportation costs are incurred on the more distant land. Since we have dealt with the first form of diminishing productivity, let us turn to the second. To eliminate the first form of diminishing marginal product of labor, we assume that each acre requires exactly z workers (which means that there are fixed proportions of factor inputs used). Moreover, let each acre, when worked, yield y bushels of wheat. The price of a bushel of wheat delivered to the central point is $\$p$ and *transportation cost per bushel* is $\$t$ per unit distance. This implies that revenue to pay labor and land per bushel at distance x from the central processing point is $p - tx$. This must equal labor cost per bushel $w(z/y)$, where z/y is workers per bushel, plus land rent. Thus

$$p - tx - w\frac{z}{y} \qquad \text{land rent} \qquad (2.2)$$

is the revenue per bushel left to be allocated to land at x. Multiplying by y (bushels per acre) yields $\$$ per acre at distance x, or Equation (2.3):

$$y\left(p - tx - w\frac{z}{y}\right) \qquad (2.3)$$

which is $\$$ per acre of land rent at distance x.

Observe that adjacent to the processing place where x is zero, rent per acre is simply revenue per acre less wage costs per acre—that is, $y[p - w(z/y)]$. Transportation costs "eat up" all of net revenue or rent when at distance x, $y[p - tx - w(z/y)] = 0$. x is the *margin of cultivation* beyond which there is negative profit from working the land in the current activity. We summarize in Figure 2.6. The linear schedule is called a *rent-distance function* or a *bid-rent schedule*. It indicates at each

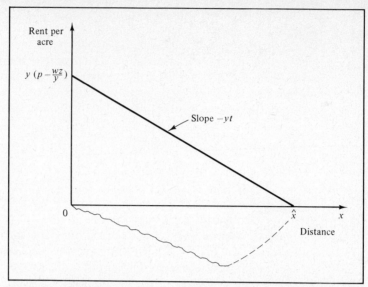

Figure 2.6 Each acre in a line is a different distance from the center. More distant land is less valuable because it is more costly to access. Rent per acre declines from the center with slope $-yt$, and beyond $\hat{x}$ land is unprofitable to use. Maximum rent occurs on the most accessible acres—namely, at the central point. The dashed line indicates that the distance $\hat{x}$ is a radius that swings forward on the page through 360°.

distance from the central processing point how much revenue is left to be assigned to the land input.

By introducing some explicit geographical detail, we are able to move from our earlier treatment of land rent as an aggregate on a parcel of land to *land rent per acre*. This was the approach used by a nineteenth-century economist, von Thunen, to analyze how best to use a large tract of land for raising diverse crops. He arrived at this principle: rent per acre at *the geographic margin between competing uses must be equal*. This is analogous to the principle that a homogeneous input should receive the same payment in every competing use if efficient use of the input as an aggregate is being achieved. For example, identical workers should get the same wage in different lines of activity if labor is being used most efficiently.

Efficient Land Use with Two Competing Uses

Consider two activities, say different crops, competing for land for production. The landowner will want to maximize the surplus, aggregate rent, or profit from using land. To this end, the owner will calculate different amounts of surplus associated with different land use patterns and select that pattern of uses which maximizes aggregate surplus. Given a single processing point and homogeneous land surrounding the point, the relevant patterns involve different concentric *annuluses* (donut-shaped areas) around the central point.

For a given radiuses x_1 and x_2 (one radius for each land use pattern), total rent is the volume under a circular "tent" formed by rotating our rent schedules 360 de-

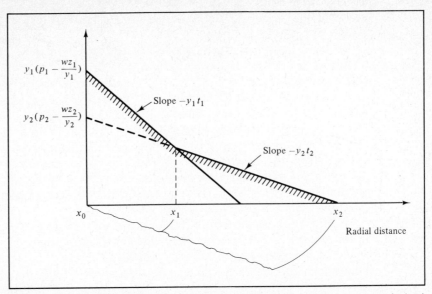

Figure 2.7 For competing land uses, activity 1 outbids activity 2 close to the center for land, and vice versa beyond boundary x_1 between the competing uses. At the boundary x_1 rents on either side are the same. Since x_1 and x_2 are radiuses, they swing forward to form circular rings.

grees. This "tent" or rent in Figure 2.7 has the following expression (which some readers may wish to ignore):

$$R = 2\pi y_1 \left\{ \left(p_1 - \frac{wz_1}{y_1} \right) \left[\frac{x_1^2 - x_0^2}{2} \right] - t_1 \left[\frac{x_1^3 - x_0^3}{3} \right] \right\}$$
$$+ 2\pi y_2 \left\{ \left(p_2 - \frac{wz_2}{y_2} \right) \left[\frac{x_2^2 - x_1^2}{2} \right] - t_2 \left[\frac{x_2^3 - x_1^3}{3} \right] \right\} \qquad (2.4)$$

where subscript 1 refers to relevant variables for a crop in the inner ring and subscript 2 refers to variables for the crop in the outer ring.

Maximizing R by choice of boundary 1, namely x_1, yields

$$y_1 \left(p_1 - t_1 x_1 - \frac{wz_1}{y_1} \right) = y_2 \left(p_2 - t_2 x_1 - \frac{wz_2}{y_2} \right) \qquad (2.5)$$

which means rent per acre at x_1 should be the same for the competing land uses on either side of the boundary at x_1. This is the principle of efficient use of land.

Maximizing R by choice of boundary x_2 yields

$$y_2 \left(p_2 - t_2 x_2 - \frac{wz_2}{y_2} \right) = 0 \qquad (2.6)$$

or rent falls to zero beyond x_2. We illustrate this equilibrium[3] in Figure 2.7.

In Figure 2.7 we have a rent-distance function in two distinct segments (the cross-hatched schedule which combines both segments is the relevant one). Observe that crop 1 can outbid crop 2 for land close to the center at x_0 and crop 2 can outbid crop 1 for land farther from the center. That is, rent is higher per acre close to x_0 by allocating land to raising crop 1 and is higher per acre beyond x_1 by allocating land to raising crop 2.

Clearly the values of the slopes of the segments in Figure 2.7 and the intercepts on the vertical axis are crucial for getting the pattern we indicate. If the intercept for crop 1 were below that for crop 2 and the slopes were the same, it would be *inefficient to produce any of crop 1*. All land should be devoted to crop 2 in such circumstances. Also with different slopes and intercepts, the allocation of crops could be reversed — it could be more efficient to produce crop 1 farther from the center.

For more than two crops or more than two competing uses, the principle remains the same: *An efficient or rent-maximizing solution involves equalizing rent per acre at the margin between competing uses.* The subsidiary principle is that the appropriate use of an area of land requires that the rent generated per acre exceed the rent from competing activities.

The equilibrium in Figure 2.7 would change as exogenous conditions changed. If, for example, labor became more efficient, z, the number of workers per acre, would decline. This would cause the rent-distance schedule to shift up, leaving the slope unchanged; consider a smaller z_1 in equation (2.5). If this occurred for crop 1 only, then the acreage devoted to crop 1 would increase at the expense of crop 2. The landowner would get more rent, and the total labor used would decline. (There would be fewer workers per acre for crop 1, but more acres of crop 1 cultivated involving more workers. Workers on crop 2 would be displaced because crop 2 would be reduced in total output.)

If land became more productive, y would increase exogenously. The intercepts and slope of the rent-distance schedule would rise. If y_1 increased, then x_1 would increase and the rent-distance schedule would rise, causing crop 1 to outbid crop 2 for some land at x_1 — consider a larger y_1 in equation (2.5). Rent from crop 1 would rise and more workers would be hired to cultivate crop 1. Some workers cultivating crop 2 would be displaced as the area devoted to crop 2 declined.

An improvement in transportation facilities would have unit distance cost, t, decline. This would flatten a rent-distance schedule (the function will have a smaller negative slope). If t_1 were to decrease for crop 1, then x_1 would increase as crop 1 "encroached" on crop 2's area and rent arising from the use of land in crop 1 would rise, as would overall rent from the land used — consider a smaller t_1 in equation (2.5).

Intermediate Goods and Mixing Land Uses

Each subarea above is devoted to one of a number of competing uses. This seems to be an appropriate description of land use for agriculture. We can also think of competing land uses for natural environments. Recreation is typically incompatible with mining activities in the same area. But we can think of subareas as "producing" different types of urban activities simultaneously, such as retailing, residential housing, business services, heavy industrial activity, and so on. In the use of natural environments, hydroelectric power generation or forestry may be compatible with recreation activities. Under some conditions, it may be efficient to mix different activities within a subarea and in other cases to keep distinct activities separate.

Mixing can occur in a subarea if the distinct activities are technologically interdependent, as occurs with intermediate goods or joint products.

Suppose each unit of industrial activity requires 0.7 units of business services and each activity requires land. Depending on the cost of transporting business services relative to the outputs of industrial activity, we can observe mixed land use in subareas, or separate land uses in distinct areas. These results can be derived by setting up a rent-maximizing model and examining how the equilibrium varies as relative transportation costs vary (see Appendix A at the end of this book).

Neoclassical Land Use Patterns

Suppose that workers travel to the fields each day from a central place and must transport themselves back and forth at positive cost. A worker's net wage, per month, say, becomes $w - tx$, where t is the round-trip commuting cost to x for a month and w is the gross wage. Now we return to our earlier case in which there are variable proportions of land and labor used to produce output or crops. Suppose there is a neoclassical production function relating output q to inputs N for labor and L for land. The adjective "neoclassical" denotes constant returns to scale in production and variable proportions with diminishing marginal products for inputs. We can analyze land use and input intensities quite generally with diagrams, some familiar from elementary microeconomic theory.

In Figure 2.8(a), we start with an isoquant for producing one bushel of wheat with variable proportions of land and labor. Under constant returns to scale, all other isoquants will be scaled-up or scaled-down versions of this unit isoquant. At different distances, x, from the central point, the effective wage rate for working the land at x is $w - tx$, or the gross wage net of round-trip traveling costs. As long as wheat is produced at x, the residual payment goes to land, leaving a price per unit of land at x of $r(x)$. Thus, in Figure 2.8(a) we can obtain a schedule of $r(x)$s by rotating the input price line along the isoquant, and a schedule of effective input intensities or labor/land ratios at different xs. These are plotted in Figure 2.8(c) and (b), respectively. In Figure 2.8(a), we have two specific input price ratios and the corresponding two points, for $x = 0$ and $x = 2$ are indicated in Figure 2.8(b) and (c).

If the isoquant were L-shaped with a sharp corner, the rent-distance schedule in (c) would decline linearly and the labor/land ratio would be the same for all x. Then we would have a situation like that in the von Thunen case. Given Figure 2.8(a), the rent-distance function must be convex as in Figure 2.8(c), and the labor/land ratio will be convex as in Figure 2.8(b). The effective wage rate declines more slowly than the land price, causing the factor proportions in Figure 2.8(b) to be observed.

With two different crops, there will be different production functions and consequently different isoquants (different unit isoquants in "location" in a land-labor diagram such as 2.8(a) and in shape). Efficient land use will once again involve these conditions: (a) the crop grown at x will bid more for land than other crops can bid; and (b) at the margin between competing uses (crops), land rent will be equal on both sides of the boundary. We sketch a possible land use pattern for three competing uses in Figure 2.9. The dashed lines are the bid-rent schedules for regions in which a crop cannot "outbid" another crop for land. The solid line is the observed rent-dis-

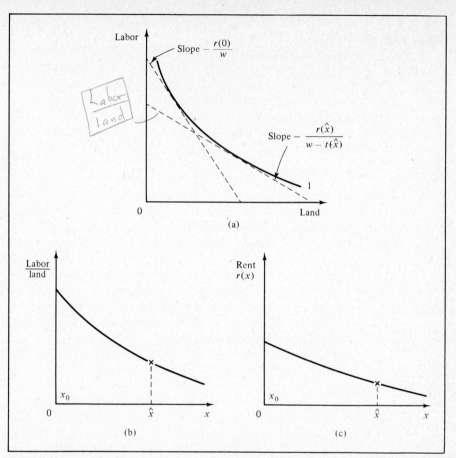

Figure 2.8 In (a) we have an isoquant for producing 1 unit of wheat using labor and land in variable proportions. Farther from the central point the effective wage rate is less, since workers pay a cost of getting back and forth to the field. Hence, different proportions of labor to land are used at different distances as shown in (b). In (c) we observe a convex rent distance schedule for this model with variable input proportions.

tance or bid-rent schedule. For example, crop 1 grown between radius 0 and x_1 cannot "outbid" crops grown beyond x_1.

At x_3, land rent has fallen to zero. Alternately, there may be a positive residual rent it falls to, say for land in a basic use such as sheep farming.

Restricting our attention to land use patterns in concentric rings or parts of rings around a central point is convenient but not essential to our argument concerning conditions for efficient land use. The notion that land has value relative to its accessibility is basic, so *transportation costs as well as intrinsic fertility or productivity play a role in determining the relative price of a particular plot*. We have illustrated this using the convenient and traditional circular geography. Charles Ellet (1839), an American civil engineer, worked out some of the basic principles of efficient land use by analyzing patterns of use around rivers, canals, and ports on coasts given transportation improvements.

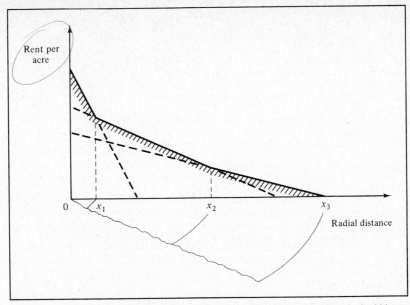

Figure 2.9 A three-competing-crop example. The solid cross-hatched line is the bid-rent schedule. Note how the efficient activity can outbid the competitive activities for its land. The overall effective rent-distance schedule is a series of flat segments with an overall convex shape.

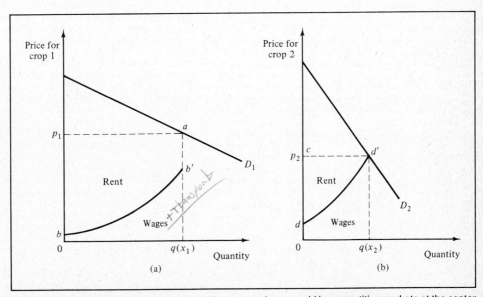

Figure 2.10 Crops from land areas with radiuses x_1 and x_2 are sold in competitive markets at the center. Here are the resulting supply-demand schedules with land use implicit. The marginal bushel of crop 1 earns positive land rent, distance ab' in dollars. The marginal bushel of crop 2 earns no rent, since it is grown at the geographic margin of land use.

Institutional Arrangements and Land Use Patterns

So far, we have treated the price of output, say wheat, as a given in our analysis of rent per acre. But suppose the demand curve for wheat was downward-sloping or had less than infinite elasticity. A government planner would maximize consumer and producer surplus from the land. Land rent is the producer surplus, and the resulting land use pattern would be similar to those above. Suppose again that we have two crops with radiuses x_1 and x_2 from the central processing point. The demand and supply curves are shown in Figure 2.10. Each crop faces a downward-sloping demand curve. Supply is shown by the curve $b'b$ in (a) and dd' in (b). These curves are based on the land use diagram of Figure 2.7. Producer surplus is land rent that does not fall to zero at the margin x_1 with crop 1 because of the presence of the second crop. Crop 1 is the intramarginal crop, and all output produced on that land earns positive rent.

Observe in Figure 2.10(b) that rent on the marginal bushel on the marginal land does fall to zero—x_2 being the distance at which rent is assumed to have declined to zero in the corresponding rent-distance diagram. Notice also that *rents per bushel are not equal at the margin between crops (distance ab' does not equal distance cd). Rent per acre is equal at the margin, not rent per bushel, and our supply and demand diagrams are for outputs of crops.*

A monopolist selling the outputs would maximize profits by setting his marginal cost equal to marginal revenue (not price) for each crop and skimming off its profit or surplus from monopoly control of the sale of the outputs (see Figure 2.11). There is both land rent and monopoly rent or surplus. Output is determined where

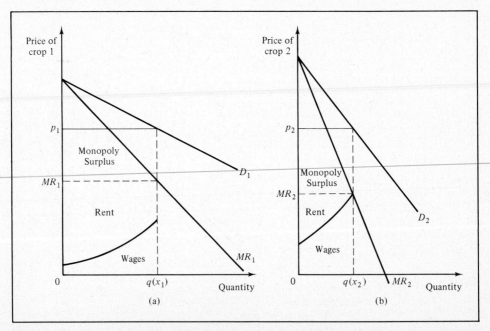

(a)   (b)

Figure 2.11 Compare this figure with Figure 2.10. Here we have monopoly in the two markets for crops. Hence monopoly surplus exists as indicated. Less of each crop will be produced and less land used. However, at the margin between uses, rent per acre will be the same in the competing uses.

marginal revenue equals wages plus land rent. At this output, $q(x_1)$, the monopolist receives price, p_1, as determined by the demand curve D_1. The selling price charged by the monopolist exceeds marginal revenue on the sale of output, as in a standard monopoly model. A monopoly surplus results.

A different land use pattern emerges under monopoly because the output of each crop has fallen relative to the nonmonopoly situation. *Less land will be used.* However, at the margin between crops, land rent per acre will be equal and land use will be determined by that activity which can bid most per acre. This reflects a general phenomenon: Monopolists use inputs efficiently, but they price their output so as to restrict the maximum welfare achievable from given resources. They generally produce less than optimal amounts at excessively high prices.

BOX 2.3
Water Allocation and the Colorado River

In the western United States the legal environment for water allocation is based on the *doctrine of appropriative water rights.* The circumstances are such that a user generally depletes the water supply available to others. In times of a shortfall, the appropriative doctrine indicates that those users who acquired rights first in time may draw on the supply ahead of subsequent users. The queue is based on history, not on a measure of the user's contribution to aggregate well-being. Actually, in times of emergency, the priority is, in order, municipal and domestic, irrigation, and finally commercial and industrial. (The *riparian water rights doctrine* descending from English common law assigns user rights to the landowner whose property borders on the water. The presumption is that one user's "consumption" of water will not affect the supply available to others on the water body.) Burness and Quirk (1980), using the Colorado River system as an illustration, point out that a competitive market in water use rights would be more efficient (yield more dollar benefits to producers and consumers for a given volume of water available) than allocation under the doctrine of appropriative water rights. In particular, they would like to see a transfer of water from the Imperial and Coachella irrigation districts to the Metropolitan Water District in Southern California. A surplus for export from one jurisdiction could be generated by basic conservation methods, such as lining irrigation aqueducts.

The Colorado River Basin comprises California, Mexico, Arizona, New Mexico, Nevada, Utah, Colorado, and Wyoming, and the annual runoff of 13.5 million acre feet (MAF) is very carefully allocated: 1.5 MAF go to Mexico as required by treaty, and the rest is consumed for agricultural, domestic, municipal, and industrial use or stored. The Colorado River Basin comprises 240,000 square miles of drainage area. This is relatively large, and, of course, the runoff has no feasible substitute to keep the southwest United States alive.

The Colorado River Compact of 1922 divided the waters of the Colorado between the Upper and Lower Basin states. Colorado, Wyoming, Utah, and New Mexico comprise the Upper Basin group while California, Arizona, and

Box 2.3 continued

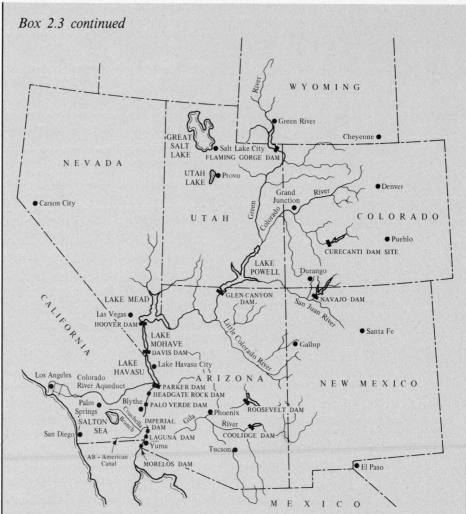

Figure B2.1   The Colorado River Basin. *Source:* Annual Report, 1975, Colorado River Board of California.

New Mexico comprise the Lower Basin group (see Figure B2.1). The compact required 7.5 MAF to be delivered to the Lower Basin states. In fact, 8.25 MAF have been received in recent years. Netting out the Mexican allotment leaves 6.75 MAF for Lower Basin use. Arizona's recent allocation is 1.2 MAF, California's is 5.0 MAF, and Nevada's is 0.1 MAF. However, the Central Arizona Project (CAP), due to be completed in 1985 will result in new allotments. Available water for Arizona will be 2.5 MAF, for California 4.0 MAF, and for Nevada 0.29 MAF. Clearly, California will suffer a most significant decline in its supply. Current action involves a program whereby the Metropolitan Water District (MWD) will spend hundreds of millions of dollars to line the All

American Canal and the Coachella Canal in order to augment the available flow. One-third of the power generated at the Hoover Dam is used to pump water up over the Palo Verde mountain range in order to reach users in metropolitan Southern California.

Source: H. S. Burness and J. P. Quirk, "Water Laws, Water Transfers, and Economic Efficiency: The Colorado River," *The Journal of Law and Economics,* 23 (April, 1980) pp. 111–134, and correspondence with Professor Quirk.

Transportation Costs and Aggregate Land Rents

The notion that relative accessibility (low or high transportation costs) of identical pieces of land implies relative value of the pieces (high or low prices for the land) has led to the doctrine that an improvement in accessibility or transportation costs should be reflected in a specific increase in land rent or the value of the land. This view has often been expressed in the phrase, "Transportation improvements are capitalized in land rents." Much attention has been devoted to this idea over many decades.

A recent discovery is that *differential aggregate rents in circular geographies are twice the size of aggregate transportation costs.*[4] Differential rents are rents in excess of those for competing uses. The measurement of these rents is based on the price at the boundary between the competing uses. Let the price of land at the boundary be r_A. This could be the price of land in agriculture onto which an urban area is encroaching. We will derive the basic result by calculating aggregate differential rents and aggregate transportation costs for our constant coefficient model. Total differential rent in Figure 2.6 is derived by sweeping the rent schedule through 360 degrees (a circle) and calculating the volume created. The value is

$$R = 2\pi y \left[\left(p - \frac{wz}{y} - \frac{r_A}{y} \right) \frac{x^{*2}}{2} - \frac{tx^{*3}}{3} \right] \tag{2.7}$$

where $x^* = (py - zw - r_A)/ty$ is the boundary which maximizes aggregate differential rent. All variables are the same as defined above. Total transportation costs are

$$T = \frac{2\pi ytx^{*3}}{3} \tag{2.8}$$

which appear in Equation (2.7) above. Now we substitute for x^*, and Equations (2.9) and (2.10) are obtained in their stark simplicity:

$$R = (M/2) - (M/3) \tag{2.9}$$

and $$T = M/3 \tag{2.10}$$

where $M = 2\pi yx^{*3}$. We have, from (2.9) and (2.10),

$$R = T/2. \tag{2.11}$$

or aggregate differential rent is one-half aggregate transportation costs.

The implication of this result is that a proportionate reduction in aggregate transportation costs results in an equal proportionate reduction in aggregate land rent. This is at odds with the traditional view that a decline in transportation costs *increases* land rent. The "one-half" rule is quite special. It holds for circular or portions of circular geographies; it deals with aggregates; it involves differential not total land rents; and it holds in equilibrium. It is a *curiosum* which alerts us to the more familiar statement that an exogenous change in transportation costs affects land rent in a way which depends on the technology, market conditions, and current values of parameters. This is another way of saying that exogenous changes in the parameters of a complex system affect endogenous magnitudes in complex ways.

We note a similar doctrine involving public sector improvements and property values. People take for granted that public sector improvements, such as a new park, will increase the value of nearby property. They then try to relate these changes in property value very precisely to the public sector improvement. One version of these efforts is the neo-Henry George literature, which relates the value of public goods to the value of land in a locality (see for example, Stiglitz, 1977, and Hartwick, 1980). The striking proportionalities observed with transportation costs above still hold for special cases. One should really look at changes in public sector improvements and property values with a case-by-case approach. This caution applies also to valuation of the benefits of improvements in environmental quality (see Chapter 13).

SUMMARY

1. Land is a basic natural resource. Its value derives from its relative fertility and its relative accessibility. The value of land appears as a surplus or residual, or a differential rent relative to the marginal unit of land that earns no surplus. From a different point of view, the value of land is the surplus or residual earned by intramarginal variable inputs—the marginal variable input producing output resulting in no surplus. This we observed at the outset when labor, the variable input, was applied to a fixed plot of land.

2. The magnitude of the surplus or rent ascribable to land is important in measuring income shares of different groups in society. Different property rights arrangements can affect the size of the surplus. In the case of common ownership there will be no surplus, since the presence of surplus induces more people to enter the "common."

3. For efficiency, different plots of land must have variable inputs working them until the marginal product of the input on any plot is the same.

4. Accessibility of land involves transportation costs, and higher-valued plots have lower transportation costs and more surplus or land rent. It is the fact that each acre is generally at a different distance from a central node that makes even land of uniform fertility an essentially heterogenous input. Each acre has distinct economic characteristics. (For circular geographies, all plots equidistant from the center have the same accessibility characteristics.) An efficient land use arrangement involves adjacent small plots in competing uses earning the same price per acre. This condition results in aggregate land rent being a maximum, a related condition for an efficient land use pattern.

5. With output in one subarea required as an intermediate good in an adjacent

subarea, the "equal land rent at the margin" condition appears, but in a slightly different guise. In this case, there is the possible pattern of the two related activities sharing small subareas—a mixed or integrated land use pattern.

6. Factor proportions, say labor to land, can vary with accessibility in a smoothly substitutable neoclassical case. This represents an extension of the classical fixed coefficient land use model dating back to the nineteenth century.

7. In the case of improvements in transportation technology increasing land rents, we observed that special formulas are relevant only for special cases and that simple quantitative laws do not hold for a wide class of particular situations.

DISCUSSION QUESTIONS

1. One can think of a commodity, office services, as produced with the inputs floor space, location, and labor. To have floor space, one can have a low spread-out building or a high one with many stories. Does high-priced land result in tall buildings or do tall buildings cause land prices to be high in cities?

2. The value of land in an urban area can usually be represented as a tent-shaped rent surface with a single peak at the city center. Given two observations, rent at the center of a nearby city and rent at the fringe of the city, calculate the annual rental income arising from land in that particular city.

3. Urban sprawl annoys some people. In Vancouver, British Columbia, urban development was stopped by law along the south and east boundaries because the land was very good for agriculture. Evaluate how such regulations affect the long-term land use pattern—density and prices, beneficiaries and losers. (*Note:* to the north of Vancouver are steep mountains, and to the west is the Pacific Ocean.)

4. Suppose labor and fertilizer (another variable input) are used to produce crops from a piece of agricultural land. How much labor and fertilizer would the landowner use if the owner seeks to maximize land rent? Explain qualitatively the determination of the rent-maximizing solution.

5. How is rent determined on plots of land of differing quality? Does it matter whether the supply of factor inputs used on the land are perfectly elastic or not? Explain your answer. Suppose the factor supply curve is perfectly inelastic. What happens to land rent on each plot of land?

6. Distinguish between private property and common property management of land with regard to their use of factor inputs and production of output. Will the common property equilibrium always result in more production from the land? Explain. What are the welfare implications of common property ownership?

NOTES

1. Consumer surplus is a dollar measure of total utility from consuming a commodity net of the money put out to purchase the commodity. Producer surplus is total revenue to a producer net of the costs of all inputs.

2. Notice that $(dB/dq) = p$, the price of wheat. This indicates that a small change in gross consumer surplus (area under the demand curve) equals the price of the commodity in question.

3. The derivation of R involves summing rent per acre over all acres or integrating over a series of infinitesimal circular rings or annuluses. Before integrating,

$$R = \int_{x_0}^{x_1} 2\pi x y_1 \left(p_1 - tx - \frac{z_1 w}{y_1} \right) dx + \int_{x_1}^{x_2} 2\pi x y_2 \left(p_2 - t_2 x - \frac{z_2 w}{y_2} \right) dx$$

and R in the text results after carrying out the integration operations. Below we maximize R by differentiating with respect to x_1 and x_2 and set the expressions equal to zero.

4. An early statement of this was Mohring (1961). See the extensive discussion in Arnott and Stiglitz (1979).

chapter 3

Nonrenewable Resource Use: The Theory of Depletion

INTRODUCTION

Nonrenewable resources include energy supplies—oil, natural gas, uranium and coal—and nonenergy minerals—copper, nickel, bauxite, and zinc, to name a few. These resources are formed by geological processes that typically take millions of years, so we can view these resources for practical purposes as having a fixed *stock* of reserves. That is, there is a finite amount of the mineral in the ground, which once removed cannot be replaced.[1] Nonrenewability introduces some new problems and issues into the analysis of production from the mine or well that do not arise in the production of reproducible goods such as agricultural crops.

A mine manager must determine not only how to combine variable factor inputs such as labor and materials with fixed capital as does the farmer, but how quickly to run down the fixed stock of ore reserves through extraction of the mineral. A unit of ore extracted today means that less in total is available for tomorrow. Time plays an essential role in the analysis. Each period is different, because the stock of the resource remaining is a different size. What we are concerned with in an economic analysis of nonrenewable resources is how quickly the mineral is extracted—what the *flow* of production is over time, and when the stock will be exhausted.

In this chapter, we determine the efficient extraction path of the resource—the amount extracted in each time period. First, we examine the behavior of the individual mine operator. We then examine how a social planner would exploit the same deposit. Finally, we develop the extraction profile of a mining *industry*. In all cases, we assume that perfect competition prevails in every market. We derive the paths of mineral output, prices, and rents over time under varying assumptions about the nature of the mining process. The competitive equilibrium over time is compared to the socially optimal extraction path.

Our initial model is very simple and abstracts considerably from reality so that we can identify and examine basic concepts. The assumptions are gradually relaxed so that we can deal with increasingly complex but more realistic models. Relaxing the assumption of perfect competition is done in Chapter 4 and of certainty in Chapter 5. In examining the mine's and industry's extraction decision, we also illustrate the effects on output and prices over time of changes in particular variables affecting the mining process. What will be the effect on extraction over time of, for example, a change in extraction costs, the introduction of setup or capital costs, different qualities of ore, a change in the discount rate, the imposition of taxes?

THE THEORY OF THE MINE

We begin with a simple model of resource extraction from an individual mine which operates in a perfectly competitive industry. The mine owner will seek to maximize the present value of profits from mineral extraction in a manner similar to that of a manager of a plant producing a reproducible good. An output level must be chosen that maximizes the difference between total revenues—the discounted value of future extractions q_1, q_2, q_3, . . . etc., multiplied by price, p, and total cost—the discounted value of dollars expended in getting each q out of the ground. The presence of the finite stock of the mineral modifies the usual maximization condition; marginal revenue *(MR)* equals marginal cost *(MC)*, in three fundamental ways. Suppose we compare farming to copper extraction. The owner of the copper mine faces an opportunity cost not encountered by the farmer. This is the cost of using up the fixed stock at any point in time, or being left with smaller remaining reserves. To maximize profits, the operator must cover this opportunity cost of depletion. For a competitive firm manufacturing a reproducible good, the conditions for a profit maximum are to choose output such that $p(= MR) = MC$. The nonrenewable resource analogue requires $p = MC$ + the opportunity cost of depletion. How then would the mine owner measure this opportunity cost? It is the value of the unextracted resource, a resource rent related to those discussed in Chapter 2.

The second feature that differentiates nonrenewable resources from reproducible goods concerns the *value of the resource rent over time.* Deciding how quickly to extract a nonrenewable resource is a type of investment problem. Suppose one has a fixed amount of money to invest in some asset, be it a savings account, an acre of land, a government bond, or the stock of a nonrenewable resource in the ground. Which asset is purchased (and held on to over time) depends on the investor's expectation of the rate of return on that asset—the increase in its value over time. The investor obviously wants to purchase the asset with the highest rate of return. However, in a perfectly competitive environment with no uncertainty, all assets must, in a market equilibrium, have the same rate of return.

To see how this is so, consider what would happen if the economy had two assets, one that increased in value 10 percent per year, the other at 20 percent per year. Assume there is no risk associated with either asset. No one would invest in the asset earning only 10 percent; everyone would want the asset earning 20 percent. The price of the high-return asset would then increase, and the price of the low-return asset would decrease until their rates of return were equalized.

What exactly is the rate of return to a nonrenewable resource? The rate of return to the mine is the resource rent — the value of the ore in the ground. When there is a *positive* discount rate, the rent is positive and rises in nominal value as depletion occurs. If the resource rent did not increase in value over time, no one would purchase the mine, because the rate of return on alternative assets would be more valuable. In addition, the owner of an existing deposit would attempt to extract all the ore as quickly as is technically feasible. Why should one hold on to ore in the ground that is increasing in value at a rate less than can be earned on, say, a savings account? Alternatively, if the value of the ore is growing at a rate in excess of what one could earn in an alternative investment, there is no incentive to extract at all. Ore left in the ground is then more valuable to the mine owner than ore extracted. To have mineral extraction then, the rental value of the mineral must be growing at the same rate as that of alternative assets.

There is one final condition imposed on the mine owner that does not occur with reproducible goods. The total amount of the natural resource extracted over time cannot exceed its total stock of reserves. We call this the *stock constraint*.

Let us draw these strands together for the first time. Suppose a mine owner has a plan of quantities extracted roughly worked out by a rule of thumb. It remains to make the extraction plan somewhat "tighter." Should he extract one more ton of ore in this year's liftings or leave it for next year's liftings. If he *takes it out this year* and gets $10 profit, he can put that profit (rent) in the bank at, say, 8 percent and have $10(1.08) = $10.80 next year. If he leaves it in the ground and *takes it out next year,* he foresees that he will get a different price and can reap a profit (rent) of $11. In this case he will make more money by deferring extraction of the extra ton until next year. (If he were to get only $10.75 upon extracting next year, it would pay to extract currently and sell the ore this year.) By doing this calculation repeatedly the mine owner arrives at the best extraction plan year by year. Let us now examine the important features of nonrenewable resource extraction in more detail.

Extraction from a Mine Facing a Constant Price

One of the earliest economic analyses of mineral extraction appeared in 1914 in an article by L. C. Gray. In Gray's model, the owner of a small mine has to decide how much ore to extract and for how long a period of time. To solve this problem, Gray made a number of simplifying assumptions. First, he assumed that the market price of a unit of the mineral remained constant (in real terms) over the life of the mine. The producer knew the exact amount of reserves in the mine (the stock) prior to extraction. All the ore was of uniform quality. *Extraction costs then depended only on the quantity removed.*

We could view Gray's mine as a gigantic block of pure copper. Price per ton is constant forever, while the marginal cost of cutting off a piece of copper rises with the size of the piece cut off. If 1 ton of copper is cut off, it will cost $500 to remove. If 10 tons are cut off at once, the extraction costs could be $10,000. The economic problem is to cut off appropriate quantities in each period in order to maximize the present value of profits available from the stock of the mineral. The model has practical appeal, because in many mineral markets we do observe relatively constant prices over long periods of time.

To determine the efficient extraction path for the mine, we start with a simple illustration. Suppose the mine will operate for two periods only. The mine owner must determine how much copper to chop off the block today and tomorrow, using the three conditions identified earlier.[2] For the two-period case, these conditions can be stated as:

1. Price $= MC +$ rent in each period (in present value).
2. Rent today $=$ the present value of rent tomorrow.
3. Extraction today $+$ extraction tomorrow $=$ total stock of reserves.

The solution is shown in Figure 3.1. Assume that the mine has a U-shaped average cost curve *(AC)* and an upward-sloping marginal cost curve *(MC)* over some output range.[3] The constant price is shown as p. Output today is designated $q(0)$, output tomorrow is $q(T)$, where T signifies the end of the mining operation—the length of time the mine operates (in this case, two periods). Given these curves and the total stock of ore, there will be a unique solution to the extraction problem that satisfies all three conditions.

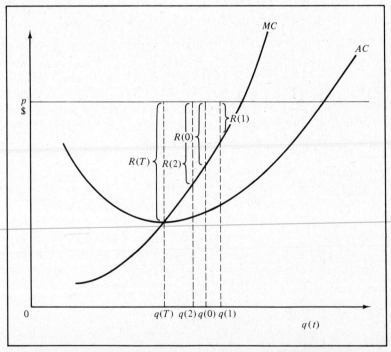

Figure 3.1   Mineral extraction in two periods when there is a constant price. The mine operator extracts the amount $q(0)$ today and $q(T)$ tomorrow. The sum of $q(0)$ plus $q(T)$ completely exhausts the mine's reserves. Rents are $R(0)$ today and $R(T)$ tomorrow, where it must be the case that $[R(0)](1 + r) = R(T)$, where r is the interest rate on alternative assets. Output levels $q(1)$ and $q(2)$ illustrate a plan that is not feasible because $q(1) + q(2)$ exceeds the total stock of reserves.

The mine owner must pick an initial output level where $p = MC + \text{rent}$. The resource rent obtained at the output level $q(0)$ is $R(0)$. This is condition 1. Notice that condition 1 defines rent as the difference between price and marginal cost. In the next period, extraction must equal $q(T)$ and the rent will be $R(T)$. It must be the case that $R(0) = R(T)/(1 + r)$, where r is the "market" interest rate or discount rate, the rate of return on any alternative asset.[4] This is condition 2. If rents did not rise at the rate of interest, extraction would not occur in both periods. If rent rose more slowly than the interest rate, the entire stock of ore would be extracted in the initial period and the proceeds of the sale invested in some other assets whose value would rise at the rate of interest (e.g., a savings account). If rent rose faster than the rate of interest, the entire stock of ore would be held in the ground until the last moment in time and then extracted. In this case, the mine is worth more unextracted because the rate of return on holding ore in the ground exceeds the return on alternative investments. Unless the rental value of the mine is growing at *exactly the same rate* as the value of other assets, extraction will either be as fast as possible or deferred as long as possible. Finally, output today and tomorrow must be chosen such that $q(0) + q(T) = S$, where S is the stock of mineral reserves. This is condition 3. For a given S, r, and p, there will be only one level of initial output and hence final output that satisfies all these conditions.

To see that $q(0)$ is unique, consider a case where the mine owner selects an initial output level greater than $q(0)$, say $q(1)$. The rent will then be $R(1)$ which is less than $R(0)$. Output in the second period must then be such that $R(1) = R(2)/(1 + r)$. This occurs at output $q(2)$. The mine owner will then have satisfied two of the three conditions (1 and 2), but notice that condition 3 is violated. The sum of $q(1) + q(2)$ must exceed S because they are both larger than previous outputs chosen. This extraction plan simply is not possible. The owner cannot extract more ore than exists in the mine. Suppose the sum of $q(0) + q(T)$ is less than S. Then the manager has ore remaining in the ground after extraction ceases, and revenue will be lost on the unextracted ore. A slightly higher extraction rate would yield additional profits.

This example can easily be extended to many periods of operation, but the same three conditions must be met. In addition, we can also tell when the mine will cease operation—how long T is. Refer again to Figure 3.1. It is not a coincidence that $q(T)$ is at the point where $MC = AC$. This point is called a *terminal condition* for the nonrenewable resource extraction problem. It has a clear economic interpretation. Consider any output level to the right or left of this point. If output in the final period is to the right of $q(T)$, the last unit of the mineral extracted will yield a marginal rent of $p - C'[q(T)]$ where $C'[q(T)]$ is marginal cost at $q(T)$. Each ton of the mineral mined in the last period will contribute an average rent of

$$\frac{pq(T) - C(q(T))}{q(T)}$$

or $p - AC$. By inspection, we can see that the average rent exceeds the marginal rent. It would therefore increase the present value of profits (rents) if the mine manager moved more tons of ore from the last period into the first period. Similarly, if marginal rent is greater than average rent at the last period ($MC < AC$), rents would be increased by moving ore in to the last period and out of the first period. Therefore, the optimal extraction plan must have the number of tons in the last period such that average rent is equal to marginal rent; that is,

$$\frac{pq(T) - C(q(T))}{q(T)} = p - C'(q(T))$$

In terms of Figure 3.1, average and marginal costs are equal at $q(T)$, and $q(T)$ is also that output which combined with $q(0)$ exhausts the mine. In the many-period case, the time to depletion will be such that all three extraction conditions are satisfied, plus the terminal condition. This will determine a unique T. Table 3.1 provides a numerical example of the efficient extraction path in a many-period situation. Price is constant at $10, and marginal cost rises at a 45-degree line from $MC = 1$ when quantity extracted in zero. In this example, 14.8 tons are extracted over seven periods, with quantity declining toward the final period of extraction: $q(0) = 3.9197$, $q(1) = 3.4117$, $q(2) = 2.853$, ... Between consecutive periods $(p - mc)(1 + r) = p - mc$ where $r = 0.1$, a 10 percent rate of interest. This is our condition that rent rises at the rate of interest. In the last period $p - mc = p - ac$, which is the condition for extracting the optimal amount in the last period (the terminal condition). Total profits evaluated in present value in period 0 are $94.4604.

Profit Maximization for the Mine[5]

Profit maximization involves making revenues large in relation to costs of production. There is a series of revenues minus costs each year or period into the future. Each instant in time is slightly different, since depletion of the stock is occurring year by year. Discounting with the current interest rate makes each annual profit value comparable to others at the date at the beginning of extraction. In the absence of discounting, recall that profit in year 8 in the future would be not comparable with profit in year 11. Each nominal value is different at any one point in time in the absence of discounting.

The conditions discussed for the mine facing a constant price will also hold in this more general model. For the mine owner, total discounted profits (the present value of profits) are

$$\pi = p \cdot q(0) - C(q(0)) + [p \cdot q(1) - C(q(1))] \left(\frac{1}{1 + r}\right)$$
$$+ [p \cdot Q(2) - C(q(2))] \left(\frac{1}{1 + r}\right)^2$$
$$+ \cdots + [p \cdot q(T) - C(q(T))] \left(\frac{1}{1 + r}\right)^T \tag{3.1}$$

Equation 3.1 is what the mine owner wants to maximize subject to the stock constraint which requires that

$$q(0) + q(1) + \cdots + q(T) \le S \tag{3.2}$$

Table 3.1 EXTRACTION FROM A MINE*

t	p − mc	mc	q	pq	ac	(p − ac)q	$\dfrac{(p-ac)q}{(1.1)^t}$
6	9	1	0	0	1	0	0
5	8.181818	1.818182	.818182	8.18182	1.409091	7.028927107	4.364410719
4	7.4380165	2.5619835	1.5619835	15.619835	1.7809918	12.83795519	8.768496134
3	6.761833	3.238167	2.238167	22.38167	2.1190835	17.63880724	13.25229695
2	6.1471211	3.8528789	2.8528789	28.528789	2.4264395	21.60645095	17.85657103
1	5.5882919	4.4117081	3.4117081	34.117081	2.7058541	24.88549665	22.62317877
0	5.0802654	4.9197346	3.9197346	39.197346	2.9598673	27.59545173	27.59545173
			14.802654				94.46040533

* A stock of 14.8 tons is extracted over seven periods in order to maximize the present value of profit (which ends up at $94.46). Price is constant at $10 and marginal extractions costs are linear and increasing. We solve by working back from period 6 to period 0. (Parameters: $r = 0.1$, $p = 10$, $mc = 1 + q$, $ac = 1 + 0.5q$, $S = 14.802654$.)

Equation (3.2) says that the sum of the quantities of ore extracted must not exceed the total stock of reserves available. The symbols used in Equations (3.1) and (3.2) are defined as follows:

p is the constant price per ton for the mineral
$q(t)$ is the quantity extracted in time t
$C[q(t)]$ is the total cost of extracting $q(t)$ tons of the mineral
t indicates the time period. Today is time 0, the next period is time 1, and so on. One can think of these periods as years
r is the discount or interest rate, which is assumed to remain constant over time
T is the number of periods over which the mine will be operated
S is the total stock of mineral reserves

All variables are interpreted in real (constant dollar) terms.

Maximizing this profit stream subject to the stock constraint on total output yields

$$p - c'(q(0)) = k$$

$$\left(\frac{1}{1+r}\right)[p - c'(q(1))] = k$$

$$\vdots$$

$$\left(\frac{1}{1+r}\right)^{T}[p - c'(q(T))] = k \qquad (3.3)$$

where c' means dC/dq and k is a constant dependent on the stock size S (k is called the shadow price of a unit of stock). The principle in action here is that the discounted value of the marginal ton taken out in any period must be the same for an extraction program to be profit-maximizing. If this were not the case, the mine operator could increase the return to the mine by shifting production to where the marginal ton earns a higher discounted value. $p - c'(q(t))$ is the value of the marginal or last ton taken out in period t. $(1/1 + r)^{t}[p - c'(q(t))]$ is its discounted value.

For adjacent periods in time we have

$$\left(\frac{1}{1+r}\right)^{t}[p - c'(q(t))] = \left(\frac{1}{1+r}\right)^{t+1}[p - c'(q(t+1))]$$

or

$$\frac{[p - c'(q(t+1))] - [p - c'(q(t))]}{[p - c'(q(t))]} = r \qquad (3.4)$$

which says that the percentage change in $p - c'$ between periods must equal the rate of interest. $p - c'$ is the *rent* on the marginal ton extracted. So we have the basic efficiency condition: *The percentage change in rent across periods equals the rate of interest.*

The terminal condition requires that the quantities chosen are those which maximize discounted total profits so that the average profit in the last period equals the marginal profit on the last ton extracted. This tells us how to terminate the sequence $q(1)$, $q(2)$, $q(3)$. This condition combined with the stock constraint makes sure that the sum of the qs equals the original stock. These two conditions are

$$\frac{pq(T) - C(q(T))}{q(T)} = p - c'[q(T)] \qquad (3.5)$$

and $\qquad\qquad\qquad q(1) + q(2) + \cdots + q(T) = S \qquad (3.6)$

These two conditions, in addition to the percentage change in rent condition, yield the profit-maximizing number of periods over which to exhaust the given stock.

Now we turn to mines with an ore quality which declines as extraction moves deeper into the mineral material. We are going to associate costs of extraction and processing with each unrefined ton, not with a "batch" of homogeneous stock as we did above. We no longer have a large homogeneous block of copper to cut away at.

Quality Variation Within the Mine

In the previous section, it was assumed that the cost of extraction rose only if more units of ore were extracted at any one time. Suppose now that the ore is not a chunk of pure copper as before, but consists of metal and waste rock. The metal is distributed throughout the waste rock in seams of varying thickness. The mine owner would like to extract from the thickest seams first, where the ratio of metal to waste rock is the highest. Suppose the deposit is laid down with richest seams on top. As the ore body is mined, the thicker seams are depleted and more waste rock must be removed to get at increasingly thinner seams. Mining costs rise per unit of metal produced simply because the metal content of the ore diminishes while the rock content increases. This means that the marginal cost of extracting and processing *each ton* of ore is different.

Extraction costs per ton shift up (increase) as subsequent amounts of ore are extracted. The flow condition for efficient extraction of the mineral (conditions 1 and 2, or Equation 3.4) is unchanged, but now holds for a single ton of ore of a specific quality (seam thickness). The mine owner can no longer slide down the marginal cost curve by extracting smaller amounts of ore over time to satisfy the conditions for efficient extraction because the marginal cost of extraction increases (shifts up) for each incremental ton of ore processed. To see what happens to the extraction path in this case, we turn to Figure 3.2.

The mine represented in Figure 3.2 illustrates a case where ore quality is continuously decreasing, and we are examining extraction over two periods of time. There are thus two curves of extraction cost per ton, one for period t and another for period $(t + 1)$, where the curve for $(t + 1)$ lies everywhere above that for period t, indicating that it will cost more to extract and process additional units of ore over time. The mine owner must determine how much ore to extract in periods t and $(t + 1)$ by following the flow condition. The quantity extracted in t must be chosen such that the rent on the last ton in the period will be exactly equal to the rent that ton could obtain if extracted in the next period, discounted by $(1 + r)$. Or, in terms of Figure 3.2, the rent on the marginal ton in the first panel of the figure is the amount ab if output is chosen at $q(t)$ and the price is $p(t)$. If the mine owner is to be indifferent between extracting the marginal ton in period t or in period $(t + 1)$, it must be the case

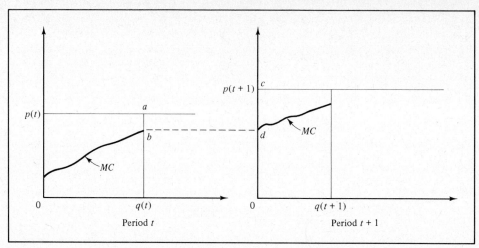

Figure 3.2 Quantity $q(t)$ in period t is set so that distance ab equals distance cd divided by $1 + r$. The marginal ton in period t gets rent ab and would get rent cd if it were extracted in period $t + 1$.

that the rent in $(t + 1)$ is equal to cd, where $cd = ab(1 + r)$. The marginal ton in period t is, we emphasize, the "least marginal" ton in period $(t + 1)$ because now every ton is of a different quality or has a different extraction and processing cost. This is what is illustrated by the higher marginal cost curve in the second panel of Figure 3.2.

The important implication of this analysis is that the market price must rise over time if extraction of lower-quality, higher-cost ore is to occur. If the mineral price does not rise to $p(t + 1)$ in the period $(t + 1)$, no extraction will occur in that period. Extraction will end with $p(t)$ equal to the extraction cost on the last ton taken out in period t. This possibility gives rise to another important distinction about the end of the mining operation. In the case of uniform ore quality, we argued that mining would cease when all the ore was removed. We can call this *physical* depletion or exhaustion.

Suppose, however, that the ore is not of uniform quality and the costs of extracting additional units rise, as Figure 3.2 shows. If the market price does not rise sufficiently to ensure that extraction proceeds from one period to another, the mine will shut down. If in period $(t + 1)$ the price is constant at $p(t)$, ore will be extracted to the point that $p(t)$ equals extraction cost. The mine is then said to have *economic* depletion in period t. It simply does not pay the mine owner to extract any ore beyond the quality indicated at $q(t)$, given the extraction cost curves and the price $p(t)$. A higher rate of return can be earned by taking the rent, ab, and investing it in an alternative asset which earns the market interest rate of r percent per year.

In a many-period model, the length of the extraction period will be determined by the time path of prices. For two prices in any consecutive periods, there will be only one value of cost per ton and hence output that satisfies the flow condition. The optimal life of the mine, the length of time to depletion (whether economic or physical), will then be determined by linking together quantities over subsequent periods until the flow condition no longer is satisfied, or the mine runs out of ore.

Mines frequently have valuable by-products. The mining of nickel in Canada yields profitable amounts of gold and platinum. It is straightforward to amend our model of the mine to incorporate this situation. Valuable rock, S_0, is defined such that for each scoop of size Q, there is $K(Q)$ of nickel and $G(Q)$ of gold. We continue to suppose that costs rise with the amount of rock, Q, processed. For p_K the net revenue for nickel, and p_G for gold, we get a revised pricing rule for optimal extraction:

$$\left(\frac{1}{1+r}\right)^t \left(p_K \frac{dK}{dQ(t)} + p_G \frac{dG}{dQ(t)} - \frac{dC}{dQ(t)}\right) = \text{constant for all } t$$

Now a weighted sum of prices net of costs increases at the rate of interest for the mine owner to be maximizing the discounted present value of profit: $dC/dQ(t)$ is the marginal cost of hoisting quantity $Q(t)$.

We have seen that when quality variation is introduced in either of two forms above that a simple rule such as "rent rising at the rate of interest" must be amended in an essential way. In other words, simple formulas are inadequate for characterizing real world extraction programs. Finally, note that because Gray's model is for a single firm, there is no discussion of the resource market and how (or if) mineral prices will rise to satisfy the flow condition and allow production to occur over time. To examine this important issue, we now turn to a model of a mineral industry.

EXTRACTION BY A MINERAL INDUSTRY
The Hotelling Model

In 1931, Harold Hotelling wrote a classic paper which examined the optimal extraction of a nonrenewable resource from the viewpoint of a social planning agency that had as its goal the maximization of social welfare from the production of minerals. The model was at the industry level rather than that of the single mine. Both Gray and Hotelling arrived at the same condition for the efficient extraction of a mineral — namely, that the present value of a unit of a homogeneous but finite stock of the mineral must be identical regardless of when it is extracted. This principle reflects conditions 1 and 2, which we call the *flow condition.* Together with the stock constraint and terminal condition, the optimal extraction plan for the nonrenewable resource can be determined at the industry level as well as for the single mine.

Hotelling viewed the problem of how to extract a fixed stock of a natural resource from the vantage point of a government social planning agency. He then showed that a competitive industry facing the same extraction costs and demand curve as the government, and having perfect information about resource prices, will arrive at exactly the same extraction path for the mineral.[6] The efficient extraction path determined by each firm acting independently in the competitive industry will yield the socially optimal extraction path. We first examine the planner's solution, and then show why it is achieved in a competitive industry. As before, a number of simplifying assumptions are made and then gradually modified to illustrate cases with practical relevance.

When we deal with an industry rather than a single mine, the mineral price can no longer be treated as a constant. Rather, it is assumed that the industry faces a negatively-sloped demand curve. The greater the industry output, the lower the price will have to be if we are to have an equilibrium in any mineral market at any given point in time. Hotelling assumed that prices would adjust so that a mineral market would be in equilibrium at every point in time; supply must always equal demand.[7] We can think of the Hotelling model as examining world production of oil, nickel, copper, or some other mineral. As before, the stock of mineral reserves is of known size, and all units of the mineral are homogeneous. We assume a unit of the stock costs c dollars to extract and refine and that this cost is constant for all units of the stock in the reserve endowment, S. Once again, it is as if we had a huge block of copper that cost \$$c$ per ton to chip off. We want to find the rate of extraction that maximizes social welfare and completely exhausts the stock. (If $c = 0$, the analysis is qualitatively unchanged. If c increases with the quantity extracted, we are back with Gray's cost assumption, which is an unnecessary minor complication at this point. See question 4 at the end of the chapter.)

The problem is to maximize society's wealth (W) or net return from mineral extraction, which is defined as

$$W = B(q(0)) + B(q(1)) \left(\frac{1}{1+r}\right) + B(q(2)) \left(\frac{1}{1+r}\right)^2$$
$$+ \cdots + B(q(T)) \left(\frac{1}{1+r}\right)^{\mathrm{T}} \tag{3.7}$$

Again, there is the resource stock constraint which requires that

$$q(0) + q(1) + q(2) + \cdots + q(T) \le S \tag{3.8}$$

$B(q(t))$ is the consumer plus producer surplus obtained in period t from the extraction of output, $q(t)$. This social surplus is simply the area under the demand curve up to quantity $q(t)$ and above the constant costs of extracting $q(t)$.

This problem can be solved in a manner analogous to that presented previously. As before, the solution requires that the flow condition, terminal condition, and stock constraint be met. The crucial distinction between Hotelling's model and Gray's is that we must examine the demand curve explicitly and derive a unique price for the resource in each period the mineral industry operates. In addition, we can make the stronger statement about the socially optimal as opposed to just the mine's efficient extraction path. We now derive the solution to the maximization of Equation (3.7) subject to the stock constraint, Equation (3.8), for a linear demand curve.

In maximizing social welfare, the planner must decide what the net benefits are of extracting some of the mineral today as opposed to tomorrow. Therefore, the planner will want to measure the change in the social surplus as one more unit of the mineral is produced today. Consider Figure 3.3. The social surplus for the last unit extracted is simply the difference between the market price and the marginal cost of extraction, c. If $q(t)$ is extracted in period t, society gains the amount for the $q(t)$th unit extracted and the amount under the demand curve and above c for all previous or inframarginal units extracted. How much will the planner choose to extract in each period?

As before, the flow condition provides an answer. To maximize social welfare, it must be the case that the net benefit to society from the last unit extracted in each

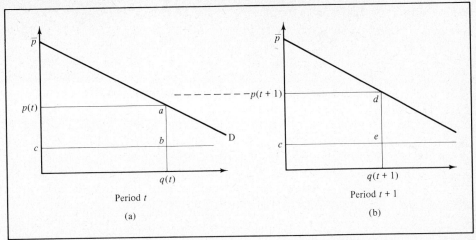

Figure 3.3 Rent per ton in period t is distance ab and rent per ton in period $t + 1$ is distance de where $ab(1 + r) = de$. Price is higher in period $t + 1$, making $[p(t) - c](1 + r) = [p(t + 1) - c]$ and this rent path yields the optimal path of q's to extract.

period is exactly equal in present value terms in each period of extraction. To do otherwise would entail foregoing the maximum benefits possible. And because the net benefit of the marginal unit extracted is simply the resource rent (ab), it must be the case that the present value of the rent on the margin in each period must be equal. For the two-period case, $q(t)$ and $q(t + 1)$ must be chosen such that

$$p(t) - c = [p(t + 1) - c]\left(\frac{1}{1 + r}\right) \tag{3.9}$$

Figure 3.3 illustrates one pair of outputs for the two periods which will satisfy this condition given D, the demand curve, and c and r. Notice the flow condition implies, as can be seen in Figure 3.3, that the mineral price must rise over time. In this model, with a stationary demand curve, the only way the price, and hence the rent, will rise is if the quantity extracted declines over time. Therefore, extraction in period $(t + 1)$ must be less than that in period t to ensure that the price rises just enough to satisfy Equation (3.9).

We can rewrite Equation (3.9) to obtain

$$\frac{[p(t + 1) - c] + [p(t) - c]}{[p(t) - c]} = r \tag{3.10}$$

Written in this form, we see that as price rises, *rent per ton grows over time at a rate equal to the rate of interest.* This is often referred to as Hotelling's r percent rule, or simply *Hotelling's rule.* We sketch the price path in Figure 3.4. How do we know the path shown is the one that maximizes social welfare? All Hotelling's rule says is that rents must grow at the rate of interest. Might there be dozens of different paths, all of which satisfy Hotelling's rule? Yes, but a unique path of output can be derived with the help of the stock constraint and terminal condition. If extraction costs are constant, the planner will want to ensure that all the mineral is removed. If any ore is left

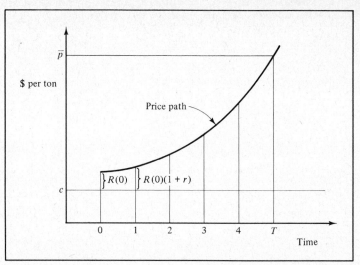

Figure 3.4 Price minus cost c is rising between periods at a rate equal to r, the rate of interest. This yields a rent path rising exponentially at rate r in the optimal program of extraction.

in the ground, the mine owner will be foregoing rents. The constant cost assumption is crucial in this argument. Each unit of ore costs the same to extract (in nominal terms); therefore, it cannot pay the planner to leave ore behind. We know that the sum of the amounts extracted in each time period must exactly equal the total stock of the mineral reserves (S).

We can also see, from Figure 3.3, that with the linear demand curve there is some price, call it $\bar{p}$, at which no one is willing to buy more of the mineral. The price $\bar{p}$ is often called the *choke price*, meaning that demand for the good is choked off at this point. Ideally, the planner would seek to have the stock of the mineral go to zero at exactly the point that demand goes to zero. Therefore, the planner would seek to have the last unit of output extracted at $\bar{p}$. To do otherwise deprives society of maximum benefits.

We can then work backward from $\bar{p}$, given the fixed stock S, to find just that initial output $q(0)$, which will, over time, decline so that rent increases at rate r and outputs sum to the stock of reserves. Only one such extraction and hence rent path exists. It will yield the largest amount of social surplus available to society and hence be the optimal plan. In addition, we can now determine the length of time the mine operates. In Figure 3.4, the point at which the price path intersects price $\bar{p}$ will determine the unique duration of the extraction profile, T. Once the price reaches $\bar{p}$, there will be no more demand for the mineral, so extraction will cease. Extraction ends at time T.

Note also that the terminal condition discussed earlier is also met at T. *The rent on the marginal ton must be equal to the rent on the average ton at T.* This condition also implies in this case that output at time T must equal zero. Table 3.2 gives a numerical example of an optimal extraction path for the industry. Rent per ton is $p(t) - c$ and for consecutive periods $(p(t) - c)(1 + r) = p(t + 1) - c$. This is the condition that rent rises at the rate of interest. The demand curve intersects the vertical

Table 3.2   AN INDUSTRY EXTRACTION EXAMPLE*

t	p(t) − c	p(t)	q(t)	(p − c)xq	$\dfrac{(p(t) - c) \cdot q(t)}{(1.1)^t}$
6	9	10	0	0	0
5	8.181818	9.181818	.818182	6.6942162	4.1565816
4	7.4380165	8.4380165	1.5619835	11.618059	7.9352906
3	6.761833	7.761833	2.2388167	15.134111	11.370482
2	6.1471211	7.1471211	2.8528789	17.536992	14.493382
1	5.5882919	6.5882919	3.4117081	19.065621	17.332382
0	5.0802654	6.0802654	3.9197346	19.913292	19.913292
			14.802654		75.20141

* A stock of 14.8 tons is extracted over seven periods resulting in the maximization of the present value of net consumer surplus. Extraction cost per ton is constant at $1 and the industry demand curve is linear. We solve by working back from period 6 to period 0. (Parameters: $r = 1$, $c = 1$, $q = 10 - p$, $S = 14.802654$.)

axis at $p = 10$, when $q = 0$. This value $p = 10$ is the *choke price*. Over seven periods, 14.803 tons are extracted. Total *profit* evaluated at period 0 in present value terms is $75.20. (We have not illustrated that in period 6; $p(6) - c = [B(q(6)) - cq(6)]q(6)$, or marginal welfare from extracting $q(6)$ equals average welfare. This is slightly tricky, since $q(6) = 0$ in order to satisfy this basic end point condition.)

Exhaustibility and Welfare: Demand Curves and Backstop Technology

What would happen if the world were to run out of oil or any nonrenewable resource one day? What does the Hotelling model tell us about this occurrence? The impact of complete exhaustion on society depends on the technology of producing and using resources in production and can be reflected in the demand curve for the resource. A crucial question is whether substitutes for the resource exist or whether the resource is so necessary to the production process of other goods that once it is depleted the other goods will also cease to be produced. Our model with the linear demand curve and choke price says that a substitute exists. The choke price is that price at which the users of the good will switch entirely to the use of the substitute good. This substitute may be another nonrenewable resource such as oil shale as a substitute for conventional crude oil, or it may be a reproducible good such as solar energy.[8] If the substitute exists, society and economic systems will not collapse when the oil runs out; they will shift to the substitute commodity.

What if there is no substitute for the depletable resource? In this situation, as the available quantities of the resource dwindle, prices would begin to rise very quickly. We can characterize this with a nonlinear demand curve, say an isoelastic curve, that does not have a positive intercept[9] (see Figure 3.5). We will not have to worry about running out of the resource in this case, because we never will in finite time. From society's viewpoint, however, this is not a very desirable situation because what it suggests is that as the resource quantity extracted gets smaller and smaller, its price will rise to higher levels. We can think of extracting oil by the bucket, then the cup, and finally by teaspoons and eyedroppers while the price climbs continuously toward infinity. This is asymptotic depletion. (*Asymptotic* means that two lines approach each other more and more closely as time passes but never touch.) This can happen in

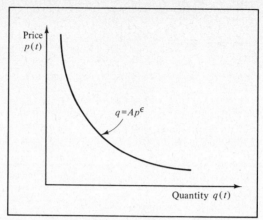

Figure 3.5 An isoelastic demand curve. As the quantity extracted diminishes, the price rises toward infinity. Exhaustion does not occur in finite time.

a mathematical model, but it is rather unrealistic. The conventional view is that exhaustion of most minerals is followed by the production of a substitute product.

We can incorporate the substitute product into the extraction model. It is common to think of the substitute product as a *backstop technology,* a technique for producing energy at a constant cost such as fusion power that becomes feasible to implement once the price for conventional oil reaches a certain level. *Feasible* here means that the producers of the backstop can cover their costs.[10] Suppose the backstop technology can provide the substitute commodity at a price of $Z per ton forever, because the substitute can be produced with constant costs. This case is illustrated in Figure 3.6.

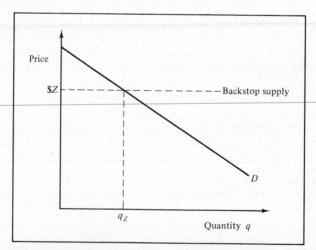

Figure 3.6 The backstop technology provides a resource substitute at $Z per ton. Rent will rise to the point at which price per ton equals $Z and the substitute will take over as exhaustion occurs at that "joining" of price and $Z.

All demands below $Z are satisfied by flows from the nonrenewable resource stock and those at $Z are supplied by the backstop technology. One can think of the demand curve in Figure 3.6 as one for energy, derived from conventional oil wells. The backstop is energy from fusion or solar power (two possible substitute goods). For a planner controlling both sources of supply—the exhaustible stock and the backstop technology—the optimal program will be to consider $Z as the choke price for conventional oil and to arrange to exhaust this oil in the Hotelling fashion, as set out in the previous section. At the moment of exhaustion, price will have risen to $Z per ton and the backstop technology brought on line.[11]

A Model of a Competitive Nonrenewable Resource Industry

We have argued that the socially optimal extraction path would be obtained if a planner organized production in the industry. Would a decentralized, competitive industry replicate the socially optimal program of extraction? Suppose there were a large number of mines or oil wells, each owned by a different person. If none of the owners coordinated their actions, we would have what is called a decentralized competitive setting. Each owner would be faced with this decision: Should I mine and sell a ton of ore this period and earn $p(t) - c$ dollars of profit, or should I wait until the next period and extract, sell, and receive $p(t + 1) - c$ dollars of profit for the ton? If the prices $p(t)$ and $p(t + 1)$ were such that Equation (3.9) was satisfied—that is, $p(t) - c = (p(t + 1) - c)/(1 + r)$, each owner would be indifferent between selling this period or next. Since all owners and deposits are identical (there are no quality differences among mines), all are indifferent.

If there was a general tendency to wait until next period by sellers, current output would fall and the current price would rise. Sellers would then find it profitable to sell now and put their rents (or profits) into an asset earning r percent. If there was a tendency to sell a lot of ore in the period, however, the current price would fall, and mine operators would be reluctant to sell until future periods. Therefore, the flow condition will be met by each firm seeking to maximize profits to ensure extraction in each period, and the market forces of supply and demand will ensure that the condition is met.

Will a competitive industry which is on an equilibrium path also satisfy the optimal terminal condition? To show that it does, we assume that the extraction and price paths were not optimal then argue that this cannot happen in the context of our model. If the price path were not the optimal path, there would be a jump in the rent up or down at the transition to the backstop technology. Consider Figure 3.7. Extraction commences at $t = 0$ with an initial price of $p(0)$. The rent in the first period, $R(0) = p(0) - c$, grows at rate r until the resource is exhausted at time T. But notice that at T, the market price of the resource appears to have risen above $\bar{p}$. This cannot occur, because with the backstop technology, no consumer will pay more than $\bar{p}$ for the resource. It therefore means that the resource will be economically depleted at time T' which is less than T.

But this cannot be a plan that maximizes profits, because ore will be left in the ground that could have been extracted. If all firms know that this price path is emerging, they will alter their extraction plans to shift production to the present. The

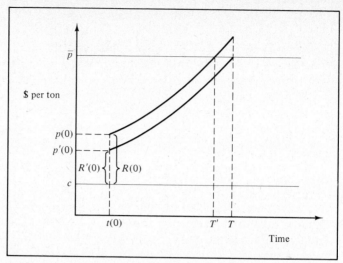

Figure 3.7 A price path with a jump down in the price at the time of exhaustion cannot occur. Extraction would be shifted away from later periods and into earlier periods to prevent economic depletion at T'.

increase in current production will lower the initial price to say $p'(0)$, which yields the rent $R'(0)$. It will grow at rate r and have exhaustion occur at precisely $\bar{p}$. A similar argument applies if the price path fails to reach $\bar{p}$, that is, firms run out of ore before the backstop technology can be implemented.

What these arguments require is that all mine operators have *perfect foresight* about the price of the mineral in all periods. To be able to see that it is profitable to shift production from one period to the other, individuals must know what the price will be. Given that mines can produce for several decades, it is difficult to imagine that perfect foresight characterizes the centralized or decentralized operation of mineral markets. Some economists have argued that market forces will ensure that a perfect foresight equilibrium will be achieved in decentralized situations, even if some participants in the market have deficient information. If person i's foresight is

---

BOX 3.1
Exhaustible Resource Prices

Heal and Barrow examined a hundred-year sample of exhaustible resource prices and found that interest rates did have a significant effect on price movements but not as in the Hotelling model. They found *changes* in interest rates were significant rather than levels and indicated their results supported a "rather more general asset market approach." They also found that the level of industrial output did not have a major influence on resource prices.

Source: G. Heal and M. Barrow, "Empirical Investigation of the Long-Term Movement of Resource Prices: A Preliminary Report," *Economics Letters*, 7 (1981), pp. 95–103.

deficient relative to person j's, j could make a profit by signing a contract to buy or sell from i in the future at specific conditions. The informational deficiencies will be competed away by the forces of profit maximization and free entry into the industry. We now consider some modifications of the basic model, but still assume that all participants act with perfect foresight. (Imperfect information is considered in Chapter 5.)

EXTENSIONS OF THE INDUSTRY MODEL
Changes in Extraction Paths Under Altered Conditions

We will show how the price and extraction paths of a competitive industry are affected by: (1) a rise in the constant costs of extraction; (2) an increase in the interest (discount) rate; and (3) the introduction of taxes. In each case, we compare equilibrium paths under two different assumptions. Diagrammatic techniques will be used to derive the results.

An Increase in Extraction Costs

In Figure 3.8, we examine the case where the costs of extraction, while still constant, are higher than initially assumed. How will these higher costs affect the extraction and price paths? In this and all subsequent cases, we look at the effects as if no extraction had yet occurred. We could modify the results if the cost (or other parameter) change occurred at some time after the mine had begun to operate. In these situations, it will matter whether the mine owner anticipated the changes or not (see

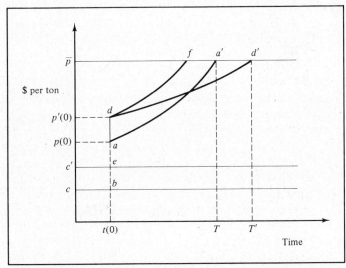

Figure 3.8 The comparative statics of an increase in extraction costs — the effect on the price path. If costs of extraction increase from c to c', the mining industry will respond by reducing output in the initial period so that the resource price rises from $p(0)$ to $p'(0)$. Production is then increased again in later periods. A higher extraction cost will lengthen the time to depletion.

discussion question 7). Suppose the initial situation is an industry facing constant costs of c and a choke price of $\bar{p}$ (see Figure 3.8). The price path that satisfies the flow and terminal conditions along with the stock constraint is aa'. Now, what would happen if costs were c' rather than c, where $c' > c$? If the industry tried to follow the path aa', it would not be maximizing profits. Along the path aa', rent will grow faster than rate r when costs equal c'. Each mine owner then decreases current output (because rents in the ground exceed returns from extraction), the industry supply declines, and the initial price, p_0, rises to p_0' in Figure 3.8.

What happens to extraction over time? If mine owners produced less output in every period when costs are c' rather than c, the price path would look like df. In this situation, the choke price $\bar{p}$ is reached when there is still ore remaining in the ground. This cannot be an optimal plan because the terminal condition is not met. What it means is that at some point in the extraction path, mines must begin to increase their rate of production, which will cause the market price to rise less rapidly than when costs were c. This will ensure that physical depletion occurs at $\bar{p}$. Thus, the path dd' results. It is important to notice that the increase in costs results in a *lengthening* of the time to depletion. The backstop is reached at T', which exceeds T.

There is an economically intuitive explanation for the effect on the extraction and hence the price path when costs change. If the cost of extraction is higher, in present value terms it will benefit each firm to postpone extraction. If firms postpone incurring the costs, the rents will be larger than if the same path as aa' is followed. Production is reduced in the early periods and increased in later periods. The present value of the mine has fallen due to the increase in costs, but the stock of ore is still physically depleted and the terminal condition is met.

A Rise in Interest Rates

Suppose that the rate of return on investing in assets alternative to mineral extraction rises. What will be the response of the mining firms? In Figure 3.9, suppose the price path prior to the increase in the interest rate is aa'. If the mine operators continued to follow this path, the mines would be earning a lower rate of return over time than available elsewhere. The way to avoid this loss is to shift production to the present. The mine owners will extract more ore in the initial period, thus driving down the market price to, say, $p'(0)$.

Thereafter, less ore will be extracted so that the rate of return on the remaining ore rises at the now higher interest rate. This means, however, that the time to depletion must fall. The extraction path dd' will start from a lower initial price than did aa' and will rise more steeply so that it hits the choke price at T', which is less than T. Any other path would not maximize the profits of the mines, given the new interest rate.

The Introduction of Taxes

Suppose the government decided to impose various taxes on the mining industry. What would be their effect on the extraction and price paths, and the time to depletion? We consider two types of taxes: a tax on the mineral rent, the difference between

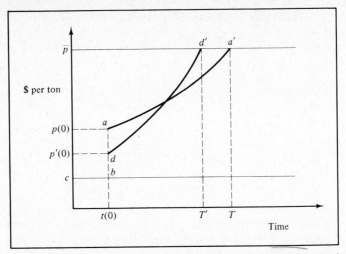

Figure 3.9 The comparative statics of an increase in the interest rate. A rise in the interest rate will increase the opportunity cost of extracting ore in the future (the present value of future rents is lower). Extraction is shifted to the present, and the initial price falls. The smaller amounts of ore remaining in the ground increase in value at a higher rate than before, so the path *dd'* is steeper than *aa'*. Depletion occurs at *T'* which is sooner than *T*, the exhaustion point under a lower interest rate.

price and marginal cost, and a royalty, a tax at a constant rate, on the value of production.[12] A rent tax will have no effect on the extraction decision of a mine already in existence. There is no change in the rate of extraction over time that can offset the decline in the present value of the mine resulting from the tax. The government will simply collect some of the mineral rent, and production will proceed in the same manner as before the tax.

To see that this is so, we present the flow condition required after a rent tax is imposed. Let α be the tax rate levied on mineral rents or profits. Then Equation (3.9) becomes

$$(p(t) - c)(1 - \alpha) = (1 - \alpha)(p(t) - c)\left(\frac{1}{1+r}\right) \qquad (3.11)$$

Because rent in each period is taxed exactly the same, the term $(1 - \alpha)$ cancels from both sides of Equation (3.11). There is no way the mine operator can avoid the tax by shifting production.

While a rent tax is said to be *neutral* or nondistorting to the extraction path because it does not alter the path, the same cannot be said about the effect of this tax on the discovery of new mines. The higher the tax rate, the less incentive there is for individuals and firms to explore for new mineral deposits. Two identical deposits with different taxes levied on their output represent two assets of quite different market value. The rent tax reduces the return from exploration—the value of the mineral in the ground—because the expected payoff from discovering a new deposit declines with the tax. We will come back to this topic in our discussion of exploration and uncertainty in Chapter 5.

Now let us examine the effect of the imposition of a royalty on the total value of mineral extraction. The government now taxes the total revenues of each mining firm at, say, rate γ. The introduction of the royalty has an effect analogous to a rise in the cost of extraction. If the firm postpones the extraction of some ore to the future, it can then reduce the effect of the royalty on the present value of its rents. To see this, we rewrite Equation (3.11) to obtain the flow condition after the royalty.

$$(1 - \gamma)(p(t)) - c = [(1 - \gamma)(p(t)) - c] \frac{1}{(1 + r)} \tag{3.12}$$

Notice that there is no way we can cancel the term $(1 - \gamma)$ from both sides of Equation (3.12). The royalty reduces the price received by the firm for each unit of mineral sold and thus, the present value of the mine. If sales are postponed, the effect of this reduction will be minimized because of the discount factor. The result is a time path of extraction similar to that shown in Figure 3.8; the initial output will fall, and price will rise. Later in time, extraction will rise again, and price will rise less quickly than in the case without a mineral royalty. Again, the time to depletion of the fixed stock is lengthened. The size of this effect depends on the magnitude of costs. If extraction cost is very small, the distorting effects of the royalty are relatively small.

Numerous other comparative static exercises can be done (see discussion problem 8). These exercises will help in understanding the model of the industry and also enable the reader to try applications of the model to some real-world events, such as the introduction of new energy taxes, a fall in the cost of producing oil from oil shale deposits, and so on. We now turn to some further extensions of the industry model that make it more compatible with real-world observations.

Declining Quality of the Stock

Suppose the mineral industry finds its stock of ore declining in quality. Deposits of poorer quality must be brought on stream as the high-quality reserves are exhausted. As in the case of the single mine, quality decline can be viewed as requiring the removal of more waste rock per unit of ore extracted to get at the thinner seams of metal. Thus the average cost of producing metal increases as more of the mineral is extracted. If each ton has a specific extraction and processing cost associated with it, and these costs rise as more mineral is extracted, the flow condition of Equation (3.9) remains the same, but its interpretation is modified.

For a *specific ton* of the mineral, the flow condition requires the rent on that ton in period t to be equal to the discounted rent on that same ton if it were extracted in period $(t + 1)$. In period t, this ton will be the marginal ton extracted, whereas in period $(t + 1)$ it will be the most inframarginal ton extracted. We illustrate the effects on the industry in Figure 3.10.

In Figure 3.10, the rent on the marginal ton in period t is ab. This same ton would obtain the rent of ge in period $t + 1$. Distance ge must be equal to the amount $ab(1 + r)$, if the owner of the marginal ton is to be indifferent between extracting in period t or period $(t + 1)$. All owners of ore inframarginal to the marginal ton earning ab at t will extract their ore at that point simply because their rent in period t exceeds

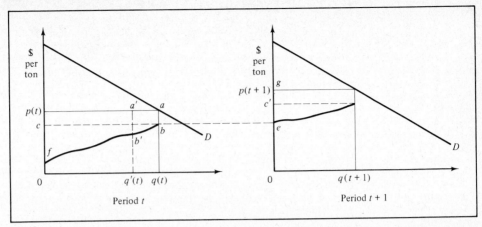

Figure 3.10 The marginal ton extracted in period t has rent per ton of ab or $p(t) - c$, and this ton would earn rent $p(t+1) - c$ in period $t+1$ or distance ge. The rate condition "causing" $q(t)$ to be the optimal level to extract is $[p(t) - c](1 + r) = [p(t+1) - c]$. fb is the rising extraction cost per ton for tons of declining quality.

the rent they could obtain by waiting until period $(t+1)$. The inframarginal ton, $q'(t)$, for example, earns a rent of $a'b'$ in period t. It would earn ge in period $(t+1)$ which is less than $a'b'(1 + r)$. The flow condition for extraction in both periods is not satisfied for this ton, and hence the ton is extracted in period t. A similar argument applies to all tons to the left of $q(t)$ in Figure 3.10.

Distance ab is the *rent* per ton. Area cbf is the *Ricardian* or *differential rent* arising from the variation in ore quality. The marginal ton of ore in period $(t+1)$ earns a rent equal to $p(t+1) - c'$. If the flow condition is then linked together for all periods, the amount of ore to be extracted at each different quality will be determined for each period. The price in each period is determined by the aggregate amount extracted; thus, the price is endogenous.

We have yet to examine the terminal condition for the problem and set the time to depletion, and hence initial $q(t)$. Because there are now many grades of ore in the industry, we must distinguish between the possibility of economic versus physical exhaustion. Assume in either case that there is a linear demand curve and choke price $\bar{p}$. If there is physical exhaustion, the output will go to zero in the last period, just as the price hits $\bar{p}$. With $q(T) = 0$, marginal rent equals average rent on the last batch of ore removed. We can then work backward to find the unique first period output that satisfies the flow and terminal condition with complete physical exhaustion.

Physical exhaustion will occur in any industry if the marginal cost of extracting the final ton is less than (or equal to) the choke price. If, however, there are ore qualities with extraction costs in excess of the choke price, economic exhaustion occurs. In this situation, the mining sequence ends when the choke price equals the marginal cost of extraction. There will be an ore grade at which mining ceases. The final quantity extracted from all mines is that which yields $\bar{p} - c = 0$. Again, we work backward from this quantity to find the initial output level that satisfies the flow condition in each period.

Deposits of Distinct and Differing Quality

Now we examine the case where each deposit has ore of a uniform quality, but differs in quality from other deposits. What is an optimal plan for exploitation of ore in this case? We can treat ore quality as signifying different costs of extraction and processing. These costs of extraction could be due to ore grade and seam thickness, as discussed earlier, or simply to the fact that deposits are located at different distances from a central market. Transportation costs give the deposits a distinct "quality"; the metal is still of uniform quality.

Consider an example of two deposits of different quality within a competitive industry. Each deposit is within itself of uniform quality. Deposit 1 has extraction costs of c_1 and an initial stock of reserves equal to S_1 tons. Deposit 2 has unit costs of c_2 and reserves equal to S_2. As long as the demand curve remains stationary, only the low-cost deposit will be exploited initially. Why? Suppose deposit 1 is the low-cost deposit. Its extraction costs are shown in Figure 3.11 as c_1. Extraction from deposit 1 commences at T_1, where the initial rent earned is the amount ab. Deposit 2 clearly cannot come on stream at T_1 because at price p_1, it will incur a substantial loss. Its extraction costs of c_2 greatly exceed the initial price.

How is this initial price set? Why isn't the initial price high enough to allow both deposits to operate? One way to see why the initial price is less than the extraction costs of the high-cost deposit is to work backward from the time when both deposits are exhausted — that is, we use the terminal condition. As long as the choke price $\bar{p}$ is greater than c_2, we know that physical exhaustion must occur. At T, $q(T) = 0$. The rent at T would be equal to $\bar{p} - c_1$ for deposit 1 and $\bar{p} - c_2$ for deposit 2 if both extracted their last ton of ore at this point. Deposit 1's rent greatly exceeds that of

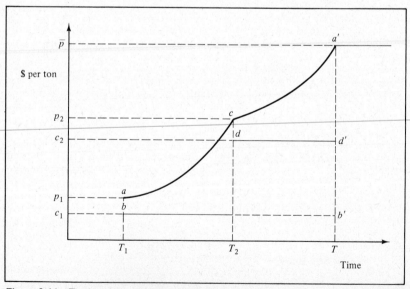

Figure 3.11 The low-cost deposit is extracted between T_1 and T_2. Upon exhaustion, the second deposit is worked until it is exhausted at time T. $\bar{p}$ is the cost of the backstop. Rents rise over each phase at the rate of interest.

deposit 2. Can we then arrange extraction in each period prior to T so that the flow condition is met for each deposit? The answer is "no" if each deposit operates simultaneously and "yes" if they operate sequentially.

Consider simultaneous extraction. The price in each period must be the same for each deposit if both are to sell any metal. There is then no way that the flow condition can be met for both firms. Working backward from T, the discounted rent cannot simultaneously be the same for each deposit with different extraction costs and the same market price. In particular, if a path such as $a'c$ is followed, rents to deposit 1 will not be falling fast enough from T. Only deposit 2 can then extract and satisfy the flow condition.

If there is sequential extraction, then for each deposit both the flow condition and terminal condition will be met, along with physical exhaustion. Working backward from T where the choke price is reached, deposit 2 will be extracted over the interval T_2 to T. T is defined by the choke price; T_2 is defined by the initial rent deposit 2 can earn to satisfy the flow condition for each period and exhaust at T. The initial rent for deposit 2, the amount cd, will be that which compounded at rate r yields the terminal rent $a'd'$ as the ore body is depleted. T_2 is also the time when deposit 1 physically exhausts its reserves.

It will not pay the owners of deposit 1 to extract once the price has reached p_2, because they know that then deposit 2 can begin extraction. If both 1 and 2 were to extract simultaneously, the market price would not rise fast enough to allow 1 to satisfy the flow condition, as noted earlier. T_2 thus marks deposit 1's terminal time and p_2 its choke price. For deposit 1, the initial price, p_1, is what results from the output level chosen to obtain rent ab. Rent ab is that amount which compounded at rate r allows deposit 1 to exhaust its reserves as it reaches p_2. The scalloped price path shown in Figure 3.11 is the result.

We know that the scalloped price path must be continuous at the point where one deposit exhausts its reserves and the other begins extraction. In Figure 3.11, the point of the scallop, T_2, does not have any jump in the price upward or downward. To qualify as an optimal path, it must be the case that price does not jump at the transition between deposits. Consider what would happen if the price did jump. Suppose the price jumped up at T_2. The operator of deposit 1 would then decrease the extraction rate from the deposit immediately before time T_2 and extract this additional amount at T_2. The increase in the total supply at T_2 causes the price to fall. Production will continue to shift to T_2 until the jump in price is eliminated.

Similarly, if the price jumped down at T_2, ore from deposit 2 would be shifted to periods right before T_2. This would cause the price to fall prior to T_2 and rise at T_2, again eliminating the jump. As long as the extraction rate can be adjusted from one period to another, the transition from one deposit to another is smooth—there is no discontinuity in the price between one instant in time and the next.

Does this multideposit variation of the basic industry model have any real world applications? Nordhaus (1973) set out a numerical example of a multideposit model for the world energy market. The common output was a BTU (British thermal unit) of energy. The different "deposits" were distinct sources of energy—oil, gas, coal, uranium, and fusion as the backstop technology. The endogenous variables in his analysis, what the model determined, were the durations of the phases of exploitation of different energy sources and the price path. He took as given demand, costs, and "deposit" sizes. A linear programming approach was used to solve for an optimal extraction program. The analysis revealed that even before the OPEC price hikes of 1973, actual energy prices were slightly above optimal prices. He attributed this discrepancy to market imperfections, including noncompetitive behavior, and various forms of government regulation and taxation. Figure 3.11 illustrates the type of price path derived by Nordhaus.

Setup Costs for the Mine and Industry

Clearing away overburden, building access roads, sinking shafts into the ground and pipes into the reservoir all represent infrastructure or setup costs—expenses that must be incurred before extraction commences. How will these setup costs affect the rate of extraction from the mine? What will happen to the industry extraction path when deposits have different setup costs? We turn now to these questions.

We first consider the effect of setup costs on the individual deposit. Two questions will be examined. How much physical capital or infrastructure should be installed in the mine or well, given that the size of the shaft or the diameter and pressure in the pipe constrain the flow of resource to the surface and hence the amount that can be sold? Once the physical capital is in place, what is the optimal extraction path? How does it differ from the path derived without considering capital requirements?

To determine the optimal size of a mine, the mine operator simply maximizes the difference between the contribution of infrastructure to the present value of mineral rents and the cost of the infrastructure. Let the capital be denoted by K. Then for capital of size K, the present value of the profits derived from the mine are $R(K)$. These profits will be the discounted value of the rent per period (revenues minus operating costs). If the amount of capital is increased, a larger flow of output, $q(t)$, could be extracted per period and the stock of reserves removed more quickly. A larger capital stock, however, increases capital costs, $C(K)$. The mine operator will then determine the value of K that maximizes

$$R(K) - C(K) \qquad\qquad (3.13)$$

If Equation (3.13) is differentiated with respect to K, the efficient condition for K is obtained: $R_K - C_K = 0$. The change in the present value of the mine due to an incremental unit of K added to the mine (R_K) must equal the marginal cost of adding that unit of capital (C_K).

Now that the optimal K has been chosen, there is a maximum amount of ore (or oil) that can be removed from the mine or well at any point in time. The capital in place acts as a capacity constraint on the mine. To see the effect of the capital choice and resulting capacity constraint on the mine's extraction path, refer to Figure 3.12.[13] We show the path of output in (a) for both the constrained mine and a mine that does not have to install capital before extraction. The unconstrained mine in a Hotelling industry will extract its maximum output in the initial period, $q(0)$, then extract decreasing amounts each period thereafter until in the last period it produces, output goes to zero. The unconstrained mine exhausts its reserves at T'.

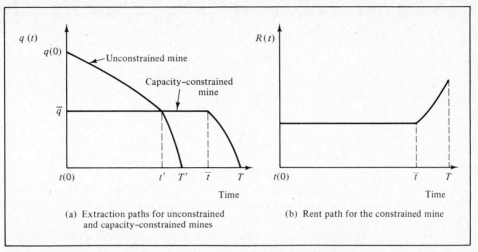

(a) Extraction paths for unconstrained
and capacity-constrained mines

(b) Rent path for the constrained mine

Figure 3.12   The effect of setup costs on the extraction and rent paths of the mine. Output and rents are constant over the time $t(0)$ to $\bar{t}$ of the mine's extraction period, for the capacity-constrained mine.

In general, the mine that must install capital and incur the setup costs will not choose an initial capital stock large enough to extract $q(0)$ because to do so would not maximize its rents. Why install a shaft large enough to remove $q(0)$ for only one period, and then have *excess capacity* over the remainder of the extraction period? Capital will be chosen such that a smaller amount of ore is extracted initially—$\bar{q}$ in Figure 3.12. Then the mine owner will produce at this maximum capacity level $\bar{q}$ for a period of time. The constant output in turn means that current (not discounted) resource price and rent (which now includes a shadow value for the capacity constraint) are constant, as shown in Figure 3.12(b).

How long will the mine produce at $\bar{q}$? The stock constraint and terminal condition again help us solve this problem. If the mine has uniform quality and constant costs, the owner will maximize profits by physically exhausting the reserves. At T, the end of the mine, output goes to zero. Typically, as is shown in the unconstrained case, the output does not jump to zero, but declines gradually. The same occurs in the constrained mine. After time $\bar{t}$, output diminishes from its constant level to hit zero at time T. If the stock of ore is the same in both the constrained and unconstrained mine, the only way the terminal condition can be met for the constrained mine is if it operates at full capacity over a period of time longer than the entire extraction period of the unconstrained mine. Thus, $\bar{t}$ exceeds T'. The area under the extraction path for both cases must be identical. The unconstrained mine will produce more than the constrained one over the interval $t(0)$ to t', less thereafter, and exhaust at T'. The constrained mine will extract a constant amount over the interval $t(0)$ to $\bar{t}$, then extract decreasing amounts until it exhausts at T, where T must exceed T'.

Now suppose different large deposits have different setup or capital costs. Each deposit will have a capital cost, $C^i(K)$, which we assume is incurred prior to exploitation of the ore. We now treat $C^i(K)$ as exogenous and *independent of the stock size or extraction costs.* This is reasonable if we are thinking of building roads, but less so for reserves of different sizes and characteristics. The assumption simplifies the analysis and illustrates the new complexities these costs can introduce.

Two new phenomena emerge. First, the industry price path has jumps down in the price at the transition between deposits. Second, the optimal plan differs from the competitive solution. The latter phenomenon occurs because setup costs introduce increasing returns to scale into the analysis.[14]

Consider how the jump in the price arises. Let us return to the two-deposit example of the preceding discussion, but add a small setup cost that occurs at the transition from deposit 1 to deposit 2. Figure 3.13 illustrates the result. As noted earlier, T_1 to T_2 is the extraction period of the first deposit, while T_2 to T represents the time of extraction for the second deposit. But if there is a setup cost to obtain ore from deposit 2, the value of extraction from the industry beyond the exhaustion of the first deposit's reserves is diminished. To counteract this new lower value beyond T_2, one can get higher rents from the first deposit by depleting it over a longer interval. This is in part because the farther into the future one can defer paying the setup costs, the lower the present value of these costs.

To postpone reaching the second deposit, less must be extracted in each period from the first deposit than was the case with no setup costs. The price of the mineral will therefore be higher in every period up to T_2, and the interval T_1 to T_2 must lengthen. At T_2, the extraction plan for the second deposit proceeds as before. Given this lengthening of the interval T_1 to T_2, the price must *jump down* at the switch from deposit 1 to deposit 2. The higher the setup costs, the greater the jump down in the price. The extraction rate from deposit 1 will be lower the larger the setup costs to reduce the present value of these costs.

The determination of the optimal path becomes much more complex if all deposits have setup costs. Prices do not link up as they did in Figure 3.11. More important, the competitive market equilibrium will no longer yield the optimal extraction path. Consider the special case of identical deposits, each with a setup cost.

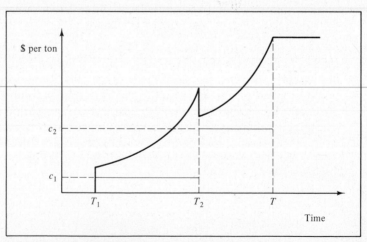

Figure 3.13 To deposits of different quality, a positive setup cost of "opening" the second deposit is added. This results in an optimal extraction path with a jump down in price at T_2, the date deposit 1 is exhausted.

From a social welfare standpoint, it is irrelevant which deposit is exploited first. However, in the firms' optimal plans, the discounted rent net of setup costs will be different for deposits entering at different times in the extraction sequence. The first deposit will get less rent than the second, the second less than the third, and so on, because early producers "pay" a higher setup cost in present value terms. The setup costs cannot be fully offset by higher initial prices when all firms must bear the costs. In a decentralized market, deposit owners will prefer to go at the end of the sequence, and there is no market mechanism to decide which deposit goes into which slot in the sequence.[15]

The reason for the breakdown of the market mechanism in the presence of setup costs is that these costs represent a form of increasing returns. The larger the deposit over which the setup costs can be spread (or the longer the time period over which they can be spread), the higher the rents to the mine owner. Small setup costs or slight increasing returns to scale cause less deviation from the familiar paths than large setup costs. Any form of increasing returns to scale leads to malfunctioning of the market as a mechanism for allocating productive resources optimally. The malfunction shows up in an unusual manner in the nonrenewable resource case.

One final point: Throughout this chapter, we have identified a mineral deposit with a mine owner or operator. This is convenient in the case of setup costs because it implies that a single coordinator incurs the costs. In a situation of many owners of small claims on a single deposit, it is difficult to see how the sharing of setup costs would be arranged. Also, for deposits with single owners, the individual last in a sequence will be induced to price as a monopolist, since all competitors will have exhausted their stocks. This again breaks down the socially optimal path. We turn to monopoly in the next chapter.

SUMMARY

1. Nonrenewable resources differ from reproducible goods because they have a fixed stock of reserves that, once removed, cannot be replaced. A unit of ore removed today means that less in total is available for extraction tomorrow.
2. The economic theory of extraction explains the flow of production over time and how quickly the resource stock is exhausted.
3. The finite stock of a nonrenewable resource alters the condition for efficient production: Marginal revenue *(MR)* equals marginal cost *(MC)* in three ways: (a) $MR = MC$ + resource rent; (b) the present value of resource rent must be constant for each period the mine operates; (c) the total amount of the resource extracted over time cannot exceed the total stock of reserves. Conditions (a) and (b) yield the flow condition, while (c) is the stock constraint.
4. Extraction from a mine facing a constant price, a positive discount rate, and extraction costs that do not increase as the stock of ore is depleted decreases in each period the ore is removed. This is physical depletion.
5. For a many-period model, the terminal condition, marginal rent equals average rent, determines the time horizon over which the mine operates.
6. Different ore qualities within the mine require the price of the mineral to rise over time for extraction to occur. If price does not rise sufficiently, the

mine will cease operating before the reserves are exhausted. This is economic depletion.

7. Extraction from a mineral industry facing a negatively sloped demand curve and constant costs of extraction will be socially optimal if the flow condition and stock constraint are satisfied. Resource rent per unit extracted will then rise continuously at the rate of interest. This is known as Hotelling's rule, and it is met if all mine operators have perfect foresight, with industry output declining over time.

8. A nonrenewable resource with a backstop technology will be extracted until the price of the resource reaches the choke price, that price at which the backstop becomes profitable to produce.

9. The following comparative static results were derived: (a) an increase in extraction costs tilts production to the future and increases the time to depletion of an ore body; (b) an increase in the interest rate tilts production to the present and reduces the time to depletion of an ore body; (c) taxes on mineral rent do not alter the extraction path of an existing mine or well, but they will affect the incentive to find new deposits; (d) a royalty on mineral production tilts production to the future and increases the time to depletion.

10. Low-cost deposits will be exploited before high-cost deposits, leading to a scalloped but continuous price path.

11. Setup costs within the mine can lead to periods of constant rates of extraction and constant prices.

12. Setup costs for the industry can lead to jumps (discontinuities) in the optimal price path.

DISCUSSION QUESTIONS

1. If the interest (discount) rate is zero, what is the value of resource rent over the extraction profile of the mine?

2. Using Gray's model, derive for a two-period case the extraction path of a mine's output assuming:
   a. Extraction costs (average and marginal costs) are linear and upward sloping.
   b. The market price of the mineral rises; the market price falls.

3. Suppose a mine has two different ore qualities in its stock of reserves. Call them block A and block B. How would the mine owner efficiently extract the total stock if the costs of extraction are constant per unit within each block, but differ between blocks? Use the Gray model.

4. In the basic Hotelling model of the industry, extraction cost per ton was constant. In order to reflect, say, diminishing returns to the extraction facilities in the industry, let cost per ton rise with the amount extracted in a period in the industry (as in the simple L. C. Gray model of the mine). Compare two programs of quantities extracted: one with constant costs and one with extraction cost per ton rising linearly with quantity extracted in a period.

5. Explain and show diagrammatically that a price path which does not reach the choke price in the basic industry model is nonoptimal and will not occur under perfect foresight.

6. In the basic Hotelling model of the industry, with constant unit extraction costs and a negatively sloped industry demand curve, technological progress in extraction can be approximated by a decline in the value of the constant extraction costs period by period. Outline how the program of quantities extracted with a 2 percent decline in unit extraction

costs period by period compares with the program of quantities extracted when unit extraction costs remain constant.

7. Derive the effect on a mineral industry's output and price path if, at some point along an optimal path, the costs of extraction rise and:
   a. The increase in costs is fully anticipated (foreseen) by the industry.
   b. The cost increase is completely unanticipated.

8. What are the effects on a mineral industry's output and price path of a fully anticipated:
   a. Increase in the total stock of ore reserves.
   b. Fall in the choke price (cost of backstop technology).
   c. Technological change that decreases the cost of extraction over time.
   d. Rightward shift in the demand curve.

9. How would the price path for a competitive industry differ if it faced an isoelastic rather than a linear demand curve?

10. Explain why the higher the setup costs a mine faces, the longer it will produce at a constant output rate and the longer the life of the mine.

NOTES

1. An important exception to the finite stock of minerals are seabed nodules. Minerals such as nickel, copper, manganese, and molybdenum have been found on the ocean floor and might be growing over a time period much shorter than the millions of years required to produce hardrock minerals, oil, and gas on land. Although the precise way in which these seabed nodules are formed is not yet clear, there is some indication that they may be cropped periodically and will re-form.

2. We do not consider here any of the capital costs associated with the development of the mine. There are no shafts to dig, pipes to install, mills to build. A later section of this chapter considers these capital or setup costs explicitly.

3. The cost curves illustrated in Figure 3.1 were chosen to show simply how the efficient extraction path is derived for the mine. We could use linear or strictly convex cost curves instead, but the discussion of the conditions for efficient extraction would not be as intuitive. If the U-shaped cost curves are used to examine mineral extraction at the industry level, there can be a problem because a competitive market equilibrium may not exist. See the industry section of this chapter and the discussion by Eswaran, Lewis, and Heaps (1983).

4. Condition 2 can also be written as $R(0)(1 + r) = R(T)$ by dividing through by $(1 + r)$. We will use both forms of the condition.

5. This is L. C. Gray's many-period model in which the length of time for exhausting the mine must be arrived at.

6. We assume there are no market imperfections of any kind in this analysis, including externalities such as pollution associated with mineral extraction, and that the market interest or discount rate is the social rate of discount as well.

7. Actual mineral markets are frequently characterized by disequilibrium caused by a variety of factors, especially imperfect competition and government regulation. We turn to these issues later.

8. Assuming perfect competition, if the substitute is a reproducible good, the choke price will equal the marginal cost of producing the good. If the substitute is another nonrenewable resource, the choke price is its marginal cost plus rent. See Figure 3.11 for an illustration of the latter case.

9. A demand curve of the form $q = Ap^\epsilon$ where ϵ is the elasticity of demand will be asymptotic to the price and quantity axes for $\epsilon < 0$. Thus, price can approach infinity and quantity

will tend to zero. For $-1 < \epsilon < 0$, the demand curve is inelastic and revenue, pq, will decline as price rises. There is no intercept on the price axis for this demand curve and hence no choke price.

10. In Chapter 5 we consider uncertainty in the introduction of the backstop technology.

11. Note that the last batch extracted from the stock will be q_z tons, as indicated on Figure 3.6. At this quantity, the rent on the marginal ton will be less than average rent on the tons in the batch. Should not more resource be brought into the end of the extraction plan from the front? The answer is "no." If a few batches of q_z tons at the end of the plan were sold at $Z, then the present value of rent on the marginal ton would be falling, because price is constant at $Z. The present value of rent per ton on these last batches would be less than on tons extracted early. This violates the principle of identical tons receiving identical rents. In the optimal plan, we are left with average rent above marginal rent for tons in the final period of extraction of the exhaustible resource.

12. There are, of course, many different types of taxes levied on mining industries. In this section we assume the tax rate is constant over time, but in many real-world examples, the rate varies considerably over time. See Dasgupta, Heal, and Stiglitz (1980) for a discussion of the effects of different types of taxes and tax rates on the optimal extraction path.

13. The discussion in this section is based on Campbell (1980). See Olewiler (1980) for a discussion of the possible nonexistence of a competitive industry equilibrium with the capacity constraint. It is possible that the capacity constraint need never bind. If it does bind at all, it need do so only in the initial period of extraction.

14. Whenever average cost curves for a firm slope down, there are some increasing returns to scale, which are a type of nonconvexity. The Gray model was presented with declining average costs. At the level of the mine, this presents no difficulties. At the industry level, however, we can expect a market failure to occur, as will be discussed.

15. This problem may be less severe in practice, because mines are discovered at different points in time. The total stock of minerals in the world is not known at any time. Development of the mine and incursion of the setup costs frequently takes place when market conditions warrant (when demand exceeds supply). In cases where mines do "wait" to go into production to minimize setup costs, the surplus rents to these mine owners at the end of the sequence are likely to be capitalized into the value of the mine or bid away by workers as higher wages and fringe benefits.

Reading 1

ECONOMICS AND GEOLOGY: ARE NONRENEWABLE RESOURCES FINITE?

What is a nonrenewable resource? We speak of it as a finite stock of some physical amount of metal, oil, gas, or other material. Is it really fixed? Why have we observed measured stocks of many minerals increasing rather than decreasing over time? What we are trying to determine is the total supply of a nonrenewable resource—the maximum amount that can be extracted.

In nineteenth-century England, economists debated whether coal consumption should continue at present levels or be saved for the future because of concern over dwindling reserves. In the previous century, the stock of wood used to generate heat had dwindled considerably. Was this a response to the abundant supplies of the new substitute, coal? Or was the coal era brought on because the stock of wood was approaching exhaustion? In 1874, a geologist from Pennsylvania State University calculated that the United States had only enough petroleum to keep kerosene lamps burning for another four years! In the 1970s, many countries considered implementing gasoline rationing to deal with the "oil crisis." But the world has not yet run out of a nonrenewable resource, and some scientists argue that we never will: "We will never physically "run out" of a mineral, because the sheer limits of the amount in place in the ground are far beyond the likely economic limits of its utilization" (Zwartendyk, 1972, pp. 8–9).

But even if we don't worry about ultimate exhaustion, measures of resource stocks are important for private and public decision-making. There are no absolute or unique measures of resource stocks. Economists differ from geologists, who differ from mining engineers in their calculations. Part of the reason for this is that people use different terminology. Are *proved* reserves the same as *measured, probable* the same as *indicated?* But even if the terminology could be standardized, the basic problem is that a mineral stock is not a well-defined or even a meaningful concept. To see the problems, consider two extreme views of what constitutes the stock of a mineral.

For the narrowest definition, the known stock of a mineral is that which can be profitably extracted given current technology, extraction costs, prices, and political factors. Once a deposit is found, test holes are drilled into the rock formations and then, by a variety of techniques, the deposit is delineated. Calculations of *total reserves* within the deposit are made based on these sample drill holes. The ore that is counted in the calculation is that *which at the time* the calculation is made is believed to be economically viable—that is, profitable to extract over the foreseeable future.

The difficulties with this technique are fairly obvious. A sample can give a very biased picture of the total. There are many examples of mines started up on the basis of reserve estimates that were not representative of the deposit. Sometimes this is good news—more is there than anticipated—but often the opposite is true: The vein disappears, the ore grades tail off too rapidly to permit extraction, and so on.

Another difficulty is that geologists and engineers do not have perfect foresight about mineral prices, costs, and technology, all of which determine whether a deposit is viable or not. World gold reserves are very small when viewed from a gold price of $35 per ounce, but much less so at $500 per ounce. The only certain measure of what a deposit contains is made after all the ore is removed and the mine shuts down. And even here there are difficulties because depletion may result from economic forces (which are not constant), not physical exhaustion.

Finally, what is counted as reserves in one country may not be in another. A 400-million-ton porphyry copper deposit in Canada with an average grade of 0.25 percent copper can be counted as a viable reserve. The same deposit would not be counted as part of Chile's copper reserves unless its ore grade was at least twice as much. Does Chile therefore have fewer copper reserves than Canada?

We have been discussing *known* deposits in the narrow definition of stocks. A very important source of the growth in mineral reserve estimates over the past fifty years has been the discovery of *new* deposits. Although geologists may have a notion that additional deposits should exist, they still have to be found if a reasonable estimate of the mineral stock is to be made.

Suppose we want to know the maximum potential stock of a mineral. We go then to the opposite extreme—the *resource base.* This is what geologists call the concentration of minerals in the earth. It is a purely geologic concept, without regard to technological feasibility or economic viability. As Brooks (1976, p. 148) explains: "Measurements of the resource base are stable, for neither individual discoveries nor depletion changes the volume significantly." However, there are difficulties even with this concept. It is fairly useful for fluids such as petroleum, because they are distinct from the rocks that surround them and are found only to some maximum depth in the earth. But for many metallic minerals, the resource base is not so easy to define. Metals in minute concentrations are in a large part of the earth and to an unknown depth. At what point do we stop counting? A number of cutoff points have been suggested, but no system has been agreed upon.

Alternative measures are to count minerals that can be extracted without crossing an "energy barrier." This implies that minerals will be counted as long as their extraction or separation from surrounding material does not use up large amounts of energy (where "large" is not defined). The appeal of the resource base is that it is a physical measure of the maximum stock of any mineral. The difficulty with the resource base as a measure of mineral stocks is that it does not indicate whether these potential supplies will ever become actual. Supply is "actualized" only when with given geological knowledge and information about extraction techniques, there is "willingness to pay" for the mineral.

An economic measure of a mineral stock lies between the narrow definition of reserve estimates based on drill hole samples and the broad measure of the resource base. The economist is concerned about not only which deposits are feasible today, but given that technology, costs, and prices are rarely constant over time, how much of the resource base will become viable reserves over time. The economist tries to draw a supply picture that incorporates effects of new discoveries, exhaustion of old deposits, and changes in prices, costs, and technologies, using statistical techniques when possible to determine supply elasticities, shifts in supply curves, and so on. The crucial thing to the economist is that the stock of reserves *will change* over time. Some reserves will come from the unanticipated discovery of new deposits; some will come from the movement of previously uneconomic resources into economic reserves due to unanticipated increases in prices, decreases in costs, and technological change.

An economic definition of reserves is illustrated in Figure 3.14. On the vertical axis, we have the expected discounted value of mineral rents (price minus unit cost). This is a slightly broader measure of mineral rents than contained in the chapter because it is an expected value. It takes into account the probability of discovering new ore bodies (which will affect the costs), the likely path of prices over time, technological change, and so on. Every ton of ore or unit of oil that can be extracted and earn a nonnegative rent will be counted as a reserve, whether it has been discovered or not. Due to differences in ore grade, there will be relatively few units of a mineral that generate high rents. Ores of lower grade (higher costs) will yield lower rents. Thus the relationship between discounted rents and mineral reserves is likely to be downward-sloping (it need not be smooth as shown, but may have wiggles or bumps). What then is the mineral stock?

The point at which this negatively sloped curve crosses the quantity axis will determine the stock of reserves. That is, where the present value of rents equals zero, the marginal ton that can be extracted is defined. Will this be a fixed stock forever? The answer depends on how good our expectations are. If we do have perfect foresight about prices, technologies, discoveries, and so on, there will be a unique relationship between rent and reserves. What is more likely is that we will be surprised—either pleasantly, in which case the reserve line shifts out and aggregate reserves rise, or unfortunately, when anticipated cost savings, discoveries, or price movements do not materialize and the curve shifts in. We expect that the reserve estimate will not be a fixed stock, but will change over time and is thus more appropriately called a flow. Figure 3.14 illustrates one hypothetical reserve estimate. (These uncertainties are examined in more detail in Chapter 5.)

So is there a unique measure of the stock of each mineral? In physical terms, "yes," if one is willing to specify some lower bound of concentration in the earth. In practical terms and for policy analysis, we are really more concerned with the *supply* of the resource potentially available for extraction. Although this supply can be fixed at points in time and extraction decisions based on a stock constraint, it is really not a stock at all, but the flow over time of resources into reserves. And as a geologist has argued: "As long as this flow can be maintained in a workable fashion, we need not worry about the absolute magnitude of the shelf inventory" (Zwartendyk, 1972, p. 11).

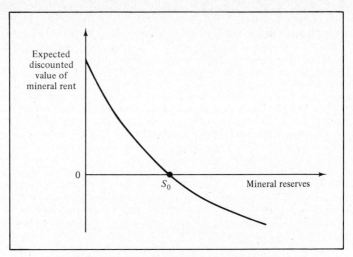

Figure 3.14 Mineral reserves as a stock and flow.

Reading 2

MINERAL INDUSTRIES OVER TIME? A "TEST" OF THE THEORY

Economic models have many functions. They enable us to understand real-world phenomena by breaking them down into manageable abstractions. Models also give rise to testable predictions about the economic activities they describe. We illustrate the use of theory to examine real-world phenomena in an examination of mineral prices over time. In a recent paper, Margaret Slade (1982) attempted to explain the price paths of a number of mineral resources over a long period of time. Once adjusted for inflation, the prices of these minerals do not look like our illustrations in this chapter. Rather, there are periods of rising and periods of falling prices, along with some periods where the price changes very little. What Slade argues is that it is changes in the cost function over time which can explain the price path of many minerals.

There are two components of the cost function, she asserts, which work in opposite directions as the industry's stocks of reserves are depleted over time. As extraction proceeds, mines typically must extract ore of increasingly lower grade. We argued that ore bodies of high quality will be mined before ore bodies of low quality. Slade finds evidence of this for many minerals. In copper deposits, for example, the average ore grade mined in the early 1900s was 5 percent. Now it is closer to 0.7 percent (Slade, p. 126). Following our model, we would expect that the decline in ore grade increases the average and marginal costs of extraction. Rising costs will then lead to rising mineral prices (see Figure 3.8).

Offsetting these cost increases due to lower ore grade is technological change. According to Slade (p. 126): "Technological developments in the early part of the century, particularly the advent of large earth-moving equipment, which made possible the strip mining of extremely low-grade ore bodies, and the discovery of froth flotation, which made concentration of low-grade sulfide ores very economical" led to a fall in many mineral prices over the early part of the twentieth century because of the decline in extraction costs brought about by these technological changes. However, the rate of technological change in many mineral extraction processes has slowed considerably in the second half of this century. Technological change appears to be less able over time to offset the cost increases due to declining ore grades. If so, we would expect costs and mineral prices to rise.

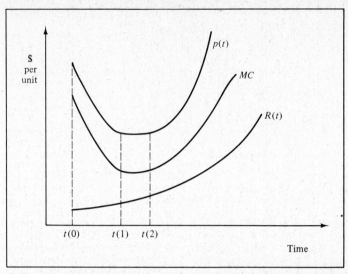

Figure 3.15   Marginal cost, prices, and mineral rent over time when marginal cost depends on the rate of technical change and ore grade. Prices initially fall because the rate of technological change offsets ore grade decline and MC falls. Eventually technological change can no longer offset cost increases due to falling ore grades, and the price path slopes up. Rents over time, R(t), are everywhere increasing to satisfy Hotelling's rule.

Slade modifies a Hotelling-type model to incorporate these assumptions about ore grade and technological advances. The model yields price, rent, and cost curves over time as shown in Figure 3.15. The path illustrated in Figure 3.15 is a stylized representation of three different regions of the price path. Over the period $t(0)$ to $t(1)$, prices are falling because the rate of technological change determines the rate of decline in ore grade. Marginal (and average) extraction costs fall. From $t(1)$ to $t(2)$, prices are stable because the two cost terms cancel one another. After $t(2)$, the rate of technological change is no longer high enough to offset the ore grade decline and the marginal cost curve increases, leading a rising price path. Notice that the mineral rent in current dollars is always increasing, so that Hotelling's rule (the flow condition) is met.

The model is then "tested" against actual prices of 12 mineral commodities for the period 1870 (or since the year of earliest available data for some minerals) to approximately 1978. Two price equations are estimated for each mineral—one where the price is a simple linear function of time, the other where price is a quadratic function of time. If the cost effects described above are a good description of mineral extraction over time, the quadratic function should fit the time series of prices better than the linear function. The linear function does not allow for changes in costs over time and therefore would be inconsistent with the cost assumption made in the theoretical model. Slade found that no discernible trend could be seen with the linear function. For some minerals, prices rose over time; in others, they fell; and in some, price was virtually constant. In the quadratic case, however, for all 12 commodities examined, the linear term was negative while the quadratic term was positive. These time coefficients were highly significant statistically for virtually every commodity. The mineral price paths do appear to be U-shaped as predicted by the model. The quadratic function is thus a better general description of the data than the linear function.

More specifically, Slade found that for every mineral, price had passed the minimum point on the U-shaped curve by 1978. There were differences among the minerals in the extent

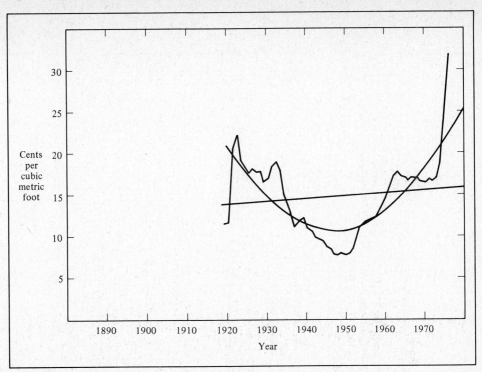

Figure 3.16 History of deflated prices and fitted linear and quadratic trends for natural gas. (*Source:* M. Slade (1982), p. 130.)

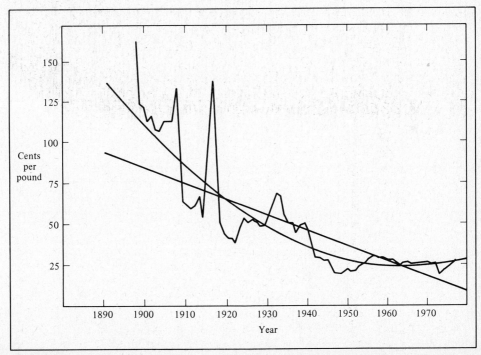

Figure 3.17 History of deflated prices and fitted linear and quadratic trends for aluminum. (*Source:* M. Slade (1982), p. 131.)

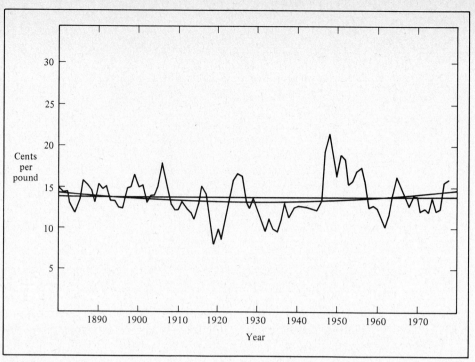

Figure 3.18 History of deflated prices and fitted linear and quadratic trends for lead. (*Source:* M. Slade (1982), p. 133.)

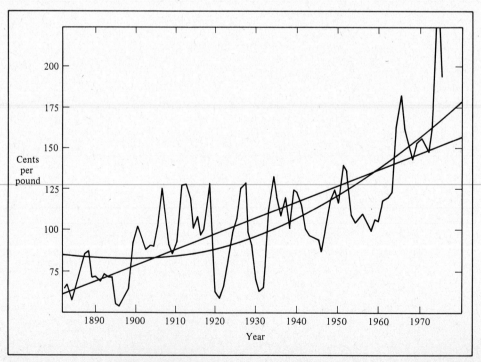

Figure 3.19 History of deflated prices and fitted linear and quadratic trends for tin. (*Source:* M. Slade (1982), p. 134.)

of the U shape and point in time when the price began to rise, which Slade attributes to the specific characteristics of each commodity. For copper, iron, nickel, silver and natural gas, a pronounced U-shaped price path was estimated. The path for natural gas is illustrated in Figure 3.16. There are three other variations. In the case of aluminum, shown in Figure 3.17, the price path is generally falling over most of the period examined. Slade attributes this to high growth rates in aluminum consumption, combined with technological advances and economies of scale. Lead and zinc, on the other hand, are metals with relatively stable demand over time and technological changes that have just offset ore grade declines. Given this information, their predicted price paths would be relatively constant, and as seen in Figure 3.18, the quadratic function fitted to lead shows very little curvature (zinc is similar). Tin, a metal that has been in use for centuries, is characterized by steadily declining consumption rates and a substantial decline in ore grade. It is not suitable for *froth flotation* and thus has been unable to benefit from that technological change. As Figure 3.19 shows, its price path, while still having a small curvature, is basically upward-sloping.

The analysis shows that the theoretical model which predicts U-shaped price paths fits the mineral data very well. When detailed information is available about the resource's consumption patterns, ore grade decline, and ability to incorporate technological changes into the mining processes, the empirical analysis will show more precisely how the general model adapts to fit these cases. The model is simple and obviously does not capture all real-world complexities. However, when "tested" against real-world observations, it performs well and shows the value of using a theoretical model to help determine empirical relationships.

chapter 4

Market Structure and Strategy in Nonrenewable Resource Use

INTRODUCTION

Perfect competition, monopoly, and oligopoly are different kinds of *market structure.* Market structure affects the levels of profits that firms attain, which in turn determine the total amounts produced and the prices obtained in the market. To maximize profits, a firm usually sets its marginal revenue *(MR)* equal to its marginal cost *(MC).* What differs among the market structures is the number of firms in the industry and their ability to engage in strategic actions.

The number of firms will determine the marginal revenue function perceived by the firm and whether strategic actions are meaningful. In the case of *perfect competition,* there are large numbers of relatively small firms, and each firm cannot affect the market price of the good it produces. In the case of *monopoly,* there is only one firm, and the monopolist thus determines the price it charges consumers.

The oligopolistic market structure is the most complex and applicable to real-world market structures. *Oligopoly* means few sellers. Each seller has some share of the market demand, but its share and its pricing actions are dependent on the actions of its rivals. In the polar cases of perfect competition and monopoly, there is no reason for firms to engage in strategic behavior because there are either too many of them and consumers perceive all firms to be identical, or there is only one and strategic behavior is not relevant. It is under oligopoly that strategy becomes important. With a small number of sellers, it is necessary to anticipate and react rationally to the observable actions of rivals if firms are to survive in the industry. The objective of this chapter is to examine the impact of market structure on the extraction path of a nonrenewable natural resource.

We will examine static equilibria under different market structures before we turn to intertemporal models. We will briefly review the market equilibrium under perfect competition versus monopoly, and then turn to some of the possible equilibria under oligopoly. We examine two different assumptions about firms' strategic behavior in an oligopoly and see the effects on the market equilibrium. These are the Cournot (or Cournot-Nash) model and the Stackelberg model.

Next, we turn to an analysis of market structure in an intertemporal setting. Again, we begin with the polar case of monopoly — contrasting it with the competitive equilibrium we discussed in detail in Chapter 3. Will the monopolist exhaust a fixed stock of reserves more quickly or more slowly than the competitive industry? We then discuss different types of oligopolistic market structure. We examine the mixed case, where the resource is supplied by a large producer (a "dominant" firm or cartel) and a "competitive fringe" (a large group of small producers). We meet the problem of dynamic consistency, two groups designing an optimal plan in isolation at the beginning of extraction and then asking whether it is rational for each group to stick to that initial plan as extraction ensues and circumstances change. We look at extraction plans for these markets with different types of sellers of the resource.

We then look at the question of how the provider of a resource substitute or backstop technology affects the extraction plans of resource owners in different types of markets and under different assumptions about the nature of the backstop technology. For example, is a monopolistic resource seller affected differently by the presence of a technology for a substitute than a perfectly competitive group? Suppose the date of arrival of the substitute can be altered at some cost to developers. When will they elect to innovate, and how will resource sellers react? We take up the important case of a "game" between innovators of a substitute and nonrenewable resource suppliers. Finally, we consider recycling as an alternative to the primary supply of a nonrenewable resource as a particular form of backstop or substitute supply. We close with an additional topic relevant to market structure — the issue of common pool problems (or externalities) in resource supply. For example, when 10 wells are sunk into an oil field by 10 competitors, each supplier's pumping draws down oil from the entire field and affects each rival's profits.

MARKET STRUCTURE IN A STATIC ENVIRONMENT

We examine different market structures to see how prices and quantities in a market are affected by both the number of buyers and sellers and how they react to the actual and anticipated actions of one another. This latter aspect is called *strategy* or *strategic behavior.* The strategy of a seller or buyer clearly depends on the number of similarly situated buyers or sellers in the market. The polar cases are the familiar competitive market, with many buyers and sellers, and monopoly, with just one seller and many buyers. For intermediate cases of a few sellers and many buyers (oligopoly), analysis has developed on almost a case-by-case basis.

Monopoly versus Perfect Competition

A monopolist can select any price it wishes on the market demand schedule because the monopolist is the only supplier of the good. The quantity supplied determines the price. The monopolist maximizes its profits when quantity is chosen so as to equate marginal revenue and marginal cost. A competitive firm also equates *MR* to *MC*, but its *MR* differs from that of the monopolist. The difference between the two market structures is that the *MR* for the monopolist is continuously declining because the monopolist views the *entire* demand curve as its own. For each additional unit sold by the monopolist, the price falls a bit, and thus the change in the revenue received *(MR)* declines. Each firm operating in a perfectly competitive market has such a small share of the total market that it can sell as much as it can produce at the equilibrium price determined in the market. The demand curve facing the competitive firm is thus *perfectly elastic* at the equilibrium price. Marginal revenue is constant and equal to the price. The profit-maximizing competitive firm sets price equal to marginal cost (see Figure 4.1).

Figure 4.1(a) shows the equilibrium for a competitive industry; Figure 4.1(b) presents the equilibrium for a representative competitive firm. Given a market demand curve, the industry supply curve is the sum of the marginal costs (above-average variable costs) of all competitive firms in the industry. The industry equilibrium is found where supply equals demand. The equilibrium price is P_c and the equilibrium quantity is Q_c. Each firm then takes P_c as given and produces where that price equals its marginal cost. For the firm shown in (b), q units of the good will be produced. In (c), marginal costs are assumed to be constant and hence equal to average costs. This assumption is made to illustrate the distinction between monopoly and perfect competition. The monopolist sets *MR* equal to *MC* to determine its profit-maximizing output level, then charges the price people are willing to pay for output Q_M. Reading off the demand curve, the monopoly price is P_M.

Facing the same marginal cost and demand curve, a competitive *industry* would produce where supply (which equals marginal cost) is equal to demand, producing Q_c' at a price of P_c'. Monopolistic control of an industry thus results in less

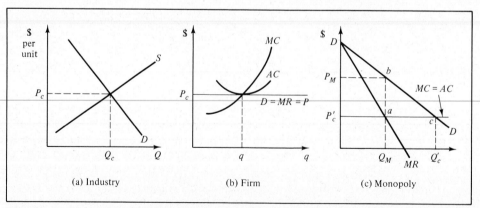

(a) Industry   (b) Firm   (c) Monopoly

Figure 4.1   In part (a) we have the competitive equilibrium for the industry, where total supply *S* equals demand *D*. The industry equilibrium determines the market price which the competitive firm shown in (b) takes as given. The competitive firm sets this price equal to its marginal costs *MC* to determine its profit-maximizing output. Price is equal to marginal revenue (*MR*) for the competitive firm. The monopolist in (c) determines its profit-maximizing output where *MR* equals *MC*. It then charges the maximum the consumers are willing to pay, price P_M. The area *abc* is the welfare loss associated with monopoly. Monopoly output is less, and the price it charges is higher than that of the competitive firm.

output than would be produced in a competitive market and charges a price that exceeds the marginal costs of production. Hence, monopoly production is inefficient. Monopoly will also affect the distribution of income, as we illustrate below.

We can calculate the allocative and distributive effects of monopoly. When the market is perfectly competitive, consumers receive a consumer surplus equal to the area under their demand curve above the marginal cost curve (recall Chapter 1). In 4.1(c), consumer surplus under perfect competition is equal to the area $P'_c cD$. Under monopoly, consumer surplus is reduced to the area $P_M bD$. The area $P'_c abP_M$ represents a loss in consumer surplus that is transferred from consumers to the monopolist. This area is thus a distributional effect of monopoly. The surplus transferred to the monopolist is an excess profit or *rent* above its costs of production. There are no rents in the competitive industry in this case. Short run rents may, of course, exist in a competitive industry, but entry of new firms to the industry will eliminate these rents over time. As long as there is no entry into an industry characterized by monopoly, these monopoly rents will persist. The rents can be interpreted as a return to whatever it is that prevents entry in the industry, for example, a patent on a production process or good, unique location, or ownership of a resource stock.

The other area of "lost" consumer surplus is the amount *abc* shown in (c). This triangle is called the *welfare cost* or *deadweight loss* of monopoly. It is a sum that is lost from the economy, not merely an amount that is transferred elsewhere. Under perfect competition, consumers gain this area. Under monopoly, *abc* is lost to the economy. The deadweight loss is the measurement frequently calculated as the cost of monopoly to the economy. If the marginal cost curve were positively sloped, the deadweight loss would consist of both consumer and producer surplus. Given the constant marginal cost curve, there is no producer surplus in this example.

Finally, what about the area $acQ'_c Q_M$? Is this another cost of monopoly? This area represents what consumers would spend on the additional units of the good produced under perfect competition. Under monopoly, consumers no longer spend $acQ'_c Q_M$, and they can therefore transfer these expenditures to some other good. This area then does not represent any social loss from monopoly.

Cournot versus Stackelberg Models of Oligopoly

We turn now to two oligopoly models and the role of strategic behavior. Let's look at the potash industry in Saskatchewan, Canada. Potash (in the form of potassium chloride) is a mineral used in fertilizers. It is a nonrenewable resource, but reserves in Saskatchewan are large enough to supply existing demand for 2,000 to 3,000 years. The resource rent derived from the "fixed stock" will be negligible for many years. A static model therefore provides a reasonable snapshot of the industry.

Although there are now some seven firms extracting potash in Saskatchewan, we will assume there are only two. This too is not a bad approximation of the way the industry operates. Over 40 percent of Saskatchewan potash capacity and reserves are owned by the provincial government, the remainder by private sector firms. We assume the private sector firms all act identically and can thus be treated as "one" firm. We denote the government firm G and the private sector firms by P.

We first examine the Cournot model. The crucial hypothesis of this model is that each seller assumes that the current quantity produced by the rival will remain fixed into the indefinite future. This is a passive or even myopic assumption, but it serves as a working hypothesis for purposes of illustration. Each seller then chooses an output to maximize its profit, assuming the other seller's output is fixed. Profit maximization by each firm, given the assumed output of the other firm, yields two equations in the quantities q_G and q_P. These equations are solved simultaneously to obtain a Cournot duopoly equilibrium. We illustrate this equilibrium with a simple numerical example:

Let

π_G be the profits of the government firm
π_P be the profits of the private firm
$p(q_G + q_P)$ is the market price when G produces q_G and P produces q_P
$C(q_G)$ is G's cost of producing q_G
$C(q_P)$ is P's cost of producing q_P

The profits of the government firm are given by Equation (4.1) and those of the private firm by Equation (4.2).

$$\pi(q_G) = q_G p(q_G + q_P) - C(q_G) \tag{4.1}$$
$$\pi(q_P) = q_P p(q_G + q_P) - C(q_P) \tag{4.2}$$

To keep the analysis simple, let unit extraction costs be constant and the same for each seller at $40 per ton of potash produced. We assume the inverse market demand curve is linear and given by $P = 100 - Q$, where Q is total industry output (q_G plus q_P). Substituting for the numerical values, we obtain

$$\pi_G = q_G[100 - (q_G + q_P)] - 40 q_G \tag{4.3}$$
$$\pi_P = q_P[100 - (q_G + q_P)] - 40 q_P \tag{4.4}$$

Each firm chooses a level of output that maximizes its profits given its assumed value of the output of the other firm. The profit-maximizing conditions are

$$\frac{\partial \pi_G}{\partial q_G} = [100 - q_G - q_P] - q_G - 40 = 0 \tag{4.5}$$

$$\frac{\partial \pi_P}{\partial q_P} = [100 - q_G - q_P] - q_P - 40 = 0 \tag{4.6}$$

Equations (4.5) and (4.6) are then solved simultaneously to find the values of q_G and q_P that are consistent with the Cournot hypothesis. We find that $q_G = q_P = 20$ tons. Each firm produces the same amount. The market price equals $60 per ton.

We can also derive the Cournot equilibrium graphically. To do so, simply solve Equation (4.5) for q_G and Equation (4.6) for q_P. The new equations are

$$q_G = 30 - q_P/2 \tag{4.7}$$
$$q_P = 30 - q_G/2 \tag{4.8}$$

These equations are then functions of known values and the output of the other firm. Equations (4.7) and (4.8) are known as *reaction functions* because they show

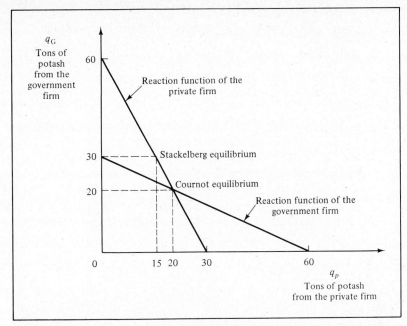

Figure 4.2 In the Cournot duopoly, each seller treats its competitor's quantity as fixed. The equilibrium is where the reaction functions of the two firms intersect. Each firm then produces an identical output of 20 tons of potash. In the Stackelberg duopoly the government firm is assumed to be the leader. It observes that the private firm is treating quantity as fixed and uses this information to gain more profit. The government firm increases its output to 30 tons; the private firm reacts along its reaction function and produces 15 tons. Total output is thus higher under the Stackelberg duopoly, which leads to a lower market price.

how each firm's output will change with a change in the output of the other firm when each firm is maximizing its profits in a Cournot model. The reaction functions are plotted in Figure 4.2. The intersection of the reaction functions yields the Cournot equilibrium; their intersection is the same thing as solving Equations (4.5) and (4.6) simultaneously.

Let's compare the Cournot equilibrium to the perfectly competitive and monopoly equilibria for the same demand curve and cost assumption. The competitive equilibrium would be where price equals marginal cost, so substituting for price in the demand curve, we have $100 - Q = 40$, or industry output Q equals 60 tons of potash. At that output the competitive price would be $40 per ton. The combined oligopolistic output (40 tons) is thus less than that of perfect competition, while the oligopolistic price is higher. A monopolist would equate MR to MC to determine output. Then $MR = 100 - 2Q$, so Q_M is 30 tons of potash. The monopoly price would be $70 per ton. Thus, limited competition in a Cournot duopoly results in more output being produced than in monopoly and at a lower price. It is in this sense that the Cournot equilibrium is seen as an intermediate case between perfect competition and monopoly.

The Stackelberg assumption regarding firms' behavior is quite different from that of Cournot. Suppose the government firm tried to exploit the fact that it had a larger share of industry capacity and reserves than any single private sector firm. The government firm can be thought of as a "dominant firm" in that it has enough "market power" to act as a leader in the industry, while the other firms act as Cournot followers. The dominant firm chooses a profit-maximizing output level, assuming the followers will take its output as given when maximizing their profits. The followers believe that the output of the dominant firm will not be affected by their decisions.

A Stackelberg equilibrium, then, consists of output levels from each firm such that their beliefs are confirmed and profits are maximized. As in the Cournot model, these behavioral assumptions are quite myopic. The existence of a Stackelberg equilibrium is dependent on the maintenance of the leader-follower beliefs.

We illustrate the Stackelberg equilibrium and contrast it with the Cournot equilibrium using the same numerical information. The profits of the dominant government firm depend on its own output and the entire reaction function of the follower, as depicted in Equation (4.8). The government firm's profit function is shown in Equation 4.9.

$$\pi_G = q_G[100 - q_G - (30 - q_G/2)] - 40q_G \qquad (4.9)$$

The government firm maximizes its profits to obtain

$$\frac{\partial \pi_G}{\partial q_G} = 100 - 2q_G - 30 + q_G - 40 = 0 \qquad (4.10)$$

Solving Equation (4.10) we find that q_G equals 30 tons. The private sector firms now maximize their profits given the output of the government firm, which means they simply solve their reaction function with q_G set equal to 30. Thus, q_P equals 15 tons. The Stackelberg equilibrium is shown in Figure 4.2. Total industry output is now 45 tons of potash, and the equilibrium price is $55 per ton. The Stackelberg equilibrium thus increases the output of the dominant leader and reduces the output of the follower compared to the symmetric case of the Cournot equilibrium. However, aggregate output rises, profit for the dominant firm rises, and the market price of potash falls.

Notice that if the private sector firms were the leader, the results would be reversed. Private firms would produce 30 tons of potash, while the government firm would produce only 15 tons. One criticism of the Stackelberg model is that it provides no rationale for why one firm is a leader and the other a follower. For some nonrenewable resources, however, the model may apply because firms do differ in their productive capacity and stocks of reserves. Firms with large reserves (and/or low operating costs and high capacities) may have the potential to dominate the firms with smaller reserves.[1] (Though our example had each firm with the same costs of production or of the same size a priori, this is not necessary for the argument. There can be asymmetric Cournot duopoly. Analogous Stackelberg solutions arise.)

All these are static models. We turn now to an examination of extraction paths for a nonrenewable resource under different market structures. But note that strategic behavior such as that in oligopoly can cause prices to lie above the marginal cost of production indefinitely in static situations. For example, an oligopolistic automobile industry can earn excess profits over long periods of time. In Chapter 3, we observed that the essence of depletion effects on nonrenewable resources was to cause price to be set above marginal extraction costs. Rents should persist as prices stay above marginal extraction costs in these industries. Oligopoly and depletability each contribute to persistent gaps between prices and marginal costs. So a thorny empirical matter arises: Are observed rents in resource industries due primarily to market structure or to the "depletion effect" of finite stocks? If to both, how much of the gap is due to each factor? One might keep this vexing question in mind as we discuss the combined effect of oligopoly and non-renewability in this chapter. There is no persuasive factual evidence.

MARKET STRUCTURE IN A DYNAMIC ENVIRONMENT
The Monopoly Resource Supplier

A monopolist that controls the entire stock of a nonrenewable natural resource in the industry will act to maximize the present value of its profits over time rather than net consumer surplus, as would a social planner. The monopolist will choose a time path of quantities extracted from the stock to achieve this result. We now illustrate the conditions the monopolist must satisfy to maximize its profits over time and see how the extraction path which satisfies these conditions differs from that of the resource managed optimally under perfect competition. As we will see, the monopolist must satisfy conditions for an intertemporal profit maximum that are very similar to Hotelling's rule, and our terminal condition established for the competitive firm.

Suppose extraction costs are zero. If $p^t(q)$ is the inverse demand curve in period t, then the present value of profit in period t will be $[p^t(q_t)q_t]/(1 + r)^t$. The present value of the monopolists' profits for a sequence of extractions over time, q_0, q_1, . . . is shown in Equation (4.11).

$$\pi_M = p^0(q_0)q_0 + p^1(q_1)q_1/(1 + r) + p^2(q_2)q_2/(1 + r)^2$$
$$+ \cdots + p^T(q_T)\, q_T/(1 + r)^T \tag{4.11}$$

As in the case of perfect competition, the sum of all the qs must not exceed the known stock of reserves, S_0. We assume that the demand curve remains stationary over time (a simplifying assumption we have maintained throughout the book). The monopolist maximizes its profits by choosing an extraction path, q_0, . . . , q_T that uses up its entire stock of reserves. The flow condition in Equation (4.12) must be satisfied at each point in time to obtain a profit maximum.

$$\left(\frac{1}{1 + r}\right)^t MR(q_t) = \text{constant} \tag{4.12}$$

From Equation (4.12), we can then derive for any two periods t and $(t + 1)$ that

$$\frac{MR(q_{t+1}) - MR(q_t)}{MR(q_t)} = r \tag{4.13}$$

Equation (4.13) requires that the percentage change in marginal revenue over time equal the rate of interest.[2] This is simply Hotelling's rule for a monopolist facing zero costs of extraction. The difference between Equation (4.13) and Hotelling's rule for the competitive firm is that MR replaces the price.

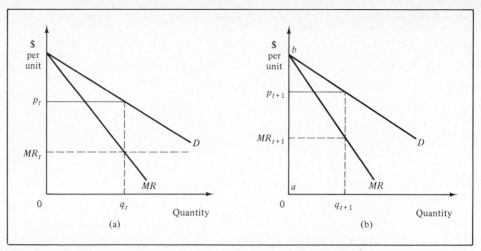

Figure 4.3 For two consecutive periods, the monopolist's marginal revenue rises at the rate of interest, $MR_t(1 + r) = MR_{t+1}$. This flow condition yields the path of quantities for each period, q_t, q_{t+1}, and so on. Note that monopoly output must fall over time to obtain the required increase in MR over time.

The intuition behind this condition for an intertemporal profit maximum is exactly the same as in the competitive case. We illustrate in Figure 4.3. Hotelling's rule or the flow condition requires output in period t and period $t + 1$ to be chosen so that $MR_t(1 + r) = MR_{t+1}$, as shown in the figure. The monopolist must also satisfy a terminal condition, as did the competitive firm, to determine the actual path of marginal revenues. Without the terminal condition, any sequence of qs that satisfies Hotelling's rule is acceptable. The terminal condition pins down the final output level and hence all subsequent outputs. The flow condition requires the marginal revenue per ton extracted to be constant in present value (or else extraction will shift to periods with higher present values). To meet this condition, output must fall over time so that the current (undiscounted) value of MR will rise.

The last ton extracted will thus yield the highest undiscounted value of marginal revenue (shown as the amount ab in Figure 4.3). Hence, the terminal condition is satisfied when $q_T = 0$ as $MR(q_T) = ab$. Formally, this outcome derives from the condition that marginal profit on the last ton should equal average profit on that ton (the analogous condition as for perfect competition). This is satisfied only when q_T equals zero and marginal revenue (the same as marginal profit here since costs equal zero) equals ab in Figure 4.3(b).

Note, however, that because the marginal revenue curve is steeper than the demand curve, the monopolist will have to decrease output in each subsequent period it operates by less than a competitive industry would. Think of the monopolist moving up its marginal revenue curve and the competitive industry moving up the demand curve in each succeeding period. Both regimes must satisfy their respective versions of Hotelling's rule, facing the same discount rate. Thus, as we will show numerically and graphically below, when the demand curve is linear and extraction costs are zero, the monopolist will extract its ore reserves more slowly than the competitive industry. The monopolist will therefore take longer to extract a fixed

Table 4.1　MONOPOLY DEPLETION OF A HOMOGENEOUS STOCK OF 7.4 TONS*

t	mr(t) − c	mr	q(t)	p(t)	(p(t) − c) · q(t)	$\dfrac{(p(t) - c) \cdot q(t)}{(1.1)^t}$
6	9	10	0	10	0	0
5	8.1818181	9.1818181	.409091	9.590909	3.5144635	2.1822052
4	7.4380165	8.4380165	.7809917	9.219009	6.4189778	4.3842478
3	6.761833	7.761833	1.1194083	8.880592	8.8216	6.6277982
2	6.1471211	7.1471211	1.4264394	8.573561	10.803225	8.9282842
1	5.5882919	6.5882919	1.705854	8.294146	12.442748	11.11588
0	5.0802654	6.0802654	1.9598673	8.040133	13.797726	13.797726
			7.401327			47.231849

* The demand curve is linear, and we solve by working back from the terminal period: $q = 10 - p$, $c = 1$, $r = 0.1$, $q = (10 - mr)/2$.

stock of ore than a competitive industry. We illustrate with a numerical example in Table 4.1.

The linear demand schedule example in Table 4.1 is based on the same demand schedule and extraction costs as our example for the competitive regime in Chapter 3. Again, we work back from the terminal time for the same six periods, but now *only half as much ore* is extracted in the same time as was the case under competitive extraction. In other words, a monopolist will take exactly twice as long to extract the same stock of reserves as would a competitive industry. The difference in the relative speeds of extraction between the two market structures led Hotelling (1931) to remark that the monopolist was a "friend of the conservationist." That is, the monopolist would run down the stock more slowly than the planner. This also implies that for the same stock size, the monopolist's initial price will be higher and rise at a slower rate than for the competitive regime.

We sketch a price and quantity path in Figure 4.4 for the competitive regime and one for a monopoly regime that illustrate these results. In Figure 4.4(a), there are two smooth price paths, one for the monopolist *(M)* and the other for the competitive industry *(C)*. Each regime has an identical stock of ore reserves with zero extraction costs (for simplicity). As in Chapter 3, we are looking at smooth price and output paths as approximations to the discrete-time model. The initial price for the monopoly regime is P^M, while P^c is the initial price for the competitive regime. Suppose both begin extraction at time t_0. $\overline{P}$ is the choke price from the linear demand curve.

In Figure 4.4(b), there are two extraction (quantity) paths corresponding to the price paths. The monopolist's output is initially lower than the competitive industry's, so the initial monopoly price must be higher. But because marginal revenue is less than price, the price path of the monopolist is flatter than that of the competitive industry (it rises more slowly). Recall that Hotelling's rule for the monopolist requires marginal revenue to "grow" at the rate of interest while for the competitive industry, it is price that grows at the rate of interest (when extraction costs are zero). The monopolist then extracts *less* in early periods than the competitive industry, but *more* in later periods when the competitive industry nears exhaustion. The monopolist exhausts its ore reserves at a later date, T^M, than the competitive exhaustion date, T^c.

We can see then that in early periods of the extraction horizon, the monopoly price exceeds the competitive price. But because the competitive price is rising faster

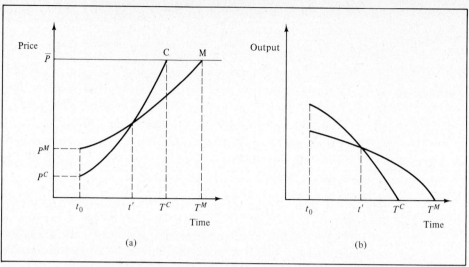

Figure 4.4   Price and quantity schedules over time for extraction under competition and under monopoly for a linear demand schedule and zero extraction costs. Monopoly extracts the same stock over a longer horizon. The monopolist produces less for all periods up to t' and charges a higher price. For periods after t', monopoly output exceeds competitive output and monopoly price is lower. The price path of the monopolist is flatter than that of the competitive industry exploiting the same stock.

than the monopoly price, at the point t', the competitive price exceeds the monopoly price (because competitive extraction falls below monopoly extraction). However, over the two time horizons for the regimes, consumers will spend more in present value on the mineral if extracted by a monopolist than under the competitive structure. Monopoly rent, which includes both resource rent *and* the excess profits of the monopolist, exceeds the resource rent accruing to the competitive industry.

Consumers are thus worse off under monopoly than with perfect competition in the sense that they are paying more for the mineral and consuming less of it in early periods. In later periods, the monopoly price is lower than the competitive price and monopoly output is higher, but these lower prices and higher outputs must be discounted back to t_0 so they are weighted less heavily than the price output combinations in early periods. Monopoly profits (including resource rent) exceed those of the competitive industry (see the last column of Table 4.1 and Table 3.2). But other welfare costs are possible.

Suppose the monopolist does not have 100 percent control of the market, and some very small firms also exist. What will happen to these firms over time? Given the monopoly price path, an individualistic "outsider" with a small deposit would be induced to extract and to "dump" its stock on the market, because the price of the mineral would be rising at less than the rate of interest. A monopolist can thus induce "outsiders" with small holdings to get rid of their stocks and in this sense strengthen its monopoly power.

The result on the relative speeds of extraction under monopoly versus perfect competition is not general. For a *constant elasticity demand* schedule, $p = \alpha q^{-\epsilon}$, marginal revenue is $p(1 - \epsilon)$. Hence, price and marginal revenue are *proportional* to one another, the factor of proportionality being constant. Monopoly and competitive extraction paths are *identical* in this case if extraction costs are zero. This can be illustrated graphically in a two-period model derived from Stiglitz (1976). The horizontal axis of Figure 4.5 measures the total stock of the deposit. Extraction must be divided among the two periods so as to deplete the stock fully. Thus, the output chosen in the first period determines the output for the second. The vertical axis on the left side measures the current market price of the resource, which is also the shadow price or rental value of the resource in the ground because there are no extraction costs. The vertical axis on the right side is the price of the resource in the next period discounted back to the present.

Hotelling's rule requires extraction to be chosen such that the discounted price for the competitive firm or marginal revenue for the monopolist is the same in each period. We assume that demand and hence MR is stationary over the two periods. The D_1 and MR_1 are the demand and marginal revenue curves for an isoelastic demand curve in the first period and D_2 and MR_2 are the curves (which depend on the discounted price) for the second period. The second-period curves are simply the first-period curves "flipped over." It is then easy to see that the competitive and monopolistic equilibrium must coincide. For the competitive firm, P_1 must equal $P_2/(1 + r)$ while for the monopolist, MR_1 must equal $MR_2/(1 + r)$. The quantity produced and price charged are the same for each type of firm. Output will be divided between the two periods by the point q'. Output in period 1 will be Oq', while output in period 2 will be $q'q''$. Because marginal revenue is proportional to demand, the

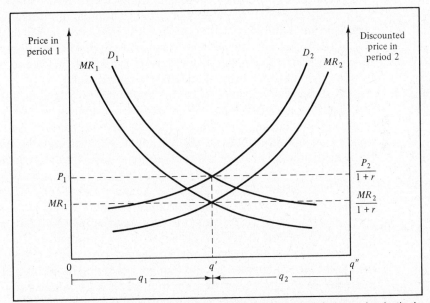

Figure 4.5 A monopolist and perfectly competitive industry both facing an isoelastic demand curve will extract the same output and charge the same price as the other in each period. In the competitive industry, price in the first period is equated with the discounted price in the second period. The monopolist equates marginal revenue in the first period to discounted marginal revenue in the second period and prices off the demand curve. Each type of industry will produce q_1 in period 1 and q_2 in period 2 to fully exhaust the stock of reserves in the two periods.

competitive and monopoly outputs coincide.[3] If we reintroduce extraction costs into the model, the monopolist will again extract more slowly than the competitive industry.

For our basic model of monopoly extraction, comparative statics indicating how paths respond to changes in parameters are much like those for the competitive industry model in Chapter 3. Working back from the time of exhaustion, we can see that an increase in the constant cost of extraction will increase the duration for depleting the stock. An increase in the rate of interest will shorten the time to depletion of the stock. Since a tax of x dollars per unit output is the same as an increase in the constant cost of extraction, such a tax will lengthen the period over which the stock is depleted. An excise tax of y percent of the price of the ore is equivalent to a flattening and lowering of a linear demand curve. This will slow extraction near the beginning of the program, and the new speed of extraction near the end will depend on the amount of flattening and lowering of the demand curve induced by the tax.[4] Industry analysts often do not concern themselves with tax effects on industry extraction in this context; they ask themselves how many mines or deposits will become uneconomic as mineral taxes rise. This is a slightly different type of "tilting" of the industry extraction path.

Dominant Firms and Fringe Sellers: A Case of Oliogopoly

Suppose a mineral industry consists of a mixture of firms, some competitive and some acting as a single monopoly or *cartel.* A number of mineral industries may be characterized in this way. For example, OPEC has been viewed as the cartel and the rest of the world as "fringe" suppliers. A less well known example is that of the IBA—a producers' association in the bauxite industry, which also faces competition from a group of fringe firms that behave competitively.

A straightforward version of this model has the cartel or dominant seller extracting from a known stock of ore at low constant extraction costs. The fringe producers are perfectly competitive and also have the same constant costs of extraction. An equilibrium involves the dominant seller setting an initial price, and exhausting its stock. The *marginal revenue net of extraction costs* of the dominant firm rises at the rate of interest. The price rise in this phase is sufficiently slow so that fringe sellers with perfect foresight await the capital gains of selling *after* the cartel has exhausted its stock. That is, fringe producers cannot extract at the same time as the cartel and still satisfy Hotelling's rule. If no large capital gain is foreseen, these fringe sellers would sell off their holdings ahead of the monopolist.

In the second phase, *rent* (price minus marginal cost) for the competitive fringe rises at the rate of interest. Each seller is maximizing its discounted profit with this approach. We illustrate a price path in Figure 4.6. In Figure 4.6, C_d is the cartel or dominant seller's constant extraction cost and C_f is the same constant extraction cost for the competitive fringe. Rent rises at the rate of interest between T_f and T, and marginal revenue less extraction cost rises at the rate of interest between T_d and T_f. Over $T_f T$ the fringe exhausts its total stock and over $T_d T_f$ the dominant seller exhausts its total stock. Such an oligopoly extraction program has been labeled a *binding contract* program because everyone agrees at the outset at T_d to follow it. It is

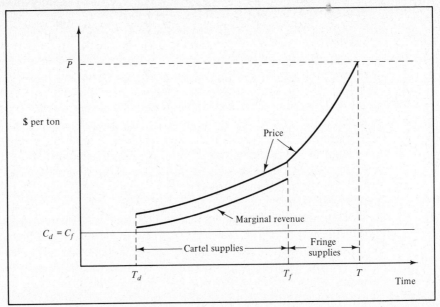

Figure 4.6 With identical extraction costs, while the monopolist (cartel) is selling, price net of costs rises at less than the rate of interest. The fringe waits until the cartel exhausts its stock. In the last phase rent (price net of extraction costs) rises at the rate of interest. The fringe exhausts at T.

as if a legal agreement were arrived at at the beginning of extraction. In addition, it is a *dynamically consistent* program because at no date after T_d is any agent induced to change its extraction plan in anticipation of greater profit.

If the constant extraction costs for the two parties, fringe and monopolist, are different, three new types of paths can emerge. First, if the cartel has high extraction costs, it will sell after the fringe has exhausted its stock. (With identical extraction costs, the monopolist exhausted its stock first in the sequence while rent was rising slower than the rate of interest.) Second, there can be intervals over which the two parties are both supplying mineral simultaneously—a Cournot situation in which the marginal revenue net of extraction costs for the monopolist is rising at the rate of interest for its part of the quantity demanded and the price net of extraction cost for the fringe is rising at the rate of interest. Third, it can pay the monopolist to sell some of its stock while rent rises at the rate of interest *in order to push down the initial price* in the complete extraction program and speed up the interval to exhaustion by the fringe.

This is like a "loss leader." One sacrifices some profit on some ore "dumped" on the market in phase 1 in order to speed up exhaustion by the fringe. Once the fringe is done, the monopolist can maximize its discounted profits on the remaining ore without the possibility of entry by rivals. The fringe here is passive. They sell as long as rent never rises over any interval at a rate faster than the rate of interest. The monopolist is "dumping" some stock early to force down the initial price. This can lead to a *dynamic inconsistency*. The optimal extraction plan set at the initial time will be departed from in a profit-maximizing fashion as extraction proceeds, and time passes. Dynamic inconsistency will be observed when a dominant seller changes extraction paths at a certain date after "announcing" it would be following "path A."

An easy illustration of dynamic inconsistency involves the case where the fringe has low constant costs of extraction, while the cartel has high constant extraction costs per ton. The binding contract equilibrium for this case involves the cartel selling some stock during the initial competitive or fringe phase of the program in order to push the initial price down and speed the fringe toward exhaustion. Price path $ECBA$ in Figure 4.7 is the relevant binding contract path. Over EC, the fringe sells alone with rent rising at the rate of interest. Rent for the fringe continues to rise at the rate of interest over BC, even though the fringe has exhausted its stock. This is a phase in which the cartel sacrifices current profit in order to push down the initial price at E to speed exhaustion by the fringe sellers.

Consider this program as an "equilibrium." In the first phase, only the fringe is producing and price moves along EC as its rent per ton rises at the rate of interest. At T_1 it exhausts its stock and price is at C. Here is the catch: At T_1, the dominant seller observes that the fringe is no longer able to produce and compete and so can set its price anywhere. Selling off any stock along BC while its marginal revenue net of cost is *not* rising at the rate of interest is not profit maximizing. So the cartel will set a new price at T_1, different from C, so that it will sell all its stock while its marginal revenue net of cost rises at the rate of interest and price ends at the choke price c_z. *Thus, there is: (a) an incentive for an agent to deviate from the binding contract extraction path,*

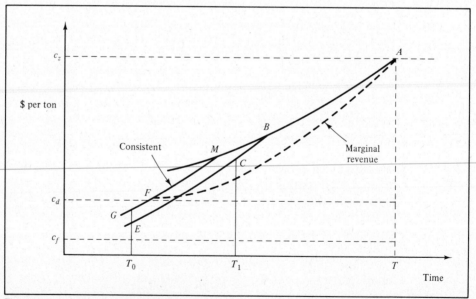

Figure 4.7 Extraction program $ECBA$ is dynamically inconsistent. The cartel sells along CB to force down the initial price at E, but at T_1 it will not be induced to follow price path CB because the fringe has exhausted its stock. Path $GFMBA$ corresponds to a consistent program. The fringe and the cartel sell simultaneously in the first phase.

and (b) no check to the cartel is actually deviating from this path. The binding contract path is not dynamically consistent; it would unravel as time progressed, and given perfect foresight, would never be followed by any of the firms in the first place.

The dynamic inconsistency can be eliminated by setting up a new path based on slightly different behavioral assumptions. In the first phase, we will have both groups selling, and the cartel will still be striving to keep the initial price low in order to have the fringe exhaust quickly. But now the cartel's effective marginal revenue net of extraction cost will be rising at the rate of interest at the same time as the fringe's rent is rising at the rate of interest! This is a Cournot-Nash situation set out in Salant (1976). It goes as follows. The fringe has an extraction or quantity path $q_0, \ldots,$ $q_t, \ldots,$ which for the moment comes out of thin air. Given the demand curve and an output level, say q_t at time t, the cartel has an effective marginal revenue schedule AB in Figure 4.8. Now the cartel sets an extraction path using its effective marginal revenue net of extraction cost, which rises at the rate of interest. Price net of fringe cost must also rise at the rate of interest if the fringe is in dynamic equilibrium. The fringe q_ts must satisfy this dynamic equilibrium for both groups. This is a Cournot-Nash dynamic equilibrium. (It is Cournot-Nash because the cartel *treats* the fringe quantities as fixed or as parameters.)

Back in Figure 4.7, *GFMBA* is a dynamically consistent path. The fringe sells alone along price path *GF*, and the two groups sell simultaneously along *FM* using the Cournot-Nash equilibrium concept. The fringe exhausts its holdings at *M*, and the cartel sells alone with its marginal revenue net of extraction costs rising at the rate of interest until choke price c_z is reached and the cartel's stock is exhausted.

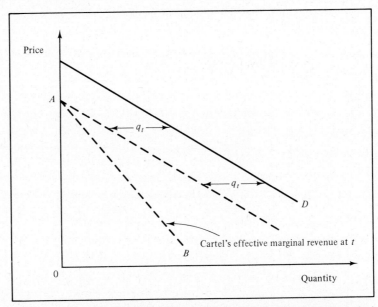

Figure 4.8 Given the fringe supplying q_t at time t, the cartel's effective marginal revenue schedule is *AB*. The schedule *AB* is used to calculate the cartel's time path of marginal revenue net of costs.

Although this new solution is dynamically consistent (neither party can deviate and make a profit given its behavioral rules), it is not in general profit-maximizing for the cartel. For example, for the cartel to take the fringe's quantity path as given is unreasonable, since the cartel is dominant and should behave in a preemptive or Stackelberg fashion. Moreover, it should optimize the stock it sells in phase 1 of the overall price path and not wait until phase 2. This was not done in the solution in Figure 4.7. Dynamically consistent Stackelberg paths are very difficult to construct, so we must leave this subject without sketching one in detail (see the discussion in Newberry, 1980). If the cartel and the fringe are operating with different discount rates — one group caring less about the future than the other — then dynamic inconsistency can also arise. For this case, Newberry (1980) makes some observations.[5]

Let us summarize. For *dynamically consistent* paths, no agent or mine owner ever wishes to depart from the optimal path once it has seen all the facts and established its future actions at the beginning of extraction. For a *dynamically inconsistent* path, optimal plans are set at the beginning of extraction, but once extraction gets under way, one party arrives at a point where it finds it profitable to depart from the previously set optimal path. *Binding contract* paths are those all extractors agree to stick to even though they might wish to change plans in the future in order to increase profits. Getting dynamically consistent paths with a dominant seller and a fringe group is very complicated when the dominant extractor is acting as a Stackelberg leader, but cases have been worked out.

BOX 4.1
Norway and the United Kingdom Sharing North Sea Oil Fields

Drilling in the North Sea along the boundary of Norway and the United Kingdom is handled as follows. In a treaty between Norway and the United Kingdom in 1965, it is stated that if a hydrocarbon find stretched over the boundary between the two countries, one should seek to unitize the interest and form a joint venture for a common development. Although the treaty does not specify how this is going to be achieved, this has been the guideline.

Every time a joint find has been made, the unitization process has commenced, and so far resulted in negotiated agreements regulating the production of the joint resources. The process can be long and tedious, and somewhat costly. The first such agreement, Frigg, was made in 1977, after about three years of negotiations. There are two main problems related to unitization: (1) How much of the reserves are in each country? (2) who will do the work?

However, it has been possible to solve these questions, and after agreements have been made, the two governments in question have entered into treaties regulating the unitized license.

There are today three such unitized fields, Frigg, Statfjord, and Murchison. Frigg and Statfjord are developed and operated from Norway, while Murchison is operated from the United Kingdom. The Frigg reserves are split in this way: 60.82 percent in Norway and 39.18 percent in the United Kingdom.

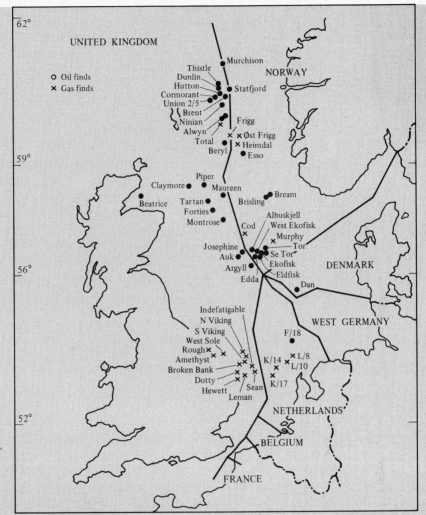

Source: R. Bailey (1978), p. 321.

Statfjord is 84.09 percent in Norway and 15.91 percent in the United Kingdom. Murchison is 74.94 percent in the United Kingdom and 25.06 percent in Norway.

The ownership can be revised every three years if any of the licensees so request. If there is a change, the ownership is revised back to day 1 in the project and redistributed among the partners both for investment and for production.

The way the unitization works is that the reservoir is looked upon as a unit. The reserves split according to the size of the reservoir in each country, and then the licensees in the licenses in question are allotted their respective shares in the reservoir. Usually, the operatorship in the unitized field is allotted to the operator in the country with the largest share of the reservoir. All investments

Box 4.1 continued

and all production is distributed to the licensees according to their share of the reservoir.

In the early 1970s, when the first joint fields were discovered, it was believed that a more free-for-all situation existed. Therefore, you will find that all the interesting blocks along the median line between Norway and United Kingdom have been licensed, in order to find out if there were joint fields. This is because one has to prove by drilling that the find is on both sides of the median line before unitization is requested. However, the licensing of blocks defines the well drilling program for the licensees, and when the border blocks were awarded, the authorities defined and made sure that all possible joint discoveries were drilled, as far as that is possible. But that does not mean that the wells are spaced in any way. The wells are drilled where seismic surveys indicate that there is any prospect of finding hydrocarbons. Where to place the wells is then part of the license negotiations and defined by prospectivity alone.

Licenses are applied for by individual companies, and license groups are put together by the government. The licensees must then undertake an agreed exploration program, which is defined in the license. The license period is 36 years, and the exploration program must be carried out in the first six years. After this period is completed, 50 percent of the licensed area must be relinquished by the license group. It can be relicensed to other groups.

BACKSTOP TECHNOLOGIES AND MARKET STRUCTURE

A crucial form of non-competitive extraction behavior is how a resource owner reacts to the different institutional forms which provision of the backstop supply can take. If, for example, resource stocks are monopolized by a cartel, then "outsiders" can influence the cartel by doing research on substitutes and announcing their discoveries. But cartel members can also do research and development on a backstop substitute, and if successful, *they* can gain control over the backstop supply. In this section, we look at how: (a) the presence of the backstop affects a monopoly (cartel) extraction plan, and (b) different market structures with which the backstop can be supplied affect the monopoly extraction plan. Our reference point will be the case of pure monopoly extraction, with price rising to a choke price (or price rising asymptotically to infinity for the case of asymptotic depletion).

A Backstop Owned by the Monopolist

When the backstop supply as well as the nonrenewable resource stock are controlled by a monopolist, marginal revenue net of unit extraction costs will rise at the rate of interest in the resource extraction phase at the outset. There will be a "ceiling" marginal revenue from the backstop calculated in the usual way.[6] We follow Hoel (1978) here and assume that the monopolist switches over to the backstop when marginal revenue from extraction equals the marginal revenue from using the back-

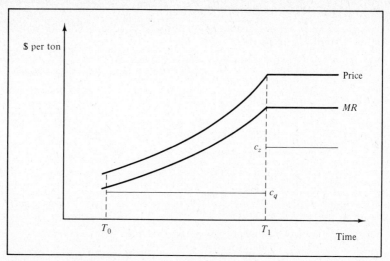

Figure 4.9 Since the monopolist controls both the resource stock and the backstop, its marginal revenue is continuous (without jumps) across the two phases. c_z is the cost of the backstop.

stop. It will never pay the monopolist to sell the mineral once the marginal revenue from mineral extraction equals the backstop marginal revenue because the marginal revenue per ton of mineral extracted cannot rise, and hence later tons earn less in present value terms.

The general implication of the presence of this backstop with its "constraint" or "ceiling" on marginal revenue is that marginal revenue and the mineral price will be lower at the instant of exhaustion than they would be if the backstop were not present. This leads to a *lengthening* of the duration of complete extraction of a fixed stock of the mineral, or an increase in the initial price over what it would be without the monopolist being faced with a backstop. We illustrate the price path in Figure 4.9. In Figure 4.9, T_1 is the date of transition from resource extraction to substitute production from the backstop; c_q is the constant cost of unit extraction, and c_z is the constant cost of providing a unit from the backstop. Exhaustion of the mineral stock occurs at T_1, with price and marginal revenue remaining constant thereafter as the backstop is produced.

A Resource Monopolist Facing a Competitive Backstop Technology

Suppose now that the backstop technology can be supplied by a competitive industry. The cost of producing the backstop is constant at c_z. What will happen to the monopolist's extraction path? We illustrate in Figures 4.10 and 4.11. In Figure 4.10, the monopolist begins extraction at T_0. Quantity extracted will be chosen such that marginal revenue net of extraction costs will rise over each interval of time at the rate of interest. The present value of marginal revenues will be constant. For the output extracted, the monopolist charges the maximum buyers are willing to pay, as represented by the demand curve shown in Figure 4.11. One can think of output falling in

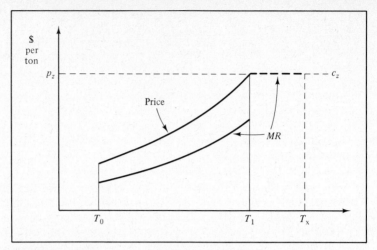

Figure 4.10   The marginal revenue jumps at T_1 as the monopoly resource owner moves to the phase in which the competitive backstop price is constant at c_z. The monopolist continues selling at c_z until he exhausts his stock at T_x and the backstop "takes over."

each subsequent period as the monopolist "moves up" its marginal revenue curve. However, as soon as output reaches q' and marginal revenue hits point b in Figure 4.11, the price will rise to the unit cost of providing the backstop good. This is also shown in Figure 4.10, where the price path intersects the line $p_z c_z$ at time T_1.

What this means is that marginal revenue net of extraction costs can no longer rise at the rate of interest after time T_1. Marginal revenue "jumps" at T_1 and output q' to c_z and remains constant thereafter until the monopolist exhausts its fixed reserves at time T_x. In Figure 4.11(b), the present value of marginal revenues is shown.

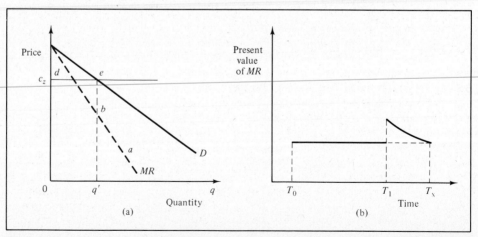

Figure 4.11   Given that the backstop technology can be produced at constant cost c_z, marginal revenue rises at the rate of interest between dates T_0 and T. At date T_1 marginal revenue jumps to c_z and falls in present value until date T_x because the current value of MR is constant at the cost of producing the backstop. Schedule $abed$ is the marginal revenue followed.

Discounted marginal revenue in the early phase of extraction will be constant. Then it will jump up and in the last phase, current marginal revenue will be constant at c_z, but discounted marginal revenue will decline as the interest rate takes effect. The present value of marginal revenue for the last ton is the same as the value for earlier tons.

With constant extraction costs per ton, the current value of marginal revenue less extraction cost at the end of the second phase, namely, at T_x when discounted to the end of the first phase (date T_1) must equal the current value of marginal revenue less extraction cost at T_1. This makes the monopolist indifferent between adding a marginal ton of mineral to the beginning of its extraction program to the end of date t. (An example is presented in Appendix D.)

However, in spite of the positive jump in marginal revenue, the high value of marginal revenue is less than the terminal value the monopolist could get without the presence of the backstop. The profit on the late phase of extraction is *reduced by the presence of the backstop.* This induces the monopolist to *defer* reaching the final extraction phase. Thus, the competitively supplied backstop causes the monopolist to raise its initial price and lengthen the time it takes to reach the last stage of extraction. Then at time T_1 (output q'), when the marginal revenue would jump to c_z, the monopolist *prevents* the entry of the backstop suppliers by pricing the mineral infinitesimally *below* c_z until the resource stock is exhausted at time T_x.[7]

Gilbert and Goldman (1978) presented this model of constrained monopoly extraction to illustrate a paradox involving limit pricing. They suggested that the monopolist's rising mineral price would induce entry by competitors. Given the entry of competitive backstop suppliers, they pointed out that the monopolist's initial price would lie *above* the price the monopolist would set in the absence of the backstop entry. Hence, the paradox — potential competition from the backstop induced *higher* prices from the monopolist, the prevailing supplier of a perfect substitute. It is also true that as the price of the backstop is *reduced,* the initial price for the monopolist's extraction is *increased.* The lower the price of the backstop, the longer the monopolist will want to defer reaching that backstop and thus the higher its initial price. Potential competition to a monopoly resource supplier through the introduction of a backstop technology can thus actually worsen consumers' well-being.

Strategic Behavior in Developing a Substitute

The element of strategy between exhaustible resource suppliers and potential substitute suppliers has been investigated in detail for the case of a developer of a substitute who can move first in a strategic game. The idea is that, for example, if an innovator of fusion power can credibly announce a date and price of providing the substitute, that innovator influences the price and pace of depletion of the exhaustible resource stock. This could be another example of OPEC versus the West if OPEC was the monopolist oil supplier and the West the "player" developing a perfect substitute such as fusion power. In such a game it turns out that if the cost of developing the substitute is not too high, it pays to perfect the technology and hold it in abeyance for an interval while additional stocks of the exhaustible resource are used up. This holds true even though it is more costly to develop the technology for producing the substitute earlier than later. Moreover, even if it were possible to implement the technology for producing the substitute earlier at no additional cost, there are circumstances in which it pays to delay implementation while some of the stock of the exhaustible resource is used up.

The details of deriving these results are intricate, but the outline of the narrative is easy to follow (see Dasgupta, Gilbert and Stiglitz, 1983, and Gallini, Lewis and Ware, 1983). First, we observe the best extraction plan for the resource cartel in the face of a fixed date of *availability* of the substitute. Then we ask at what date the substitute supplier would actually make its innovation available, given that the substitute costs more to develop if the date of availability is brought forward.

There are three distinct "response paths" of the cartel to a known date of availability of the substitute. The first is early availability of the substitute at price $\bar{p}$. We observed in the limit-pricing example that if the substitute is available at the outset, it pays the cartel to let price rise to $\bar{p}$ and exhaustion ensue some time later, the last part of the stock being sold at a constant current price infinitesimally below $\bar{p}$. The same argument holds for dates of availability up to T_1 in Figure 4.12(a). T_1 is the time that the cartel would choose to sell the resource at the constant price $\bar{p}$ per ton. Suppose next there is moderate delay in the availability of the substitute. For dates of availability beyond T_1 but less than T_2, in Figure 4.11(b), it pays the cartel to let the price rise above $\bar{p}$ until the substitute is available at T and then to sell off the remaining stock at the price of the substitute, $\bar{p}$. For dates T beyond T_2, the cartel will have an extraction plan where exhaustion occurs at the instant the substitute is made available at price $\bar{p}$. Again, the resource price rises above $\bar{p}$, but at time T the resource stock is exhausted. There is no simultaneous extraction of the mineral and presence of the backstop as in the intermediate case. Notice in Figure 4.12(b) and (c) that the cartel must *lower* its initial price to obtain these price paths.

We summarize. Given a fixed date T of availability of the substitute at a known price p, three distinct responses from the cartel are profit-maximizing. The appropri-

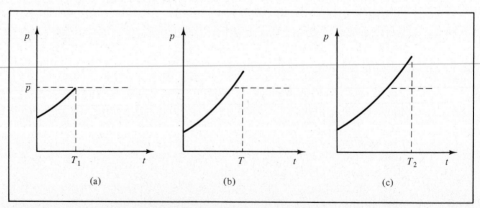

Figure 4.12 T is the known date of innovation of the substitute for the resource. For early innovation ($T \leqq T_1$), we have a price path sketched in (a). For late innovation date T, ($T \geqq T_2$), we have the path in (c) with no resource sold at price $\bar{p}$. For the intermediate innovation date, we have as in (b) price rising above $\bar{p}$ for an interval and then some stock sold at price $\bar{p}$.

ate response depends how far into the future the date T is. The two basic responses involve either no sales at prices above p (case a — early availability of the backstop) or no sales for an interval of time at price p (case c — a later availability of the backstop). In cases b and c, the price of the resource thus rises temporarily above what will be the price of the backstop good. The reason this can occur is that implementation of the backstop is not until a later date. The difference between the "intermediate" and "late" availability is whether the resource stock is depleted (late case) or not (intermediate case) when the backstop is available.

So far, we have looked simply at arbitrary dates of availability. What is the optimal date for the substitute developer to make its product available to resource users? This presumes that the developer's announcement of a date is made at the beginning of the game (at time $T = 0$). That is, the developer's announcement must be *credible* and given at the onset of the game (the first mover). The cartel responds by announcing its optimal extraction plan. The solution to the game is that it is optimal to make the substitute available for use slightly beyond T_1. This holds true even if at no cost it could be made available earlier. If it were made available earlier, then the cartel would pursue the extraction plan in Figure 4.12(a). For dates beyond T_1, it pursues the plan in Figure 4.12(b) or (c). An announcement of availability before T_1 forces the cartel to raise its initial price of the resource.

This optimal action of the part of the substitute developer is what we argued for intuitively at the outset of this section. First, it often pays to develop a substitute and make it available, but not use it for an interval. This action forces the resource extractor to respond in a particular fashion. Second, even if the substitute were available earlier than T_1 at no extra cost, it pays the developer to hold availability to date T_1. This model has strong implications for, say, the development of energy resources other than fossil fuels. Even though we do not anticipate using these alternatives for a while, research and development today may result in lower prices for conventional fuels.

Now consider some revisions of this model. First, suppose that rather than the substitute developer announcing first, each player commits itself to a future action *simultaneously* at time zero. It turns out that even with this option, the cartel will find it optimal to follow the announced action of the substitute developer (see Dasgupta, Gilbert, and Stiglitz, 1983, p. 1446). Second, suppose there is a competitive race to develop the substitute in the resource-importing country, in which the winner has sole rights to use of the new substitute technology. It turns out that now it is optimal for the cartel to maintain prices higher than they would be otherwise in order to deter substitute development (see Dasgupta, Gilbert, and Stiglitz, 1983, p. 1447). Third, if there is competition in the resource-supplying country for the patent on the new technology, the cartel will preempt rival developers. We assume that resource users do not engage in research and development for this case (see Dasgupta, Gilbert, and Stiglitz, 1983, p. 1447).

This gives a hint of how strategic "play" by resource users can affect paths of exhaustible resource use. The results above have been worked out in relatively simple contexts; realistic "play" will be harder to unravel. For example, the resource stocks are of known size and of standard quality in this analysis, which clearly is not true in real-world situations.

Recycling as an Alternate Source of Supply

If all the world's copper were extracted from the ground and oceans, it would still be possible to acquire copper for some time by bidding it away from existing users and recycling it. An active market with a stable price could develop in recycled copper if new demands for copper are not growing too rapidly. Recycling in this sense is a special kind of backstop technology. As primary copper prices rise, it can become less costly for users to develop recycled metals rather than pushing extraction into lower-quality ore bodies. This type of recycling is impossible with minerals which are burned up in use, such as oil, coal, uranium, and natural gas. This makes the markets for durable versus combustible minerals different.

BOX 4.2
Recycling

Rapidly rising energy prices in the 1970s put recycling on a more cost-competitive basis with new production of such products as aluminum, steel, and paper than it had been earlier. For example, between 1970 and 1981 the percentage of the production of aluminum recycled worldwide increased from 17 to 28, and in the United States alone, from 17 to 32 percent. And yet in the United States in 1981, more recyclable aluminum in the form of beverage cans was thrown away than was produced in Africa in both primary and secondary smelters. There is, moreover, an active international trade in scrap with, for example, large amounts of Norwegian scrap aluminum ending up in smelters in Italy. The Soviet Union recycled and exported only 10 percent as much aluminum as it consumed in 1979. The incentives have been lacking for recycling. There, gross rather than net production figures are often considered the index of success.

Recycling forest products is also an expanding activity. Between 1970 and 1980, recycled paper as a percentage of total consumption grew worldwide from 21 to 25 and in the United States from 21 to 27. In Canada, the figure was constant at 19 percent. However, international trade in waste paper has grown in the same period from almost nothing to 10 percent of all waste paper collected. In South Korea, 40 percent of the fiber used in paper production is derived from imported waste paper. The United States is the major exporter, accounting for about 85 percent of net sales. A subtle part of the "price" of recycled products is the implicit cost of collecting the waste material. For example, for residents to separate their garbage into glass and metal, paper products, and other material can be inconvenient or personally costly. Small changes in the way products are handled and packaged could make the process of separation less irksome. In Islip, New York, inspectors were assigned to patrol garbage at the curb and to fine people who did not separate the material.

Steel has long been recycled as dramatic pictures of autobody compactors indicate. Currently, about 25 percent of world consumption each year is recycled steel. For the United States, the figure is 35 percent and for the Soviet

Union, the rate is 17 percent. Certain furnaces operate more effectively with scrap. The open hearth furnace generally uses about 45 percent scrap, the basic oxygen furnace about 28 percent, while the electric arc furnace operates well with 100 percent scrap as "fuel." The electric arc furnace can produce steel with 75 percent less energy than other processes and has a lower capital cost. Use of this smelting technology has grown dramatically around the world. This is the ideal furnace for recycling, also.

Source: William U. Chandler, "Materials Recycling: The Virtue of Necessity." Worldwatch Paper 56. Washington, D.C.: Worldwatch Institute, 1983.

MARKET STRUCTURE AND COMMON POOL PROBLEMS WITH OIL AND GAS RESOURCES

Certain nonrenewable resources such as oil and gas seep away from one underground pool or reservoir to another in the same field as rates of extraction vary from one location to another above ground. This seepage is a form of externality or failure of property rights to be defined over the entire reservoir. One reservoir owner can increase its share of the marketable mineral by drawing oil from a neighboring reservoir without paying for the oil. Generally, this externality will lead to inefficiently rapid extraction of each reservoir in a preemptive battle.

Rapid extraction can take the form of working existing wells at rapid rates or by drilling more wells than is efficient and working those wells at less than efficient rates. In either case, the end is to extract more rapidly than would be done in the absence of seepage. Not only is extraction excessive, but the total stock recovered from all fields will fall, because the ultimate size of the recoverable stock is inversely related to the *rate* of extraction. Moreover, with a small number of extractors, overly rapid extraction leads to downward pressure on current prices. In the special case where firms are small and ignore the effect of "preempted" seepage on current price, the seepage externality will be less pronounced in its effect on extraction programs. Very rapid extraction can be inefficient because some oil gets left underground unnecessarily.

All seepage from under one well to another could be avoided if each firm could instantly exhaust its stock at the outset and store the oil above ground. This situation is physically impossible and can be ruled out as well by introducing above-ground storage costs. One can view these man-made storage facilities as the external cost of seepage, because without seepage there would not be a race to extract and oil could be stored free underground.

A straightforward way to introduce seepage into our models is to have stock of firm i disappear or appear as firm i's holdings fall short of or exceed the average size of its neighbor's holdings of stock. Given extraction, firm i's stock can be reduced in two ways—via direct extraction by firm i or by seepage:

$$\dot{S}_i^u = -q_i(t) - \alpha[S_i^u(t) - MS_{(j\neq i)}^u]$$

where $\dot{S}_i^u$ is the instantaneous change in i's stock size at a point in time
$q_i(t)$ is what firm i is currently extracting
S_i^u is i's current stock underground
$MS_{(j \neq i)}^u$ is the mean size of its neighbor's stocks underground
α is a technical coefficient relating the seepage flow to the difference between i's stock size and its neighbor's stock size

In the small group case, each firm realizes that whatever stock a rival has or acquires from seepage will affect the market price path. Assuming that these effects are fully anticipated, we are then in a Cournot world where rivals' paths are known and fixed in equilibrium.[8]

The *flow condition* on extraction for firm i in such a model is (see Sinn, 1982):

$$\frac{\dot{\lambda}_i}{\lambda_i} = r + \frac{C'(A_i)}{\lambda_i}$$

where λ_i is the value of a barrel of oil in the ground
r is the interest rate
$C'(A_i)$ is the marginal cost of storing an extra barrel of oil in above-ground tanks

This condition is much like one involving heterogeneous stocks. The capital gain on a barrel left in the ground must exceed the rate of interest in order to compensate the firm for maintaining stocks in storage. (Storage costs play the role of rising extraction costs in a model with heterogeneous stocks.)

For the special case of n identical firms and a market demand curve with elasticity η, the rate condition becomes

$$\frac{\dot{p}}{p} = r + \alpha \left[1 + \frac{1}{\eta(n-1)} \right]$$

where p is price per barrel and some mineral is still underground. The terminal condition involves asymptotic depletion of each owner's stock at a rate which is the same for each identical firm.

The solution involves an initial phase with rapid extraction (rapid relative to the rate with no seepage). Some of the oil or gas extracted is sold on the open market by each firm, while the rest is stored. During this phase, the value of the loss to firm i from a barrel that has seeped away equals the cost of storing an extra barrel in above-ground tanks. In the second phase, below-ground extraction ceases as stocks are exhausted. The oil stored above ground is used up in the usual intertemporal program except that there are now costs of storage incorporated. Unit storage costs should rise as the stock in tanks is run down, since fixed storage tanks must be maintained with progressively less oil in them. We sketch the solution in Figure 4.13, which is due to Sinn (1982).

In Figure 4.13, the current stock of oil, whether above or below ground, is measured on the horizontal axis. Current extraction and/or delivery to market is measured on the vertical axis (S is in millions of barrels and $R(t)$ is in barrels). Time moves along the lines in the direction of the arrows. Starting with the same overall

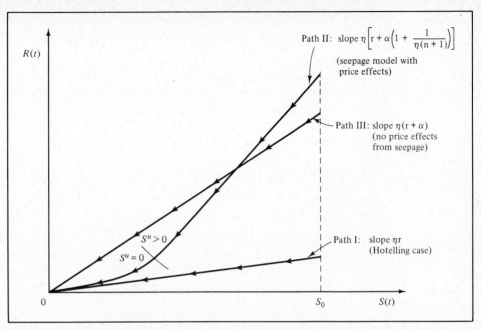

Figure 4.13 $R(t)$ are deliveries from mines and/or stored stock above ground. $S(t)$ is the current size of the stock. Time is indicated by arrows. Three regimes are indicated with the same initial stock S_0, paths I, II, and III. Path II, the schedule with seepage and price effects, involves an early phase of exhaustion of mines. Stored ore in the first phase is exhausted in the second phase. The Hotelling case (path I) has less extraction for any stock size, and there is no storage for this case of no seepage.

underground stock of S_0 divided among firms, there are three possible paths. In the standard Hotelling model with no seepage (path I), less oil or gas is extracted and/or delivered at each date than when there are seepage and storage costs that affect oil prices (path II). Exhaustion of underground stocks occurs in the seepage path at the line cutting at 90 degrees. Deliveries are then made from stored oil.

The third case is shown by path III, where there are no price effects from "captured" seepage. Price effects arise when each seller realizes that its production is having some perceptible affect on the current price. This path is also everywhere inefficient in the sense that the rate of extraction and/or deliveries always exceeds that for the case of no seepage (path I, the Hotelling case).

To see these "overextraction" results, observe that for any value of S, deliveries R, measured on the vertical axis, are larger when there is seepage than for the case with no seepage. (Time will be moving at different rates along the different schedules, so that we have extraction and/or delivery rates related only to current stock sizes, not to similar calendar dates. Starting with the same S_0, each program will be carried out over infinite time, but rates of change in R will differ over time.)

The traditional solution for an externality like seepage is to assign property rights to the field. This is called *unitization*. The different reservoirs in the field are assigned to a single owner or are managed by a government agency that prorations the allowable extraction of oil or gas in the field among the different owners. If a government manager assigns the extraction rights, the efficient Hotelling solution can be achieved. Unitization by a firm instead of a public authority would create a local monopoly and could involve the misallocations associated with that noncompetitive form of organization.

Our analysis has turned heavily on the presence of storage and the costs of storage. This is a convenient way to introduce a constraint on very rapid extraction of the stock. An alternative approach would involve no storage costs but extraction costs that rose very rapidly with the amount currently extracted. The result would still have an inefficiency arising from the "racing" in extraction by firm i to avoid loss from seepage.

BOX 4.3
Avoiding Excessive Drilling and Overly Rapid Extraction in Alberta

The Energy Resources Conservation Board (ERCB) of the Alberta Government regulates the spacing of wells and rates of extraction, including, of course, rates from pools with common property characteristics. This is called prorationing. With regard to well spacing, the standard for oil pools is one well per section. (A section is an area 1 mile square.) These guidelines can be amended in certain circumstances. For example, if the productivity of an oil pool is 15 barrels per day with one well per 1/4 section, it could take a couple of hundred years to drain the reservoir if it is a large pool. In this case, the producer can apply to the ERCB to arrange for a denser configuration of wells. For high-productivity pools of, say, 400 barrels per day, the ERCB would not usually permit more than one well per 1/4 section. (A barrel is 31.5 U.S. gallons.)

Overly rapid extraction by competitors drawing from a single pool is controlled by regulators. Maximum efficient rates are assigned by the ERCB to a pool. If for one pool with two producers this rate was set at 500 barrels per day, each producer would be permitted to extract 250 barrels per day. In the event that there was excess capacity in the system, the allowable rates would be reduced by the ERCB. "There is little or no room for subterfuge in this process," the ERCB reports, "because all oil pipelines are designated common carriers which has the effect of turning refiners into common purchasers." The antidiscrimination regulations for common carriers prevent favorable treatment for a producer who might be extracting more rapidly than it has been permitted by law.

An alternative approach to excessive drilling and pumping by competitors in the same field is unitization. Many states have laws encouraging this single control or ownership in a common pool. The advantage over prorationing is that it leaves the incentive to extract completely with the owner. This has proved especially important in the matter of the secondary recovery of oil. Under unitization, the incentive to invest heavily in secondary recovery methods exists, whereas it does not under prorationing. In this latter case, severe problems in coordinating investment would be required. Certainly, prorationing to a large extent solves the common property problem in oil pools.

> Libecap and Wiggins (1984) cite a report that estimates that 100,000 unnecessary wells were not drilled at an annual saving of $10 billion because of prorationing in Texas, Louisiana, New Mexico, and Mississippi in the late 1940s.
>
> *Source:* Energy Resources Conservation Board, Calgary, Alberta, Canada, personal communication.)

SUMMARY

1. The interval of extracting a known stock can be longer when the stock is controlled by a monopolist rather than a group of perfect competitors.
2. With a dominant resource seller "sharing" the market with a fringe group of perfect competitors, dynamic inconsistencies can arise. The dominant seller can be motivated to reverse its stated optimal policy as time passes for inconsistent cases.
3. Costs of extraction are important in the determination of optimal extraction programs. The presence of the substitute or backstop can affect extraction programs under different market structures.
4. When the timing of development of the technology for producing the substitute is endogenous, cases of "sleeping patents" can arise—cases in which a new technology is invented before it is planned to put it into use.
5. Recycling is a special type of technology to replace extraction from natural deposits.
6. Spillover effects of one firm's extraction activity on another affect the pace of depletion of a deposit.

DISCUSSION QUESTIONS

1. Suppose the SUN Company sees that it can perfect a solar power system to produce energy at the equivalent of an oil price of $30 per barrel (U.S.). It will be such a good system that oil producers will be obliged to respond by keeping their price below $30 per barrel. Should the government subsidize the SUN Company? Should the government force oil prices above $30 per barrel by taxes and tariffs and leave the SUN Company on its own?
2. Consider two scenarios: (a) the earth must make do with fossil fuels for all time, and (b) fusion power, a constant cost perpetual supply, comes on stream in the year 2020. Compare the price of oil today if (a) is true and if (b) is true.
3. Evaluate a policy of regulating each competitive extractor from a common pool of oil with one of legislating unitization (legally encouraging one owner of the pool).
4. Suppose the inverse demand curve for nickel is given by the equation $P = 10 - 0.5Q$ where P is the market price and Q the total output from the industry. Unit costs of extraction are constant and equal to $2 per pound. Assume a static model.
   a. Suppose that nickel is produced by a large number of competitive firms. What is the equilibrium price and output for the competitive industry?
   b. Suppose now that the industry is controlled by a monopolist. Compute the profit-maximizing output and price a monopolist would charge. Explain verbally and compute the allocative and distributive effects of monopolization of the nickel industry.
   c. How would your answers to parts (a) and (b) change if extraction costs were given by the

equation for total costs *(TC)*, $TC = 2Q + 0.5Q^2$? Does the welfare cost of monopoly rise or fall compared to case (b)? Explain.

5. Prove graphically or algebraically that the Nash-Cournot equilibrium for two firms yields a smaller aggregate output than a Stackelberg equilibrium in a static model. Explain intuitively why this is so.

6. a. Derive and explain the price and output paths for a monopolistic versus competitive mineral industry facing identical constant unit cost curves and a linear demand curve. Which regime will exhaust its ore reserves first? Explain why.

b. Derive the price and output paths assuming the monopolist begins extraction before the competitive industry. What will be the relationship between the monopolistic and competitive price over the extraction periods?

c. How will your results change from case (a) if the demand curve is isoelastic?

NOTES

1. For a more detailed discussion of the oligopolistic structure of the potash industry, see Flatters and Olewiler (1984).

2. If extraction costs per ton are constant at $\$c$, then the flow condition is $\{[MR(q_{t+1}) - c] - [MR(q_t) - c]\}/[MR(q_t) - c] = r$. If the interest rate changes in a known way into the future, r will be subscripted to be r_{t+1} to indicate which interest rate is in effect.

3. The relationship between the speed of exhaustion and varying elasticities of demand has been investigated by Lewis, Matthews, and Burness (1979), and Lewis (1976). In this latter note, there is a two-period example in which the monopolist extracts more of the fixed stock in the first period than is socially optimal. In this sense, the monopolist can extract more rapidly than the planner for certain cases. Conditions that guarantee such results are not provided.

4. For the treatment of minerals of heterogeneous quality, the reader will observe strong parallels between monopoly and simpler cases of extraction under competition. The arguments of Chapter 3 can be applied to the monopoly case here.

5. For the case of heterogeneous stocks held by the cartel and the fringe, Gilbert (1978) has outlined a scenario, but dynamic consistency was not investigated. The model above has homogeneous stocks, a simpler situation to analyze.

6. In some cases, the monopolist might "sit on" its backstop and exhaust its mineral stock in the usual way. Innovation of the backstop technology will be delayed. See Dasgupta, Gilbert, and Stiglitz (1983) and the discussion in the text.

7. If the stock is sufficiently small, there may be no early phase of rising prices. The entire stock would then be depleted at the backstop price p_z. Demand must be inelastic for the usual reason that a decline in price lowers total revenue at that point in time.

8. Costs are crucial here. If each firm assumed that what it lost from seepage today could be made up later by rapid extraction, no inefficiency would arise. Kemp and Long (1980) have developed such a model.

chapter 5

Uncertainty and Nonrenewable Resources

INTRODUCTION

Though people cope with uncertainty in going about their daily activities, including their economic activities, formal analysis of this coping as a branch of the science of behavior is fairly rudimentary. Economics relies on the notion that in the face of uncertainty, people select an action so as to maximize their *expected* (roughly speaking, "average") utility. To determine the socially optimal exploitation of a nonrenewable natural resource, the social planner maximizes expected social welfare (expected consumer and producer surplus). This is an ex ante exercise—decisions are made prior to the resolution of the uncertainty. As time passes, the uncertainty is generally resolved, and the results of the action can be seen ex post, or after the dust has settled.

Uncertainty arises in important areas in nonrenewable resource use. There is uncertainty about stock size or about how much ore is in the ground, uncertainty about how successful research and development will be in discovering substitutes for exhaustible resources (uncertainty about the cost and date of arrival of the backstop technology), uncertainty about payoffs from exploration for new stock, and uncertainty about the actions of rivals. *Risk* can be viewed as the cost uncertainty imposes on people obliged to take actions.

The general issue addressed here is, How does the presence of uncertainty affect the appropriate course of action? This can be broken down into two parts: (a) What do optimal extraction programs look like when there is uncertainty, and how do they compare with certain programs? (b) How does increased uncertainty affect optimal actions? The latter is a type of comparative statics and has been labeled the *analysis of increased riskiness*. Our emphasis will be on the first issue, but the analysis of increased riskiness will be discussed in various sections of the chapter.

First, we sketch the way economics has come to analyze uncertainty in economic life. We then examine different kinds of uncertainty in the analysis of exhaustible resources: stock size uncertainty, and uncertainty as to the cost and date of arrival of the backstop technology. With uncertainty present, we analyze how more or less uncertainty affects optimal extraction plans. The next section looks at the process of exploration for new reserves of minerals and how discoveries of new ore bodies can reduce uncertainty and change the return from mining a stock of ore. Exploration is a somewhat distinct topic, since it involves acquiring information or altering uncertainty by purposeful activity.

ECONOMICS AND UNCERTAINTY

How does an individual evaluate an uncertain prospect? Consider the uncertain payoff—say on the stock market. Suppose you have a chance of earning a capital gain on the sale of a stock of $100 with probability .2 and $300 with probability .8. What this means is that there are 2 chances out of 10 that you will earn $100, and 8 chances out of 10 that your earnings will be $300. The *expected payoff* of this situation in dollars is ($100 × .2) + ($300 × .8) = $260, which we can treat as a certain payoff for purposes of comparing certain and uncertain prospects. Since the value to an individual of an uncertain prospect of $100 with a probability of .2 and $300 with a probability of .8 is generally different than the value of a sure $260, economics has developed *expected utility theory* for comparing these payoffs.

The expected utility of the uncertain prospect is $.2U(\$100) + .8U(\$300)$ where $U(\cdot)$ is the individual's utility of income. This magnitude is then compared with $U(\$260)$—that is, the utility of a certain value of $260. If people have diminishing marginal utility of income, then the uncertain prospect of an average payoff of $260

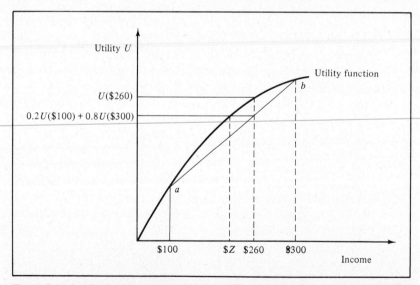

Figure 5.1 A utility function concave in income. The shape implies aversion to risk. The certain income of $260 yields more utility than the uncertain prospect of $100 with a probability of .2 and $300 with a probability of .8. The distance $260 − $Z is the premium required for the individual to be indifferent between the uncertain prospect and a certain $Z.

will be treated as less desirable than the certain $260 (see Figure 5.1). The axiom that individuals dislike uncertainty is embodied in this framework in: (a) utility of income is concave (to reflect diminishing marginal utility of income), and (b) by treating expected utility of income as a key magnitude in the calculation an individual is assumed to make when faced with uncertainty in making choices.

The expected utility of the uncertain gain, $.2U(\$100) + .8U(\$300)$, is read off the straight line ab that connects the two values, $U(\$100)$ and $U(\$300)$, at the income level of $260. The vertical gap in Figure 5.1 between the $U(\$260)$ and $.2U(\$100) + .8U(\$300)$ reflects the relative undesirability of the uncertain prospect. This gap is measured in terms of utility. The horizontal gap between $260 and Z is called the *risk premium* and represents the extra dollars ($260 − Z) an individual must be compensated with to be indifferent between a certain Z and an uncertain prospect of $100 with a probability of .2 and $300 with a probability of .8. The person must be "bribed" with ($260 − Z$) in order to "like" the uncertain prospect as much as the certain Z.

The degree or amount of uncertainty is associated with the "spread" around the mean payoff. The *variance* is one measure of spread, and for the problem above is calculated as $.2(\$100 − \$260)^2 + .8(\$300 − \$260)^2 = \$6400$. If two uncertain prospects have the same mean payoff but different variances, the one with the higher variance is said to be more risky and yields less utility to a risk-averse individual. The risk premium depends on the curvature of the utility function of income. The more "concave" the utility function, the greater the individual's degree of aversion to risk, and the larger the risk premium.[1]

The focus of study in the economics of uncertainty is what action a person takes in the face of uncertainty and how that action is affected by increased uncertainty. A rational agent is assumed to choose an action in the face of uncertainty so as to maximize his or her expected utility. After the action is decided and executed, uncertainty is resolved as time passes. It may well be that an individual will devise a new action after the uncertainty has been resolved, but we take as given that an action must be arrived at *before* the uncertainty is resolved by time passing. (Of course, it is sometimes optimal to take no action until the uncertainty is removed. This is one definition of procrastination. But not all situations can be handled by such a strategy.)

Consider an individual planning to allocate $1,000 of investment funds between ($1,000 − I) of bonds yielding a certain return R_0 and I of mining equities yielding an uncertain return of R_1 with probability π and R_2 with probability $(1 − \pi)$. Given a utility function of income $U(\cdot)$, the person will divide the $1,000 between equities and bonds so as to maximize $\Omega = \pi U(R_1 I) + (1 − \pi)U(R_2 I) + U[R_0(\$1,000 − I)]$. I is put into the equities which will yield either R_1 or R_2 per dollar invested a year from now. The first-order condition $\dfrac{d\Omega}{dI} = 0$ yields the investment rule: Choose I to satisfy Equation (5.1).

$$\pi U'(R_1 I)R_1 + (1 − \pi)U'(R_2 I)R_2 = U'(R_0(\$1,000 − I))R_0 \qquad (5.1)$$

where $U'(Y)$ is the marginal utility of $\$Y$ of income. The expected marginal utility of an extra dollar in equities must equal the marginal utility of an extra dollar in bonds.

Conditions will be required on rates of return R_0, R_1, and R_2 to ensure that not all the $1,000 goes to one investment possibility alone (a corner solution).

When confronted with more uncertainty (mean uncertain income remaining the same but variance increased), does the agent put more or less money into the uncertain prospect? The answer is established by general arguments in Rothschild and Stiglitz (1970). For our example of how much to put into risky mining equities, we get the result that expected returns are concave in I, and increased risk implies that less will be allocated to equities, the uncertain prospect, and more will be invested in bonds, the certain prospect.

Does uncertainty prevent Pareto optimal outcomes from occurring? Under stringent assumptions, "no." A crucial assumption is that each agent must be able to "neutralize" uncertainty by obtaining insurance against undesirable outcomes. A futures market is an indirect market for insurance. For example, a futures contract in copper gives the purchaser the right to buy copper in a subsequent year at a price specified today. But futures and insurance markets do not exist for all investment opportunities, and those that do operate typically do not extend for long periods into the future. The lack of futures markets or their limited duration means that welfare optimums will not be reached. Uncertainty may thus lead to a "market failure."

The presence of uncertainty that cannot be fully insured against means that people are worse off than in a certain environment. Government actions that reduce uncertainty and/or improve the operation of markets providing insurance are warranted. We return to government policy issues in Chapter 14; we turn now to topics in uncertainty about mineral extraction.

UNCERTAINTY CONCERNING STOCK SIZE

How is an extraction plan to be made if the amount of available stock is unknown? We do not assume complete ignorance on the part of the agent concerning stock size; rather, we assume he or she has a prior notion of how large the stock is — a degree of ignorance represented by an *estimate* of stock size. The estimate is subject to error. Suppose the prior notion is that the stock size might be 150 tons with probability .8, or 95 tons with probability .2. This prior notion can be based on a preliminary geological study. (One can update by investing in more information, perhaps by carrying out more geological study, but generally not without cost.) We take the state of information represented by the prior notions as given in this section.

Suppose we are in an industry with planners following Hotelling's rule. The planners' priors are 150 tons with probability .8, and 95 tons with probability .2, as above. How does the planner arrange a plan of extraction? Say an arbitrary plan is devised, and extraction proceeds by some rule. At the instant the 95th ton is removed, the planner will see whether there is zero remaining, or 55 additional tons. So at the instant the 95th ton is removed, the problem changes to one of certainty — a certain zero tons or a certain 55 tons. If it is zero, the planner switches to the backstop technology (if present), and if it is 55 tons, this stock is exhausted in a familiar Hotelling fashion. It is also the case that the first 95 tons are known with certainty, and we should follow a Hotelling path with rent rising at the rate of interest for that branch. The problem reduces to one of linking two phases — the 95-ton phase and the zero- or 55-ton phase. This problem reduces to choosing an initial price or quantity to extract at the beginning of the extraction plan.[2] After the initial price is selected, the rest of the problem involves phases where the rent rises at the rate of interest, and a last phase that involves working backward from the backstop cost.

We illustrate in Figure 5.2. Suppose an initial price p_0 is somehow arrived at and 95 tons are extracted between T_0 and T_1. At T_1, the switch is made to the remaining 55 tons (schedule ef) or to the backstop if zero tons remain. Along ab, rent rises at the rate of interest, and along ef, rent rises at the rate of interest. Fifty-five tons are extracted along ef between T_1 and T. By varying the decision variable p_0, given the demand schedule, we vary the present value of rent on the first 95 tons and the date we get to the second phase at T_1. Lowering the initial price (increasing initial ore extracted) reduces the present value of rent on the first 95 tons and speeds up the time it takes to get to the phase at T_1. The marginal tradeoff of these two magnitudes gives us the optimal value for the initial price at T_0. The actual formula maximizes expected surplus and combines the consumer surplus at b, the instant before T_1, with additional rent at e, the instant after T_1.

The "certainty" stock after T_1 is the mean value $(0 \times .2) + (55 \times .8) = 44$ tons. Our uncertainty problem should be compared with a problem of a certain 95 + 44 = 139 tons. Because discounted surplus is concave in stock size, the discounted surplus for a certain 44 tons exceeds the mean surplus from zero tons with probability .2 and 55 tons with probability .8. (Recall the basic argument in the previous section and Figure 5.1.) The uncertain remaining stock after T_1 yields less expected surplus than the certainty equivalent stock (44 tons). The optimal plan is to *defer what is less valuable,* given the discount rate. This is done by raising the initial price over its value under certainty. Hence *uncertainty leads to a higher initial price than would be observed under certainty.*

Let us return to the link between phases at T_1 in Figure 5.2. Normally, price paths with uncertainty satisfy a zero arbitrage condition at points like T_1. The price per ton just before T_1, say $p(T_1^-)$ just equals the expected price per ton just after T_1, namely, $[p_z \times .2 + p_{55}(T_1^+) \times .8]$. This indicates that profits cannot generally be

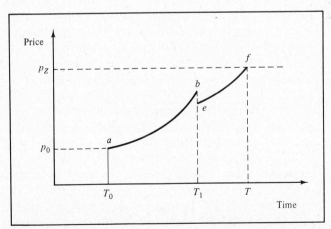

Figure 5.2 Rent rises at the rate of interest along *ab* until 95 tons are extracted. If no more ore is discovered, price jumps to p_z. If 55 more tons show up at time T_1, then price path *ef* is in effect with rent rising at the rate of interest with a new starting value for price at *e*.

made by transferring a ton from one phase to the other. This is what *zero arbitrage* means. Paradoxically, our optimal initial price in fact results in $p(T_1^-) > [p_Z \times .2 + p_{55}(T_1^+) \times .8]$. This condition is "directing" agents to move their holdings in the second phase, $T - T_1$, into the first phase. Positive profits will result (profits from intertemporal arbitrage).

There is an *externality involving information* in this problem. Removing ore in the first phase yields information about future ore availability. Mining yields ore plus information, and the price path reflects this joint product from mining. The optimal path will not be a market path because of the profitable arbitrage possibilities. This information externality precludes socially optimal plans being the same as free or decentralized market paths.

What will be the resolution of this market failure? Formally, we can make information available by an exploration process separate from the extraction process. Dasgupta and Heal (1979) introduce a probe-drilling process that resolves all uncertainty in the first phase. Since their process is independent of extraction or time passing as extraction takes place, they obtain the familiar zero-profit arbitrage condition across links between phases. In actual situations, extraction may well proceed more rapidly than would be socially optimal, since there are externalities and extraction does indeed yield valuable information in addition to ore. Once stock size is known, the resulting extraction path can be made to yield more profit, welfare, and so on, than when plans are unfolding into the unknown stock sizes. Information is valuable in this sense.

Our representation of the unknown stock size by two possible states is a convenience. Formally, nothing changes for more than two possible states, although exposition becomes messier. A slightly different approach is to have an infinity of possible states. Again nothing formal changes, although different mathematical techniques would be required (see, for example, Loury, 1978).

In a problem where there are many states (possible stock sizes), the trend in prices can be downward over a period of time. We could have a sawtooth pattern, as in Figure 5.3. Here the downward trend in prices results from successive "lucky" discoveries—more ore in fact is available than was anticipated. A pattern like that in Figure 5.3 would result when the prior beliefs about the stock were pessimistic, but discoveries kept being made. If beliefs were that more ore would be discovered, prices would start low and the trend on average would be upward. Clearly, how prior beliefs are arrived at is crucial to the evolution of the path of resource prices. The generally downward trend in resource prices in the period 1890 to 1950 can in part be attributed to unwarranted pessimism about future discoveries. As new discoveries were in fact made, strong downward pressure on prices resulted.

These price paths are quite different from the Hotelling price path, which predicts steadily rising exhaustible resource prices. The assumption of certainty in the Hotelling models appears severely to restrict their predictive power. Models with uncertainty also have areas where measurement or quantification is almost impossible, so incorporating uncertainty properly leads only to the prediction that price paths will be difficult to predict. For example, in carrying out an empirical study given a background of uncertain stock sizes, some estimate of prior beliefs about stock size must be incorporated. Arriving at these estimates is very difficult. With

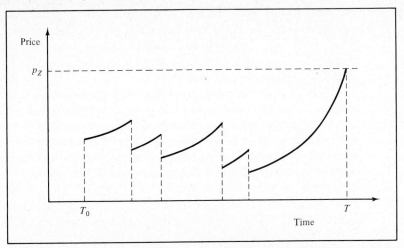

Figure 5.3 The trend in observed prices can decline over long periods if new discoveries of ore are made which were not anticipated. Finiteness of the stock implies that prices must ultimately rise.

finite stocks and positive demand at any price, prices will eventually rise in a Hotelling-like fashion, but there may be periods of declining prices before a final and inexorable rise.

Two Deposits of Unknown Size

If a planner is confronted with a multiplicity of deposits of unknown size, in what sequence should he or she arrange to mine them? Even for only two deposits, Robson (1979), found this problem impossible to work out in general, since it involves switching back and forth between deposits. He chose to consider the simpler case of one deposit of known size and one other of unknown size. His analysis revealed that it was always optimal to exploit the unknown deposit first. In place of a mathematical argument, a straightforward logical one shows why this is so: Extraction from the deposit with an unknown stock reveals information about the size of the deposit. It is always better to obtain this information *before* exploiting the known stock, because the information is costless — it is revealed as the deposit with the uncertain stock is mined. Let's examine the argument in more detail.

Suppose the uncertain deposit is the same as the one in the previous section: 95 tons with probability .2 and 150 tons with probability .8. Suppose the certain deposit has 100 tons. If it were optimal to extract from the certain deposit first, we would have a problem formally identical to the one in the previous section — a single deposit of uncertain size. That is, in the first phase, one would extract the certain 100 tons plus the next 95 tons or a "certainty branch" of 195 tons. In the second phase, information would be revealed whether zero tons or 55 tons remained. An optimal initial price could be worked out for this artificial single-deposit case. Now for the trick.

In the first phase, 195 tons were extracted along a regular Hotelling path. It makes no difference if first 95 tons came out of the uncertain deposit and then 100 tons came from the certain deposit, or vice versa. The problem does not distinguish.

But if the 95 tons were extracted from the uncertain deposit first, the planner would then know whether 55 or zero tons remained in that deposit. Then a new second phase should be devised with either the 100 tons or 155 tons remaining. But by extracting the 100 tons first from the certain deposit and then the 95 tons from the other, this information is wasted.

The optimal plan is to exploit the uncertain deposit first and then have a second phase with either 100 or 155 tons, as illustrated in Figure 5.4. The same problem arises at T_1 with respect to profitable arbitrage, as we observed for the case of a single uncertain deposit. It is profitable to move tons from the second phase to the first because of the positive information externality from working down in the mine and discovering its actual size. The socially optimal solution is *not* a market solution, as we noted.

We can in fact solve some cases where there are two deposits of uncertain size with the analysis above. We will make them identical to avoid the delicate problem of which to start exploiting first. Let there be deposits 1 and 2, each of size 95 tons with probability .2 and 150 tons with probability .8. Suppose the optimal initial price has been given, and let extraction begin with deposit 1. Since there are 95 tons at least, extraction proceeds in a Hotelling fashion, with rent rising at the rate of interest. As the 95th ton from deposit 1 is extracted, we determine whether deposit 1 has zero or 55 additional tons. If it is zero, we have one uncertain deposit left and we know how to extract that optimally. We proceed to the next deposit. If there are 55 additional tons, we are in a world of a certain deposit with 55 tons and an uncertain one of either 95 or 150 tons. Again, the remaining uncertain deposit is exploited next to obtain information about its ultimate stock. Once the initial price is determined, we have an optimal

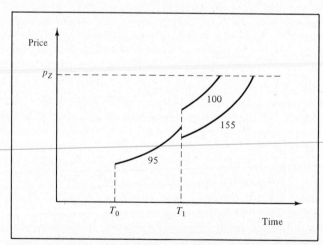

Figure 5.4 Rent rises at the rate of interest from time T_0 until 95 tons are extracted. Then it is discovered whether 55 additional tons are available in the uncertain deposit. If so, the 155 price path is in effect. If not, the 100 tons from the certain deposit are extracted along the 100 price path. The planning solution illustrated differs from a competitive market path because positive arbitrage possibilities exist across the switch at T_1 for the planning solution.

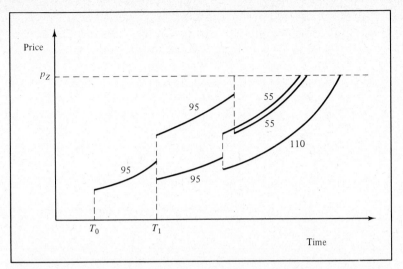

Figure 5.5 Two identical but uncertain deposits. An optimal extraction program requires switching deposits as soon as knowledge of the first deposit is realized. We then have one certain and one uncertain deposit remaining, given two states for each deposit.

extraction plan fully specified. This price setting is done to maximize expected welfare or expected discounted consumer surplus.

We illustrate in Figure 5.5. Given a p_0, optimally chosen, how do we know that the solution we outlined above and have sketched in Figure 5.5 is optimal? Working backward from the backstop price p_Z should convince us. The top branch in Figure 5.5 is optimal, since it is a single uncertain deposit situation. The bottom branch beyond T_1 is optimal, since it is a case of one certain deposit and one uncertain deposit. If the overall solution is optimal each subbranch must be optimal, and we can infer that we have indeed arrived at the optimal extraction program in Figure 5.5. The labels on the price segments refer to tons extracted along the segment in question.

If the deposits were not identical, there is no simple rule indicating which to start with. To know which deposit to start with requires a comparison of values for complete alternative programs, not just alternative segments for each deposit. Complicated problems with many states (possible sizes) and many deposits do not have obvious extraction program patterns like the one in Figure 5.5. One conclusion we can state is that even with two deposits, there can be complicated switchings between deposits in the optimal extraction program, and simple solutions will be the exception rather than the rule.

UNCERTAINTY AND BACKSTOP TECHNOLOGIES

Fusion as a source of energy is said to have no effective fixed stock of reserves. If it becomes available, fusion will be able to replace other energy sources, such as coal, oil, uranium, and gas. At what cost will it become available for commercial use? If fusion is the backstop energy supply, how will uncertainty about its long-run cost

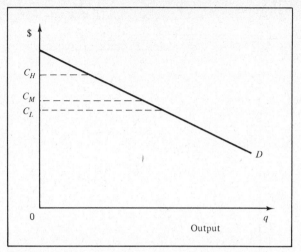

Figure 5.6 C_M is the mean or certain backstop constant cost (and price). The two uncertain prices are C_H (high) and C_L (low).

affect the extraction paths of alternative sources of energy? We deal with the situation in which the actual cost becomes known at the instant the stock of conventional fuels is exhausted. The date of the "arrival" of the backstop is related to the speed of exhaustion. (In the next section we consider the case of a known cost of the backstop, but an uncertain date of availability.)

The basic issue is, other things being the same, does uncertainty per se speed up or slow down exhaustion of the known stock in a planned optimal extraction program? Changes in duration of exhaustion show up as different initial prices for the extraction program. The initial price rises or falls as uncertainty appears. Uncertainty means here that the mean or average cost of the backstop stays the same (at the certainty value), but the variation in cost about the mean occurs. Let the uncertain cost assume value C_H with probability π and value C_L with probability $1 - \pi$ for $0 < \pi < 1$. The average cost or certainty value is $C_M = \pi C_H + (1 - \pi)C_L$.

As Figure 5.6 shows, with certainty the optimal plan has the initial price chosen, so that the stock is exhausted at the moment the price rises to C_M. We assume that there are zero costs of extraction, a homogeneous stock of known size, and the planner controls the exhaustible resource and the backstop technology. The issue with an uncertain cost is whether to set the initial price of the resource so that exhaustion occurs at a price above or below C_M. At the moment exhaustion occurs, the actual value of the cost of the backstop is revealed, and price moves to that cost level. A jump in price will occur with uncertainty. What we will observe is that uncertainty leads to the *initial price being set higher* than it would be under certainty.

To see this, consider the problem of extracting the stock under uncertainty about the cost of the backstop. The problem is to choose p_0 to maximize

$$W = R(p_0) + \pi e^{-r(T-T_0)} R_H[T(p_0)] + (1 - \pi)e^{-r(T-T_0)} R_L[T(p_0)] \qquad (5.2)$$

where $R(p_0)$ is the present value of consumer surplus obtained from the resource for a Hotelling path starting with price p_0 and consuming the stock.

$R_H[T(p_0)]$ is the present value of consumer surplus evaluated at time T (when the backstop with the high cost is started in use) for the interval T to infinity, given that time T depends on when the stock is used up and extraction started at price p_0.

$R_L[T(p_0)]$ is the same as above except for the low cost backstop cost

Now W is maximized simply by choice of p_0. Marginally "lower" p_0 implies that the stock is exhausted faster and expected surplus from the backstop is reached faster. Marginally "higher" p_0 implies that the stock is used up over a longer horizon and the surplus from the backstop regime is pushed into the future. Because $R_H(\cdot)$, $R_L(\cdot)$, and $R_M(\cdot)$ are concave in cost C, the expected surplus will be less than the certainty surplus $(R_M(T) > [\pi R_H(T) + (1 - \pi)R_L(T)])$. (This is analogous to an uncertain income yielding less utility than the certain mean income we discussed above.) Thus uncertainty lowers the future (expected) surplus with the backstop compared with certainty and induces the planner to use the stock of resource longer at the margin. Uncertainty leads to a higher p_0 *and a longer period of resource stock use before the backstop takes over.*

A more realistic case would have the cost of the backstop revealed at a known date in the future. At the date the cost is revealed, the problem becomes one of exhausting the remaining stock along a certainty path—say one of two branches if there are two uncertain values for the backstop at the outset (see Figure 5.7). The average cost, $\bar{c}$, is also indicated; T is the known date at which the actual or realized of

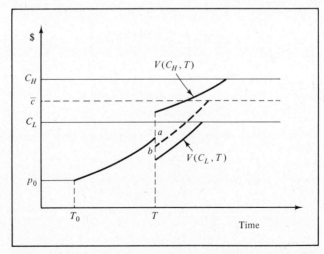

Figure 5.7 $\bar{c}$ is the mean cost of the backstop's two uncertain values. Information arrives with certainty at date T indicating whether the backstop cost is C_H or C_L. A certainty plan is followed to C_H or C_L after date T. At the outset, date T_0, the uncertain cost induces the planner to increase the initial price P_0 over what he would set in the absence of uncertainty.

the two costs is revealed. Let $V(C_H,T)$ and $V(C_L,T)$ be the discounted realized rents on the two branches from date T to the exhaustion of the stock. Let $V(c,T)$ be the discounted realized rents on the path to the mean of the costs, $(1 - \pi)C_L + \pi C_H = \bar{c}$.

The concavity of $V(\cdot)$ yields the result $V(c,T) > \pi V(C_H,t) + (1 - \pi)V(C_L,T)$. The uncertain cost makes the mean of the values of the last two extraction paths less than the certainty equivalent path. Hence uncertainty at T_0 induces a planner to weight extraction between T_0 and T slightly more than he or she would without uncertainty. The "tilting" is accomplished by raising the initial price and getting more per ton between T_0 and T than would be gotten in the absence of uncertainty. Hence the downward jump at T. In other words, uncertainty leads to an increase in the initial price, p_0.

BOX 5.1
Stockpiling

Currently the United States is stockpiling 100,000 bbl of oil a day in empty salt mines. The spot price (about $30 per bbl in 1983) is paid, and maintenance costs of $1.50 are required. Arranging for storage capacity costs between $3.50 and $5.00 per bbl. The size of the oil reserve in 1981 was 120 million barrels, yielding a stock to annual consumption ratio of .016, lower than the comparable figure for strategic metals in the U.S. reserves. The motive for acquiring strategic reserves in the United States is to avoid a severe supply disruption and the (a) associated price jump that results from a supply cut and (b) the possibility of severe dislocations in the production of essential commodities such as hardened steel.

U.S. STRATEGIC RESERVES

Commodity	Government stock/ annual consumption
Chromite	5.43
Cobalt	5.25
Tungsten	5.15
Manganese	4.99
Tin	3.33
Mercury	3.21
Chromium ferroalloys	2.17
Platinum group	1.15
Manganese ferroalloys	1.04
Bauxite	1.01
Lead	0.76
Zinc	0.58
Molybdenum	0.38
Nickel	0.22
Copper	0.09

Source: Charles River Associates, "Public and Private Stockpiling for Future Shortages," Cambridge, MA, 1976.

With national strategic stockpiling, there's a large element of prudence in the face of potential war. Stockpiling has also taken place over the centuries in anticipation of disruptions due to poor harvests: Recall Joseph in the Bible advising the pharoah to expect seven lean years and to initiate stockpiling. Food stockpiling is still a major issue in international discussions. The specter of famine in the face of poor harvests globally haunts everyone. A reserve of 18 to 20 million metric tons of food is required to meet the needs of South Asian nations in the event that five consecutive years of bad harvests occurred around 1980, says one observer. The cost of this stock would be about one-tenth of India's GNP.

A third motive for stockpiling primary commodities is to smooth price paths and possibly to assist in transferring wealth from consumers in developed countries to producers in Third World countries. In 1976, the UN trade group, UNCTAD, called for international stockpiling agreements in 17 commodities to promote the goals mentioned. Even without explicit wealth transfers incorporated in such schemes, *international* stockpiling agreements have been difficult to maintain for the same reason that a cartel is unstable. One producer often produces more than its quota, and the agreement unravels as prices decline.

Source: S. Devarajan, "Stockpiles: A Review of the Literature and the Experience" (mimeo, Harvard University, June 1981).

Uncertain Date of Arrival of the Backstop Technology

If the date of arrival and cost of the backstop technology are known, then the optimal extraction plan will be to exhaust the stock at the moment of arrival of the backstop. Price of the resource will rise above the cost of the backstop as exhaustion is imminent. If this date becomes uncertain and the social implications of a period of no supply are catastrophic, exhaustion will be planned for the latest possible date of arrival of the backstop. If the date of arrival turns out to be "early," the remaining stock will be sold off over a certainty path, with price rising to the backstop price.

In Figure 5.8, a T_L is the "low" or early date of arrival with probability π. This date is assumed to be realized in Figure 5.8(a). Price rises from p_0 at the rate of interest, the backstop arrives at T_L, price jumps to follow a certainty path slightly below p_Z, and the stock is sold off to be exhausted at T_X. In Figure 5.8(b), the late date T_H is realized. The price p_0 is set so that exhaustion occurs at this latest of possible dates of arrival of the backstop. (The same initial price holds for the case of the early realized arrival of the backstop.) The certainty date for this problem would, of course, be the mean time $T_M = \pi T_L + (1 - \pi)T_H$. Under certainty, exhaustion would be planned for that date. Since $T_H > T_M$, *uncertainty has led to a higher initial price than under the certainty path abc and a longer period over which it is exhausted.* The price of the stock rises above p_Z until the backstop is introduced at time T_H and the initial stock is exhausted. In the appendix to this chapter we derive a Hotelling rule for

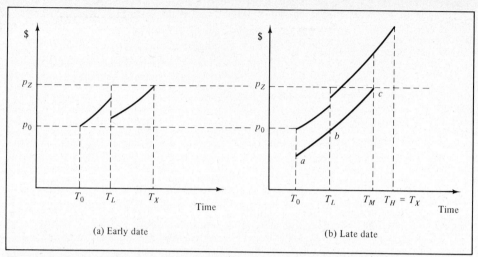

Figure 5.8 The two dates of arrival of the backstop are T_L (low or early) and T_H (high or late). If the early date is realized as in (a), price jumps down at T_L and rises to the backstop cost P_Z. If the late date is realized, price rises above the backstop cost until the stock is exhausted at the instant the backstop appears. Price then drops to P_Z as in (b).

the case of an uncertain date of arrival of the backstop in which the backstop can arrive at any point in time in the future.

Suppose there is some possibility that the backstop may never arrive: there is a positive probability that the time of arrival is infinity or that the cost is infinity. If it is catastrophic to be without any supply, a reasonable plan must involve never exhausting the stock, using less and less indefinitely. The term *option value* has been introduced to describe outcomes of uncertain but irrevocable decisions. Suppose a mineral is discovered in the rocks at Yosemite Park in California and the main park is turned into an open pit mine. Yosemite Park cannot be recreated. This is the kind of decision we are dealing with, given an essential resource that may never have a substitute. The formal analysis of option values involves proceeding cautiously or paying now to keep options open. The bottom line is that an optimal plan involves keeping supply in reserve or having a precautionary supply available (see Chapter 13).

Option Value of Minerals and Coping with Price Uncertainty

An owner of a deposit can sell a ton of ore today at a known price or tomorrow at generally an unknown price. How should the owner deal with this future price uncertainty? He might buy insurance against a future decline in prices if he could, but such markets do not exist. An alternative approach is to create his own insurance by selling claims today for delivering new ore at a fixed price in a future period. Such a claim is called an *option* for future delivery of a ton at a fixed price. The deposit owner protects himself against future market price uncertainty by selling these options. We get a new Hotelling rule incorporating this future price uncertainty and options sold. Let us see this with a two-period example.

The deposit owner can extract and sell for the current price of $8 per ton today or wait until next period and face a market price of either $12 or $9 per ton. To remove the uncertainty or insure against the low future price, the deposit owner sells y options in the first period that promise to deliver y tons in the future period at $10 per ton. Each of these y tons can then be sold for $12 if that is the future price, or held for sale in a subsequent period. The option owner will not exercise his option to purchase if $9 is the market price. The option lapses. Losses in period 2 from selling the newly delivered tons is $(12 - 10)y$ or $2y$. A Hotelling rule or intertemporal arbitrage condition will have the deposit owner indifferent between selling his ton in the current period or the future period.

$$\$8 = \frac{\pi[\$12 - \$2y] + (1 - \pi)\$9}{1 + r} + yp^0$$

where p^0 is the price of an option in the current period and π is the probability that the $12 market price is realized in the second period. The left-hand side is the return from extracting a marginal ton today and the right-hand side is the return from selling y options today and the marginal ton of ore in the next period. $(1 - \pi)$ is the probability that the $9 future market price is realized; r is the riskless interest rate. In a zero-risk environment, $\pi(\$12 - \$2y) = (1 - \pi)\$9$ regardless of the value of π. Hence $y = 3/2$, and the current price of the option p^0 depends on the value of the riskless interest rate r.

The deposit owner is in the business of selling ore *and* options. Each ton considered for extraction is linked to a contract to deliver other tons if the high price is realized. p^0 is what the deposit owner is willing to pay currently to acquire reserves for possible sale in the subsequent period. He does not pay the market price for extra tons because he may not have to deliver them in the next period.

EXPLORATION FOR NEW RESERVES
General Issues and Externalities

Exploration is a method of reducing uncertainty. Even when an ore body has been discovered, exploratory drilling is often carried out in order to reduce uncertainty as to how much ore is available and how it is distributed. Exploration has another dimension: It is the method of finding ore, and along with extraction can be viewed as an intrinsic part of the process of getting ore to market. In fact, if we abstract from the uncertainty linking exploration inputs to the stock discovered, exploration can be viewed exactly as we viewed extraction costs. Pindyck (1978) has provided the details of such an approach.

Rather than viewing $c(z)$ as the costs of extracting and processing a ton of ore of quality z as we did in Chapter 3, we can treat $c(z)$ as the cost function of discovering ore with a difficulty-of-discovery value of z. In other words, the models of minerals of heterogeneous quality can be interpreted as models of rising costs of discovery of ore. But the element of uncertainty is absent in these models, and as are certain important aspects of exploration.

The uncertain payoff of exploration can lead to excessive searching and a dissipation of rents from the ore body, once it is discovered. Inventors, for example, race to be first to patent a new product or process, and the racing itself can lead to excessive amounts of R&D relative to what might be done in different institutional environments. See Loury (1979) for an example.

We can illustrate excessive exploration. Suppose it is known that there is a deposit with discounted rents R in a square area with, say, 9 leases. The deposit is in one of the 9 squares (see Figure 5.9). If leases are set up the way we have them illustrated and the law requires that the leases be worked without delay, and one firm can only have one lease, exploration will occur in each of the 9 leaseholds. The probability of success for each leasehold is 1/9th. One exploration will be successful, with payoff R. Total exploration resources used up will be $9K$, where K is the cost of exploration per leasehold. The total payoff is R. The social payoff is $U(\$R - 9K)$, where $U(\,\cdot\,)$ is the utility of net revenue from the mine discovered.

If one firm were allowed to explore the entire grid, presumably at a less demanding pace, it would explore on average *half* the small squares before the discovery was made. The average cost would be $4.5K$ and the payoff R, with net social payoff of $U(\$R - 4.5K)$. This is higher than for the decentralized, rushed case above. Some observers allege that *all* rents are dissipated by exploration activity. This seems to be an extreme and probably unwarranted view; any entrepreneur engaged in exploration will incur exploration expenses up to the point that the expected dollar return from another dollar spent on exploration equals that expenditure. That is, at the margin there are zero profits from exploration. Expected return takes the form of additional marketable ore discovered at the margin.

Let us for the moment agree that mineral rents are dissipated by exploration to the extent that this zero marginal profitability condition for exploration is satisfied. This still leaves ample room for *total rents* minus *total exploration* costs to be positive. There is no presumption of excessive mineral rent dissipation by exploration activity, although there can be different amounts of dissipation when institutional leasing arrangements vary, as we noted in the example of the 9 subareas. A lease is a temporary ownership right. Exploration will be conducted on owned land like agri-

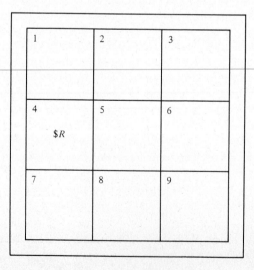

Figure 5.9 A grid is superimposed on an area containing a single deposit with discounted rent R in subarea 4. Exploration is required to discover the location of the deposit.

cultural activity on owned or leased farmland. If there are no ownership arrangements prior to discovery of a deposit, the setting is like the fishery (see Chapter 8), and excessive exploration activity can be anticipated as firms race to lay first claim to new deposits. To the extent that leasing arrangements can minimize the "racing" element of exploration, rent dissipation will be reduced.

In certain cases, a tax on resource rents would leave the extraction path unchanged. In our discussion, the tax seemed to have neutral impact. However, since exploration activity varies with expected mineral rent anticipated to be earned, *a tax on rents will at the margin discourage exploration.* A distortion of the optimal time path of extraction by tax may have small efficiency costs compared with the social cost represented by exploration activity curtailed as a consequence of a tax downstream on future rents. In order to balance the government's desire for tax revenue from mineral extraction with the repression of exploration induced by taxes on mineral rents, analyses have been carried out on schemes in which the exploration firm pays a fee to the government for the right to explore a certain site and then a royalty per ton on what is discovered and mined. If a mine is discovered, the tax on ore extracted is not punitive. If a mine is not discovered, the incentive to explore is not snuffed out by high right-to-explore fees.

The government diversifies its revenue base by getting part of its revenue from taxes on rent of ore discovered and part on the right to explore an area. Fine-tuning of the parameters (area allowed, right-to-explore fee, tax rate on ore extracted) of this contract can lead to a desired amount of exploration, mining, and government revenue. See Crommelin, Pearse, and Scott (1978) for a discussion of the issues in the context of oil and gas leases in Alberta, Canada.

Our discussion suggests that excessive exploration can result when mineral lands are an open-access resource. But it is possible that there may be too little exploration. Consider the case of a gold rush, which is an example of an exploration externality in action. If person *j* finds gold, other people infer that there may be other profitable sites nearby, and they rush to try to locate and exploit the nearby sites. The cost of search borne by person *j*, perhaps a lifelong prospector, is not incurred by the other people who rush in. The followers receive a free ride on the information acquired by person *j*. We assume that, on average, too little exploration occurs in such environments. Each prospector balances personal costs and expected profits from a gold strike at the margin on searches.[3] If an individual can appropriate only a small fraction of the rewards from a strike, then too few individuals will be exploring relative to an optimal allocation.

The gold rush phenomenon is a manifestation of one individual capturing only a fraction of the rewards from successful exploration. The size of areas one can stake a claim to is crucial, since the externality we are discussing involves areas nearby a successful discovery that also yield profitable mines in addition to the one found first. Large claim areas can internalize some of the externality, but large areas may be inadequately explored by one individual with exploration rights. One way to improve matters is for those who rush in subsequently to be charged an entry fee that is transferred to the original discoverer. This will induce more prospectors to enter the exploration sector initially, since they can expect higher average returns from a successful discovery in a new area.

BOX 5.2
Bidding for Mineral Rights

Bonus bidding involves submitting a bid for a mineral tract. The highest bid wins the tract and the government receives the amount bid as its revenue. Oddly enough, under reasonable assumptions about diverse firms making competitive bids, the government will not end up with, on average, all of the rent from the resources in the tract. This is because there is a subtle "spillover" of information about the value of the tract by the process of auctioning the tract.

The *naive approach* for a bidder is to evaluate the tract and receive information or signals which might be a seismic reading and conclude that the value of the tract was, let's say, $V given the signals plus or minus an error term arising from the variance, say, of the distribution of "signals" and values. A bid of $V would be made. However, if, say, 10 bidders are involved for a tract and Mr. Eue wins, it suggests that his signal indicated the richest value for the tract. But by definition his reading must have been high and in the upper part of the distribution relating signals to values. If Mr. Eue keeps winning auctions, he will be bidding consistently above the mean value of the tracts and he will lose money in the long run, since presumably the average bid of 10 bids is close to the market value of a tract. This has been labeled "the winner's curse."

The *sophisticated approach* is to estimate the value of the tract and scale down the bid to allow for the "bias in winning" noted above. If all bidders follow an adjustment procedure, the average bid will be lower than the average value of the tract. Reese solved some hypothetical auctions on the computer using the sophisticated approach above and found that the government received at best about 90 percent of the rent (10 percent accruing to the firms bidding). Generally, the more firms that were in the auction, the larger the share of rent that accrued to the government. Also, the lower the degree of uncertainty about the value of the tract, the more rent could be captured by the government. This opens the door for increased exploratory work by the public sector, improving welfare.

Consider one auction of many held in the United States, as reported in the *Wall Street Journal* (April 14, 1976). On April 13, the first nine auctions were held for tracts in the Gulf of Alaska. The sum of winning bids was $572 million (the record then was an auction for offshore Louisiana tracts totalling $6.5 billion). A group comprising Texaco, Inc.; Allied Chemical; Celanese's Champlin Petroleum Company; and Diamond Shamrock Corporation paid the most for a tract—$62.8 million. Another group bid $62.3 for this tract. Exxon won 25 of 53 tracts it bid for, spending $47 million in total. Shell won 29 of the 41 tracts it bid for, spending $148 million. It placed $232 million in bids.

Source: D. K. Reece, "Competitive Bidding for Offshore Petroleum Leases," *Bell Journal of Economics* 9, 2 (Autumn 1978), pp. 369–384.

There is another externality and possible market failure associated with exploration — an *information* externality. Private inside information about potential stock sizes leads to unusual pricing phenomena because the price ends up transmitting the private information. Price then plays the two roles, one of signaling the relative value of a ton of ore and the other of signaling how much uncertain stock remains.

Suppose person *i* has discovered for certain that the largest of two uncertain stock sizes will be realized. She can sign contracts today to deliver ore in the future at today's price, weighted by the probability of the large stock size occurring. This is called a *contingent contract*. The price and delivery date are agreed to in advance of the uncertainty being cleared up for all buyers and sellers. If the informed person signs too many contracts, people will suspect she has inside information about stock sizes and the current price will be driven down, eliminating the profit the insider was hoping to realize.

If the insider is satisfied with a small profit, she must expect other speculators to become informed at some cost by the same route so they can also make a profit. But this entry of competing speculators will drive down the current price, and the speculative profit will be eliminated. If each speculator foresees this, no one will purchase inside information (presumably by private geological surveying). But if no one is striving for this "inside" speculative profit, there is room for one person to do it and make a substantial profit. The point is that inside information, once acted upon for personal gain, will show up in price changes and be revealed free of charge to all who observe current price movements. The incentive to become privately informed is strong if no one else follows suit. If everyone follows, the incentive is eliminated, and no single person will become privately informed of stock sizes!

This is a cautionary tale in the logic of the price system. In real situations there is much extraneous information being capitalized in actual price movements, so we might not inevitably observe market failures due to information externalities in prices (see Dasgupta and Heal 1979, Chapter 4, for further discussion of this type of information externality.)

Exploration and Risk Pooling

Let us return to our 9-square example in Figure 5.9. Suppose we indeed have 9 separate firms exploring, each in its designated territory. Each firm has an expected profit of $m = \frac{1}{3}R - K$. The variance in the profit is $\frac{8}{9}(0 - m)^2 + \frac{1}{9}[(R - K) - m]^2$. If all 9 individuals or firms joined a syndicate or pooled their plots and proceeded with 9 probes, each member would get $\frac{1}{9}R$ for certain and be responsible for putting up $\$K$. Expected profit per firm is the same with pooling as with individualistic exploration, but now the individual firm's variance of profit is zero. Each firm's expected payoff is a certain $\frac{1}{9}R - K$.

Pooling of uncertain prospects can reduce risk (variance, in many cases). Since risk is considered a cost, reducing it can improve welfare. This is the logic behind mutual funds, investment syndicates, and exploration consortiums. Exploration companies frequently act as a syndicate in order to take advantage of risk pooling or risk reduction. The cost to a firm of pooling is that it earns only the average profit and cannot "win big."

Exploration of a Known Deposit of Unknown Size

Is there an optimal amount of exploration for new stock? If, to find the same deposit, there is a cheaper method, then we have a clear case of excessive exploration. It also makes little sense to explore for stock in amounts greatly in excess of current needs, since those same discoveries can presumably be made in the future when ore is needed. This presupposes that the prior views on the total stock to be discovered are widely shared. To the extent that views of future total stocks vary widely, it probably makes sense to explore more in advance of use, because then current extraction activity can be tailored more closely to aggregate stocks. More information in this case leads to revised current extraction plans and larger total welfare from the stocks ultimately exploited.

Let us consider this in a slightly different context — namely, exploration as a means of refining views about uncertain stocks. With regard to an optimal level of exploration activity, we should stick with the working rule of discovering new stock at least cost. Above, we considered a stock of unknown size. We represented it as having two tentative sizes: 95 tons with probability .2, or 150 tons with probability .8. Exploration in this situation can be viewed as learning before 95 tons are extracted how much is in the ground. There are two types of learning: revising prior views on the probabilities as new information becomes available, or learning the full details. Sinking exploratory probes into a deposit is a way of gaining information about its size or a way of revising prior views on ultimate size. Such probes are costly. Suppose that by spending K on such probes, we could learn exactly how much ore was in our hypothetical deposit. (The ultimate value of the deposit will be reduced by the K expended, of course.) If the probes were sunk at the outset, the actual size would be revealed and a certainty extraction path would be pursued. The gross value of the deposit would be

$$Z = .2R(95) + .8R(150)$$

where $R(\cdot)$ is the rent obtained for an extraction path under certainty with $(\cdot)$ tons of stock. Z is larger than the value of the deposit with uncertainty or without the costly probes. (The value of the deposit with uncertainty is the discounted value corresponding to the uncertainty path illustrated in Figure 5.10.) Thus, removing uncertainty or revision of prior views has a positive value and is in fact defined as *the value*

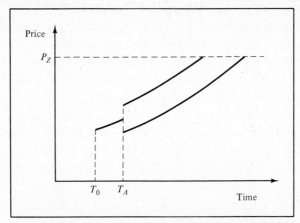

Figure 5.10 At time T_A, news arrives of the exact size of the uncertain deposit. If 55 more tons will become available, the price drops and the bottom price path is realized after T_A. Otherwise the remaining ore, up to 95 tons, is depleted along the top price path.

of information. Now, the present value of K expended on the probes could be reduced if it were deferred, since the interest rate is positive. And the value of information would decline slightly too, since it was coming later in the extraction program. We illustrate a hypothetical date T_A in Figure 5.10. There, T_0 and T_A (the date of arrival of the information on actual stock sizes) are fixed. An optimal plan reduces to the choice of an optimal initial price (and quantity) for the extraction program. *The rate of extraction cannot speed up or slow down the date of arrival of the information in this model.* Once the information arrives, the rest of the extraction program is in an environment of certainty. At T_A, the price just before the information arrives *equals* the expected price just after the information arrives (the midpoint between the two paths starting at time T_A). There is no externality of the kind where mining changes the timing of the arrival of information.

As T_A is moved forward in time, the value of the extraction program rises — but so does the present value of K, the cost of getting the information. At the optimal date, the gains and losses from a *marginal change* in the date will be equal. Rent dissipation will be reflected in the change of the *total* value of the deposit less the *total* cost of information and also will be dependent on the date of sinking the probes (during the exploration). In fact, at the "optimal" date, the total cost of information may exceed the total value of the deposit, and then it is better to proceed with full uncertainty and without the probes.

BOX 5.3
High Oil Prices Have Diverse Effects on the
Economies of Exporters and Importers

At first glance, the setting of the price of oil by oil-exporting nations appears to coerce oil-importing nations. The price setters' interests are assumed to lie with relatively high prices for oil, and the importers are the losers. However the situation is more complex than this: There is a wide area of gray in place of the supposed black and white. One way to see the complexities is to note that the exporters set a *nominal* world price for oil and economies adjust to produce a new *real* price of oil—the real price being, roughly speaking, the commodities purchasable by the value of oil sold. Rapid changes in relative commodity prices in the world via perhaps different rates of inflation and in exchange rates between currencies can result in a new nominal price of oil being "high" or "less high" in real terms. The channels of response to the initial high nominal price are crucial. For example, there is substantial recycling of OPEC revenues via the international financial system back to industrial countries such as those of Europe which import much oil—as much as 50 percent was recycled in the 1970s, Chichilnisky and Heal report. This cushions a decline in demand and in economic activity in the industrial countries. Then less-developed countries without oil have received loans from oil exporters and increased their investments substantially (from 16 to 24 percent of their GNPs, Sachs estimates in *Brookings Papers* 1981). These new investments would be in large part for products from the industrial countries, a plus for these producers.

Higher real prices for an exhaustible resource usually induce searches for substitutes and in turn lengthen the interval over which the stock is available. This can be viewed as an indirect benefit of high prices to oil-importing countries. A more complex indirect benefit is on the internal characteristics of the *importing country*. The higher resource prices induce substitution away from high resource-using commodities by consumers and induce producers of all commodities to substitute relatively cheaper capital and labor for resources. Prices of capital and labor will rise, and income can rise. This is the *substitution effect*, and it can largely mitigate the *wealth effect*, which is the loss in purchasing power to people in importing countries who must export more of their wealth in order to pay for the more expensive resource imports. Chichilnisky and Heal (1983, p. 45) indicate: "At low resource prices, when the substitution effect dominates, the importing country will gain from an increase, and at high prices, when the wealth effect dominates, it will gain from a reduction" in oil prices it must pay.

For partly developed countries such as Mexico which are *oil exporters*, the substitution effects can induce lower wages from higher-priced oil exports and more unequal income distribution. This has been emphasized by Chichilnisky (1983) in a number of papers. She classifies a country as having a dual structure when its industrial sector is very capital-intensive and its traditional sectors very labor-intensive. Countries with dual structures can have wage earners end up worse off from an increase in the price of its oil or primary resource exports. Another effect of high prices on exporters is the upward pressure on the exchange rate. This makes manufactured goods more expensive to foreigners and can lead to major contractions in the demand for and output of manufactured goods from countries with a booming natural resource export sector. The deleterious effects on the manufacturing sector have been labeled "the Dutch disease," and the analysis of the internal adjustments required for new natural resource exporters such as England, Norway, and Holland is called "the economics of a booming sector." Chichilnisky has touched on some key aspects; Corden (1983) contains a careful survey of other aspects.

Of course, higher export prices will benefit exporters if demand for the commodity is inelastic. But the elasticity depends on the speed at which substitutes are brought on line or developed. Smaller, lighter, more efficient automobiles are one form of substituting for higher oil prices. Since 1973, the longer-run price elasticity of oil has proved much more elastic than was predicted in 1974.

Sources: Chichilnisky, G. (1983). "Oil Prices, Industrial Prices and Outputs: A Simple General Equilibrium Macro Model." Columbia University Discussion Paper; Chichilnisky, G., and G. Heal (1983). "Trade and Development in the Eighties: A Report to the Secretary General of UNCTAD" (mimeo); Corden, M. (1983). "The Economics of a Booming Sector." *International Social Science Journal* 35, 3, pp. 441–454.

SUMMARY

1. Much of the activity of mineral extraction takes place with limited information. As extraction proceeds there is limited information about stock sizes currently being worked and about future increases in aggregate stocks, limited information about the availability of substitutes being brought on stream by technological developments, and limited information about future demands[4] and actions by rival suppliers.
2. Extraction paths are affected by the presence of uncertainty. In many instances, uncertainty leads to a marginal reduction in the value of future activity and a marginal deferring in the date of reaching those uncertain contingencies. Current prices are pushed up as extraction slows down in the face of uncertainty.
3. Exploration is a means of reducing uncertainty, generally at a cost. Prior views about the degree of uncertainty can be changed by introducing new information. But the cost of exploration must be netted from the value of what is discovered. Thus exploration activity "eats into" future rents and leads to varying amounts of rent dissipation.
4. The amount of rents dissipated by exploration activity depends on the institutional arrangements for exploration rights and taxes. Under extreme conditions, almost all rent might be dissipated by costs of exploration.
5. Joint exploration ventures are a device for risk pooling or for reducing risk to individual firms.

DISCUSSION QUESTIONS

1. Suppose a person faces the following alternative. She can put $1,000 in the bank today and receive $1,200 at the end of the year. Alternatively, she can invest in speculative gold mining stocks that cost $1 per share. She must buy at least 1,000 shares. If gold is found after one year, her stocks are worth $2,000. If gold is not found, her stocks are worth $100. What investment strategy will she follow if:
a. Her subjective probability of a gold strike is .1 (one chance out of 10)?
b. Her subjective probability of a gold strike is .01 (one chance out of 100)?
Assume she is risk-averse.

2. A person is offered $20,000 with probability .1 or zero dollars with probability .9. Suppose his utility of income takes the form $u = \log y$, where y is income. Calculate a sum of money given under certainty which the person would be indifferent to compared with the result under uncertainty. What is the premium or "bribe" that must be promised to this person in order to have him accept the uncertainty rather than a sure $2,000 (=$20,000 × .1 + $0.0 × .9)?

3. Explain why, when the size of a nonrenewable resource stock is uncertain, the optimal price path is scalloped (there is a discontinuity at the date the uncertainty is resolved), and why the initial price of the resource is greater than the price that would prevail without uncertainty. Why won't the private market obtain this optimal price path? Explain the role of arbitrage.

4. There are two deposits of copper, one with a known total reserve of 1 million tons, the other with an unknown total reserve. From which deposit is ore extracted first, and why? Does it matter what the extraction costs are for each deposit?

5. Uncertainty about the date of arrival or the cost of a backstop technology will always raise the initial price of a nonrenewable mineral over its price under certainty. Is this statement true, false, or uncertain? Explain your answer.

6. A person could explore for gold in northern Quebec with no prior knowledge of the rock structure or with an accurate geological survey map put out by the government. Can we evaluate in dollars how much the map is worth to this explorer? Sketch how we might proceed.

7. Explain the externalities involved in the exploration process and why private markets cannot internalize these externalities to reach the optimal level of exploration. What types of government policies could deal with these problems?

8. In a world of certainty, when it costs money to find new reserves of ore, it makes no sense to hold reserves or to explore for more than today's needs. Discuss this contention. What considerations determine the size of reserves held by mining companies under uncertainty?

NOTES

1. A function of the elasticity of marginal utility at a point is the Arrow-Pratt measure of relative risk aversion. The higher the value, the more risk-averse an individual is said to be. That measure is η where I is mean income and $\eta(I) = -\dfrac{yu''(y)}{u'(y)}$, the elasticity of marginal utility.

2. It is presumed that the first 95 tons cannot be dug up at the outset and the planner made instantly aware whether zero or 55 tons remain. We have not, however, explicitly introduced costs that preclude this action.

3. Recall the famous value of gold sequence in the flophouse in *The Treasure of Sierra Madre.* (John Huston, *The Treasure of the Sierra Madre,* p. 61, ed. James Naremore, Madison: University of Wisconsin Press, 1979):

HOWARD *(the old man):* "Why's gold worth some twenty bucks per ounce?"

MAN *(after a pause):* "Because it's scarce . . . ."

HOWARD: "A thousand men, say, go searching for gold. After six months one of 'em is lucky—one out of the thousand. His find represents not only his own labor but that of the nine hundred ninety-nine others to boot. Six thousand months or fifty [sic] years of scrabbling over mountains going hungry and thirsty. An ounce of gold, mister, is worth what it is because of the human labor that went into the finding and the getting of it."

MAN: "Never thought of it just like that . . ."

HOWARD: "There's no other explanation, mister. In itself, gold ain't good for anything much except to make jewelry and gold teeth."

4. Weinstein and Zeckhauser (1975) have investigated uncertainty as to future demands; see Pindyck (1980) for a quite different approach. Hartwick and Yeung (1985) report on the *preference* of the resource extracting firm for uncertainty of the price of output in the future.

chapter *6*

Economic Growth and Nonrenewable Natural Resources

INTRODUCTION

Although we have been talking about the nonrenewability of mineral resources, we have yet to examine what the impact of actual exhaustion of mineral resources might be on an economy. Does it mean economic deterioration and collapse? Or will new materials, backstop technologies, and other factor inputs smoothly substitute for the depleted supplies of oil and other minerals? To answer these questions, we must examine the implications of nonrenewability over the very long run. We must see how an economy grows over time and what role nonrenewable resources play in this process. Before dealing with these issues, we briefly report on whether we *are* running out of nonrenewable resources.

A substantial amount of work has been devoted to determining just how scarce nonrenewable (and other natural resources) have become over time. The object of this work is to try to define and estimate "measures" of natural resource scarcity. Do we, for example, look at the relative prices of minerals and other commodities over time to see if minerals are becoming more scarce? Are extraction costs over time a better signal of scarcity? What about measures of the value of the resource in the ground—the resource rent? We will see that each measure proposed has its strengths and weaknesses.

But even if we could define and calculate precise measures of resource scarcity, we would then have to know how to interpret these numbers. If resources are becoming more scarce, will it mean that the economy cannot produce as many goods and services over time? Or will capital and labor and other factor inputs be substituted for the declining stocks of minerals? Will technological change be rapid enough to maintain output even with smaller stocks? We cannot answer all these questions, but we will discuss ways in which resource use can be modeled as part of the production and growth processes of an economy and illustrate some possible time paths of resource use, given the stocks remaining, and output produced.

First, we review measures of natural resource scarcity and report on some of the empirical findings of those calculating these measures. Next, we see how nonrenewable resources can be combined with other factor inputs to produce goods and services throughout the economy. We observe how the demand for natural resource flows is derived from the demand for "final" goods. This leads us to a discussion of economic growth and how nonrenewable resources affect such growth. Normative theories of economic growth are our focus. From a specified "desirable" path of consumption over time, we see how capital and resources can be combined to obtain this path. We find that a variant of Hotelling's rule also guides us (along with a rule about optimal savings) in determining how capital is substituted for resources. The interest or discount rate is again an important variable, and we see what happens to capital versus resource use when the discount rate (and some other parameters of the model) change. We then briefly discuss some notions of how to make resource use equitable over time—the concept of intergenerational equity. We conclude this section with a brief discussion of how population growth, pollution, and technical progress can affect economic growth, then note what issues a positive theory of economic growth would consider.

The final section of this chapter examines models that try to project economic growth over long periods of time when resources are finite. Jay Forrester and Dennis Meadows were pioneers in systems modeling of growth in the early 1970s with their "limits to growth" work. Before evaluating that work, we will look at the basic ingredients of these models, how projections can be made, and what different trends indicate. Finally, we discuss economists' criticisms of the system models of the limits to growth.

NATURAL RESOURCE SCARCITY

The publication of reports evaluating the effect of natural resource use on economic growth in the early 1970s and the "energy crisis" of the mid-1970s focused public attention on the issue of the available long-term supply of many natural resources, and on the role these resources play in the production of goods and services. Our intention here is to examine some proposed methods to measure whether or not nonrenewable natural resources are becoming more scarce. Scarcity is at the heart of economics. By *natural resource scarcity,* we mean what must be given up to obtain an additional unit of the resource—the opportunity cost of exploiting the resource. Ideally, we should incorporate both private and social opportunity costs of resource exploitation. Not only are capital, labor, and other market factor inputs used to exploit the resource (private opportunity costs), but so are some nonmarket environmental resources (social costs).

Social costs may include the degradation of the natural environment and use of common property resources such as ground water and air in the production of the resource in question. We will not incorporate the social opportunity costs of nonrenewable resource extraction here, although they should be taken into account. (We discuss this issue further in Chapters 12 and 13.)

While our focus is on nonrenewable resources because we have yet to examine renewable and environmental resources in detail, we do want to point out that the literature we cite covers some renewable resources, such as forestry, fisheries, and agricultural land. Although recent work has centered on the nonrenewable sectors, it may turn out that some of our so-called renewable resources are indeed more scarce than resources which have finite stocks. The reasons for this are complex and include the ill-defined property rights to some renewable resources and certain government policies. We will examine some of the issues surrounding the exploitation of the forest in Chapter 11.

Concern with the long-term supply of natural resources is not new; it dates back to the work of Malthus. In the 1950s and 1960s a number of studies were done to examine the availability of certain natural resources in response to the great consumption of these products during World War II. The report of the Paley Commission in 1952 and the very important work of Barnett and Morse in 1963 were done in this period. Barnett and Morse found little cause for alarm. For the period they examined, 1870 to 1957, only forestry indicated any apparent increase in scarcity. The evidence for the agricultural and mineral sectors suggested that these resources were becoming *less* scarce. Barnett and Morse attributed the increased availability of mineral commodities to three general factors (and one specific to the United States, greater imports of minerals). These include: (1) the substitution of more plentiful lower-grade resources for less abundant high-grade resources; (2) the discovery of new mineral deposits; and (3) technical changes in exploration, extraction, processing, and all phases of natural resource production and use, which allowed output of these resources to increase while the real marginal costs of production declined. In an update of the Barnett and Morse work to include data up to 1970 made by Barnett (1979), he still found no relationship between increased scarcity of mineral resources and time.[1]

Some reasons why effective supplies of these resources had increased over time are noted by Smith and Krutilla (1979). First, as high-grade deposits are depleted, the low-grade sources substituted are typically found in greater abundance. Second, as a mineral resource becomes more scarce, possible increases in the rate of appreciation of its price are dampened or offset by substitution of other resources. Third, increases in mineral prices stimulate exploration for new deposits and encourage recycling of nonfuel minerals. Fourth, technical changes reduce the costs of extracting and processing nonrenewable minerals and make previously uneconomic deposits viable (see Box 3.1 in Chapter 3).

Will these factors continue to affect resource supply favorably? We do not know. There is some evidence, for example, that the supply of various ores does not increase uniformly as their grade is reduced, but follows a bimodal or more complex distribution. Who can predict technical change or the potential for continued substitution possibilities? The work on resource scarcity is based on past observations, trends, and expectations about the future. But no one can foretell the future; we can only develop concepts that let us use information about the past to make predictions. Economists assume this is what people do and also assume that the underlying structure of our predictive models does not change. Because we cannot cover all aspects of natural resource scarcity here, we refer the reader to a comprehensive survey of the important issues in the collection of papers (and their references) in Smith (1979).

Measures of Natural Resource Scarcity

As we noted above, natural resource scarcity should reflect what must be given up to obtain one more unit of the resource. A number of different measures have been proposed to estimate scarcity. We examine three: (1) the real unit costs of extraction, (2) the real price of natural-resource-intensive goods, and (3) resource rents—the value of the resource in the ground. Our discussion is based on the work of Barnett and Morse (1963), Brown and Field (1978, 1979), and Fisher (1979, 1981).

Real Unit Costs

The principal measure of scarcity used by Barnett and Morse is *unit cost,* which they define as $(\alpha L + \beta K)/Q$. L is labor, K is reproducible capital (which does not include the value of natural resources), and Q is the output of the extractive industries. The terms α and β are weights used to aggregate inputs. Table 6.1 summarizes their estimates for unit cost for minerals and other natural resources.

The rationale for the unit cost approach is simple. If lower-quality resources are exploited over time, increasing scarcity will be reflected in the increased use of capital and labor (both assumed to be of constant quality) that is necessary to produce a *given* level of output. The Barnett and Morse data suggest that unit costs were falling and at an increasing rate, except in the case of forestry (where the results are somewhat ambiguous). By their measure, resources were becoming more abundant, not more scarce.

The main advantage claimed for this measure is that it incorporates technological change, which relaxes resource constraints and allows output to be extracted at lower unit cost. Brown and Field argue that technological change can make the unit cost measure ambiguous. Technological change is not the only reason why unit costs will change, and there is no guarantee that declining unit costs imply decreased scarcity.

The relationship between technical change and extraction costs is complex. For example, as physical depletion approaches, it may well be that unit costs rise as deposits become harder to find. Or the quality of the new deposits may be low and

Table 6.1 INDEXES OF LABOR AND CAPITAL INPUT PER UNIT OF EXTRACTIVE OUTPUT

	Total extractive		Agriculture		Minerals		Forestry		Fishing
	A	B	A	B	A	B	A	B	A
1870–1900	134	99	132	97	210	154	59	37	200
1919	122	103	114	97	164	139	106	84	100
1957	60	87	61	89	47	68	90	130	18

Note: A: indexes of direct unit extraction costs. B: indexes of unit extraction costs relative to nonextractive goods.

Source: H. J. Barnett and C. Morse, *Scarcity and Growth: The Economics of Natural Resource Availability* (Baltimore, Johns Hopkins University Press for Resources for the Future, 1963) pp. 8, 9, 172.

substantial increases in capital and labor may be required to exploit a given quantity of ore. But it may also be the case that the effort to find these new deposits will result in technological changes that reduce exploitation costs. Brown and Field cite an example from Norgaard (1975), who found that technological change in the drilling of oil wells had offset a large part of the decline in the quality of the resource. Unit costs of extraction were far less than they would have been if the technological changes had not occurred. It is possible that unit costs will fall right up to the point at which a resource is physically exhausted if technological change offsets the physical properties associated with depletion. The point is simply that no clear signal can be inferred from the unit cost measure.

The measure has other weaknesses as well; one is the elasticity of substitution between the resource and other factor inputs. Suppose there is an increase in the rental price of a mineral. Those using the mineral will seek to substitute lower-cost factor inputs in their production processes if this is possible. Less of the mineral will be extracted. The unit cost of extracting the mineral can rise as a result, and the increase in unit costs will be larger the greater the substitution possibilities. Brown and Field illustrate this result using a constant elasticity of substitution production function. If the measure is signaling more scarcity but the economy finds it easier to deal with scarcity by substitution, then the measure is not very meaningful for practical policy prescription. Market processes would appear to be ensuring continued production of goods and services over time.

The unit cost measure also has practical problems. To compute the measure, the inputs such as capital and labor must be aggregated. Aggregation, especially of capital, always presents difficulties. Due to data problems, Barnett and Morse had to aggregate over different stages of the manufacturing process for their labor series, but output was from the extractive level. Unit costs are also a backward-looking indicator: They measure the costs that have been incurred and do not typically incorporate expectations of decision makers about what costs will be in the future. We noted above that people will make decisions based on both past observations and beliefs about the future. These beliefs or expectations may turn out to be wrong, but they are the basis on which actions are made. A measure that incorporates expectations should give a more accurate picture of actual scarcity.

The Real Price of the Resource

The second measure of resource scarcity is the one preferred by many analysts: the real price of the extracted resource. But although conceptually better than the unit cost approach, this measure too has weaknesses. Its great strength is that it is the easiest to compute. Resource prices are readily available over long time periods, and there are a number of indexes with which to deflate the price. It is a forward-looking measure because expectations about future supplies, costs, technological changes, and so on will be reflected in the market price of the resource. The most troublesome problem is that the choice of the deflator or numeraire used to calculate real prices influences the results.

The relative price of minerals can be calculated with respect to the prices (or price index) of other factor inputs (capital and labor), to indexes of prices of interme-

Table 6.2a THE RELATIVE PRICES OF MINERALS AND LABOR (1900 = 100)

	1900	1920	1940	1950	1960	1970
Coal	459	451	189	208	111	100
Copper	785	226	121	99	82	100
Iron	620	287	144	112	120	100
Phosphorus	—	—	—	130	120	100
Molybdenum	—	—	—	142	108	100
Lead	788	388	204	228	114	100
Zinc	794	400	272	256	125	100
Sulfur	—	—	—	215	145	100
Aluminum	3,150	859	287	166	134	100
Gold	—	—	595	258	143	100
Crude petroleum	1,034	726	198	213	135	100

Source: From W. D. Nordhaus, "The Allocation of Energy Resources," *Brookings Papers on Economic Activity,* no. 3 (1973) pp. 529–570.

Note: Values are price per ton of mineral divided by hourly wage rate in manufacturing. Cited in Brown and Field (1979), p. 225.

diate goods (wholesale price indexes), or to price indexes of final goods and services (consumer price indexes or implicit GNP deflators). We would not expect to get a uniform result over time because these indexes do not always move together. And there is no agreement on the best index to use.

Brown and Field present two tables taken from Nordhaus (1973) and Jorgenson and Griliches (1967) to illustrate the point; see Table 6.2. Part *a* shows the prices of eleven mineral commodities at the refined level deflated by a manufacturing wage rate; part *b* shows the same commodities deflated by the price of capital. Although not all years are presented for the data in *b*, we can see that the real price measures are not consistent. The Jorgenson and Griliches data indicate that coal, lead, and zinc be-

Table 6.2b REAL PRICE OF SELECTED MINERALS USING THE PRICE OF CAPITAL AS A NUMERAIRE, SELECTED YEARS, 1920–1950

	1920	1940	1950
Coal	340	195	413
Copper	170	125	129
Iron	216	149	146
Phosphorus	—	141	170
Molybdenum	—	—	186
Lead	292	211	298
Zinc	301	281	335
Sulfur	—	—	281
Aluminum	647	297	217
Gold	—	615	337
Crude petroleum	547	205	278

Source: Taken from D. Jorgenson and Z. Griliches, "The Explanation of Productivity Change," *Review of Economic Studies,* vol. 34 (July 1967) pp. 250–282; U.S. Bureau of Census, *Historical Statistics of the United States, 1789–1945* (Washington, GPO, 1949); U.S. Bureau of Census, *Long-Term Economic Growth 1860–1965* (Washington, GPO, 1966); and U.S. Bureau of Census, *Statistical Abstracts of the United States, 1974* (Washington, GPO, 1974). Cited in Brown and Field (1979), p. 226.

came more scarce from 1920 to 1950, and that phosphorus is added to this list for 1940 to 1950. However measured in the same years, the Nordhaus data indicate that *all* the commodities were becoming less scarce. Other indexes would presumably give different results.

It can also be misleading to look at real resource prices (or any measure of natural resource scarcity) only at specific years or only for a few years, and then draw inferences about resource scarcity from these observations. The real price calculations illustrated in Table 6.2 look only at one price per decade. Fisher (1981) presents data on the real prices of the same nonfuel minerals examined in Table 6.2 (crude petroleum is omitted) for the years 1969 and 1979. In Table 6.3 we have recalculated Fisher's numbers for 1969 and 1979, using data from the United States Bureau of Mines, and we have added the figures for 1982.

Fisher's interpretation is that with the exception of copper and sulfur, the dominant impression is that most real prices have risen substantially. He suggests that even though the evidence is sketchy, the numbers may indicate that the real prices of these resources have ceased their downward trend and are now rising because cost-saving technological change has stopped and new discoveries are declining. This may well be the case—but look at the figures for 1982. With the exception of sulfur, there is a decline or no significant change in the real prices of all other nonfuel minerals. If, then, we looked only at the years 1979 and 1982, a very different impression of the scarcity of these minerals might emerge.

Did the minerals suddenly become *less scarce* from 1979 to 1982? No. In 1979, most mineral commodities were riding the boom in resource prices created by the increases in oil prices in the 1970s. It takes time for any mineral supplier to respond to price increases. Capacity must be expanded, reserves brought on stream, and so on. By 1982, a lot of new capacity did come on stream (indicating that these resources were not becoming more scarce and perhaps were less scarce than in previous years). But by 1982, most of the world was also in a severe recession, with very low aggregate demand for minerals (and other natural resources). Mineral prices fell not just because supply rose, but because there was very little demand for steel, automobiles, and other goods using these commodities.

One simply cannot look at selected years to make inferences about scarcity. If

Table 6.3   REAL PRICES OF SELECTED NONFUEL MINERALS, 1969, 1979, 1982

Mineral	1969	1979	1982
Copper	$0.45/lb	$0.40/lb	$0.25/lb
Iron	$10.09/ton	$10.61/ton	$10.69/ton
Phosphate rock	$5.77/metric ton	$8.20/metric ton	$8.35/metric ton
Molybdenum	$1.77/lb	$2.58/lb	$1.32/lb
Lead	$0.14/lb	$0.22/lb	$0.09/lb
Zinc	$0.14/lb	$0.16/lb	$0.11/lb
Sulfur	$25.00/metric ton	$23.66/metric ton	$36.17/metric ton
Aluminum ingots	$0.25/lb	$0.25/lb	$0.25/lb
Gold	$38.98/oz	$130.52/oz	$125.60/oz

Notes: All prices are deflated by the United States producer price index for all commodities, not seasonally adjusted, 1967 = 100. Mineral prices are from U.S. Bureau of Mines, *Mineral Facts and Problems*, 1980 edition, Bulletin 671.

we must "explain away" the price increases by referring to events that do not pertain to resource scarcity as such, then the real price (or any measure) is not going to be very meaningful. Looking at real prices over a long period of time may be more meaningful, but there is still the problem that there may be no significant relationship between prices and time and that the price movements reflect much more than scarcity.

Other problems with the real price are that the market prices of the minerals will include any distortions which exist in these markets: government policies such as taxes, subsidies, quotas, and strategic stockpile strategies, and other factors such as the structure of the market and the influence of labor unions. These distortions are not constant over time nor identical for all minerals examined. Thus, the real price data may be reflecting all sorts of economic changes *not* associated with scarcity per se. Still other problems cited by Brown and Field are analogous to some of those for unit costs—complication of interpretations of the measure when there is technological change and substitution of other commodities for the mineral. These difficulties aside, many analysts continue to use real price as a measure in evaluation of resource scarcity.

Brown and Field have also provided some examples contrasting the unit cost with the real price method. The numbers they present on an aggregate of all metals for the period 1890 to 1970 are shown in Figure 6.1. Both measures of resource scarcity indicate a generally downward trend up to 1970. Despite the problems associated with using either the real price of the resource or unit costs of extraction, for the numbers derived by Brown and Field the two measures give similar results overall. Whether these two measures track other resources similarly remains to be shown.

Resource Rents

The final measure we consider is that of the rental value of the resource *in the ground.* Our theoretical work in previous chapters has focused on resource rent, and we argue (along with others) that conceptually it is the most appropriate measure of scarcity.[2] (We need not reexamine the way in which resource rent changes over time in response to impending depletion, the presence of backstop technologies, uncertainty, and changes in underlying parameters such as extraction costs and the discount rate.) Rents are superior to market prices because they correctly incorporate the effects of technological change and substitution possibilities. The market price will understate scarcity when substitution among factor inputs is possible, because the price rises less rapidly than the rents. The market price will also be affected by the share of the resource input relative to other inputs. If the resource has a small share, the price of the finished good will not be affected as much by a decline in the mineral supply as would a good with a high mineral content.

There are, however, some problems involved when resource rents are used as a measure of scarcity. Rents are affected by government policies as well as market imperfections. As we saw in Chapter 4, a monopolist extracting a nonrenewable resource will earn both monopoly and resource rents. While in theory it is possible to distinguish between the two types of rents, in practice it is quite difficult. The large rise in rents earned by oil producers in the 1970s cannot be attributed solely to growing scarcity; the noncompetitive behavior of OPEC is certainly an important

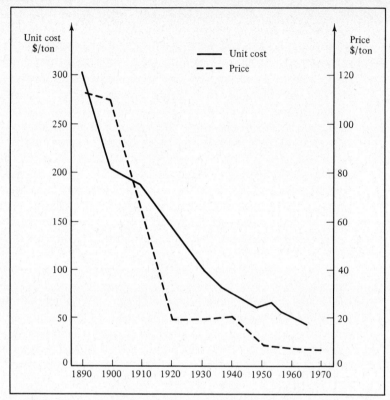

Figure 6.1 Price and unit cost for all metals, 1890–1970. *Source:* G. M. Brown and B. Field (1979) "The Adequacy of Measures for Signalling Natural Resource Scarcity" in V. K. Smith ed., *Scarcity and Growth Reconsidered,* Baltimore: Johns Hopkins University Press for Resources for the Future. Copyright, Resources for the Future, Inc.

factor. Thus the principal difficulty with resource rents as a measure of the scarcity of minerals is practical: They are difficult to measure because they require substantial amounts of firm-specific data.

To get around this problem, some economists have used the *cost of discovering new deposits* as a proxy. The argument is that exploration dollars will be spent (on the margin) as long as the expected gain from finding the resource equals the marginal cost of exploration. The expected discovery value of the resource stock is simply the present value of its expected rents. The advantage of using exploration costs is that they are easier to calculate. The disadvantages are that most estimates are only average, not marginal, costs, and that the measures will also incorporate any distortions that exist in the exploration process. For example, in Canada exploration for oil and gas is heavily subsidized by the tax policies of the federal government.

Devarajan and Fisher (1982) have presented estimates of the average real exploration costs for oil and gas in the United States from 1947 to 1971 (see Table 6.4). They show an upward trend. Uhler (1979) has calculated the costs of finding oil and gas reserves for deposits in Alberta, Canada. His results suggest that it is becoming more costly to discover oil, but that the results are less clear for natural gas. We thus have different measures across countries. There are a few estimates of resource rent for nonfuel minerals, but they do not calculate rents over time. Cairns (1981), for example, looked at the rents from nickel production by Canada's (and the world's) largest nickel producer, Inco. Slade (1982) examined rents from copper deposits. Both found that most of the rent derived from differences in ore quality, not from the fixed supply of the resource itself.

But estimation of resource rent remains important not just as an aid in measuring resource scarcity over time, but because the measures are very useful in formulating government tax and regulatory policies, and can be used to test theoretical models of resource extraction.

Table 6.4 AVERAGE REAL EXPLORATION COSTS FOR U.S. OIL AND GAS, 1946–1971

Year	Cost*
1946	0.568
1947	0.527
1948	0.291
1949	0.323
1950	0.497
1951	0.748
1952	0.827
1953	0.692
1954	0.628
1955	1.036
1956	0.789
1957	0.653
1958	0.950
1959	1.449
1960	1.213
1961	1.509
1962	0.98
1963	1.35
1964	1.26
1965	0.98
1966	1.65
1967	1.39
1968	0.14
1969	1.78
1970	1.24
1971	1.38

*Dollars per equivalent barrel of oil discovered (average 1947–9 dollars). To combine oil and gas discoveries, physical units were aggregated on the basis of market value.

Source: F. M. Howell and H. A. Merklein (1973) "What It Costs to Find Hydrocarbons in the U.S." *World Oil,* pp. 75–79, as cited in Devarajan and Fisher (1982).

Concluding Comments

There are some difficulties with all measures of resource scarcity. They are inapplicable to common property resources—fisheries and environmental resources such as air, water, and some natural environments. The rental value does not work because common property exploitation of a resource results in the dissipation of rent. The market price will not reflect the externalities associated with common property (see Chapter 8). The measures are difficult to interpret. Because people cannot determine the future, they often form expectations about what will occur. These expectations will influence extraction decisions, which will in turn influence the measures of resource scarcity. Often our expectations are wrong, and thus what was anticipated does not happen. Finally, none of these measures incorporates social valuations of resource exploitation and use.

Although there has been much work done on resource scarcity using the measures described above, it is not clear to us (and others) that these measures are useful in deciding what actions to take if we agree that a resource is becoming more scarce. What we want to know is how scarcity affects our general welfare: What will happen to the goods and services we are able to produce and consume? Simply knowing that a resource is becoming more scarce does not tell us whether or not the aggregate welfare

---

BOX 6.1
"Commodity Prices Plunge, Severing Link with Growth"

An article from *The Economist* (reprinted in *The Australian,* August 16, 1984) suggests that certain natural resources, particularly minerals, may be becoming less important in the production of goods and services over time. This may be due to greater substitution possibilities. Fiber optics are being used instead of copper wire in telecommunications; plastics are used instead of zinc in automobiles, and so on. Recycling will affect primary production of commodities such as aluminum and copper. The industrial structure in developed economies is also changing. Mineral demand may fall over time once the aggregate capital stock of a country reaches a certain level and population growth declines. There are only so many factories, railway tracks, roads, houses, and so on needed when an economy is in a "steady state," with zero population growth. Machines and automobiles will have to be replaced when they wear out, but the demand for minerals is much smaller when they are used for replacement as opposed to building up a country's capital stock. The decline in mineral use may also reflect a shift in the composition of goods and services in a developed economy. The recent high growth period in the United States (and other countries) has been largely in the service sectors of the economy, not sectors which use a lot of minerals. An interesting question is whether the economic growth in countries now going through rapid industrialization (such as Korea and Malaysia) will absorb the mineral output that used to be bought by the OECD countries.

of individuals will change. It does not suggest that governments should, for example, attempt to conserve that resource.

Other measures can provide some information about the importance of a particular commodity. Unfortunately, they are all for goods with well-defined markets. For resources with well-functioning markets, one measure of importance is the elasticity of substitution. It gives us an idea of how readily one factor input can be substituted for another in the production of a particular good. If a resource has many good substitutes (and it is not valued for its own sake or its contribution to environmental stability), then do we care if we run out of it? There are many instances where one resource has been substituted for another to produce essentially the same product. As Box 6.1 on commodity prices suggests, there is growing evidence that many minerals are no longer needed in large quantities to produce the goods and services in great demand today and into the future. Perhaps, as is also suggested by Brown and Field, we should be focusing our attention on substitution possibilities and the importance of the resource in our economy rather than on measures of the scarcity of the resource in isolation. This focus has been used in the case of energy resources, as we will see in Chapter 7, and for some other minerals as well. But much work remains. Scarcity measures are a first step in the process of determining what is happening to natural resource production over time. Additional information about how the resource is used in the economy is required before we conclude that increasing scarcity, if it exists, is a social problem. We turn now to a more abstract discussion of how natural resources can enter into the production process and how they can affect the economy's ability to produce goods and services over time.

BOX 6.2
Resource Use in Selected Industrial Countries

In spite of the fact that the proportion of national output accounted for by the manufacturing sector varies very little among industrial countries, there is considerable variability in resource use, as the data in Table 1 indicate. The United States was using more than 2.5 times the aluminum per capita, compared with the United Kingdom for example. The same is true for phosphates. Germany was using twice as much magnesium per capita relative to the United States. When the figures were aggregated, Kay and Mirrlees (1975) found the United States to be consuming, in per capita terms, twice as much resources as the Netherlands and about 60 percent more than the United Kingdom.

Which commodities or sectors use the most resources is also highly variable. Using the United States input-output table, Kay and Mirrlees investigated the percentage of the selling price of a commodity attributable directly and indirectly to selected natural resources. In other words, 36 percent of the selling price of a streetcar can be attributed to the steel used in its construction. The input-output tables permit us to measure the intermediate input as well as the final or directly observed input. The values in Table 2 include both final and intermediate inputs and thus provide a comprehensive measure of the resources embodied in a commodity. Relatively large users of an input will

Box 6.2 continued

Table 1 INDICES OF SELECTED NATURAL RESOURCES CONSUMED PER CAPITA IN SELECTED COUNTRIES, 1969
(United Kingdom = 100)

Country	Iron	Copper	Aluminium	Lead	Zinc	Tin	Nickel	Magnesium	Phosphates	Potash	Aggregate
United States	156	105	261	84	117	81	108	299	252	197	158
United Kingdom	100	100	100	100	100	100	100	100	100	100	100
Germany	143	111	151	104	126	67	103	608	168	197	134
France	103	87	104	80	91	60	108	74	388	276	100
Italy	82	59	69	55	60	36	52	37	109	38	74
Netherlands	91	41	59	76	51	107	8	22	99	111	77
Sweden	164	123	145	138	91	14	344	62	214	180	156
Denmark	103	14	20	81	47	52	3	—	311	423	77
Canada	115	148	150	64	106	67	107	100	222	125	121
Japan	139	96	115	38	113	72	113	55	84	78	125

Source: O.E.C.D. *Statistics of Energy;* British Steel Corporation, *Statistical Handbook; Metal Statistics;* National Accounts of O.E.C.D. Countries; *U.N. Annual Bulletin of Statistics,* as cited in J. A. Kay and J. A. Mirrlees, "The Desirability of Natural Resource Depletion." In D. W. Pearce and J. Rose, eds., *The Economics of Natural Resource Depletion.* London, Macmillan, 1975, Table 9.2.

Table 2 PERCENTAGE OF THE TOTAL VALUE OF SELECTED PRODUCTS ACCOUNTED FOR BY DIRECT AND INDIRECT USE OF SELECTED RESOURCES IN THE UNITED STATES, 1969

Aluminum		Chemical and fertilizer minerals	
Metal foil	28.4%	Fertilizers	11.6%
Electrical industrial goods	7.0	Industrial chemicals	3.4
Sheet metal work	6.3	Agricultural chemicals	2.7
Tanks and components	5.7	Plastics	1.5
Trucks and trailers	4.9	Misc. chemical products	1.0
Trailer coaches	4.1	Paints	0.9
Coal		**Copper**	
Federal electric utilities	17.6	Small arms and ammunition	7.7
State and local utilities	6.9	Pipes, valves, and fittings	6.5
Metal barrels, drums, pails	1.5	Transformers	3.7
Fabricated plate works	1.3	Motors and generators	3.3
Railroad and streetcars	1.3	Welding apparatus	2.8
Sheet metal work	1.2	Switchgear	2.4
Lead		**Petroleum and natural gas**	
Storage batteries	24.5	Refined petroleum products	53.0
Small arms and ammunition	8.4	Gas utilities	27.8
Paints	1.4	Industrial chemicals	6.2
Printing trade machinery	1.2	Air transport	5.2
Metal foil	1.1	Agricultural chemicals	5.0
Industrial chemicals	1.1	Paints	4.2
Steel		**Zinc**	
Fabricated plate works	39.8	Miscellaneous hardware	2.6
Railroad and streetcars	35.7	Storage batteries	2.2
Sheet metal work	34.1	Small arms and ammunition	1.0
Safes and vaults	34.0	Household laundry equipment	0.7
Metal stampings	29.8	Commercial laundry equipment	0.6
Fabricated metal goods	25.9	Electric housewares	0.5

Source: J. A. Kay and J. A. Mirrlees, "The Desirability of Natural Resource Depletion." In D. W. Pearce and J. Rose, eds., *The Economics of Natural Resource Depletion.* London, Macmillan, 1975, Table 9.5.

observe larger price increases as particular resources become scarce. Kay and Mirrlees remark: "When we know that lead mostly goes into car batteries, we realise that if we want to conserve lead it is a good deal easier and more effective to design a car that does not need a lead-acid accumulator than to halve economic growth."

ECONOMIC GROWTH AND DEPLETABLE RESOURCE USE

Resources are a factor input which, when combined with other factor inputs, produce goods and services. We will derive a demand curve for resources from the demand for the goods and services they produce, and that demand will then be related to the demand for other factor inputs. Then we can trace what can happen to resource use over time when there is another factor input—capital.

The Derived Demand for Nonrenewable Resource Flows

Our hypothetical economy produces one good — say fiber — which can be consumed or set aside to provide machines for producing fiber in future periods. Fiber is produced in our economy with machines and fuel mined from nonrenewable resource stocks of known size. Thus, in any period fuel and machines produce fiber, and our people can consume the fiber or fashion it into new machines. This will be our economy. How fuel and machines can be combined is crucial to the productiveness of our economy. A *production function* defines the feasible ways of producing fiber with fuel and machines in any period. Examples are the Cobb-Douglas form of the production function

$$Q = K^{\alpha}R^{1-\alpha} \tag{6.1}$$

or the *CES* (constant elasticity of substitution form)

$$Q = [aK^{-\rho} + (1 - a)R^{-\rho}]^{-1/\rho} \tag{6.2}$$

where Q is the output of fiber in tons per period
K is the amount of machines yielding a flow of productive services proportional to K per period
R is the input of fuel in tons per period
α, a and ρ are positive constants where $0 < \alpha < 1$ and $0 < a < 1$.

The production function specifies ways of combining inputs to get output — ways that represent known techniques. A production function is like a set of procedures for producing a homogeneous output, say gravel from rock. Depending on whether there is an abundance of labor relative to machines, a different procedure for producing gravel will be used. The production function with two inputs is often illustrated by sketching its level curves or *isoquants,* as in Figure 6.2.

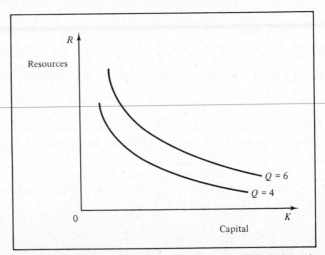

Figure 6.2 These two *isoquants* indicate the technological possibilities for combining capital, K, and the natural resource fuel, R, to produce quantities of output, $Q = 4$ and $Q = 6$, respectively. These are two of a family of isoquants for producing different physical amounts of output (called fiber in the text).

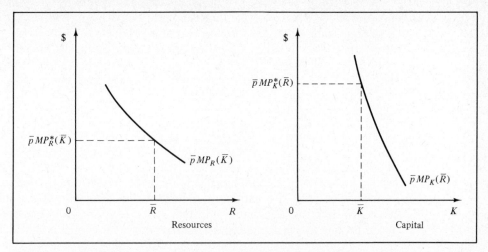

Figure 6.3 Two demand curves for inputs R and K, respectively, used in producing a quantity of fiber being sold at price $\bar{p}$ per ton. These demand curves are called *value of marginal product schedules*. Note the position of each schedule depends on the level of use of the other input.

Given a demand for Q at price p per unit of fiber, there must be demands for inputs K and R to produce the Q. These demand curves for a competitive economy are called the *value of marginal product schedules* and look like the familiar demand curves for final products (see Figure 6.3). The marginal product of an input i is the increment in Q which results from one additional unit of i being fed into production. Given K held constant at say $\bar{K}$, the marginal product of R (the first derivative of the production function with respect to R) will be negatively sloped as R varies, as in Figure 6.3, and similarly for the marginal product of K, given R held constant at, say, $\bar{R}$. When each marginal product schedule is multiplied by p, the price of a unit of Q, we have the value of marginal product schedules illustrated. These are the demand curves for inputs derived ultimately from the demand for Q at price p.

In our economy with the single multipurpose output called fiber, its price can be set at unity and the prices of inputs defined with respect to this price of output. (This is called *normalizing* all prices so that the price of fiber is the numeraire.)

The input demand schedules are interdependent. Any change in the use or quantity demanded of one input shifts the demand schedule for the other. Holding output constant,[3] the extent of the shifts in these curves can be measured by the *elasticity of substitution* inherent in the production function. This elasticity is reflected in the amount of curvature of an isoquant — the closer the isoquant is to a straight line, the closer the elasticity is to infinite. For the two inputs, capital and resources, this elasticity[4] is given by the formula:

$$\frac{\text{percent change in the ratio } K/R}{\text{percent change in the ratio } MP_R/MP_K} \tag{6.3}$$

This shifting of input demand schedules is important because with nonrenewable resources, we expect an inevitable decline in the magnitude of resource flows available for production. As stocks of oil are depleted, less will be used each year. The shifting of input demand curves will occur in the process of economic growth or decline. Can we tell how these demand curves will shift over time? A version of Hotelling's rule, defined in terms of marginal products, in part governs the time path of resource use and hence affects the use of capital as well. It must be the case that

$$\frac{MP_R(t+1) - MP_R(t)}{MP_R(t)} = MP_K(t+1) \tag{6.4}$$

across periods, or

$$\frac{P_R(t+1) - P_R(t)}{P_R(t)} = P_K(t+1)$$

where, as we noted, marginal products are prices of inputs expressed in terms of the output, fiber. (We treat extraction costs of fuel as zero without essential loss to the analysis.) In terms of demand schedules, as we have shown in Figure 6.4, since the resource flow $R(t)$ is changing, the demand curve for capital is shifting and this will lead to a subsequent shift in the demand curve for resource flows. For our example below with a Cobb-Douglas production function, K increases over time, causing the demand curve for R to shift to the left, and R decreases over time, causing the demand curve for capital to shift also to the left. The arrows in Figure 6.5 indicate how prices and quantities demanded change over time as the demand schedules shift.

In this example, each demand schedule shifts to the left over time, the price of resource flows rises and $R(t)$ declines, and the price of capital (its rental price) declines and $K(t)$ increases. This illustrates how the demand schedule for resource flows is related to other variables in the economy and will certainly not remain stationary as the economy develops. We turn now to the demand for output, the engine that drives the demand for our two inputs.

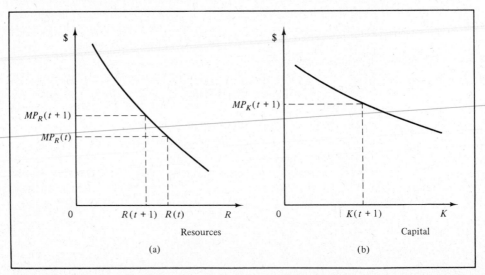

Figure 6.4 A condition for efficient depletion of a known resource stock is that its price (here MP_R) should rise at a rate equal to the return on capital (here MP_K). The time path of resource use, $R(t)$, $R(t+1)$, $R(t+2)$, etc., follows. This percentage change in resource price rule was earlier labeled Hotelling's rule.

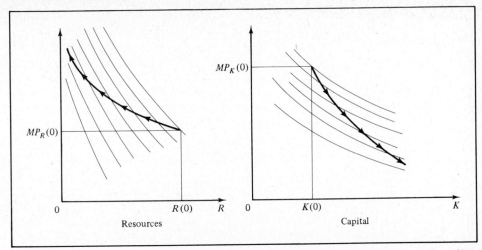

Figure 6.5   The time paths of prices (*MPs*) and input use are traced out in the paths with arrows. Also over time in our numerical example, we have shifts in the input demand schedules to the left as time passes. Note that the price of resources continually rises as less are used each period and the price of capital declines as more is accumulated and used in production. *R*(0) and *K*(0) are initial values of resources and capital, respectively.

Normative Models of Economic Growth with Depletable Resources

Our fiber-producing economy exists because fiber output is required by individuals for consumption. However, a balance must be struck between consumption today and consumption tomorrow, since overconsumption today will leave less fiber for expanding capacity needed for consumption tomorrow. The capital stock must be increased to enhance production opportunities for the future, and nonrenewable resources must be managed so that there will be fuel available for future production of fiber. The issue then is to balance consumption and investment today so that future production will be satisfactory.

Two general approaches have analyzed the trade off between current consumption and future consumption, period by period: *positive* and *normative*. In the positive approach, which we discuss below, a particular savings rule is proposed, and then implications of the rule for economic growth are determined. Resource use in this type of approach is governed by an intertemporal efficiency condition—a variant of Hotelling's rule.

Now our focus is the normative approach. A particular path of consumption over time is selected as the most desirable, and a savings and resource use program is established to fulfill the requirements of this path. Clearly such a path must be practical; it cannot be unrealistically large in consumption possibilities period by period. A traditional approach of the normative type is to arrange to maximize the discounted present value of future utilities period by period from consuming fiber. We then find how much investment in new capital goods must occur and how natural resource flows must be used so that the maximum of the discounted utility of consumption is achieved. Specifically, we find a path of capital stocks $K(1)$, $K(2)$,

$K(3), \ldots, K(N), \ldots$ and resource stocks $S(1), S(2), \ldots, S(N), \ldots$ such that

$$W = U[C(0)] + \beta U[C(1)] + \beta^2 U[C(2)] + \cdots \beta^N U[C(N)] + \cdots \quad (6.5)$$

is a maximum. $U(\cdot)$ is the utility of consumption and β is the discount factor. $\beta = 1/(1 + r)$ where r is the discount rate. For any two periods, t and $t + 1$, $C(t) = f[K(t),R(t)] - [K(t + 1) - K(t)]$ and $R(t) = S(t) - S(t + 1)$ where $S(t)$ is the nonrenewable resource stock at time t, $C(t)$ is total consumption of fiber at time t, $f[K(t),R(t)]$ is the production function relating inputs to output of fiber, and $K(t + 1) - K(t)$ is the investment resulting in additional capital goods at time t. (We abstract from the depreciation of produced capital goods without losing the essentials of the analysis.)

Maximizing W requires that the derivatives of W with respect to $K(t)$ and $S(t)$ must equal zero for all periods. This gives us simultaneous, nonlinear, recursive equations in (6.6) and (6.7). (Recursive means relationships in one period are algebraically intertwined with relationships in adjacent periods).

$$\frac{f_R[K(t + 1),R(t + 1)] - f_R[K(t),R(t)]}{f_R[K(t),R(t)]} = f_K[K(t + 1),R(t + 1)] \quad (6.6)$$

$$\beta U_C[C(t + 1)]\{f_K[K(t + 1),R(t + 1)] + 1\} - U_C[C(t)] = 0 \quad (6.7)$$

where $f_R(\cdot), f_K(\cdot)$, and $U_C(\cdot)$ are derivatives with respect to R, K, and C, respectively. Equation (6.6) is a new appearance of Hotelling's rule, and Equation (6.7) is a relation involving the marginal utility of consumption, the marginal product of capital, and the discount factor. Equation (6.7) is called a *Ramsey optimal savings rule.*

Complete optimality requires that the initial choices of $K(1)$ and $S(1)$ result in the highest value for W and in so doing satisfy conditions at the horizon of the program (the transversality conditions, in mathematics). That is, given $S(0)$ and $K(0)$, we chose $S(1)$ and $K(1)$ and solve for $S(2)$, $K(2)$. We can then solve for $S(3)$, and $K(3)$ in our time-recursive pair of equations and so on for $S(t)$ and $K(t)$ into the future.

Using a Cobb-Douglas form $K^\alpha R^{(1-\alpha)}$ for the production function and a constant marginal utility consumption function $\frac{1}{1 - v} C^{1-v}$ $(0 < v < 1)$, we have computed some time paths for consumption, output, capital, resource stock, savings, rents for resources, and prices.[5] An optimal program is a sequence of $K(t)$s and $S(t)$s that make discounted utility from consumption, W, a maximum. The optimal program is not a steady state, since resource stocks keep dwindling in order to provide fuel for production.

For some hypothetical values, we "solved" the model on the computer to illustrate the time paths of $K(t)$, $R(t)$, output, consumption, savings, resource rents, and prices. We chose some initial trends for $K(t)$ and $S(t)$ and let the system evolve according to our optimizing relations in Equations (6.6) and (6.7). This procedure does not in general produce optimal paths, since the correct initial trends are special values that are extremely difficult to determine. Our hypothetical base path illustrates what an optimal program resembles: $R(t)$ declines more and more slowly, $K(t)$ rises, and consumption declines. The price of fuel rises and that of capital goods declines.

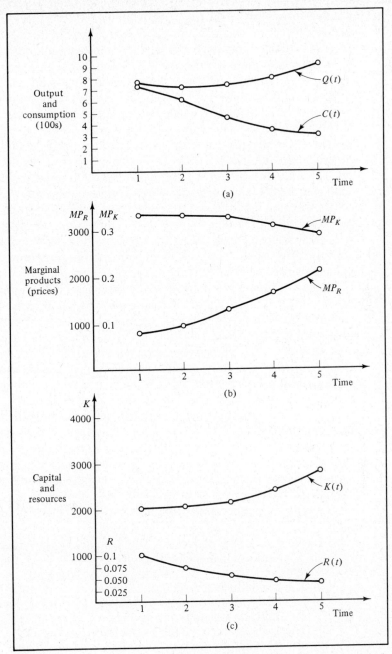

Figure 6.6 Time paths of key variables generated on the computer for a growth model.

In Figure 6.6(a), the base case, we observe consumption steadily declining and output dipping down initially and then rising. In Figure 6.6(b), the price (marginal product) of fuel is rising and that of capital goods is declining. In Figure 6.6(c), we observe that fuel used declines gradually and capital accumulation accelerates. The parameters used in our base computer run and reported in Figure 6.6 are $v = .5$, $\beta = 1/(1 + r) = .683$, $\alpha = .9$, $S(0) = 1$, $S(1) = .9$, $K(0) = 2000$, $K(1) = 2001$.

A complete analysis of how resource use and other input demands respond to new conditions (changes in technology or tastes) or changes in parameters involves re-solving the problem for a new optimal program. Rather than follow this exhaustive approach, we have made do with sticking with our original initial trends in $K(t)$ and $S(t)$ and observing how the paths are altered, given new values for a selected parameter. Three parameters were perturbed separately in three revised runs of the model. The three are the share of capital in production in the production function (namely, α), the discount factor β, and the parameter in the utility function (namely, v).

Our intuition is that an increase in v, the elasticity of marginal utility, which is defined as the percentage change in marginal utility due to a percentage change in consumption, would make an increment in consumption, C, in any period less valuable, since marginal utility becomes more negative. This would tend to even out the stream of $C(t)$s across periods in the absence of discounting. In the presence of discounting, relatively larger increments in $C(t)$ would be made later in the program, when the effect of discounting was stronger. Hence an increase in v is expected to lower inputs, output, and consumption today in favor of more of all tomorrow. In fact, we observe the $C(t)$ path declining relative to the base path in the early periods.

With regard to the discount rate, we expect a high value to make current consumption relatively more valuable compared with later consumption, and thus for early values of $C(t)$ to rise. We observe this to be the case.

A rise in the coefficient α for capital in the production function [and a decline in that for resources, namely $(1 - \alpha)$] is like technological progress for capital goods and the opposite for resource flows. Other things being the same, x units of capital will contribute more to output than before the rise in α, and vice versa for resource flows. Thus the change in α would be expected to lower the early path of $K(t)$ and raise it for $R(t)$ as the model strives to maintain the base path with the new parameter. We observed this in our computer run; here are the details of the experiments.

1. The elasticity of marginal utility. The increase in this parameter (from .5 to .52) results in higher time paths for $R(t)$, $K(t)$, output, savings, and resource rents and a lower time path for resource stock $S(t)$.
2. The discount factor. The increase in this parameter (from .683 to .684) results in higher time paths for resource stocks $S(t)$ and lower time paths for $K(t)$, output, consumption, savings, and resource rents.
3. The share parameter in the production function. The increase in this parameter from .90 to .92 results in higher time paths for the resource stock, output, and consumption, and lower time paths for $K(t)$, savings, and resource rents.

The model is analyzed in mathematical detail in appendix F.

Investing Resource Rents and Intergenerational Equity

Suppose people do not discount consumption that occurs in the future, but treat each year as the same as the rest. In terms of the model, this means that $\beta = 1$. One rationale for this type of behavior is that current generations want to ensure that there will be a sufficient supply of goods and services available for their descendants. What will happen to resource use in this case? Suppose then that $v = 0$, which means $U(C) = C(t)$. The optimal growth model described above now generates the rule that all resource rents should be saved and invested in new machines, dollar for dollar. This rule implies that consumption and output in each period of time will be *constant* and *positive*. The level of output and consumption depends on $S(0)$ and $K(0)$. In certain cases, they can remain positive over *infinite time*. How is this possible, given a finite stock of resources at the initial date?

Resource stocks are run down asymptotically, and resource use becomes infinitesimally small as time passes. However, resources continue to be used and reserves remain positive because capital goods are accumulated rapidly enough to compensate for the continually declining use of resources and keep output from collapsing. Note that the Cobb-Douglas production function, $Q = K^\alpha R^{1-\alpha}$, has the property that each input is *essential*. That is, if either K or R is zero, output is zero. This means that a strategy of running the resource stock to zero and attempting to continue production after the resource is exhausted is not feasible when R is essential. An optimal plan must cope with the finiteness of the resource stock and the unboundedness of the future.

When consumption remains positive and constant forever and the population is unchanging over time, per capita consumption remains positive and constant forever. This result leads to a type of intergenerational equity in the sense that no generation consumes more goods than another. Moreover, the strategy of saving all resource rents, the current value of minerals removed from the ground, and investing them in reproducible capital goods such as buildings and machines connotes reciprocity across generations. The following generation has less of a mineral stock to work with but more reproducible capital. The value of the diminution of the stock equals the value of the extra buildings and machines. As it turns out, the savings rule *does* imply intergenerational equity.[6]

Rather than investing[7] in durable reproducible capital goods such as buildings and machines, investment could be made in extra research and development and/or education. Assuming that these investments paid off in increased future production, a similar intergenerational equity result is valid. New productive knowledge can be a substitute for new machines and buildings. Thus we can see why intergenerational equity might still be valid if the investment is in knowledge rather than buildings and machines (see Robson, 1980).

The result also suggests a role for government policy. Will private markets generate the optimal amount of "saving" of resource rents and invest enough in capital goods? If decision-makers extracting nonrenewable natural resources base their actions on a social discount rate of zero (and no other distortions exist), optimal saving should occur. However, it is possible that decision-makers *do* discount the future, and the amount of saving of resource rents will then not be optimal. Government policies to encourage the optimal saving of natural resource rents could include a tax on resource rents. Government can then invest the rents it collects in capital projects. See Box 6.3 on investing resource rents in Alberta and Alaska. Another possible government action is the nationalization of the resource industry, which has occurred in many countries.

BOX 6.3
Accumulating Exhaustible Resource Revenues in Special Funds

In all states in which oil is extracted, local governments are involved in one way or another. At a minimum, the governments license the companies doing the exploration and extraction and reap some royalties on the amount extracted. At the other extreme, a branch of government is the company doing the exploration, extraction, and marketing. For example, Norway's dominant actor in the oil business is Statoil, the government company; in Mexico, it is Pemex; in the United Kingdom, it is British National Oil Company (BNOC); and Canada has its Petrocan, a government company dominant in retailing but also active in exploration and production.

    The allocation of revenues accruing to the governments is an issue. One approach is simply to make taxes, personal and excise, relatively low and to finance public expenditure with resource revenues. This has two apparent drawbacks. First, it is felt that too little provision is being made for future generations. Since the resource stock will be exhausted, the current generation has an obligation to provide for future generations that will be without the wealth in the ground. Second, lower taxes attract immigrants, and implicit surpluses represented by the lower taxes are dissipated by the newcomers. This is especially true for states within nations, such as Texas and Alaska in the United States or Alberta in Canada, where immigration is not directly controlled. Rather than lowering taxes, some states have established special funds into which resource royalties are directed. These funds are invested, and the principal and interest will be available to future generations. The accumulated principal represents a stock of wealth above ground in place of part or all of the depleted resource stock below ground.

    Alberta and Alaska established such special funds in 1976. In Alberta, 30 percent of oil and natural gas royalties were placed in the Alberta Heritage Savings Trust Fund, and in Alaska, 25 percent of oil royalties were put in the Permanent Fund. The rest of the royalties and resource taxes were used for current government expenditure. (Thus other taxes are lower for citizens in those states in spite of special resource funds being established.) The issue confronting governments is what to do with the capital and interest from the funds. In 1983 the Alberta Heritage Fund stood at 13.2 billion Canadian dollars, and the Alaska Permanent Fund at 4.02 billion U.S. dollars. The choice has been narrowed down to one of whether to invest in local industries and to try to enlarge the industrial base of the state, or to invest in the open international market in a portfolio of equities and bonds. In the case of Alberta, the former action has been designated "province building." The catch is, of course, that local investments may turn out to have a lower long-run rate of return compared with open market investments. This may be especially relevant if new, risky, competitive, high-tech industries are invested in heavily. Moreover, is there any guarantee that more wealth will be preserved from the resource royalties with a special government fund than if royalties were dispersed to residents each year as a special "dividend"? Individuals regularly save and invest. A decentralized approach may spread risks better rather than having all eggs in one basket. But the concern is that individuals will squander the dividends in consumption, rather than putting them in investments that will provide output for their children.

Since future generations do not vote, one might expect their interests to be slighted in difficult times. The economic slump in the early 1980s in Alberta induced the government to cut the transfer of resource revenue to the fund from 30 to 15 percent. In addition, the Alberta government decided to use the full investment income from the fund for 1983 for general government expenditures. The fund will grow more slowly in the near future.

Sources: "The Alberta Heritage Savings Trust Fund," a symposium in *Canadian Public Policy,* special number, 1980, pp. 141–280; and communication with the Alberta and Alaska governments.

Population Growth, Pollution, and Technical Progress

Sustaining a positive consumption level over infinite time with a finite, essential nonrenewable resource is possible. But the level of consumption may be low, and there may be no scope for sustained increases in $C(t)$ as time passes. We assumed population was constant in the analysis above. In such a framework positive population growth, which is the realistic assumption, implies inevitable collapse in per capita consumption, in a familiar Malthusian scenario. The standard explanation of why in fact Malthus's predictions did not come about is that technological improvements kept per capita output increasing at least as fast as per capita consumption. The introduction of population growth and technological progress into the one-sector model has been carried out by a number of individuals. Beckmann (1975) labeled his treatment "The Limits to Growth in a Neoclassical World," and his model can be viewed as an economist's response to the systems analysis published as *World Dynamics* by Forrester (1971) and *The Limits to Growth* by Meadows et al. (1972).

If we introduce population growth into our model, the production function is expanded to make labor another input into production; a time path for population growth is introduced; and welfare is evaluated explicitly in terms of per capita consumption. Thus the production function becomes

$$Q = K^\alpha R^\beta L^{1-\alpha-\beta} \tag{6.8}$$

where L is the quantity of labor in production and is usually set as equal to population size. For a path of population growth, a frequent working hypothesis is that population (and the labor force) grows geometrically at a constant rate n, or

$$\frac{L(t+1) - L(t)}{L(t)} = n \tag{6.9}$$

The utility of discounted per capita consumption $C(t)/L(t)$ is to be maximized. We see at once that a rising population has advantages and disadvantages for the general welfare. A larger labor force means that there is a larger input into production; but a larger population means that aggregate consumption must be spread over more people.

Technical progress has the effect of making a constant quantity of one or more inputs yield more output. Neutral technical progress makes all inputs proportionately more productive as time passes. (We abstract from the process of investing in research and development in order to get an improved technology.) Suppose γ is the technical improvement factor. In period t, the inputs are multiplied by γ^t, and in period $t + 1$ the inputs are multiplied by $\gamma^{t+1} > \gamma^t$. The rate of technical progress would be $((\gamma^{t+1}/\gamma^t) - 1)$.

Pollution can be viewed in a variety of ways in these aggregate models. We can assume that specific inputs become less productive over time (reverse technical progress), or that a specific allocation of output to consumption is being lost or "evaporated" in "transit." Finally, pollution can be a commodity which, when consumed, yields negative utility.[8] Let us simplify matters by treating pollution as negative technical progress that is neutral. This makes our γ^t a *net* figure combining the positive aspect of technical progress and the negative aspect of pollution increasing over time at an exogenous rate.

In this new model, with population growth, technical progress, pollution, and nonrenewable resources, whether collapse of the system occurs turns on whether net technical progress is rapid enough to counteract the growth in population. If net technical progress is rapid enough, per capita consumption can grow over infinite time, even with a finite stock of an essential, nonrenewable resource. The latter is run down asymptotically, and resource use period by period gets very small but never goes to zero. Stiglitz (1974, p. 128), for example, observes that to sustain a constant level of per capita consumption, the rate of resource-augmenting technical progress must exceed the population growth rate. (*Resource-augmenting* technical progress means that the same physical amount of resources yields more output in the production process as time passes.)

Positive Approaches to Economic Growth with Nonrenewable Resources

The normative approach we took above involved choosing a path to maximize some criteria of welfare. In positive approaches, we simply say: This is the rule people use in deciding how much to save each period; what does it imply for paths of growth? Of course, associated with any positive approach is an "inverse" problem in which some measure of welfare can be devised which the rules associated with the positive approach actually maximize, but this is not the primary focus of attention. For example, saving resource rents in each period is a positive approach by our definition, but it turns out to be a strategy to yield the highest per capita consumption along one path among constant consumption paths. So it is also an optimal growth path. The central issue is, given a savings rule, how does growth evolve over time?

The simplest rule involves *saving a constant fraction of output each year* and allocating the resources saved to new capital goods. With nonrenewable resources, is sustained growth in per capita consumption possible? Not without technical progress. With a high enough rate of technical progress, growth is possible even with an increasing population and a finite stock of nonrenewable resources.

The interpretation of optimal growth is that someone is in fact optimizing across periods. This may be a planner or many individuals behaving in the same way so that it appears as if a planner were in charge. Since individuals are not infinitely long-lived, what interpretation is sensible? If individuals have identical offspring who spring to life on the death of their parents, they will carry on and it will appear as if one person were in fact living forever. An alternative approach is to have individuals living for a lifetime, producing offspring in their middle years, and passing wealth on at death. This is an *overlapping generations* model: People are explicitly not behaving as if they lived forever, so the fiction of treating the economy as if it were under the control of a planner is not valid. Overlapping generations models behave quite differently from optimal planning models and are distinct from positive models.[9]

LIMITS TO GROWTH

In the introduction to this chapter, we asked if the finite stocks of some natural resources spelled catastrophe for world economies. A number of researchers have addressed this question. In this section, we begin with a discussion of the types of models used to evaluate changes in economic and social systems over time. We will see what arithmetic and geometric trends mean and what restrictions these trends imply for large systems models. Then we evaluate the approach taken in *The Limits to Growth*.

Projections and Predictions

The appeal of making predictions by projecting trends in key variables seems deeply rooted in the human mind. Since the future is in one sense unknowable because of uncertainty, predictions may dampen anxieties. But predicting future paths of economic variables over decades has not become more reliable, even with computers capable of processing vast quantities of data. Social systems are just too complex, and this shows up in numerous and subtle "feedback loops" (Jay Forrester's term). For example, we cannot project population growth paths without analyzing paths of future food output and how shortfalls of food production affect population growth. These are the dynamic interdependencies that show up in any dynamic, simultaneous equation system. Above we focused on a system involving the simultaneous development of the nonrenewable resource stock and the stock of producible capital goods. As early as 1939, economists became familiar with the complex behavior that simultaneous dynamic equations could display when Samuelson presented his analysis of the multiplier and the accelerator. The careful dissection of past trends became a central activity in economics, and the implications of such trends for future short-term projections was probed. But their limited success in using medium-term trends for short-term future projections restrained economists from making long-term predictions based on explicit models.

The most famous prediction in this area is surely that of Malthus, who indicated that unless the procreative behavior of people was altered, human life would settle at subsistence because: "Population, when unchecked, increases in a geometrical ratio. Subsistence increases only in an arithmetical ratio. A slight acquaintance with numbers will show the immensity of the first power in comparison of the second" (Malthus, 1959, p. 5). This sort of doomsday scenario has been revived periodically since Malthus's day. The conservation movement in the United States early in this century was basically neo-Malthusian, and the Club of Rome has spread a variant of this doctrine in recent years.

At the most aggregate level, of course, Malthus's prediction cannot be denied. The surface of the earth is finite, and incessant population growth can only bring about a collapse of civilized life. The issue then becomes: How will the details of this catastrophe work themselves out, and are there social mechanisms that will come into play which will both curtail population growth and preserve prosperity for future residents on the planet? For example, urbanization and high income levels are associated with relatively low birth rates. So modernization or economic development may be one mechanism that will result in a decline in population growth rates. This would be a *built-in stabilizer,* to borrow the jargon of macroeconomists. Political upheaval and coercive population control programs are another possibility. But just what do these projections tell us? Are they meaningful exercises, or simply a sophisticated version of "star gazing"? Before we deal with these questions in the context of the limits to growth models, let us examine some details of trends that imply arithmetic and geometric growth.

A Trend Displaying Arithmetic Growth

Suppose the United States has decided to stockpile copper for use in a national emergency. If 1 million pounds is stored each year, the stockpile will be observed to grow arithmetically. An equation for arithmetic growth is $S = A + Bt$, where S is the stock and A and B relate the passage of time to the stock. For our copper stockpiling case, let $A = 0$ and $B = 1$ million. As t changes from 1 to 2 to 3, S grows by 1 million pounds per period. $S = A + Bt$ is called a linear equation because its graphic representation is a straight line (see Figure 6.7).

Suppose S were an industry's output and comprised the outputs of three firms, so that $S(t) = s_1(t) + s_2(t) + s_3(t)$. How do the components behave? We cannot have $S_i = A + Bt$ for any or all i. (If one component were $s_i = A + Bt$, the other components must be zero.) A measure of *growth* (not the rate of growth) is the slope B, since it equals the change in S as time changes. The components cannot each have larger growth parameters than the industry value, since the sum will eventually grow faster than the industry schedule already given. For each firm we can have $s_i = A_i + B_i t$, where $A_1 = A_2 = A_3 = A$ and $B_1 + B_2 + B_3 = B$. Then the sum of the components will grow as $A + Bt$.

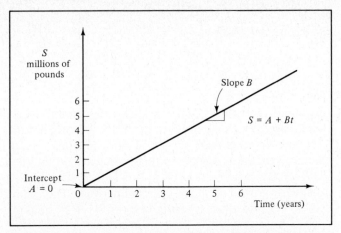

Figure 6.7 Arithmetic growth: There is a constant increment for each period of time. (The increment is not related to the current size of S.)

In Figure 6.8, we see that the projected trends will not sum to the value for the aggregate if these restrictions on the components are not satisfied. Thus there are basic constraints on trends in the components that must be met given a *projected trend for the aggregate:* accounting restrictions on trend projection, and what we might call behavioral restrictions. Food use and population growth are obviously related, though perhaps in complex ways via markets that involve prices and incomes. Sen (1981) has been emphasizing that the link between famines and aggregate shortages of food is not tight. He sees many famines resulting from sudden shortages of purchasing power rather than sudden collapses in food production. Do we, for

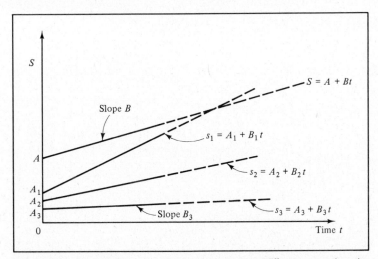

Figure 6.8 Three components of a total can grow at different rates than the total forever if $B_1 + B_2 + B_3 = B$. Hence given a growth rate of the total, the components are constrained to follow certain time paths. If $A_1 + A_2 + A_3 = A$ also, then the sum of the components will grow as $A + Bt$. This is arithmetic growth.

example, expect a leveling off in food production if population growth ceases? The link between these two variables is obviously complex when details are sketched in.

Geometric Growth

Geometric growth is like the familiar case of compound interest on a bank account (see Chapter 1). At the end of a year, $10 has grown to $10(1 + r)$, where r is the rate of interest. After two years, the $10 has grown to $[10(1 + r)](1 + r)$, since the interest in the first year earns interest in the second year. After 12 years, the $10 has grown to $10(1 + r)^{12}$, where $(1 + r)^{12}$ means $(1 + r)$ multiplied by itself 12 times. This is geometric growth at rate of r percent per year. The value after, say, 8 years is $V(8) = 10(1 + r)^8$, and after 9 years is $V(9) = 10(1 + r)^9$, making a growth rate in $V(t)$ of

$$\frac{V(9) - V(8)}{V(8)} = \frac{10(1 + r)^8[(1 + r) - 1]}{10(1 + r)^8} = r \qquad (6.10)$$

We illustrate the graph of this growth process in Figure 6.9. In Figure 6.9(a), the example of $10 growing by compound interest is presented. The familiar exponential or explosive path characterizes geometric growth. As time passes, $V(t)$ gets very large, since growth is at rate r and is said to be *exponential growth*. Since such schedules sweep up to the northeast so quickly, the alternate presentation in Figure 6.9(b) is often used. The variables are transformed by taking logarithms and then plotted with logged values of $V(t)$ on the vertical axis and time (not in logarithms) on the horizontal axis. The slope indicates the rate of growth, with larger values of r corresponding to steeper straight lines in Figure 6.8(b). (The line is straight because r is constant.)

If growth is compounded *instantaneously* (by the minute, say) at the annual

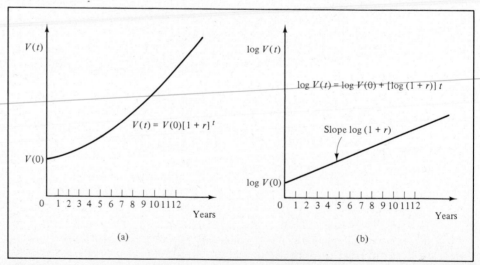

(a)   (b)

Figure 6.9 Geometric (exponential) growth: Growth is "compounded" each period as interest accumulates in a bank account. The increment in V is proportional to the current size of V. In (a) we have the familiar exponential growth schedule. If we take common logs, we have the picture in (b). Log $V(t)$ grows linearly with time.

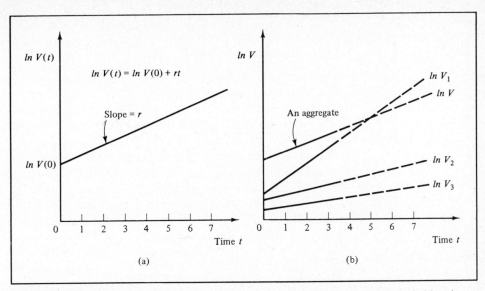

Figure 6.10 Continuous geometric (exponential) growth expressed in natural logarithms. In (a) we have one variable growing at a constant rate r. In (b) we have an aggregate growing at a constant rate. The components cannot grow at different rates forever in order for the components to sum to the aggregate at each point in time.

rate r, then after 5 years $10 grows to $10e^{5r}$ and after 12 years to $10e^{12r}$, where e is a constant like $\pi(e = 2.718)$. Needless to say, whether we compound annually at the interest rate r or instantaneously at the annual rate r, the answer should be similar. For $10 growing at 5 percent over 10 years, the two approaches yield $16.49 and $16.29 (the latter for noncontinuous compounding). The graphic representation of the growth of $V(0)$ with continuous compounding at annual rate r is the same as that for the case of compounding annually; see Figure 6.8(a). However, when natural logarithms are taken of $V(T) = V(0)e^{rT}$, we get $\ln V(T) = \ln V(0) + rT$ when ln stands for natural logarithm or those with base e rather than base 10, as with common logarithms. The graph is shown in Figure 6.10(a). Note that the slope is now the interest rate. Steeper slopes indicate more rapid growth in $V(t)$ as the interest or growth rate is larger.

If V is, say, industry output, and $V = V_1 + V_2 + V_3$, we observe in Figure 6.10(b) that there are accounting constraints on the growth paths of the components of V. No component can grow faster than the growth rate in V without "swamping" the other components and in a sense becoming V itself. Rosenbluth (1976) has emphasized that as long as the growth rates of the components differ from one another (and necessarily differ from the rate of S itself), *an average rate of growth of the components must show retardation over time.* For example, if the sum is growing at 8 percent per year and there are two components, S_1 and S_2, growing today at 10 and 6 percent, respectively, in the future the two growth rates must be, say, 10 and 4 percent. Otherwise the aggregate will be growing at faster than 8 percent! This follows from basic arithmetic, although it seems at first to be a paradox. (The slopes of the components in our diagram must change over time in order to accommodate this change in growth rates.) Clearly, simple trend projection is at the most basic level an exercise requiring much careful qualification.

BOX 6.4
Doubling Your Money (or the GNP)

Suppose you put $100 (or K) in the bank at 8 percent interest compounded. How long does it take to double in value if left in the bank? *Answer:* 70 ÷ 8 = 8.75 years. At 5 percent? *Answer:* 70 ÷ 5 = 14 years. And so on for any interest rate. *70 ÷ (the interest rate) = (the number of years to double the initial value) has been called the "growth rule of thumb."*

    It is devised from the following equation: $Ke^x = \$2K$. The answer is $x = rT$, the rate of interest multiplied by the time it takes to double K with continuous compounding at an annual rate of $r\%$. x equals about .70. Hence for any value of r or T, one can solve for the T or r that doubles the initial K.

The Limits to Growth Approach

A model designed for projecting past trends for many decades into the future was presented in Forrester's *World Dynamics* (1971) and applied or implemented in *The Limits to Growth* (1972). We refer to the second model as the LTG model (for limits to growth), and to the approach underlying the model as the LTG approach. The model

> . . . was built specifically to investigate five major trends of global concern— accelerating industrialization, rapid population growth, widespread malnutrition, depletion of nonrenewable resources, and a deteriorating environment. These trends are all interconnected in many ways, and their development is measured in decades or centuries, rather than in months or years. With the model we are seeking to understand the causes of these trends, their interrelationships, and their implications as much as one hundred years in the future. (Meadows et al., 1972, p. 21)

The authors dismiss the extrapolation of past trends as demonstrably inadequate for making reasonable projections. They introduce the idea of *feedback loops* as the phenomena preventing simple extrapolations from being actually observed in the future. For example, the growth of population has a positive loop—more people imply more births, so growth is not arithmetic—and also a negative loop—more births imply more deaths, so that all individuals do not get added to the population year by year. Some disappear by death. "Since every real population experiences both births and deaths, as well as varying fertility and mortality, the dynamic behavior of populations governed by these two interlocking feedback loops can become fairly complicated."

Feedback loops are sketched for population, capital, agriculture, and pollution. Let us reflect on the industrial capital loop for a moment. The positive loop turns on output from current capital and other inputs being available for investment in new capital in the future. The negative feedback loop accounts for capital's tendency to depreciate because it is subject to wear and obsolescence. The loops governing development in the key subsectors are intertwined, making for a balance of simultaneity in functional relationships with considerable subsector autonomy. As in an organism, the parts have an autonomous and an interdependent quality—in the human body, the liver is physically separate from other tissue and organs and is also connected to other organs via bodily processes. A sketch of the subsectors and the loops suggests the model's great complexity. The components can be analyzed in a conventional piece-by-piece fashion, but the totality evolves in ways that must be tracked with a computer. The use of computer simulations, a principal tool of systems analysis, is the method underlying the LTG approach.

First, then, the loops are isolated and specified, and numerical values relating the variables are inserted. The links between the loops are also isolated and numerically specified. Then the initial values are set for key variables, and the model is "turned on" on the computer. Time paths are generated like the time paths we have set out earlier in this chapter and in previous chapters—some of them generated on the computer in much the same way as the LTG model. Some additional calibration of the model would be required, since many links involve social and economic relationships that have not been analyzed with statistical methods (in economics, for example, statistical inference is done in the subdiscipline of econometrics).

The LTG modelers were able to get their complex model to track or replicate observed paths in key variables from the years 1900 to 1970. They let the model track on into the future with the specific loops and links that had interacted to generate the observed time paths. This gave a prediction of what the future would be like *if* (a) the loops and links were specified correctly and (b) there were no change in the underlying socioeconomic processes and constraints that governed the model. We have reproduced the LTG base run in Figure 6.11, with the researchers' comment below.

Note that food and industrial output per capita fall after the year 2000 to levels below those throughout the twentieth century. Population swamps other variables, so that per capita magnitudes decline in a manner reminiscent of the Malthusian scenario of 1800. Since the base case is so miserable in the long run, the modelers then changed the model to try to generate more attractive futures. These more attractive scenarios were to provide a basis for new policy prescriptions that would lead to a better future than that associated with the base case. The LTG model includes additional computer-generated time paths based on altered loops and links representing new policies.

The publication of the report of the LTG model in *The Limits to Growth: A Report for the Club of Rome's Project on the Predicament of Mankind* in 1972 attracted much attention in the press and in the academic community. The underlying message was this: Here is a scientifically based picture of the future derived with the assistance of high-speed computers. That future is dismal without radical changes in the world's socio-economic-demographic system.

Negative criticism came from many sources. Academic economists made the case that (a) the predictions broadly defined were not new; (b) the methodology was not new; and (c) the empirical underpinnings were not taken from the best sources or were untenable. The first general criticism reminded observers that the base case of the LTG model was much like Malthus's dismal predictions of 170 years earlier: Uncontrolled population growth will push living standards down to undesirable levels. This apocalyptic view glossed over certain essential mechanisms that could

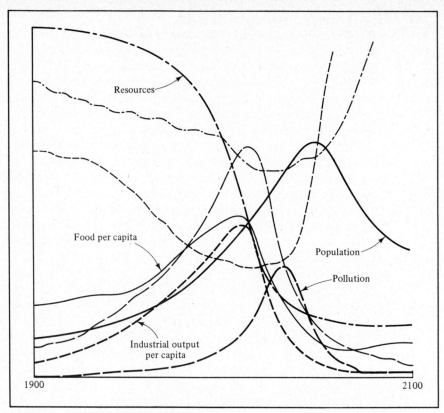

Figure 6.11   This is an illustration of the output from the Limits to Growth (LTG) Model. This is the "Standard Run" or evolution of existing trends from 1970 as the authors viewed the situation. *Source: The Limits to Growth: A Report for the Club of Rome's Project on the Predicament of Mankind,* by D. H. Meadows, D. L. Meadows, J. Randers, W. W. Behrens, III. A Potomic Associates book published by Universe Books, N.Y., 1972.
    The "standard" world model run assumes no major change in the physical, economic, or social relationships that have historically governed the development of the world system. All variables plotted here follow historical values from 1900 to 1970. Food, industrial output, and population grow exponentially until the rapidly diminishing resource base forces a slowdown in industrial growth. Because of natural delays in the system, both population and pollution continue to increase for some time after the peak of industrialization. Population growth is finally halted by a rise in the death rate due to decreased food and medical services.

slow population growth without coercion by governments. Moreover, as resource stocks such as petroleum reserves were depleted, prices would rise and in part induce conservation and the development of substitutes. *The role of prices was ignored in the LTG model,* and the substitution of other inputs for nonrenewable resources was assumed to be quite limited. These are the most serious shortcomings of the LTG model.

    Nordhaus (1973) argued that the modeling of social processes, particularly in economics, by system of difference or differential equations was not new. Having unanticipated time paths for variables in such models was also not new. Economists are trained to expect that the direction of change in a variable depends on the magnitudes in many interrelated components. For example, an increase in the price of a commodity may increase or decrease total revenue; it depends on the elasticity of demand. Was the size of the LTG model a novelty? Huge macroeconomic models of, say, the U.S. economy developed in the 1960s as computers were developed to process the data. But these models were used to project time paths only a few years into the future, largely because longer-term projections had proved so inaccurate. These macroeconomic models generally incorporated fine-scale processes, whereas the LTG model was immensely aggregative at the world level and was not fitted to known time paths at a high level of statistical "goodness-of-fit." This is always a difficulty in science.

The fitting of macroeconomic models in econometrics is done entirely differently from the fitting of the LTG model to the time paths of variables between 1900 and 1970. The LTG model lets the eye be the judge, whereas the macroeconomic models require that statistical tests of goodness of fit be passed. Thus, to say that the LTG model's base case is valid because the model tracked the time paths of key variables from 1900 to 1970 is not acceptable. The fit is crude, and the projections must be treated as crude as well. Ultimately, we do not need a computer to tell us that continued rapid population growth in the world will lead to less food per person and to lower industrial output per person. The broad picture is probably clear; the timing of the developments is difficult to predict. Bob Dylan's admonition, "You don't need a weatherman to tell you which way the wind is blowing," seems appropriate here.

The third type of criticism was that the numerical specifications of processes in the feedback loops and links was inaccurate. Consider the following comment on the LTG model:

> One of its main modes of "collapse" is resource depletion. The main reason for this is the assumption of fixed economically-available resources, and of diminishing returns in resource technology. Neither of those assumptions is historically valid. The relative cost of minerals has remained roughly constant, and has not increased over the past eighty years as a consequence of diminishing returns. And new economically exploitable reserves are being discovered all the time. . . . If one also includes the possibilities of improvements in recycling, and of further economy in the use of resources in industry, then we can conclude the following: If the sum of the annual rates of increase of resource discovery, of recycling, and of economy of use in industry add up to more than around 2%, then the resource mode of collapse in the model will be avoided and there will not be any net drain on "available" reserves. (Page, 1973, pp. 41–42)

This criticism[10] is representative of those of the detailed specification of feedback loops and links in the LTG model. Critics proceeded to revise the formulations in the LTG model as published, and amended versions of the model did not end in collapse. In particular, if advances in technological, economic, and sociopolitical activities are made continually at appropriate rates, world economic and population growth can continue well beyond the year 2100, which was the cutoff point in the LTG analysis. Alternatively, if there is simply a one-time revision in the assumptions about improvements in conditions in the model, collapse is simply deferred.

In performing the sensitivity tests, the critics we have quoted also found the model to be quite unstable in the sense that small changes in key parameters could prevent collapse. (Cole, et al., 1973, p. 130). In the short term, it is of interest to note that resource use grew considerably slower than total output in industrialized countries in the post-1945 economic expansion. For example, in the United Kingdom gross national product grew by 67 percent between 1950 and 1969, while resource use grew in value by 49 percent. For the United States, the comparable figures are 105 percent for gross national product and 67 percent for resource use (Kay and Mirrlees, 1975, Table 9.1).

BOX 6.5
Mining in Polar Regions

Exploitation for minerals in the polar regions is one of the last frontiers on earth. In the 1970s and 1980s, Alaska's oil has been successfully tapped and mines have been brought into production in Greenland and in Canada's north [The Black Angel lead-zinc mine in Greenland (1974), the Polaris lead-zinc mine on Little Cornwallis Island in Canada (77° N) in 1982; and the Lupin gold mine in Canada (65° N) in 1983]. Much of this activity is learning by doing, and has a payoff in improving production techniques in other areas of extreme ice conditions and cold. Rich mineralization is a necessary condition for a mine, but accessibility makes the deposits economically viable. In these new mines in the far north, a worker is flown out for rest and relaxation about every eight weeks, recreation facilities are provided on the site, much processing is done in underground chambers, and plants and buildings are largely completed in the south and sited at the mine location.

No mines have been started in Antarctica, although exploration has been going on for oil in the Bellinghausen, Waddell, and Ross seas, and for minerals on the land. Matters are complicated because no one has sovereignty over the continent or parts of the continent. There are no clear property rights. The continent is divided into zones of influence and is administered by a consortium of interested nations (16 in 1983) with an executive committee called the Scientific Council for Antarctic Research (SCAR). The current arrangement dates from 1961 and is in effect until 1991. SCAR meetings are not open to the public. Large-scale geological investigations have been going on for decades. That Antarctica was a component of the supercontinent of Gondwanaland provides a frame of reference. This supercontinent comprised Africa, Australia, India, New Zealand, Antarctica, and South America. Geological formations with rich mineral areas extend into Antarctica from South America and South Africa and this leads observers to expect valuable deposits on the polar continent. There are areas not covered by the ice cap with conditions similar to those in Canada's Arctic where mining has recently been undertaken successfully. However, mining through the ice cap would be much more difficult, since in places the ice mass creeps continuously over the land, many kilometers below.

Source: Maarten J. de Wit, *Minerals and Mining in Antarctica: Science and Technology, Economics and Politics.* New York: Oxford University Press, 1984.

Making long-term projections of key variables for the world on the basis of detailed simulation models slowed after the debate over the merits of the LTG approach simmered down, but the dismal Malthusian scenario continues to be discussed by futurologists, politicians, and ordinary citizens. Models continue to be developed in order to make projections, but for long-term planning the effort is directed to models of specific sectors operating as a unit, all interconnected with feedbacks, as in the LTG model. Models of world energy supply and demand or world food supply and demand are examples.

SUMMARY

1. Different approaches to the measurement of the scarcity of nonrenewable resources include changes in extraction and processing costs, changes in the real market price of the resource output, and changes in resource rents. Each approach has conceptual as well as measurement difficulties. And for many natural resources, the measures generally do not indicate increasing scarcity over time.

2. Measures of natural resource scarcity are a first step in analyzing whether or not individuals will be worse off over time as a result of continued use of these resources. Even if a resource is deemed to be growing "more scarce," society is not necessarily worse off if: (a) other inputs are good substitutes for the resource in question; (b) the goods produced with the resource have good substitutes.

3. In a simple growth model of an economy with depletable natural resources, different aggregate production functions can be incorporated and the model solved for an optimal path of consumption, investment, and resource use over time. A Hotelling-like rule governs the use of resources and other factor inputs. The demand schedule as well as prices for resource flows change systematically as the economy evolves. Resource use is linked to the demand for a final product by consumers. Demand for this final product depends essentially on the desire for current consumption relative to future consumption. Future consumption requires current savings to provide for investment in future capacity. It is ultimately the inclination for current relative to future consumption that determines the position of the demand schedule period by period for flows of resources.

4. It is possible in special cases for consumption to remain constant at a positive level forever even though essential nonrenewable resources are being used up. The resource stock would be depleted asymptotically in this case. Moreover, a policy of investing period by period the value of nonrenewable resources currently extracted in new productive capital or capacity will result in consumption remaining constant. This leads to a type of intergenerational equity: What the current generation used up in nonrenewable resources it "deposited" above ground as new capital goods, which will produce goods and services for subsequent generations.

5. Economywide models should be viewed as highly aggregated prototype models of an economy. They are too aggregated and lacking in key behavioral submodels to be used in prediction exercises. The *Limits to Growth* (LTG) model was developed for prediction and has an exhaustible resource subsector. Thus the LTG model is a distant cousin to the neoclassical aggre-

gative growth models. The claims of the developers of the LTG model of predictive power provoked critics into a detailed critique of the work; in many ways, the model was found wanting. Economists have avoided making grand predictions, at least on the basis of widely disseminated and explicit models. Decades of work in econometrics has made them circumspect about expecting accurate forecasts.

DISCUSSION QUESTIONS

1. Suppose we found that the real average costs of extraction for a natural resource were rising over time. Can we then conclude that the natural resource in question is becoming more scarce? Explain.

2. Suppose the real price of a natural resource and its rental value were falling over time. Does this always mean that the natural resource is becoming less scarce? Explain.

3. To know what a high-cost energy future will be like, we need only examine economies in those parts of the world where energy is scarce today. Evaluate this argument. Are there different valid interpretations of the word *scarce?*

4. Suppose we can characterize the aggregate production of goods and services in the economy by a CES production function where the factor inputs are resources (R) and capital (K). Does this function imply that the resources are "essential"? Explain. Suppose the elasticity of substitution of capital for resources is rising over time. You can think of a new CES function for each year. What will then happen to aggregate production in the economy over time as the fixed stock of a nonrenewable resource is depleted?

5. In an economy with no international trade, aggregate output Y equals that part consumed, C, that part invested, I, and government activity, G ($Y = C + I + G$). If a person reported that C is to grow at 4 percent this year, I at 6 percent, and G at 3 percent, what will Y grow at? How could you calculate Y's growth rate?

6. Price changes in basic inputs will guide the world economy away from sudden collapse. Evaluate this argument. Would the history of the price of wood burned for heat in England and/or Western Europe provide a guide to future prospects for a scarce essential input?

NOTES

1. Smith and Krutilla (1979) make the important point that although the work of Barnett rejects the hypothesis of increasing natural resource scarcity over time for minerals, the statistical model used does not allow us to conclude that there is any statistically significant relationship between the relative price of resources (in terms of other goods or factors) and time. The relationship may vary considerably over time, and this instability means that the trend regressions between real prices of resources (the measure used by Barnett) and time may not be telling us very much.

2. Not everyone agrees with this assertion. Barnett and Morse (1963) dismissed resource rent because it does reflect all the changes in economic environments. We disagree. Fisher (1981) presents some conceptual difficulties the interested reader can examine.

3. If we relax the assumption that output remains constant, then a change in the quantity demanded of one input will influence the demand for the other via output and possibly scale effects as well as pure substitutability effects. A production function is said to exhibit constant returns to scale if a proportionate change in all inputs results in the same proportionate change in output. Increasing returns to scale are manifested when the proportion-

ate change in inputs results in a larger proportionate change in output. Decreasing returns to scale is the opposite quality. Given the demand for output, a shift in the quantity demanded of an input will change the demand for the other input via substitution effects and most probably scale effects if nonconstant returns to scale are present. Our examples of production functions in the text all display constant returns to scale. The parameters were set to achieve this result.

4. The elasticity of substitution for our Cobb-Douglas example above is 1, and for the CES production function it is $\tau = \dfrac{1}{1+\rho}$, a constant that can assume values between zero and $+\infty$. If this elasticity is zero, the isoquants are L-shaped.

5. The two recursive nonlinear equations are, upon substituting with our specific functions above,

$$\left\{(1-\alpha)\left[\frac{K(t)}{S(t)-S(t+1)}\right]\right\}^{\alpha}\left\{\left[\alpha\left(\frac{K(t)}{S(t)-S(t+1)}\right)^{\alpha-1}+1\right]\right.$$
$$\left.-\left[(1-\alpha)\left(\frac{K(t)}{S(t)-S(t+1)}\right)^{\alpha}\right]\right\}=0$$

$$\beta\left\{\alpha\left[\frac{K(t)}{S(t)-S(t+1)}\right]^{\alpha-1}+1\right\}\{K(t+1)^{\alpha}[S(t+1)-S(t+2)]^{1-\alpha}$$
$$-[K(t+2)-K(t+1)]\}^{-v}=C(t)^{-v}$$

6. We are given three basic relations governing the time path of the economy.

$$C(t)=f[K(t),R(t)]-\dot{K}(t) \quad \text{(accounting relation)}$$
$$f_R/f_R=f_K \quad \text{(efficiency condition, Hotelling variant)}$$
$$\dot{K}=Rf_R \quad \text{(saving-investment rule)}$$

where a dot indicates differentiation with respect to time, and f_R and f_K are derivatives of $f(\cdot)$. Differentiating the first and third equations with respect to time yields

$$\dot{C}=f_K\dot{K}+f_R\dot{R}-\ddot{K}$$

and

$$\ddot{K}=f_R\dot{R}+R\dot{f_R}$$

Substituting for $\ddot{K}$ yields

$$\dot{C}=f_K\dot{K}-R\dot{f_R}$$

and substituting for $\dot{K}$ from the savings rule and for $\dot{f_R}$ from the efficiency condition yields $\dot{C}=0$, or consumption remains constant over time. Solow (1974) established that for α in the Cobb-Douglas production function large enough ($0<\alpha<1$), a finite $S(0)$ could maintain $C(t)$ positive and constant into the infinite future. That the above savings-investment rule was implicit was pointed out by Hartwick (1977), and generalizations to economies with many inputs and outputs have been established by Dixit, Hammond, and Hoel (1980). That this approach works for renewable resource models was emphasized by Hartwick (1978).

7. This rule holds even when reproducible capital goods are subject to steady depreciation at a constant rate. Investment then goes partly to new capital goods and partly to replace depreciated goods.

8. Beckmann (1975) inverts the pollution problem by making the environment a produced and directly consumable commodity. He leaves population growth out of his analysis but does focus attention on natural resource depletion, technical progress, and environmental

enhancement in an economy with a Cobb-Douglas production function and a logarithmic utility function. See our discussion of the tradeoff between pollution control and technological change in Chapter 13.

9. Pearce (1975) presents a brief discussion of an overlapping generations model.

10. In fact, Alexander King, a founding member of the Club of Rome, which commissioned the study *Limits to Growth,* recently stated: "The minerals section was the weakest part of our projections" (Toronto *Globe and Mail,* November 22, 1983, p. 3).

chapter 7

Issues in the Economics of Energy

INTRODUCTION

The 1970s saw tremendous changes in world energy markets that have had major effects on world economies. Some people have called these events an "energy crisis." In this chapter we see why energy resources have been the natural resources most studied in the 1970s and early 1980s, why and what type of "crisis" emerged, and the effects on prices and outputs of goods and services and incomes of individuals. We will see in what sense there was a crisis, whether the crisis is over, and what types of government policies have been used to deal with the changes in energy markets. Our initial focus is on one energy resource — oil. It is the energy resource that precipitated the crisis, and on which much research has been done. Other nonrenewable energy resources, such as natural gas, coal, and uranium, will enter into some of our discussion, but we cannot focus on them all in one chapter on energy. We begin with a discussion of the major events in the energy markets in the 1970s.

From 1973 to 1974, the price of crude oil quadrupled over its level in 1972 and supplies of crude oil from the Middle East were cut off to the United States, parts of Europe, and other parts of the world. In 1979–80, the oil price doubled over its 1978 level. These are the bare bones of what has been come to be known as the energy crisis of the 1970s — a rapid escalation in the price of an energy resource.

We begin our analysis of this crisis with a discussion of the events that gave rise to the price increases in 1973–74 and 1979. Our discussion in this section draws from the work in Griffin and Teece (1982) and Griffin and Steele (1980). Then we examine the short-run effect of an increase in oil prices, and the potential long-run supply of energy, focusing first on the role of OPEC and then on the response of non-OPEC energy supplies to the increase in the oil prices. In the next section we examine the impact of higher energy prices on the demand for energy. Finally, we cover some government policies designed to deal with the energy crisis.

The chapter divides easily into two parts. Part 1 is concerned primarily with issues of energy supply; part 2 focuses on energy demand and policy.

We begin our story with the formation in 1960 of the Organization of Petroleum Exporting Countries — OPEC. OPEC originally consisted of five oil-producing countries: Saudi Arabia, Iran, Iraq, Kuwait, and Venezuela. These countries observed that economic rent was being generated in the sale of oil and that their share of the rent was low relative to that obtained by the international oil companies, governments of the consuming countries, and the consumers themselves. Griffin and Teece note that in a number of European countries, gasoline prices at the retail level were in excess of $30 per barrel of oil, due largely to gasoline taxes. The price of extracting a marginal barrel from, say, Saudi Arabia was at the time between 10 and 20 *cents* per barrel (and is still less than one dollar for Saudi Arabia). One goal of the founders of OPEC was to obtain a larger share of these rents than it had in the past.

OPEC countries were concerned about their rents for two reasons. First, they collected rents largely in the form of taxes levied on the international oil companies who owned the oil deposits in the OPEC countries. OPEC's tax receipts had declined since 1957 because taxes were based on the profits of the companies, and the price of oil had been falling. The decline in prices was due to increased competition in oil markets. A number of new firms had entered the market since 1950 and had driven the share of the Seven Sisters — the major oil-producing companies — from 98.3 percent of the market in that year to 89 percent by 1957 (and 76 percent by 1969).[1] The difference between the market price of oil and the taxes paid to the producing countries encouraged the entry. In 1950, for example, the market price was $1.80 per barrel, the payment to the producing country $0.60, leaving a difference of $1.20. The producing countries then made matters worse by trying to increase their tax revenues by requiring the oil companies to increase production.

When formed, OPEC did not possess much market power. Oil from OPEC countries supplied less than one-half of non-Communist world demand in 1960 due to the large reserves in countries such as the United States. Figure 7.1 illustrates the relationship between spare capacity (maximum supply minus demand) and consumption beginning in 1955. Although consumption was growing steadily from 1955 to the mid-1960s, so was excess capacity. The United States alone had in 1960 a productive reserve capacity of over 2 million barrels per day, an amount sufficient to meet its needs and that of many of its allies in the event of a shutdown of Middle Eastern oil. Any attempt by OPEC at this time to influence prices by cutting allowed production from its wells would not have been very successful.

But conditions were changing in world oil markets. The economic boom of the late 1960s resulted in a large increase in oil consumption (see Figure 7.1 and Table 7.1). At the same time, the share of world production from countries outside the Middle East was dropping. This was due in part to the depletion of some of the oil reserves in these countries. Spare capacity had peaked by 1965, and now began to decline. Meanwhile, OPEC was pursuing some new policies that were not successful in the 1960s but became important in the 1970s.

OPEC tried in 1965 to set annual growth rates of oil exports for each member.

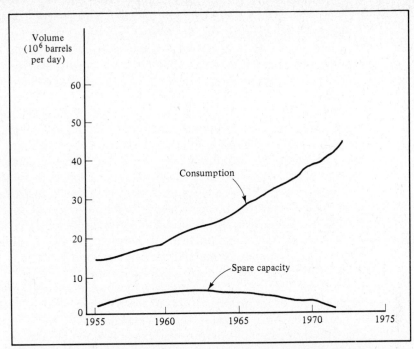

Figure 7.1 World crude oil spare capacity and consumption (excluding Communist countries). *Source:* Statement of G. T. Piercy, Exxon Corporation, before the Senate Foreign Relations Subcommittee on Multinational Companies Hearing, Washington, D.C., February 1, 1974, as cited in Griffin and Teece (1982), p. 6.

Table 7.1   WORLD OIL CONSUMPTION: 1973–1981

(Millions of barrels per year)

	1973	1974	1975	1976	1977	1978	1979	1980	1981
North America									
Canada	594	617	593	591	618	616	661	650	593
Mexico	189	218	222	251	279	292	309	371	405
U.S.	4,521	4,420	4,512	4,851	5,297	5,351	5,305	4,869	4,507
Total	6,240	6,136	6,056	6,510	6,999	7,007	6,994	6,592	6,143
South America	1,124	1,126	979	1,051	1,066	1,128	1,167	1,147	1,107
Europe	5,940	5,640	5,066	5,530	5,527	5,634	5,942	5,401	4,767
USSR	2,616	2,806	2,963	3,044	3,169	3,400	3,447	3,579	3,636
Africa	315	319	361	374	402	417	428	477	530
Middle East	896	893	841	921	995	1,019	1,050	989	957
Far East									
China	368	447	489	573	623	685	682	684	639
Japan	1,797	1,747	1,641	1,676	1,737	1,710	1,740	1,617	1,440
Total	2,979	2,996	2,917	3,129	3,362	4,370	3,565	3,470	3,304
World total	20,344	20,148	19,404	20,789	21,756	22,315	22,838	21,891	20,679

Note: Totals for North America and the Far East include consumption from other countries not listed. Europe includes all European countries except the USSR.

Source: United Nations, *Yearbook of World Energy Statistics,* selected years, figures converted from metric tons to barrels as cited in Institute of Gas Technology, *Energy Statistics* 6, third quarter, 1983.

This was the first time OPEC attempted to act as a cartel by allocating allowable production among members. Individual members resisted these controls because they interfered with domestic sovereignty over oil production. This is a standard problem in the operation of a cartel: how to get members to agree to an allocation rule for production. Production controls did not work, and so they were abandoned in 1967.

Nationalization of concessions was started in the 1960s, although no oil deposits were actually nationalized until after 1970. In 1968, OPEC announced that it sought to maximize its oil revenues and to obtain effective control of the oil companies' operations. It introduced the doctrine of "changing circumstances," which allowed cancellation of concession agreements, changes in taxation arrangements, and changes in the profit rates of the concessionaires. None of these "powers" were used in the 1960s, and the doctrine was not thought to be a threat to the major oil companies. A change in OPEC actions and in perceptions of its potential power came in 1971, when Algeria nationalized its oil resources. Other oil-producing countries announced timetables for nationalization, but none occurred until after 1973.

OPEC did succeed in obtaining an increase in tax revenues from oil companies in the 1960s. Figure 7.2 shows the level of tax receipts of producing countries relative to the price of oil for the period 1948 to 1980. Beginning in the 1960s, the taxes began to rise (although the biggest increases were after 1970). OPEC accomplished this by changing the price of oil on which the taxes, then income taxes, were based. The price used before 1960 was the market price, which as noted above had been falling. After 1960, OPEC succeeded in changing to a *tax reference price*—an artificial price established by agreement with the oil companies. The tax reference price was set above the market price. The oil companies agreed to this practice because at that time, the taxes they paid to host countries resulted in equivalent tax credits in their tax homes. The oil companies were no worse off (but the governments of the oil companies' home countries saw their tax revenues decline).

After the tax changes, OPEC members received a slightly larger share of the rents from oil extraction, but it was not until the late 1960s that OPEC's potential for a very much larger share was realized. Throughout the 1960s, political unrest in the Middle East was growing. Wars between Arab countries and Israel occurred, along with a rise in the strength of nationalistic factions in Arab countries. In 1967 the Suez Canal was closed, which disrupted oil shipments to consuming countries. At the same time, world demand for oil was rising. One country took advantage of this situation.

Libya, located on the Mediterranean, could avoid shipments through Suez. In 1969, Libya's monarchy was overthrown by radical Arabs who began to extract more rents. In 1970, Libya successfully persuaded some oil companies to increase the tax reference price under threat of nationalization. This paved the way for further oil price increases by OPEC countries. In 1971, OPEC obtained an increase in the reference price from $1.80 to $2.18 per barrel, with an agreed escalation of 7.5 cents per barrel each year thereafter to 1976 (see Table 7.2). It also obtained an increase in the tax rate from 50 to 55 percent. The oil companies agreed to these changes under threat of embargo. OPEC countries then found that the real value of the tax increase was being dissipated by high rates of inflation in the United States. In 1973 OPEC met with oil companies to seek an increase in the reference price to $5.15. Griffin and

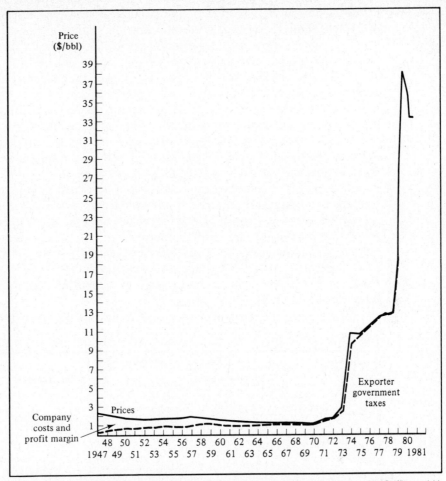

Figure 7.2 Actual market prices and exporter government taxes. *Source:* J. M. Griffin and H. Steele, *Energy Economics and Policy* (New York: Academic Press, 1980), p. 96; and *Petroleum Intelligence Weekly,* October 20, 1980, p. 11, as cited in Griffin and Teece (1982), p. 8.

Teece note that the intent at this time was not to influence the world price per se, but simply to increase its share of oil rents.

The Arab-Israeli War in 1973 changed matters fundamentally. Once the war broke out in October, OPEC ceased bargaining with the oil companies and used oil as a weapon in the war. OPEC announced an increase in the tax reference price, implemented cutbacks in production, and put an embargo on oil exports to the United States and the Netherlands. Panic resulted. The price of oil traded rose from under $3 a barrel to over $10. Governments of consuming countries began examining ways to deal with this tremendous increase in the price of a commodity that was essential to the production of many goods and services. The profits of oil companies rose tremendously. Again, OPEC saw its share of the rents decline and responded in 1974 by raising the tax reference price to $10.50. The tax reference price then became the lower bound for the market price of oil.

And now OPEC also began to think seriously about nationalization. Beginning in 1974, as Figure 7.3 indicates, the oil-producing countries began to acquire ownership of their oil. At present, the major oil companies extract the oil under contract, but generally do not own the actual reserves.

The period 1975 to 1978 was relatively quiet on the oil front. The nominal price of oil rose 10 percent in September 1975, 5 percent in December 1976, and 5 percent in June 1977. However, these increases represented a decline in the real price from a high in 1975 due to high rates of inflation in most countries (see Table 7.2). During this period, Saudi Arabia sometimes cut back its output to help maintain the price. Other oil producers (such as Libya, Iraq, and Nigeria) engaged in price discounting. These actions indicate some discord and instability among cartel members. But the internal arrangements of the cartel were again superseded by political events — this time the revolution in Iran and the subsequent war between Iran and Iraq. Once again oil supplies were disrupted, and the price of oil began to rise steeply. By 1980 the price was over $32 a barrel. OPEC's internal relations were not harmonious during this period, foreshadowing the events of recent years. There were disputes about how much the cartel prices should rise and what production levels members should adhere to. Saudi Arabia increased its share of total OPEC output, as did Iraq and Indonesia.

Since 1981, nominal and real oil prices have fallen. We will analyze the re-

Table 7.2   OIL PRICES FOR U.S. DOMESTIC SUPPLIES AND IMPORTED OIL, 1970–1983

| | Average prices per barrel (U.S. $)* | | | | | |
| | Nominal prices | | | Deflated prices† | | |
Year	Imported	U.S. Domestic	U.S. Composite	Imported	U.S. Domestic	U.S. Composite
1970	$ 1.80	$ 3.54	$ —	$ 1.97	$ 3.87	$ —
1971	2.24	3.55	—	2.33	3.70	—
1972	2.48	3.55	—	2.48	3.55	—
1973	3.62	4.01	—	3.42	3.79	—
1974	12.52	7.18	9.07	10.88	6.24	7.88
1975	13.93	8.39	10.38	11.09	6.67	8.25
1976	13.48	8.84	10.89	10.19	6.68	8.23
1977	14.53	9.55	11.96	10.37	6.82	8.54
1978	15.57	10.61	12.46	10.35	7.05	8.28
1979	21.67	14.27	17.72	13.26	8.73	10.84
1980	33.89	24.23	28.07	18.99	13.58	15.73
1981	37.05	34.33	35.24	18.99	17.59	18.06
1982	33.55	31.22	31.87	16.22	15.09	15.41
1983‡	29.35	28.90	29.02	13.61	13.40	13.46

* Imported oil prices represent for the years 1970–73: posted prices of Arabian Light 34° Gravity, crude oil, FOB RAS Tanura, as cited in Foster Associates *Energy Prices 1960–73* (Cambridge MA: Ballinger, 1974). For the years 1974–83, they are U.S. refiners acquisition costs (average price paid) of imported crude oil, as cited in U.S. Department of Energy, *Monthly Energy Review,* selected issues. Domestic prices are for a four-source average of U.S. refiners' acquisition costs of crude oil from domestic sources from Foster Associates for 1970–73 and an average of all refiners' acquisition costs for the period 1974–83 from the U.S. Department of Energy. From 1973 to 1981, most domestically produced oil faced a price ceiling. Composite prices are a weighted average of domestic and imported oil prices, as cited in U.S. Department of Energy, *Monthly Energy Review.*

† The deflator is the GNP implicit price deflator for the United States, 1972 = 100, as cited in U.S. Department of Commerce, *Survey of Current Business,* monthly, selected issues.

‡ Average of first 11 months.

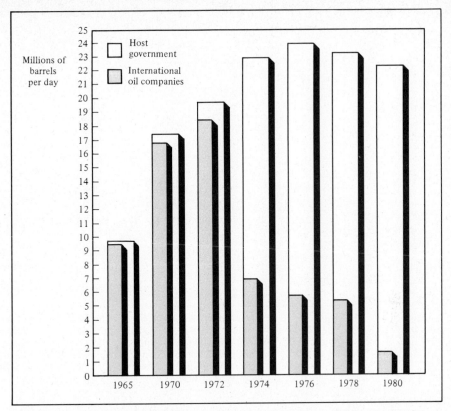

Figure 7.3   International oil companies' equity interest in Middle East crude oil production. *Source:* OPEC *Statistical Yearbooks* for 1965–1978. 1980 estimate based on earlier announced plans of producing governments. Reprinted from J. M. Griffin and D. J. Teece (1982), *OPEC Behavior and World Oil Prices.* London: George Allen & Unwin, p. 10.

sponse in energy markets to the OPEC price increases of the 1970s in detail later in the chapter; we now note briefly the effects. High oil prices have stimulated the supply and reduced the demand for oil. These events combined with the recession of 1981– 1983 have led to a significant decline in the demand for oil. OPEC has found its market power eroding and its members' ability to compromise threatened. In 1983, OPEC had a number of emergency meetings to try to agree on a price of oil. Oil prices fell from close to $40 per barrel on the spot market to around $28 per barrel, and it looked for a time as though the cartel would dissolve. The question we must ask is this: Will the cycle be repeated if political events again disrupt oil supplies? Does OPEC continue to have a significant effect on the world price of oil? We do not know the precise answer, but we will examine the economic effects of a sharp rise in the price of oil.

SHORT-RUN EFFECTS OF ENERGY PRICE INCREASES

Suppose it is October 1973 in the United States. OPEC has just announced its embargo of oil. What is the effect of this embargo? Figure 7.4 illustrates the short-run static effects of the reduction in output of oil. We examine only the market for oil—a

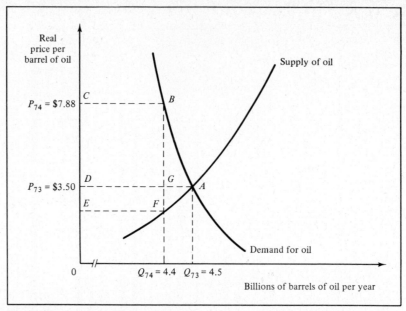

Figure 7.4 Short-run effects of the embargo on oil to the United States, 1973–1974. The embargo reduces oil supplies to the United States, resulting in a decline in oil consumption from 4.5 to 4.4 billion barrels of oil from 1973 to 1974. The average price of oil to U.S. consumers (deflated) rises from $3.50 to $7.88 per barrel. Welfare costs are the area *ABF*. Income is redistributed from oil consumers to oil producers by the area *BCDG*, which is approximately $19.3 billion in 1973–1974.

partial equilibrium analysis. There will, of course, be repercussions in other markets, but we postpone discussion of some of these effects to the section on long-run implications of the increase in oil prices.

Figure 7.4 presents a hypothetical demand curve for oil. We assume the supply curve represents the aggregate supply of oil. We have illustrated a relatively inelastic demand curve and a supply curve that is more elastic, as this characterizes the situation in 1973. Suppose the oil market is initially in equilibrium at point *A*, where supply equals demand. Consumption of oil in the United States is 4.5 billion barrels per year, while the real price of oil is around $3.50 per barrel (see Tables 7.1 and 7.2 for the numbers used in this example). OPEC then imposes the embargo against oil sales to the United States. This results in a reduction in aggregate oil consumption in the U.S. to 4.4 billion barrels in 1974. The new equilibrium in 1974 is at point *B*, with the equilibrium real oil price equal to $7.88 per barrel. The *price elasticity of demand* determines by how much the price increases, given the cutback in production. We have illustrated an inelastic demand curve. The price rise associated with the embargo is thus quite large relative to what would occur if the short-run demand for oil were more elastic. We have assumed that demand is inelastic in the short run (we later provide some numerical estimates of the price elasticity in Table 7.11) because for many uses of oil, it is impossible to furnish substitute fuels in the short run.

What are the welfare costs of the embargo? They are the area *ABF*. Oil consumers lose their consumer surplus—the area *ABCD*. Oil producers gain the area

BCDG in increased revenues, but lose the producer surplus equal to *AGF*. Before the nationalization of oil reserves in OPEC countries, the oil producers receiving the increased revenues are the international oil companies. After nationalization, OPEC receives the surplus. There is thus a redistribution of profits among oil producers. The welfare cost is then the sum of lost consumer surplus net of producer profits plus lost producer surplus. However, the loss of consumer surplus represents not only a welfare cost, but *a significant redistribution of world income.* Consuming nations will suffer a loss of real income equal to the lost consumer surplus, while OPEC (and all other oil producers) will gain income due to the higher price of oil (net of its relatively small loss of producer surplus *AGF*). The magnitude of these effects is quite large.

We can approximate the welfare costs and redistributive effects of the embargo. The loss in consumer surplus is equal to the rectangle *BCDG* plus the triangle *ABG*. The rectangle can be measured by the difference in real oil prices in 1973 and 1974 ($7.88 − 3.50 = $4.38) times the total amount consumed after the embargo, or 4.4 billion barrels per year. We get a loss of $19.3 billion per year. The triangle can be approximated by the formula 1/2 base times height. The base is the difference in aggregate consumption or 0.1 billion barrels from 1973 to 1974, while the height is the difference in the deflated prices — $4.38. The total consumer surplus loss is thus $19.7 billion over the period 1973–74. The gain in producer revenues is the area *BCDG* net of the lost producer surplus *AGF*. Without knowing where point *F* is, we cannot calculate the lost producer surplus, but note that it will be small relative to the other areas measured.

Oil producers thus gain $19.3 billion over the period, while oil consumers lose the same amount. This represents a significant transfer of income and subsequently wealth as the oil producers' revenues are invested. In summary, the dollar net gain to producers from the embargo is area *BCDG* minus *AGF*. The dollar net loss to consumers is area *ABCD*. This leaves area *BCDG* as a *transfer or redistribution* from consumers to producers and area *ABF* as *deadweight loss* or a net subtraction resulting from the embargo.

This analysis has been based on the embargo — a unilateral reduction in output. Recall that OPEC subsequently increased the tax reference price to $10.50 per barrel, which became the effective floor price of oil in 1974. One can think of OPEC, then, as acting more like a monopolist — using the embargo and threat of sustained production cutbacks as a means of maintaining the price of oil above competitive levels. Once the embargo was lifted, OPEC could continue to sustain a high price for oil by restricting supply to world markets. The world oil market is thus converted from one which was relatively competitive to one which is more monopolistic.

LONG-TERM EFFECTS OF HIGH OIL PRICES: SUPPLY EFFECTS

Our first topic in this section is the possible strategies followed by OPEC over time. Will oil prices be maintained at high levels? What extraction paths can OPEC follow? We discuss two hypotheses about OPEC's objectives and resulting activities. First, we assume that OPEC is a dominant firm facing a fringe of competitive oil suppliers — a model familiar from Chapter 4. In this model, OPEC is assumed to maximize the present value of its profits, as would a cartel acting cohesively. We then present an alternative assumption about OPEC's objectives and behavior—namely, that it seeks to maintain a target level of revenues from oil extraction to finance desired expenditures in member economies. Their actions are not those of a unified cartel. The two models give different predictions about the behavior of OPEC over time and the subsequent effect on the supply of oil.

Possible OPEC Actions: The Wealth-Maximizing Model

Our first view of OPEC suggests that the embargo of 1973–74 and subsequent OPEC actions indicate that OPEC successfully cartelized the world oil market and based its actions on the objective of maximizing its net wealth—the present value of the profits from oil extraction. Several variants of the cartel model have been proposed. We will discuss the work of Pindyck (1978) because it is representative of the types of models encountered in the wealth-maximizing approach and contains a numerical simulation of the price path of the cartel.

The model is that of the dominant firm—in this case a group of producing countries organized into OPEC—determining its profit-maximizing price path when constrained by the presence of a fringe of suppliers who behave competitively. OPEC seeks to act monopolistically by setting marginal revenue equal to marginal cost plus resource rent, but it cannot follow a pure monopoly path because of the fringe. The model is essentially that explained in Chapter 4. Pindyck does not consider any of the practical problems of operating a cartel, such as allocating production among members. We will discuss some of these issues when we see how well the model has explained OPEC behavior over time. When testing the model against the real world, its assumptions must be kept in mind. A crucial assumption of the model is that OPEC has perfect information about all the relevant parameters it needs to solve the maximization problem—the price elasticity of demand, the price elasticity of the non-OPEC oil supply, and so on. There are also no surprises in the model, no unanticipated events that alter oil supply. We know that many of these assumptions are not consistent with events of the past five years. However, it is the basic objective of OPEC, maximizing its wealth, that we wish to contrast with other possible objectives, not all the details of the model.

As noted, the objective of the cartel is to select a price path that maximizes the present value of its profits over a long period of time. The model unfolds as follows. We begin with a total demand relationship for oil, where with real oil prices, P_t

$$TD_t = f_1(P_t, Y_t, TD_{t-1}) \tag{7.1}$$

Y_t is a measure of aggregate income among oil consumers and TD_{t-1} is the previous year's demand for oil. One could also include the price of energy resources which are substitutes for oil in the specification of Equation (7.1). Pindyck assumes that these substitute prices are fixed over time and he therefore omits them from the aggregate demand curve.[2] In the simulation exercise, TD_t is given by Equation (7.2):

$$TD_t = 1.0 - .13P_t + .87TD_{t-1} + 2.3(1.015)^t \tag{7.2}$$

The total demand curve is assumed to be linear and based on demand of 18 billion barrels per year at a price of $6 per barrel. The short-run price elasticity of demand at that price is .04; the long-run elasticity is .33. If the price of oil were $12 per barrel, the elasticities would change to .09 and .90, respectively. The last term in the demand equation allows for an exogenous rate of growth of demand of 1.5 percent per year. This corresponds to a long-run income elasticity of .5 and a 3 percent real rate of growth of income.

The cartel does not supply the entire market, but competes with fringe producers. The demand curve facing OPEC is then the *net* demand curve, D_t, given by the difference between total demand for oil *(TD)* and the amount of oil supplied by the competitive fringe (S_t). Thus

$$D_t = TD_t - S_t \tag{7.3}$$

The fringe supply is a function of the price of oil, the output of the fringe in the previous period, and cumulative extraction, CS_t. Cumulative extraction is given by

$$CS_t = CS_{t-1} + S_t \tag{7.4}$$

and represents the effects of depletion of reserves over time. As cumulative extraction rises, the fringe supply curve shifts to the left. The supply curve of the fringe is then

$$S_t = f_2(P_t, S_{t-1})(1 + a)^{-cs_t/s} \tag{7.5}$$

where S is average annual production from the competitive fringe, and a reflects the rate of depletion. In the simulation, Equation (7.5) becomes

$$S_t = (1.1 + .10P_t)(1.02)^{-cs_t/7} + .75S_{t-1} \tag{7.6}$$

When the price of oil is $6, the competitive supply is approximately 6.5 billion barrels per year. The supply equation (7.6) then implies a short-run price elasticity of supply of .09 and a long-run elasticity of .35. These elasticities rise to .16 and .52 when the oil price is $12 per barrel.

Equation 7.7 presents OPEC's objective function:

$$\text{maximize } W = \sum_{t=1}^{N} [1/(1 + r)^t][P_t - m/R_t]D_t \tag{7.7}$$

N is set between 40 and 60 years so that the problem approximates an infinite horizon. The parameter r is the discount rate that is set at either 5 or 10 percent. P_t is the real price of oil in each time period, while m/R_t is the average costs of production: m is a parameter that represents the initial cost of extraction, while R_t is the cartel's reserves in any period t.

This formulation of average cost allows Pindyck to incorporate depletion into the objective function for OPEC without explicitly adding a resource stock constraint. As reserves decline, the average costs of extraction rise. When the reserves approach zero, average costs approach infinity. This formulation simplifies the numerical calculations. OPEC's initial reserves are assumed to be 500 billion barrels (an estimate of proved reserves) and m is set at 250 so that the initial average cost of extraction is assumed to be $0.50 per barrel.

Reserves are defined by the difference between its reserves in the previous period and the amount of oil demanded from OPEC—its net demand. The relationship between reserves and demand for oil is shown by Equation (7.8):

$$R_t = R_{t-1} - D_t \tag{7.8}$$

We now have all the ingredients to solve the cartel problem. OPEC selects a price path that maximizes its wealth, W. As can be seen by the equations above, the presence of the fringe means that OPEC does not face the aggregate demand curve for oil, but the net demand curve where the supply of the fringe is netted out. The competitive fringe takes the price set by OPEC as given and determines its output in each period as given by Equation (7.6). In a perfectly competitive model, as we know from Chapter 3, each supplier chooses an output path so as to satisfy Hotelling's rule. Pindyck's formulation of Hotelling's rule is given by Equation (7.9):

$$P_t = (1 + d)P_{t-1} - dm/R_{t-1} \qquad (7.9)$$

where m is the marginal cost of extraction and d the discount rate. To compute the price path for the competitive model, an arbitrary price is chosen for the initial period; then Equations (7.1), (7.2), (7.3), (7.5), and (7.9) are solved simultaneously. This process is repeated with different values of the initial price until demand and reserves become zero simultaneously.

The price paths for the cartel model versus the competitive model under two different discount rates (5 and 10 percent) are shown in Figure 7.5. The price path when OPEC acts as a dominant firm lies above that of the competitive path until the end of the twentieth century. OPEC immediately more than doubles the oil price over the competitive price when the discount rate is 5 percent, or raises it 9 times over the competitive price when the discount rate is 10 percent. The competitive price rises continuously to the year 2010, while the cartel price declines from 1975 to 1979, then

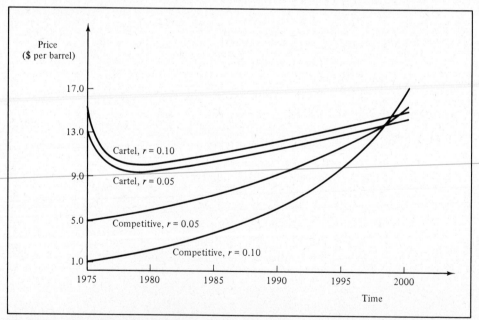

Figure 7.5 The paths of real oil prices over time under two different market structures. The paths labeled cartel, $r = 0.05$ and $r = 0.10$, reflect Pindyck's simulations with OPEC as a dominant firm facing a competitive fringe under a discount rate of 5 and 10 percent. The paths labeled competitive reflect the simulations when the oil market is perfectly competitive under the same two discount rates.

rises slowly thereafter. This result arises from the adjustment lags incorporated in OPEC's net demand function. Without the lags, the cartel price path would rise monotonically, as does the competitive path.

Because it takes the market time to adjust to the higher price set by OPEC, the cartel can increase its profits by setting the price high initially, then gradually lowering it as demand shifts to other sources of oil. Note that the slope of the price path under the cartel is less than that of the competitive path after 1979. This is what we also found in the theoretical models of Chapter 4.

The effects of different discount rates are as discussed in Chapter 3. With a high discount rate, the competitive price is lower because extraction in the initial periods rises relative to extraction in later periods. The price path is then steeper than that with $d = .05$, and exhaustion of the reserves would occur sooner. With the discount rate of 10 percent, the competitive price in 1975 would be $1.55. Pindyck notes that this price is in the vicinity of the pre-1974 price of oil in the Middle East. He offers this as evidence that "prior to 1974, OPEC producers set output levels competitively using a high discount rate" (p. 243).

Finally, Pindyck computes the gains to OPEC from cartelization. The gains are the net present value from determining the price of oil over time as a dominant firm divided by the net present value of extraction under perfectly competitive conditions. These gains are computed at 5 and 10 percent discount rates, for the period 1975 to 2015 (or when reserves are exhausted), and for the first five years (1975–1980). Not surprisingly, OPEC gains are largest when the discount rate is 10 percent and only the first five years are measured. The ratio under these circumstances is 5.78. Under the least favorable conditions to OPEC ($d = 5$ percent and the period 1975–2010 is used), the ratio is 1.54. Even when the elasticities, initial reserves, and shape of the demand curve are modified, the ratios change very little.

What can we say about how well Pindyck's model predicts actual behavior of OPEC? We know, of course, that the price of oil took a jump in 1979–1980. This was a surprise, and Pindyck's model could not anticipate the shift because there are no supply shocks of this sort incorporated in the model. But even if we ignore unanticipated political events, is the wealth-maximizing model a reasonable description of the behavior of OPEC members?

Criticisms of the wealth-maximizing model fall into two basic categories: problems with the analytical structure of the model, and the basic assumption of economic rationality on the part of OPEC. Wealth-maximizing models can be quite complex to solve, as we have seen in earlier chapters. These models are abstractions of the real world and must simplify behavior to obtain solutions. Consequently, it would be surprising if such a model accurately predicted *all* actions taken by OPEC and their effect on the world oil market. There is simply too much left out to give us a close prediction of year-to-year events. However, if the underlying assumptions about OPEC's objectives are valid, the model can yield reasonable predictions of prices and outputs over time.

Simplifying assumptions can be altered to incorporate such things as changes in elasticities or the rate of growth of GNP over time, new sources of non-OPEC supply, and different expectations about the future. These changes make the models more difficult to solve, but would give a range of possible predictions. There is a substantial amount of modeling of world oil markets that incorporate some of these assumptions. For a discussion of some of the models, see Gately (1984) and the Energy Modeling Forum (1982). However, we are still left with the uncomfortable fact that *any* result can be generated with the appropriate assumptions. What we want is a general type of model that yields consistently reliable predictions.

This is where the second criticism of the wealth-maximizing model arises. Some observers argue that the reason these models do not explain the facts well beyond the late 1970s is not because of the specific values of parameters chosen or the particular assumptions about adjustments to price and output changes over time, but because of the underlying objective function assumed for OPEC. The wealth-maximizing model, the critics claim, simply implies more economic rationality than is consistent with OPEC's actual behavior. Too many observations over the period 1973 to 1983 are inconsistent with wealth maximization. For example, there is little evidence that OPEC has ever actually *set* prices or been able to apportion production quotas among its members. The embargo in 1973–74 simply restricted sales to the United States and other consuming countries, it did not allocate sales of individual OPEC members.

Similarly, it is argued that the increases in the world price of oil have largely come about because of aggregate supply and demand conditions. This does not mean that OPEC does not influence world supply; it does. *What is implied is that OPEC took advantage of existing world conditions, it did not create them.* For example, by 1973 world demand for oil had risen considerably since the mid-1960s. Non-OPEC supply had stagnated over the period; OPEC supply had risen by 10 percent per year from 1969 to 1973. But as Gately (1983) argues, this increase in output could not be sustained even with its substantial reserves. The oil market was very tight even before the 1973 Arab-Israeli War. Thus, it is asserted that the price rise in that period reflected excess demand more than the emergence of the monopoly power of OPEC.

We will examine a variant of this viewpoint — one that argues that what OPEC was doing was satisfying internal revenue objectives rather than maximizing wealth. But before we turn to this approach, we will look at OPEC's actions after 1973 to see how closely they are predicted by the wealth-maximizing model.

A model such as that of Pindyck does well in predicting the price path of oil from 1974 to the second price shock in 1979 (recall Figure 7.5). After the initial jump in the price from the competitive to the monopoly level, the real price falls somewhat over the next five years. While the magnitude of the decline in the real price in Pindyck's simulation is not quite the same as what actually occurred, the shape of the price path *does* reflect the actual path. The real-world price of oil fell over the period 1975–1978 by about 6 percent. For the price path calculated by Pindyck, the price of oil fell by about 4 percent over the same period. But, as noted above, the wealth-maximizing model did not predict the doubling of oil prices in 1979–80, although such an increase would be consistent with the wealth-maximizing model. It may reflect a move by OPEC to exploit the Iranian situation and further increase its share of oil rents. There is some evidence to support this belief: Saudi Arabia cut its output in January 1979 from 10.4 to 8.0 million barrels per day. The spot price of oil rose from about $20 per barrel in January 1979 to over $31 per barrel in February.

Others view the 1979–80 events as evidence that OPEC did not effectively control world oil markets. Supply and demand without a cartel such as OPEC, it is argued, can explain the increase in the price of oil. The loss of Iranian oil is a political change, not one orchestrated by OPEC. The market simply responded to the reduction in supply as would a competitive market—the equilibrium price of oil rose. Support for this argument comes from the way OPEC adjusted its prices during this period. The OPEC price increases typically came *after* prices rose on the spot market. Thus, it is argued, OPEC merely responded to market conditions, it did not create these conditions. In addition to the Iranian conflict, another factor contributed to excess demand in this period. A number of oil-consuming countries were aggressively increasing their strategic stockpiles of oil. These purchases obviously put pressure on the price of oil.

What about recent events—the period from 1980 to 1984? Beginning in approximately 1981, a severe recession affected most of the world. World oil demand fell by 20 percent (compared to a 6 percent decline in the period 1973 to 1975). But this decline in demand was spread unevenly across oil producers. Demand for oil produced by OPEC fell by about 45 percent (compared to a 15 percent decline in demand in 1973 to 1975).

A number of factors contributed to the decline. The recession, of course, affected the aggregate demand for oil. Conservation measures and substitution of alternative energy sources also contributed to the reduction in world oil demand. The increased supply of oil from non-OPEC countries in response to the very high prices of oil in 1979–80 contributed to the loss of OPEC's market share. Indeed, as noted above, OPEC reduced its official prices in 1983 for the first time since 1973. Before the OPEC price was lowered, however, the spot price had already fallen 20 percent below the OPEC price, and there was widespread price cutting among OPEC members. Today OPEC's solidarity and market power seem much dissipated.

Possible OPEC Actions: The Target Revenue Model

An alternative explanation for the behavior of OPEC and events in the world oil market is presented by Teece (1982). His basic argument is that OPEC does not seek to maximize its wealth. Rather, each member of OPEC attempts to match its oil revenues with the desired level of government expenditures within that country. Most of the oil deposits were nationalized in the 1970s. Thus, the decision-making body is no longer the private corporation, but government policy-makers. Teece makes the reasonable assumption that governments will have a different set of objectives from those of the private sector producers. In setting oil revenues equal to desired government expenditures, a very different extraction profile will emerge from OPEC countries over time. Teece argues that a backward-bending supply curve of OPEC oil will result.

When oil prices are high, revenues from oil production will be large. If an OPEC country already has sufficient revenues to meet its domestic expenditure needs, it will not expand production. Indeed, it is likely to reduce production, because it does not require the revenues. But, one asks, why don't OPEC countries simply invest the proceeds from oil sales in foreign assets? The answer, Teece says, is that many OPEC countries do not like to acquire large amounts of foreign capital for political, economic, and religious reasons.

Politically, it may be risky to OPEC producers to invest abroad. They fear expropriation of their assets, especially after the Iranian crisis, when the United States froze Iranian assets for some time. A number of countries restrict the amount OPEC producers are allowed to invest. In the United States, there was a public outcry in the 1970s when OPEC countries were purchasing interests in banks and other sectors. Leaving oil in the ground, it is argued, is a much less risky investment. There are also fundamentalist Islamic sects that oppose acquisition of foreign assets on religious grounds. It is not viewed as appropriate to make one's living off dividends and interest payments on investments abroad. Thus, the argument goes, each OPEC country may acquire a certain amount of foreign assets, but will not continue to produce simply to buy assets once its domestic expenditure requirements are met.

Suppose now that the oil price has fallen, say due to a decline in aggregate demand for oil due to a recession. OPEC producers will find their oil revenues declining. They will have an incentive to *increase* production to try to maintain revenues sufficient to cover their domestic expenditure requirements. Increases in production will tend to further dampen the price of oil. OPEC is, however, constrained in how much it can increase output by the productive capacity of its oil wells. So in the short run, output will tend to increase to full capacity and stay there until and if new capacity is added. What one would then tend to observe, after the decline in oil prices, is a period of stable prices (until some other exogenous change occurs).

Teece uses the term *absorptive capacity* to describe the amount of returns from oil production OPEC countries require. More specifically, absorptive capacity is the amount of investment that can be made at an acceptable rate of return. Let's examine his model more closely to see what this means and how the backward-bending supply curve is obtained. The basic model is the following: Suppose that oil is the dominant export industry. The oil producers — the government of the country — set domestic investment requirements, and then set production goals to generate the revenue to meet the requirements.[3] For simplicity, assume that the government determines the desired level of domestic investment expenditures based on a marginal efficiency of investment schedule (MEI). Figure 7.6 illustrates an MEI schedule. Suppose the rate of return on investment, r, is given at r^*. Given the MEI, the desired level of investment is then I^*. Investment could, of course, be determined in a more sophisticated fashion; the MEI curve is used merely for illustrative purposes.

Given I^*, an isorevenue curve can be defined in terms of oil production and price; see Figure 7.7. The isorevenue curve I^*/Q shows combinations of oil prices and output that yield I^* revenue from the export of oil. Although only one isorevenue curve is shown in Figure 7.7, there will be a unique curve for any desired level of investment. Figure 7.7 also shows the demand curve for the oil. The intersection of the demand and the isorevenue curves then determines the amount of oil supplied to international markets, Q^*, at a price of p^*. The isorevenue curve is thus a type of supply curve up to the quantity that represents full capacity in oil production. The demand curve illustrated is fairly elastic because we are examining the demand for

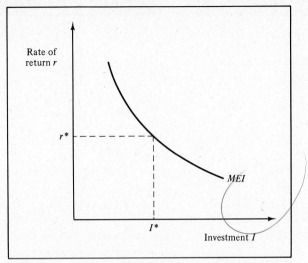

Figure 7.6 The marginal efficiency of investment schedule shows the desired level of investment, I^*, given a rate of return, r^*.

one country's oil. It is not perfectly elastic due to the location of the country, the quality of its oil, or other characteristics.

Suppose now that a higher investment target I^{**}, is desired. The isorevenue curve will shift from I^*/Q to I^{**}/Q, as shown in Figure 7.8. If the demand curve is stationary, we find that the oil producer will expand output to try to obtain sufficient revenues to pay for the new investment. Suppose, however, that the maximum capacity of oil production is given by Q'. Oil production will thus increase to Q', but

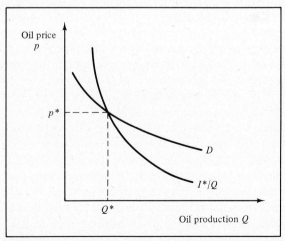

Figure 7.7 The intersection of an isorevenue curve, I^*/Q with the demand curve for oil from an OPEC country determines the quantity of oil the country produces, Q^*, at a price p^*.

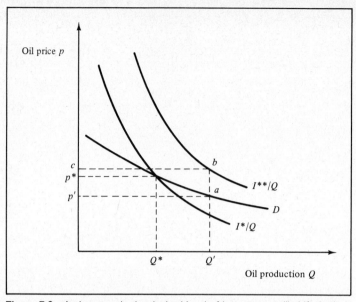

Figure 7.8 An increase in the desired level of investment will shift the iso-revenue curve from I^*/Q to I^{**}/Q. Oil production will rise to Q', which is the maximum capacity for oil output in the country. If the demand curve is stationary at D, *the price of oil will fall from p^* to p'*. The area $p'abc$ shows the shortfall in revenue needed to finance investment expenditures. Output and price will remain constant at Q' and p' until capacity is increased, or another exogenous change occurs.

the price will fall from p^* to p'. Revenue will be less than the target by the amount $p'abc$. The oil producer will continue to produce at this level until new capacity can be installed or some other exogenous change occurs.

Notice that the supply curve of oil from this country will now be vertical at Q'. If demand does not shift, the price will remain constant at p'. Thus increases in the desired level of investment by an OPEC producer may result in a reduction in the price of its oil and a stable price for some time thereafter.[4] This result has some implications for future oil production from OPEC and the effect on oil prices.

Let's see now what happens when the demand for oil rises, as was the situation prior to the first oil shock in 1973–1974. Figure 7.9 illustrates this case. Suppose the demand for oil rises due to increased income in consuming countries. The demand curve shifts from D_0 to D'. Given a stationary isorevenue curve, the price of oil will rise from p_0 to p'. When it does, the OPEC producer will respond by cutting oil production from Q_0 to Q'. Rising demand puts pressure on prices when an excess demand is created. But rising prices increase oil revenues. The only way the OPEC country can stay on its revenue target is to reduce output. If the MEI were to shift to the right as oil prices rise, a new isorevenue curve would result. It is then possible that output of oil will increase when demand shifts. The oil supply curve would then be positively sloped, as is the usual assumption (try this exercise yourself). However, if there is no change in the MEI and the producer seeks to remain on the isorevenue curve I^*/Q, output will fall when the price of oil rises.

We have illustrated the supply curve for just one OPEC country, but if enough OPEC producers behave similarly, the supply curve of OPEC oil will bend backward. Figure 7.10 illustrates one such supply curve, S. If demand is growing over time, oil production will first rise, then fall once the supply curve bends back, as shown by the demand curves D_0, D_1, and D_2. These demand curves have been drawn elastic enough so that there is only one intersection of the demand with the supply curve. But given the backward bend of the supply curve, it is possible that there may be two points at which supply equals demand. If so, the price of oil will be unstable over the region between the two equilibrium prices. Let's see what the model implies about OPEC's behavior. We present some evidence from the 1970s and 1980s that is consistent with the model.

First, the model suggests that OPEC need not be a cartel in the traditional sense. Cartels typically restrict output to drive up the price of a good. OPEC may cut output when prices are high in response to revenue objectives. The reduction in output exacerbates the pressure on prices, and a vicious cycle may result. The point is that the cycle need not begin with OPEC operating as a cartel that restricts output. Note also that there will be fewer problems with cartel stability. There is no incentive for members of OPEC to cheat on any cartel agreement to supply a particular amount of output to the market *if* the producers are on the backward-bending portion of the supply curve. Increasing one's output simply makes meeting the revenue objective more difficult.

This point is important, because there has yet to be conclusive evidence that OPEC has been able to maintain the price of oil through collusive action. If the

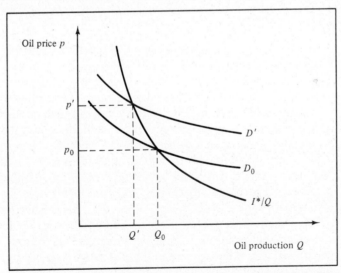

Figure 7.9 A shift in demand for oil from D_0 to D' will lead to an excess demand for oil at the initial price of p_0. The price of oil will then rise, and as it does, the OPEC producer obtains revenues in excess of that needed to finance investment expenditures of I^* (assuming no change in the iso-revenue curve). The OPEC member then reduces output from Q_0 to Q' so as to maintain revenues consistent with investment expenditures. The final equilibrium price is p'.

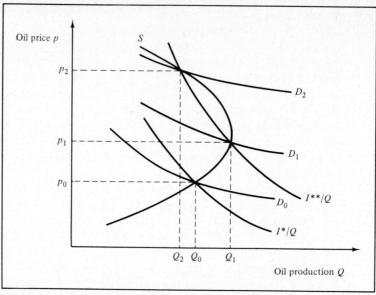

Figure 7.10 A backward-bending supply curve of oil from an OPEC country. As demand for oil rises over time, oil production and prices will rise if target revenue requirements also rise. This is shown by the shift in demand from D_0 to D_1 and the shift in the isorevenue curve from I^*/Q to I^{**}/Q. Output and prices increase. Once revenue targets are met, the OPEC country reduces its output when rising demand puts upward pressure on prices. If demand shifts again to D_2, but revenue targets do not change, output declines from Q_1 to Q_2, while price continues to rise from p_1 to p_2. The backward-bending portion of the supply curve arises once the revenue targets are met.

wealth-maximizing model is more descriptive of OPEC behavior, collusion is required. In practice, many of OPEC's actions do not seem to be consistent with observations of other successful cartels. Teece argues there is no evidence that OPEC sets production quotas for its members. Some argue that the international oil companies effectively prorate OPEC output, but the evidence for this is not conclusive. One or two countries in OPEC may negotiate a price and the rest of the members may sometimes follow. OPEC, according to Teece, has been really setting only one price, the price for Saudi Arabian light 34° API. This is the "marker" price on which other prices are based, but based loosely. Other OPEC members are free to set their own prices. And indeed, if we now examine the prices charged by different OPEC members, a wide divergence is observed. This is what Teece's model predicts.

There is no reason to expect all OPEC members to behave identically in this model. That is another one of its strengths. The output or oil price charged by an individual member depends on its absorptive capacity and where the country is on its supply curve. Countries with high absorptive capacities may tend to expand output as the price rises because they have not yet reached their target isorevenue curve. Teece argues that absorptive capacity will depend on political and religious factors, which vary by country. The economic factors that affect absorptive capacity include the per capita oil revenues of the country. Countries with large oil revenues per capita will be more constrained than those with small per capita oil revenues.

Table 7.3 presents world production of oil and Table 7.4 groups OPEC countries by their possible absorptive capacity. Although Table 7.4 is approximate, it does suggest what types of actions might be taken by each country facing a particular oil price. In the period 1980–1981, when oil prices were at their peak, one would expect the countries with low absorptive capacity to have greater excess capacity in oil production than countries with higher absorptive capacities. This is what Teece found, as shown in Table 7.5. Countries in group I (low absorptive capacity) represented over 63 percent of the excess capacity in 1981, while the group III countries (high absorptive capacity) represented only about 16 percent of the excess capacity. The difference in crude oil prices among OPEC members may also reflect differences in absorptive capacity, although other, more complex, features of the Middle East political situation are at work, as Teece notes (see Teece's paper and that by Moran, 1982, in the same volume for an interesting discussion of these issues).

What does the revenue constraint model suggest about oil prices and output from OPEC in the future? Assuming there is no disruption in supply for political reasons, and OPEC countries do not expand their existing capacity, Teece sees a period of relatively stable or even declining real oil prices. Refer back to Figure 7.8. The recession of 1981–1983 and the effects of the oil shocks of 1973–74 and 1979–80 working through economies over time has dampened oil demand considerably, and demand for OPEC production considerably. The fall in the real price of oil may stimulate OPEC producers to increase their output subject to their capacity constraints. The price would then remain stable until new capacity is installed or something else changes.

At the same time, OPEC countries are experiencing an increase in their government expenditures. Part *a* of Table 7.6 shows the rates of growth of OPEC countries' government expenditures over the 1970s compared to the rates of growth of oil revenues, while part *b* shows the ratio of foreign assets to oil revenues held by selected OPEC countries. With government expenditures growing over time, additional revenue will be needed to finance these expenditures. The revenue can come from increased oil production or returns on investment. But because investment in foreign assets is somewhat limited (and returns are not as high as in the early 1980s, when interest rates were very high), much of the additional revenues must come from oil. Hence, the prediction that oil prices (barring political upheaval) will remain relatively constant as OPEC countries maintain or increase oil production.

We thus have two quite different predictions coming from the wealth-maximizing model and the revenue-constraint model. The wealth-maximizing model suggests that the real price of OPEC oil will rise over the next 10 to 15 years following a path set by a dominant cartel constrained by a competitive fringe. The revenue-constraint model suggests that real oil prices will remain relatively constant. Neither model explicitly considers the effect on oil markets of increases in supply from non-OPEC oil producers and from alternative forms of energy. We turn now to a discussion of price-induced effects on energy supply.

Effects of Rising Oil Prices on Energy Supply

Our discussion above focused on views of the role of OPEC in the world energy market. In this section, we examine more generally the effect a rise in oil prices has had on supplies of energy resources. The discussion will assist us in predicting the

Table 7.3 WORLD OIL PRODUCTION: 1973–1982
(Millions of barrels per year, crude oil)

	1973	1974	1975	1976	1977	1978	1979	1980	1981	1982‡
North America										
United States	3,361	3,210	3,057	2,976	3,009	3,178	3,121	3,129	3,129	3,165
Canada	655	614	522	480	481	478	545	523	468	499
Mexico	165	210	262	293	358	450	537	687	818	1,002
Total*	4,244	4,103	3,921	3,828	3,933	4,192	4,284	4,420	4,488	4,737
South America	1,640	1,484	1,227	1,218	1,203	1,209	1,304	1,251	1,249	1,192
Europe	276	280	342	454	641	764	951	1,019	1,073	1,224
USSR	3,153	3,372	3,606	3,819	4,010	4,200	4,303	4,432	4,475	4,471
Middle East										
Saudi Arabia	2,776	3,092	2,586	3,143	3,358	3,030	3,479	3,623	3,588	2,366
Iran	2,139	2,193	1,953	2,153	2,065	1,913	1,156	537	473	1,022
Kuwait	1,104	937	763	788	718	801	914	612	411	302
Iraq	737	721	826	884	856	935	1,269	969	335	292
Total*	7,761	7,972	7,179	8,105	8,114	7,748	7,881	6,712	5,698	4,770
Africa										
Libya	794	557	540	709	753	724	765	669	417	455
Nigeria	742	825	651	759	761	700	846	770	526	474
Total*	2,149	1,982	1,808	2,158	2,282	2,217	2,427	2,230	1,705	1,656
Far East										
Indonesia	494	501	477	550	615	597	580	577	583	488
China	375	475	549	622	685	761	776	775	740	745
Total*	1,056	1,149	1,208	1,397	1,542	1,624	1,674	1,640	1,621	1,571
Oceania	142	146	137	145	151	155	153	145	153	142
World Total†	20,422	20,491	19,427	21,125	21,876	22,110	22,977	21,849	20,463	19,764

* Total includes countries not listed in table.

† Numbers may not add to world total due to rounding.

‡ Data for 1982 estimated from period 1/82 to 8/82. Source for 1982: *World Oil.*

Source: United Nations, *Yearbook of World Energy Statistics,* selected years. Converted from metric tons to barrels, as cited in Institute of Gas Technology (1983) *Energy Statistics* 6, No. 3.

Table 7.4   OPEC COUNTRIES: 1978 POPULATION, RESERVES, AND REVENUES PER CAPITA*

	Population (millions)	Proved reserves (MMB)	Output (1000 B/D)	Reserves: years (at 1978 output rate)	Revenue from oil exports (US$m.)	Revenue per inhabitant (US$)
Group I (low absorptive capacity)						
Saudi Arabia	6.89	153,100	8,059	52.05	38,736	$ 5,622.06
Libya	2.73	25,000	1,982	34.58	9,490	3,476.19
Kuwait	1.18	70,100	1,865	102.98	9,575	8,114.41
Qatar	0.23	5,600	485	31.63	2,315	10,065.22
United Arab Emirates	0.83	32,425	1,832	40.49	8,658	10,431.33
Subtotal	11.86	286,225	14,223	54.00	68,774	
Share of total	3.7%	65.70%	48.96%		51.5%	
Avg. revenue per inhabitant†						5,799
Group II (moderate absorptive capacity)						
Iran	36.64	62,000	5,264	32.27	21,766	594.05
Venezuela	13.1	18,200	2,163	23.05	9,187	701.30
Iraq	12.65	34,500	2,629	35.95	11,008	870.20
Algeria	17.25	6,000	1,225	13.42	6,015	348.70
Subtotal	79.64	120,700	11,281	26.00	47,976	
Share of total	24.6%	27.71%	38.83%		35.9%	
Avg. revenue per inhabitant†						602
Group III (high absorptive capacity)						
Nigeria	91.17	18,700	1,910	26.82	9,318	102.20
Indonesia	141.28	10,000	1,637	16.74	7,439	52.65
Subtotal	232.45	28,700	3,547	22	16,757	
Share of total	71.7%	6.59%	12.21%		12.6%	
Avg. revenue per inhabitant†						72
Total	323.95	435,625	29,051		133,507	

* Excludes Ecuador and Gabon.

† Subtotal revenue divided by subtotal population.

Source: J. M. Griffin and D. J. Teece (1982), *OPEC Behavior and World Oil Prices.* London: George Allen & Unwin, p. 70.

path of energy prices and output over time. We consider the impact of higher oil prices on oil production from non-OPEC countries and on the supply of other nonrenewable energy resources such as natural gas, coal, synthetic oils from tar sands and oil shale, nuclear energy, and renewable energy resources such as solar, geothermal, hydroelectric power, and biological sources of fuel.

Estimation of Supply Curves of Nonrenewable Resources

An estimate of the supply curve for a nonrenewable resource is essential if we are to determine the responsiveness of supply to changes in the price of the resource in question and to changes in the price of substitute resources. But modeling the supply of a nonrenewable resource is more difficult than determining supply of reproducible goods, because the supply of a nonrenewable resource is not as well defined as that of

Table 7.5   OPEC COUNTRIES: 1981 PRODUCTION AND SHORT-RUN EXCESS CAPACITY (1000 B/D)[a]

	Capacity		Production			
	Installed[b]	Maximum sustainable[c]	Available[d]	Latest post-embargo peak	Current (JFMA 81)[e]	Short run excess capacity[f]
Group I (low absorptive capacity)						
Saudi Arabia[i]	12,500	9,500	9,500	10,200 (Jan.81)	10,209	0
Libya	2,500	2,100	1,750	2,210 (Mar.77)	1,612	598
Kuwait[i]	2,900	2,500	1,500	2,990 (Dec.76)	1,471	1,519
Qatar	650	600	600	610 (Dec.75)	501	109
United Arab Emirates	2,570	2,415	1,630	2,260[g]	1,601	659
Subtotal	21,120	17,115	14,980	18,070	15,394	2,885
Share of total	52.5%	51.1%	51.6%	49.5%	62.9%	63.4%
Group II (moderate absorptive capacity)						
Iran	7,000	5,500[h]	3,500[i]	6,680 (Nov.76)	1,650	—
Venezuela	2,600	2,400	2,200	2,950 (Jne.74)	2,214	736
Iraq	4,000	3,500	3,500	3,500 (Jne.79)	825	—
Algeria	1,200	1,100	1,000	1,160 (Dec.78)	938	222
Subtotal	14,800	12,500	10,200	14,290	5,627	958
Share of total	36.8%	37.4%	35.1%	39.1%	23.0%	21.0%
Group III (high absorptive capacity)						
Nigeria	2,500	2,200	2,200	2,440 (Jan.79)	1,840	600
Indonesia	1,800	1,650	1,650	1,740 (Mar.77)	1,629	111
Subtotal	4,300	3,850	3,850	4,180	3,469	711
Share of total	10.7%	11.5%	13.3%	11.4%	14.1%	15.6%
Total	40,220	33,465	29,030	36,740	24,490	4,554

[a] Excluding Ecuador and Gabon.

[b] Installed capacity, also called nameplate or design capacity, includes all aspects of crude oil production, processing, transportation, and storage. Installed capacity is generally the highest capacity estimate.

[c] Maximum sustainable or operational capacity is the maximum production rate that can be sustained for several months; it considers the experience of operating the total system and is generally some 90–95 percent of installed capacity. This capacity concept does not necessarily reflect the maximum production rate sustainable without damage to the fields.

[d] Available or allowable capacity reflects production ceilings applied by Abu Dhabi, Kuwait, Iran, and Saudi Arabia. These ceilings usually represent a constraint only on annual average output, and thus production may exceed the ceilings in a given month. These ceilings are frequently altered and not always enforced.

[e] Production estimates are the average for January, February, March, and April 1981 as reported in *Monthly Energy Review*, U.S. Department of Energy, Energy Information Administration, August 1981.

[f] Except in the case of Iran and Iraq this is calculated by subtracting current production from the latest post embargo peak. In the case of Iran and Iraq it is assumed that there is no excess capacity because of the dysfunctional effects of revolution and war.

[g] This figure is composed of the following: Abu Dhabi 1,930 (Jul. 1975), Dubai 370 (Jul. 1979), Sharjah 60 (Dec. 1974).

[h] The precise loss in sustainable capacity remains uncertain.

[i] This figure represents the upper end of the range of available capacity, according to government statements.

Sources: International Energy Statistical Review, CIA, April 28, 1981, and *Monthly Energy Review*, U.S. Department of Energy, August 1981, as cited in Griffin and Teece (1982), pp. 72, 73.

reproducible goods. For reproducible goods, supply is the output or outputs derived from the inputs.

Intertemporal issues are not always crucial to the analysis because the supply process can be repeated indefinitely. Statistically, supply curves can be derived in a number of ways from production functions, profit, and cost functions. The supply of a nonrenewable resource, while in principle the same as that for a reproducible good, is more complex because of the fixed supply of the reserves of a given deposit and

Table 7.6a   RATES OF GROWTH OF OIL INCOME AND GOVERNMENT EXPENDITURES
(Annual averages in percents)

Country	Oil income*	Government expenditure†	Time period
Kuwait	31.2	38.2	1972–79
Libya	29.8	20.0	1972–78
Qatar	116.0	50.0	1972–77
Saudi Arabia	46.5	42.7	1972–79
United Arab Emirates	43.7	39.0	1972–79
Algeria	41.5	22.3	1972–79
Ecuador	49.6	20.0	1972–79
Indonesia	57.7	38.9	1972–78
Iran	43.1	40.5	1972–78
Iraq	65.0	35.7	1972–79
Nigeria	36.9	33.6	1972–78
Venezuela	20.0	24.3	1972–78
Simple average	48.41	33.76	1972–79

* *OPEC Bulletin*, January 1981.

† *OPEC Statistical Bulletin*, 1979.

Source: Griffin and Tecce (1982).

because the resource must typically be discovered through the exploration process. Nonrenewable resource supply will depend not only on such factors as the current price and cost of factor inputs, but on the rate of change in prices anticipated over time, future costs, discount rates, future discoveries of new reserves, and the remaining stock of the resource in the ground. The question is, then, is there a unique supply curve for a depletable natural resource, or rather a set of curves that shift over time that can be determined by looking at the entire process of supply? The latter is probably more descriptive of supply, but it is not easy to describe and measure the supply process.

Table 7.6b   SELECTED OPEC PRODUCERS FOREIGN ASSETS, OIL REVENUES, AND TOTAL FOREIGN ASSETS AS A PERCENTAGE OF ANNUAL REVENUES, 1979
(In U.S. dollars, millions)

	Foreign assets*	Revenues from oil 1979	Foreign assets divided by annual revenues 1979
Iraq	17,500	11,008	1.589
Iran	15,900	21,766	.730
Kuwait	40,000	9,575	4.177
Libya	6,344	9,490	.668
Qatar	4,267	2,315	1.843
Saudi Arabia	75,000	38,736	1.936
United Arab Emirates	12,707	8,658	1.467
Total	171,718	101,548	1.691

* *Middle East Economic Survey*, April 18, 1980.

Source: Griffin and Tecce (1982).

The supply process for a nonrenewable resource consists of four distinct but related phases: (1) acquisition of property that may contain the resource; (2) exploration for and the possible discovery of resource deposits; (3) development of productive capacity; and (4) extraction and processing of the resource. Modeling any of these relationships or all simultaneously is a difficult task. The four phases are totally interdependent (not recursive), because a change in a parameter in any one phase can affect actions in all other phases. For example, a change in the price of oil to consumers will affect not only the supply of oil from phase 4, but the inputs and outputs from the preceding phases as well. If we are concerned only with very short-run analysis, then the supply of the resource from phase 4 can be the focus. But if we want to know what will happen over time, all phases must be examined.

But even if we examine the supply from phase 4, assuming there is a known stock of the resource, depletion effects must be included. No such depletion effects occur with reproducible goods. The problem with much of the early work on quantitative estimates of nonrenewable resource supply is that only the extractive phase (4) was examined and depletion effects were not explicitly incorporated. More recent work has attempted to include not only depletion, but the other phases as well.

If we want to model the supply process fully, there are a number of conceptual and statistical problems. The simultaneous nature of the process means there is an econometric problem of identification of the system. It is difficult to measure, for example, the responsiveness of final output from the mine or well due to a change in the price of the resource. The direct effects of the price change must be separated from the effects on discoveries, development of new capacity, and so on. This also means that the supply elasticities obtained (own price and the cross price) must be interpreted with care.

What kind of supply elasticities are desired? The short-run price elasticity should show the proportionate change in output of, say, oil due to a change in the price of oil, holding fixed all other prices. When there is more than one phase to the mineral supply process, this implies holding constant all endogenous variables from the phases other than the one in question. A long-run price elasticity will then measure the adjustment in quantity supplied when all the variables held constant are allowed to adjust in response to the price change. It is obvious that the short-run and long-run elasticities are different, but how does a researcher measure these elasticities?

Typically, one phase of the supply process is examined — for example, exploration or extraction. A price elasticity of supply is determined for that phase, holding all else constant. This approach may be useful for detailed discussions of the phase in question, but it does not explain mineral supply. Alternatively, what is called a *reduced form expression* is estimated. This is a single equation that incorporates features of all the phases. The elasticity can be calculated from the value of the coefficient on the price term in the equation, but then the influences of the various phases are combined in an unspecified way. To have the most meaningful elasticity, a model of the supply process consisting of the four phases treated simultaneously is needed.

One of the crucial aspects of modeling supply is measurement. Measures are needed of the inputs and outputs for each phase, prices, costs, and the interest rate.

None of these variables is easy to determine. We will focus on some of the issues in trying to determine output. Let's look first at the output of crude oil from the well. Crude oil may appear to be a homogeneous good, but it is a good with many characteristics, such as sulfur content, location, and viscosity. Will estimates of supply be very inaccurate if we treat oil as a homogeneous good? It depends in part on whether the combination of characteristics stays the same over time and at different extraction rates.

If we deplete, say, all the low-sulfur oil that is easy to extract in 10 years, then our supply curve of oil will be quite different after this period. Estimates of supply based on a large share of low-cost oil from large reservoirs in the total amount extracted will give misleading predictions of future supply once the low-cost oil is gone and high-cost oil from smaller reservoirs dominates.

But not only does oil have characteristics that may change over time, it is not necessarily the only output from a well. Oil and natural gas are frequently found together—they are *joint products* in some deposits. This presents a number of complications when one tries to determine elasticities of supply.

Prior to the 1970s, much natural gas was found when explorers were looking for oil. It is difficult to specify a functional relationship for gas discoveries when they are found by accident. The responsiveness of gas discoveries to the price of gas may thus be negligible if one is looking at data prior to 1970, but positive thereafter.

Natural gas has another complication. It must be connected to a pipeline to be extracted (or a plant that can liquify it). The amount of gas extracted from a given region over a given time period may be explained by when the pipeline was connected to the region (and the factors associated with pipeline construction and contracts between gas producers and the pipeline), not simply by changes in the price of gas, costs of extraction, or the price of oil. Prices of energy resources will be important, but the price elasticities measured at any point in time may be biased by the presence or absence of the pipeline.

If we want to measure the output from phase 2, exploration and discovery, what is it? Exploration inputs may yield discoveries of new oil, gas, or other energy resources. They may also yield information about where resources are *not* located—that is, dry holes. Does one simply count as output only the reserves that were discovered? There may be some market value for the information about dry holes, but it is difficult to measure (recall our discussion in Chapter 5 about the value of information in exploration).

But even if we simply count reserves discovered as the output from exploration, more practical difficulties exist. Reserves reported at the time of discovery are often what is practical to extract *at that time*—that is, given current prices, costs, and technology. Costs, prices, and technology all change over time. Additional reserves of oil, gas, coal, and so on can be counted whenever the price of the resource rises, even if no additional exploration occurs. A good deal of research being done on these issues attempts to incorporate these complications. For example, Uhler (1983) has put together a data set for oil and gas reserves discovered in Alberta over approximately the last 20 years that differentiates between initial reserves and appreciations in reserves—additions to the reserves made over time. This distinction enables us to look at economic conditions at the time the discovery is made and contrast them with conditions when appreciation of reserves occurs. This type of data should yield better predictions of supply elasticities from the exploration phase.

We could continue with more practical difficulties, but we conclude this section with a brief listing of some of the other measurement and associated problems. Measuring the inputs into the phases of the supply process is complicated by the lack of markets for many of the inputs. In particular, reserves in the ground are an input into the extraction of the resource. These reserves typically do not have a market price, so an imputed or shadow price must be calculated. Cost data for other inputs are often difficult to obtain and frequently highly aggregated. The aggregation may not present a problem when we are concerned with elasticities for the entire supply process, but difficulties may emerge when there are changes over time in the factor inputs used in each phase. Price of the final output are also complicated by the presence of many prices—OPEC prices, spot market prices, contract prices, and so on. Posted prices frequently differ from transaction prices. Taxes and other forms of government intervention will also distort the market prices observed, which means that scarcity prices or shadow prices should be calculated.

Once all the data issues are resolved, we must still contend with the statistical properties of the relationship—for example, the functional form, role of expectations, incorporation of error terms, cross-equation restrictions, aggregation, identification, and so on. Mineral supply, because of its complex nature, simply presents a large number of econometric difficulties. To date, the imperfect numbers themselves are less important than the increased understanding of the actual process of supply that has emerged from empirical studies of energy supply.

Specific Energy Resources

When there is an increase in the price of oil, there will tend to be increases in the supply of not just oil, but all energy resources that are substitutes for oil over time. Each of the four phases of supply for a nonrenewable energy resource will be affected. Figure 7.11 illustrates what may happen in, say, the market for resource-bearing land.[5] We draw a supply curve which is relatively inelastic to indicate that there may be few areas available for exploration in certain countries. The increase in the price of oil shifts the demand curve for this land to the right from D to D'. More land will be demanded to search for new deposits of oil, natural gas, tar sands, coal, shale oil, and uranium. How much additional land is used for exploration and at what price depends, of course, on the elasticities of each curve.

The quantity of land used in equilibrium then becomes an input into the exploration and discovery phase of mineral supply. Land, along with other inputs, may yield new discoveries that ultimately get developed and turned into producing deposits if the market price of the resources covers the costs of production, including any resource rent. The prices of all energy resources that are good substitutes for oil will tend to rise when the price of oil increases. We can expect more of these resources to flow into energy markets. The process takes time, however: Estimates of the interval between land acquisition and ultimate production of a fossil fuel range from 5 to 20 years. If there is a lot of excess capacity in the energy system at the time the oil price rises, then additional supplies will be forthcoming somewhat faster. However,

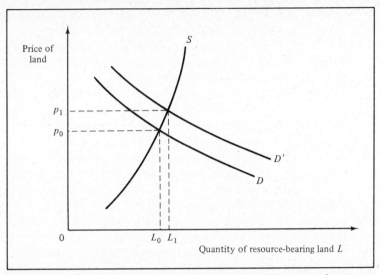

Figure 7.11   The effects of an increase in oil prices on the amount of resource-bearing land purchased. The rise in oil prices increases the demand for land, shifting the demand curve from D to D'. The quantity of land purchased rises somewhat from L_0 to L_1. The elasticity of the land supply curve determines the size of the increase $L_0 L_1$. An inelastic curve, as shown, leads to a relatively small increase in land purchases and a relatively large increase in the price compared to a more elastic supply curve.

in the 1973–74 period, for a variety of reasons, this excess capacity did not generally exist. This is why we concentrate on long-run responses.

An increase in the price of oil has another effect on energy markets. The higher prices will stimulate research and development (R&D) for new technologies for exploration, extraction, processing, and use of energy resources. Some aspects were taken up in Chapter 5. Griffin and Steele (1980) list five possible effects of R&D activities.

R&D may: (1) increase the probabilities of discovering concentrated and low-cost energy deposits (a number of geologists disagree); (2) increase production from existing reserves (or supplies of renewable resources) due to, for example, increases in recovery rates; (3) promote greater efficiency in processing energy by industrial and other intermediate users; (4) increase efficiency in the transmission of energy — reduce heat loss, improve thermal efficiency, especially in electric power generation; and (5) increase the efficiency of the energy-using appliances and structures that comprise the final demands for energy products.

We will concentrate on the price responsiveness of energy resources to rising oil prices and the possible effects of R&D on energy supply, enhanced recovery from existing reserves, or increased supplies of the resource. We will look at a number of energy resources individually.

Crude Oil   After the first oil price shock in 1973–74, a substantial increase in exploration for new oil deposits occurred all over the world. Drilling of exploratory wells increased not only in regions where conventional oil deposits had been found in the past, such as Texas and Alberta, but in more exotic regions such as the Arctic, the North Sea, and other offshore locations. A number of new deposits have been discovered, some of them substantial. Table 7.7 shows world oil reserves over the period 1973 to 1982 for the major oil-producing regions. Over the period, reserves fell somewhat from 1974 to 1977, but were sharply higher in 1978 over their 1974 level (by over 9 percent for the world total, but about 14.5 percent for non-OPEC oil). From 1980 to 1982, reserves continued to rise. Now, of course one must be careful with these measures of proved reserves, but the point is that oil reserves, particularly in non-OPEC countries, were rising.

However, while the amount of oil discovered did rise as a result of the increase in the price of oil, some analysts feel that few large conventional deposits remain undiscovered. There may be considerable oil beneath the ocean floor, but extraction is proving to be quite costly, and it is not clear that oil from these deposits will be able to compete with other energy resources on a cost basis over time. Griffin and Steele report ranges of estimates of potential reserves offshore between 40 and 120 billion barrels. With current oil prices around $29.00 per barrel, some of these deposits are quite close to the margin of profitability. After many years of exploration, one significant oil discovery was reported in May 1984 in the Canadian Arctic. It will be more than 10 years before its oil reaches the marketplace. Again, costs of extracting oil from these deposits, even if sizable, are high. New pipelines must be constructed and/or methods of shipping the oil through the frozen waters improved.

What about the effects of technological change on oil supply? Technological change can lead to new drilling techniques and/or decrease the costs of existing techniques. This is especially important for offshore and Arctic drilling. The potential for increased recovery from conventional (onshore, non-Arctic) oil deposits may be considerable. Griffin and Steele note that according to the American Petroleum Institute, the original oil in place in all fields in the United States is estimated at 450 billion barrels. Of that, 115 billion barrels have already been extracted, and the estimate of remaining proved reserves—oil that can be extracted at current prices and technology—is about 30 billion barrels (about 32 percent of the oil in place).

With some breakthroughs in the recovery of this oil, a substantial amount could be added to proved reserves. For each 1 percent increase in additions to reserves, 4.5 billion barrels of oil could be extracted and brought to market. The area where technological improvement is needed is in tertiary recovery techniques. These techniques, which involve thermal injection (such as steam), are not cost effective at current oil prices. Secondary recovery (injection of water) is currently being used, and was used even prior to the 1973–74 increase in oil prices.

Natural Gas Exploration for natural gas increased dramatically after 1974, as did new discoveries and additions to reserves of existing deposits. In Alberta, for example, discoveries and appreciation of reserves averaged 4,500 billion cubic feet over the period 1968 to 1973. In the following six years, the average rose to over 6,600 billion cubic feet, an increase of over 46 percent. Proved gas reserves worldwide are given in Table 7.8. Over the period 1973 to 1982, proved reserves rose by more than 60 percent. Not all these reserves can be readily tapped; a major constraint in the use of natural gas has been the location of pipelines. But there are substantial reserves, and if

Table 7.7 PROVED OIL RESERVES: 1973–1982
(Millions of barrels)

	1973	1974	1975	1976	1977	1978	1979	1980	1981	1982
North America										
Canada	7,674	7,171	6,653	6,257	5,971	6,856	6,806	5,986	6,656	6,400
Mexico	2,847	3,087	3,431	7,279	10,428	28,406	30,616	44,161	48,084	48,084
United States	35,300	34,250	32,682	30,942	29,486	27,804	27,051	29,805	29,426	29,675
Total*	46,332	45,161	43,437	45,143	46,551	63,824	65,223	80,623	84,755	84,682
South America	20,073	24,729	24,782	25,126	23,630	25,737	25,855	26,271	26,723	31,788
Europe	19,160	17,538	19,834	18,233	18,641	14,818	17,978	20,836	18,770	18,490
USSR	47,500	56,341	58,878	59,900	59,000	58,438	59,787	82,000	85,000	86,054
Middle East										
Saudi Arabia	96,922	103,480	207,857	110,187	110,400	167,066	163,384	164,220	164,813	165,000
Iran	68,000	68,050	50,108	48,130	46,863	44,966	40,558	39,936	39,432	38,410
Kuwait	72,969	70,890	70,219	71,800	72,000	71,400	68,530	68,023	67,680	67,500
Iraq	35,675	35,124	35,000	35,165	35,338	34,392	35,000	34,080	33,700	33,408
Total*	316,703	339,253	309,547	309,119	306,622	363,340	309,719	358,068	359,440	357,513
Africa										
Libya	23,208	23,000	24,000	24,493	25,327	27,204	26,446	25,788	25,859	25,403
Nigeria	18,250	13,652	13,000	12,241	12,243	12,273	11,634	11,295	20,000	19,526
Total*	56,087	52,030	53,324	50,437	54,617	58,892	57,252	53,498	63,669	63,940
Far East										
Indonesia	11,500	12,000	12,000	11,500	8,297	9,824	11,003	10,540	9,976	9,542
China	14,800	14,800	17,242	18,000	18,026	20,025	19,250	19,000	18,500	18,200
Total*	31,514	31,411	33,858	34,949	31,497	35,254	36,211	36,507	36,883	36,400
Oceania	2,430	2,615	2,475	2,880	2,774	1,937	2,099	2,067	1,810	1,727
World total†	539,788	569,079	546,135	545,787	543,332	621,752	574,125	659,870	677,050	680,593

* Totals include countries not listed.

† Numbers may not add to world total due to rounding.

Source: World Oil, selected issues. As cited in Institute of Gas Technology (1983), *Energy Statistics* 6, No. 3.

Table 7.8 PROVED NATURAL GAS RESERVES: 1973–1982

(10^9 cubic feet)

	1973	1974	1975	1976	1977	1978	1979	1980	1981	1982
North America										
Canada	52,457	56,708	56,975	58,282	59,472	81,974	88,549	88,400	90,988	92,000
Mexica	10,812	11,185	11,924	19,410	27,868	58,935	61,217	64,511	75,352	75,352
United States*	249,950	237,133	228,200	216,026	208,878	200,302	194,917	199,021	209,434	212,576
Total*	316,213	309,028	301,099	301,718	302,227	347,230	356,701	366,007	393,246	397,245
South America	61,582	62,462	62,923	65,726	74,603	79,624	86,271	84,453	90,367	98,475
Europe	159,802	161,915	165,977	157,486	156,688	147,760	155,738	180,392	174,696	171,309
USSR	649,800	699,800	710,000	781,000	774,900	813,645	909,300	1,077,110	1,377,000	1,495,000
Middle East										
Saudi Arabia	56,126	59,861	62,290	63,759	65,700	97,871	65,861	116,170	113,393	114,000
Iran	376,164	374,400	374,794	375,000	373,400	371,955	371,104	371,094	370,000	369,489
Qatar	7,954	7,808	47,808	58,799	58,737	41,510	59,975	59,818	60,000	59,831
Total*	581,781	575,702	605,462	616,333	616,197	629,784	675,318	732,994	733,957	737,363
Africa										
Algeria	100,000	100,200	115,500	115,499	122,500	95,549	99,186	98,820	123,550	130,000
Nigeria	48,380	50,244	52,225	51,419	51,649	51,775	50,718	49,840	48,346	48,911
Total*	189,665	190,823	209,608	200,048	214,141	189,977	191,516	196,126	220,560	232,178
Far East	68,297	65,949	72,306	87,970	108,611	138,513	153,823	151,787	166,463	168,608
Oceania	34,898	32,267	36,554	34,700	34,475	35,542	35,698	35,454	23,338	22,409
World total	2,062,038	2,097,946	2,163,929	2,244,981	2,281,842	2,382,075	2,564,365	2,824,323	3,179,627	3,322,587

* Totals include countries not listed.

Source: World Oil, selected issues. As cited in Institute of Gas Technology (1983), *Energy Statistics 6,* No. 3.

oil prices do not decline, it is likely that much of the gas will be brought to market.

About 80 percent of the gas in place is now being recovered with primary techniques, so there is less scope for significant additions to proved reserves due to technological change. There are, however, some known gas deposits that cannot be exploited by existing drilling techniques. New techniques would enable exploitation of these deposits. Additional gas would also be available to many more markets with the extension of pipelines.

Synthetic Crude Oil   Synthetic crude oil can be produced from oil shale deposits, tar sands, and liquification of coal. Gas can also be obtained from coal. These energy resources are primarily in the developmental stages. A few prototype plants exist to produce oil and gas from these resources, but they have yet to show their technical and economic feasibility. With the recent decline in the price of crude oil, many of these projects have been canceled or have had their development slowed. There are vast reserves of these resources, but their exploitation awaits the discovery of methods of reducing the costs of extraction and processing.

Oil shales   Oil shales are sedimentary rocks containing matter that can produce oil. They are found in the United States and the USSR in abundance; smaller reserves exist in Brazil, Canada, Zaire, China, and elsewhere. An estimate cited in Hagel (1976) puts the oil content of the shale deposits in the United States at 1.8 trillion barrels, with 129 billion barrels in the most readily recoverable form. When one compares this to the 30 billion barrels of proved conventional oil, the shale oil deposits seem worthy of investigation.

Unfortunately, there are a number of difficulties in the development of these resources. First, the capital and operating costs of producing oil from shale are quite high. Griffin and Steele note the capital cost of constructing a relatively small plant (50,000 barrels per day) can run from $1.2 to 2.8 billion (1978 U.S. dollars). The estimates for the cost per barrel of producing oil from shale range from $11.70 (1977 dollars) to over $23 (1978 dollars) per barrel. Thus, at current oil prices the shale oil is not very competitive. Its extraction and processing costs are high compared to the costs of conventional oil and gas, but as we will see below, these costs correspond to those for other methods of producing oil synthetically.

There are also environmental problems associated with the extraction and processing of oil shale. It must be strip mined and requires large amounts of water in processing. Processing also contributes to air and water pollution. The shale oil found in the western states of the United States is where water is scarce, and where other uses exist for the land under which the deposits are located. Additional water resources would be needed, and environmental and land use issues must be resolved before large-scale production can begin. It is unlikely, given conditions existing into the mid-1980s, that any significant production of oil will come from shale.

Tar sands   While oil shale deposits are solid, the oil contained in *tar sands* located primarily in Canada and Venezuela is liquid, but very thick. The United States has small reserves. Reserves of tar sands are large, estimated at around 1 trillion barrels of oil in Canada (see Feick, 1983). However, given existing technology, only about 70 billion barrels represent reserves of crude that can yield 20 billion barrels of upgraded synthetic oil. New techniques may increase reserve estimates to 250 billion barrels of oil.

At present, two tar sands plants are operating in Canada. One, a small plant operated by Suncor (previously Sun Oil), began production in 1967 and produces 45,000 barrels of oil per day. The other, the Syncrude operation, began production in 1978 and as of 1983 was upgrading its capacity from 109,000 to 130,000 barrels per day. Another project, Alsands, was being developed by a consortium of private firms with the participation of Canadian governments. The project has been put on indefinite hold due to the decline in world oil prices and rapidly escalating costs. The Syncrude plant was constructed for $2.5 billion (1978 Canadian dollars). The estimate to complete Alsands was $13 billion for a 140,000 barrel-per-day plant. The operating costs per barrel of oil produced range from $13 to $16.

The major problems with oil production from tar sands are the high capital costs and environmental degradation (due to strip mining and sulfur emissions from processing the tar sands). Feick (1983) argues that the plants need not be as large as Syncrude or Alsands. Scale economies could be obtained even with a plant producing 50,000 to 70,000 barrels per day, thus lessening the need for massive capital expenditures.

Coal   Coal has been used for energy for centuries. It is the most abundant readily available energy resource in the United States and many other countries, with reserves sufficient to sustain present levels of consumption well into the twenty-first century. U.S. reserves of coal were about 3.2 trillion short tons in 1976 (Hagel, 1976), with about 150 billion short tons recoverable at current technology. World reserves of coal are between 9 to 12 trillion short tons.

While coal is by far the most abundant nonrenewable source of energy in the world, its share in total energy production in most countries has been declining through much of this century because of the increasing use of the more convenient, cleaner, and less environmentally damaging oil and natural gas resources. The coal extracted in the eastern United States has a high sulfur content, which contributes greatly to air pollution when coal is used as a fuel for electric power plants (see Chapter 13). Western coal has a lower sulfur content but must be strip mined and thus causes another set of environmental problems. The costs of extracting coal are also rising over time due to the depletion of thicker seams of deposits.[6] Coal is, however, less expensive than domestic crude oil of comparable energy content, although transportation costs for coal add greatly to its price to the final consumer.

It is doubtful that coal will ever regain its dominance in many energy markets (unless severe supply disruptions of oil and gas occur) due to its bulk, inconvenience, and pollution problems. However, there are techniques that can turn coal into synthetic crude oil or gas. The technology for coal gasification is currently more advanced than for that of coal liquification, according to Griffin and Steele.[7] The capital costs of constructing a gasification plant producing 250 million cubic feet of gas per day would be between $1 and 1.5 billion (1978 dollars). The cost of the gas would be between $2.70 and $6.70 per million BTUs. But because electric utilities would be the major buyers of this gas, it is unlikely that gas produced from coal can compete with natural gas at current or expected natural gas prices in the near future. The estimate of capital costs for a coal liquification plant range from $1 to $3 billion for a 40,000 to 50,000 barrel-per-day operation. This translates into oil between $20 and $30 per barrel (1978 dollars), again well above the current price of oil.

Nuclear Energy   The energy resource that has received more R&D dollars (mostly funded by government revenues) and public subsidies is nuclear power.[8] Unfortunately, the high expenditure on nuclear energy has not yet resulted in any cost-saving breakthroughs that make this source of electricity competitive with power plants fired by fossil fuels (at the existing prices of oil, gas, and coal) and current forecasts of the growth in energy demand over the next 5 to 10 years. We cannot go into the details of the nuclear power story over the past 30 years, but refer you to a number of studies.[9]

The situation as of 1984 is that nuclear energy has a very uncertain future, at least in the United States. At present, no new nuclear power plants are under construction in the United States. Several plants completed in the past year have been unable to obtain operating permits due to failure to conform to safety and environmental regulations. Numerous technical problems are yet unresolved, as well as serious environmental and health and safety problems (such as the disposal of radioactive wastes and the proliferation of fissionable material). Delays by regulators in approving new plants became long, and after the Three Mile Island incident, confidence in the ability of regulators to supervise safety procedures was shaken. Capital costs are extraordinarily high for both light and heavy water commercial reactors.

In other countries (Europe for example), nuclear power is somewhat less controversial and planned to provide an increasing share of electric power over the next 10 to 20 years. There are some differences in the technology used between the United States and say Canada or France, as well as the fact that electric power companies are operated by the government in the latter countries, but are privately owned in the United States (see the references cited above for more details).[10] France produces a large percentage of its electricity from nuclear power stations and has a very active research program including investigations of fusion reactors.

Solar Energy   We turn now to a discussion of *renewable* energy supplies, which are all basically derived from solar energy. Some analysts feel that renewable supplies are the great hope for the future. Indeed, Lovins and Lovins (1983) argue that more new energy has come from renewable sources than from all nonrenewable sources combined. They estimate that in 1983, 8 percent of the energy supply in the United States comes from renewable resources.

There are a number of ways in which solar energy can be harnessed on earth. The major ways are to capture solar heat, and in photovoltaic cells. The sun is a giant fusion reactor. It supplies about 1 kilowatt of energy per square meter at the earth's surface during the day. Its primary advantages are that it is renewable, and that it has a minimal impact on the environment and the health and safety of living things. If decentralization of energy generation is seen as a desirable activity, then solar energy has another advantage because it is generally most effective on a relatively small scale — space heating in residences and small commercial establishments.

Its disadvantages are its current cost. Griffin and Steele note that to supply 50 percent of an average home's space heating requirements, a solar operation would cost $15,000 to $20,000. This number may be somewhat misleading, however, because there are many ways to reduce the costs of solar power. Solar collectors are not yet mass-produced, and there is hope that large-scale production of the components will bring down unit costs. Also, passive solar operations may be combined with other energy-saving activities, such as increased insulation, at lower cost than that estimated above.

Photovoltaic cells are a promising use of solar energy because they convert this energy directly to electricity. Although electricity generated in this manner is currently quite expensive (Griffin and Steele cite a cost of $12 to $15 per watt compared to 30 to 40 cents for fossil-fuel-fired power plants), some technical changes may greatly reduce these costs. If so, an optimistic forecast is that solar cells could produce

---

BOX 7.1
Hydro Power Is One of Canada's Leading Natural Resources

There are economic rents in hydroelectricity generation. Whenever price exceeds marginal cost of production, we have a rent. The world price of oil can be translated into a world price for a kilowatt-hour of electricity and this can serve as a basis for calculating rent from producing electricity with water power. Recent calculations by Bernard, Bridges, and Scott [1982] place rent per kilowatt hour in 1979 Canadian dollars at $25.88 in British Columbia, $5.30 in Manitoba, $5.09 in Ontario, $9.94 in Quebec, and $11.28 in Newfoundland (Churchill Falls project). The province of Quebec has an abundance of hydroelectricity produced by the government-run company, Hydro-Quebec. Currently (March 1, 1983) Quebec consumers pay $21.85 U.S. for 500 kilowatt-hours. In New York City the price is $72.45; in Chicago, $34.62; and in Houston, $40.65. Current production (26,400 megawatts) is adequate for all the needs of New York and New Jersey, though 75 percent is consumed in Quebec. Exports to New England at a price 80 percent of the average cost of oil will bring in $5 billion U.S. over the next 11 years. A 1982 contract with New York will gross $17 billion over 13 years.

Hydro-Quebec is the largest company in Canada in terms of assets ($23.1 billion U.S. in 1982) and profits ($800 million). It also is bigger than any private or public utility in the United States, including the recently created subunits of American Telephone and Telegraph. Finding markets is not easy. Importers do not want to rely on a foreign supplier into the distant future. Quebec has recently attracted the French aluminum maker Pechinay by offering very low electricity prices until 1990.

Source: J.-T. Bernard, G. E. Bridges, and A. Scott, "An Evaluation of Potential Canadian Hydro-Electric Rents," UBC Resources Paper No. 78, 1982, and *New York Times,* January 29, 1984.

3 to 4 percent of the electric power in the United States by the year 2000 (Griffin and Steele).

A number of other sources of energy come from the sun. *Hydroelectricity* is indirectly a solar product. The sun evaporates water that returns to the earth as rain, resulting in the renewable cycle of water rushing down rivers. Hydroelectricity is relatively more important in some countries than others. For example, in Canada hydroelectricity supplies approximately two-thirds of the total electricity produced. In the United States, hydroelectricity represents a much smaller share of electricity generated.

Although hydroelectricity comes from a renewable resource, the power it generates is typically seen as limited because of the scarcity of good sites for the construction of dams. Most of the good sites have been taken, and development of new sites sometimes involves substantial tradeoffs between land use and environmental degradation. Hydroelectricity produces no air pollution and little thermal pollution, but it does damage ecosystems, fisheries, and affects recreational uses of the natural environment. In the United States, there is opposition on environmental grounds to further construction of hydroelectric dams, and many feel it is doubtful that more electricity can be generated by this technique.

Another promising solar product is *biomass energy* — the fuel that is produced from plants (ethyl alcohol or methane gas). A number of countries, notably Brazil, are actively cultivating crops to convert into gasohol for transportation and other uses. There is of course one of the oldest energy sources — wood — in this category as well. While biomass energy is renewable, plants are relatively inefficient in converting solar energy into fuel. Plants cultivated in water, such as the water hyacinth, are the most efficient. Another interesting plant is the rubber plant, which produces hydrocarbons directly. Biomass energy may contribute an increasing share of energy in years to come. Other solar energy sources include wind power, solar thermal conversion (giant collector mirrors concentrating heat which is transmitted to a heat exchanger), and ocean thermal conversion.

Finally, miscellaneous energy resources which at present contribute small amounts to total energy production include energy from waste recovery — burning garbage and collecting methane from sewage — geothermal energy, peat, tidal power, fuel cells, and hydrogen. These are typically viable in relatively few locales or are expensive and present difficult technical problems.

BOX 7.2
Biomass Fuel in China

More than 85 percent of the energy used by rural households in China comes from burned biomass fuels, largely crop by-products, fuelwood, and animal wastes (see Table 1), according to Robert Taylor (1983). But population pressures have led to shortages of fuelwood, crop, and animal wastes. About one-half of the fuelwood used is collected from "legitimate" areas — pruning and

Box 7.2 continued

Table 1   CURRENT RURAL HOUSEHOLD ENERGY CONSUMPTION IN CHINA

Fuel	Physical quantities (10^6 tons)	Energy (10^6 TCE)	Percentage of total
Crop by-products	266	129.2	44.4
Fuelwood	180	115.7	39.7
Coal	53	37.9†	13.0
Dung	10	5.5	1.9
Kerosene	1	1.5	0.5
Electricity	—	1.0	0.3
Biogas	—	0.6	0.2
Total	—	291.4	100.0

Sources: Individual fuel consumption figures are taken from the All-China Exhibition on Rural Energy, Beijing (September 1982); and Wu Wen, Chen En-Jian, and Li Nianguo, Guangzhou Institute of Energy Conversion. "Our Views to the Resolution of China's Rural Energy Requirements" (paper prepared for the Joint CAS–NAS Science Policy Conference, August 1982). The total energy consumption figure is consistent with the figure of 290 million TCE resulting from a survey conducted by the China Energy Research Society in 1979.

* *Note:* TCE is tons of coal equivalent.

† Chinese coal has an energy content of about 5,000 kcal per kilogram, whereas the international standard for 1 kg of coal equivalent is 7,000 kcal.

thinning of timber forests and plantings for fuelwood purposes. The other half is taken illegitimately. Areas are stripped of trees, grasses, and brush, leaving behind barren hillsides that can quickly erode and create other environmental problems.

In response to these illegitimate harvests and pressure for more fuelwood, the Chinese government in 1980 announced a plan to quadruple the fuelwood supply by 1990. Fuelwood will be increased primarily by the creation of private fuelwood lots, as well as increased plantings in collective forests. Households will be given certificates granting them ownership of the *trees,* with the right of

Table 2   FORESTED LAND AREA IN CHINA

Forest classification	Area (10^6 ha)	Percentage of total
Timber	98.00	80.5
Economic	8.52	7.0
Protective	7.85	6.4
Fuelwood	3.67	3.0
Bamboo	3.15	2.6
Special	0.67	0.5
Total	121.86	100.0

Note: Economic forests represent forests that provide fruits, nuts, edible oils, and other cash crops. Special forests are used for esthetic or experimental purposes.

Source: 1976 General Forestry Survey data, issued by the National Forestry Bureau. See *Zhongguo Nongye Dili Zonglun* (A General Treatise on the Agricultural Geography of China), Beijing, October 1980 [JPRS, *China: Agriculture,* no. 78054 (May 8, 1981), p. 182].

family inheritance of these certificates. Ownership of the land will remain with the rural collectives. The trees must be planted by a specific deadline, but then families may use, sell, or give away any wood and brush grown. By 1981, almost 3 million hectares of land had been distributed to households for the cultivation of fuelwood. This represents an amount almost equal to all fuelwood lots previously planted (see Table 2). According to Taylor, the success of the program will depend on a high level of government support and assistance in supplying seedlings, selecting species, and providing technical assistance. If successful, the woodlots will provide not only energy, but will also help prevent environmental degradation of other lands.

Source: R. P. Taylor, "Fuelwood for China," *Resources,* February 1983, pp. 10–11.

So there are many sources of energy as alternatives to OPEC oil. The new technologies that are being developed have been given a price-induced boost from the increase in oil prices in 1973–74 and again in 1979–80. It is still too early to predict exactly how much energy can be derived from unconventional sources of supply, but it is clear that the supply of conventional fuels (oil, natural gas, coal) has been stimulated by the price shock. Most developed economies today are less dependent on OPEC oil than in 1973, and the trend is to decrease the dependence on OPEC still more in the years to come. We should add a caveat to this, however.

If the price of oil remains at its current level, many of the alternative energy supplies and even high-cost conventional supplies will be uneconomic to produce. There is thus the possibility that countries such as the United States will increase their dependence on OPEC oil in the near future. In 1985 the United States is a net debtor in capital flows for the first time in more than 75 years. However, if decision-makers fear a repeat of the events in the 1970s, alternative energy sources ought not to be scrapped at this point. Continued R&D may be the prudent policy. We return to policy issues later; now we turn to the other side of the energy market—demand.

THE DEMAND FOR ENERGY

Supply represents only half of the market for energy products. If we are to examine the impact of oil price shocks such as those that occurred in the 1970s, we must also know how the consumers of energy respond to exogenous increases in the price of oil. We begin our discussion of energy demand with a question. How important is energy to an economy? Hogan and Manne (1979) examine this question by presenting a metaphor—elephant stew. Suppose a stew consists of one elephant and one rabbit. What will it taste like? The elephant or the rabbit? The elephant is the aggregate economy, and the rabbit is energy used as an input into the production of goods and services. The elephant clearly dominates the stew, but could one bad rabbit spoil the flavor?

To answer this question, we need to know the importance of energy as an input into the economy and the degree to which other inputs can be substituted for it when energy prices rise. We begin with a very simple approach by looking at energy as one homogeneous input and the aggregate production of goods and services in the economy as measured by the gross national product (GNP). This is obviously a big oversimplification, but it illustrates the important point about the need to determine empirical measures of the degree to which the economy can adjust to changes in energy prices. We then discuss more complex models.

The Importance of Energy in the Economy

In the United States in the 1970s, energy represented about 4 percent of total GNP when measured in terms of 1970 prices (Hogan and Manne, 1979). If the price of energy had remained constant in 1970 dollars (and no energy-saving or energy-using technological change had occurred), over time we would expect to see the demand for energy growing roughly at the same rate as GNP, and energy's 4 percent share would be maintained over time. But suppose the real price of energy doubled. What would happen to GNP over time? Let's assume for the moment that the mix of inputs used to produce goods and services remains constant even with the large increase in energy prices. The increase in energy prices will then mean that an additional 4 percent of GNP must be allocated to energy costs, so that GNP would decline by 4 percent. This is not a small number. The GNP of the United States in 1982 was $1,477 billion. A 4 percent decline amounts to a loss of over $59 billion — which means higher unemployment and associated problems. Under this simple calculation, it looks as if the bad rabbit is spoiling the stew.

But the simple story is not accurate. It is most unlikely that the input mix would remain constant with the doubling of energy prices. The only case in which this occurs is if the elasticity of substitution between energy and other factor inputs is zero (see Chapter 6 for more discussion on the elasticity of substitution). What is far more likely is that the mix of factor inputs will change in response to higher energy prices. While in the short run there will be limits to the amount of substitution among inputs that can occur, over time virtually all factors can adjust to the higher energy prices. What is important are the estimates of the degree to which other factor inputs can be substituted for energy and the substitution possibilities *among* different energy sources. Measuring these substitution possibilities is our focus here. First, however, we note how important the elasticity of substitution is in predicting the impact of increases in energy prices on aggregate production in an economy.

We illustrate the importance of input substitution using numbers derived by Hogan and Manne. Their example is in terms of a reduction in the amount of energy consumed.[11] Suppose energy consumption were reduced by 14 or by 50 percent (due, for example, to an embargo on oil or a tax on energy consumption). Table 7.9 shows for different elasticities of substitution (or what is commonly measured empirically, the price elasticities of demand for energy inputs), the percentage reduction in GNP that would occur. The effects of a reduction in energy used is very dependent on the elasticities. If the elasticity of substitution is very low, .1, a 50 percent decline in energy consumption would reduce GNP by over 27 percent. If, however, the elastic-

Table 7.9　PERCENT REDUCTION IN GNP DUE TO A DECLINE IN ENERGY USE AT DIFFERENT VALUES OF THE PRICE ELASTICITY OF DEMAND FOR ENERGY

Percent reduction in energy	Price elasticity of demand/elasticity of substitution				
	0.1	**0.2**	**0.3**	**0.5**	**0.7**
14%	0.6	0.3	0.2	0.1	0.1
50	27.7	9.2	4.3	1.9	1.2

Source: Hogan and Manne (1979).

ity is .7, GNP would fall by 1.2 percent. The numbers for a 14 percent decline in consumption are, of course, much smaller.

The point is simply that we need good estimates of the substitution possibilities between energy and other inputs to analyze changes in energy markets. Unfortunately, there is no agreement among economists and other energy analysts about "the" correct substitution elasticity. In addition, we might be interested in *income* elasticities of demand. Table 7.10 summarizes some of these elasticities, but we will not deal explicitly with their estimation. We concentrate on several studies that present some of the most recent thinking on energy demand.

Table 7.10　ESTIMATES OF THE INCOME ELASTICITY OF DEMAND FOR ENERGY BY TYPE OF FUEL

Energy type	Short run	Long run
Residential demand for electricity		
Range of estimates	0.07 to 2.00	0.12 to 2.20
Mean estimate using average prices	0.08	0.60
Mean estimate using marginal prices	0.16	1.12
Commercial demand for electricity		
Range of estimates	0.10 to 0.72	0.80 to 1.38
Industrial demand for electricity		
Range of estimates	0.06 to 0.87	0.51 to 0.73
Residential and commercial demand for natural gas		
Range of estimates	−0.03 to 0.05	0.07 to 2.18
Mean estimate using average prices	—	1.36
Mean estimate using marginal prices	—	0.09
Demand for gasoline		
Range of estimates	0.16 to 0.58	0.72 to 1.74
Mean estimates	0.39	1.09
Transportation fuels other than gasoline		
Truck fuel		1.74
Bus fuel		0.285
Rail diesel fuel		0.144
Airline jet fuel		1.46
Residential and commercial demand for fuel oil		
Two estimates available	0.50 and 1.26	1.33 and 1.70

Note: All estimates significant at the 0.05 level and represent the results of different econometric studies.

Source: Studies cited in Bohi (1981).

Price Elasticities of Demand for Energy

There are a number of approaches taken to estimate the effect of changes in energy prices on the demand for energy. Some studies look at particular fuels consumed in various markets—for example, the demand for oil by industry or in the transportation sector, or the demand for electricity by households. We will not discuss these microeconomic studies, but simply provide Table 7.11, which summarizes some of the price elasticities of demand by fuel and end use. See Bohi (1981) for a discussion of the issues, methodologies, and conceptual problems involved in estimating energy demand, price, and income elasticities, and an evaluation of many of the studies done in the 1970s.

Other energy demand studies look at more aggregate levels of the economy, treating energy as an individual input used in combination with capital, labor, and materials to produce output. These are frequently referred to as KLEM models, named for the inputs capital *(K),* labor *(L),* energy *(E),* and materials *(M).* We will focus on these aggregate studies.

Most aggregate studies of energy demand specify an aggregate production function to obtain estimates of the price elasticity of demand for the factor inputs. While most of these aggregate production studies are based on static models, a few dynamic models are now appearing. We discuss one such dynamic model here.[12] A dynamic

Table 7.11 SUMMARY OF INFORMATION ON PRICE ELASTICITIES OF DEMAND BY FUEL AND SECTOR

Fuel and sector	Estimates in the literature*		Conclusions about the estimates	
	Short-run†	Long-run*	Short-run†	Long-run‡
Electricity				
Residential	−0.06 to −0.49	−0.45 to −1.89	−0.2	−0.70
Commercial	−0.17 to −0.25	−1.00 to −1.60	Uncertain	Uncertain
Industrial	−0.04 to −0.22	−0.51 to −1.82	Uncertain	Between −0.5 and −1.0
Natural gas				
Residential	−0.03 to −0.40	−0.17 to −1.0	−0.10	0.5
Commercial	−0.03 to −0.40	−0.17 to −1.0	Uncertain	Near −1.0
Industrial	−0.07 to −0.21	−0.45 to −1.5	Uncertain	Uncertain
Electric utilities	−0.06	−1.43	−0.06	Uncertain
Gasoline	−0.11 to −0.41	−0.36 to −0.77	−0.2	−0.7 or more elastic
Fuel oil				
Residential	−0.13 to −0.3	−1.1 to −1.76	Uncertain	Uncertain
Commercial	−0.07 to −0.2	−1.1 to −1.76	Uncertain	Uncertain
Industrial	−0.11 to −0.22	−0.8 to −2.82	Uncertain	Uncertain
Electric utilities	−0.10	−1.50	−0.10	Uncertain
Coal (steam)				
Industrial	−0.10 to −0.49	−0.49 to −2.07	Uncertain	Uncertain
Electric utilities	−0.09 to −0.46	−0.67 to −1.15	−0.09	Uncertain

* Excluding outlying values related to regions or end uses.

† Refers to a response period of one year.

‡ The response period is indefinite, but is generally interpreted to be less than 10 years.

Source: D. Bohi (1981), *Analyzing Demand Behavior, A Study of Energy Elasticities,* Baltimore: Johns Hopkins University Press for Resources for the Future. Copyright, Resources for the Future, Inc.

model measures the full adjustment of all factor inputs to a change in the price of any input (or to changes in aggregate output). A static model does not contain any description of investment (changes in the capital stock over time) and therefore cannot predict fully the economic changes resulting from, say, an energy price shock. Dynamic models are much more complex and many employ fairly restrictive assumptions about investment and production over time. The dynamic work we discuss is that of Pindyck and Rotemberg (1983), hereafter referred to as P-R.

P-R specify and estimate a KLEM model in which firms are assumed to have rational expectations and maximize the expected sum of profits discounted over time. This means that the firms minimize the expected sum of discounted costs, where the cost function is the dual to the production function.[13] The resulting first-order conditions of cost minimization are estimated along with the cost function and equations that represent the share of each input in total costs. The estimated equations describe the production technology and yield estimates of both short-run and long-run elasticities of demand.

The short-run elasticities measure the percent change in the demand for input i given a percent change in the price of input i (the own-price elasticity) or change in the price of input j (the cross-price elasticity). Optimal factor demands over time are computed using simulation. P-R are unable to solve for the optimal paths of factor demands in the full stochastic version of the model. This type of dynamic problem is very difficult (sometimes impossible) to solve. The model solved assumes that firms respond to some known set of values (such as factor prices). Changes in the price of energy are then introduced, and the model is repeatedly re-solved.

The model is applied to data developed by Berndt and Wood (1975) for the total use of capital, labor, energy, and materials for U.S. manufacturing annually for the period 1948–1971. Although the data do not cover the 1970s, when the energy shocks were occurring, Pindyck defends his data set by noting that it has been carefully constructed and corresponds to the data used in other studies of energy demand so that comparisons can be made between the dynamic and static approaches. It would be very interesting to see what would happen to P-R's estimates if the data set were extended to include the entire 1970s.

P-R calculate the price elasticities of demand for the factor inputs for two versions of the model. In the first, three time periods are identified: the short run, where energy and materials can adjust to changes in factor prices; the intermediate run, when labor also adjusts; and the long run, in which all factors adjust. In the second version, labor is also treated as a flexible factor input in the short run, so only two time periods are identified, short and long run.

We report the results for only the first version. The interpretation of the short-run price elasticities is equivalent to their usual meaning in other studies—namely, the percentage change in the demand for that factor, assuming the other fixed factors remain constant. However, the intermediate and long-run elasticities must be interpreted with some care because of the way in which the model is "solved." In computing these elasticities, firms are implicitly assumed to ignore the variance of future prices in responding to price changes. This means that their response to the price changes is best interpreted as a description of the technology.

Table 7.12 reports the computed elasticities for the first version of the model.

Table 7.12 ELASTICITIES FOR MODEL WITH CAPITAL AND LABOR QUASI-FIXED

	Elasticity of Demand			
	E	*M*	*L*	*K*
A. Short-run elasticities (*E* and *M* adjust)				
e	−.3616	.0254		
m	.3616	−.0254		
Q	1.2106	1.2556		
L	−1.3685	−.3774		
K	.4683	−.1375		
B. Intermediate-run elasticities (*L* also adjusts)				
e	−.5791	−.0345	.1589	
m	.1347	−.2614	.6239	
Q	−.1854	.87063	1.0201	
w	1.0713	.2760	−.7892	
K	.4579	−.1403	.0075	
C. Long-run elasticities (*L* and *K* also adjust)				
e	−.9914	.0914	.1521	−.9001
m	1.3064	−.8121	.6535	3.9272
Q	.4905	.6634	1.0312	1.4758
w	1.0256	.3094	−.7836	−.0998
v	−1.3406	.4108	−.0220	−2.9271

Source: Pindyck and Rotemberg (1983).

All the own-price elasticities are negative, as they should be. The own-price elasticity of energy is −.36 in the short run. This is very close to the number obtained by Berndt and Wood (1975). That study used time-series data, so P-R's and Berndt and Wood's results are consistent with the interpretation of time-series data as yielding short-run elasticities. The long-run elasticity is −.99, which is close to the result obtained by Griffin and Gregory (1976), who used a cross-section data set.

The value for the long-run own price elasticity of energy is high relative to a number of the static estimates and almost equal to 1. This means that for each percentage point the price of energy rises, the demand for energy will fall by 1 percent. At the beginning of the oil shock, many analysts assumed that the demand for oil (or energy in general) was very insensitive to changes in its price. P-R's study and the actual response of demand suggests that far more substitution is possible. Energy and capital are complements in the long run, as are capital and labor. Berndt and Wood (1979) also find complementarity between energy and capital, but not between capital and labor.

P-R explain the complementarity as a function of the production structure of their model. However, there is growing acceptance of the capital-energy complementarity. Note as well that capital is very sensitive to changes in its own price, with a long-run elasticity of −2.93, and to changes in output. These numbers are consistent with the changes in investment over the business cycle and also consistent with the possible effects of the second oil shock on investment.

P-R then use their parameter estimates to show how the economy adjusts over time to an unanticipated increase in the price of energy and an unanticipated decline in output. Figures 7.12 and 7.13 illustrate their results. In Figure 7.12, the price of energy increases unexpectedly in year 1 (1971) by 10 percent, and is expected to remain at the higher level thereafter. If all factor inputs were in a steady-state equilibrium in 1971, the figure shows the percentage changes in inputs used over time. Both capital and energy use drop, while labor and material demand rises. This follows from the complementarity of capital and energy and the substitutability between energy and labor and energy and materials. Capital declines more gradually than energy demand because of adjustment costs in capital (a quasi-fixed factor). However, there is substantial disinvestment in the first two to three years.

Energy use can adjust in the short run, thus the large initial drop. By about the seventh year, most of the adjustment has been made. These simulations assume no technological change occurs. It is a distinct possibility that higher prices of energy will induce technological change in the use of both capital and energy. A rise in the energy price may then lead over time to a different time path of capital and energy use.

Figure 7.13 illustrates the effect of an unanticipated recession. Once the recession occurs, however, it has an anticipated and actual duration of two years. Output declines by 5 percent in the base year (1971), then remains at the lower level for two years. At the end of the second year, output returns to its previous level. This is an interesting simulation, as it is similar in spirit to the recession of 1981–1983. There is little decline in the capital stock in this case, due to the expectation that the recession is limited. Net investment, however, declines sharply, as does employment and the use of materials. Energy use falls relatively little because of the limited change in capital stock. Most of the effect of the recession thus falls on labor and materials, as was the case in the recent recession.

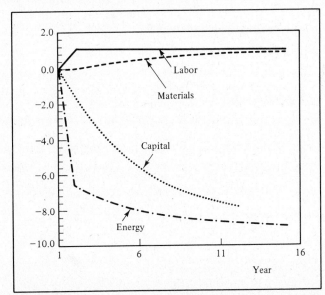

Figure 7.12 A 10 percent unexpected increase in energy prices in year 2 and effects on factor input use over time. *Source:* Pindyck and Rotemberg (1983).

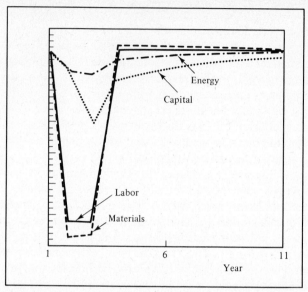

Figure 7.13 A 5 percent unexpected decline in output beginning in year 2 and lasting until year 4, when output returns to its initial level. The duration of the recession is both expected and occurs. Effects on factor-input demands are shown. *Source:* Pindyck and Rotemberg (1983).

P-R's study is interesting because of its dynamic nature and because it reconciles some of the differences in elasticity estimates derived in various studies. However, like all KLEM models, it suffers from a number of difficulties. We list these and direct the reader to Bohi (1981) and Berndt, Morrison, and Watkins (1981) for more detailed discussion of the issues.

1. The model is highly aggregated. Outputs and inputs are aggregated across firms and industries. This may distort a number of sector-specific changes.
2. Technological change (assumed to be Hicks-neutral in P-R's paper) is not modeled explicitly. As noted above, increases in the price of energy may have effects on both the supply of energy products and the way energy is used.
3. The data do not include the periods when actual adjustments to energy price shocks were occurring.
4. Will the estimates of the elasticities change when the additional years of observations are added? Some feel the elasticity estimates are too optimistic. Work by McRae and Webster (1982) finds for the static models some instability in the elasticity estimates when the data after the oil shock are included.

Energy Consumption and Conservation over Time

The Pindyck and Rotemberg model is a sophisticated, dynamic model which predicts that energy demand will be relatively responsive to changes in the price of energy. But the data for which price elasticities were calculated ends in 1971. Is there any evidence that energy demand has responded to the oil price shock, and if so, how? We now briefly report the figures for oil and other energy consumption since the first oil price shock in 1973–74, then provide simple economic rationales for what has occurred. We focus on events in the United States.

Since the oil price shock of 1973–1974, there have been three major trends: a large decrease in oil consumption, a significant decline in the growth rate of total energy consumption, and a shift in the mix of energy fuels used away from nonelectricity energy supplies (oil, gas) to electricity. Let's review what has happened so far and why the process may continue. Refer back to Table 7.1. With the initial price shock, oil demand did not decline significantly until the late 1970s, but then the decreases were large. From 1978 to 1981, for example, world oil consumption fell by almost 25 percent, and oil demanded from OPEC countries fell by almost 40 percent (from 31 million to 19 million barrels per day). In general, it now takes far less energy to produce the economy's goods and services than it did before the oil shocks.

The amount of energy required (measured in BTUs) to produce $1 of GNP was 20 percent less in 1982 than the amount needed to produce that same dollar in 1973. And by most indications, energy's share has continued to decline. Figure 7.14 shows the growth rates of an aggregate measure of energy consumption for the period 1960–1972 versus 1972–1982. The decline in growth rates of energy use is considerable in all sectors. The most significant decline is in the industrial sector, where energy consumption has gone from a positive growth rate of over 3 percent to a negative rate of over 1 percent—a decrease of 4.8 percentage points. In the residential/commercial and transportation sectors, growth has declined from over 4 percent

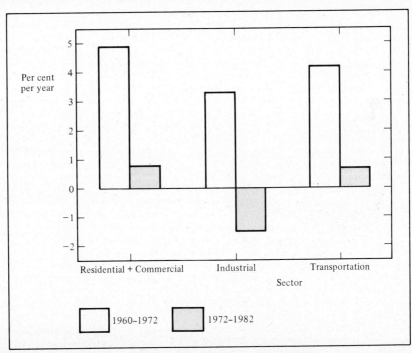

Figure 7.14   Primary energy growth rates. *Source:* Hogan (1983).

to under 1 percent for the same periods. These rates are for the entire period (1972–1982), and if numbers for the late 1970s–early 1980s were examined separately, the decline in consumption would be more dramatic. Figure 7.15 illustrates the shift in the use of energy fuels from nonelectric uses (oil primarily) to electricity. The shares of electricity in aggregate energy consumption have approximately doubled since 1960 in all sectors.

The explanation for these events is a relatively straightforward application of elementary economic theory. The real price of oil rose tremendously in the 1970s. Consumers began reducing energy consumption in general and also began shifting out of oil and into other energy fuels. The relative rise of electricity as an energy fuel can be explained simply by the observation that electricity prices have risen by less (in real terms) than the prices of nonelectric fuels.[14] Reductions in energy consumption and the substitution process take time, because energy is used with durable capital goods. Capital goods take time to wear out, and consumers will not instantly scrap the durable equipment the minute the oil price rises. Automobiles, for example, require gasoline. The stock of cars existing in 1973 was not very fuel efficient; average fuel economy then was 13.1 miles per gallon. By the 1980s, average fuel economy is expected to be over 25 miles per gallon. If the number of miles driven does not change

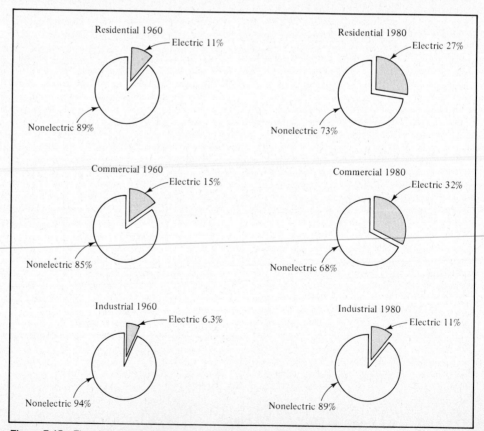

Figure 7.15   Electric and nonelectric energy shares. *Source:* Hogan (1983).

significantly between 1973 and 1985, the increased efficiency in gasoline consumption in the automobile represents a significant decline in oil requirements.

Other uses of oil reflect similar changes. Use of oil for home heating has declined due to the use of more efficient furnaces, greater insulation, and the shift to other energy fuels (electricity and natural gas). Industrial use of oil has declined due to conservation, the development of more efficient energy-using equipment, and the shift to other relatively less expensive and/or more abundant fuels (particularly renewable energy resources). The increase in energy efficiency is just beginning to be felt, with more improvements expected. Innovations on the immediate horizon include windows that capture more solar heat than they lose, refrigerators using one-eighth as much electricity as a standard model, jet airplanes twice as fuel-efficient as the current fleet, moderately priced heat exchangers, and so on (Lovins and Lovins, 1983).

Hogan (1983) argues that we are just beginning to see the readjustments in energy use coming from high oil (and other energy prices). He argues that the entire 1970s and early 1980s was a period of disequilibrium. Energy consumers, given a capital stock with a relatively high energy intensity, were in the process of trying to reduce energy use. In each year, some of the capital stock would be retired due to depreciation, and the new capital installed would typically be far more energy efficient. But the replacement of capital takes time. Suppose, for example, firms use a straight-line depreciation rate for capital of 10 percent per year. It would take until 1983 for all the capital stock to be replaced after the first oil price shock.

Of course, some capital is depreciated in less than 10 years, some in much more. What we are talking about is the process of investment—a complex subject beyond the scope of this book. Many factors, particularly macroeconomic variables such as interest rates, influence investment. The energy price shock had an effect on GNP, employment, interest rates, imports, exports, exchange rates, and so on. The substitution process will continue, and barring any future supply shocks in energy markets, a new equilibrium will be established at a generally lower growth rate of energy consumption.[15] Hogan (1983) argues that the process of adjustment will continue into the next two decades. If so, a relatively optimistic picture emerges from the energy demand side. We now turn to some policy implications of the oil price shock and its aftermath.

ENERGY POLICY AND THE ENERGY CRISIS

Did the large increase in oil prices in the 1970s require the implementation of particular government policies? We examine three interpretations of events in the 1970s and the type of government policies they suggest may be in the public interest. We cannot examine all possible government policies dealing with energy supply and demand, so we concentrate on several that correspond to the different viewpoints about the so-called energy crisis of the 1970s.

The first viewpoint suggests that the real energy crisis is ahead. What will constitute the crisis is the impending physical scarcity of oil, which some forecast as early as the late 1980s. The fear is that alternative energy resources will not be available to meet demand when the oil runs out. That is, private markets will not respond sufficiently over the next decade to bring alternative energy sources to market when needed. Those who promote this viewpoint might advocate policies that encourage exploration for new reserves of oil and gas and promote research and development into provision of alternative energy sources. Policies that encourage conservation of existing energy supplies would also be consistent with this viewpoint. Incentives to use less energy might include higher energy taxes or subsidies for using alternative sources such as solar power. An economic rationale for these measures is that individuals place a higher discount rate on future energy consumption (and GNP) than is socially desirable.

The second viewpoint argues that the crisis is really a national security problem for energy-consuming nations. When countries that are net importers of oil are dependent on politically unstable regions for a substantial proportion of their needs, an energy crisis will occur when the producing countries turn off the taps, as they did in 1973–1974. Policies advocated to deal with this sort of political crisis are somewhat similar to those suggested by the first viewpoint. They would encourage substitution of more abundant sources that are available domestically or from "trustworthy" suppliers. *Energy self-sufficiency* is a term that has been used to describe these policies. An economic rationale for government intervention is that the price of energy supplies from politically unstable regions typically does not incorporate the risk that supply may be cut off. (Stockpiling was discussed in Chapter 6.) Consumption of these risky fuels is then greater than is socially desirable.

The third viewpoint is that the crisis is artificial and due to the monopoly power of OPEC. It is a crisis brought about by market structure, not by physical scarcity. This viewpoint is linked to the second because monopoly power makes sense only if consuming nations are dependent on OPEC supplies. But the policy prescriptions can be different. If monopoly power is the problem, then the desirable policy is to make oil markets more competitive. This may be difficult to do if the consuming countries have no legal jurisdiction over the cartel and if the international oil companies themselves have little say in the determination of OPEC policies. An alternative policy is to insulate consumers from the monopoly price by putting a price ceiling on oil. This policy also is advocated for macroeconomic stabilization. Sudden increases in oil prices have severe impacts on aggregate output, prices, and employment. A price ceiling (or ceiling gradually rising to the world price) allows an economy some "breathing room" in coping with high monopoly prices.

Each of these viewpoints has some merit. In our view, a combination of the three characterized events in the 1970s, and may indeed apply throughout the 1980s. But note how complex this makes policy determination. For example, if one believes that physical scarcity is the most pressing problem, then policies that encourage supply and discourage demand are the logical choice. If, however, monopoly power of OPEC is viewed as the most significant problem, price ceilings seem advisable. But if it turns out that physical scarcity *is* on the horizon or security of supply a concern, price ceilings encourage consumption and may reduce the time to exhaustion of reserves. Before we examine some specific policies, let us summarize our findings from previous sections of this chapter as they relate to the three viewpoints.

After examining the possible activities of OPEC, the effect of rising oil prices on the supply of and demand for energy, what can we now say? First, the energy crisis of the 1970s was not one of actual scarcity of resources. Countries such as the United States had declining production from domestic energy resources prior to 1973 and increasing dependence on OPEC for oil. OPEC oil was in general available at less cost than domestic oil, for a variety of reasons. The declining availability of other energy resources (such as natural gas) was due not to depletion, but to complex domestic regulatory policies (see Chapter 14). Further evidence in support of the contention that no actual scarcity caused the crisis is the increase in reserves of energy resources obtained after the price increases. This does not mean that in the future there will be no shortage of energy resources, but simply that the events in the 1970s cannot be interpreted as due to resource scarcity per se. Thus the second viewpoint, the reliance of the United States and other countries on unstable political regions, does seem to have some merit.

There is debate about whether the crisis was the result of OPEC's cartelization of a substantial portion of the world oil supply or simply a fortuitous (for OPEC) combination of political events and short-run excess demand for oil. If the backward-bending supply curve model of Teece is a better explanation of OPEC's behavior than the wealth-maximizing cartel model, the argument that the crisis was the result of monopoly power has less appeal.

Calling the events of the 1970s a crisis is perhaps too strong a term. Certainly there were adjustments, and even very painful adjustments. It is a good lesson in the economics of the difference between short- and long-run adjustment to an unanticipated change. The short-run effects of the embargo and price increases in oil were to create excess demand for many energy resources. Over time, however, both supply and demand have adjusted. Demand for oil has declined considerably since the first shock, but it has taken time. Supplies of additional energy resources have now come on stream, as have innovations in energy efficiency, but these have also taken time. Thus in the 1970s the events in energy markets may well have appeared to be a crisis — but they were a short-run crisis.

As the first viewpoint suggests, the real crisis may come in the future, when reserves of conventional energy resources such as oil decline more dramatically if development of alternative energy resources does not materialize. There will also be environmental tradeoffs in the continued extraction of existing energy reserves and the development of new ones. Let's turn now to some actual policies that have been used or advocated. Again, we concentrate on oil, but note policies applied to other fuels. In each case, we will briefly describe the policy used or contemplated, then examine its effects on oil production, consumption, imports, and welfare costs.

Price Ceilings

Price ceilings on oil have been used by Canada and the United States and other countries over varying periods of time in the 1970s and 1980s. In the United States, price ceilings on oil produced domestically were introduced by Congress in 1973. The legal apparatus for implementing price ceilings was the 1971 wage and price control package of the Nixon administration. The Emergency Petroleum Allocation Act passed by Congress in 1973 simply extended these controls to domestic supplies of oil. Almost from the start, the price ceilings were seen to have undesirable effects on

U.S. oil markets. Shortages occurred, and the government was faced with the task of designing methods of rationing the available oil. President Ford extended the controls in 1975, and the new legislation introduced more complex regulations (for example, the distinction between the vintage of oil—old oil versus new). It became widely recognized during the Carter administration that price ceilings were not in the nation's interests, and decontrol began in 1979. The decontrol was to be phased in gradually and completed by September 1981.

Meanwhile, the second oil shock hit in 1979, and people were again lining up for gasoline and worrying about the supply of home heating oil. The domestic price of oil in the United States was at this time about half of the world price. Rationing schemes were again contemplated but not needed, as the oil markets began to respond to the high prices of the 1970s—a process we have described in detail. When President Reagan took office in January 1981, he announced immediate decontrol of oil. But by this time the domestic price had reached $32 per barrel, while the world price was about $36. Most of the adjustment had occurred prior to the actual final decontrol. Oil prices peaked in March 1981, and the oil market went from excess demand to excess supply.

The two rationales in support of price ceilings are to prevent macroeconomic destabilization in an economy and to protect consumers from monopoly prices. The macro rationale is complex, and we merely note the basic point.[16] A large increase in oil prices acts as a supply shock to the economy. The aggregate supply of goods and services shifts to the left. This will lead to a decrease in GNP and hence employment, and an increase in the price level. The government is then faced with a policy dilemma. It can introduce countercyclical policies that moderate the effects on output and employment, but these policies may increase inflation and interest rates. A price ceiling on oil moderates the size of the supply shock and the need for other measures. There are difficult questions of what to do over time if the rise in the world oil price is permanent. One approach is simply to control prices, and then gradually allow them to rise to the world price.

The second rationale is to protect consumers from OPEC's monopoly power and redistribute income away from oil producers to oil consumers. High oil prices reduce real incomes of individuals and lower their standard of living. As we have seen, demand for energy will adjust to high prices, but changes in consumption take time and money. In the short run, people are adversely affected. Figure 7.16 illustrates the price ceiling used in the United States and the income transfer from producers to consumers.

The supply curve of OPEC oil is shown as S_F. It is assumed to be very elastic at the prevailing world price of oil, P_W. The supply of oil from the home country, say the United States, is S_H. It is much less elastic due to the smaller reserves of oil and higher costs of extracting additional units of oil over time. Demand for oil by the home country is represented by D_H. In an unregulated market, the price would be P_W and domestic consumption of oil would be equal to Q_T. Of this total, $0Q$ would be supplied from domestic oil producers, and QQ_T would be supplied by imported oil. The producer surplus to domestic producers is the area ABC. A price ceiling on oil produced domestically at P_D will reduce the price paid by consumers of oil from P_W to an average or blended price of oil P_A. The average price is the weighted average of

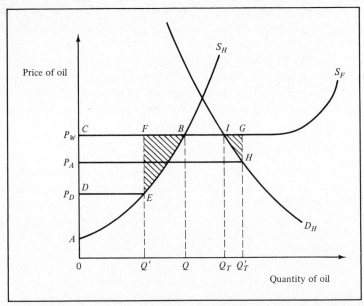

Figure 7.16 Effects of a price ceiling on domestic production of oil. Production of oil from domestic sources will fall from $0Q$ to $0Q'$ with a price ceiling of $0P_D$. Domestic consumption increases from $0Q_T$ when oil prices are set at world levels, P_W, to $0Q'_T$ when consumers face an average price of P_A, which blends imported oil and domestic oil. Imports rise from QQ_T to $Q'Q'_T$. The welfare costs of the ceiling are the areas BEF and GHI representing underproduction of domestic oil and overconsumption of oil, respectively.

the oil consumed from domestic and foreign sources, where the prices P_W and P_D are the weights. At price P_A, oil supplied from domestic producers will now fall from $0Q$ to $0Q'$, while imported oil will rise from QQ_T to $Q'Q'_T$. Producer surplus is reduced by the amount $BCDE$ to ADE, with most of the gain going to consumers. Income is thus transferred to consumers in the form of lower prices per unit of oil consumed.

There are a number of problems with the policy. First, oil consumption rises. If there is any reason to seek conservation of oil supplies and to induce substitution among different energy resources, a price ceiling will be counterproductive. Second, oil production from domestic sources is discouraged; domestic producers no longer receive the world price of oil. There will be less incentive to explore for new reserves and to increase recovery from existing deposits. If we are worried about security of supply, the price ceiling increases dependency on foreign oil and decreases supplies of domestic oil. Shortages will then occur if the supply of imported oil is restricted. Suppose, for illustration, that no imported oil is available. If the price ceiling remains in effect at P_D, excess demand will be equal to $Q'Q'_T$, and nonprice methods of rationing the available domestic supply required. The welfare loss from the price ceiling is shown by the triangles BEF and GHI. The area BEF represents the social loss due to underproduction of domestic oil, while GHI measures the social loss due to overconsumption of oil. Griffin and Steele (1980) estimate the value of these welfare costs at \$1.16 billion for area BEF and \$0.75 billion for GHI for 1977.

If we leave aside the macroeconomic difficulties associated with a supply shock, most economists are critical of the use of price ceilings to redistribute income. The ceilings introduce distortions into a market that interfere with the most efficient use of productive resources. There is no doubt that many people would suffer if oil prices were raised to the world level, but there are alternative means of ensuring that those least able to bear the costs of higher fuel prices would be helped (income transfers, for example). And, as noted above, if the energy crisis partly reflects concerns about future resource availability and security of supply, price ceilings are not a wise choice.

Policies to Reduce Dependence on Oil Supplies

Suppose we seek to reduce our dependence on oil as an energy resource, in part to deal with any impending physical scarcity of oil and to reduce dependence on supplies from politically unstable regions.

A number of policies could be used to encourage greater conservation of energy resources. These include rationing of output, fuel and other energy use taxes, regulations such as temperature controls in public buildings, subsidies (tax credits) for the purchase of energy-efficient appliances and other capital goods, and R&D into ways to use energy more efficiently. A number of these policies have been used over the past 10 years with varying success. However, the Reagan administration has canceled public support for many R&D programs on energy sources other than nuclear energy and has eliminated a number of the conservation measures introduced by the Carter administration (see Hogan, 1984, for additional discussion of these points). The rationale is that private markets can undertake an efficient level of R&D without government intervention. This rationale is disputed by a number of economists who argue that there will be an underinvestment in R&D due in part to the inability to capture the returns from new information that is easily disseminated in the market place. The subsidy to nuclear energy is also a questionable use of public funds, given the disappointing performance of that industry.

Policies to increase domestic energy supplies have been discussed above. Higher oil prices will stimulate exploration for new reserves of oil and gas, alternative fuel sources, and new technologies. As with conservation, there is some argument for government support of R&D for alternative energy sources. Long-term contracts with "friendly" suppliers are a possible policy for small countries. For large countries, it is unlikely that it would be cost-efficient to obtain much oil in this manner. Suppliers writing long-term contracts will seek a premium in the price to insure against price increases. And the supply curve of oil available from "secure" countries is undoubtedly upward-sloping. Thus, the more oil contracted, the higher the price. There is also the risk that world oil prices will fall and the holder of a long-term contract will be committed to purchasing oil at higher prices than available elsewhere. Long-term contracts are a form of insurance and as such might be purchased, as long as the cost of the contract does not exceed the expected loss from insecure supplies. For a country such as the United States, it is unlikely that the expected loss could exceed the price of the long-term contract. Other policies include reserve capacity—paying producers of oil to store their oil in their wells until needed in an emergency—and international sharing agreements among consuming countries. Again, these are unlikely to contribute much oil to U.S. assured supplies due to limitations on the amount of oil available under these policies and/or the high costs of the policies.

A policy currently in place but controversial is the *strategic oil reserve*—a stockpile of oil which is to be stored in salt domes along the Gulf Coast. The U.S. Congress authorized this strategic stockpile in 1975, but the government has been slow to obtain reserves. The authorization was for 1 billion barrels of oil, with a goal of reaching 500 million barrels by 1980—but there was no general agreement on the best way to acquire the reserves. One fear is that if too much oil is purchased over a short interval, the price will rise. By 1982, the stockpile was at about 300 million barrels. Although the Reagan administration does not support the policy on the ground that private markets can accomplish the same task, the current plan is to reach 500 million barrels by 1985 and 750 million barrels by 1989.

A number of theoretical and empirical papers have been written by economists on the concept of a strategic stockpile. See, for example, Nichols and Zeckhauser (1977), and Wright and Williams (1982). While there is no general agreement on the efficacy of a stockpile, a number of economists do feel it is justified because the private market will not supply a socially optimal amount of stored oil due to the presence of a large number of distortions in energy markets. But there are also a number of concerns. The first is just how much the stockpile will cost to obtain and maintain (including the opportunity costs of storage). Estimates range from storage costs of $2.50 to $3.00 per barrel up to $50 to $70 per barrel. It is also unclear whether the salt domes are a secure facility in terms of safety from sabotage, chemical changes in the oil, and the amount of oil that could be recovered. There are also concerns about exactly how the oil would be used in an emergency. So one hesitates to depend on this policy alone to obtain self-sufficiency. It may turn out to be extremely costly to obtain, maintain, and ultimately use. Strategic stockpiles for other minerals have been accumulated and sold off again over time, and it is not clear that their value to society has exceeded their costs.

Finally we come to a policy—which has received much attention by economists and some government officials—a *tariff* on imported oil. There are a number of rationales for a tariff. First, it will discourage consumption of oil, encourage conservation, and stimulate domestic production (and exploration). Second, it will provide revenue to the federal treasury—revenue needed in times of high deficits. Third, a tariff may be able to capture for consuming countries some of the rents from oil producers. A tariff in this case operates like a tax on land. Rents are transferred from the landowner to the government (recall the discussion in Chapter 2). A tariff is not, however, politically popular because it does increase the price of oil to consumers. While no explicit legislation to implement a tariff existed in 1984, various policies are said to be under consideration by the Reagan administration.

Let's examine the allocative effects of a tariff and its welfare costs. Figure 7.17(a) shows the effect of the tariff on domestic production and consumption of oil. S represents the supply of oil produced domestically; D is domestic demand. Suppose that a perfectly elastic supply of oil can be imported at price P_W. The equilibrium price before the tariff is then P_W, $0Q$ is total oil consumed, with $0Q_H$ supplied from domestic producers and $Q_H Q$ imported. A tariff of $$t$ per barrel of oil raises the price of oil to consumers to $P_W + t$. Demand will fall to Q', domestic supply will increase to

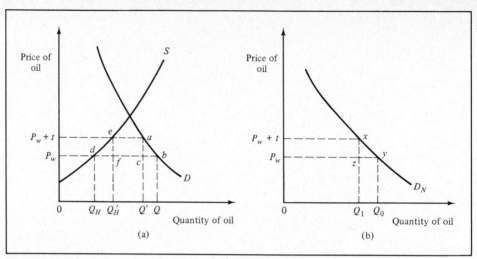

Figure 7.17 The effect of a tariff on imported oil. A tariff of $$t$ per barrel of oil increases oil prices to consumers. Consumption of oil will fall from $0Q$ to $0Q'$. Domestic oil production will rise from $0Q_H$ to $0Q'_H$. The taxing government gains tariff revenues equal to *eacf*. Loss of consumer surplus equals $P_w + tabP_w$. The welfare cost of the tariff is area *abc* plus *def*. In (b), OPEC producers' sales decline from $0Q_0$ to $0Q_1$, with a loss of rents equal to $P_w + txyP_w$.

Q_H', and imports will fall by the amount $Q'Q$ (to $Q_H'Q'$). Consumers are worse off in the short run because they lose consumer surplus equal to $P_wbaP_w + t$. The taxing government gains tax revenues equal to *acfe*. Domestic producers gain the area $P_w + tedP_w$. The welfare costs of the tariff are the areas *def* and *abc*.

OPEC's losses are shown in Figure 7.17(b). Let D_N be the net demand curve for OPEC's oil — that is, total demand less the amount supplied by non-OPEC producers. The tariff increases the price consumers of OPEC oil pay from P_W to $P_W + t$, as in Figure 7.17(a). Demand for OPEC oil falls from Q_0 to Q_1. The loss to OPEC is the area $P_W + txyP_W$, of which the amount $P_w + txzP_w$ is transferred to the government of the taxing country.[17]

The tariff looks like a reasonable policy except for its impact on a consumer's well-being (and possible adverse effects on world trade). Over time, the loss to consumers might, however, diminish if new energy resources are developed in response to the higher prices of oil. The reliance on OPEC is reduced. However, if new energy resources are not developed to replace the declining supply of U.S. reserves of oil, the tariff will simply speed up eventual dependence on OPEC as domestic supplies are depleted more rapidly. Thus, some combination of tariff plus policy to encourage alternative energy supply would seem desirable.

The policy debate over energy is far from over. This discussion has provided some examples of alternative policies, how they might work, and whether or not they are consistent with different viewpoints on what has constituted the energy crisis.

SUMMARY

1. The factors leading to the first oil price shock in 1973–74 include the emergence of OPEC, the shift in world oil markets from excess supply to excess demand, and political unrest in the Middle East. Then there were a fall in real oil prices from 1976 to 1978, the second (unanticipated) oil shock in 1979 – 80 with the Iranian revolution, the world recession of 1981 – 1983, and a subsequent decline in nominal energy prices in 1983.

2. There are two hypotheses about the objectives and actions of OPEC in the 1970s and early 1980s: the wealth-maximizing model and the revenue-target model.

3. In the wealth-maximizing model, OPEC is assumed to act as a dominant firm or unified cartel facing a fringe of competitive suppliers. OPEC sets prices and outputs of its members to maximize the present value of cartel rents over time, given information (and perfect foresight) about reserves, discount rates, costs, and demand. Fringe producers simply take OPEC's prices as given and supply oil to satisfy Hotelling's rule. The simulated price path for the cartel lies above a price path for a perfectly competitive oil market for a long period of time. The gains to cartelizing the oil market — the present value of cartel rents — exceed the present value of competitive rents.

4. The alternative hypothesis is the revenue-target model — the backward-bending supply curve of oil. This model suggests that OPEC members do not maximize the present value of their oil rents, but try to maintain oil revenues consistent with domestic expected government expenditures and investment demands. If oil prices rise, oil revenues rise as well. When the oil revenues exceed the target expenditures, the OPEC member will reduce its oil production, which in turn leads to further price increases. If expenditure targets exceed oil revenues (and investment earnings), production will be increased up to the capacity limit of each producer. Oil prices may then fall, to remain constant until conditions change.

5. A number of observations about OPEC behavior are consistent with this model. These include the lack of evidence that production quotas have been used (these quotas would be needed to ensure cartel stability, but are not required in the revenue-target model) and differences in behavior among OPEC members with different revenue targets (for example, excess oil capacity in countries with low revenue targets).

6. Rising oil prices have effects on non-OPEC energy supplies. But the supply process for a nonrenewable resource is difficult to measure.

7. A number of different energy resources are available: increased reserves of oil and gas, coal, synthetic fuels, nuclear energy, and renewable energy resources.

8. Measuring energy demand and the price elasticity of demand for energy products in the economy can be done by means of a dynamic model that yields estimates of short-run and long-run elasticities.

9. The rationales for government intervention into energy markets and examples of energy policies include creating incentives to substitute from scarce oil supplies to more abundant fuels, ensuring a secure supply of energy resources, and compensating consumers for the noncompetitive behavior of oil producers. The policies considered are a price ceiling on domestically produced oil, various measures to increase energy self-sufficiency (including conservation measures, increased research and development into energy supplies and utilization, and strategic stockpiling), and a tariff on imported oil. The price ceiling redistributes oil rents from producers to consumers but

encourages consumption of oil, discourages domestic production, and increases reliance on foreign oil supplies. The tariff, on the other hand, reduces demand for oil, reduces oil imports, and stimulates domestic oil production, but makes consumers worse off. No single policy is capable of handling all aspects of the energy problem.

DISCUSSION QUESTIONS

1. An economist friend reports that the house he bought has a very large furnace and that in this substituting of capital for fuel oil, he heats his house cheaply. Evaluate this reasoning. What sort of capital is a good substitute for fuel in heating buildings?

2. Retrofitting means altering existing equipment to make it more energy-efficient. North America has reduced energy use in industry per unit of output produced greatly in the 1970s. What are some prime candidates for retrofitting in industry?

3. Derive graphically and explain verbally how a wealth-maximizing cartel such as OPEC would react to:
   a. A decrease in extraction costs of the competitive fringe.
   b. An increase in the reserves of the competitive fringe.
   c. A shift in the demand curve for oil to the left (demand decreases).
   You may want to refer back to the oligopoly models in Chapter 4.

4. Suppose OPEC countries set oil production each year based on their individual revenue targets. Derive the supply curve of oil for a country with a large revenue target. Derive the supply curve of oil for a country with a small revenue target. How will each type of country respond to an:
   a. Increase in the demand for oil.
   b. Decrease in the demand for oil.
   c. Increase in its revenue target.

5. What are the allocative and distributive effects on an oil-consuming country of:
   a. An embargo on oil.
   b. Monopolization of a competitive domestic oil market.
   c. A tariff on imported oil.
   d. A price ceiling on domestically produced oil.
   e. Large purchases of domestic oil for a strategic stockpile.
   f. Subsidization of exploration and development expenditures for domestic oil producers.
   g. Discovery of a technique that makes electricity production from fusion possible and very cheap.
   Treat each case separately. Assume that the oil-consuming country has a positively sloped supply curve for its domestic oil and can import foreign oil at a constant world price (initially).

6. Some observers emphasize that the nuclear power generation industry has not been cost-effective because much of its early very expensive development was funded under government research and development programs. Utility companies have not had to pay these expenses. Is there a role for government in nuclear research, or should private industry fund the research and development? Explain.

NOTES

1. See Griffin and Teece (1982), p. 5, for the market shares of the Seven Sisters, which consist of Exxon (then Esso), British Petroleum, Shell, Gulf, Standard Oil of California, Texaco, and Mobil.

2. This assumption can be interpreted as suggesting that the only constraint on the cartel's pricing is the supply of oil from the competitive fringe. No other form of backstop technology is explicitly introduced. Pindyck assumes that no backstop such as shale oil or oil from tar sands would come into production until the real price exceeds $20 per barrel. In his simulations, the price does not exceed $20 until well into the twenty-first century. Of course in practice, as we note below, many energy resources are currently being substituted for oil in a number of the markets where oil is used (such as natural gas in home heating). Inclusion of prices of substitutes would enrich the model but complicate it due to the need to disaggregate aggregate demand for oil into demand by various markets.

3. Teece refers to investment expenditures in his model, but speaks as well about other government expenditures. Investment can include both domestic investment in infrastructure and local industry or foreign investment. But, as argued above, the amount of foreign investment might be limited. Presumably governments of OPEC countries seek oil revenues not just to meet domestic investment requirements, but also for other forms of government expenditure, including transfer payments. In what follows, we speak of these revenue requirements in terms of investment expenditures, but assume that the expenditures can be broadened to include other categories.

4. The model illustrated is static. An interesting exercise would be to examine a dynamic version of this model when investment and the choice of capacity are made and adjusted over time.

5. This discussion could apply to any energy resource, renewable as well as nonrenewable. For example, the supply curve shown could be for the cultivation of plants that will be turned into ethyl alcohol for combustion. It could even describe the supply curve of solar power, which is unlimited but may still be thought of as upward-sloping because of the capital goods required to convert the sun's rays into useful power.

6. See the paper by Zimmerman (1977) for an empirical estimate of the effect of depletion on the average costs of extracting coal and the implications for public policy.

7. See Gallini (1982) for an interesting discussion of the possible output paths of liquified coal over time under different assumptions about oil prices, environmental regulations, and other factors.

8. Griffin and Steele (1980) list the ways in which nuclear power has been subsidized. These include all R&D expenditures, the cost of enriching uranium, the disposal of radioactive wastes, and insurance to utilities operating nuclear power plants. Even with these subsidies, nuclear power plants cost far more to construct and operate than conventional power plants except at very high and sustained levels of electricity production.

9. See Joskow (1982) and the references therein for a discussion of the issues surrounding the use of nuclear power. See Denton (1983), who is director of the Office of Nuclear Reactor Regulation for the U.S. Nuclear Regulatory Commission, for a somewhat different viewpoint.

10. Fusion is another nuclear energy source that is an appealing idea, but very far from practical application. Formidable technical problems must be solved before fusion can be used to produce electricity. Its appeal is the virtually unlimited supply of one of its key inputs—hydrogen from sea water—and its minimal pollution. Most observers feel we are decades away from any energy production from fusion.

11. Hogan and Manne (1979) analyze the effect of a tax on energy consumption designed to reduce aggregate use of energy (due to conservation objectives, environmental protection, national security, etc.). They examine the effect of such a tax on GNP. It is this portion of their example we use.

12. See Berndt, Morrison, and Watkins (1981) for an evaluation of different dynamic models of energy demand.

13. For any well-behaved production function there is an associated cost function which is the dual to that production function. There are numerous formal economic analyses of duality, but we can grasp the ba... recalling the relationship between profit maximization and cost mi... efficiency conditions arise when a firm maximizes its profits subj... inputs (a budget constraint) as when a firm minimizes its costs su... level of output. The empirical studies of demand typically estima... demand for factor inputs that are obtained from particular ... using the properties associated with duality.

14. We discuss natural gas co... ter 14 when we examine the regulation of this energy res...

15. All this assumes that the rea...

16. For an elementary discussion ... nomic model, see Lipsey, Purvis, and Steiner (1984) f... ...is, Sparks, and Steiner (1983) for the Canadian poli...

17. This is a partial equilibrium a... ...ty effects of a tariff on oil on international trade mo... ...n this subject. Also see Bergstrom (1982) for a mo... ...hich an excise tax can extract oil rents.

chapter 8

The Economics of the Fishery: An Introduction

INTRODUCTION

Fish have long been an important source of food and other products for people and animals. Table 8.1 shows the total U.S. landings and value of fish and shellfish from 1960 to 1980; Table 8.2 provides figures on employment in the fishing industry in the United States from 1960 to 1979. Average annual catches of major fish species from Pacific waters off Canada are given in Table 8.3. As the tables show, quantity, value, and employment in the fishing sector has generally increased over the years. Although in most developed economies commercial fishing industries — the harvesting, processing, and marketing of fish — do not represent a large share of GNP, commercial fishing can be an extremely important source of employment and income in particular regions. Anderson (1982) notes, for example, that in 1980 the fishing industry in the United States contributed $7 billion to GNP, which is less than one-third of 1 percent of the total. But in Alaska, fisheries account for about 13 percent of the total state product. In Canada, about 14 percent of the gross domestic products of Newfoundland and Prince Edward Island originate in commercial fishing and fish processing.

We will be concentrating on commercial fishing, but note that in North America, as well as in many other countries, sport fishing is also an important industry. Sport fishing generates millions of dollars of revenue in industries supporting this form of recreation — boating, hotels, tourism. Indeed, the revenues from sport fishing may exceed those from commercial fishing in many regions.

In less developed countries (LDCs) fishing is typically even more important to the economy than in developed countries. Many fishing industries in LDCs involve individuals fishing on a small scale for personal consumption and limited sales. But

243

Table 8.1   U.S. LANDINGS OF FISH AND SHELLFISH, 1960–1980

Year	Millions of pounds	Millions of dollars (current)	Average price per pound, cents (current $)	Average price per pound, cents (deflated)*
1960	4,942	$ 354	$ 7.15	$10.41
1961	5,187	362	6.98	10.08
1962	5,354	396	7.40	10.49
1963	4,847	377	7.78	10.87
1964	4,541	389	8.57	11.79
1965	4,777	446	9.34	12.57
1966	4,366	472	10.81	14.08
1967	4,055	440	10.85	13.73
1968	4,160	497	11.95	14.47
1969	4,337	527	12.15	14.01
1970	4,917	613	12.47	13.65
1971	5,018	651	12.97	13.49
1972	4,806	748	15.56	15.56
1973	4,858	937	19.28	18.22
1974	4,967	932	18.76	16.30
1975	4,877	977	20.02	15.94
1976	5,388	1,349	25.03	18.92
1977	5,200	1,500	28.85	20.58
1978	6,100	1,900	31.15	20.71
1979	6,300	2,200	34.92	21.37
1980	6,500	2,200	33.85	18.97

* The average price per pound is deflated by the United States Consumer Price Index, 1972 = 100.

Source: For all but deflated values: Department of Commerce, National Marine Fisheries Service, *Fisheries Statistics of the United States,* various issues, as cited in Anderson (1982).

as noted in Panayotou (1982), these small-scale fisheries accounted for about *one-half* the world's marine catch used directly for consumption in 1980, and employed about 10 million fishermen. The policy issues in LDCs may be quite different from those in industrialized countries, but the basic economic models we develop in this section are applicable to both small-scale fisheries in Southeast Asia and larger fisheries in the United States. We will illustrate a number of interesting problems unique to the fishing industry, regardless of size and location.

There are two key issues: First, fish are living creatures, with their own biological "production function." Fish cannot be produced in the same way as a washing machine or a loaf of bread. People can influence, but not completely control, the reproduction and growth of fish populations. Their habitats—lakes, rivers, and oceans—are large areas which typically cannot be farmed in the same manner as agricultural land.[1] To understand commercial fishing industries, one must know about the biological characteristics of fish and their interaction with their habitat. But incorporation of biological characteristics into economic analysis is difficult because there are so many unknowns in the biology and ecology of fish populations. In the beginning, we must abstract from these complexities to build economic models that enable us to examine problems of interest.

The second major issue is the effect common property ownership has on the economics of harvesting a fish population. As noted in Chapter 1, fish are an *open*

Table 8.2 EMPLOYMENT IN FISHERIES INDUSTRIES, 1960–1979

Year	Fishermen	Processing, wholesaling
1960	130,431	93,625
1961	129,693	92,115
1962	126,333	90,993
1963	128,470	87,252
1964	127,875	83,976
1965	128,565	86,864
1966	135,636	88,748
1967	131,752	88,624
1968	127,924	88,742
1969	132,448	84,820
1970	140,538	86,813
1971	140,392	90,771
1972	139,119	91,268
1973	148,884	93,792
1974	161,361	91,118
1975	168,013	92,310
1976	173,610	91,863
1977	—	96,041
1978	—	—
1979	184,000	93,054

Source: *Fisheries Statistics of the United States,* various issues, as cited in Anderson (1982).

access resource. In the absence of regulation, a person is free to harvest as many fish as possible given his or her ability and the costs of fishing. Open access or common property rights give rise to a host of economic problems — overfishing, even extinction of fish species; inefficient use of factor inputs; low returns to fishing industries. These problems have led to extensive regulation of most fishing industries.

In this chapter we will examine and develop economic models of harvesting

Table 8.3 AVERAGE CATCHES OF MAJOR SPECIES OF FISH IN PACIFIC WATERS OF CANADA

Species	Units	Average annual catch
Salmon[a]	Millions of pounds	155
Herring[b]	Thousands of metric tons	54
Halibut[c]	Millions of pounds	8
Other groundfish[d]	Thousands of metric tons	29
Shellfish and others[e]	Millions of pounds	20

[a] Includes commercial, sport, Indian catches, average for years 1971–1980.

[b] Average for years 1971–1980.

[c] Catch by Canadian fishermen only, average for years 1977–1980.

[d] Average for years 1976–1980.

[e] Average for years 1976–1980, includes about 6 million oyster harvest (a mariculture/fanned) product.

Source: Pearse (1982).

fish. This task requires incorporation of biological factors and an analysis of the open access problem. First, we develop the basic biological and economic model of the fishery. We examine issues such as what determines the size of a fish population. Will open access to a fishery lead to an economic equilibrium different from the one reached if private property rights existed? Then we cover a more advanced topic, the dynamics of a fishery — the effects of discounting future harvests and how an equilibrium is reached over time. This section contains somewhat more complex material, and the mathematics may be skimmed in favor of the concepts. The final section provides some examples of when a fish species may be extinguished by harvesting under open access. Our discussion of fishing continues in Chapters 9 and 10: Regulation of fishing industries is the topic of Chapter 9, and Chapter 10 presents some specialized topics in fisheries, extensions of the simple models presented in this chapter.

A MODEL OF THE FISHERY

A *fishery* consists of a number of different activities and characteristics associated with fishing, including the types of fish to be harvested and the types of vessels and gear used. There may be many species of fish being harvested by a variety of different vessels. Vessels may be able to switch easily among different types of fish or not. To simplify our analysis, we assume that a fishery is a particular region where one type of fish, crustacean, mollusk, or sea mammal, is harvested by homogeneous vessels all originating from a particular port. In Chapter 10 we will look at more complex fisheries, where interdependent species are harvested.

There are many different types of marine animals — lobsters, salmon, halibut, whale, flounder, bluefin tuna. We will henceforth refer to all marine animals as "fish" regardless of whether they are fish, mammals, or mollusks. Biologists differentiate between two major classes of fish. *Demersal* or groundfish are those that feed on ocean or lake bottoms and typically do not range over a wide area, such as lobster, crab, flounder, and cod. *Pelagic* species are the tourists — free-swimming fish that can migrate over a wide area in the ocean. Commercial pelagic species include tuna, herring, and sea mammals such as whales.

The distinction between demersal and pelagic fish is important not only when discussing fishing techniques, but also because property rights for the different species can be quite different. Demersal fisheries, because of their relatively fixed location, are frequently more amenable to the imposition of private property rights than the pelagic fisheries. It may be possible to assign private property rights to species such as salmon, which migrate from salt to fresh water, during the period they are in fresh water, but not when they are in the oceans.

Because there are so many differences among fish that can affect the optimal economic harvest of each species, we will confine ourselves here to an abstract model so that fundamental points common to all fisheries can be studied. Some of the complexities — for example, the age distribution of the fish — will be discussed in Chapter 10.

Fish are not minerals; they are living creatures that reproduce, grow, and die. This is what we mean by a *renewable* resource. There may be a limit to the number of fish that can be supported in a particular habitat at any point in time, but harvesting a fish and removing it from the population does not mean that the total stock of fish at the next instant in time will necessarily be smaller.

But as with nonrenewable resources, it is important to distinguish between stocks and flows in the fishery. The *stock* or population of fish is either the number of fish or the *biomass,* the aggregate weight of the fish population measured at a point in time. There will be a number of fish of different ages, sizes, and weight represented in this biomass, but we do not distinguish among individual members of the stock. The *flow* is the change in the stock over an interval of time, where the change results from biological factors, such as the entry of new fish into the population through birth (called recruitment), growth of existing members of the population, and natural death, and economic factors, such as harvesting the species. Here is the difference between fish and nonrenewable resources: The stock of fish can be changing over time even if *no harvesting* takes place. The stock will grow in number and/or weight as new fish are born and existing fish increase in size. The stock will diminish as fish die naturally or are removed by predators, including humans.

Before examining these concepts in a simple model of the fishery, we reemphasize one important similarity between renewable and nonrenewable resources noted in Chapter 1. Renewable resources can be fully exhausted or extinguished. If too many fish are harvested over some time period and their ability to reproduce is reduced, the stock may decline over time. When, for example, many females are harvested before they have a chance to lay eggs, the population falls. If harvesting is so great as to prevent *any* new births over time, the species will become extinct.

Large harvests of blue whales (relative to their population) up until the 1960s drove them almost to extinction simply because there were so few whales that they had difficulty locating one another and reproducing. Their continued survival is still in doubt. We examine the conditions under which extinction can occur later in this chapter.

The model presented below will illustrate four important concepts:

1. The simple biological dynamics of a fishery
2. How harvesting affects the population
3. How conditions of open access affect the harvest and the fish population
4. The socially optimal harvest and the open access harvest

Fishery Populations: Biological Mechanics

Suppose we are examining a lobster fishery along the Maine coast. We have consulted a biologist about the reproductive and growth characteristics of the lobster. The biologist estimates that the region is capable of supporting a maximum of 30 million pounds of lobster each year. If the population begins to exceed that number, the lobsters will have to compete with one another (and other species) for scarce food supplies, and their numbers will decline. If no harvesting takes place in this fishery, we would expect to find approximately 30 million pounds of lobster residing off the coast at each point in time.

But we want to know more. We also need information about the growth of the species. For most fish species, including crustaceans such as lobsters, we typically assume that the growth rate of the stock taken as a whole depends on its size — the population or its biomass. This is a simplifying assumption, but it characterizes many species, especially demersal fish.[2] With small populations births will tend to out-number deaths because of the large food supply. But as the biomass or stock size increases, deaths will begin to rise as food per creature diminishes. The growth rate will decline. The stock may ultimately get so large that deaths will equal births, and the growth rate will fall to zero. We can summarize all this information graphically and mathematically.

Let $X(t)$ be the stock of fish at time t, which throughout this and the next chapter we measure as the biomass. How will this stock grow or change over time? Let $dX(t)/dt$ denote the change in the stock over a short interval of time, t.[3] In the algebra that follows, for simplicity we will suppress the dependence of all variables on time. Let Equation (8.1) describe the instantaneous growth of our lobsters before any harvesting occurs.

$$dX/dt = F(X) \qquad (8.1)$$

$F(X)$ is the instantaneous rate of growth in the biomass of the fish population in question. It can also be thought of as a biological production function for the fishery, or the biological mechanics. It indicates for each stock or biomass X the net increase over a small instant of time in the natural size of the population. This net natural growth (or relative rate of surplus growth, from Hannesson, 1978) is due to increases in the biomass — new fish entering the stock through birth, physical growth of the fish existing in the stock at each time t, minus decreases in the population through natural mortality. For a hypothetical population of identical members, it is number of births less number of deaths.

$F(X)$ is often represented with the logistic function, which yields a parabola when $F(X)$ is plotted against X starting from a stock size of zero. The logistic function is illustrated in Figure 8.1 and can be represented mathematically by:

$$F(X) = rX(1 - X/k) \qquad (8.2)$$

In Equation (8.2), r represents the intrinsic instantaneous growth rate of the biomass, and is equal to the rate of growth of the stock X when this stock is close to zero, while k is the *carrying capacity* of the habitat. We can think of k as the maxi-mum population or biomass the habitat can support. We assume r and k are parame-ters (fixed values) given to us by fisheries biologists. Although k is assumed to be fixed for our model, in more general models it would be sensitive to stochastic variables determined by a number of environmental factors, such as epidemic disease, oil spills, water temperature, and the presence of predators. Equation (8.2), then, reflects our earlier intuitive explanation.

Starting at a small but positive stock, the biomass will at first grow rapidly. Growth will reach a maximum, then decline until the biomass reaches its maximum carrying capacity. Notice that the net growth in the population can be identical at different levels of the stock. In Figure 8.1, we can see that a net growth rate of $F_1(X)$ can be obtained with a small population X_1 or a large population X_2. Intuitively what is happening is as follows: At X_1, births greatly outnumber deaths because the popula-

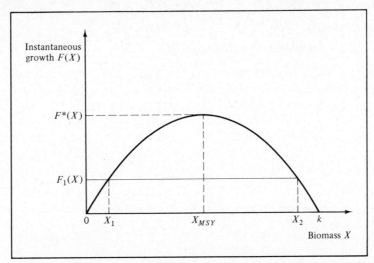

Figure 8.1 Each point on the growth curve represents a sustainable yield of fish for a given stock of fish, X. The point k is the equilibrium stock size that is reached without any human predation and is called the carrying capacity of the habitat. The point X_{MSY} is the stock size which corresponds to the maximum sustainable yield from the fishery. If the population were reduced to this level, the fish stock would grow at its maximum potential yield, $F^*(X)$.

tion is small and food is ample. The stock is small, though net births over deaths can be a large proportion of this stock. At X_2, births slightly outnumber deaths, and the average size of the population is large.

Using Figure 8.1, we can find a biological equilibrium for the species. We define a *biological equilibrium* as the value of the fish stock X for which there is no growth in the fish population or biomass—that is, the flow, $dX/dt = F(X)$, is equal to zero. Simply by examining Figure 8.1, we can see that there are two possible values of X for which there is no growth of the biomass. If X is equal to zero, there are no fish and therefore no growth. The more interesting equilibrium is where the growth curve crosses the X axis at the point we have labeled k. As noted in Equation (8.2), k is the carrying capacity of the habitat. The species will therefore be in a biological equilibrium whenever $X = k$. To see mathematically why this is so, simply set $F(X)$ equal to zero in Equation (8.2) and solve for X. The notion of a biological equilibrium will be a reference point for our simple model with a homogeneous biomass comprising a single species. We will now add harvesting to the model, assuming the fish population begins in a biological equilibrium at point k. The objective is to find a new equilibrium for the fishery.

BOX 8.1
Logistic Growth of Species

The logistic growth curve captures the familiar S-shaped growth of individuals and numbers in a group. Growth is slow at the outset, with a few members of a group in existence, speeds up for an interval, and slows down at a "saturation level." The saturation level is referred to by ecologists as the *carrying capacity* of the environment. Growth is less than exponential (the biotic potential) because of *environmental resistance.* See the lower portion of Figure B8.1. Our familiar stock-yield curve in the upper part of the figure has equation

$$\frac{dx}{dt} = rx\left(1 - \frac{x}{k}\right)$$

where k is the carrying capacity, r is the *intrinsic rate of increase,* and dx/dt is the instantaneous rate of growth corresponding to stock size x. If we integrate this equation, we get the logistic growth equation

$$x(t) = \frac{k}{1 + ce} - rt$$

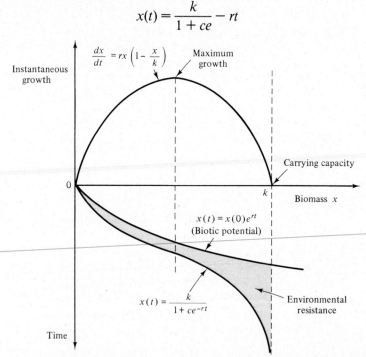

Figure B8.1 Relationship among schedules of stock-yield (the inverted bowl) logistic growth (the S-shaped curve) and biotic potential (explosive growth). The carrying capacity introduces a crowding or saturation element which constrains exponential growth from persisting beyond the very early stages of the growth in numbers of a species. ($C = (k - x_0)/x_0$). Note we have drawn the logistic growth curve for the initial population x_0 near 0. We could have made x_0 large and plotted a schedule of stock decline using our basic logistic equation.)

Table 1 SOME INTRINSIC RATES OF INCREASE

Species and environmental conditions	Intrinsic rate of increase (r) per female per year	Size of population after one year starting with a pair (2e)
Insects		
Sitophilus oryzae at 29°C	39.6	3.16×10^{17}
Sitophilus oryzae at 23°C	22.4	10.68×10^{9}
Sitophilus oryzae at 33.5°C	6.2	996
Tribolium castaneum at 28.5°C and 65% humidity	36.8	19.20×10^{15}
Mammals		
Microtus agrestis	4.5	180
Rattus novegicus	5.4	442
Man	0.0055	2.011

Source: Roger Dajoz, *Introduction to Ecology,* trans. A. South. London: Hodder and Stoughton, 1977, p. 180.

where $c = (k - x_0)/x_0$, which is the S-shaped schedule of stock size plotted against time in the bottom part of the figure. In the absence of a "saturation" or "negative feedback" from crowding or environmental resistence, the stock would grow exponentially at rate r along the line labeled biotic potential. Thus the logistic equation combines in a subtle way exponential growth constrained by crowding effects induced by the carrying capacity being approached.

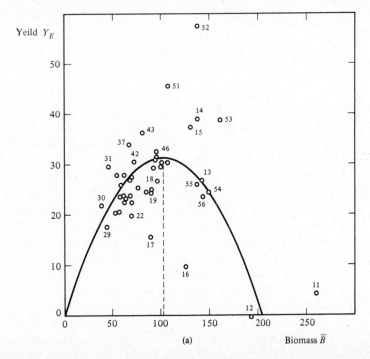

(a)

Box 8.1 continued

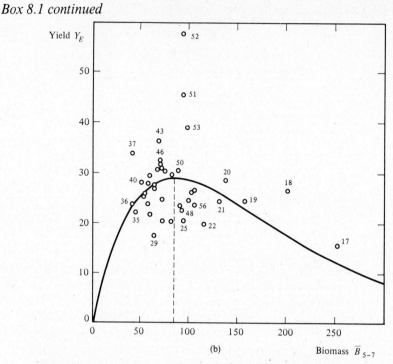

Figure B8.2 Two fitted yield-biomass (stock) schedules for data on the Pacific halibut, years 1910–1957. In (a), we have yield plotted against current mean biomass whereas in (b), we have yield plotted against the mean biomass 5–7 years earlier. (*Source:* W. E. Ricker (1975), *Computation and Interpretation of Biological Statistics of Fish Populations,* Bulletin 191, Ottawa: Environment Canada, Fisheries and Marine Service, Figure 13.2, p. 324.)

In Table 1 we have the intrinsic growth rates of two types of insects (one breeding at three different temperatures) and three mammals. We also indicate the size the populations would grow to starting with two individuals in one year. In Figure B8.2, two yield-biomass schedules are presented for Pacific halibut.

The Bionomic Equilibrium in a Simple Model

So far, we have not introduced any economic decision-making into the model. We will now examine the role played by the economic activity of harvesting. We first assume that harvesting is a costless activity. We do not yet worry about how harvest rates are chosen; no discounting of harvests that occur in the future is made. We use this simple case to develop some important concepts that connect biological and economic factors. We derive what has been called a *bionomic equilibrium*—an equilibrium that combines the biological mechanics with economic activity. In Figure 8.2, three rates of harvest are shown. We will see how different harvesting rates will affect the fish population, given the biological mechanics postulated above.

The three different rates of aggregate harvest for an instant in time are shown in

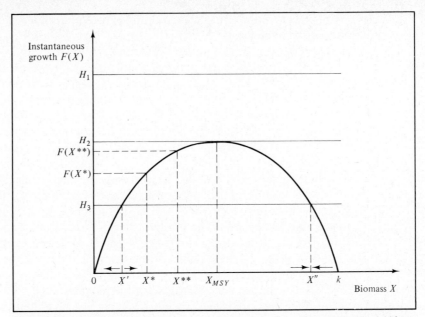

Figure 8.2 The effect of three different annual harvest rates on the sustainable yield from the fishery are shown. A harvest of H_1 will extinguish the fishery because H_1 is everywhere larger than the growth rate of the fish stock, $F(X)$. A harvest of H_2 leads to the maximum sustainable yield from the fishery. A harvest of H_3 results in two equilibriums, X' and X'', but only X'' is a stable equilibrium. This means that for any stock of fish to the right of X' if the harvest is H_3, the stock will reach X''. For any stock size to the left of X' given H_3, the species will be extinguished.

Figure 8.2 as H_1, H_2, and H_3. Assume the lobsters are in a biological equilibrium at k. Consider catch or harvest levels of H_1 and H_2 pounds. As drawn, H_1 represents a level of harvest that lies everywhere *above* the biological growth function, $F(X)$. What this means is that more lobsters are removed at each point in time than are being reproduced. It should be obvious that no fish population can survive for long if more are harvested than are replaced by new births and growth of existing members of the population. The fish population will therefore decline to zero if this level of harvest is maintained season after season. This is an extreme example of *mining* the fishery — driving it to extinction.

Suppose now that the instantaneous rate of harvest is H_2. We can see that H_2 touches the growth function $F(X)$ at its maximum point. X_{MSY} is the maximum sustainable yield from the population, the point where the "net growth" or surplus growth is at a maximum. Given our logistic biological production function, we see that the MSY occurs at exactly one-half the carrying capacity, k. If the population is initially at point k, then $dX/dt = 0$. In the next instant, if H_2 pounds of lobster are harvested and these levels of harvest are maintained, the stock will gradually fall to $k/2$, which is X_{MSY}. The remaining biomass of lobsters will grow at the maximum rate because food and space are more ample than at k.

At the MSY stock, the largest *sustainable* harvest can occur. That is, the process of catching H_2 pounds of lobster per unit of time can continue indefinitely (as long as no other exogenous changes occur). In a very simple economic model, in particular one with no harvesting costs or discounting of future revenue from fishing, the MSY is the most desirable equilibrium for the fishery. This equilibrium generally is not an economic optimum, as we will see. Note finally that if the initial population were to the left of X_{MSY} initially, a harvest of H_2 would deplete the stock. If, for example, the stock were X^* when harvesting began at rate H_2, net growth would be less than the harvest. The population must then decline, because the population of X^* *cannot be sustained* at a harvest rate of H_2: The harvest exceeds the incremental growth of the biomass given by $F(X^*)$. In the next instant if H_2 is again harvested, the stock will decline further. If harvesting continues at rate H_2, the population would eventually be depleted.

A harvest set at H_3 pounds per season is an interesting case. There are two possible equilibriums for the fishery, the two points at which H_3 intersects the fishery production function, $F(X)$, at X' and X''. Which one is likely to occur? Suppose harvesting has just begun in the lobster fishery. We are thus at point k, the habitat's carrying capacity. If the stock is initially at k and H_3 is taken at each point in time, the equilibrium point, X'', will be approached from the right. If H_3 is taken, then as the diagram shows, H_3 exceeds $F(X) = 0$ at k, and the population declines. That is, the harvest exceeds the net natural growth of the biomass.

But once the population reaches X'', there will be no tendency to move from this point because the natural growth rate exactly equals the harvest. The fishery will yield H_3 pounds of lobster each instant, while the stock size will remain at X''. This is another example of a *sustained yield* harvest; sustained, because H_3 can be removed at each point in time and the lobsters will remain at a population of X'' (Recall that the harvest of H_2 yielding X_{MSY} was the *maximum* sustained yield. The point X'' is simply a particular sustained yield, not the maximum). The difference $(k - X'')$ is the reduction in the stock of lobsters from their biological equilibrium at k.

Now suppose that when harvesting begins, the stock is not at level k, but somewhere between X' and X''. What will the equilibrium be? Suppose, for example, the stock is at the level X^*. The rate of harvest H_3 is now less than the natural growth in biomass at X^*, which is shown in Figure 8.2 as $F(X^*)$. The species will grow in size in the instant by the difference between $F(X^*)$ and H_3. At the beginning of the next instant, the additional lobsters will increase the stock from X^* to X^{**}, where $(X^{**} - X^*)$ is equal to $[F(X^*) - H_3]$. At X^{**}, the harvest rate of H_3 is again less than the biological growth, $F(X^{**})$, and again the stock will increase in size. This process continues until the equilibrium at X'' is reached. Thus any stock size that lies to the right of X' will ultimately yield an equilibrium at X''.

We call X'' a *stable* equilibrium. This means that if there is a slight movement in the stock size to the right or to the left of X'', the system will ultimately return to an equilibrium at X''. This is what we have just shown by seeing how the system behaves when the population is to the right or the left of X''. The arrows in Figure 8.2 toward X'' show that it is a stable equilibrium.

Suppose now that the population lies to the left of X'. This could be due, for example, to a toxic chemical spill that has wiped out much of the lobster population, or abnormally warm water temperatures that have interfered with their ability to spawn. If harvesting continues at rate H_3 per year, we can see that the species will be extinguished. The natural growth rate to the left of X' lies everywhere below H_3. Each period, fewer and fewer new lobsters enter the population because existing ones are captured before they get a chance to reproduce. Eventually all lobsters will be caught, and the fishery will cease to function.

Finally, what would happen at point X'? If the stock just happens to be X', given the rate of harvest H_3, this will be an equilibrium, but one which is *unstable* because a slight movement of the stock to the right or to the left of level X' will lead to a new equilibrium. If there is a slight increase in the stock, the equilibrium will eventually reach X''. If there is a slight decrease in the stock, the equilibrium will eventually fall to zero. To illustrate that X' is unstable, the arrows are directed away from it in Figure 8.2.

We can summarize the effects that harvesting has on the fish population over time in the following equation:

$$dX/dt = F(X) - H(t) \tag{8.3}$$

Equation (8.3) says that the change in the fish stock over a small interval of time will be given by the difference between the biological growth function and the amount of harvesting in that time interval. This equation can be solved for an equilibrium in which the fish stock does not change — that is, its growth rate is equal to the rate of harvest. This is called a *steady-state bionomic equilibrium.* If we are given a harvest rate, say H_2 from Figure 8.2, the steady-state equilibrium will occur where $F(X)$ is equal to H_2. Thus, dX/dt will equal zero. Only when the growth of the stock is exactly equal to the harvest will there be no change in the size of the stock over time. In Figure 8.2, we saw that H_2 intersected $F(X)$ at the population level X_{MSY}. This is the steady-state maximum sustainable yield, a bionomic equilibrium.

Harvesting under Open Access

In the discussion above we arbitrarily picked three harvest rates to illustrate the principle of a steady-state equilibrium in the fishery when economic and biological factors interact. Each equilibrium derived above is a bionomic equilibrium. No assumption was made about the economic nature of the fishing industry or about how the harvest rate was chosen. Now we will derive the bionomic equilibrium when there is *open access* to the fishery, and then contrast the common property equilibrium with a socially optimal equilibrium. We continue to assume no discounting of the value of future harvests.

We first define a *harvest function* for the industry. We assume that the industry is perfectly competitive and each firm in the industry takes all prices, including factor prices, as given and constant over time. These assumptions mean that the demand curve for fish facing each firm is perfectly elastic, as is the supply curve of factor inputs. These simplifying assumptions can be modified readily, and we'll do so in later sections.

As before, let $H(t)$ indicate the level of harvest at time t. This is the output of an aggregate production function which we will call a harvest function. We assume that $H(t)$ depends on two inputs: $E(t)$ and $X(t)$. Mathematically,

$$H(t) = G[E(t), X(t)] \tag{8.4}$$

E is a variable known as *fishing effort*. Effort can be thought of as some combination of the familiar inputs in economics—capital, labor, materials, and energy. These inputs are combined to yield an aggregate measure of effort—for example, man-hours per trawler over 50 feet in length, or seiner nets per person per trawler. In other words, effort is an *index* of factor inputs. Continuing our example of the lobster fishery, here industry effort will be measured by the total number of lobster traps set.

The other factor input in the production function is the stock of fish at time t, $X(t)$. The harvest function is dependent on the stock of fish for the obvious reason that no fish can be caught if none exist, and that more fish will be caught with a given level of effort, the more there are or the larger the stock in the region.

We can look at the interaction between E and X graphically in two ways. First, we can consider how the harvest changes when more effort is added to a fixed stock of fish. Then we can see how the harvest changes when we increase the stock of fish, keeping effort constant. Figure 8.3 shows a simple example. Suppose the stock of fish equals X. The harvest function is the curve $H = G(E,X)$. As more lobster traps are added to this fixed stock the harvest will rise, but at an ever-decreasing rate. This is the well-known principle in economics of the *diminishing marginal product* of the variable factor (effort in this case) that is combined with a fixed factor (the stock of fish). The fixed stock of fish should be interpreted as a steady-state fish population discussed in the previous section—that is, one that can be sustained indefinitely at a particular level.

Now suppose the stock of fish is higher than X, say X'. At the higher stock, there will be a greater harvest for each unit of effort utilized.[4] This is shown in Figure 8.3 by the curve $H' = G(E,X')$. For a given level of effort, say E_0, H fish will be caught when the stock is X, and H' will be caught if the stock is X'. The marginal product of effort

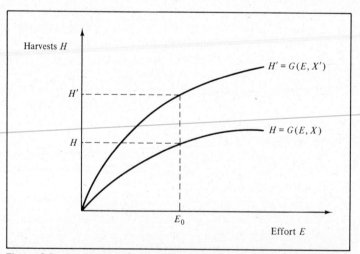

Figure 8.3 Two harvest functions for the fishery are shown assuming the stock of fish is held constant. The biomass caught depends on the amount of effort E and the fish stock X. If the stock of fish is assumed first to be X, the curve H shows the possible harvests as E increases. If we then have a larger fish stock X', the harvests as E rises are shown by H' which lies above H. This means that for a particular amount of effort, say E_0, more fish can be caught, the larger the stock available.

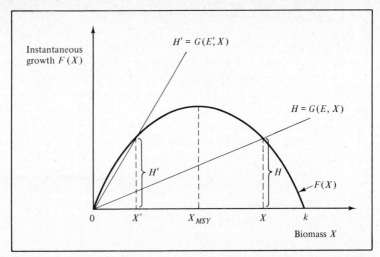

Figure 8.4 Steady-state harvests for given levels of effort as a function of the fish stock are shown. If effort is increased from E to E', the steady-state population falls from X to X', but the catch stays the same (H equals H'). Effort levels which give rise to a harvest function that intersects the biological production function to the left of X_{MSY} are inefficient in this model because the same harvest can be obtained with much less effort.

thus slopes downward given a particular fish stock, with slightly more effort resulting in proportionately smaller harvests. This concept will be useful in defining the equilibrium reached under open access to the fishery, and we will come back to it below.

Let us now see how a fixed level of effort combined with different stocks of fish affects the harvest. We can now determine the steady-state bionomic equilibrium. Figure 8.4 illustrates some possible cases. Suppose we take a given level of effort, E. The harvest will then be an increasing function of the fish stock. We assume for simplicity that this harvest function is linear. A particular amount of fishing effort will yield a larger harvest, the larger is the population of fish. The steady-state equilibrium will be, as before, where there is no change in the fish population, $dX/dt = 0$. This requires that $F(X) = H(t)$. Graphically, the equilibrium is defined where the harvest function, H, intersects the $F(X)$ function. The steady-state equilibrium is at a stock level of X, which yields a harvest of H. So far, the results are quite similar to those above. But now see what happens when we increase the amount of effort, say, by increasing the number of lobster traps set from E to E'.

The increase in the number of traps set causes the harvest function H to pivot upward to H'. Now the new harvest function intersects the biological growth function at a fish stock of X', which yields a steady-state harvest *exactly the same* as the harvest with only E traps. However, the fish stock, X', is *much lower* than the stock X. These results reflect the interaction of biological mechanics and economics. We will explain first intuitively then more formally what is happening in this case.

Suppose the fishery starts in a biological equilibrium at k. There is no harvesting. Now some fishing firms enter, and traps are set. (We will discuss what determines entry of fishing firms more formally below). We are at a point such as X with harvests at H. Now more firms enter, and more traps are set. The harvest function pivots upward, and for a while more effort yields greater harvests. But notice that these increased harvests will decrease the stock of fish. Because of the shape of the biological function, harvests will increase until the steady-state equilibrium is where the stock of fish is at its maximum sustainable yield (imagine the intersection of a harvest curve at the top of the $F(X)$ function). Further increases in effort will pivot the harvest function until its intersection with the biological growth function is *to the left* of the MSY. The catch thereafter declines. As more fish are caught, the stock size falls, and it becomes more difficult to catch those remaining. The catch per unit of effort thus falls, and the total catch may decline for an effort level greater than E'.

Another way to look at the result is that if the stock size were larger, less effort would be required to catch the same number of fish (compare E to E'). *It is clearly inefficient from an economic viewpoint for a fishing industry to operate to the left of the MSY stock level in this model because more effort than necessary is used to catch a given amount of fish.* The important question is whether an equilibrium would exist in this model to the left of the MSY biomass. We will see under what circumstances such an equilibrium would occur when there is open access to the fishery.

Suppose lobsters are an open access or common property resource: No one has exclusive rights to harvest a particular quantity of lobsters or owns a stock of lobsters thought to reside on a particular section of the ocean bed. Anyone with a boat and lobster traps can attempt to capture lobsters. First, let's define the total revenues and total costs for the industry, and then see what determines industry equilibrium.

Suppose the unit cost of harvesting lobsters is constant. It costs c dollars per unit of effort, where as before we measure effort by the number of traps set. In Figure 8.5, total costs are shown by the curve TC, which is linear with slope c (ignore for now the total cost curve TC'). Total revenues are given by the price of lobsters per pound times the number of pounds harvested *(PH)*. Let the price per pound be constant, and set equal to 1. This normalization of the price allows us to determine the steady-state harvest and stock of lobsters in an open access equilibrium as well as the equilibrium level of effort. Total revenue *(TR)* will simply be the harvest determined by Equation (8.4).

Refer back to Figure 8.4. Suppose we start at a biomass of $X = k$, with zero pounds of lobster harvested. As effort is introduced, the stock of lobsters falls. Harvests at first rise as the industry moves up the biological production function. They reach a maximum, then fall again. The total revenue curve with $P = 1$ is thus *exactly the same* as the biological production function, $F(X)$. This means that once we know the equilibrium level of total revenue, we know the equilibrium harvests. Given the harvests, we can determine the steady-state stock that sustains these harvests.

The open access or common property equilibrium for the lobster industry will be determined where total revenues equal total costs. For which stock is this so? Consider a level of effort such as E' in Figure 8.5(a). At E', total revenues exceed total costs, and excess profits or rents exist. Because there are no barriers to entry — no one in the fishery can exclude another from setting traps — firms will enter the fishery. Effort will enter or rise. Entry will continue as long as total revenues exceed total costs and rents exist. When $TR = TC$ at point A in Figure 8.5(a), rents to the fishery equal zero, and economically rational firms will expend no effort beyond this point. No new effort will come in to the fishery. The common property equilibrium for the fishery will employ E^0 units of effort.[5]

Another way to look at the common property equilibrium is shown in Figure

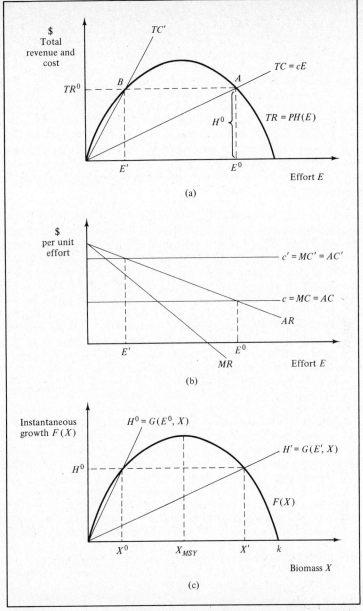

Figure 8.5 A common property equilibrium for a fishing industry occurs where $TR = TC$. Note in (a) and (b) that all curves are functions of effort (not harvest). If unit costs equal c, the equilibrium is at point A in (a). E^0 units of effort will be used, yielding a total revenue of TR^0. If the price of lobsters is normalized to 1, the total revenue is also the total harvest. (b) illustrates that the common property equilibrium is where the average revenues (as a function of effort) equal the marginal cost of effort and thus that marginal cost of effort exceeds marginal revenue. (c) illustrates the steady-state harvest in a common property equilibrium, H^0, that results in a steady-state stock or biomass of X^0. If unit costs rise to c', the common property equilibrium is at a point B in (a), with E' effort. This new equilibrium also yields a steady-state harvest of H^0, but with less total effort than when average costs $= c$. The sustained stock (c) is then X'. A common property equilibrium is economically inefficient because $MC > MR$. It can also be biologically inefficient if the equilibrium is to the left of the MSY stock.

8.5(b). Here, we derive the industry's average revenue *(AR)* and marginal revenue *(MR)* curves as a function of effort from total revenues *(AR* is *TR/E,* while *MR* is *dTR/dE*). As explained before, both *AR* and *MR* are negatively sloped, with *AR* lying above *MR.* The open access fishery will be in equilibrium when *AR* equal *MC.* With constant unit costs, *MC* simply equals *c* (and is thus also equal to *AC*). Notice that at the equilibrium level of effort, E^0, *MR* is less than *MC* and is negative. In the open access equilibrium, *MR* will always be less than *MC* and may be negative.

What is the common property harvest? With our assumption that $P = 1$, we can see in Figure 8.5(a) that harvests are given by TR^0, which equals a harvest of H^0. We now look at Figure 8.5(c), which illustrates sustained harvests at different stocks of lobsters. Measuring H^0 vertically, we find that H^0 in biomass can be taken at each unit of time at two different stock levels, X^0 and X'. Because the common property level of effort, E^0, lies to the *right* of the maximum sustainable total revenues, we know that the harvest function in Figure 8.5(c) must be to the *left* of the maximum sustainable yield in terms of biomass. Our harvest function is thus H^0.

The same harvest could be achieved with E' units of effort. But as long as total costs equal *TC*, E^0 will be used leading to a harvest function such as $H^0 = G(E^0, X)$ in Figure 8.5(c). To achieve a steady-state harvest of *H* with a lower level of effort, total costs would have to be *TC'* in Figure 8.5(a). Unit costs would then be *c'*, which as shown in Figure 8.5(b), exceed *c*. The common property equilibrium would then be at point *B*, and E' traps would be set. Notice that *TR* and hence harvests are *exactly the same* at point *B* as at point *A*. Because unit costs *c'* exceed *c*, less total effort will be used in the industry. The common property equilibrium thus lies to the left of the maximum sustainable revenue. In Figure 8.5(b), *AR* now equals *c'*. And in Figure 8.5(c), we find that *H'* is the new harvest function which yields the same steady-state harvest as was the case with E^0 effort, but at a larger sustainable stock of lobsters, X'. What Figure 8.5 illustrates is that two levels of effort yield the same harvest. The level of effort chosen under common property depends on where *TC* = *TR*. For *TC* curves different than those shown in Figure 8.5(a), the harvest will of course change.

The common property equilibrium can also be defined in terms of average and marginal costs of harvest. This is quite simple. We know the *CPE* (common property equilibrium) is where *TR* = *TC*. Given our assumptions, the equilibrium condition can be written as *PH* = *cE*. Dividing by *H*, we see that $P = cE/H$ — that is, price equals the average cost of the harvest. Firms will enter the fishery under open access as long as price exceeds average cost.

To summarize, two points can be made about the common property equilibrium in the fishery. First, the common property equilibrium occurs where *TR* = *TC*, which implies that *AR* = *AC* of effort. Thus *MR* is less than *MC* of effort. Second, a common property equilibrium may be both economically and bioeconomically inefficient. It is *economically inefficient* because efficiency requires that *MR* = *MC*, but we have just shown that *MR* < *MC*. *Bioeconomic efficiency* can be interpreted as any equilibrium which is to the left of the maximum sustainable yield in terms of biomass (or to the right of the maximum sustainable total revenues). If an equilibrium occurs to the left of the MSY biomass, it indicates that the same harvest could be taken at a higher sustained biomass.

In terms of our example, if unit costs of effort are *c*, bioeconomic inefficiency will occur because the common property equilibrium lies to the left of the MSY biomass. If unit costs are c', the common property equilibrium is not bioeconomically inefficient. But all common property equilibriums are economically inefficient. Let us also repeat: The equilibriums described here are all steady-state in that they can be repeated indefinitely. But they are also static. Future revenues are not discounted, and we have not discussed the time paths of adjustment to equilibrium.

The Industry Supply Curve for a Common Property Fishery

We can now use the model developed above to derive an industry supply curve for a common property fishery.[6] The supply curve will be derived graphically. In Appendix G, the supply curve is derived algebraically. We want to know what will happen to the steady-state lobster harvests at different prices of lobster. In Figure 8.6(a), three total revenue functions are shown. TR_0 is derived assuming the price of lobsters is \$0.50 per pound. TR_1 assumes the price is \$1 per pound (as in Figure 8.5), and at TR_2 the price is \$2. We again assume unit costs of effort are constant and equal to c and total costs given by the curve TC. The common property equilibrium can then be derived for each different price of lobster.

When the price is \$0.50 per pound, the common property equilibrium is at point A in Figure 8.6(a), where E_0 traps are used. The common property harvest for E_0 traps is read off the TR_1 curve. Recall that when $P = 1$, TR also defines harvests uniquely. Therefore H_0 pounds of lobster will be harvested when the price per pound is \$0.50. In Figure 8.6(b), the industry supply curve is derived. The point A' corresponds to the common property harvest of H_0 at $P = \$0.50$. Similarly, when the lobster price is \$1 per pound, point B in Figure 8.6(a) is the common property equilibrium, E_1 effort will be used, and the harvest is H_1. In Figure 8.6(b), B' is the point on the supply curve representing this harvest at a price of \$1 per pound. Notice that the supply curve is positively sloped, as is the usual case over the range from A' to B'.

However, see what happens when price of lobster doubles yet again to \$2 per pound. The common property equilibrium is at point C in Figure 8.6(a), with E_2 traps and a harvest of H_2. The corresponding point on the supply curve is C'. Notice now that the common property harvest of H_2 is *less than* that of H_1. The supply curve for lobsters harvested under open access is therefore *backward-bending.*

Can we determine where the supply curve begins to have a negative rather than a positive slope? The supply curve will bend backward for all harvests to the right of the maximum sustainable revenue (the left of the MSY biomass). This follows from the nature of the bionomic equilibrium. Once the MSY revenue is passed, moving toward the right from $TR = 0$, harvests fall as effort rises. Effort will rise when the fish price rises. So at high fish prices, it is most likely that the industry will be on the backward-bending portion of its supply curve.

We can now examine equilibriums in the market for lobsters. Suppose our lobster market is in equilibrium where demand equals D_0 and supply equals S_0, as shown in Figure 8.7. The equilibrium price will be P_0 and the quantity sold H_0. Now suppose demand shifts to the right to D_1 because the incomes of consumers have risen. People now substitute lobster for chicken. The new equilibrium is at P_1 and H_1. Both price and consumption have risen. If incomes rise yet again and demand shifts to D_2, the market equilibrium will now occur to the left of the MSY harvest in Figure

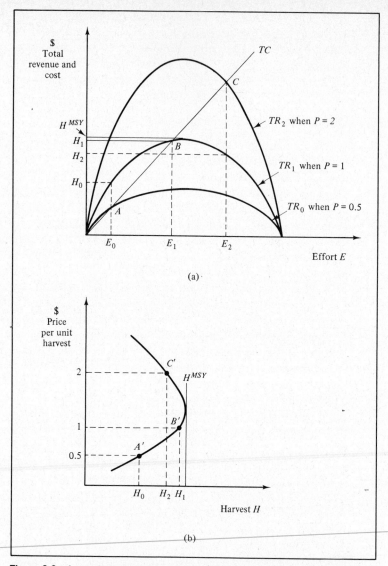

Figure 8.6   A steady-state supply curve is derived for the open access fishery. If the price of fish rises, the steady-state harvest will rise as long as the harvests are to the left of the maximum sustainable total revenue (or right of *MSY* stock). Once the maximum sustainable total revenue has been reached, further increases in the price will lead to greater effort, but smaller harvests. Harvests for each level of effort are read off the total revenue curve when $P = 1$ in (a).

8.7. The price of lobster will continue to rise, but the quantity harvested and hence sold falls. It is possible that the demand curve could continue to shift upward and to the right. Lobster harvests would continue to fall while the price rose, and the stock could be depleted to very low levels. But this depletion is unlikely, because lobsters are by no means an essential good.

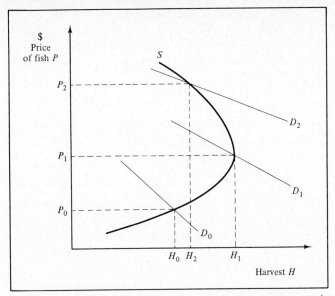

Figure 8.7 Equilibrium in a fish market with an open access supply curve. If demand shifts from D_0 to D_1, both harvests and the price of fish rises. But for shifts in demand beyond D_1, no further increase in harvest is possible. Therefore the price of fish will rise, but the catch will decline.

Socially Optimal Harvests under Private Property Rights

One should suspect by now that unlike mining, the pursuit of private interests in the fishery will not yield a socially optimal allocation of resources. The reason is the lack of private property rights in the fishery. Because no agent has the *exclusive right* to the resource (or a portion thereof), a market failure or common property externality exists. To examine the nature of the market failure, let's look more closely at the common property industry equilibrium derived above.

Our discussion thus far has focused on the behavior of an open access industry. In contrasting the common property equilibrium with the social optimum, we want first to look at the behavior of each firm in the industry. Given the assumption of constant costs of effort, we cannot predict the number of firms. If cost curves were U-shaped a unique equilibrium could be defined, but there are problems associated with whether an equilibrium exists with U-shaped cost curves. (We encountered this problem in the discussion of mineral extraction.) There is, however, an important implication of the common property equilibrium for the fishing firm.

Under open access to the fishery, each firm receives the *average product* of the industry's total effort. That is, the catch per lobster trap is determined by the total harvest divided by the total number of traps set. A firm does not capture the marginal product of its effort; rather, it harvests the industry average product, which must lie above marginal product. But by harvesting the average product, each firm imposes *external costs* on every other firm. We can show this algebraically. Each firm treats the stock X as exogenous when actually the action of firm, i, leads to a lower equilibrium stock *and* slightly higher harvest costs for every boat. This follows because harvesting H pounds with a higher stock requires less effort than with a lower stock. From Figures 8.5 through 8.7, we know that the total harvest from the fishery will be equal to the average product of effort times the amount of effort used (with $P = 1$, average revenue equals average product). We write this relationship in Equation (8.5):

$$H = AP_E \cdot E \qquad (8.5)$$

Consider what would happen to the harvest with a marginal increase in effort —one firm sets an additional lobster trap. If we differentiate Equation (8.5) with respect to E (the marginal change), we find that

$$dH/dE = AP_E + E(dAP_E/dE) \qquad (8.6)$$

The term dH/dE can be interpreted as the marginal product of effort (over the long term). Thus, Equation (8.6) says that the marginal product of effort equals the average product of effort plus the term $E(dAP_E/dE)$. This latter term shows the change in the harvest per unit of effort due to the use of an additional unit of effort. It is negative because an increase in effort reduces the sustainable fish stock, X. The lower the stock (or biomass), the lower the catch per unit effort. All firms in the industry are then affected by the marginal change in effort.

But because the effect *per firm* is relatively small, each firm ignores the term $E(dAP_E/dE)$. Each firm perceives the marginal product of its effort to equal the average product before that increment in effort was added. The firm ignores the effect an increase in the number of traps has on the stock of fish and hence on the harvests of other firms. The term $E(dAP_E/dE)$ therefore reflects an externality we call the *stock effect*. In other words, for each increment in effort, firms actually receive the industry average product of effort *minus* the stock effect. But because the stock effect is felt by all firms, no single firm takes it into account when deciding how much effort to use. All firms act symmetrically. The industry equilibrium is where the value of the average product of effort equals marginal cost, not where the value of the marginal product of effort equals marginal cost. Marginal and average product differ by the amount of the stock effect. The stock effect is ignored in the steady-state common property equilibrium, and this is the economic inefficiency.

Another externality arises in our steady-state model under common property in addition to the stock effect: congestion. In our simple model, harvesting costs per unit of effort were assumed to be fixed. What is more realistic is the general model where harvesting costs depend on the amount of total effort in the fishery and the stock of fish. For each additional unit of effort employed, harvesting costs rise because of congestion. Vessels have to line up in the fishing grounds. There can be conflicts among vessels with regard to equipment. Trawlers can tear the buoys off lobster traps or pots. Nets of different vessels can become entangled. These congestion costs will be ignored in the open access fishery. Under private property, they will not. In the next section, we examine additional inefficiencies that arise in an intertemporal model of the common property fishery.

What is the socially optimal equilibrium for our model? Suppose the lobster grounds could be divided up so that each firm in the industry had the exclusive right

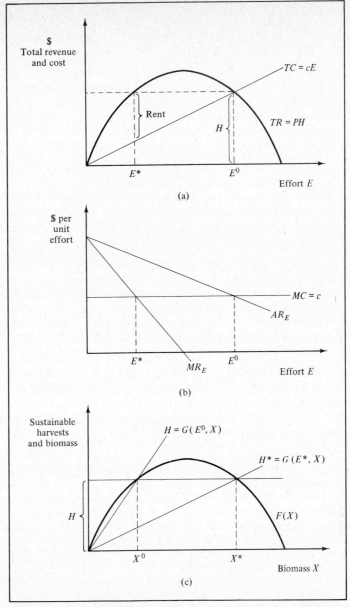

Figure 8.8 A private property equilibrium is compared to the common property equilibrium. If the fishery is managed by a sole owner, profits will be maximized where $MR = MC$. The private property equilibrium uses effort E^*, which is less than the common property effort of E^0. But the harvest H is identical in both cases, given the total cost curve TC. Rent is maximized under the private property equilibrium, dissipated under the common property equilibrium. The private property equilibrium is both economically and biologically efficient, while the common property equilibrium is economically inefficient and may be biologically inefficient as well. Biological inefficiency of the *CPE* is illustrated in this figure with the sustainable biomass to the left of the *MSY* biomas.

to trap lobsters in a particular region. If there were a large number of firms, each with a private property right such that the industry behaved competitively (takes all prices and factor costs as given), and no other imperfections or externalities existed, the assignment of private property rights to the lobster grounds would guarantee a social optimum.[7] We continue to assume that the discount rate is zero. A firm possessing private property rights will choose the level of effort that maximizes its long-run sustainable profits.

The profit-maximizing level of effort is where *marginal* revenue equals *marginal* cost; the difference between total revenue and total cost is at a maximum. If, for example, one firm "owned" the lobster fishing grounds, there can be no entry to those grounds without that firm's consent. The firm will then limit the number of traps set to that which maximizes its profits. The efficient amount of effort is E^*, shown in Figure 8.8(a) and (b), where $MR = MC$. The sole owner would choose E^* traps to maximize the rents from the fishery, where rents are the difference between total revenue and total costs. The fishery itself is now a factor of production that earns a return — rent.

We can compare the private property equilibrium (PPE) to the common property equilibrium (CPE) described in the previous section, maintaining all our previous assumptions (constant unit costs, $P = 1$, and PPE is competitive). In Figure 8.8, the CPE uses E^0 effort (setting $TR = TC$ or $AR = MC$). It is thus clear that with the CPE, more effort will be used than with a PPE, given the same cost and revenue curves — E^0 exceeds E^*. Given unit costs c, it also turns out in this case that the harvest under both ownership regimes is exactly the same. This need not be the case, of course.

With different TC curves, the optimal harvest could be greater or less than the common property harvest. But in our case, we can see from Figure 8.8(c) that the common property harvest is indeed biologically inefficient, while the private property harvest is not, given the same total cost curve for each ownership regime. The sustained stock under private property is X^*, which exceeds the common property stock, X^0. There is no stock externality under private property because the sole owner fully incorporates the effect each increment in effort has on the biomass and hence the harvest. Under private property, the value of the marginal product of effort is set equal to the marginal cost of effort, where the MP includes the stock externality.[8] Appendix G derives algebraically the supply curve under private property.

BOX 8.2
Lobsters

Can we use the simple model derived in this section to analyze a particular fishery? Bell (1972), using the Schaefer model presented in the text, has examined the New England lobster fishery. He estimated a harvest function for the open access fishery — the average product of effort as a function of parameters reflecting environmental carrying capacity of the fishery, a "catchability coefficient" which shows for each unit of E how much sustainable yield of biomass will be harvested, effort, and water temperature (an exogenous variable affecting lobster biomass). Bell found, using time series data from 1950 to 1966, that

$$\left(\frac{H}{E}\right)_t = -48.4 - 0.000024E_t + 2.13°F$$
$$\qquad\quad (-1.43) \qquad (-3.37) \qquad (2.58)$$
$$R^2 = .96 \qquad D.W. = 2.05$$

where H is the annual landings of northern lobster, E the annual number of traps fished, °F the mean annual seawater temperature, Boothbay Harbor Maine. t statistics are given in the parentheses.

To use this average product of effort relationship to derive both the common property and private property equilibrium for the fishery, the average product equation is solved or normalized for a particular water temperature. Bell chose the temperature in 1966, as it was close to the average temperature for the past 65 years to 1966. Inserting this temperature (46 °F) and multiplying by E, we find that

$$H_t = 49.4E_t - 0.000024E_t^2$$

This harvest function can then be used to solve for the common and private property equilibriums. Assuming the industry's total cost curve is a linear function of effort, Bell calculated the average costs of effort for 1966 at $21.43 per trap (where effort includes measures of capital and labor used per trap). Bell assumes that demand for lobster is perfectly elastic at the 1966 price per pound of $0.762.

Given this information, we can now solve for the common property equilibrium. (Bell derives long-run marginal and average costs as functions of the harvest and solves for a CPE where $P = AC$, and for a PPE where $P = MC$. This is equivalent to our solution in terms of effort). We know the CPE for the industry is where $TR = TC$ of effort or the $AR = MC$ of effort. Substituting for all values, we find that

$$.762(49.4 - 0.000024E_t) = 21.43$$

and $E_t = 891,000$ traps in the common property equilibrium

Substituting this effort level, we find a harvest of about 25 million pounds of lobster. The actual number of traps set and the harvest in 1966 was 947,000 and 25.6 million pounds. The theoretical model thus fits reasonably well the observations in the fishery. It would seem that the lobster fishery off New England was approximately near a common property equilibrium.

What does the model predict the private property equilibrium would yield? To have a private property equilibrium, marginal revenue (as a function of effort) must equal the marginal cost of effort. Solving for the PPE using Bell's numbers, we find that the number of traps set would be 443,000, with a steady-state harvest of 17.2 million pounds. The common property equilibrium in 1966 thus used more than twice the number of traps than is efficient. Was the CPE biologically inefficient as well? No. Bell finds that both the CPE and PPE are to the left of the maximum sustainable total yield (the right of the MSY biomass). The MSY harvest is 25.5 million pounds with about 1 million traps set.

FISHERY DYNAMICS

In this section we introduce a positive discount rate into the analysis, examine the resulting steady-state equilibrium assuming the fishery is optimally managed, and compare this *dynamic* equilibrium with the *static* common property and private property equilibriums derived above. We also introduce more complex assumptions about the way in which fishing firms enter and exit the industry. Up to now, we have concentrated on the dynamics of the fish population and made arbitrary assumptions about when firms entered the fishery. Now we look at an open access equilibrium under a specific assumption about the entry and exit of firms. We also analyze paths toward a possible steady-state equilibrium.

In this section we discuss aspects of *getting to an equilibrium,* not simply different types of equilibriums. We will discuss all concepts verbally and graphically, provide a numerical example, and present an example of dynamic analysis for a fishery. (Some readers may wish to skim the material in this section.) Of significance is the derivation of a bionomic equilibrium when harvests occur over a number of years. The value of each future harvest will be discounted back to the beginning of the plan for harvesting. Before beginning the analysis, we discuss intuitively the effect discounting has on the steady-state harvest and the fish stock.

The Discounting of Future Harvests

The model of the optimally managed fishery above assumed that no discounting of the revenue and costs of future harvests was made. One period was assumed to be identical to the next. This assumption means that individuals are indifferent between receiving a dollar today or a dollar tomorrow. Or, in terms of the fishery, one dollar of profit from fishing is valued the same whether it is earned this year or next. Although there are some who argue that the appropriate social discount rate is zero, most economists assume that a preference for dollars received today rather than tomorrow should be reflected in the computation of a socially optimal policy. It is the inclusion of the discount rate that distinguishes the *static* steady-state equilibrium from the *dynamic* steady-state equilibrium. What are the effects on the optimal fishery equilibrium when the discount rate is positive?

Let's first see what the inclusion of the discount rate means under common property and private property ownership. Under the open access fishery, the discount rate is effectively infinite. Long-run profits would increase in the fishery if entry could be reduced today to let the fish stock rise. But no single firm has any incentive to reduce its effort because if it did, other firms would reap the benefits without incurring any loss in current revenue. Other firms might also increase their effort and thus offset the positive effect on the stock. When is an infinite discount rate, all the static and dynamic equilibriums coincide.

In a private property equilibrium where dynamic effects are considered, the discount rate will typically lie between zero and infinity. Throughout this section we will assume that the discount rate used by holders of a private property right will be equal to the social discount rate. This need not be true in practice, but it enables us to argue that the PPE will be socially optimal. When the discount rate is positive, the static and dynamic private property equilibriums will not coincide.

With a positive discount rate, the owner of the fish stock faces an intertemporal tradeoff. Harvests tomorrow are simply worth less than profits today. A firm may not be willing to operate with a large fish stock and low harvests today in anticipation of rising future harvests. The higher the discount rate, the more impatient the individual is for harvests today. Therefore, the larger the discount rate, the less the difference between the CPE and the PPE. The sharp distinction between the CPE and PPE derived in the static model becomes less sharp in a dynamic model with high discount rates.

We now present a dynamic model of a fishery that is being managed optimally by a government agency or a competitive sole owner. We note briefly how a monopolist would behave. Assume that the objective function of society is to maximize the present value of the *net benefits* from the fishery by choosing a harvest rate $H(t)$ that maintains a steady-state biomass or fish population X. There are three ingredients to this problem. First, let $U[H(t)]$ be defined as the total benefits derived from the harvesting of fish. This function can be interpreted in a number of ways, depending on who is maximizing the net benefits from fishing.

If we are talking about a government maximizing social welfare, $U[H(t)]$ can be interpreted as the sum of consumer plus producer surplus. Net benefits are then $U[H(t)]$ minus harvesting costs. If a sole owner is exploiting the fishery, where the owner may be operating in a competitive market or as a monopolist, then $U[H(t)]$ is the profit function for the owner. We will concentrate on the optimal harvest from the viewpoint of *a government doing the maximizing.* The results will be identical for the competitive sole owner with private property rights, so we can compare the results in this section with those above. We will note the difference in the solution for the case of the monopolist.

Next, we have to specify what the harvest, $H(t)$, depends on. We assume, as in the previous section, that harvests are a function of fishing effort, E, and the stock of fish, X. Thus, $H(t) = G(E,X)$. In this model, $H(t)$ need not be a steady-state or sustainable harvest. If the harvest exceeds the sustainable yield from the fishery, the stock of fish will decline over time. If the harvest is less than the sustainable yield, the population will rise over time. We examined this situation in our simple model above.

The next ingredient is the cost function for harvesting fish. We assume a very general cost function. The cost curve is assumed to depend on the amount harvested, $H(t)$, and the stock of fish, $X(t)$. We have then $C = C[G(E,X),X(t)]$. Thus effort enters the cost function through the harvest function. We further assume that harvesting costs rise when there is an increase in the harvest ($\partial C/\partial H > 0$), while harvesting costs for a given H fall when there is an increase in the stock of fish ($\partial C/\partial X < 0$). The latter condition follows from our biological model, where we argued that it is easier and thus cheaper to catch $H(t)$ of fish, the larger their stock.

Finally, the biological mechanics must be incorporated into the problem. We require that in equilibrium the fish population must be sustainable — the change in the fish stock, dX/dt, must be equal to zero. When there is harvesting, the net growth of the stock over time must be exactly equal to the harvest over the same interval. As before, we assume the biological mechanics $F(X)$ can be represented by a logistic function (Equation 8.1). Thus, $dX/dt = F(X) - H(t) = 0$ is an equilibrium condition for the planning problem. The condition has been written thus far in a continuous time framework; we have been looking at the fishery over a small interval of time. Let us instead work explicitly with distinct time periods.

We examine the fishery from one period, say a year, to the next. The two approaches are the same when we let the discrete periods get smaller and smaller. Let us then rewrite the biological mechanics in a discrete form as

$$X(t + 1) = X(t) + F[X(t)] - H(t) \qquad (8.7)$$

Equation (8.7) can then be rewritten in terms of $H(t)$ to obtain

$$H(t) = F[X(t)] - [X(t + 1) - X(t)] \qquad (8.8)$$

That is, the harvest in period t must equal the difference between the growth in the fish population at t, $F[X(t)]$, and the change in the stock from one period to the next. If the fishery is in a steady-state equilibrium where $X(t + 1) = X(t)$, $H(t)$ will equal $F(X)$. If the stock changes from one period to the next, the harvest will not be equal to the growth of the stock. Equation (8.8) simply specifies mathematically what we have argued verbally above.

The determination of the optimal fishery equilibrium can now be stated.[9] We assume that the government manager seeks to determine a sequence of harvests, $H(t)$, where $t = 0,1,2, \ldots n, \ldots$, which maximizes

$$
\begin{aligned}
W = U[H(0)] - C[H(0),X(0)] + (1/1 + r)\{U[H(1)] - C[H(1),X(1)]\} \\
+ \cdots + (1/1 + r)^n\{U[H(n)] - C[H(n),X(n)]\} + \cdots \qquad (8.9)
\end{aligned}
$$

subject to

$$H(t) = F[X(t)] - [X(t + 1) - X(t)]$$

for
$$t = 1, \ldots, n$$

Notice now we are solving for an optimal harvest and steady-state stock, not for effort as we initially did in determining the common and private property static equilibriums. To solve this problem, we can substitute the constraint representing the biological mechanics into the objective function for each t, then differentiate the expression with respect to the stock of fish in each period. To find the optimum, each derivative is then set equal to zero. The resulting equilibrium condition for any two periods, t and $t + 1$, is

$$
\frac{[U'(t + 1) - C'(t + 1)] - [U'(t) - C'(t)]}{U'(t) - C'(t)} + \frac{[U'(t + 1) - C'(t + 1)][F'X(t)]}{U'(t) - C'(t)}
$$
$$
- \frac{C_X[H(t),X(t)]}{U'(t) - C'(t)} = r \qquad (8.10)
$$

The term U' is the additional benefit received from harvesting an additional fish or pound of fish in period t or period $t + 1$. This derivative will be equal to the price of fish if a government manager or competitive sole owner is operating the fishery. (It is equal to marginal revenue if a monopolist is managing the fishery.) C' is the marginal cost of harvesting an additional pound of fish in period t or $t + 1$. $F'[X(t)]$ is the marginal product of the fish stock, or the change in the biomass in the period t. C_X is the marginal cost of harvest due to a change in the stock of fish in period t. Finally, r is the social discount rate.

Equations (8.8) and (8.10) together govern the time path of the stock of fish, $X(t)$, the time path of the harvest, $H(t)$, and determine as time extends far into the future the optimal steady-state equilibrium values of the harvest, H^*, and the fish population, X^*. We will interpret Equation (8.10), then show how it simplifies for the case of our harvested fishery in a steady-state equilibrium. This dynamic steady-state equilibrium will be compared to the static one. We then show how the equilibrium changes under different assumptions about the discount rate and harvesting costs. We will next examine possible paths to a steady-state equilibrium for a specific example—the North Pacific fur seal.

Equation (8.10) can be interpreted as a "rule" which, combined with Equation (8.8), governs how X and H (and costs and benefits) evolve over time. Given a historical value of the stock $X(0)$, there will be a unique initial harvest $H(0)$ which will result in the fishery evolving to its steady-state or bioeconomic equilibrium. At the steady state, harvests and stock size remain at their equilibrium levels indefinitely, period by period. Let us examine each term in Equation (8.10). (It is analogous to the Hotelling rule from Chapter 3.)

The first term in Equation (8.10) is the percentage capital gain (or loss), the increase in net benefits or profits received from the fishery from periods t to $t + 1$. The capital gain is measured as a percentage of the net benefits to the fishery. The capital gain or loss term will be non-zero when the fishery is *on a path moving toward or away from the steady-state* values of H and X. If there is a capital gain (the value of the fish "asset" is increasing over time), it will pay the operator to shift harvests to the future—that is, to decrease harvests today to allow the stock to build up and reap larger gains in the future. This procedure is like mining where ore is kept in the ground if the rental value of the mineral is growing at a rate in excess of the interest rate. Here we are keeping fish in the ocean. If there is a capital loss, the value of the fishery falls from this period to the next. Harvests today should therefore rise, and the stock will decline.

If there is neither a capital gain nor a loss, we will have a steady-state. There is no change in the net benefits from one period to the next when there is no change in the amount harvested from one period to the next. In the steady-state, the numerator of the expression is zero and the term disappears. Let us define $V(t + 1)$ be equal to $[U'(t + 1) - C'(t + 1)]$ and $V(t)$ be equal to $[U'(t) - C'(t)]$, then in the steady-state $V(t + 1) = V(t)$. For a government fisheries manager $U[H(t)]$ is the area under the demand curve and $U'[H(t)]$ is price per unit harvested. For the owner with private property rights, $U' = P$. Then $V(t) = P(t) - C'(t)$ is the *rent* per unit of harvest.

Rent for the government manager or sole owner is the difference between price and marginal cost. For the monopolist, $U' = MR$, and rent is the difference between marginal revenue and marginal cost. Rent in the fishery is like rent in the mine. For nonrenewable resources, the percentage capital gain term was crucial and never went to zero because the stock and "harvest" (extraction) changed period by period until the reserves were depleted. The same sort of thing occurs in the fishery along the optimal path. The difference between the mine and the fishery is that in the fishery a steady-state can exist where the harvests and stocks of fish remain constant over time.

For the mine, no such steady-state exists because ore is steadily depleted until reserves are exhausted.

The second term is the value of an additional unit of biomass recruited to the fishery. The term $F'[X(t)]$ shows the growth in the fish stock in physical terms if the population is at X in the period t. This term is weighted by the ratio $V(t + 1)/V(t)$, to put it into dollar terms and thus make the physical change comparable to the net benefit measure of the first term. We call this expression the *marginal stock effect*. It reflects that effect the fish population has on the future growth of the fishery, valued by the net returns to the fishery. If the fishery is on a path to the steady-state, as before $V(t + 1)$ will not equal $V(t)$. The fish stock will be increasing or decreasing. At the steady-state $V(t + 1) = V(t)$ the stock is constant, so the weighting factor will simply be equal to 1, and the term reduces to $F'[X(t)]$.

The third term captures the stock externality described in the previous section. If an additional unit of the fish stock is harvested, the marginal cost of harvesting rises. Conversely, if the stock is larger, the marginal costs of harvesting are reduced. Recall that in the social optimum or competitive equilibrium with private property rights, the effect of the stock on the costs of harvest will be incorporated into the analysis. This is the term that does it. This cost is again weighted by the net benefit in period t, $U'(t) - C'(t)$, or simply $V(t)$. Note that the stock externality will be present whether the fishery is on the path to the steady-state or at the steady-state.

Equation (8.10) thus says that along a potentially optimal path, a rate of harvest must be chosen such that the sum of the capital gain plus the marginal stock effect minus the stock externality must be set equal to the interest rate. When the fishery is at a steady-state, Equation (8.10) reduces to

$$F'[X(t)] - C_X(t)/V(t) = r \qquad (8.11)$$

where $F'(X(t)$ is the marginal biological productivity of the stock of fish and can be either positive or negative; $C_X(t)$ is the stock effect on fishing costs and will be negative; and $V(t)$ is the rent or net surplus on the marginal quantity harvested at t.

Let's examine the steady-state equilibrium. In particular, we will see how the equilibrium changes for different values of the discount rate and different costs.

Equation (8.11) cannot tell us exactly where the equilibrium stock of fish will be without having quantitative estimates of the terms in the equation. To see this, we rewrite Equation (8.11) as

$$V(t) = C_X(t)/(F'[X(t)] - r) \qquad (8.12)$$

where $V(t)$ is the difference between price and marginal harvest costs for the optimally managed fishery or competitive sole owner, or the difference between marginal revenue and marginal cost for the monopolist. Price will exceed marginal cost in the steady-state because the fish stock will generate a rent. Thus the right-hand side of Equation (8.12) must also be positive in the steady-state.

We know by assumption that $C_X(t)$ is negative. Increases in the stock decrease the cost of harvesting a particular catch. The interest rate is positive. Thus to have the right-hand side of Equation (8.12) be positive, it must be the case that r is greater than $F'[X(t)]$. $F'[X(t)]$ is the slope of the sustainable yield curve (the biological production function). This value can be positive, negative, or zero. *So it is possible that the steady-state equilibrium can be to the right or the left of the MSY,* given our introduction of discounting or interest rate effects.

Now let's compare the dynamic steady-state to the static steady-state. The comparison is straightforward. In the static case, the discount rate is zero. We could thus resolve Equation (8.9) with r equal to zero, or simply note that r vanishes from the steady-state condition in Equation (8.11). The steady-state condition then becomes

$$V = C_X/F'(X) \qquad\qquad (8.13)$$

where the ts have been dropped for simplicity. Equation (8.13) implies for the sole owner or the government that the price of fish equals marginal costs of harvest plus the marginal stock effect. For the monopolist, marginal revenue equals marginal costs plus the marginal stock effect. This was our condition for rent maximization in the previous section. We know that the *static* steady-state equilibrium must therefore be at a fish population that is to the right of the MSY stock. Price or MR are positive. C_X is negative, and therefore $F'(X)$ must be negative. The equilibrium must lie on the decreasing portion of the biological production function. One error in doing the static analysis where r exceeds zero is that we rule out the possibility of an optimal equilibrium to the left of the MSY stock of fish. When is this error likely to be large? The higher the interest rate, all else equal, the greater the possibility that $F'(X)$ can be positive.

Now suppose we let r move toward infinity. In this case, the right-hand term of Equation (8.12) vanishes, and we are left with the condition that $U' = C'$. *This is the common property equilibrium,* where no stock effects are incorporated into the determination of the optimal harvest and stock of fish. The condition for a steady-state dynamic equilibrium is thus the general case. The static PPE is a special case with $r = 0$, while the common property equilibrium is a special case with r equal to infinity. Before turning to a discussion of the paths to the steady-state, let us consider another simplification.

Suppose we return to the assumption made in our preliminary static model that *the costs of harvesting fish are independent of the size of the fish stock.* If we maintain the assumption that r is positive, we can see that the steady-state equilibrium must now lie to the left of the MSY population. Refer back to Equation (8.11), where the term C_X is now zero. The equilibrium condition now becomes simply that $F'(X) = r$. If r is positive, then $F'(X)$ must be positive, and the steady-state equilibrium must occur to the *left* of the MSY. Figure 8.9 illustrates this case. We simply set the slope of $F(X)$ equal to the interest rate. The steady-state equilibrium is thus independent of both the price of fish (or marginal revenue) and the cost of harvest.

Notice that in the cases examined above, where r is not infinite, price (or U' or MR) is never set equal to marginal cost. This is because of the stock effects involved in harvesting fish — the harvest affects the stock of fish, and the stock of fish in turn affects the cost of harvest. Two terms reflect the stock effects — namely, $F'(X)$ and C_X. The optimal management of the fishery over time must incorporate these effects.

We will illustrate some of the cases examined above with a numerical example.

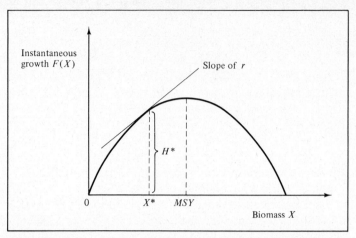

Figure 8.9 The steady-state equilibrium when the marginal costs of harvest are independent of the stock of fish. The equilibrium requires $F'(X)$, the slope of the biological production function to be equal to r, the discount rate. If r is positive, then $F'(X)$ must also be positive, and the equilibrium must be to the left of the *MSY* biomass (and harvest).

We solve for the socially optimal equilibrium assuming a positive but finite discount rate, then show what happens when the discount rate is equal to zero or approaches infinity.

Suppose the demand curve for flounder is perfectly elastic at a price p. Let the total cost of harvesting flounder be given by $C = wH/mX$, where w is the unit harvesting cost per firm per season, H is the harvest, m is the technology of harvesting or the "catchability coefficient," and X is the stock of flounder. Total costs thus increase as the harvest rises and the stock of flounder falls. The biological mechanics, as in Equation (8.7), are given by

$$X(t + 1) = X(t) + F[X(t)] - H(t)$$

In this example, we let $F[X(t)] = X(t)\{a - b[X(t)]\}$, where a and b are parameters. This is the logistic growth relation for the stock. Our steady-state relation requires that $F(X) = H(t)$. This will occur where $X(t + 1) = X(t)$. We then take our steady-state value equation, (8.11):

$$F'(X) - [C_X/(P - C')] = r$$

where for this case $F'(X) = a - 2bX$, $C_X = -wH/mX^2$, and $C' = w/mX$. We find in the steady-state that

$$(a - 2bX) - (-wH/mX^2)/[p - (w/mX)] = r$$

Substituting for $H = F(X) = X(a - bX)$ into this expression, we obtain the quadratic equation

$$2bX^2/a + (r/a - 1 - wb/apm)X - rw/apm = 0$$

Let us now solve this expression for the steady-state solution, given some hypothetical values for the parameters in the problem. For $a = .5$ and $b = .1$, the stock corresponding to the maximum sustainable yield (X^{MSY}) is 2.5 tons, while the biological equilibrium stock (X^E) in the absence of harvesting is a/b, which is equal to 5. We now examine three cases with harvesting.

Case A   The socially optimal harvest, X^*, where we let $p = 1$, $w = 6$, $m = 4$, and $r = .05$, is equal to $(1.2 + 1.62)/.8 = 3.12$. Hence, X^* exceeds X^{MSY}. This is what we expect when harvesting cost depends on stock size. In our cost function above, total costs and marginal costs fall as stock size rises. Therefore, larger stock sizes will increase the present value of the harvest.

Case B   Under open access to the fishery, the equilibrium conditions change from our steady-state equation above to $p = AC$, where $AC = w/mX$ for this example. For the same parameter values, the common property equilibrium stock, X^C, is 1.5, which is less than the MSY population. The common property equilibrium is thus in the biologically inefficient range of the stock size. Note we can also see that in the socially optimal solution, as the interest rate approaches infinity we obtain the common property equilibrium. Intuitively what occurs with r very large is that the future is irrelevant and optimization is done myopically, period by period.

Case C   Suppose now that the price of flounder approaches infinity. The optimal stock, X^*, would then approach $(a - r)/2b$. Now if r equals zero, the optimal stock is $a/2b$, which is the MSY. If the discount rate is positive, the optimal stock will be less than the MSY. In other words, in that case, with high prices the presence of discounting ($r > 0$) leads to steady-state stocks on the biologically inefficient branch, but not too far down the inefficient branch if r is relatively small. A positive r implies that harvests "today" are more desirable than harvests "tomorrow," and this impatience leads to the setting of X^* below X^{MSY} for high prices.

Our example shows that two factors typically prevent the optimal harvest from being at the maximum sustainable yield—the discount rate and stock effects on harvesting costs. If these terms are positive, an MSY harvest is most unlikely. However, in case C we saw that the MSY harvest is socially optimal when the price of fish is very high and the discount rate is zero. Intuitively what is happening is that very high prices (large demand) make the cost effects of the fish stock insignificant. At lower prices, harvest costs are more important. Because the marginal cost of harvesting fish depends on the steady-state stock of fish, it is generally desirable for the firm to operate where there is a stock of fish higher and a harvest lower than the MSY. The value of having a large harvest is offset by the high marginal costs of having a low population. This cost effect has a bigger impact on the fishery, the lower the price of fish.

The optimal steady-state equilibrium involves the interest rate and cost effects working simultaneously. In some cases, only one effect will be dominant. The interest rate effect tends to lead to an equilibrium to the left of the MSY, while the cost effect pulls the steady-state equilibrium to the right of the MSY. But unless both effects are absent or they just offset each other, the MSY is not the optimal steady-state equilibrium.

Dynamic Paths in the Fishery: The North Pacific Fur Seal

Let's return to Equation (8.10), the condition for a steady-state equilibrium in our dynamic model and the condition that must be satisfied along a path that leads to the steady-state. We will examine the paths to a possible equilibrium. Again, let $V(t) = U' - C'$. We will proceed by treating time as a continuous variable. When $t + 1$ and t are separated by an "instant," we can look at the change in V over this instant by taking the derivative of V with respect to time, $dV(t)/dt$. Let us define this derivative of V as $\dot{V}(t)$. Then the change in $X(t)$ over an instant of time is given by $\dot{X}(t)$. We can then rewrite our basic dynamic value Equation (8.10) in continuous time as

$$V[F'(X)] - C_X = rV - \dot{V} \qquad (8.14)$$

If we solve for $\dot{V}/V$, we find

$$\dot{V}/V = r - F' + C_X/V \qquad (8.15)$$

We have suppressed the time subscripts to avoid clutter.

It is Equation (8.15) which must be satisfied at each instant along the optimal path to the steady-state equilibrium. Equation (8.15) should look familiar; recall the condition for the optimal extraction path of the nonrenewable mineral as given by Hotelling's rule (Equation 3.10). In that expression, the percentage change in rent had to be equal to the interest rate at each point in time for there to be optimal extraction of a nonrenewable resource. Equation (8.15) is a generalization of the simple Hotelling rule which allows for the possibility of a growing resource stock rather than one which simply diminishes over time. We can see why this is so.

The fundamental distinction between renewable and nonrenewable resources is that for the latter, $F'(X) = 0$. There is no growth of the fixed stock (except perhaps over millions of years). The term C_X, the change in marginal harvesting costs due to a change in the stock of fish, will be present in the case of minerals when extraction costs per ton vary with location in the deposit.[10] With the terms $F'(X)$ and C_X set equal to zero, we have $\dot{V}/V = r$, which is identical to Hotelling's rule.

Let's now examine some possible paths to the steady-state equilibrium. Rather than examine a general model, we illustrate a particular example taken from Wilen (1976). The model Wilen uses simplifies much of the complexities of the fishery, but it clearly shows the interaction of the biological mechanics with the dynamics of entry and exit of firms. The industry in this case is one of historical interest, the North Pacific fur seal fishery.

Wilen's model examines seal harvests from the late 1800s to the early 1900s. The fishery existed in the Pacific Ocean along the northwest coast of North America. Harvesting of fur seals occurred in two phases of the seal's annual migratory and reproductive cycle. Fur seals migrate relatively long distances, going up the west coast of North America from mainland United States to the Bering Strait. They also settle on land to mate. Harvesting that occurs when the seals are on land was long governed by regulations of both the Canadian and the U.S. governments. When harvesting occurred during the migratory phase, a common property situation generally existed. A number of countries, including Canada, the United States, the Soviet Union, Japan, and Great Britain took part in the harvests. Our concern is with these pelagic harvests.

In the period from the late 1880s to the early 1900s, there was virtually open access to the pelagic seal fishery. A large number of vessels entered the industry at the beginning of this period, and at first large catches were made. After a few years, catches plummeted and vessels began exiting the fishery. By 1898, the Canadian fleet had shrunk to one-half its size in 1896. At this point, the Canadian fleet owners made an effort to save the industry. They formed a single firm, the Victoria Sealing Company, to exploit the fishery as a monopolist. U.S. fishing effort was withdrawn by the end of the 1800s due to a ban by the U.S. federal government on pelagic sealing. From 1901 to 1910, a single Canadian firm had almost complete control over the fishery. However, the Japanese entered the fishery in increasing numbers, and by 1909 the fishery was thought to be in danger of collapse. An international agreement signed by Canada, the United States, Japan, the Soviet Union, and Great Britain in 1911 prohibited all pelagic harvests and allowed only males to be harvested on land. The treaty is still in force today.

A number of interesting economic questions arise from the fur seal industry. We will look at the period from 1880 to 1900 using a dynamic bioeconomic model. The objective is to use the model to predict the steady-state equilibrium when there is open access to the fishery and to trace possible dynamic paths to that equilibrium. The question asked by Wilen is whether or not the fishery would have collapsed under open access. This involves two questions. Does a steady-state equilibrium exist that involves both positive seal stocks and positive fishing effort? Second, without government regulation, would the industry find the dynamic path that leads to this steady-state equilibrium? Would it follow an efficient path, such as the one described by Equation (8.15)?

To answer these questions, Wilen developed a simple model of the seal fishery. The biological aspect of the model is virtually identical to the approach taken in this chapter. The economic portion focuses on the conditions for an industry equilibrium with open access — namely, that an equilibrium will occur when there is no incentive for firms to enter or exit. This will occur when there are zero rents from the fishery.

The seal population is assumed to have a quadratic growth function, $F(X)$, that looks like Figure 8.1. The equation for this function is given by

$$\dot{X} = F(X) = X_t(a - bX_t) \tag{8.16}$$

In this equation, a and b are parameters that represent the natural growth rate and net reproductive capability of the species. Equation (8.16) is again our logistic equation for the fishery. With harvesting, the change in the population is again given by $\dot{X} = F(X) - H(t)$, as we have assumed throughout this chapter. A very simple harvesting relationship is then assumed:

$$H_t = AE_tX_t \tag{8.17}$$

A is a technological parameter, and E_t is again effort, which in Wilen's model is represented by the number of sealing vessels in the industry.[11] Substituting Equation (8.17) into the condition for the steady-state, we find that

$$\dot{X} = aX_t - bX_t^2 - AE_t X_t = 0 \tag{8.18}$$

There will be an equilibrium if $X_t = 0$ (extinction) or if there are no harvests (the natural biological equilibrium), in which case E_t equals zero. To have a steady-state equilibrium with positive seal stocks and harvests requires an interior bionomic equilibrium where $\dot{X} = 0$, which implies that $F(X) = H(t)$. Solving Equation (8.18) for X_t, we find this equilibrium stock at:

$$X_t = (a - AE_t)/b \qquad (8.19)$$

Examining Equation (8.19), we see that a sustained population and thus harvest depends on the parameters a, b, A, and the level of effort, E_t. We now have to determine the *number of vessels* that will exist in the industry. This is where economic assumptions enter.

Wilen assumes that an economic equilibrium occurs when there is no entry or exit into the fishery. The condition for entry or exit is given by

$$\dot{E} = s(P_t H_t - TC_t - \alpha_t)/E_t \qquad (8.20)$$

The variables are defined as follows: P is the unit price of a harvested seal, and is assumed to be constant in each period. TC_t are the total industry operating costs of harvesting seals, assumed to be equal to cE. α_t is a cutoff rate of return for the industry, where this cutoff is equal to the opportunity cost of capital, r, multiplied by the number of vessels in the industry (E), so $\alpha = rE$. The term s is an industry response parameter which indicates how quickly effort (vessels) responds to excess profits. Quite simply, then, whenever the right-hand side of Equation (8.20) is positive, positive profits per unit of effort (per vessel) exist, and more vessels enter the fishery.

When excess profits are negative, vessels exit. Note that the discount rate appears in Equation (8.20) in the form of the opportunity cost of capital (r). If asset markets work perfectly, then we expect r to be equal to the private discount rate used by owners of fishing vessels. It is what these individuals forego when investing in their vessels rather than alternative forms of capital. But there is no reason to expect r to be equal to the social discount rate. The analysis examines the common property equilibrium, not the social optimum. Incorporating all the assumptions listed above into Equation (8.20), we obtain

$$\dot{E} = s(PAX - c - r) \qquad (8.21)$$

Industry equilibrium occurs when there is no entry or exit—that is, $\dot{E}$ is equal to zero. Setting $\dot{E} = 0$ in Equation (8.21) and solving for X, we find

$$X_t = (c + r)/PA \qquad (8.22)$$

We now have an equation for the level of seal population that will lead to a steady-state equilibrium in the industry. Note that this population depends only on the parameters, c, r, P, and A, not on the number of vessels. This follows from the simple assumptions in the model. However, as we will see, the model is still powerful enough to explain much of the behavior of the industry and the seal population. We should also note that in a more complex (and more realistic) model, both p and c are not likely to be constant. If this is so, the dynamics become more complex.

The two equations which are necessary to solve for a steady-state bionomic equilibrium and to indicate the possible paths to this equilibrium are given by Equations (8.19) (biological equilibrium) and (8.22) (industry equilibrium). Figure

8.10 graphs these two equations as functions of X_t and E_t. The diagram in Figure 8.10 is called a *phase* diagram. The curve $\dot{X} = 0$ shows combinations of vessels E and seals X for which there is a bionomic equilibrium where $F(X) = H(t)$ — the net growth of the biomass equals the harvest. The curve $\dot{E} = 0$ shows combinations of E and X where there will be no entry or exit from the industry — the number of vessels will be constant. Notice that X_t is a decreasing function of E_t in the biological equilibrium, which we would expect. In the industry equilibrium, X_t is dependent on the ratio of c to P but is independent of E. The location of the two curves depends on the parameters identified previously.

The steady-state equilibrium for the seal fishery is where the two curves intersect. This is shown as point F in Figure 8.10. A steady-state equilibrium exists where there are positive levels of seals and vessels. It is possible, however, that the curves do not intersect in the interior of the phase plane. For the seal fishery over the period in question, the values for the parameters are such that an interior solution does exist. Using Wilen's numbers, in the open access phase of the fishery the steady-state equilibrium would have occurred at slightly more than 582,600 seals, with around 90 vessels actively fishing. This implies a maximum harvest of about 79,000 to 89,000 seals.

The question is whether the industry would have reached this common property equilibrium or whether the fishery would have been extinguished by excessive entry of vessels and overfishing before the equilibrium was reached. To answer this

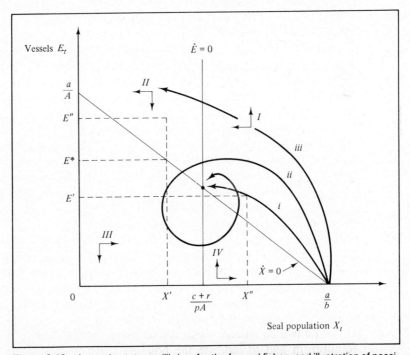

Figure 8.10 A steady-state equilibrium for the fur seal fishery and illustration of possible dynamic paths. Paths *i* and *ii* converge to the equilibrium, but path *iii* does not.

question, we need to examine the possible paths to (or away from) the steady-state equilibrium. We must describe the simultaneous motions of X_t and E_t when they are not at their steady-state values. This motion of X_t and E_t can be described mathematically, but we will explain intuitively what is happening.

The arrows in Figure 8.10 tell us how X_t and E_t will tend to change when the fishery is not on the steady-state equilibrium curves. Let's first examine the movement of X_t when it is not on $\dot{X} = 0$. Suppose the fishery is at X'. At X', E^* vessels would be needed to have the net natural growth of the seal population equal to the harvests. Suppose there are only E' vessels. Then the biomass harvested is less than the net growth of the seals over the time period in question, and the seal population will rise. The horizontal arrow below $\dot{X} = 0$ points to the right to indicate this increasing stock of seals. Conversely, if the fishery is at X' but there are now E'' vessels harvesting seals, the stock of seals will fall over time because the harvest exceeds the growth of the stock. The horizontal arrows above $\dot{X} = 0$ thus point to the left.

Now suppose there are E' vessels fishing. To have a steady-state industry equilibrium, the fish stock must equal $(c + r)/PA$ seals. If, however, there are only X' seals, not enough will be caught for the industry to cover its costs (including the opportunity cost of capital). Exit from the industry will occur. This is shown by the vertical arrow pointing downward to the left of the $\dot{E} = 0$ line. Conversely, if the population of seals is X'', firms will be earning excess profits and entry will occur. This is shown by the vertical arrows pointing upward. In the figure, then, we have four different sets of arrows. Each set describes the movement of the variables X_t and E_t when not at the steady-state equilibrium. We have labeled the quadrants I, II, III, IV. Let's now see what happens out of steady-state equilibrium.

Suppose the fishery starts in a steady-state with no harvesting of seals. We begin at point a/b on the X_t axis. Now fishing vessels enter. We illustrate three possible dynamic paths emanating from the point a/b. In path i the industry converges smoothly to the steady-state equilibrium. Path ii shows an oscillating path that ultimately reaches the equilibrium. Path iii leads to the extinction of the seals. Which path will occur? It depends on the values of the parameters in the model.

Path i will occur whenever s and b are relatively low and/or a is relatively high. This means that the response of the industry to profits or losses is relatively sluggish, but the seals have low mortality rates and reproduce lustily. Path ii would tend to occur when both s and a are relatively high. The industry responds very quickly to excess profits or losses, but the seal population is very resilient. There will be large swings in both X and E, but these ultimately dampen, and the equilibrium is approached.[12] Finally, path iii could appear when s is high but a is low (relative to b), PA is high, and $c + r$ is low. This means that the $\dot{E} = 0$ curve will be quite close to the origin. When vessels first enter the fishery in response to the high profits, their harvests so decimate the seal population that recovery is impossible. The seals cannot reproduce fast enough to sustain their population, and extinction occurs.

What actually happened in the Pacific fur seal fishery in the late 1800s? Wilen calculated values for the parameters and predicted that path ii would result. He then looked at the actual figures for E_t and X_t for the period 1882 to 1900.[13] The path that resulted is shown in Figure 8.11. The actual path looks very much like the theoretical path shown as path ii. We will never know if the industry would have reached this

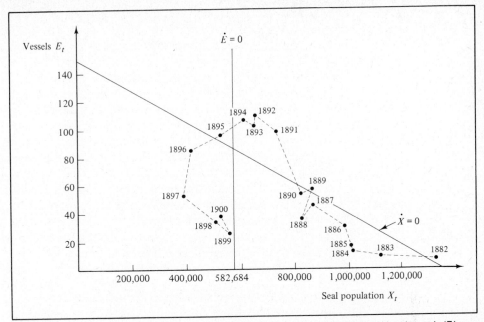

Figure 8.11   Estimates of the stock of fur seals (X_t) and the stock of vessels harvesting the seals (E_t) over the period 1882 to 1900. Notice that the path taken by the two stocks is very similar to the path labeled (ii) in Figure 8.11. It appears as if the path may have been converging to the steady-state equilibrium. *Source:* Wilen (1976).

equilibrium, because the Canadian firms were monopolized at the turn of the century. Again note that the steady-state equilibrium is not an optimal equilibrium; it is still the common property solution.

Wilen computes the rents that were foregone as a result of open access to the fishery. They were substantial, which suggests that monopolization of the fishery would pay off. It also suggests that some form of government intervention would be required if the monopoly solution was socially unacceptable (we know that monopolists generally produce less and charge more than is socially optimal). But what Wilen's analysis does indicate is that extinction is not an inevitable outcome under common property.

BOX 8.3
Extinctions: Past and Present

Vernon Smith has made use of a version of the model of human predation of a species in analyzing the extinction of the megafauna some 10,000 years ago. He argues that the large herding animals such as mammoth, bison, camel, and mastodon, which became extinct, presented low hunting cost relative to kill value. The common property nature of these animal stocks removed an incentive to harvest conservatively. Wastage killing is evident in some ancient sites. The slow growth or long maturation of these animals also made them vulnera-

Box 8.3 continued

ble to extinction. Small stocks did not grow rapidly once they were hunted intensively.

The commonly accepted cause of the extinctions was climate change and a reduction in grassland areas. Smith contends, however, that human predation was the cause. There is clear evidence that man hunted the animals in question; spearheads have been found among the bones. Human migration to North America coincided with the extinctions. Lastly, Smith sees the types of spearheads discovered as being refined for big game hunting. Eighty genera in continental North America vanished about 10,000 years ago, and 49 of these had adult members weighing over 110 pounds. It was this group that Smith argues was hunted to extinction like the passenger pigeon in our own era.

Direct human predation is today a small part of the phenomenon of species extinction. The problem now is one of having the habitats of species destroyed by the encroachment of settlement and forestry activity. For example, in East Kalimantan, Indonesia, logging was started in 1970 and the habitat

Table 1   EXTINCTIONS OF SPECIES IMPLIED BY THE GLOBAL 2000 STUDY'S PROJECTIONS

	Present species (thousands)	Projected deforestation	Loss of species	Extinctions (thousands)
Low deforestation case				
Tropical Forests				
Latin America	300–1,000	50	33	100–333
Africa	150–500	20	13	20–65
S. and SE. Asia	300–1,000	60	43	129–430
Subtotal	750–2,500			249–828
All other habitats Oceans, fresh water, nontropical forests, islands, etc.	2,250–7,500		8	188–625
Total	3,000–10,000			437–1,453
High deforestation case				
Tropical Forests				
Latin America	300–1,000	67	50	150–500
Africa	150–500	67	50	75–250
S. and SE. Asia	300–1,000	67	50	150–500
Subtotal	750–2,500			375–1,250
All other habitats Oceans, fresh water, nontropical forests, islands, etc.	2,250–7,500		8	188–625
Total	3,000–10,000			563–1,875

Source: U.S. Council on Environmental Quality and the Dept. of State, *The Global 2000 Report to the President,* Penguin, N.Y., 1982.

of the orangutan is being ruined. In 10 years, the local human population jumped from 1,000 to 8,000. Much concern is focused on plant species today, and it is in tropical forests where diversity is greatest. It is estimated that less than half of the plant and animal species have been catalogued. But the diversity is thought to be important in ecological balance, and any major change in the balance involves unknown consequences for future human welfare. Natural preserves have been created in most areas of the world, but encroachment by squatters is a major problem. Politicians are reluctant to be severe with very poor families. The unquantified value of future biological diversity is not a practical point for rallying support from citizens for protecting natural reserves. It is an instance in which the beneficiaries of large-scale preservation of the species are the future generations, and their voices are not heard in current debates. UNESCO has encouraged the allocation of special areas to natural reserves by itself designating areas throughout the world as important in the drive to preserve species from extinction. More than half of extinctions since A.D. 80, the year the European lion died out, have occurred since 1900. Ten percent of the 22,250 plant species in the continental United States have been listed as "endangered" or "threatened" by the Smithsonian Institution. Some recent projections are presented in Table 1.

Besides natural reserves protected by law, two other approaches to preserving species are (1) legal requirements that new projects must not result in a threat to a species, and (2) treaties outlawing trade in many species. With regard to the former, in the United States alterations to a project have often been worked out to preserve some threatened animal or plant. However, the difficulty with bans on trade in certain plants and animals is that many countries are not signatories to the principal treaties.

Sources: Erik Eckholm, "Disappearing Species: The Social Challenge." Worldwatch Paper #22. Washington D.C.: Worldwatch Institute, 1978, and V. Smith, "The Primitive Hunter Culture, Pleistocene Extinction, and the Rise of Agriculture." *Journal of Political Economy,* 1983, 4 (August 1975), pp. 727–756.

What, then, do these dynamic models tell us? A dynamic steady-state equilibrium and paths to that equilibrium (if it exists) can be defined under any property rights scheme. Values of parameters essential to industry and biological equilibrium are required. The parameters of the model will also help determine what sorts of regulations will expedite the movement to the steady-state equilibrium. Static models cannot determine the paths to the equilibrium and may give an inaccurate picture.

In a static model, effort in a CPE is always greater than is socially optimal. In a dynamic model, the PPE and CPE levels of effort might be quite close when interest rates are high. Effort may have to fluctuate in a dynamic model to achieve efficiency. This does not occur in a static model. One must therefore be careful in prescribing policies for the fishery based solely on static analysis. However, it is often difficult to obtain enough information about the fishery to do a thorough dynamic analysis. The gains from doing dynamic analysis may not be large if not enough is known about the fishery.

EXTINCTION OF FISH SPECIES

There is a large literature on extinction. See, for example, Berck (1979), Clark (1973a, 1976), Smith (1977), and Hartwick (1982). In this section we highlight a case in which the extinction of a renewable resource is possible. In most such cases, extinction would only occur if the fishery were characterized by open access—that is, lack of private property rights is the major problem. However, as we saw in our discussion of the dynamics of the fur seal fishery, common property does not necessarily lead to extinction.

What are the critical features of a fishery that can cause extinction? We focus on two. First, the biological mechanics may be such that a species becomes extinct if the population sinks below a critical biomass or number of individuals. In our simple logistic model, extinction will occur only when the last fish is caught. It is hard to imagine cases where costs would remain constant as fishing firms search for that last fish (or pair of fish). For some species, extinction can occur if the population is reduced below some critical level. In these cases, survival of a sufficient number of individuals is required to ensure that enough new members are born to maintain the population. This type of biological mechanics tends to occur in species with few births per female—for example, sea mammals such as whales. For other fish, reproductive capacity is not the issue, as one fish can produce millions of offspring (shrimp, for example).

Extinction also depends on the economic characteristics of the markets for the resource and the technology of harvesting as our box on extinction illustrates. Extinction is possible when the costs of harvesting are independent of the stock, and price of the fish increases significantly. In this situation a harvest function $H = G(E, X)$ can be tangent to the fishery production function $F(X)$ at the origin even without threshold effects. Entry of more and more vessels trying to catch ever fewer fish can lead to the extinction of the species. Although the assumptions required to have extinction in this static case are somewhat implausible, especially the assumption that costs are independent of the stock of the fish, the case does illustrate that cost and demand conditions are important in determining whether it can be privately profitable to keep on harvesting right to extinction.

To have extinction, it has to be the case that the price must always exceed the marginal cost of harvest. We should note that for particular discount rates, under certain cost and demand conditions, it may be socially optimal to extinguish a species if society does not value the species for its own sake (that is, no social value is put on preservation of a species even if it has no commercial value). Indeed, some species may have a large negative value to society—mosquitoes, parasites, and viruses. Extinction of these species would then be socially desirable. *Common property per se is not the cause of extinction in these cases.* We now examine an example of near extinction that illustrates the interdependence of the biological and economic features noted above—the blue whale.

The Bioeconomics of the Blue Whale: A Case of Near Extinction

Rather than assuming that the production function for the fish species is characterized by a smooth quadratic curve, we now consider a case where there is a minimum

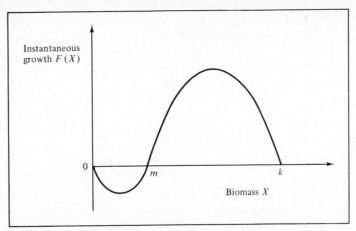

Figure 8.12 A biological production function when a threshold level of fish stock is essential for survival of the species. If the biomass (or population) falls below *m*, reproduction is less than natural mortality, and the species gradually dies out.

sustainable stock size, which we denote *m*. As is shown in Figure 8.12, the left-hand side of the biological production function equals zero at *m* rather than at a population of zero, as before. If the biomass reaches *m*, there are not enough of the species to have reproduction exceed natural mortality, and it will gradually die out. This is shown by the production function dipping below the *X* axis until the population hits zero. Given these biological mechanics, if the fishery is characterized by open access (common property), extinction becomes a likely outcome.

Suppose we have an open access fishery where the demand schedule for the fish is rising over time. The initial common property equilibrium is, say, at a stock level well above the critical threshold. Suppose rising incomes cause demand to increase. The price of fish rises, harvests increase, and the fish population falls. If the demand curve shifts up enough, the common property equilibrium may occur below the threshold, and the species will become extinct. The population need not be reduced to zero when there are threshold effects. If there is any uncertainty in the location of the threshold, extinction would seem to be even more plausible in this common property environment.

In addition, it need not be shifts in demand that are the culprit. Over time, the costs of harvest are likely to fall. This has happened in practice with the use of sophisticated capital equipment such as sonar. More recently, satellites are being used to track pelagic species, and the information about the location of the fish is fed instantaneously to shipboard computers. These new techniques may offset the higher marginal harvesting costs that would normally result from a lower stock of fish. However, it is not shifting demand or falling costs alone that contribute to the extinction possibility. Open access is the key element, as we see in the case of the blue whale. The socially optimal management of the fishery would in general lead to the maintenance of a population above the critical threshold.

The blue whale is the largest creature in the world. It was harvested for many years, but the peak harvests occurred in the period from 1928 to 1938.[14] Up to 26,000 whales were caught in a single year in this period. Little whaling was done during

World War II. The postwar catch declined steadily, until by the beginning of the 1960s the species was almost extinct. Even today, there is uncertainty as to whether the blue whale will survive. What factors led to near extinction of the blue whale? We focus on two: the minimum stock size of its growth curve, and the economics of whaling.

Whales are, of course, a pelagic species, and no property rights to the species existed until 1964, when an international agreement among whaling nations prohibited their capture. Whalers attempted to harvest as many blue whales as possible, given the costs of effort. The question, like that addressed with the fur seals, is this: Would open access lead to a sustainable stock of whales and thus a sustainable harvest? To answer this, the profitability of the whaling industry must be examined.

What happens to profits as the catch declines? One might expect that, as in the case of the seals, as the catch declines costs rise faster than the value of the catch. Boats would then exit from the industry, and the species would recover. But, whaling boats do not specialize by species. This is one reason why a number of whale species are endangered. Whaling boats will go from species to species until the aggregate whale population is so low that costs cannot be covered by revenues. The products of the blue whale — oil, blubber, meat, ambergris (used in making perfumes) — are all readily obtainable from other whale species. Thus, blue whales were harvested along with other species; they were the preferred catch because of their size. It is the costs of harvesting any type of whale that are important in the industry, not the costs of harvesting the blue whale alone. The economics of whaling did not protect them, and the biological mechanics are such that the species cannot survive unless sufficient numbers survive.

By the early 1960s, public attention was focused on this irreplacable natural resource. An international agreement that prohibited the capture of any blue whales was signed. Their population was so low at that time that survival was in doubt. Thus the obvious policy response to preserve the species was to call a moratorium on the harvests. Was this the optimal economic policy?

Spence (1974) says "yes."[15] Even if we do not measure the social value of preserving the species, the economic optimum will correspond closely to the broadly interpreted social optimum. A calculation of the optimal economic harvest must incorporate both industry profits and biological mechanics. Spence computes the optimal steady-state population and the associated sustainable harvest. From his calculations, the steady-state stock with no harvesting at all is about 136,000 whales. The maximum sustainable yield (MSY) is 9,890 whales at a sustainable population of 45,177. Given his assumptions, the optimal population would be about 67,000 whales, with a sustainable catch of 9,000 per year. Notice that the optimal harvest is less than the MSY harvest, while the optimal population is larger.

What was the whale population in the 1960s, when international regulation began? Spence estimates that the stock of whales was about 1,639 in 1960. Although the number of whales critical for survival was not known, most observers felt that the population at that point was very close to the critical threshold. What, then, was the optimal regulatory policy? A moratorium on whaling. The species had to be allowed to grow at its natural rate until the steady-state equilibrium was reached. *Any* harvesting of blue whales would drive the industry away from the steady-state and toward extinction. Harvesting would reduce the value of the blue whale industry. Given estimates of the costs of whaling and the value per whale, Spence calculated that the harvest of blue whales would have to be prohibited for at least nine years. That calculation was based on very sketchy information about the recovery rate of the species; it was possible that the moratorium would have to last much longer to ensure the survival of the species and the continuation of the industry. At present, no commercial harvests of the blue whale are permitted.

The policy prescription for the blue whale — a moratorium — presents a difficult problem. What will happen to the factor inputs over the period when no harvesting is allowed? In the case of whaling, the vessels may just shift to other whale species. This creates another regulatory problem. If the other species are not protected, they too may be in danger of becoming extinct. Thus, regulations to deal with one case may merely shift the factors of production into another common property fishery. It is the lack of property rights that is the fundamental problem. Are there, however, cases where extinction will occur even with optimal management of the fishery?

Socially Optimal Extinction

Are there any situations in which it is socially optimal to extinguish a renewable resource? There are combinations of values for the social discount rate, the price of the fish, the costs of harvest, and the reproductive rate of the population for which extinction is optimal, but it is very unlikely that all the necessary conditions will be met. If the social discount rate is very high, indicating that individuals do not care much about the future, the price of fish is high, and marginal harvesting costs are unaffected by declining stocks, it is possible that the optimal steady-state equilibrium occurs at a fish stock below the threshold necessary to sustain the population. However, we can think of no cases in which a commercially valued species was exhausted in a fishery managed by a sole owner or regulated by government. The assumption that marginal costs do not depend on the remaining stock of fish is simply not consistent with fact in most fisheries. It is also difficult to imagine cases where the social discount rate has been high enough to make the value of the fishery negligible in the future.

Extinction of many plant and animal species has occurred, largely as a by-product of economic activity that did not put a social value on these living things. As we will see in Chapter 12, this type of extinction is the classic example of an externality for which social intervention is required. Extinction thus remains a phenomenon that is due to open access to the fishery.

SUMMARY

1. Fish populations are renewable natural resources that are often harvested under conditions of open access. This lack of property rights to the fish can lead to overfishing, inefficient use of factor inputs, low returns to fishing industries, and even the extinction of species.
2. To analyze the economics of the fishery, a biological production function for the species is needed. In a simple model, the stock of fish is assumed to grow over time according to a logistic function which relates the net growth of the

population to its size or biomass. Each point on the biological production function shows a sustainable yield of fish. If no harvesting occurs, there will be a natural or biological equilibrium where the net increase in biomass is equal to zero. This equilibrium occurs at the maximum carrying capacity of the species' habitat — where the biological mechanics $[dX/dt = F(X)]$ equal zero. The biological production function has a maximum sustainable yield (MSY) at a population level of one-half the maximum carrying capacity for the model of logistic growth.

3. When harvesting is introduced, a steady-state bionomic (bio-economic) equilibrium occurs when the net growth in the fish stock is exactly equal to the rate of harvest. The fishery can then continue indefinitely in this position of sustained cropping of fish.

4. Under conditions of open access to the fishery, a common property equilibrium will occur where the average revenue with respect to effort (where effort is an index of fishery inputs) is equal to the marginal cost of effort — an economically inefficient equilibrium. This equilibrium gives rise to the following problems: (a) A common property equilibrium will use more effort in catching a given harvest than is socially optimal. (b) Economic rent from the fishery will be lost. (c) Fishing firms fail to incorporate the effects of their actions on the stock of fish (a stock externality) and on the harvesting costs of other firms in the same fishery (a crowding externality). A smaller sustainable stock of fish will typically exist in a common property equilibrium than in a socially optimal equilibrium. (d) Bioeconomic inefficiency may result if the common property equilibrium is to the left of the MSY biomass.

5. The optimal path to a dynamic fishery equilibrium is one where the harvest rate is chosen such that the net return to investing in the fishery equals the social discount rate. The net return to investing in fish incorporates the sum of: (a) the capital gain from holding the stock from one period to the next; (b) the stock externality; and (c) biological growth from one period to the next.

6. In a dynamic model, the steady-state harvest and level of effort occur where the rent from the fishery (price minus the marginal cost of the harvest or marginal revenue minus marginal cost) net of the stock externality equals the discount rate. In a static model, the optimal steady-state equilibrium will be to the right of the MSY stock. In a dynamic model, with a positive but not infinite discount rate, the equilibrium can be to the right or the left of the MSY. The higher the discount rate, the more likely an equilibrium is to the left of the MSY.

7. If the discount rate equals zero, the static and dynamic private property equilibriums coincide. If the discount rate is infinity, a common property equilibrium exists and the static and dynamic equilibriums are the same. Only if the discount rate is zero, harvesting costs are zero, and the price of fish is very high will the optimal equilibrium be the MSY harvest and biomass.

8. A study of the possible dynamic paths of the fur seal industry in the late 1800s determines the common property equilibrium, given assumptions about the fish population, its biological mechanics, and industry conditions (exit and entry). Dynamic models combine the behavior of the fish stock with the behavior of firms to find a path of harvests and stocks over time that is most likely.

9. Extinction of a fish species can occur when the population is reduced below a critical threshold and/or because of open access. To have extinction, it must be the case that the price of fish must exceed the marginal cost of harvesting.

DISCUSSION QUESTIONS

1. Suppose the biological mechanics for a fishery are given by the equation $F(X) = aX - bX^2$, where X is the biomass of the fishery, and a and b are biological parameters which are assumed to be constant. What is the MSY biomass? What is the biological equilibrium of the fishery when there is no harvesting? Suppose harvesting of this species is always equal to H tons per instant of time, where H is less than the MSY biomass. Determine the bionomic equilibrium and explain how a steady-state equilibrium will be obtained: (a) starting from the biological equilibrium; and (b) starting from a point to the left of the MSY biomass.

2. Determine graphically the common property equilibrium level of effort and harvest for a fishery. Derive the industry supply curve for this fishery. Then (a) show what happens to the supply curve when the unit costs of effort rise; (b) when the unit costs of effort fall. (c) Show what happens to market equilibrium (supply equals demand) when demand shifts, say, due to a change in tastes (people like fish more than they did in the past).

3. Derive the common property and the socially optimal equilibrium when the supply curve of effort is positively sloped (the costs of effort rise as more effort is required). Explain the difference between the common property and private property equilibriums. Do any of the fundamental results derived for each equilibrium change? Explain.

4. Suppose the demand curve for flounder is given by $P = 400 - 3H$, where P is the price of flounder and H is the harvest in thousands of pounds. Let the *sustainable catch* given by $H = a_1 E - a_2 E^2 = 0.6 E - 0.0015 E^2$, where E is the level of effort. Unit costs are assumed constant and calculated to be about \$200 per unit of fishing effort. Given this information, compute graphically: (a) the common property harvest and level of effort; (b) the private property harvest and level of effort, assuming a competitive firm owns the fishery; and (c) the private property harvest and level of effort, assuming a monopolist owns the fishery. Show your solutions algebraically and graphically.

5. Explain the difference between the static and dynamic steady-state equilibriums of a fishery characterized by: (a) open access; (b) private property rights in a perfectly competitive market structure. Will a private property equilibrium ever be at the MSY biomass? Explain.

6. Under what conditions might a fish species be extinguished? Explain.

NOTES

1. There are some fish "farms" in lakes and off coastal waters where certain species of fish are grown like domestic farm animals. For example, in parts of the southern United States, crayfish are grown in coastal regions. Oysters, a case we examine in Chapter 9, are also frequently farmed in well-defined "beds" off the coasts of the United States, Canada, and elsewhere. Salmon farming is being developed off Canada's east and west coasts.

2. This model was developed by Schaefer (1957) and is often referred to as the Schaefer model. Also see Gulland (1974) for more biological details. Obviously, many more complex features enter into the determination of the growth rate than are given in the simple model described here. However, biologists tell us that stock size is a major determinant of growth and can be used as a proxy for other variables that affect the species over time. The implicit assumption is that each member of the stock (as measured by weight) produces

some offspring each season. The aggregate weight of the offspring thus depends on the aggregate weight of the current stock. Clearly, two stocks of the same weight could have different numbers of fertile members, and thus two seemingly identical stocks would have quite different net additions over time. Moreover, even two identical stocks could have different growth rates due to environmental factors. We return to these issues in Chapter 10; our simplified biological mechanics will be the working model for this chapter.

3. This is a continuous time model. Alternatively, we could look at the change in X over a discrete period, say a year, as $X(t + 1) - X(t)$. In practice, the discrete version makes more sense because fishing occurs over specific periods of time—a day, a week, or a fishing season. However, the continuous time version is easier to represent graphically and algebraically in most cases. Both yield approximately the same results, so in general we will use the continuous version here.

4. Mathematically, we assume for Equation (8.4) that $G(0,X) = 0$, $G_E > 0$, $G_{EE} < 0$, $G(E,0) = 0$, $G_X > 0$, G_{XX} is uncertain, and G_{EX} also uncertain. In the figures relating harvests to stock size (for a given amount of effort), we assume $G_{XX} = 0$ for simplicity.

5. In this example, with constant average and marginal costs, we cannot determine the number of firms in the industry. The problem is the same as that with any competitive industry facing constant costs.

6. This derivation is adapted from Hannesson (1978).

7. Alternatively, we could have derived the social optimum from the government's maximization of the sum of consumer plus producer surplus. With no market imperfections, the private property equilibrium is the social optimum.

8. The graphic solution discussed above can also be shown using simple calculus. The objective of the sole owner is to maximize profits by choosing a level of effort, E^*, subject to the constraint imposed by the biological mechanics, $dX/dt = 0$. Mathematically, the problem is to

$$\text{max social welfare} = pG(E,X) - wE + \lambda[F(x) - G(E,X)]$$

by choosing a level of E. To find the optimum, the equation above is differentiated with respect to E and X, and the resulting first-order conditions set equal to zero. These first-order conditions are:

$$pG_E - w - \lambda G_E = 0$$
$$pG_X + \lambda[F'(X) - G_X] = 0$$

If an interior solution (non-zero) exists, then it requires that $dX/dt = 0$, or $F(X) = G(E,X)$, and that

$$G_E + (G_E G_X)/[F'(X) - G_X] = w/p$$

Now how does this equilibrium differ from that of common property? First, note that in a steady-state equilibrium that is socially optimal, the real wage, w/p, equals the marginal product of effort, G_E, not the average product of effort, as in the common property equilibrium. The term $(G_E G_X)/[F'(X) - G_X]$ represents the effect an additional unit of effort has on the steady-state harvest (and thus fish stock), and in turn the effect of the decrease in the steady-state stock on the growth of the fish population over time. It is the stock externality noted in the text. The common property equilibrium does not incorporate this stock effect at all. Because the stock effect is negative, the common property equilibrium must have a higher level of effort and lower level of the fish stock than is socially optimal.

9. To solve the continuous time model, more advanced mathematics is required. We can solve the problem using the calculus of variations or control theory. We do not require

these techniques here; those wishing a more complete mathematical treatment should consult Clark (1976) and Dasgupta (1982), and the references in those texts.

10. The term C_X will also be nonzero for nonrenewable resources when the marginal costs of extraction rise as the stock of the mineral declines. This is true in the case of, say, oil, where as oil is pumped from a well, the natural pressure remaining in the well diminishes and it will take more costly recovery methods (pumping in brine) to recover additional units of oil. The fundamental difference between minerals and fish is the growth term, $F'(X)$, which is not meaningful in the case of minerals.

11. There are conceptual difficulties with the harvesting function assumed in Equation (8.17): No limit is placed on the harvest as additional units of effort are employed. But we know that, as X goes to zero, no amount of effort will yield a positive harvest. See Spence (1974) for a simple harvest function that eliminates this problem.

12. A variant of this path is the ever-cycling system. The boats and seals may simply cycle forever around the equilibrium point but never reach it.

13. There are many difficult problems empirically in the analysis, as one might expect. Data are sparse, and many simplifying assumptions had to be made. Nonetheless, the calculations show how the dynamic model can be used.

14. Information on the blue whale is taken from Spence (1974) and some of the references cited therein.

15. See, however, the discussion of the blue whale in Hannesson (1978) based on a paper by Clark (1973b). For different social discount rates, Clark calculates the optimal stock level, sustainable yield, and the number of years a moratorium on harvesting blue whales is necessary to obtain the optimal stock, given an initial common property equilibrium of 7,000 whales. The optimal stock is very sensitive to the discount rate. For relatively low discount rates, the optimal stock is below the MSY level. This feature, combined with relatively low harvesting costs due to versatility of whaling vessels, implies that extinction may be socially optimal (ignoring any social value of the species). If the discount rate exceeds 5 percent and costs are sufficiently low, extinction is economically efficient. This result is much less likely with other species.

chapter 9

Regulation of the Fishery

INTRODUCTION

The economic rationales for regulating the fishery are very clear. In the last chapter we saw that the common property equilibrium: (1) Was economically inefficient because the value of average, not marginal, product with respect to effort is set equal to the marginal cost of effort. Excessive amounts of effort are therefore used for a given harvest. (2) Could be bioeconomically inefficient with a steady-state stock of fish to the left of the MSY biomass. (3) Could lead to extinction of the species. (4) Dissipated all the rent to the fishery and could contribute to low incomes of workers in the fishery. Economic policies to remedy these problems should thus: (1) find methods of rationing the amount of effort in the fishery; (2) find methods of regulating the harvest to maintain efficient stocks of fish; and (3) recognize that any policy implemented may affect the distribution of income through the reduction of effort and by generating rents.

Regulation of a fishery is a complex task. We will focus on policies which in theory could improve the economic efficiency with which factors of production are utilized in the fishery. We note as well some of the practical issues of implementing policies and effects on the distribution of income and generation of rents. In this chapter we use the basic model examined in Chapter 8 to examine the possible ways in which the fishery can be regulated to achieve an efficient equilibrium. Then we examine policy objectives of governments, some regulations enacted, and the effects of these regulations on particular fisheries. In most actual cases, regulation has done very little to eliminate the inefficient use of factor inputs. Much existing regulation in the fishery is designed to sustain the fishery and increase the incomes of fishermen, not to reach a socially optimal equilibrium. There are bound to be conflicts of interest among different groups. What is beneficial to particular individuals in the fishery is costly to others; what is good for consumers may reduce incomes in the fishery. Governments have to be responsive to these interests. This is a major reason why it is so difficult to find cases where fisheries have been regulated so as to maximize social welfare.

How do we analyze the regulation of any fishery? First, we assume a policy target must be set. Here we first assume that the target is to reach the optimal harvest and level of effort, and thus steady-state stock of a particular fish species. Later we look at actual cases where the target may be different. Second, methods of reaching the target must be found. We evaluate alternative devices in terms of their ability (administratively and in theory) to reach the optimum target. We examine taxes on the harvest or on effort, quotas on the catch or effort, licensing of vessels or fishermen, and the assignment of private property rights.

In each policy examined we assume that the regulators know the growth function of the species and how individuals in the fishery will behave. This is often not the case in practice. The ecology of fish species can be highly complex and not amenable to precise statistical analysis. It is hard to examine the interaction of different species and their habitat when everything happens below water. This is especially true for the pelagic species, which range over large tracts of the ocean.

In most regulatory environments, the growth function is estimated from the actual catch and amount of effort used at different points in time. There are obvious problems with this technique, as we will see. But it is not just the stock of fish we have imperfect information about; regulators must also contend with the unpredictable behavior of the individuals working in the fishing industry. There are many examples of policies that looked good on paper, but failed to reach their objectives because the individuals being regulated did not act the way they were expected to.

THE ECONOMICS OF FISHERY REGULATION

We begin this section by defining the tax on the fishery which will convert a common property equilibrium to one which is socially optimal. We do this first for the somewhat more complicated dynamic model in which a positive discount rate is assumed, and then turn to a graphic analysis of particular taxes and quotas on the fishery. For the graphic analysis, we concentrate on the static steady-state equilibrium and do not explicitly deal with the discount rate. As we saw in Chapter 8, the static steady-state coincides with the dynamic steady-state only if the discount rate is zero. A positive discount rate will modify the precise results, but will not change their qualitative nature. The essence of the different regulations can be seen using the static model.

The Optimal Taxes on the Fishery

The condition that determines the optimal steady-state harvest in our dynamic model of the fishery is given by Equation (9.1).[1]

$$P = C' + C_X/[F'(X) - r] \qquad (9.1)$$

where all terms are as defined in Chapter 8. P is the price of fish, which we continue to assume is constant. C_X is the marginal stock effect on harvest costs. $F'(X)$ is the incremental effect of the stock on potential harvest.

These terms reflect the effect an additional unit of fish harvested today has on future harvests. A fish left for tomorrow may lower harvest costs, leave a larger population to reproduce, and thus lead to greater harvests in the future. But these costs have to be weighted by the opportunity cost of time, r, the discount rate. The higher the discount rate, the less important are these stock effects because individuals would rather have large harvests today than a higher sustained harvest over time. C' is the marginal cost of harvesting an additional unit of biomass. The optimal steady-state harvest must thus be chosen where price net of the stock effect is equal to the marginal cost of harvesting. We now want to compare the equilibrium implied by Equation (9.1) to the common property equilibrium.

As seen in Chapter 8, the industry harvest in a common property equilibrium will be set where the price of fish is equal to the average cost of harvest (which is equivalent to saying the average revenue product from effort equals the marginal cost of effort), that is:

$$P = cE/H \tag{9.2}$$

The common property equilibrium (CPE) occurs because of the free access to the fishery and continued entry persisting when total revenues exceed total costs ($P > AC$ of harvest or AR of effort). Our problem is how to convert a common property equilibrium to one that is socially optimal.

One way is to impose a tax on the fishery. An *optimal tax*—one which is levied on the open access fishery to yield an efficient equilibrium—can be imposed on effort or on the harvest. In this section, we first note the components of such a tax on the harvest algebraically in the context of our dynamic model. We then illustrate optimal taxes on the harvest or effort graphically, using our steady-state static model. Compare Equations (9.1) and (9.2). We see that they differ in two respects: The marginal stock effect is absent in Equation (9.2) and price there is set equal to the average, not marginal, cost of harvest.

The reason the marginal stock effect is zero in the open access case is that the discount rate is effectively equal to infinity. Under open access there may be no fish to harvest in the future, therefore no individual in the fishery cares about the effect of harvests today on the growth of the biomass or the costs of tomorrow's harvests. The optimal tax on each unit of fish harvested is $C_x/[F'(X) - r]$, evaluated at the socially optimal harvest. Rent per pound harvested is made positive by this tax. Tax per unit harvested equals rent per unit harvested. This tax will reduce the value of the harvest to each firm. As total revenues decline, less effort will be employed in the fishery. Some factors of production will leave because they are not covering their opportunity costs. What this tax effectively does is to force fishing firms to incorporate the effect their actions have on the stock of fish—to prevent overfishing.

In the absence of discounting or interest rate effects, the appropriate tax equates the marginal revenue product of effort to its marginal, not average, cost. Figure 9.1 illustrates this tax. We have drawn marginal and average costs of harvesting fish as derived in Chapter 8. Suppose the price of fish is P. In the open access case the harvest

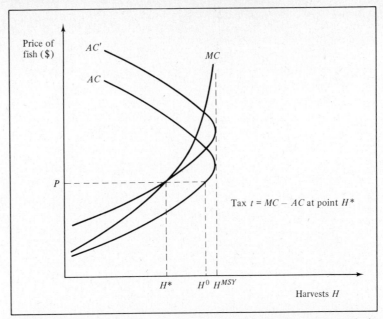

Figure 9.1 The optimal harvest is determined where the price of fish equals the marginal cost of the harvest. This occurs at a harvest of H^*. The common property equilibrium is where price equals the average cost of the harvest. This occurs at $H°$. A tax equal to the difference between the marginal cost of the harvest and the average cost of the harvest at the optimal harvest will yield the optimal harvest in an open access fishery. The tax shifts the average cost curve from AC to AC' for the fishery. Setting price equal to AC' yields the optimal harvest H^*.

will be H^0, but the optimal harvest is H^*, which is less than H^0 in this case. The harvest is too large under open access (but of course it could also be too small at a different initial price level). The tax on the harvest equal to $C' - cE/H$ means that each firm will be choosing a harvest *as if* it were on its marginal cost curve. For if we subtract $(C' - cE/H)$ from average cost, cE/H, we are left with marginal cost C'.[2]

Graphically, the tax can be interpreted as causing the firm's average cost curve to shift up to AC', where the vertical distance of the shift is equal to $C' - cE/H$ at the harvest H^*. With the constant price, the firms, still operating in an open access environment, will equate P to AC' and thus reach the optimal harvest H^*.

So far we have focused on the optimal tax on the harvest from an open access fishery. We turn now to a graphic examination of the different ways in which the optimal harvest and level of effort can be obtained. We will examine the steady-state equilibrium, not the paths of evolution of H and X to the equilibrium. We examine taxes and quotas on both effort and the catch. Recall that although we assume the growth function for the fishery and behavior of fishing firms is known, this is rarely the case in practice. Every policy studied below will be imperfect if these functions are not known. In some cases, the "cost" of an imprecise calculation of the optimal amount of effort and catch will be higher than in others. We will indicate when this is so.

A Tax on the Catch

The government fishery manager has just computed the optimal taxes discussed above in consultation with a fishery biologist who has provided information on the growth function of the fish, $F(X)$. The government is prepared to levy a tax equal to the marginal stock effect plus the difference between marginal and average costs of harvest on the fishing firm. How will the manager impose the tax? Above, we noted that the tax would be levied on the harvests. One way to view the tax is that every pound of lobster that is landed now yields a price to the fisherman net of the taxes.

In the preceding section, we illustrated the tax on the average costs of the harvest. Alternatively, we can look at the effect of the tax on effort. The tax on the catch reduces total revenue received for each unit of effort employed in the fishery. Figure 9.2 illustrates the situation. Before the tax, each firm in the industry faced a total revenue function given by $TR = PH$, where H, the harvest, is dependent on the amount of effort and the stock of fish. Total costs are dependent on the unit cost of effort, which is assumed to be constant, and the amount of effort used; $TC = cE$. The tax now means that for each fish sold, the price received is net of the tax, t, or $P' = (P - t)$. Total revenue is therefore $(P - t)H$. This is shown by the curve TR' in Figure 9.2.

Firms still equate total revenue to total cost (the open access condition remains), but if the tax has been set appropriately, the new equilibrium point will be at the optimal amount of effort, shown as E^*. The total value or rents from the fishery will be maximized. The value of the fishery is Y^* if effort is set equal to E^*. The government captures the rent in the form of the tax revenue equal to $(Y^* - Y')$. Fishing firms receive the amount Y'. Thus, the optimal tax generates the rent to the fishing ground that was lost under open access. But it need not improve the income of fishermen; indeed, it may lower aggregate income from fishing, as we see below.

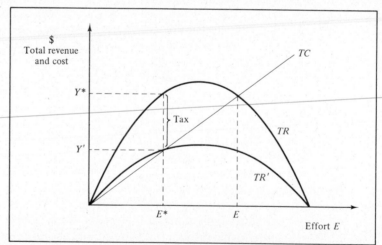

Figure 9.2 An optimal tax (t) on the catch will reduce the revenue to the fishery for each unit of effort employed. Before the tax, firms will enter an open access fishery until total revenues (TR) equal total costs (TC). The amount of effort used in the common property equilibrium is E. The tax reduces total revenue to TR', where $TR' = (P - t)H$. Firms now set $TR' = TC$, yielding the optimal amount of effort E^*.

Notice that with a tax, the government is in effect sharing some of the risks involved in fishing with the fishing firms. A tax is levied only when fish are caught. There are no costs for the firm to pay "up front." Firms should incorporate the tax in their decision-making, but they will not incur any costs of this policy until they see their return reduced at the time of sale. The effect of the tax may thus be quite different from other forms of regulation—namely, license fees or quotas, which require payment before the harvest occurs.

The tax on the catch looks very appealing in theory. It allows fishing firms to act independently, it doesn't involve monitoring of fishing effort, and it can lead to the social optimum. Fishing firms still act as if they had open access to the fishery, but the tax forces them to reduce effort and harvests to the optimal level. In practice, however, we seldom observe taxes on the catch. Why not? There are a number of administrative and political problems with a tax on the catch.

Suppose the tax is set at the wrong level. The government cannot determine the optimal tax and simply guesses at an amount that it thinks will decrease effort sufficiently to move the fishery toward the optimal steady-state. If the fish species is in no immediate danger of extinction, the nonoptimal tax will still lead to a reduction in effort. This reduction may be too much or too little, but as long as the tax can be revised as data on the catch and the fish population are revealed, the system may ultimately reach the optimum. This is not to say that costs will not emerge. A tax set too high may create large amounts of unemployment in the fishery—a situation that has serious income and political implications. If there is some uncertainty about the viability of the fish stock, an inappropriate tax may not reduce effort enough, and the species could be extinguished.

Note as well that the optimal tax will depend on exogenous variables such as the price of fish, or more generally, the demand for fish and the biological characteristics of the fishery. We have assumed that these exogenous variables do not change, but in practice they can fluctuate quite a lot. Over time, the demand for fish may rise due to changes in income and tastes. Fishery population dynamics can be affected by environmental factors, changes in predators, and so on. The "optimal" tax must account for all these factors at each point in time. Altering the tax to incorporate changes in exogenous variables may be straightforward in theory; in practice, it is difficult to change any governmental policy, including taxes. What is optimal today may not be optimal tomorrow. This makes it very difficult to advocate taxes as a means of correcting a common property fishery. We will encounter this problem again in our discussion of environmental resources in Chapters 12 and 13.

A tax on the harvest is very difficult to implement. Landed fish can be sold in a variety of different markets—to packers, to restaurants, to individuals from the backs of pickup trucks, and in different countries. It would be difficult for a government to make sure the tax was paid in each case. Fishing firms may have a big incentive to evade the tax, and may find it easy to do so. Unlike other types of taxes (the retail sales tax, withholding tax on personal income), which are more difficult to avoid, a tax on the catch would be relatively difficult to collect. The tax may also interfere with the government's ability to formulate good fishery policies. This is because harvests are often the main source of biological and economic information and hence help determine the optimal tax rate. The regulator may think that the tax is working to reduce effort, when in fact the tax induces firms to underreport harvests and sell the unrevealed catch illegally.

A tax on the catch can create unemployment. Aggregate effort will typically fall if the tax is effective. Those remaining in the fishery are no worse off, but some will have to exit. If there are high costs of finding alternative forms of employment (whether these costs are real or perceived), these individuals will be worse off than before the tax was imposed. The government will be pressured to not impose the tax or, if implemented, to compensate those who lose. Recall that the government is collecting the rent from the fishery, so it is feasible to compensate losers. But this may still not appease those displaced by the tax. In many countries, fishing communities have a lot of political power and may thus prevent the implementation of policies that threaten them. The commissioner investigating the West Coast salmon fishery for the Canadian government was heckled and booed by fishermen when he conducted hearings. His crime was to propose a tax on the salmon harvest. There are still no taxes on the salmon harvest in Canada.

A Tax on Fishing Effort

Rather than tax fish as they are landed, suppose the government decided to tax effort in the fishery. Will this form of tax lead to an optimal harvest? In theory, yes. Figure 9.3 illustrates two types of optimal tax on effort. The first is a *head tax*—a tax of a particular amount levied on each operator in the fishery. An example of this type of tax is a license fee. Each firm (or boat) must pay the government a particular sum if it wishes to fish. The tax must be paid before any amount of effort is used in harvesting fish, but the tax is independent of the actual amount of effort employed by each firm. Let's see how the head tax alters each firm's total cost function.

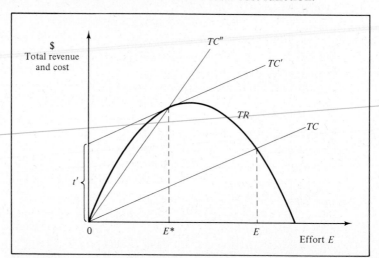

Figure 9.3 Two taxes on effort are shown. A head tax equal to t' shifts the original TC curve to TC', where $TC' = wE + t'$. Open access firms equate TC' to TR, and the optimal amount of effort, E^*, results. A unit tax on effort equal to t'' will pivot the TC curve to TC'', where $TC'' = (w + t'')E$. The optimal amount of effort is achieved where $TC'' = TR$.

In Figure 9.3, before any taxes are levied, each firm has a total cost function that is given by TC, where TC is equal to cE, the unit cost of effort (c) times the amount of effort used. The common property equilibrium is originally at E (where $TR = TC$). The optimal amount of effort is E^*, where $MR = MC$. The optimal head tax equal to t' will shift the firm's TC curve to TC', where $TC' = cE + t'$. The firm still equates total revenue to total cost, but in this case they are equal where total costs, TC', are tangent to TR. Thus the tax has led to the optimal amount of effort, E^*. Notice that the fee must be levied in each period the firm operates. We are describing a steady-state fishery, and this means that the costs shown by TC' must be repeated each period. If the license fee is paid only once, the cost curve will return to TC in the next period. The fee will have become a sunk cost that no longer has an effect on the marginal amount of effort employed in the fishery.

The second form of tax on effort is levied on each unit of effort employed, in each period that it is employed. With a tax equal to t'', the original total cost curve TC then pivots to TC'', where $TC'' = (c + t'')E$. The tax has no effect if no effort is used, so the total cost curve continues to pass through the origin (unlike the curve with the head tax). If the optimal tax is chosen, again the total cost curve will intersect the total revenue curve at the optimal amount of effort, E^*.

The most serious difficulty with any tax on effort is defining effort. We have talked about levying such a tax in theory, but how exactly is this tax to be imposed? Effort is an index of the capital, labor, and materials used by the fishing firm. When it comes to imposing a tax on this index in practice, how can it be done? It is not difficult to impose the tax on certain types of effort; government managers routinely license boats and even individuals. The problem is that unless all forms of effort are taxed, fishing firms have an incentive to avoid the effects of the tax by substituting types of effort that are not taxed for those that are.

Suppose there is a tax on the boat. Clearly, we'd want to make that tax depend on the size of the boat, because it is generally possible to harvest more fish, the larger the size of the vessel. But what if the equipment on the boat is not taxed? We would then see small boats top-heavy with electronic equipment, nets, and people. If individuals are licensed but vessels are not, large fleets owned by one person can result. If the government tries to tax all forms of effort, an incredibly complex and extensive set of taxes would be necessary. The government is likely to spend more than it collects in taxes trying to figure out what type of untaxed equipment fishing firms will substitute for taxed items each year.

The problem with taxes in general is that they may not have a predictable effect on the amount of effort in the fishery and hence on the harvest. They act on firms' ex ante decision making. That is, they represent a reduction in the firm's net returns ($TR - TC$) from fishing. In theory, this reduction in net returns should reduce the effort used by each firm. Mobility out of fishing generally has not been rapid; many individuals do not perceive alternative forms of employment to be desirable. If so, large taxes (which may mean that all firms take losses in the short run) would be necessary to induce these individuals to reduce their effort. Governments are averse to levying any tax, especially high taxes.

We turn now to the other type of regulation in the fishery — quotas or quantity controls on the harvest and/or amount of effort in the fishery. These are by far the most prevalent form of regulation in fishing industries.

A Quota on the Catch and Effort

Let's first consider a quota on the catch alone. Suppose the government has found that the fish stock is threatened. If harvests are not reduced to a particular level, the species may become extinct and the fishery will vanish. This is a strong case for a *quota* on the harvest. Quite simply, the government limits the number (or biomass) of fish that can be caught in a given time period. In the case of the blue whale we saw in Chapter 8, that the quota was zero: firms were prohibited from harvesting any whales. Most fisheries are not in such an extreme situation, although the blue whale is by no means unique.[3]

Typically, before the fishing season begins, a quota or total allowable catch (TAC) is established for the species. The TAC is based on information about the fishery in the past — the harvests and estimates of the remaining stock — and may also reflect biological and economic modeling. Factors such as expected recruitment for the period (or past period), water temperature, catches of related or predator species, and so on are taken into account. Then the fishery is opened up and boats are allowed to enter and harvest the species until the TAC is reached. Once the TAC is met, the fishery is closed.

The quota can lead to the optimal harvest as long as the government is sure about the size of the fish stock and how it changes over time. But the quota will *not* lead to an efficient amount of effort in the fishery unless the quota is optimally rationed among individual firms. This can be shown quite simply. Figure 9.4 illustrates a biological production function, $F(X)$. Suppose the government wishes to restrict the harvest each period to level $\bar{H}$. We can see that a steady-state equilibrium

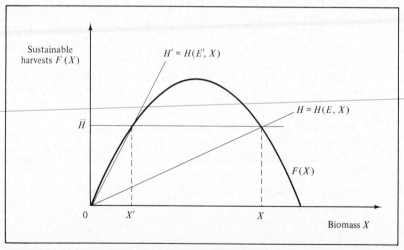

Figure 9.4 A quota on the total harvest from a fishery will not achieve the optimal amount of effort. A quota on the catch set at $\bar{H}$ restricts the harvest, but does not prevent the excessive use of effort. Two sustainable stocks, X' and X, and two levels of effort ($E' > E$) are compatible with a harvest of $\bar{H}$. If costs warrant, the common property equilibrium could be at X', using large amounts of effort.

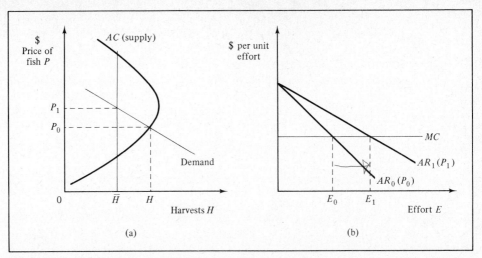

Figure 9.5 A quota on the total harvest from an open access fishery may lead to a higher price for the species. In (a), if the demand curve is downward-sloping, restricting total harvests to $\overline{H}$ will lead to an increase in the price of fish from P_0 to P_1. In (b), the rise in the price of fish from P_0 to P_1 will shift the average revenue curve as a function of effort from AR_0 to AR_1. The new common property equilibrium is then at a higher level of effort, E_1. The higher price thus induces more entry, which leads to greater congestion externalities and excess capacity in the fishery.

could be achieved at two different stock levels, X' and X, which correspond to different amounts of effort $(E' > E)$. With only the total harvest controlled and not entry, there is no way to prevent large amounts of effort being expended trying to catch the allowed limit. There is no guarantee that E' is the optimal amount of effort. The actual common property equilibrium will, of course, depend on costs (which may change with the imposition of the quota).

A quota on the total harvest may in fact exacerbate open access problems. Suppose the quota restricts the harvest, and the reduction in the harvest leads to an increase in the price of the species, as illustrated in Figure 9.5. In (a), with the fishery facing a demand curve D, the initial common property equilibrium yields a harvest of H at price P_0. If the quota restricts harvests to $\overline{H}$, price will rise to P_1. Vessels from other fisheries may then enter in response to the higher prices in the regulated fishery. This is shown in Figure 9.5(b). The rise in the price of the fish shifts the average revenue curve (as a function of effort) from AR_0 to AR_1. The CPE is then where the marginal cost of effort equals AR_1. This means that effort will rise from E_0 to E_1.

Fewer fish will be harvested with more effort. The quota may simply lead to more firms fishing for more valuable fish in a shorter period of time. Firms will rush to catch the quota as quickly as possible to prevent others from getting the fish first. All the open access problems occur as they did before the imposition of the quota — but in a shorter time period. Congestion externalities are likely to be rampant as vessels crowd in to get their share of the quota. Excess capacity in processing and retailing sectors may be needed to handle the large tonnages that are dumped on the market over a short time interval. The quality of the fish may decline if boats stay out in the fishery for longer periods to try and catch as much as possible before the limits are reached. Clearly, a quota on the harvest can lead to many inefficiencies.

What is needed is a means of allocating the quota among the fishing firms—in a sense, establishing a private property right to a particular harvest. A quota specific to a firm can lead to efficient use of effort within that firm. If each fishing firm has a guarantee that it can catch so many tons of fish each period, then the firm will act to minimize the cost of harvesting its allowable catch. Economic efficiency can be obtained. As long as the fish stock is abundant enough to ensure that each quota can be filled, each owner of a quota has no reason to put an excessive amount of effort into catching the fish. The open access character of the fishery is eliminated.

But simply assigning a quota to a firm does not guarantee that the most efficient firms are doing the harvesting. Whether economic efficiency occurs depends on how the quota is distributed and whether it is transferable and divisible. As we now see, there are two methods of allocating quotas—one by arbitrary administrative procedures and the other through market mechanisms.

First, assume that the government simply apportions the quota among the existing firms so that each is entitled to catch, say, h fish, where $h = H/E$. Alternatively, the government could apportion the quota on the basis of previous catches per firm. Those with historically large catches would be allowed a larger quota than firms which had caught relatively few fish. Some boats may not get a quota, or may get one so small that fishing does not pay. The arbitrary nature of these types of distribution schemes can politicize the fishery and create high administrative costs. If the quotas are nontransferable, economic efficiency will not in general be achieved. There is no guarantee that the firm receiving the quota is the one with the lowest costs of harvest. To see what may happen when a quota is distributed on arbitrary or political bases, reflect on quotas on agricultural products and their documented effects on inflating food prices.

As noted above, an individual quota establishes a property right to the fish harvested. These rights will then have value. If quotas are divisible and transferable, others could bid for them, and the holder of the quota would be able to capture some of the rents from the fishery. The firm could sell or lease part or all of the quota to another firm, just as it could a piece of land, and receive the discounted future profit from the use of the quota. This may mean that over time, an arbitrary distribution of quotas should lead to an efficient use of effort and harvest.

Firms with low costs could bid more for a quota than those with high costs. If the original holder of a quota was a high-cost firm, it would do better to sell its quota and move to another industry. Even if quotas are given away in an economically inefficient manner, if they are divisible and transferable, economic efficiency may ultimately be achieved. If quotas are not transferable, inefficiencies will persist. New firms with new and less costly technologies may be prevented from entering the fishery. Quotas may not benefit consumers. An effective quota will generally raise local prices consumers pay, and a decline in the industry will occur if the fish have good substitutes or foreign competition.

Another way to apportion quotas is to auction them off to the highest bidder. Firms will offer the present value of the potential profits from having the quota. If the quota restricts the total catch below what it would be under open access, these profits will be positive. They are the rent from the fishery, and the government will collect these rents from the sale of the quotas. They become public revenue. Auctioning should lead to an impact in the fishery per se similar to free distribution, as long as quotas are divisible and transferable and no imperfections exist in the market for fishing rights. Under auctioning, however, much of the rent is transferred to the government or public domain. Under a free distribution scheme, the rents are captured by those lucky enough to acquire initially some of the quota. The income distribution effects are markedly different. Moreover, free distribution usually means that the political process is involved and fairness can get little attention. Obviously, there are many more complexities involved in the sale or free distribution of a quota, as we will see below.

Are there any rationales for the imposition of a quota on effort alone? An example of a quota on effort is the licensing of vessels. Let's first see how a quota on effort would achieve the optimal amount of effort and the optimal harvest. Suppose that an index of effort can somehow be accurately measured. The government fisheries board then solves for the socially optimal amount of effort, E^*. In Figure 9.6, E^* would be set where the slope of the total cost curve (the MC of effort) is tangent to the TR curve. No effort beyond E^* would be allowed in the fishery. This will yield the optimal harvest, because once E^* is achieved, the efficient harvest function is obtained.

Of course, this simple graphic representation omits all the difficult problems with a quota on effort. As with a tax on effort, the most severe problem is how to measure and then restrict each component of effort. Should the quota be placed on boats, people, equipment, or all of those? In practice, there are many different quotas on the various factor inputs that make up effort. Fishing firms have responded to quotas on one component by substituting factors that are not restricted. Government fisheries managers must then try to make the quotas as specific as possible. Regulations may be administratively very costly, and they must be altered frequently to reflect current conditions. There also remains the problem of how to implement the quota. Will it be sold or given to the firm? Will the quota be transferable and hence

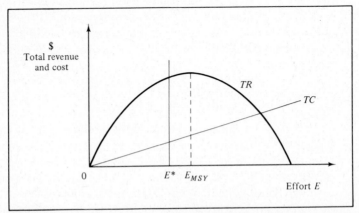

Figure 9.6 A quota on effort is imposed at E^*, where E^* is determined by equating MR to MC. If effort could be measured, the quota would restrict effort to the efficient level and result in an efficient harvest.

acquire a market value of its own (regardless of whether it was initially sold or given to the holder)? On what basis does the government restrict effort? These are the same problems taken up in the discussion of the quota on the harvest.

In practice, quotas on effort occur for a variety of reasons. Sometimes quotas are imposed because a specific impact on the fish population is desired. For example, if the government managers wish to prevent the capture of a certain age class of fish (a cohort), restrictions on the size of the nets used in the fishery may be imposed to prevent the capture of fish below a certain size. All effort (and harvests) may be banned when biologists know that the species is reproducing. These restrictions may aid in the maintenance of the species, but they are difficult to design and enforce.

Before turning to our examples, we look at one further way in which an optimal allocation of resources to the fishery can be accomplished — turning the fishery over to a sole owner. We look at one example of government-backed sole ownership — the cooperative.

Sole Ownership of the Fishery: The Cooperative

A *cooperative* is the self-administration of the fishery by the individuals doing the fishing. The government legally sanctions such organizations. The cooperative decides on quotas or other forms of control among its members, rather than taking orders from the government. To prevent overfishing, a government manager may set a total allowable catch each year and ensure that it is being met. The government biologist would also ensure that the total allowable catch is consistent with preservation of an optimal stock of fish.

The crucial decision of the cooperative is how many members to have and how to assign quotas to members. If the co-op is too large, each member would earn low profits. If the organization is too small, outsiders may be induced to demand compensation from the government for not being allowed to enter the industry. Cooperatives have been used in a number of fisheries — for example, the Bay of Fundy herring fishery.

We turn now to fishery regulation in practice. We look at U.S. management objectives and activities, then examine some specific fisheries in different parts of the world, looking at the type of regulations used and their impact on the fishery and the fishing effort.

FISHERY REGULATIONS IN PRACTICE

Our objective in this section is to illustrate the impact of various regulations being used in different fisheries on variables of interest such as effort, the harvest, incomes to workers in the fishery, the sustainable stock, and the quality of the harvest. We will, when possible, also indicate the costs of the regulations — their financial cost, and the costs in terms of potential misallocation of resources. We hope to give an indication of whether the benefits to society of regulating the fishery justify the financial and economic costs incurred in the regulatory process.

Before looking at particular cases, we discuss briefly the apparatus for regulating fisheries between 3 and 200 miles off the U.S. coast — the fishery management councils. We then consider in more detail three fisheries and how they are or are not regulated: (1) oyster fisheries off the Atlantic and Gulf coasts of the United States, (2) a sardine fishery in Spain, and (3) the Pacific halibut fishery of the United States and Canada. We need first to make some basic points about regulation in general.

First, regulation is costly. Governments must establish some sort of fisheries department with personnel to evaluate the fishery, and design and implement the policies. Once the policies are in place, the fishery must be monitored to ensure that the regulations are being followed and to see if any changes must be made. Although we have no precise estimates of the costs, we do have a tentative figure which suggests that large sums can be spent. In a study of regulation in the Canadian fisheries, Scott and Neher (1981) reported that the budget of the federal Fish and Marine Programme was $325 million in 1978. And these figures do not include the expenses of Canadian provinces on fishery regulations. Presumably, most of these funds would not be spent if fisheries were not regulated and subsidies were not paid to fishermen.

Are the expenses warranted? What is the value of the excessive amount of effort in the industry and perhaps excessively high harvest costs; the low harvests in many fisheries and thus foregone incomes that would be received under efficient management? We have no aggregate numbers, but some of the cases below will give estimates of foregone revenues and excessive costs when the fishery remains under open access. (See Box 9.1.) In these cases, the costs of open access are much larger than the costs of regulation. The second point is that there is no guarantee that regulatory agencies will use economic criteria. This is clearly brought out in the case of the Pacific halibut and in the practices of some of the U.S. fisheries management councils.

BOX 9.1
Measuring the Welfare Cost of Free Entry in a
Lobster Fishery

Estimates of the social cost of unrestricted entry to two lobster fisheries in eastern Canada were developed by Henderson and Tugwell (1979). They found these losses from unrestricted entry to be about 20 to 30 percent of the current market value of harvests in the areas. The loss was represented to a considerable extent by excess resources devoted to harvesting. While catch fell by 10 to 40 percent, effort or resources fell by 60 to 70 percent in the hypothetical switch from unregulated entry to optimally regulated entry. Let us observe the results for one area, Miminegash. They found the stock-yield equation to be

$$X(t + 1) - X(t) = X(t)[1.27024 - 0.00039X(t)]$$

and estimated a harvest equation as

$$H(t) = 2.51E^{0.48}X^{0.44}$$

where E is effort measured in hundreds of traps, $X(t)$ is the stock at time t, and $H(t)$ the harvest. The price obtained by fishermen was $370 per thousand pounds, and opportunity cost per hundred traps was $390. The results obtained are presented in the following table.

Box 9.1 continued

	Optimal solution	Free entry	Observed 1959–1963
Lobster stock (thousand lb)	2,450	1,125	1,273
Lobster catch (thousand lb)	801	936	1,094
Effort (traps)	122	365	—
Ratio: catch/stock	0.33	0.83	0.86
Shadow price of future stock	68	—	—
Optimal tax/thousand lb catch	225	—	—
Annual resource savings:			
Dollar value of traps saved			
Less value of diminution in catch	$180,470	—	—

Source: J. V. Henderson and M. Tugwell, "Exploitation of the Lobster Fishery: Some Empirical Results." *Journal of Environmental Economics and Management* 6 (1979), pp. 287–296.

Fisheries Management Councils in the United States

In 1976, the Fisheries Conservation and Management Act, FCMA (also referred to as the Magnusan Act), established the right of the U.S. federal government to manage the fish stock lying from 3 to 200 miles off all U.S. coastlines.[4] Fisheries within 3 miles are under state jurisdiction, and of course those outside the 200-mile limit are in international waters. Before passage of the act, virtually no management of fisheries beyond 3 miles had occurred.

The act established several objectives for the management of fisheries to be applied nationally. First, conservation and management measures were to prevent overfishing while achieving sustainable optimal yields. *Optimal* was interpreted as that yield which maximizes the country's benefits from food production and recreational fishing, as prescribed by the MSY biomass and modified by economic, social, and ecological factors. Fisheries were also to be managed to promote efficiency and minimize costs in utilizing the fish resources, but economic criteria were not to be the sole objective of management. At first glance, the objectives would seem to be very close to an economist's objective function for optimal fishery management incorporating distributional and ecological factors. However, because the stated objectives are qualified by the words "when practicable," some ambiguity is introduced into the interpretation of the act.

Eight regional fisheries management councils were established to implement the FCMA. Table 9.1 lists the councils and the fish species they manage. If a particular species is important in more than one area, the councils of the regions affected are to manage the fisheries jointly. The major task of the eight councils is to draw up a plan to determine the optimal harvest and how the harvest will be accomplished. The administrative procedures of the councils are complex. And other agencies, such as the U.S. Coast Guard, U.S. State Department, and the Commerce Department's National Marine Fisheries Service are involved in the management programs. Council members comprise appointees by secretaries for natural resources (or equivalent persons) from each state in the council's region (50 percent of membership); the

Table 9.1   REGIONAL FISHERIES COUNCILS

Council	States	Species
New England	Maine, New Hampshire, Massachusetts, Rhode Island, Connecticut	Atlantic groundfish, Atlantic herring, sharks, sea scallops, swordfish, redfish, billfish, bake, pollock, red crabs, American lobster
Mid-Atlantic	New York, New Jersey, Pennsylvania, Delaware, Maryland, Virginia	Surf clam and ocean quahog, Atlantic mackerel, butterfish, squid, sharks, bluefish, swordfish, scup, dogfish, billfish, other flounder, sea bass, tile fish, sea scallops
South Atlantic	North Carolina, South Carolina, Georgia, Florida	Billfish, coastal migratory pelagics, sharks, swordfish, corals, spiny lobster, tropical reef fish, calico scallops, sea scallops, shrimp, coastal herring
Caribbean	Virgin Islands, Puerto Rico	Spiny lobster, shallow water reef fish, swordfish, migratory pelagics, mollusks, billfish, corals, deepwater reef fish, bait fishes, sharks, rays
Gulf	Texas, Louisiana, Mississippi, Alabama, Florida	Groundfish, calico scallops, shrimp, coastal migratory pelagics, reef fish, corals, squids, spiny lobster, sharks, stone crab, sponges, billfish, coastal herring, swordfish, tropical reef fish
Pacific	California, Oregon, Washington, Idaho	Salmon, anchovy, groundfish, pink shrimp, billfish, herring
North Pacific	Alaska, Washington, Oregon	Tanner crab, Gulf of Alaska groundfish, king crab, high sea salmon, scallops, Bering Sea groundfish, Bering Sea clam, Bering Sea herring, Bering Sea shrimp, corals, dungeness crab, shrimp, snails
Western Pacific	Hawaii, American Samoa, Guam	Billfish, bottomfish, precious corals, seamount resources, spiny lobster

Source: L. G. Anderson, "Marine Fisheries" in P. R. Portney, ed., *Current Issues in Natural Resource Policy* (1982), Washington, D.C.: Resources for the Future. Copyright Resources for the Future, Inc.

remaining members are interested and knowledgeable members of the public (nominated to the council by the governor and secretary of commerce of each state). In practice, the "public" consists largely of representatives from the fishing industry and includes very few professionals such as economists or biologists.

Councils range in size from 8 to 16 people. Attached to each council is a professional staff that does include economists, lawyers, biologists, and so on. This staff may provide technical reports and assist the council in drawing up plans. Some councils also turn to outside consultants and universities for help in formulating plans, and still other councils use task forces or draw up the plans themselves. We cannot generalize about the nature of the plans or their impact on the fishery. However, we will make a few observations about the plans, then turn to some examples.

In principle, each council is to establish operational management objectives, then identify various means of implementing these objectives (harvests, effort allowed, and so on). In practice, Anderson (1982) notes that many plans look as if they were drafted first, and then objectives consistent with the plans appended. As of 1981, no council had completed plans for all species under its jurisdiction. In the plans developed thus far, it appears that distributional issues are a more important objective than economic efficiency. In one case, economic efficiency was even ruled out by a council vote (cost minimization was not seen as a desirable objective). This is perhaps not surprising, given the strong representation of fishing firms on the councils. Economic efficiency is a fairly complex objective, requiring definition in operational terms (the optimal tax, the number and nature of individual quotas). People are often more comfortable working with physical objectives, such as restrictions on the total harvest and equipment. "Fairness" is also seen as an important objective, necessary to thwart any lawsuits by aggrieved parties losing out as a result of the management plan.

To get a flavor of the types of plans implemented, let's look at two cases examined by Anderson (1982). The Mid-Atlantic Council established a plan for the Atlantic surf clam and offshore quahogs in the late 1970s. The surf clam was a heavily fished species, harvested under open access. The quahog had not been fished heavily at this time, but presumably could be harvested with the same fleet that captured the surf clam. The plan established *annual and quarterly quotas* on the *total harvest*. Because the clam fleet was several times larger than that needed to harvest the total catch allowed, a moratorium on new vessel entry was imposed. There were no reductions in the vessels currently harvesting the clams. The plan also controlled the days per week and hours per day that vessels could harvest, and restricted harvests in areas where young clams resided.

Economic theory predicts well the impact of this type of management plan. The regulators found that the fleet harvested the allowable catch very quickly. Vessels were first allowed to fish four days per week. That limit was later reduced to one day (24 hours) per week. The fishery thus had considerable *excess capacity,* and firms were clearly not minimizing their costs compared to a more efficient management scheme. Without a reduction in effort (number of vessels), economic efficiency could not be obtained. The council considered individual quotas, but could not implement them because of inadequate historical data on harvests. It considered basing individual quotas on harvests in a subsequent year, but recognized that this would lead to excessive harvests on which to base the quotas. No other techniques were attempted.

In the New England Council, the management plan initiated in 1977 for yellowtail flounder, haddock, and cod also consisted of a quota on the total harvest of each species. It did not restrict entry to these fisheries. The groundfish fisheries to which these species belong are very complex. Different stocks of flounder and cod reside in various locations. The fleet harvests a variety of different fish in addition to those mentioned above, and many of the species are biologically interdependent. To be fair to the council, devising management plans for these fisheries is difficult. However, its plan was a disaster.

With the annual quota, the harvest was taken early in the year and fishermen were furious about the restriction on the catch. In the second year of the plan, the council allowed two harvests in response to these complaints (the quota was filled twice), but this was obviously not a long-run solution. Quarterly quotas on the catch were tried, with similar results. Then quotas based on vessel size were introduced.

Thus the council shifted from a quota on the catch to one based on effort. The results were predictable: Boats incurred high harvesting costs because they frequently had to return to port before they filled their holds. As many of the costs of fishing (gasoline, time to fishing site) are relatively fixed, it meant lower profits, especially for large boats with quotas less than their capacity. Owners of small boats felt aggrieved because they were frequently affected by adverse weather and often missed filling their quota.

The quota was revised again and this time based on the size of the crew. Large crews then appeared on each vessel. Additional regulations were then established for each type of fish and by size of boat. Finally, the whole regulatory system became so complex and unmanageable that it was abandoned. As of 1981, these fisheries were regulated mainly by restrictions on the mesh size of the nets (to allow fish of a particular size to escape) and closed areas protecting juvenile fish. The new regulations are far from "optimal," but at least they can be implemented and administered. No taxes (except on foreign vessels) were used in these cases, or were individual quotas used. These regulations did not eliminate open access to the fisheries.

BOX 9.2
Fisheries Regulation in the U.S. Pacific Northwest

In the United States, the federal government regulates fishing activity beyond 3 miles and up to 200 miles from the coast under the 1976 Fishery Conservation and Management Act (FCMA). The coastal states regulate activity within the 3-mile zone. The FCMA is the code which permits the United States to control access to fish stocks, especially access by non-U.S. boats. In a case study of regulation under the FCMA of fishing in the Pacific Northwest region, Young (1981) estimated a cost of about $20 million for enforcement of the regulations in 1978. Sanctions in the act take the form of fines of up to $25,000 per infraction and possible seizure of vessels and contents of the holds.

Day-to-day regulation in the Pacific Northwest involves the daily publication of a Fleet Disposition Report (FDR) by the Coast Guard in Juneau, Alaska. During the peak season, there can be 300 foreign fishing vessels in the region. The Alaska Patrol (ALPAT) vessels can then identify fishing vessels and check on the printout when it was last boarded. ALPAT strives to board each foreign vessel at least once every 90 days. Regulations monitored are permit holding, equipment restrictions, season/time limits, area restrictions, species restrictions, correct logs, and national quotas. Young speculates that a more effective enforcement could be carried out by posting a government officer on each vessel at all times. He sees this costing in 1978 an extra $3 million. Do regulators become captives of those supposedly being regulated? Not in the Pacific Northwest fishing region, Young contends.

Source: Oran R. Young, *National Resources and the State.* Berkeley: University of California Press, 1981.

The Oyster Fishery

Oysters are a demersal species. After a brief period in which the oyster larva are free-swimming, they settle down as adults and permanently fix themselves to material on the ocean floor, such as rock and shell deposits. The oyster resides in the intertidal zones off many seacoasts or in inland rivers and bays.[5] The productivity of an oyster bed is related to exogenous variables such as water temperature, salinity, and parasitic disease, as well as the size of the stock itself (which is, of course, affected by harvests) and the amount of suitable material on the sea floor. This material, called *cultch,* consists of rocks, shells, or anything the oyster can attach itself. Cultch can be treated as a variable input into the oyster fishery. If cultch is added to the fishery, more oysters find it a desirable home, and the productivity of the bed is enhanced. A barren sea floor can be turned into a thriving oyster bed with the addition of cultch. But a thriving oyster bed can also be decimated if cultch is not maintained. Cultch is thus an input that can be controlled by humans.

In an open access oyster bed, there is no incentive for any firm or individual to add cultch to the bed. The fruits of that person's effort will be shared by all who harvest oysters from the bed. This is yet another externality that arises from open access which we have not yet examined. Agnello and Donnelley (1976) call this a "grounds quality" externality. Under open access, no individual has any incentive to invest in activities that increase the productivity of the fishery. Many more oysters could be harvested with the provision of more cultch, but less than the optimal amount of cultch is provided under open access.

The presence of this externality gives rise to the possibility that the optimal management of an oyster fishery *need not* result in a decline in the amount of effort used to harvest the oysters. One of the issues in regulating the fishery is that unemployment typically results. This can cause economic and political problems if the unemployed factors of production are immobile. But it is possible that, once an oyster bed is converted to private property management, an investment in cultch will be made, the productivity of the oyster bed will be increased, and no decline in effort will result. The increased output from the oyster bed eliminates the need to lay off factor inputs. The argument is simple, and can be seen graphically in Figure 9.7.

Assume that there is an infinitely elastic supply of labor to the fishery at a real wage of w. For a fixed stock of capital (oyster equipment such as hand or power rakes), the average and marginal product of labor (the other effort input) can be derived in the usual fashion. Under open access, the average and marginal products of labor used to harvest oysters are shown as AP and MP. If the bed were then turned over to private property, cultch would be added. The average and marginal product curves would shift out. Each unit of labor will now catch more oysters than before because more oysters will attach to the added cultch. In Figure 9.7, the new curves are shown as AP' and MP'.

The use of labor will also change when the fishery is converted to private property. Under open access, the common property equilibrium would employ L individuals, given the wage rate w. The equilibrium occurs where the real wage rate intersects the AP curve. If no investment in cultch is made, the private property

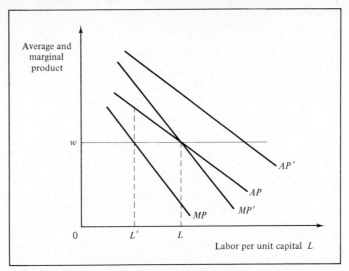

Figure 9.7 Under open access to an oyster bed, no incentive to invest in the productivity of the bed exists. The common property equilibrium with a real wage of w uses L units of labor per unit capital. When the oyster bed is managed by a sole owner, cultch is added to the oyster bed and the marginal and average product curves shift out, reflecting the higher productivity of the fishery. Under private property, the new equilibrium is where $MP' = w$, but again, L units of labor are employed. No decline in labor is observed in this example when the fishery changes from open access to private property management because increases in the productivity of the fishing grounds occur.

equilibrium would occur at point L', which is to the left of point L. The traditional result would then be reached: The rent-maximizing equilibrium leads to a decline in effort used in the fishery. But the addition of cultch may offset the decline in effort. If the AP and MP curves shift to AP' and MP', the private property equilibrium uses *exactly the same amount of labor* as the common property equilibrium. The curves shown in Figure 9.7 are not the only case that could occur, but they illustrate the point that the removal of the grounds quality externality mitigates the decline in effort that occurs when an open access resource is converted to private property.

What is the evidence in the oyster industry? Oysters are a good test case because they are harvested under both private property management and open access. Off the Atlantic and Gulf coasts of the United States, each state controls access to its oyster beds. There is a mix of property rights across the states. In some states, most of the oyster beds have been leased to individuals who basically have full control over the bed. In other states, most oyster beds are open to anyone.

Agnello and Donnelley (1976) attempted to estimate the average product of labor from an oyster bed under common versus private property management to see if the argument above has any empirical validity. They estimated the average product of labor (total harvest per state/number of people harvesting) as a function of property rights and biological and economic characteristics. The property rights variable

Table 9.2   REGRESSION RESULTS FOR
THE AVERAGE PRODUCT OF
LABOR IN OYSTER FISHERIES

Variable	Coefficient	t value
PR	44.70*	2.94
K	7617*	3.76
MSX	−4032†	−1.75
L	−7.50	−0.94
A	1.71	0.53

* Denotes significance at the 99% level.

† Denotes significance at the 95% level.

Note: PR is the property rights variable; K is the index of capital; MSX is a dummy variable for the presence of oyster parasites; L is the labor input fitted from a first-stage regression; A is the amount of land in the oyster bed.

Source: Agnello and Donnelley (1976).

is a ratio ranging from 0 to 1 which shows the percentage of the oyster catch by weight harvested under private property to the total catch in each state studied. A value of 1 indicates that the entire harvest is obtained from private property beds. The property rights ratio ranges from a low of .04 in Mississippi and Texas to a high of .98 in Connecticut and Delaware. A biological characteristic—the presence of oyster parasites that periodically infest the beds—is incorporated by using a dummy variable. The economic variables are the capital intensity of the industry—an index of capital quality (the use of dredging vessels to total vessels), the amount of labor used, and the amount of seabed land used.[6]

A linear equation that fits the average product of labor to the economic and biological variables is estimated for a data set that pools a cross-section of 16 states with a time series over the period 1950 to 1972.[7] Their results for the variables of economic interest are shown in Table 9.2. The regression supports the arguments presented above. The property rights variable (PR) is positive and highly significant. The greater the degree of private property management of the oyster beds, the higher the average product of labor. Conversion of an oyster bed to private property may thus make it possible to produce more oysters and not create unemployment.

The other variables all have the signs expected in theory. Capital (K) is positive and significant. The biological disease variable is negative and significant. Labor and land have the right sign (positive), but are not significant. The authors of the study suggest that this is because the two variables are highly correlated with each other, that very little variation in labor was observed over the sample (more support for their hypothesis?), and that land was measured inaccurately.

Agnello and Donnelley cannot tell directly whether the oyster catch is larger under private property than common property (due to statistical problems), but they do solve for the increase in the value of output per person that results when the oyster bed is managed under private property. Their estimate is $995 (1976 dollars) per year. If the supply of labor to the fishery remains constant at 14,000 people per year, then the total output gain under private property would be over $13.9 million annually. Another estimate put the value of the actual loss in employment that would result from complete privatization of oyster beds at $667,000. So even if some decline in labor occurred, it is nowhere near the gains made. No figures are presented for the costs of the privatization method — leasing the beds to a sole owner — but it is hard to imagine that these costs would offset the gains in the value of the fishery under private management.

What does this example tell us? The oyster case is perhaps the most straightforward one we examine. Because oysters do not move, it is relatively simple and cheap to convert the open access resource to a private property resource. Well-defined beds can be enumerated, and each owner then farms the bed. There are no complex catch or equipment requirements. Each owner simply "pays" for the right to manage the resource. This comes as close to our optimal management objective and practice as we'll find in these cases. The other important point is that privatization need not result in a decline in the amount of effort in the fishery, if the productivity of the fishery rises. But is this form of regulation feasible in a more complex fishery — say for a pelagic species? To examine this question, we turn to our second example, a sardine fishery in Spain.

BOX 9.3
Lobster Harvesting Regulations in Massachusetts
and Canada's Maritime Provinces

The contrasts in the approach to the regulation of lobster harvesting are striking between the jurisdictions off Massachusetts and off Canada's Maritime Provinces (New Brunswick, Nova Scotia, Prince Edward Island, and Newfoundland). In the Canadian situation, the waters or seabed are divided into 14 precisely defined zones; the length of open season is legislated; the minimum size of lobster caught and the maximum number of traps to be set per license holder is decreed. The largest trap limit is 375 in any zone. Enforcement is carried out by federal fishery officers, and the regulations are legislated by *federal* authorities. In Massachusetts, the *state* government is in charge, and the regulatory environment is more loosely structured. There is no law on season length or number of traps set. Most lobstering occurs in May through November. Permits are issued each year to the first 80 names on a list. An additional 20 permits are allotted to commercial fishermen under special circumstances. Until recently, Boston Harbor lobstermen have fished from 2,000 to 3,000 traps, but a self-imposed trap limit of 800 has been agreed upon by local fishermen there.

The Massachusetts Division of Law Enforcement has 20 agents in coastal areas. There has been criticism from marine resource user groups that this is not adequate. Reassignments have been made during peak harvesting periods. In addition, 15 agents from the Division of Marine and Recreational Vehicles are deputized to enforce marine fisheries laws and assigned to coastal areas.

Source: Correspondence with the Division of Marine Fisheries, Commonwealth of Massachusetts, January 1984, and *Lobster Fishery Regulations,* dated August 16, 1983, Fisheries and Oceans Ministry, Government of Canada.

Spanish Sardines

This case was investigated by Gallastegui (1983). It illustrates the way in which theory may be used to calculate the optimal equilibrium for a particular fishery, contrasts the optimal equilibrium with the existing common property equilibrium, then shows how the optimum can be reached. The study shows the costs of common property exploitation and the way in which a tax on the harvest (or effort) could be used to eliminate these costs. We do not know the costs of regulating the fishery, or whether the taxation schemes evaluated would be administratively feasible. But the study does indicate the potential gain from taxation in a fishery that is not amenable to the imposition of private property rights because the sardines (small herring) are pelagic.

The fishery in question is in the Gulf of Valencia on the eastern coast of Spain. The sardines do move around the area, but apparently do not venture far outside the region. All the sardines harvested are landed in two ports. Sardines are harvested only at night from March to December, and only when there is no full moon. No harvests occur on Sundays. This means, in effect, that harvests occur about 24 days per month in the season. The data used in the fishery pertain to the period from 1956 to 1969, when there was open access to the fishery. Gallastegui used a dynamic model of the fishery to calculate the optimal harvest and amount of effort.

Effort in this fishery is measured in terms of candlepower per dark day, because one of the most important inputs is the light potential of the equipment used to attract the sardines to the boats. The other major inputs are sonar equipment (if present), and of course time spent fishing. The author has assumed that the entire night is used, even if the time is spent searching for the fish. This seems reasonable, as one effect of open access would be that more time would be spent looking for fish, the smaller the population. We know already that with common property populations typically will be smaller than those under optimal management.

The harvest and stock of sardines are determined under open access and then recalculated for a regime of optimal management. The model used is similar to that presented in Chapter 8. No data on the sardine stock are available, so the author calculated the stock from data on the amount of effort and the catch. Suppose the harvest function is given by $H_t = F(X_t, E_t)$. If the harvest and the effort values are known, a point on the biological production function $F(X)$ is found. For different harvests and catches, the production function can then be mapped out. In Gallastegui's paper a more complex harvest function is presented, but the concept is the same.

Obviously, there are a number of difficulties with this approach. There may not be enough variation in harvests and effort fully to map out the biological function. The data on H and E may also be poor. Fishing firms may not reveal accurate information to government authorities. Estimates of the biological mechanics may have to be revised as the data change. The technique nonetheless provides a way by which numerical calculations of the stock can be made. And it is the most common method used by government fisheries managers to calculate $F(X)$.

The author then uses data on the sardine fishery in an econometric model to determine the steady-state harvest, stock, and amount of effort under optimal management. The values depend on three unknown terms: the social discount rate, the real unit cost of effort, and a parameter that reflects the rate of growth of the marginal product of effort. The author uses different hypothetical values for these terms. The

Table 9.3 STEADY-STATE EQUILIBRIA IN A SARDINE FISHERY IN SPAIN AT DIFFERENT DISCOUNT RATES: THE SOCIALLY OPTIMAL CASES VERSUS THE COMMON PROPERTY EQUILIBRIUM

| | Optimal equilibria discount rates | | | |
Variable	0%	3%	8%	Common property
Stock (tons)	35,065	34,415	33,450	17,750
Harvest (tons)	7927	8088	8321	10,624
Effort (candlepower units per day)	390	403	425	886

Note: Each case above assumes that the unit cost of effort is 11.84 pesetas, the instantaneous rate of growth of the marginal product of effort is .000523, and the scale parameter estimated from the fishery production function is .6103. Numbers have been rounded up to the nearest unit.

Source: Based on C. Gallastegui, "An Economic Analysis of Sardine Fishing in the Gulf of Valencia (Spain)," *Journal of Environmental Economics and Management* 10 (1983), pp. 138–150.

common property harvest, stock, and effort are determined from the common property equilibrium (the average product of effort equals the real unit cost of effort). In Table 9.3, the common property equilibrium is contrasted with optimal equilibriums at different discount rates and a particular marginal product of effort. Table 9.4 shows how these values change at different unit costs of effort, and Table 9.5 lists the actual historical data.

These tables illustrate a number of points about the fishery under different forms of ownership. First, as is not surprising, the common property equilibrium always uses more effort and has a lower stock than the optimum. The higher the discount rate, the larger the optimal harvest and amount of effort and the lower the optimal stock. Why is this true? Under open access, the discount rate is effectively infinite. As the discount rate increases, the optimal equilibrium approaches the common property equilibrium. However, for this sardine fishery the discount rate would have to be substantially higher before the optimal equilibrium was anywhere close to the CPE.

Table 9.4 shows the sensitivity of the harvest, stock, and effort to changes in the

Table 9.4 EFFECTS OF REAL COST OF EFFORT ON THE STEADY-STATE VALUES OF THE STOCK, HARVEST, AND AMOUNT OF EFFORT

Real cost of effort	Optimal values			Common property values		
	Stock	Harvest	Effort	Stock	Harvest	Effort
0.00	13,790	10,533	1,085	—	—	—
4.00	21,200	10,423	765	4,460	7,753	1,926
6.00	24,530	10,039	675	7,450	9,254	1,544
11.84	33,450	8,321	425	17,725	10,625	897
14.20	36,950	7,437	350	22,250	10,320	729
16.00	39,260	6,800	306	23,200	10,210	697
20.00	44,850	5,111	207	33,100	8,404	433
30.93	59,156	—	—	49,000	3,731	140
40.00	59,156	—	—	58,850	118	4

Note: Numbers have been rounded up to the nearest unit.

Source: C. Gallastegui, "An Economic Analysis of Sardine Fishing in the Gulf of Valencia (Spain)," *Journal of Environmental Economics and Management* 10 (1983), p. 146.

Table 9.5   DATA FOR A SPANISH SARDINE FISHERY

Year	Catch (metric tons)	Effort
1956	9,447	516
1957	10,269	551
1958	9,070	533
1959	9,932	627
1960	6,857	780
1961	5,192	756
1962	10,951	756
1963	11,100	804
1964	10,057	688
1965	4,060	492
1966	4,020	378
1967	4,092	503
1968	4,327	572
1969	5,289	878

Note: Numbers have been rounded up to the nearest unit.

Source: C. Gallastegui, "An Economic Analysis of Sardine Fishing in the Gulf of Valencia (Spain)" *Journal of Environmental Economics and Management* 10 (1983), p. 140.

unit cost of effort, assuming the discount rate is 8 percent. We see that below a real cost of 4, the common property equilibrium will result in complete extinction of the stock, but not so with the social optimum. At a very high unit cost, above 30, no harvests are made in the optimal case and the fishery is at its maximum population level; but under the CPE, harvests still occur.

Table 9.5 shows that the actual open access harvests tended to fluctuate somewhat. The period from 1956 to 1959 and again from 1962 to 1964 would all be years of overfishing compared to the optimum (at each discount rate). In every year except 1966, the open access effort was far above that suggested by the social optimum for any unit cost above 11 pesetas (1 peseta equaled .0063 1984 U.S. dollars). After 1964, the stock was apparently decimated enough that sardine effort was shifting toward other fisheries—namely, anchovies.

Using these figures, Gallastegui computed the resource savings that would arise if the fishery were managed optimally. These savings are the reduction in effort needed to harvest the sardines net of the lower total value of the catch, assuming the price of sardines remains constant. If the catch from this region has any impact on the sardine market, the price may rise as the harvests fall, and these revenue effects would not be as large. The savings in effort at a discount rate of 3 percent are about 54 million pesetas per year. The loss in revenue from decreased harvest is about 24 million pesetas, leaving a net gain of about 30 million pesetas. Effort must fall by 228 units, which would mean, if effort is immobile, a foregone earnings of about 25 million pesetas. The *net* social gain from optimal management would then be about 5 million pesetas (about $300,000 U.S.) if all the unemployed effort was immobile and fully compensated for its loss.[8]

How could the optimum be reached? First, a three-year moratorium would be needed (assuming a perfectly elastic supply of effort) to build the stock of sardines up to the optimal level. The moratorium is the fastest way to rejuvenate the stock and can be shown to be the optimal dynamic path. Once the stock is at the optimal steady-state level, a tax on the catch or a tax on effort would be necessary to deal with the open access problem. It is unlikely that any property rights assignment would work in this case because of the pelagic nature of the fishery, and perhaps the difficulty of enforcing private property rights.

The tax on the catch must reflect the stock effect of the fish population and the difference between marginal and average cost at the optimum. Gallastegui computed the required tax to be 3,856 pesetas per ton. The 1971 price of sardines was 9,440 pesetas per ton, so the tax would mean a net price to fishing effort of 5,594 pesetas. Total tax revenue collected by the government would be over 31 million pesetas. Total revenue to the fishery would fall from around 100 million pesetas to 45 million pesetas, where these numbers are based on the CPE versus optimal equilibrium in Table 9.3 at a discount rate of 3 percent. Thus the total loss of revenue (as noted above) equals the reduction in total revenue to the fishermen net of government tax revenues, 24 million pesetas.

The author does not discuss whether an optimal tax could be levied in practice. Given that all sardines harvested are landed at two ports, it suggests that a landing tax may be administratively feasible. Imposition of the moratorium may be more difficult, as three years is a long time to go without any fishing income. However, Gallastegui notes that if the supply curve of effort has a positive elasticity of 2, then the moratorium need last only one year, and no decline in effort is needed to obtain the optimum. Spanish policy-makers would thus want to estimate this supply curve before implementing a moratorium. And, as noted before, moratoriums have been imposed in other fisheries (see footnote 3).

What regulations have been imposed on the sardine fishery? The Spanish government has in the past few years established some regulations for pelagic fisheries in the Mediterranean. In 1979, the number of hours each vessel can fish daily was restricted. Minimum vessel capacity was set at 25 gross registered tonnage. Previously, vessels of 10 to 15 tons were prevalent in the fishery. These regulations thus represent attempts to limit effort. The light intensity of lamps was limited to 2,200 candlepower, and fishing at depths below 25 meters was forbidden. Minimum size restrictions on the fish harvested were also imposed. These are measures to protect the species and reduce the harvest. Penalties for violating the regulations were introduced, but it is not known if these have been effective. Thus, like fisheries in North America, it appears that neither taxes nor individual quotas have been imposed on this open access fishery.

These two cases show the value of converting to private property and the theoretical possibility of implementing an optimal tax to achieve economic efficiency in the fishery. But as suggested in the discussion of current U.S. regulatory policies, it is rare to find a case where economic efficiency has been the objective of regulatory policy. There are many examples of regulatory failure. To illustrate what can go wrong with regulation, we next examine a fishery with a long history of regulation and problems resulting from regulation—the Pacific halibut.

The Pacific Halibut

Halibut have been commercially harvested off the West Coast of the United States and Canada since the late 1880s.[9] The fishery originally extended from Santa Barbara, California, to Nome, Alaska. Over the years, the stock has been depleted in the southern portion of the region, so the fishery is now concentrated on the continental shelf off the coast of British Columbia in Canada and Alaska. Harvests peaked in the 1920s at around 70 million pounds, then decreased to about 30 million pounds in the 1930s.

Halibut are the largest flat fish. Their weight and hence commercial value increases substantially over time. A 4-year-old halibut may weigh only 3 pounds, but a 20-year-old can weigh more than 100 pounds. Halibut reproduce only after the male is between 7 and 8 years and the female 12 or older. This makes the species vulnerable to overfishing. If a large proportion of juvenile halibut are harvested, the population can be decimated. The long growing period means that it can take many years for the population to rebuild to commercially viable levels. Because the fishery has *always* had open access, it is not surprising that the stocks have been threatened with severe depletion.

The threat to the population was first recognized in the early 1920s. In 1923, a commission, first called the International Fisheries Commission, renamed the International Pacific Halibut Commission (IPHC) in 1953, consisting of both Canadian and U.S. participants, was set up to regulate the fishery. Its objective was to obtain the *MSY stock* and *harvest*. The initial regulatory device was a three-month closure. But this policy was inadequate to protect the stock, so in 1930 the commission was given greater power to control harvests. Quotas on total harvests, equipment restrictions, and closure of nursery areas were implemented.

The quota on the total catch is still in place today, although its precise form has been somewhat modified. The quota is announced prior to the beginning of the fishing season each year and implemented by means of a limitation on the number of days that halibut can be harvested. The quota was first assigned to the entire fishery, but has since been broken down into different seasonal openings in defined areas.

The equipment regulations stipulate that only long lines (which are in fact long fishing lines with hooks placed at different intervals) are permitted in the fishery. The commission had no authority to regulate entry. Any number of vessels of any type were permitted into the fishery, and there has been no licensing of boats or people until very recently. As we will see, these regulations have not protected the stock of halibut and have led to excessive amounts of effort used to catch a declining harvest. Before examining these effects more closely, we need some other facts about the fishery.

A large number of age classes are harvested simultaneously. This has meant that the harvests have tended to be more stable than, say, in salmon fisheries, where only particular age classes are harvested and therefore the catch is more sensitive to environmental factors that affect the stock. The vessels harvesting halibut range considerably in size from small boats needing only one or two people to larger vessels with a crew of eight or nine. The number of small boats entering the fishery has increased dramatically since the early 1970s, due to two factors. First, regulation in other Pacific fisheries—namely salmon—has released vessels to the halibut fishery.

In the salmon fisheries in British Columbia, vessels must be licensed. Because the licenses are restricted and thus have a market value, owners who cannot afford the license have shifted to the less restricted halibut fishery. Second, the price of halibut rose considerably in the early 1970s as a result of increases in demand. Prior to this time, the industry had seen a gradual reduction in effort because of dwindling harvests and rising harvesting costs. But the increase in the price offset these factors, and entry surged.

Table 9.6 shows the prices, harvests, and a measure of effort in the halibut fishery from 1970 to 1981. Small boats represented the largest increase in effort, and began to take an increasing share of the catch. Before 1970, small boats accounted for between 5 and 10 percent of the harvest. By 1976, they took more than 20 percent. But the high entry rates in the 1970s was not solely in the small boat class. In 1975, a total of 304 vessels exceeding 5 tons fished the two regulated areas. In 1978, just three years later, 530 vessels of the same size fished the same areas.

Compounding all these factors is one more problem in the halibut fishery: harvests of halibut by those seeking other fish. Fishing firms from both Canada and the United States, as well as from Japan, fish for other species in the same waters. It is impossible to prevent the harvest of halibut by mistake, given the fishing techniques (trawling). These "by catches" must be thrown back, but about 50 percent of the halibut die in the process. It has been estimated that about 2 million pounds of halibut are lost each year from these by-catches. When the total harvest is around 21 million pounds annually, the by-catches are significant.

They can have an even more severe impact on the stock of halibut. In the early 1970s, foreign vessels were harvesting other species of fish in areas where juvenile halibut also resided. The mortality of these halibut had a much larger impact on the stock than would a by-catch of mature adults who had already reproduced. One

Table 9.6 HALIBUT PRICES, HARVESTS, AND EFFORT, 1970–1982

Year	Price per pound*	Landings in U.S. waters (millions of lb/year)†	Effort: skates (thousands/day)‡
1970	$0.39	54.9	17.35
1971	0.37	46.6	12.02
1972	0.64	42.9	21.90
1973	0.83	31.7	20.22
1974	0.78	21.2	14.78
1975	0.89	27.6	18.00
1976	1.06	27.5	22.29
1977	0.98	17.5	22.31
1978	1.05	17.5	24.55
1979	1.62	21.2	—
1980	0.99	19.0	—
1981	1.02	26.6	—
1982	0.86	32.6	—

* Prices are average annual ex vessel nominal prices per pound, as reported in Orth et al. (1981), Stokes (1983), and National Marine Fisheries Service, *Fisheries of the United States,* selected years.

† Landings are in millions of tons dressed weight for 1970–1976, as reported in Orth et al. (1981), and millions of tons round weight as reported in National Marine Fisheries Service, *Fisheries of the United States,* 1977–1983.

‡ Effort is measured in skates per day, as cited in International Pacific Halibut Commission (1976), and IPHC *Annual Reports,* selected years, 1977–1980.

estimate is that the incidental kill rate is close to 20 million pounds annually. Biologists estimate that these by-catches were the most important cause of a significant decline in the halibut stock beginning in the late 1960s.

What are the effects of the halibut regulations on the fishery? Again, economic theory can predict the results. Recall that a quota on the catch alone will not reduce effort. This is exactly what has happened in the halibut fishery, but the problem is exacerbated by the entry of more vessels from other fisheries. The economic impact of the regulations has been considerable overcapacity in the fishery, high harvesting costs, and low incomes. Since quotas on the total catch were first imposed over 50 years ago, the following chain of events has occurred.

The catch was limited by restricting the time period in which halibut could be harvested. With no control over effort, the existing stock of vessels simply fished more intensively during the restricted season, then were idle or migrated to other fisheries in the closed season. But whenever the harvest was reduced (and demand for halibut was either constant or increasing), the price of halibut would rise, and the expected average return would rise (in common property, firms are still setting average revenue from effort equal to the marginal cost of effort).

Entry was encouraged. Boats would catch the quota more quickly, which then required a shortening of the season. The large increases in halibut prices due both to declining halibut harvests and increases in the price of other species in the 1970s has greatly increased the entry and required substantial reductions in the length of the season. In 1975, the season was 128 days in each of two areas harvesting is allowed. By 1978, the season was restricted to 23 days in one area and 32 days in the other. In 1982, the seasons ranged from 5 to 60 days, depending on the area.

Entry was also encouraged by the increased harvests over the period from 1930s to the 1950s. The regulations did appear to increase the stock to about its MSY.[10] This increase in the stock, as we have earlier argued, decreases the average cost of harvests (more fish are around), which again encourages entry. A large influx into the fishery occurred by 1950. Effort rose from 384 regular boats (the larger boats) and 1,903 people in 1931 to 820 regular boats with 4,077 people in 1951. This represents an increase of over 100 percent in both boats and people over the period. The harvests rose as well, but by only 27 percent. Crutchfield (1981) estimated that two-thirds of this effort was totally redundant. That is, one-third of the vessels could have caught the entire quota in a season of 6 to 9 months.

If somehow entry could be limited to this number, many advantages would occur. With entry limits, the season could be lengthened. Boats and people would not have to be laid up or search for alternative useful activity. The fleet could be used far more efficiently. With the geographic quotas and limited seasons, the fleet is currently used inefficiently. Too many vessels crowd into an area during the season. With a season of less than a month, the problem is clear. Boats are scurrying out to catch as many fish as they can in the short period allowed. This not only increases the costs of harvest for each vessel (crowding externalities), but increases the processing costs and reduces the quality of the fish.

Because the entire annual harvest is caught in a short period, large processing and storage capacity is required. If the harvest were spread over a long period, a far smaller (and less expensive) processing capacity would be required. Virtually all the halibut must be frozen and stored. The value of the catch is then lower than it would be if the harvest were spread more uniformly across the year. More fish could be sold as "fresh," commanding a higher unit price. The quality is reduced because vessels tend to stay in the fishery as long as possible; trips back to port take up precious time. With minimal storage capability on the vessels, fish spoils.

Returns to both labor and capital are also greatly reduced with a quota on the total catch, as the theoretical model predicts. No rents exist. Crutchfield estimated that labor was earning less than its opportunity wage in the late 1950s, and although no data are provided for the present, it is hard to imagine that any improvement has been made, considering the large influx of effort into the fishery in the 1970s. The return on investment in the vessels was between 3.9 and 4.8 percent before depreciation, hardly the opportunity cost of capital. If an optimal number of vessels could be achieved, the return on capital would be approximately 8 to 10 percent, and the return to labor would double. Rents would then exist.

Costs of harvesting are also higher no doubt because it is difficult to replace worn-out and technically obsolete capital with such a low rate of return. If effort were restricted, a more efficient fleet could be utilized. The equipment restrictions may also be preventing the most efficient techniques from being used, although Crutchfield feels that the efficiency loss from the restriction to long lines is not too large.

Finally, and perhaps most important, there is no guarantee that the quotas have protected the stock of halibut. Mortality has been so high in the 1970s, especially because of the by-catches, that the continued survival of the fishery is in doubt. What has the halibut commission been doing all this time? Why didn't the regulatory failures lead to new policies? There are some reasons. First, the goal of the IPHC was to achieve the MSY stock and harvest, not to achieve an economic optimum. As long as the stock was protected, the economic costs were not incorporated into the objectives of the commission. There is evidence that commissioners worried implicitly about economic factors but were hampered politically in doing anything about them. Crutchfield argues that the commission was afraid that if restrictions on effort were imposed, the IPHC would be seen as lackeys of the industry, imposing regulations to generate rents (profits) to the most vocal groups in the fishery that would be allowed to remain. Sticking to biological objectives is a much safer political strategy. When a fishery is international, it is difficult to enact policies to satisfy both countries.

But the whole halibut fishery has been changing since the imposition of the 200-mile limit. Up to 1978, Canadians and Americans were allowed to fish in each other's territorial waters. With the new limits, each nation has now prevented the other from fishing in its territory. U.S. fishermen were banned from Canadian waters in 1979, and Canadians were to exit U.S. fisheries by 1980. Because Canada took about two-thirds of its catch from U.S. waters off Alaska, the 200-mile limit has had a severe impact. However, each nation obtained exclusive rights to its respective halibut stocks and could limit entry. Both countries are now in the process of implementing policies that do affect entry. Pearse (1982) explains what has happened in the Canadian halibut fishery.

The Canadian government implemented a license and compensation scheme in 1979 to deal with the displaced fishermen. Halibut licenses were distributed to all vessels that had reported landings of at least 3,000 pounds in 1977 or 1978. Licenses cost $10 annually and were transferable. Those fishing in U.S. waters who also had licenses to harvest other species were offered compensation for their halibut equipment and a vessel grant if they did not maintain their halibut license. Alternatively, they were given a vessel and equipment conversion grant to enter the sablefish fishery.

Fifty-four Canadian vessels were excluded from Alaska, and of these, 16 surrendered their halibut licenses while the rest received a license. In the B.C. halibut fishery as a whole, about 331 vessels received licenses, and 400 fishermen were excluded because they did not meet the requirements. Those excluded were largely part-time fishermen who harvested in total less than 20 percent of the catch. Shortly after the licenses were issued, appeals were allowed on the grounds of financial hardship (and other factors). These appeals were successful, and 100 more licenses were issued. Because of the minimal requirement for a license, by 1981 the B.C. halibut fleet comprised 422 vessels. Prior to the introduction of "limited entry," 100 vessels operated in the fishery.

As well, the stock of halibut available in Canadian waters has declined. The quota in 1982 was 5.4 million pounds and catch rates were very low, with no significant change in the landed price ($1.25 per pound in 1982). The fishery was therefore in dire straits: low harvests, overcapacity, and high operating costs. Pearse recommended the adoption of a system of transferable catch quotas assigned to areas and distributed to individual fishermen now in the fishery. Equipment restrictions (no trawling) would still apply to protect immature fish. The fishing season was not to be curtailed; fishermen are free to take their quota whenever they want. Pearse's suggestions were received with enthusiasm by halibut fishermen and were implemented in 1983.

Using economic analysis, we can make some predictions about the effect of the individual quota on the operation of the fishery. First, the harvest should be taken much more efficiently. Each individual holding the quota now has a guaranteed catch (subject to the availability of halibut). There is no need to compete with hundreds of other vessels in a particular area over a short interval of time to get a share of the harvest. Factor inputs can then be arranged efficiently.

Transferability of the quota should ensure that the most efficient operators remain in the fishery. The quotas will quickly command a market value, and only those whose expected profits from fishing equal or exceed the market value of the quota should remain. Others will sell their quota. Of course, the original holders of the quota will receive a rent in the form of the market value of the quota. This is one reason why Pearse also advocated a royalty on the harvest. Pearse does not mention divisibility of the quota. Presumably, given the state of the fishery preceding 1983, the quotas are not large, so the market for quotas should not be badly distorted due to indivisibilities. If the quotas were large, the market for their exchange could become imperfectly competitive. Quotas may also have to be adjusted yearly if biological conditions warrant.

A potential problem is that those fishing for halibut may operate in other fisheries as well. Because halibut have been relatively unprofitable in recent years, there may still be some tendency to harvest one's quota in a short period of time, and then go catch other species. Crowding externalities may still exist, along with problems with processing and storage. One possible modification of the scheme may be to have the individual quotas specified for each season. Effort would then be spread out over a longer time period. Of course, the important related problem is that regulation in one fishery, halibut in this case, can cause effort to spill over into other fisheries. The problem of the by-catches from fleets trawling for other species also remains, although Pearse recommends allowing salmon trawlers who do not hold halibut licenses to be allowed to purchase them. By-catches will then not be wasted.

Presumably, there is still an incentive to not report harvests in excess of one's quota. But due to processing requirements, halibut cannot be sold "illegally" as easily as species such as lobsters. Given the enthusiasm of the fishermen for the Canadian scheme, they may play by the rules and not cheat on their quotas. Their understanding of the problems with open access so long endured in the fishery should provide an incentive to stick to their quotas.

SUMMARY

1. Two types of government policy that can achieve an optimal steady-state harvest and amount of fishing effort are taxes on effort or harvests, and quotas on effort and harvests.
2. The optimal fisheries equilibrium in a dynamic model can be achieved with a tax on the catch equal to $C_X/[F'(X) - r]$ per pound harvested. The tax forces firms to take into account for each unit of the stock harvested today the effect on future harvests. A fish left for tomorrow may lead to a decrease in harvesting costs and leave a larger population to reproduce. But these benefits have to be weighted by the discount rate—the opportunity cost of time.
3. An optimal tax on the catch, levied when the harvest is landed, will reduce the total revenue to the firm. The firm operating under open access will still equate total revenue to total costs, but the total revenue curve will have shrunk until it is tangent to the total cost curve at the optimal amount of effort. An optimal tax is difficult to compute due to continuous changes in exogenous factors such as environmental conditions, demand, and costs, and difficult to implement. Firms have a large incentive to evade the tax by landing their catch away from government tax collectors. The tax is rarely used to regulate fisheries.
4. Taxes on effort can be imposed as head (or entry) taxes or as taxes per unit of effort used in the fishery. The optimal effort tax will increase the total costs of fishing until they intersect the total revenue curve at the optimal amount of effort. The most serious problem with taxes on effort is ensuring that all components of effort are covered by the tax. If labor is taxed but not capital, firms can avoid the tax by substituting capital for labor. The optimal amount of effort will not be reached. Taxes on effort would be costly to administer because government regulators must attempt to keep track of all the components of effort.
5. A quota on the total catch will restrict harvests, but will not lead to the optimal amount of effort in the fishery. A quota given to individuals or firms to catch a specified amount of fish can lead to the optimal amount of effort and harvest if the quota is transferable and divisible. Each holder of the

quota has a private property right to the fish and can therefore choose a cost-minimizing amount of effort to harvest the allotment.

6. Since 1976, the United States has been regulating fisheries within its 200-mile limit through fisheries management councils. One objective of these councils has been to achieve an optimal harvest, where optimal suggests that economic efficiency is to be considered. Thus far, few actual regulations have been passed that are based on economic efficiency. Many still use inefficient quotas on the total catch and on various components of effort.

7. Oyster fisheries in the United States represent an example where assignment of property rights can increase the stock of the species by improving the productivity of the fishing ground. Under private management, firms have an incentive to invest in the grounds. Aggregate use of effort then need not fall, even when the fishery is managed optimally. The decline in effort that would occur under private management is offset by the increase in the productivity of the fishing grounds.

8. After a three-year moratorium on harvesting sardines in a particular Spanish fishery, an optimal tax on the harvest would allow the species to recover from overfishing and allow profitable exploitation with much less effort than in the common property equilibrium.

9. In the United States and Canada, halibut have been regulated by area quotas on the total catch since the 1920s. The quota has been unsuccessful in limiting entry to the fishery, and has resulted in excessive amounts of effort (overcapacity), low returns to capital and labor, and no guarantee that the stock will not be depleted to levels that threaten viability. A quota on the catch assigned to individual fishermen is the policy recommended to reduce effort, increase the returns to effort, and protect the stock from excessive harvesting. This type of individual quota is being implemented in British Columbia and is being considered in the United States.

DISCUSSION QUESTIONS

1. Explain graphically and verbally how a tax on (a) the harvests and (b) effort yields a socially optimal equilibrium in the open access fishery. Explain some of the practical difficulties of imposing taxes on fisheries.

2. Explain graphically and verbally the effects of a quota on the total catch versus an individual quota for a portion of the catch on effort in a fishery.

3. What would be the effects of a quota on effort and on the harvest in an open access fishery?

4. If the demand curve for a particular species of fish moves out over time as consumer incomes and population increase, will costs of harvest generally rise, leaving no rent or high profit, or will the costs not rise significantly? What elements affect the trend in costs?

NOTES

1. Those who read the previous chapter will recognize Equation (9.1) as Equation (8.12), where $V(t)$ is equal to $P - C'$ and terms have been rearranged.

2. Note if the price of fish is very high, the common property harvest is less than the optimal harvest. The tax will then increase the harvest by decreasing effort, so the equilibrium moves to the right-hand side of the MSY biomass (left of the MSY harvest). For each price, a different optimal harvest and hence tax per unit of harvest must be defined.

3. For example, a moratorium was imposed from 1972 to 1974 in the Icelandic herring fishery because the species had been overfished and the stock had collapsed.

4. See the Fisheries and Conservation Act of 1976, Public Law 94-265 (amended by Public Law 95-354 and 96-61), Title III, Section 301(a). For a more detailed discussion of the act, see Anderson (1982).

5. This information is taken from Agnello and Donnelley (1975).

6. Notice that they do not incorporate the biological mechanics directly. There is no stock effect in the relationship. The authors do not discuss this, but we suspect the omission is due to lack of data on the stock of oysters.

7. Because of simultaneity problems, a two-stage least squares regression was performed. In the first stage, labor was regressed on production variables and a measure of the opportunity wage (the wage rate of production workers in manufacturing). The fitted labor variable from this regression was then used in the average product relation

$$APL_{it} = f(X_{it}, D_{it}, Z_{it}, e_{it})$$

where i is the state, t the year, and X the vector of production variables discussed above, except that the labor variable is from the first-stage fitted equation. D and Z are binary shift variables for the cross-section and time series, respectively. These are necessary control variables in the pooled regressions. The final term, e_{it}, is the error term, which is assumed to have a zero mean and constant variance and be independent across observations. No evidence of autocorrelation or heteroskedasticity was found.

8. It should be noted that much of the effort is not likely to stay unemployed because it can be used in another fishery—anchovies. Because anchovies are also harvested under open access, it means that the Spanish authorities must be concerned not only about the sardine fishery, but also about anchovies.

9. Information on the halibut fishery is taken from Crutchfield (1981), Pearse (1982), and Stokes (1983).

10. There is some debate about this point due to imprecise estimates of the stock in early periods. The stock was estimated from data on effort and harvests. Because effort was not measured accurately, some observers think the stock estimates in the 1930s were too low, making the estimates of the recovery of the stock by the 1950s too high.

11. Pearse (1982) also recommended a royalty fee (tax on the catch), but this was not implemented.

chapter *10*

Special Topics in the Economics of the Fisheries

INTRODUCTION

This chapter introduces some special topics in fisheries economics. It builds on the previous chapters, but in some sections the arithmetic manipulations are more complex than before. Three topics are examined. First, we reexamine our biological assumptions and note the variety of biological production functions that can arise for different species. Different biological conditions usually require regulations that must be tailored to the species. We examine the steady-state equilibriums for two particular examples—salmon and shrimp. In addition to differences in the biological mechanics for many species, there may also be complex interactions among species. The analysis of the optimal harvest can be much more complex when there are multiple species in an area. For example, a "trash" species may be preying on a commercially desirable species. In this case, it may pay to harvest the trash species to improve the growth and hence harvests of the desired species. We examine the optimal equilibrium in a fishery with this type of predator-prey relationship.

In the next section, we examine international disputes concerning a fish stock. When two nations separately plan to exploit a single fishery, they must form conjectures about the reaction of one to the other. This means that a game-theoretic structure may be an appropriate tool in the analysis of these fisheries. We present a simple illustration of international competition and cooperation in the exploitation of a single species fishery. An example of this in practice is the "cod war" between Iceland and Great Britain.

Finally, three kinds of uncertainty in the fishery are noted: uncertainty in the stock-yield relationship, in the input-harvest relationship, and in the market demand for the fish. We report briefly on what others have discovered.

VARIETIES OF BIOLOGICAL BASICS

We focused on the classic logistic sustained-yield growth function in the previous two chapters. Clearly, there are many variations possible in the biological mechanics. We have already discussed the case where a minimum stock size was necessary to ensure survival of the species. In this section we touch on some other variations in the biological mechanics and how they can affect the optimal harvest.

Our model of the fishery developed in the preceding two chapters is most applicable to relatively short-lived species where net growth depends on aggregate biomass rather than factors such as the age structure of the population, or exogenous environmental factors such as water temperature and currents. A number of models have been developed to analyze fisheries with different biological characteristics. The Beverton-Holt model, for example, looks at the age structure of a fish population and can analyze the effect of different types of equipment (mesh size of nets) on the sustainable yield. The basic notion is that the sustainable yield relationship will change depending on the age class (or size of fish) harvested. The model applies to long-lived species such as cod and haddock, where a number of age classes are harvested simultaneously (see Beverton and Holt, 1957, and Hannesson, 1978, for more details).

In this chapter, we examine two cases where the aggregate biomass is not a good predictor of the growth of a particular species over time. For salmon, the number of fish able to spawn is a better determinant of the growth of the population than biomass. With shrimp, environmental factors are more important than biomass or number of individuals, and it may not be meaningful to talk about a long-run steady-state equilibrium. We then turn to multiple-species fisheries and an examination of an interdependent species in a predator-prey relationship.

Salmon

Weight or biomass has been our approximation of the stock of fish. We assumed that the net growth of the stock was dependent on the aggregate biomass. Any harvest from the stock then takes a mixture of age classes — fish of different sizes and weights. In the case of salmon, this type of population dynamics does not give a good approximation of the growth over time of the stock size. For salmon, age and the number of fish in different age classes (cohorts) is more important in determining the size of the stock over time than aggregate biomass. What is crucial to the growth of a salmon population is the number of fish able to spawn in each period. Biomass in period $t + i$ is not related to biomass in period t as precisely as the numbers spawning in period $t + i$ to the numbers spawning in period t, where i is the interval between birth of a particular cohort and its return to fresh water to spawn.

Escapement is the term given to the numbers of salmon that have survived the harvest in period t and will thus be able to spawn. In a fishery of this kind, maintenance of a steady-state population depends on the number left to spawn.

There are a number of different types of salmon. Our discussion focuses on the Pacific salmon, which consists of a number of species — sockeye, chum, pink, coho, and chinook. Each species has different biological characteristics and susceptibility to fishing equipment, but they all have the common characteristic that at a particular age (which varies by species) they return to the freshwater river or stream where they were born, spawn, and then die. Atlantic salmon, by comparison, do not die after they spawn.

The key feature of Pacific salmon fisheries is that the stock is available for harvest for only a short period of time. The commercial salmon harvests occur as the fish are returning upstream to spawn.[1] Harvests occur before spawning because the fish deteriorate rapidly in weight and commercial quality the closer they are to the spawning grounds. Typically, then, only one or two age classes will be exploited in a given season. The relationship on which to focus is between the number of fish that will spawn and the subsequent fish born from that age class that will return to spawn (and thus be available for harvest) in i years.

The relationship between spawning fish and new age classes is complex. See Crutchfield and Pontecorvo (1969) and Larkin (1966) for more details. Figure 10.1 is a simple illustration of the biological mechanics before harvesting occurs. On the horizontal axis is the number of fish that can spawn in period t. These spawning fish are those born $t - i$ years ago and have survived life in the ocean to return to their spawning grounds. On the vertical axis is the number of fish born to those spawning in period t that are expected to survive all the rigors of their environment and will return to spawn i years later (i ranges from 2 to 6 years). $F(N)$ shows the relationship

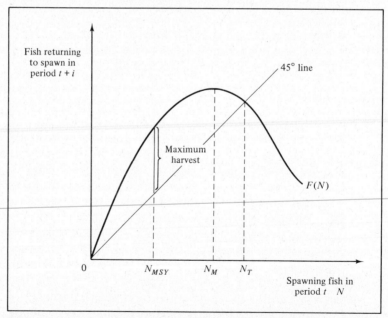

Figure 10.1 Simple biological mechanics for a salmon fishery. The fish spawning in period t determine the numbers which will return to the river to spawn in period $t + i$. The 45° line shows where the number of fish spawning in t exactly equals the number spawning in $t + i$. A harvest of the fish spawning in period t which yields no net change in the stock of salmon from t to $t + i$ is given by the distance between $F(N)$ and the 45° line. The *MSY* harvest is shown. This figure is the basis of the quadratic relationship between yield and effort for a salmon fishery.

between the number spawning in t and the number returning to spawn in $t + i$. The curve rises, reaches a maximum, then declines again.

The biological reasons for the shape are as follows. If few "parents" spawn, of course, few fish will be born and survive to spawn again. The larger the spawning population up to a size of N_M, the greater the number surviving to an age of i. There will be a relatively large number of eggs laid and hatched, and a population substantial enough to survive the rigors of the environment. But once the population of spawning fish exceeds N_M, those of the next generation surviving decline. Although many eggs will be deposited and hatched, relatively fewer hatchlings will survive than when fewer eggs are laid. The reason is that spawning grounds become overcrowded, increasing the mortality of the new recruits due to scarcity of food and other causes of mortality that depend upon density. Hence, the $F(N)$ function has a maximum, then declines.

A 45° line has also been drawn. Along the 45° line the number of spawning fish exactly equals the number of fish returning in i years. The distance then between the 45° line and $F(N)$ lying above the 45° line is the number of fish that can be harvested in period t while still providing for replacement of themselves in period $t + i$. That is, the difference between $F(N)$ and 45° is the harvest that can be taken at different populations which yields a biological equilibrium with no change in the size of the stock. The maximum harvest (the MSY yield in physical terms) can be taken where the distance between the 45° line and $F(N)$ is the largest — where the slope of $F(N)$ equals 1. This occurs at a population of spawning fish equal to N_{MSY}. The same relationship can be repeated each year with different age classes of salmon.

Thus we have the same type of relationship between sustainable yield of a fish species and a measure of the stock of the species. The difference between salmon and, say, the demersal species represented by our aggregate biomass model is that we must talk about distinct age classes for salmon and spawning parents, rather than the aggregate biomass. But if we look at the relationship between a sustainable yield of salmon and the number of fish spawning, we obtain the usual quadratic shape seen with our simple biological mechanics. That is, the $F(N)$ curve from zero to N_T in Figure 10.1 lying above the 45° line shows the sustainable harvests possible for different numbers of spawning fish. This means that the relationship between the sustainable harvest and *effort* should look the same as in our simple model.

Figure 10.2 provides an illustration. Assuming the price of salmon is constant, the total revenue *(TR)* function is quadratic. Assuming unit costs of effort are constant, total costs of effort *(TC)* are again linear. The common property and private property equilibriums are shown in the figure, and the distinction between the two equilibriums is the same as before. In the CPE, more effort is used than in the PPE, given the costs and price of fish.

In using a figure such as 10.2, we must interpret the relationships with care. We are looking at particular age classes of salmon available for harvest, not aggregate biomass. In addition, exogenous factors can have a big impact on salmon age classes. Salmon are affected by environmental hazards such as changes in food supply and the presence of predators, but they also must contend with man-made hazards. Hydroelectric dams may impede their travel upstream. Salmon habitats are threatened by pollution from residential areas and from industries such as mining and forestry.

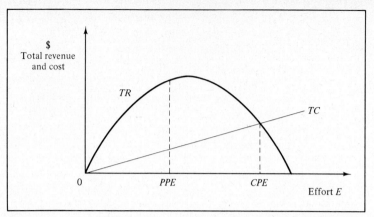

Figure 10.2 The CPE and PPE for a salmon fishery, assuming a constant price per pound of salmon and constant unit cost of effort. The fishery shown is for a particular age class, not the aggregate biomass of the fishery.

Thus there can be considerable variation in the actual population available for harvest in any given year. The yield-to-effort relationship is thought to be less stable than that for fish species typified by the aggregate biomass model. These features of the salmon fishery thus create special problems for fisheries management.

We cannot go into detail on the various policies applied to open access salmon fisheries (see Crutchfield and Pontecorvo, 1969, and Pearse, 1982, for information on past and present policies). The basic management problem is that it is possible to harvest any particular age class very extensively because the fish swim through confined regions — rivers — to spawn. In theory, an entire age class of one or more species could be extinguished by putting nets across important spawning rivers. Earlier in this century, many salmon populations were decimated by the construction of hydroelectric dams and blockage of spawning rivers (before fish ladders were installed and perfected).

Regulation has generally come in three forms: restriction of the equipment used (size and type of nets, prohibition of particular items); area closures (high seas salmon harvests are prohibited to U.S. and Canadian commercial fishermen); and time closures for the spawning rivers. British Columbia has also experimented with a licensing scheme for vessels. There are, in addition, a number of policies implemented by governments to protect the species and their habitats. These include the construction of fish ladders at dams and hatcheries. But taxes have not been used, and none of the policies has attempted to achieve the "optimal" economic harvest.

The regulations have by and large led to economic inefficiency and high costs in harvesting salmon, and have not prevented overfishing — harvests in excess of an economic optimum. Although damage to salmon habitats has taken its toll on the species, ineffective regulation of the fisheries and the resulting excessive harvests have reduced spawning stocks far below their maximum economic potential. New policies have been recommended by, for example, Pearse. It is too early, however, to predict the effect any of these policies might have on salmon stocks. Thus salmon represent a different type of biological mechanics and challenge to fishery management.

Environmental Factors in Fishery Biological Mechanics

There is no meaningful long-run, steady-state yield in many fisheries because the population in any period depends on ecological conditions—water temperature, currents, disease, new predators, pollution—that have prevailed over the life cycle of the species, not the population in the previous period. In each period, the population is determined largely by exogenous factors rather than biological mechanics. That means that at a particular point in time—say one fishing season—only short-run functions can be drawn for the fishery. Species whose biomass is greatly affected by environmental factors include shrimp and anchovies.

Suppose the stock can be measured at the beginning of the fishing season. It is then possible to analyze the optimal harvest *for that period.* The usual sort of total revenue and total cost curves can be drawn relating the harvest to the amount of effort used. But it may not be meaningful to analyze the fishery using the dynamic model. The stock must be reevaluated each period that harvesting is to occur, and a new set of short-run curves defined.

Moreover, if the fish feeds on an erratic stock of another species, the harvest will also be highly variable. That is, if the cycles in the "food" are unpredictable, there will be stochastic variations in the population of the harvested species. If the cycles in the food are known, the optimal harvest of the commercial species is much simpler. The fish must then be harvested in different intensities over the cycle.[2]

The dangers from open access to a fishery with an unpredictable stock in each period can be substantial. Disease, fluctuations in water temperature, food supply, and presence of predators can lead to large swings in the stocks. If there are excessive amounts of effort at work harvesting the species and a bad year occurs, the population can be driven close to extinction. This occurred in the anchovy fishery off the coast of Peru in the early 1970s. The fishery was decimated because of open access and the unpredictable exogenous factors—namely, El Niño—a warm ocean current (see the reading at the end of the chapter).

Optimal harvesting practices require careful monitoring of the stock before each fishing season. If exogenous factors are such that a bad year for the stock exists, effort should be curtailed. Regulating this type of fishery is difficult and costly, in part because of the different levels of effort that may be needed each year. But the costs of allowing open access and risking extinction may be even higher.

Interaction among Species

Biological interaction of different fish species can take place in many ways.[3] Each species can benefit from having more of the other on hand. This is called a *commensal* situation. Alternatively, each can suffer from a greater presence of the other. We then have a *competitive* situation. There can also be cross-effects, such as a predator-prey relationship in which one species benefits from the presence of the other (eats it), while the other species suffers (is eaten). From an economic perspective, the presence of another species can make harvesting more or less easy because the costs of harvesting a particular species may be affected by the presence of the stock of another species. If both species are valuable, harvesting one might yield the salable by-product—the other species captured simultaneously.

We examine the case in which two species interact in a predator-prey situation. We first consider the biological mechanics, then turn to the determination of an optimal harvesting program. There are many examples of predator-prey situations. For example, many species eat shrimp in their larval stage and can greatly affect important commercial harvests. Sea mammals such as sea lions, harbor seals, and killer whales feed on salmon. In this section, we look at a predator-prey model using sharks and tuna as our fictitious example. We choose these species for heuristic reasons — it is not difficult to remember which species is the predator and which is the prey.

Suppose then we have two species — tuna and sharks. Tuna are a commercially desirable species, but they are eaten by sharks which in general have less commercial demand.[4] Tuna have a stock size of $X(t)$ and are eaten by sharks, which have a population of $Y(t)$. Sharks' natural mortality is at the exponential rate d. The change in the population of sharks over any two periods, t and $t + 1$, is defined by Equation (10.1).

$$Y(t + 1) - Y(t) = Y(t)[-d + c'X(t)] \qquad (10.1)$$

where c' is a parameter which reflects sharks eating tuna, and d is the "decay" of the shark species in the absence of tuna to eat. Tuna achieve a steady-state stock $X = a/b$ through their natural growth in the usual logistic pattern, but are "harvested" by sharks by the amount $cY(t)X(t)$, given a stock size $X(t)$ and c, the parameter that measures the intensity of sharks "harvesting" tuna. The change in the tuna population over time is then given by Equation (10.2):

$$X(t + 1) - X(t) = X(t)[a - bX(t) - cY(t)] \qquad (10.2)$$

where a and b are the parameters of the biological production function for the tuna.

In an equilibrium without human predation, $X = d/c'$, and $Y = (a - bX)/c = (ac' - bd)/cc'$. In this steady-state equilibrium, the predator "harvests" cXY per period or $d(ac' - bd)/(c')^2$. Recall that sharks will die out without tuna, but tuna will grow to their carrying capacity in the absence of sharks. We have an equilibrium with sharks living off the net growth in the tuna at a stock size of $Y = (a - bX)/c$, which is equal to $(ac' - bd)/cc'$. We illustrate in Figure 10.3. In Figure 10.3(a), we have our familiar single-species stock-sustainable yield schedule for the tuna, assuming no predation occurs. When there is predation, the tuna stock will fall to d/c' and the sharks are eating $[d(ac' - bd)]/(c')^2$ each period — the vertical distance between the X axis and the $F(X)$ function at d/c'.

In Figure 10.3(b), we show the shark's biology. Sharks eat enough tuna to remain at a steady population. Tuna are also in equilibrium, with their net growth eaten by the sharks. That means when sharks are eating enough tuna, there is no growth in the stock of tuna. Natural increase and predation by sharks cancel out. In (b), no one harvests sharks, so there is no excess of births over deaths; no vertical part in (b) is positive. Births match deaths at the equilibrium stock size. The biological mechanics of the two species are quite different, but they interact to yield a steady-state with both species having positive stocks.

We now introduce optimal fishing (by people) into the analysis. Assume that the tuna are commercially more valuable than the sharks. We will show that it will be socially desirable to harvest sharks so that the steady-state population of tuna will rise

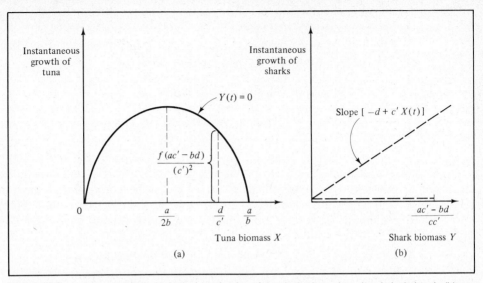

Figure 10.3 In (a) we have the biological mechanics of the desired species when in isolation. In (b) we have the mechanics for the preying species. With no human predation, a steady-state emerges with the stock of Y at $\dfrac{ac' - bd}{cc'}$ and X at d/c'. The predator Y species consumes the net increment in the X species each period.

and more tuna can be harvested. This optimal solution requires that *the harvesting of sharks be subsidized — that a bounty be paid.* The government fisheries manager will try to maximize social welfare over time from the harvest of both species. The objective function the manager maximizes is given by Equation (10.3):

$$
\begin{aligned}
W = \; & B^H[H(0)] - C^H[H(0), X(0), Y(0)] + B^L[L(0)] - C^L[L(0), X(0), Y(0)] \\
& + \beta\{B^H[H(1)] - C^H[H(1), X(1), Y(1)] + B^L[L(1)] \\
& - C^L[L(1), X(1), Y(1)]\} + \beta^2\{B^H[H(2)] - C^H[H(2), X(2), Y(2)] \\
& + B^L[L(2)] - C^L[L(2), X(2), Y(2)]\} + \cdots +
\end{aligned} \tag{10.3}
$$

where $B^H(H)$ is the gross consumer surplus associated with a harvest of H tons of tuna — the high valued species

$\quad\quad B^L(L)$ is the gross consumer surplus associated with a harvest of L tons of shark — the low valued species

$\quad\quad C^H(\cdot)$ is the cost of harvesting H tons of tuna when the two stocks of fish are present at their indicated sizes

$\quad\quad C^L(\cdot)$ is the cost of harvesting L tons of tuna when the two stocks of fish are present at their indicated sizes

$\quad\quad \beta$ is the discount factor which is equal to $1/(1 + r)$, where r is the social discount rate

Let's rewrite the biological dynamics for each species in the more general form shown in Equation (10.4):

$$
\begin{aligned}
X(t + 1) - X(t) &= G[X(t), Y(t)] \\
Y(t + 1) - Y(t) &= Q[X(t), Y(t)]
\end{aligned} \tag{10.4}
$$

Equation (10.4) shows general representations of the interactions between the two species. Previously, we had a specific case where sharks died at an exponential rate without tuna dinners. Now, the two species simply interact in some unspecified way. The harvests from fishing firms are then given by

$$H(t) = G[X(t), Y(t)] - X(t+1) + X(t)$$
$$L(t) = Q[X(t), Y(t)] - Y(t+1) + Y(t) \qquad (10.5)$$

We then substitute Equation (10.5) for $L(t)$ and $H(t)$ in Equation (10.3) to obtain a W which is to be maximized by choice of tuna and shark stocks (and hence, harvests) in each period, 0, 1, 2, . . . , that follows. This is readily done by differentiating Equation (10.3) with respect to X and Y, then setting the resulting first-order expressions equal to zero. The solutions yield the relationships for an optimal extraction program over time.[5] Rather than write down the solution, which must hold at each point along the optimal path, let's assume that we have a steady-state equilibrium with positive values for X and Y. In the steady-state, the stocks of tuna and sharks must satisfy Equation (10.6) simultaneously

$$(p - C_H)(G_X - r) + (q - C_L)Q_X - C_H - C_L = 0$$
$$(q - C_L)(Q_Y - r) + (p - C_H)G_Y - C_H - C_L = 0 \qquad (10.6)$$

where p and q are market prices for a ton of tuna and sharks, respectively; r is the discount rate; and the other terms are partial derivatives of the cost and production functions. For the following, we assume that q, the shark price, is positive, but the analysis would be the same even if q were equal to zero.

For the *special case* of $G(X,Y)$ and $Q(X,Y)$ given by our predatory-prey biological dynamics above, and assuming that the total costs of harvesting each species are *not* interdependent—that is, $C^H(H,X) = wH/mX$ and $C^L(L,Y) = wL/nY$—then these two steady-state equations in (10.6) become, respectively,

$$p(a - bX) - pcY = (r + bX)[p - (w/mX)] - c'Y[q - (w/nY)]$$
$$q(-d + c'X) = cX[p - (w/mX)] + r[q - (w/nY)] \qquad (10.7)$$

Observe that the left-hand sides are steady-state harvests if multiplied by X and Y, respectively (in dollar terms). The terms $[p - (w/mX)]$ and $[q - (w/nY)]$ are the rent per ton from the harvest of tuna and sharks, respectively, where rent, as before, is the difference between price and marginal cost per ton. This indicates that $rX[p - (w/mX)]$ and $rY[q - (w/nY)]$ are the rental value of the respective stocks in flow terms multiplied by the discount rate. A steady-state solution must have the left-hand side of the first equation in (10.7) positive, because as we saw in Chapter 8, rents are positive for a desired species in an optimally managed fishery.

To see what the steady-state stocks and harvests are in the optimal equilibrium, we solve Equation (10.7) by inserting some assumed values for the parameters. These two equations can be combined to form a polynomial equation in X^3. For parameter values: $a = .5, b = .1, c = .6, d = 1, r = .05, w = 6, c' = 1, m = 6, n = 50, p = 1$, and $q = .5$. The two equations of (10.7) are plotted in Figure 10.4. Only the solution, $X = 2.24$ and $Y = .040$, is economically meaningful. The other positive solution for the steady-state stocks results in a negative harvest of sharks.[6]

We illustrate both the biological equilibrium without harvesting and the so-

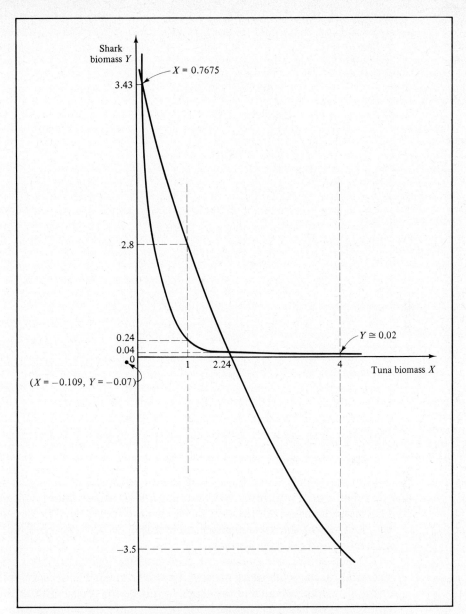

Figure 10.4   A sketch of the two equations in X and Y yielding our solution of Y = .04 and X = 2.24. Of the three sets of roots, only the one we have noted makes economic sense.

cially optimal equilibrium in Figure 10.5. The biological equilibrium is shown in (a), while the optimal equilibrium with an active fishing industry is shown in (b). Without human predation, the stock of sharks is large and the tuna stock is small relative to the situation illustrated in Figure 10.5(b). The much smaller stock of sharks that occurs with human predation implies that the sharks are eating much less of the net growth in the tuna population (.402 tons of tuna are consumed by sharks in the biological

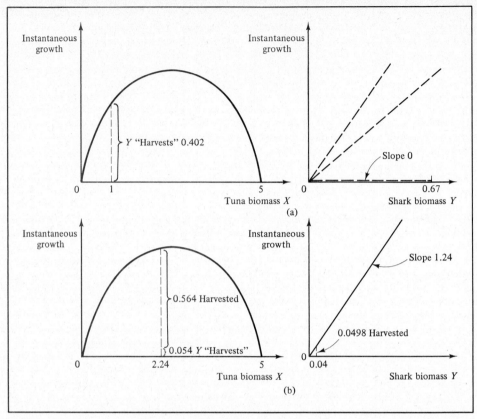

Figure 10.5 In (a), we have the situation with no human intervention. In (b), humans harvest .564 of the *X* species and .0498 of the *Y* species. Observe the large changes in steady-state stocks after human intervention. The *Y* stock drops more than tenfold, and the *X* stock more than doubles.

equilibrium versus .054 in the economic equilibrium). The larger sustainable stock of tuna that results with human predation on both sharks and tuna leads to a sizable commercial harvest of tuna — namely, .564 tons per season. With commercial fishing, .05 tons of sharks are caught each season in order to keep that species from expanding and consuming tuna.

Because the commercial value of sharks is low, a subsidy or bounty will be necessary to have the shark species harvested under the socially optimal arrangement. The optimal value of the shark subsidy is the social value of the rent per ton from the shark harvest. The shark rent per ton is $[q - (w/nY)]$, or with our parameter values, -2.485. The negative sign indicates that a subsidy is necessary, because in an unregulated fishery no sharks would be harvested. The higher the price of sharks, of course, the lower the required subsidy. If the price exceeds the harvesting costs, no subsidy is required. To achieve the optimal harvest of tuna, a tax is required which is also set equal to the rent per ton of tuna harvested at the optimum. The tax is thus set equal to $(p - w/mX)$, which would be equal to .559 for our parameter values. (If the shark rent is positive, its harvests must also be taxed). With our solution, the tax on the tuna yields revenues which exceed the subsidy to the sharks, so there is a surplus for the fishery managers that can offset administrative costs.[7]

What the optimal policy does is thus subsidize the shark harvests to reduce their population and prevent sharks from eating as much tuna. The tuna population will then increase to a point where a sizable harvest can be taken by human fishing effort. Without the harvest of sharks, the available tuna harvest would be much lower, and although sharks would be better off, people would be worse off. In an optimally managed fishery, the rents per ton are "shadow prices" indicating the relative values of the different tons harvested at the optimum.

In practice, it would be very difficult to regulate a predator-prey fishery. In an open access setting, the regulator must first calculate the optimal solution and find the optimal tax and subsidy per ton. These taxes and subsidies must be levied on entering firms. The administrative and monitoring problems examined in Chapter 9 will apply in this case as well. But the regulator cannot easily tell how changes in the fishing environment are affecting the equilibrium stocks without extensive recomputation. These computations are necessary in a single-species fishery as well, but with a predator-prey relationship the measurement is more complex.

But even if we leave aside the practical problems associated with imposing and enforcing optimal regulations over time, could the regulatory agency even deal in theory with changing economic conditions in the fishery? Suppose the social discount rate or the unit costs of harvesting fish rose. In the predator-prey model, would the regulator be able to determine the optimal response? In his analysis of this problem, Solow (1977) found that the effects of a change in the discount rate or unit costs on the optimal steady-state harvest (and fish stocks) could not be determined unambiguously for a general model. Algebraic investigations yielded results with different possible signs. Numerical values were needed to get definitive results. This awkward outcome led him to comment: "It's an excellent example of the conflict between complex ecology and simple economics."

Although we cannot get general comparative static results for the effect of changes in parameters on the steady-state equilibrium, we can calculate results for specific parameter values. Given our "base equilibrium" from the parameters above, we changed separately the interest rate r, a parameter in the cost function for harvesting tuna, m, and the similar parameter in the cost function for harvesting sharks, n. The results are shown in Table 10.1.

From our base equilibrium, an increase in the interest rate decreases the opti-

Table 10.1 COMPARATIVE EQUILIBRIA IN THE PREDATOR-PREY MODEL

Change in	Change in			
	Tuna biomass	Shark biomass	Tuna harvests	Shark harvests
Discount rate (r)	−	+	−	+
Cost of Tuna Harvests ($1/m$)	+	+	−	+
Costs of Shark Harvests ($1/n$)	−	+	−	−

mal tuna stock and tuna harvest while it increases the optimal shark harvest and stock. These results do not have much intuitive appeal and are quite different from the single-species case. Normally, an increase in the discount rate leads to an increase in the harvest and a decrease in the stock, because the present value of waiting for larger harvests in the future by letting the stock build up today is reduced. What appears to be happening here is that the decline in the tuna harvest makes more tuna available for shark food. Thus tunas decline and sharks rise, making more sharks available for harvest. But why the asymmetry between the shark and tuna harvests? Intuition is not always reliable when the number of interactions between variables increases. Simulation becomes necessary.

The cost effects are more straightforward and intuitively plausible. A rise in the cost of harvesting tuna decreases tuna harvests, but increases shark harvests. Both stocks rise as a result. Firms shift to harvesting the lower-valued shark species as the rent per ton on tuna harvested falls. The tuna stock rises because fewer are caught and more sharks are caught. The shark stock rises because there are more tuna to eat (even though more sharks are caught). Finally, a rise in the cost of harvesting sharks decreases the harvests of both species. A fall in shark harvests leads to a fall in the stock of tuna (more sharks remain to eat them). This results in a smaller tuna harvest and an increase in the stock of sharks.

We wish to emphasize that these results do depend on our parameters and will change when other values are chosen. An alternative equilibrium would be one with free entry and no subsidy for the harvesting of trash fish. In this case, the price of both species would equal their average harvest cost. For tuna, $p = w/mX$, and for sharks, $q = w/nY$. For our model and base-value parameters, $X = 1$ and $Y = .24$, with a tuna harvest of .256 and shark harvest of zero. These tuna values are slightly below half those for the socially optimal case. The shark stock is six times larger. The price of sharks might be zero in actual cases, and with no government intervention, the desired stock may be very low and the fishing activity quite small.

We have considered a detailed case of one type of biological interdependency: sharks preying on tuna. Other cases and numerical examples would change the results, although in general, we would expect human predation to increase the stock of the prey and reduce the stock of the predator. In our example, the tuna stock more than doubled in size when optimal human predation was introduced, while the shark population was reduced to about 1/17th of its original size. It's possible that for very low commercial value of the predator, extinction would result. There are examples of near extinction in predator-prey relationships among mammals as a result of human harvests of the predator. Wolves are known to prey on commercial species such as sheep and cattle when their "natural" prey such as deer are scarce. A bounty on wolves in some areas has decimated wolf populations. These actions may have been misguided ecologically and socially (preservation of species may have social value), but the actions were taken to increase the stock of the commercial species to increase their harvests. Other examples of this sort exist.[8]

Before turning to our next topic, note that we have analyzed only biological interactions. It is also possible that harvesting costs are affected by the presence of both species. For example, we assumed that tuna and shark harvesting costs were independent of the stock of the other species. Suppose these costs were instead functions of each other's stocks. In our previous example, the total costs were wH/mX for tuna and wL/nY for sharks. If there are cost interdependencies, the functions could be written as wHY/mX and wLX/nY, respectively. In this situation, the costs of harvesting tuna are higher the larger the stock of sharks, and similarly for harvesting sharks. Introducing such interdependencies complicates computation of our equilibriums, but the model may then more closely capture the details of certain fisheries. The comparative static computations are no less complex. Anderson (1977) refers to these cost effects as technical interdependencies that may be present along with the biological interdependencies examined here.

BOX 10.1
Lamprey and Lake Trout

A profitable lake trout fishery in the Great Lakes (Ontario, Erie, Huron, Michigan, and Superior) was almost eliminated between 1930 and 1960 by the arrival of a predator species, the lamprey. This latter species migrated from the ocean into the lower Great Lakes; a sea lamprey was first observed in Lake Erie above Niagara Falls in 1921. By 1946, they had migrated, in part by piggybacking on the hulls of ships, into the colder upper Great Lakes. Canadian and American harvests of 15 million pounds of lake trout annually fell to 300,000 pounds in the early 1960s as a result of the lamprey invasion. This is a case in which subsidized harvest of the trash species, the lamprey, was necessary in order to make harvests of the desired species, the lake trout, profitable.

"Harvesting" of the lamprey took the form of destroying the young lampreys, known as ammocoetes. Lampreys spawn only in certain streams. Once these were isolated, a specially tested toxicant, TFM (3 triflourmethyl-4 mitro-

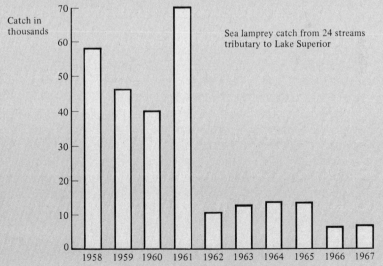

Figure B10.1 Sea lamprey and trout. *Source:* Department of Fisheries of Canada, "Lamprey Control in the Great Lakes". Ottawa, Queen's Printer 1968.

> *Box 10.1 continued*
>
> phenol), was applied with special pumping systems. Of 2,000 Canadian streams tested for spawning, only 105 were used by lampreys. Large streams were first treated in 1959, and by 1962 only 20 percent of the early stock remained (see Figure B10.1). A large program of restocking of lake trout was initiated in 1958, with 20 million planted in Lake Superior by 1968.
>
> Although not commercially exploited in North America, lampreys have been eaten for many years and are considered a delicacy in some parts of the world. Imports to North America have been taking place for many years. However, in the Great Lakes the lamprey was the trash species, and it was necessary to subsidize its harvest.

INTERNATIONAL FISHERIES
A Two-Country Model

Until the 200-mile coastal boundaries were imposed by many countries in the late 1970s, most major fishing grounds were exploited by vessels from two or more nations. Under a regime of open access, the equilibrium should be the same as if one nation were in control. The flags on the boats would be of no importance; too much effort and too small a stock size relative to the optimum results. Suppose, however, that a fisheries department in each nation wanted to control the number of boats used by its nationals in a fishing ground outside its territorial limits. What plan might it devise? How would this plan differ from a plan coordinated by all nations exploiting a particular fishery?

Consider a two-country illustration with each government fishing department acting in isolation. Suppose Iceland and Great Britain both fish for cod in the North Sea. Iceland makes an assumption about England's program of harvests into the indefinite future. That is, Iceland makes a conjecture about how much cod English boats will harvest period by period into the future. This is an abstract approach, but it introduces the concept of a *strategic game*. Games can be quite complex, especially when they occur in a dynamic environment such as our fishery model.

We assume that cod reside in a single-species fishery, so the biological environment is the same as our simple model of Chapters 8 and 9. The only difference is that the harvests are now divided among Iceland *(I)* and Great Britain *(B)*. Several equilibrium concepts will also be introduced—a noncooperative equilibrium in which Iceland and Britain do not get together to plan their harvests, and a cooperative equilibrium in which they do. We first set up the social welfare problem each government manager solves, then show the differences between the two equilibriums.

The steady-state relationship for the cod population is given by Equation (10.8):

$$X(t + 1) - X(t) = F[X(t)] - H^I(t) - H^B(t) \qquad (10.8)$$

where $X(t)$ is the current stock of cod, $F[X(t)]$ is the natural growth in the stock, and $H^I(t)$ and $H^B(t)$ are Iceland's and England's current harvests, respectively. Suppose first we are viewing the problem of determining the optimal harvest from the perspective of a fisheries manager in Iceland who believes that English harvests in each period are going to be at a particular level. This is a conjecture made about the competitive environment Iceland operates in. It must determine its own harvests, based on its beliefs about English harvests. Iceland then selects its own harvests in all periods, $n = 0,1, \ldots$, to maximize the present value of cod harvests. Equation (10.9) shows Iceland's objective function:

$$
\begin{aligned}
W^I = \; & B^I[H^I(0)] - C^I[H^I(0),H^B(0),X(0)] \\
& + \beta\{B^I[H^I(1)] - C^I[H^I(1),H^B(1),X(1)]\} \\
& + \beta^2\{B^I[H^I(2)] - C^I[H^I(2),H^B(2),X(2)]\} \\
& + \cdots \\
& + \beta^t\{B^I(t)] - C^I[H^I(t),H^B(t),X(t)]\} \\
& + \cdots
\end{aligned}
\tag{10.9}
$$

The variables are analogous to those defined above—namely, $B^I(.)$ is the area under the demand curve for fish in Iceland; $C^I(.)$ is Iceland's cost of harvesting H^I cod *given* that England's cod harvests are H^B and the stock of cod is X; and β is the discount factor $1/(1 + r)$. Suppose England's harvests are identical in every period. Then a steady-state for Iceland must satisfy Equation (10.10):

$$
p^I - MCH^I = [MCX^I/(F_X - r)]
\tag{10.10}
$$

where we must also have that $F(X) = H^I + H^B$—that is, the growth in the cod stock equals the harvests of both countries. p^I is the price of cod in Iceland, taken from the demand schedule for cod in that country. MCH^I is the marginal cost of harvesting cod in Iceland, given England's constant catch H^B and the stock size X. MCX^I is the effect of a marginal increase in stock size X on the cost of harvesting H^I by Iceland, and F_X is the effect on cod growth due to an increase in the stock size X. To have a steady-state, the harvests of both Iceland and England must be constant over time. If the fisheries manager in England does the same calculation with the same demand and cost schedules, there will be the analogous relationship required for a steady-state equilibrium given by Equation (10.11):

$$
p^B - MCH^B = [MCX^B/(F_X - r)]
\tag{10.11}
$$

Both Equations (10.10) and (10.11) should look familiar. They are very similar to the equation for a dynamic steady-state equilibrium presented in Chapter 8. The difference is the dependence of each country's costs on the harvests of the other country.

We can now solve for the equilibrium stock size X and the harvests in each country. Suppose, first, that each country plans its harvests without consulting the other. If both countries assume the harvest of the other is given and this indeed occurs, the steady-state equilibrium that results is called a Nash-Cournot or noncooperative equilibrium. There will exist a pair of harvests, H^I and H^B, such that Equations (10.10) and (10.11) are satisfied simultaneously. A numerical example is presented below.

Now if the two countries coordinate their fishing plans by jointly determining the optimal harvest and stock of cod, the relationship for the optimal steady-state equilibrium becomes Equation (10.12).

$$
p^I + p^B - MCH = MCX/(F_X - r)
\tag{10.12}
$$

We can solve this for stock size X and harvests $H^I = H/2 = H^B$. For the case of a linear demand schedule which is identical in both countries, $p = A - BH$, and $F(X) = X(a - bX)$, and costs given by $C^I = [w(H^I + H^B)]/mX$ and $C^B = [w(H^I - H^B)]/mX$, we find that:

1. Rent from the fishing ground is always higher for the cooperative arrangement.
2. The stock size is always smaller for the cooperative arrangement, but it can be on either side of the stock corresponding to the maximum sustainable yield. The total harvest is generally higher for the cooperative solution (both solutions yield equilibrium stocks to the right of the stock corresponding to the maximum sustainable yield. See the appendix to this chapter).
3. Aggregate welfare is always highest under the cooperative arrangement

The first two results are established by the algebraic solution for the noncooperative and cooperative problems. The last result holds because the cooperative arrangement jointly maximizes social welfare for two countries. There is no constraint operating on the objective function of each, where that constraint is the harvest of the other country. An unconstrained maximization problem always leads to at least as high a value of the variable being maximized as does a constrained problem. (Think about how high a consumer's welfare would be without a budget constraint.) In the joint problem, the countries are constrained by the biological mechanics and usual marginal conditions, but they are not constrained by each other's independently chosen harvests.

The following example illustrates these points. Suppose the demand curve for cod in each country is linear and is given by $p = 1.4167 - H$. The total cost of harvesting cod in each country is $C = w(H^I + H^B)/mX$, with $w = 6 = m$. Marginal cost is w/mX. The biological mechanics are $F(X) = X(1 - .1X)$. Given these assumptions, the solutions are:

1. For the cooperative equilibrium: $X = 6$, and the total harvest is 2.4, with each country getting a harvest of 1.2 tons.
2. For the Cournot or noncooperative competitive equilibrium: $X = 6.588$, and the total harvest is 2.2478, with each country getting a harvest of 1.1239 tons.

The assumption that each party takes the other's harvest as fixed (the constraint) is a simple introduction to strategic behavior and merely provides a flavor of types of international conflict possible in fisheries. Other strategic settings might have one country dominant in the decision of how much to harvest. Highly aggressive strategies might result in cyclical activity in which one country is dominant, the other displaces it, and so on. Steady-state equilibriums will be different in each situation.

It is not the case that the results obtained here will be repeated in other situations. If, for example, there are three countries exploiting a fish stock and only two of them coordinate their harvests, then it may not be the case that the welfare of the two cooperating countries rises compared to the noncooperative case. Similarly, it may not pay a country to cooperate, as it may do better by staying out of an agreement and "preying" on the other countries' harvests. The point is that each case of international fishing must be examined and the pecularities of the situation incorporated into the model.

One final point. Like the cartels in the nonrenewable resource sectors, it is very difficult to set up and enforce cooperative agreements in the fishery, especially if the species being harvested is pelagic and there are many ports where the catch is landed. Enforcement may be virtually impossible if any country has an incentive to cheat on the agreement. Countries have a very difficult time even setting up these agreements. Canada and the United States are still disputing fishing treaties on their east and west coasts where their 200-mile limits overlap. There is a growing literature on strategic games in the fishery that is interesting and complex.[9] Whether this analysis can be applied in its current state to international fisheries disputes is an open question.

UNCERTAINTY IN THE FISHERY

Cases of *uncertainty in the reproductivity of the stock* and in the payoff or catch from a specific amount of resources used in harvesting have been reported in some detail in Reed (1979), Smith (1980), and Lewis (1981), respectively. There are few general results in this literature. For example, both Smith and Lewis used numerical examples to derive their particular results.

Smith finds that by introducing randomness in lobster reproduction, the results of Bell (1972), which were developed for a certainty environment, are not greatly changed. However, Smith points out that Bell's specification of costs may not be reasonable and that more plausible values for costs result in much less waste of resources in the common property equilibrium than suggested by Bell. For the case of uncertainty in the "reproductivity" of whales, however, Smith indicates that current estimates of the stock under a certainty regime are 8 percent higher than they would be if uncertainty were incorporated.

Lewis makes the *catch for a given level of effort in harvesting* uncertain. He then examines the implications of different types of harvest cost functions in this uncertain environment. He solves for the socially optimal equilibrium where the risk preferences of the government manager are also considered. With declining average harvesting costs, cyclical policies are optimal. In such cases, there is much harvesting and stock depletion, followed by no harvesting and stock replenishment. Then another burst of harvesting occurs; stocks are depleted, then rebuilt, and so on.

"Averaging" and ignoring the details of uncertainty can yield almost optimal policies for the case of increasing average harvesting costs. But this course of action is inadequate for the case of declining average harvesting costs. With increased risk aversion by the manager, effort is spread more evenly over the potential population sizes that might arise probablistically. Finally, there is the question of increases in uncertainty or mean preserving spreads. More uncertainty leads to less effort in harvesting and smaller average catches. In the risk-averse case, effort is increased for small populations of fish and decreased for large populations. In the latter case, the government manager reduces the riskiness of returns from harvesting.

In a longer unpublished study, Lewis considered uncertainty in the price the government manager could expect, but has not reported his results in his papers. For the case of rising average harvest costs, we presume that increased price uncertainty would lead to a reduction in effort and a smaller average harvest. This is because a certain income stream of X dollars is more desirable than an uncertain stream with an average of X dollars. Uncertainty in the fishery is an active subject for research, and no doubt more results will be forthcoming.

SUMMARY

1. The biological mechanics for salmon should be based on spawning fish (escapement) rather than the biomass. The biological relationship is then between spawning fish in period t and the age class that returns to spawn in period $t + i$, where i is the interval spent before spawning. Although the sustainable yield from the salmon fishery will look like that from our simple model based on aggregate biomass, the interpretation is different. Each year, one or more age classes are harvested as the salmon travel upstream to spawn.

2. The biological characteristics of the salmon create special management problems. Governments must ensure in an open access fishery that too many salmon are not harvested as they pass upstream. To date, salmon fisheries have largely been regulated with equipment restrictions, area and time closures, and some licensing of vessels. The regulations have led to inefficient harvests and have not protected various species from overfishing.

3. In many species, exogenous factors, including the weather, water temperature, disease, and predators, can be a more important determinant of the total population at each point in time than the biomass. Short-run biological relationships are more meaningful than long-run functions. Optimal harvesting policies for this fishery must be flexible, allowing for large harvests in "good" years and small harvests in "bad" years. The possibility of extinction is high when there is unrestricted open access to this kind of fishery.

4. In a predator-prey model, the social optimum involves harvesting the predator to allow more prey to survive and be harvested by people. To achieve the optimum, a subsidy on the predator will be required when its commercial value (rent) is low. A tax on the prey is required to obtain the optimal harvest and amount of effort.

4. In a complex predator-prey model, comparative static results of a qualitative nature are difficult to obtain. Numerical simulation is required to get definitive results.

5. In a model where two countries compete for a particular fish stock, a cooperative fishing policy between the countries will lead to more rent from the fishery, higher aggregate welfare, but possibly a lower sustainable stock than when the two countries compete for the fish (the noncooperative equilibrium).

6. When there is uncertainty in the reproductive capabilities of the stock or the relationship between effort and harvesting, the optimal steady-state equilibrium may be significantly different from that under certainty. Numerical simulation is typically used to derive the results because of their sensitivity to the specification of the harvesting cost function and biological mechanics.

DISCUSSION QUESTIONS

1. How can an open access salmon fishery be managed to obtain an efficient harvest and level of effort? Explain the particular biological features of the salmon fishery that distinguish it from the basic logistic model of fishery net growth.

2. International fishing organizations that plan global quotas on harvests are unstable. The more effective they are, the more advantageous it is for a single country to remain outside the organization. Evaluate this claim. Are there examples which come to mind?

3. Ecological complexity is the principal barrier to planning appropriate harvests for fish. Once quotas are in effect, stock sizes are often quite different from those anticipated. Is this a valid contention, or might one instead contend that if binding quotas are maintained, the ecology will look after itself? Do examples come to mind?

4. The snail darter is a tiny fish threatened with extinction when its habitat was being disturbed by a dam-building project. How should we evaluate the value of the snail darter to society?

NOTES

1. People sport fishing and certain fishing fleets foreign to the United States and Canada do catch salmon in the ocean.

2. For an example of this type of fishery, see Flaaten (1983). Also see Blumo et al. (1982), who have developed a simulation model of the pink shrimp fishery in the Gulf of Mexico. Seawater temperature is taken into account in the biological mechanics. The growth of weekly age classes of shrimp is calculated. Optimal policies for the fishery are contrasted with existing regulatory practices proposed by the area's fishery management council.

3. Ecologists distinguish eight types of species interaction: (1) neutralism—no interaction between cohabiting species; (2) competition—mutual negative interaction, as in competing for scarce common feeding or breeding grounds; (3) mutualism—symbiotic relationships in which each species needs the other to survive (such as bacteria and host); (4) cooperation—an elected symbiotic relationship such as occurs for mutual defense against predators; (5) commensalism—one species benefits and the other neither benefits or suffers (phoresis is the transport of a small species by a larger one); (6) amensalism—one species suffers and the other, the inhibitor, is unaffected; (7) parasitism—one species, generally smaller, inhibits growth or reproduction of the host species; (8) predation—one species kills the other to obtain food. See Dajoz (1977), pp. 151–153.

4. Some consumers consider shark very desirable, but we will ignore this complication. In this example, we assume that sharks *only* eat tuna. If they don't eat enough tuna, the shark population begins to decline. This is not realistic, but simplifies the analysis and allows us to illustrate the basic points in a predator-prey relationship using names of well-known species of fish.

5. The problem is analogous to that solved in Chapter 8, the dynamics of the fishery.

6. See Solow (1977), pp. 217–220, for further comments on possible solutions. A steady-state solution need not exist for this problem.

7. Observe that the harvest of sharks exceed stocks. This is both biologically and arithmetically possible. For example, if each pair of sharks has five offspring per period, then three can be harvested and the stock can remain constant.

8. Clark (1976), pp. 303–311, presents a model in which every harvest of the two species caught results in quantities directly proportional to their stock sizes. The fishing firms cannot vary the mix of species caught. For an open access or common property solution, he argues that extinction of one species is a plausible outcome.

9. See, for example, Lewis and Cowans (1982), and Levhari and Mirman (1980).

Reading 1

The Anchovy Crisis

An article by Idyll (1973) in *Scientific American* tells the story of the anchovy and the complex set of biological conditions that, combined with overfishing, led to its demise in 1973. The small Peruvian anchovy resides in a complex ecosystem off the coast of Peru. It is a key organism in an aquatic food chain that starts with microscopic diatoms and phytoplankton, on to small crustaceans, small fish, including the anchovy, and then larger fish and sea birds that feed on the anchovy. The anchovy was, however, the species that captured a very high proportion of the total energy from the food chain. The maximum sustainable stock of this anchovy is probably around 15 to 20 million metric tons.

Although anchovies can spawn at any time during the year, the peak spawning periods are from August to September and to a lesser degree in January and February. The natural life span of an anchovy is short—about three years. The female can reproduce when she is a year old and is capable of producing over 10,000 eggs. At two years, she can produce around 20,000 eggs. Life is not easy for an anchovy, however; natural mortality is high. Anchovies require food almost immediately upon hatching, and if environmental conditions are such that food is scarce, most new recruits will die. They are also preyed upon by copepods (who are themselves eaten by larger anchovies) and by sea birds known as guano. Only about 1 percent of all anchovy larvae survive one month after they hatch. This is why millions of eggs must be produced each period to ensure the survival of the species.

The anchovy's habitat is also somewhat precarious due to periodic shifts in ocean currents. Most people are now familiar with the phenomenon known as El Niño, a reversal in the Pacific Ocean currents that happens periodically for unknown reasons. When El Niño hits the Pacific coast of South America, it greatly increases the water temperature and may lead to torrential rains in a normally very arid climate. These environmental changes spell disaster for the anchovy and many other species. It's not quite clear what exactly leads to the high mortality of the ocean species.

It could be the warmer water temperature that decimates the microorganisms upon which anchovies and other creatures feed. During conditions of El Niño, massive numbers of fish, squid, sea turtles, and even small sea mammals die. The guano birds that feed on these creatures also die or fly away. The decaying creatures release hydrogen sulfide from the water and lead to a phenomenon called El Pintor (the painter). The water becomes filled with microscopic plants called dinoflagellates which turn the water to shades of red, brown, and yellow. This phenomenon is known elsewhere as *red tide.* At high concentrations, these plankton blooms are toxic. Why El Niño leads to El Pintor is not quite clear. It could be the higher water temperature or the sluggish current that does not disperse the plants as quickly as normal.

Anchovies are used in the manufacture of fish meal that is used to feed domestic livestock and fish oils. It was a very valuable product for Peru. In the early 1970s, Peru was the world's largest fish-producing country, with fish products accounting for almost one-third of its foreign exchange earnings. The anchovy harvest was around 10 to 12 million metric tons per year until disaster hit in 1973. The industry was a classic case of open access. Although regulations had existed since the 1960s, they appear to have been designed merely to maintain the MSY anchovy stock. No limitations of effort appear to have existed (or worked, if they did exist). Idyll notes that the anchovy fleet off Peru was so large that it could harvest the equivalent of the annual U.S. catch of yellowfin tuna in *one day,* or the U.S. salmon catch in two and a half. To harvest 10 million metric tons of anchovies annually, 75 percent of the fleet would be sufficient.

What happened to anchovies in 1973 illustrates the necessity to monitor environmental conditions and regulate effort accordingly. Because of the periodic presence of El Niño and the

Table 1   THE PERUVIAN ANCHOVETA FISHERY,
1959–1978

Year	Number of boats	Number of fishing days	Catch (million tons)
1959	414	294	1.91
1960	667	279	2.93
1961	756	298	4.58
1962	1,069	294	6.27
1963	1,655	269	6.42
1964	1,744	297	8.86
1965	1,623	265	7.23
1966	1,650	190	8.53
1967	1,569	170	9.82
1968	1,490	167	10.26
1969	1,455	162	8.96
1970	1,499	180	12.27
1971	1,473	89	10.28
1972	1,399	89	4.45
1973	1,256	27	1.78
1974	—*	—	4.00
1975	—	—	3.30
1976	—	—	4.30
1977	—	—	0.80
1978	—	—	0.50

* Missing data not currently available.

Source: Colin W. Clark, "Bioeconomics of the Ocean." *Bio-science* 31, (3) (March 1981), p. 233, Copyright © 1981 by the American Institute of Biological Sciences.

characteristics of anchovy reproduction and survival, *the stock of anchovies at any given point in time is not a good predictor of the growth of the species.* The number that survive in any season depends more on environmental factors than the biomass. This, combined with excessive effort and imprecise regulations, led in 1973 to the virtual extinction of the anchovy fishery. The story is simple, although some biological puzzles remain unexplained.

El Niño appeared in 1972. By June of that year, the anchovies had just about disappeared and the total harvest for the year was about 4.5 million metric tons, or about one-third to one-half of the harvests in preceding years. The stock was apparently only one to two million metric tons. El Niño continued until the spring of 1973. Anchovy harvests in 1973 were even less than in 1972, as shown in Table 1. Catches were way below the quotas set. Even with rapidly rising prices for fish meal (due to the energy price shock and commodity boom of the 1970s), there were not enough anchovies to warrant the use of effort in the fishery.

Idyll was unsure of the fate of the Peruvian anchovy over the long run. The table suggests some recovery in the catch from 1974 to 1976, then a sharp decline in 1977–78. If enough anchovies could survive both El Niño and the harvests, the species would rebuild if harvests were severely curtailed. But this required a change in the regulations, restrictions on effort, a more thorough monitoring of environmental conditions, and regulations that change quickly to reflect the environmental conditions. In the presence of El Niño, the appropriate policy would have been to curtail the harvest sharply. Even 3 to 4 million tons may have been too much. Without these regulatory responses, the anchovy fishery may not survive, and with it will go other species (the guano birds) and the livelihood of many people.

chapter *11*

Forestry Use

INTRODUCTION

A forest is a capital good, like a mineral deposit or a stock of fish. It is a renewable resource that relies on both natural regeneration and replanting by forest managers to produce new generations of trees. Many species of trees are very long-lived and may take over 100 years to reach their maximum size. Unlike the steady-state fishery, in forestry the stock and that year's increment — the entire tree — are harvested after a period of time, not just the increment. On a plot of land used in forestry, a cycle is observed: trees cut, trees grown, trees cut, trees grown, and so on. The period between one cut and the next is often called the *rotation period* and is the center of analysis in the economics of forest use.

What is the optimal rotation period, and why and how does it vary from place to place and time to time? We take up these matters in this chapter. For example, in remote areas where harvesting costs inclusive of transportation costs are higher than in more accessible areas, will the rotation period be longer or shorter? How does the discount rate, and differences in harvesting or planting costs or fertility of the land affect the rotation period?

We then review the links between a price-taking firm in forestry and the industry price and quantity. Since separate plots are harvested in cycles, there can be large quantities somewhat suddenly delivered to market. Middlemen and/or the use of inventories of forest products may be required to bring about smooth flows of timber for market demanders. Alternatively, a monopolistic, vertically integrated forestry operation, or a manager of large tracts of public forests, might arrange for smoothing of deliveries. The large firm or managers of public forests would control many plots of land on which marketable timber were grown. They could affect the total quantity delivered per unit of time and thus affect the price. The determination of the efficient rotation period on the many plots of land would be affected by the market conditions and method of smoothing deliveries.

Most "traditional" economic models assume that a forest is grown on a tract of bare land at the outset. In practice, the *natural* forest appears with a distribution of tree ages, different species, and different growing conditions for each species. We will see how the given state of a natural forest can influence the pattern of cutting and replanting. In some cases, selective cutting of age classes will be the most profitable strategy. In other cases, the forest will be clear cut. We will also consider situations in which the forest is cleared or "mined" to make way for other activities. There may also be situations in which no trees are harvested because the environmental or recreational value of the forest exceeds the value of the harvested timber. We then discuss some aspects of taxing forestry operations and some issues associated with property rights to the forest.

Finally, we consider some examples of forestry practices and public policy. We focus on the activities of the managers of the public forests in the United States—the U.S. Forest Service—and try to see why the yield per acre from the private forests generally exceeds that from the public forests. What objectives do public managers follow? Does the inclusion of social benefits from the forest, such as wilderness preservation and wildlife management, recreational use, and other typically non-market activities, play a large role in the management of the public forests? Or are public managers simply following rules for forest use that are not consistent with economic efficiency? In the United States, an important policy concern is not whether the country is running down its stock of productive timber at too fast a rate, but rather whether trees are being left in the ground too long. In contrast, forests in some other parts of the world are threatened by excessive cutting and insufficient reforestation—for example, the destruction of tropical forests and insufficient reforestation in parts of Canada.

We begin with a brief discussion of the biological basics of trees and forests.

BOX 11.1
Forest Product Use in the United States in the Long Run

Total timber harvested in the United States peaked just after 1900. Wood was a primary fuel well into the nineteenth century in the United States and remained essential for rural homes into the 1930s. Lumber, the next major use of wood, was especially prominent in the late nineteenth and early twentieth centuries, since it was the major building material. Plywood has become a major user of wood in the past 50 years. The new major use of wood harvested is pulp for making paper. It was as recent as 1900 that paper production from wood fiber became a large industry. Now per capita consumption of wood processed as pulp is about the same as wood processed as lumber. Figure B11.1 indicates per capita consumption of timber products and Figure B11.2 shows the utilization of wood harvested.

Box 11.1 continued

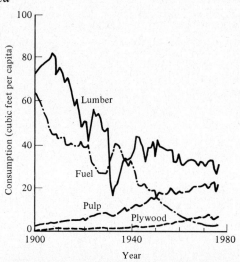

Figure B11.1   Per capita consumption of timber products, by major product, United States, 1900 to 1976. *Source:* Clawson (1979).

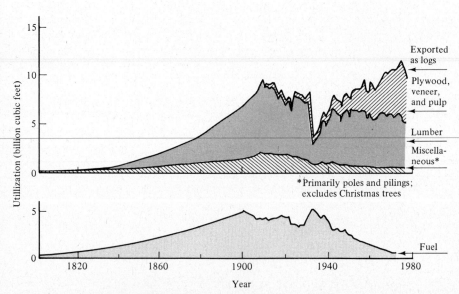

Figure B11.2   Total utilization of U.S.-grown wood (in roundwood equivalent), by major form of use, 1800 to 1975. *Source:* Clawson (1979).

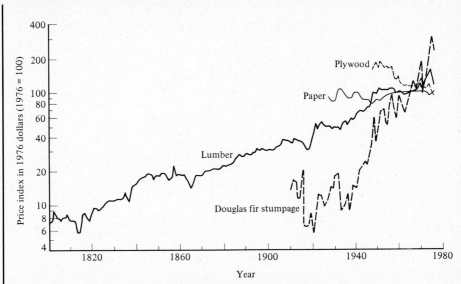

Figure B11.3 Price indices, in terms of 1967 prices (1967 = 100) for lumber, paper, plywood, and Douglas fir stumpage, for years of record, 1800 to 1975. *Source:* Clawson (1979).

The trend in the price (adjusted to constant dollars) of forest products has varied, as Figure B11.3 indicates, with plywood declining since the 1930s, paper remaining constant, and lumber rising slightly. In the long run, the price of lumber has risen fifteenfold since 1810. Stumpage is the standing tree in the forest, and we note a fairly steep trend in the price of Douglas fir stumpage since 1940. Because the price of end-use products of fir has not increased as much over this period, we can infer that the price of land in forest use has risen significantly since 1940. The declining trend in plywood prices reflects technological improvement in the process of producing plywood since the price of the wood input has increased. Also, paper production has apparently experienced substantial technical improvement.

The forest as recreation environment has become much more in demand over time. In the mid-1920s total recreation visits to the national forests were about 6 million, whereas in the mid-1970s the number had risen to about 200 million.

Source: Marion Clawson, "Forests in the Long Sweep of American History." *Science* 204 (June 15, 1979), pp. 1168–1174.

SOME BIOLOGICAL BASICS OF TREES AND FORESTS

As a tree grows, the amount of wood usable for commercial harvests changes over time. The typical schedule of the tree's growth over time is sketched in Figure 11.1.

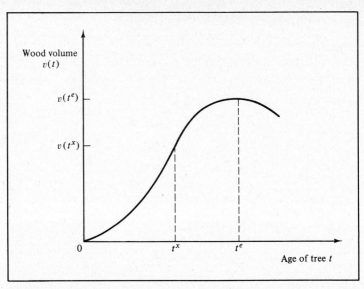

Figure 11.1 The growth cycle for a representative tree. A forest stand with trees of identical age can also have a similar shape to this schedule relating wood yield to tree age. The maximum wood volume is obtained when each tree is t^e years old. Beyond t^x, the growth rate slows.

We have the volume of wood in the tree, $v(t)$, growing over time, until a maximum is attained at date t^e. Time here is interpreted as the age of the tree. Beyond this point the tree begins to decay from old age, disease, insect predation, fire, or wind, and collapses eventually. Wood volume develops slowly in the early stages, as the tree takes root, and then beyond t^x speeds up. It slows toward date t^e, when the maximum volume is achieved.

This volume-age schedule can be altered by arranging for the optimal density of trees on a plot, by fertilizing the land, and by other activities such as thinning of trees and pest repression. The schedule can shift in a variety of ways in response to human intervention. This is part of forestry cultivation and management, also known as *silviculture.*

Figure 11.2 shows the relationship between timber volume and age for a stand of Douglas fir in a particular region up to 160 years. Beyond 160 years, these trees may continue to grow very slowly. Some stands have reached an age of 400 years. The data generating the curve shown in Figure 11.2 (and subsequent figures on the Douglas fir) are shown in Table 11.1. Note that we are talking about a stand of trees, not a single tree, but the growth relationship for the stand is similar to that for the single tree. However, there can be much mortality of individual trees as the stand ages. In one example, a stand of Douglas fir at age 40 had 1,233 stems per hectare and 492 stems at age 80.

On a plot of land of a given size, many trees can be grown so that there will be an aggregate $V(t)$ schedule representing the sum of many separate $v(t)$ schedules. In the absence of any interaction effects, $V(t)$ will simply be $Nv(t)$, where N is the number of trees. But it is unrealistic to assume $V(t) = Nv(t)$, since the density of trees and other *(handwritten margin notes: "Vol / age", "dV/dt", "du(t)/dt / v(t)")*

Table 11.1 TIME-GROWTH-VOLUME RELATIONSHIPS FOR DOUGLAS FIR, SITE CLASS II, SITE INDEX 180[a]

Age (years)	Volume standing trees over 5.0 inches d.b.h.[b] (cu ft)	Mean annual net growth to age[c] — Volume (cu ft)	Mean annual net growth to age[c] — As % of volume at age	Change in mean annual net growth over decade (cu ft)[d]	Increase in standing volume over preceding decade — Total[e] (cu ft)	Increase in standing volume over preceding decade — Average annual volume (cu ft)[f]	Increase in standing volume over preceding decade — As % of volume at end of decade[g]
	(1)	(2)	(3)	(4)	(5)	(6)	(7)
20	1,190	59.5	5.0	—	—	—	—
30	3,600	120.0	3.3	+60.5	2,410	241	6.69
40	6,400	160.0	2.5	+40.0	2,800	280	4.38
50	8,850	177.0	2.0	+17.0	2,450	245	2.77
60	11,050	184.2	1.7	+ 7.2	2,200	220	1.99
70	12,850	183.6	1.4	− 0.6	1,800	180	1.40
80	14,500	181.2	1.2	− 2.4	1,650	165	1.14
90	15,900	176.7	1.1	− 4.5	1,400	140	0.88
100	17,100	171.0	1.0	− 5.7	1,200	120	0.70
110	18,000	163.6	.9	− 7.4	900	90	0.50
120	18,800	156.7	.8	− 6.9	800	80	0.43
130	19,450	149.6	.77	− 7.1	650	65	0.33
140	20,000	143.6	.71	− 6.0	650	65	0.32
150	20,650	137.7	.67	− 5.9	550	55	0.27
160	21,150	132.2	.63	− 5.5	500	50	0.24

[a] Fully stocked acre, trees of same age; volumes are stem volumes, exclusive of bark and limbs, between stump and 4 inch top; stump height equals d.b.h. for trees up to 24 inches d.b.h., and 24 inches for larger trees. Figures rounded to nearest 50. Management at "natural" level—fire control, but no thinning, no fertilizing.

[b] d.b.h. means diameter breast high.

[c] Column 2 is column 1 divided by age; column 3 is column 2 as percent of column 1.

[d] Column 4 is difference between volumes in previous and current age in column 2.

[e] Column 5 is difference between volumes in previous and current ages in column 1.

[f] Column 6 is column 5 divided by 10, to put decade differences on an average annual basis.

[g] Column 7 is column 6 divided by column 1.

Source: Basic data in column 1 compiled by P. A. Briegleb, Pacific Northwest—Forest Range Experiment Station. All other figures derived from these data, as cited in M. Clawson (1977), *Decision Making in Timber Production, Harvest, and Marketing,* Washington, D.C.: Resources for the Future, Research Paper R–4. Reprinted by permission.

factors affects each one's growth. For simplicity, we will posit a particular $V(t)$ schedule on a plot of land of fixed size for the time being. It will resemble the $v(t)$ schedule for the individual tree, except that it will be "blown up" by approximately the number of trees located on the plot of land. We are assuming here that all trees on the plot of land are identical in type and age at any point in time. This is certainly a common feature of most cultivated forests and may be a reasonable approximation for some natural forests that evolve through changes of type of tree.

The volume-age schedule in Figure 11.1 can be *rewritten* in terms of the annual increase in volume schedule in Figure 11.3. Figure 11.3 resembles the yield-biomass schedule in the discussion of the fishery. The increment in volume is a maximum at wood volume $v(t^x)$ and age t^x. Note, however, that commercial forestry involves harvesting the tree and replanting if profitable, not harvesting the increment in the

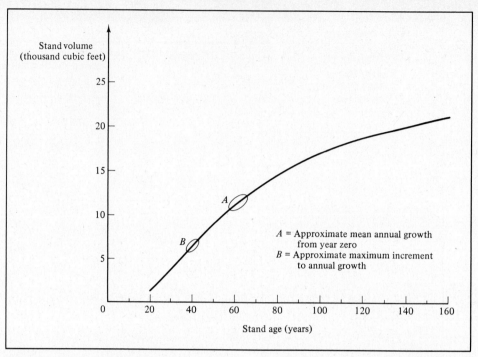

Figure 11.2 Volume of standing timber 5.0 inches or more d.b.h., by stand age, Douglas fir, in a particular site. *Source:* Clawson (1977).

volume (or mass), as was the case with the sustained-yield fishery. The increment in the volume or stock of fish represented new standard-sized fish in our basic model, whereas here the increment in the volume of a tree represents a slightly larger tree. One does not harvest timber by shaving off part of a growing tree!

The same type of relationship for an actual stand of Douglas fir is shown in

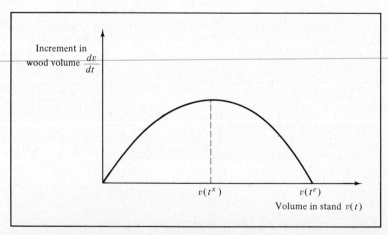

Figure 11.3 This schedule is derived from Figure 11.1. Instead of age, the increment in wood volume at different ages is plotted against the volume of wood in the tree or stand of trees.

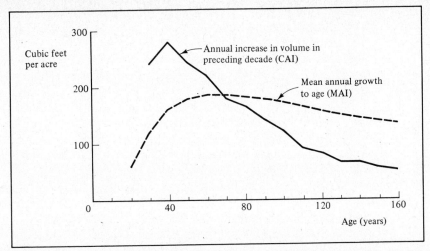

Figure 11.4 Annual growth by age and in relationship to standing timber volume, Douglas fir, in a particular site. *Source:* Clawson (1977).

Figure 11.4 in the dotted curve labeled "annual increase in volume in preceding decade." This curve has also been called the *current annual increment (CAI)*, where annual here means 10-year intervals. The CAI curve here shows the marginal changes in the volume of timber in the stand from one decade to the next. The data for the curve are derived in column 4 of Table 11.1. The CAI is thus an incremental growth relationship as a function of time. The maximum of the CAI, which occurs at around 40 years, is shown as area *B* in Figure 11.2. Area *B* thus reflects the maximum slope of the age-volume relationship.

Precise measurement of growth relationships in forestry is not possible because many factors can affect tree growth. But around the peak of the growth relationship (CAI), the tree volume changes very little, so that approximations of the growth relationship are possible. The tree can be harvested over a fairly long interval of time without the time elapsed significantly affecting its volume. A number of possible management schemes for a given tract of land are thus possible, as we shall see.

The dashed curve in Figure 11.4, called the mean annual growth to age, is obtained from column 2 of Table 11.1. This curve is also known as the *mean annual increment (MAI)*. The MAI measures the average increase in timber volume from one decade (or year) to the next. The maximum of the MAI is called the *culmination of the mean annual increment (CMAI)*. Note that the CMAI occurs at around 60 years and that the CAI intersects the MAI at this point. The CMAI is also shown in Figure 11.2 at area *A*, approximately where the slope of a line from the origin to the age-volume relationship is the steepest. In economic terms, we can think of the CAI as a marginal product curve and the MAI as an average product curve. Actual forestry management practices are generally based on the MAI relationship.

THE OPTIMAL ROTATION PERIOD FOR THE FIRM

When is the best time to harvest a tree or stand of trees? In practice, it depends on many factors, such as the final use of the harvested trees; whether we begin with bare land or a mature forest; cost, productivity, and demand conditions; and leasing or ownership arrangements. If, for example, a forest is to be used for pulp to make paper, the size of the stems and trunks is not important, but the volume of wood is. If the product is large timber beams, then the trees must be large enough in dimension to yield these beams. Larger trees also fetch a higher price per board foot than do smaller trees.

We will abstract from these complications for the moment and concentrate on the timing of a timber harvest, beginning with a tract of land on which trees must first be planted. We begin with an economic model of the optimal time to cut a stand of trees of uniform age and growth characteristics. Once the stand is harvested, saplings will be replanted and the cycle begun again. We seek the economically efficient rotation period over an infinite number of cycles of planting, harvesting, replanting, and harvesting. We then contrast the efficient rotation period with an alternative method of managing the forest: the single-rotation model.

To obtain the economically efficient sequence of rotations, the objective is to organize the forest to maximize the present value of a stream of net benefits. This involves choosing a date to harvest and replant time after time. The interval could be varying or constant. We assume that the harvesting and replanting occur within the same period of time—say one year. Present value in this model is the dollar benefit from a series of plantings, harvestings, plantings, and so on into the infinite future. The objective is to maximize the present value of the land in growing trees. If the land is to be used for, say, houses 50 years hence, a different optimal forestry plan is required.

Two types of direct costs are associated with maximizing the net present value from the forest. First, the costs of planting, silviculture, harvesting, storage, transportation to market, and so on—the actual costs of managing a forest. The second cost is the interest foregone while waiting to harvest the trees—the money that could be obtained if the trees were cut sooner in time and reinvested either in growing more trees on the land or in alternative enterprises. The value of the land on which the trees grow is an indirect cost. Land receives the residual income—the rent—from raising and marketing the forest, the income remaining after all planting, maintenance, and harvesting costs have been paid.

In our central model, we incorporate site clearing and planting costs, harvesting, and later delivery costs. By working with present discounted values, we have incorporated costs of delaying cutting. Land or site rent will be the residual.

Suppose, then, that it costs a fixed amount of D to plant a unit of land (say an acre), and c per million board feet of wood to harvest the trees.[1] The cost in present value of the first "round" in the infinite cycle is

$$D + cV(T_1 - T_0)e^{-r\cdot(T_1-T_0)} \tag{11.1}$$

where T_0 is the date of planting and T_1 the date of harvesting. Recall that the term $e^{-r\cdot(T_1-T_0)}$ transfers harvests costs from the harvest date back to the beginning of the "cycle," or back to planting date T_0. Let p be the revenue per million board feet sold upon harvesting, which we assume is constant in this competitive forest industry. Each forest manager faces a perfectly elastic demand curve that is stationary over time. Then the profit in present value (land owner's benefit) from planting and harvesting is

$$(p - c)V(T_1 - T_0)\, e^{-r(T_1 - T_0)} - D \tag{11.2}$$

Note we have removed the multiplicative symbol ($\cdot$) in Equation (11.2) and subsequent equations to avoid clutter.

Upon harvesting, the land is replanted at cost D and a new round is undertaken, then a third round. We have then the complete present value

$$\begin{aligned} W = & [(p - c)V(T_1 - T_0)e^{-r(T_1 - T_0)} - D] \\ & + e^{-r(T_1 - T_0)}[(p - c)V(T_2 - T_1)e^{-r(T_2 - T_1)} - D] \\ & + e^{-r(T_2 - T_0)}[(p - c)V(T_3 - T_2)e^{-r(T_3 - T_2)} - D] \\ & + \cdots \end{aligned} \tag{11.3}$$

Now we can assert that the intervals $(T_1 - T_0), (T_2 - T_1), (T_3 - T_2)$, and so on *must be the same*. The reason is straightforward but subtle: Once T_1 is arrived at, the remaining problem can be made identical to the original problem by relabeling dates. Once one cycle is completed, the problem is the same as before. This is because the horizon is always infinity! Let the intervals between planting and harvesting be written now as I. We call this interval the *rotation period*. Equation (11.3) becomes with these intervals, I,

$$\begin{aligned} W = & [(p - c)V(I)e^{-rI} - D] + e^{-rI}[(p - c)V(I)e^{-rI} - D] \\ & + e^{-2rI}[(p - c)V(I)e^{-rI} - D] \\ & + e^{-3rI}[(p - c)V(I)e^{-rI} - D] \\ & + \cdots \\ = & [e^{-rI}(p - c)V(I) - D]\left(\frac{e^{rI}}{e^{rI} - 1}\right) \end{aligned} \tag{11.4}$$

We have made use of the formula $[1 + e^{-rI} + e^{-2rI} + e^{-3rI} + \cdots] = \left[\dfrac{e^{rI}}{e^{rI} - 1}\right]$ in

obtaining Equation (11.4). The forest manager then maximizes the value of the forest land, as represented by Equation (11.4), by choosing a rotation interval I. The manager sets $dV/dI = 0$. This yields the condition

$$\frac{dV(I)}{dI} - rV(I) = \frac{r}{p - c}\, W^* \tag{11.5}$$

where W^* is the optimized value of the problem and equal to the right-hand side of Equation (11.4) with I equal to I^*. W^* is the capital value of the land used in forestry. rW^* is the *land or site rent* or flow value of land in its optimal land use.

There is a straightforward diagrammatic representation of our important formula or equilibrium condition in Equation (11.5). We rewrite that equation as

$$\frac{dV(I)}{dI} = rV(I) + \frac{r}{p + c}\, W^* \qquad \text{should be} \; - \tag{11.5a}$$

The term $dV(I)/dI$ on the left-hand side of Equation (11.5a) is the increment in wood volume in the forest plot achieved by delaying the harvest (increasing the rotation interval) by an instant. Because of the age-volume relationship of a stand of trees, as shown in Figure 11.3, the increment in wood volume will be an inverted bowl, as shown in the top half of Figure 11.5. The right-hand side of Equation (11.5a)

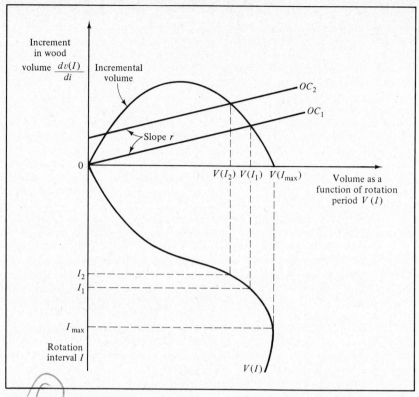

Figure 11.5 Three different solutions to the problem of choosing a rotation period are shown. The standard outcome (represented in Equation 11.5a) is captured by line OC_2, indicating harvest value $V(I_2)$ each period and rotation interval I_2. If the interest rate r were zero, then the interval I_{max} is the solution. With unlimited land (rent on land driven to zero), schedule OC_1 is the solution.

consists of two terms: $rV(I)$ and $rW^*/(p-c)$. These terms reflect the opportunity cost of holding the trees $[rV(I)]$ and land $(rW^*/p - c)$ another instant of time rather than harvesting them and replanting or using the land for other activities; r is the market rate of return. If we graph the right-hand side of Equation (11.5a) as a function of $V(I)$, we obtain a straight line with a slope r and a positive intercept equal to $rW^*/p - c$. One such line is shown in the top half of Figure 11.5, labeled OC_2 (for opportunity cost).

To find the optimal rotation interval, we must find the value of I which solves Equation (11.5a). To find I graphically, we solve first for $V(I)$.[2] In Figure 11.5, $V(I)$ is determined in the top half and I in the bottom half. Suppose first that $r = 0$; there is no discounting of future harvests, no rate of return on alternative investments. Then simply by examining Equation (11.5a), we see that $dV(I)/dI$ must equal zero. In terms of Figure 11.5, we find $dV(I)/dI$ equals zero at two points—the origin and $V(I_{max})$. If forestry operations exist, then $V(I_{max})$ is the solution; $V(I_{max})$ is the maximum wood volume. This can also be seen in the bottom half of Figure 11.5, which shows the relationship between volume $V(I)$ and the rotation period for the stand (flipped over on its side). If we drop a line straight down from $V(I_{max})$ to the $V(I)$ curve, we find the line intersects the curve at its maximum point. The rotation period is then I_{max} (for maximum sustainable yield). Thus, if interest rates are zero, the efficient rotation period is found where tree volume is at a maximum.

Suppose now that r is greater than zero, but $W^* = 0$. This means that land has no implicit value; its return or rent will be zero. Land rent could be zero if land was available in unlimited supply. Then from Equation (11.5a), we see that $dV(I)/dI = rV(I)$. There will be no intercept in our line reflecting opportunity costs of deferring the harvest. In Figure 11.5, the value of $V(I)$ which solves Equation (11.5a) is found where the line OC_1 intersects the incremental volume curve. This yields the volume $V(I_1)$. Again, dropping a line from $V(I)$ to the $V(I)$ curve in the bottom half of the graph, we find the efficient rotation interval, I_1.

Finally, let's look at the most general case, where both r and W^* are positive. The opportunity cost of deferring the harvest is now shown by line OC_2 and the volume of wood which yields an equilibrium is $V(I_2)$. The efficient rotation period is I_2. (Notice that I_2 is the shortest rotation period of the three cases. The intuitive explanation for this result is that the opportunity costs of deferring a harvest in a sequence of harvests are greatest when r and W^* are positive.)

Another way to see the efficient rotation period is to rewrite Equation (11.5) as

$$\frac{d}{dI}[(p-c)V(I)] = r[(p-c)V(I) + W^*] \qquad (11.5b)$$

This reformulation puts both sides of the equation into money value terms. The efficient rotation period is then found when the rate of change in the value of the forest equals the rate of return that could be earned by converting the harvested trees and land into money capital.

We have not yet said anything about the socially optimal rotation period versus the rotation period resulting from private management of the forest. Our three cases can illustrate when socially and privately determined rotation periods coincide, and when they do not. There are a number of possible cases. If the social discount rate is positive and equals private discount rates, and land rent is positive, then an equilibrium such as I_2 [and $V(I_2)$] is socially optimal. If, however, private discount rates exceed social discount rates, the rotation period for the private firm would be shorter than is socially optimal because the private OC line would be steeper (and have a larger intercept) than the social OC line.

There might also be a difference between the value a private firm places on land versus society's view of land. Society may wish, for example, to incorporate recreational use and wildlife and ecological preservation into its valuation of the land, whereas private enterprise may not. (Try altering the OC curve to see how this divergence between private and social values affects rotation periods.) Imperfect competition can also be present. So there can be a number of reasons why the rotation period that is socially optimal can diverge from the efficient rotation period determined by the firm. These divergences suggest a role for government intervention—a topic we return to later in the chapter.

Another Approach to the Choice of Rotation Period

A naive approach to the choice of I might be the maximization of the value of the forest over a single cycle—*one rotation period.* Presumably the same thing will be maximized in the next period, and so on. For the single period, the problem is to choose I to maximize

$$[e^{-rI}(p-c)V(I) - D] \tag{11.6}$$

The rotation period I that maximizes Equation (11.6) must satisfy the optimality condition (11.7):

$$\frac{dV(I)}{dI} = rV(I) \tag{11.7}$$

Let's contrast Equations (11.7) and (11.5). It is quite easy to see that Equation (11.7) yields exactly the same equilibrium as illustrated by I_1 and $V(I_1)$—that is, where OC_1 equals the incremental volume curve. The interval between harvests is thus shorter in the infinite-rotation model than the single-rotation case for a given interest rate, r. In the single-rotation model, no account is taken of the net benefits of future harvests—the land tied up in trees. Trees are held to an older age to obtain more valuable timber, but the possible revenue from subsequent harvests is not taken into account. Profits are thus lost. The single-rotation decision rule is inappropriate for a forest firm that will continue to grow trees on a plot of land beyond the first rotation period. The rule is more appropriate if, after one cycle, an alternative use of the land is sought. And if the rotation period in the infinite period model is quite long, the difference between it and the single-rotation period approach may be small.

Rotation Periods in Different Environments

Suppose that two areas had land of different fertility. Would a planting-harvesting cycle be longer in the least fertile area? Or suppose one region was less accessible than another or had higher transportation costs. Which one would have a longer planting-harvesting cycle? Other questions that come to mind are how a program of efficient planting and harvesting responds to an increase in harvesting costs, an increase in planting costs, or an increase in the discount rate.

The question of differences in fertility across regions or plots of land devoted to forestry is a question of how I^* responds to a new $V(I)$, forestry growth function. To be specific, let $V(I)$ be the standard logistic growth function

$$(a/b) / \left[1 + \left(\frac{a/b - V_0}{V_0} \right) e^{-aI} \right]$$

a function similar to that seen in the fishery. An increase in the parameter a can be viewed as an increase in fertility. Solving for dI^*/da reveals that *locations with increased fertility will have shorter rotation periods.* (This result is a reflection of our particular specification of the model and may not be general; see Appendix I.) A numerical example is graphed in Figure 11.6. Roughly speaking, increased fertility is represented by our S schedule in the bottom panel of Figure 11.5 moving up a certain

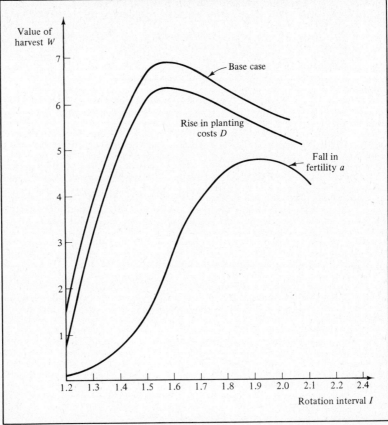

Figure 11.6   Schedules show the value of harvesting trees at different rotation intervals. The optimal rotation interval is where the value of the harvest is at a maximum. Under the base case, this occurs at 1.6. If fertility *(a)* decreases from 12 to 10, the rotation interval rises to 1.9. If planting costs *(D)* rise from 4 to 40, the rotation interval increases slightly.

percentage for each age, *I*. Thus if *I* were unchanged with improved fertility, more wood would be harvested. But why not have the best of both worlds and harvest with a slightly smaller *I*? We still get more wood than before the increase in fertility, but we get the wood sooner as well!

Suppose now that planting costs, *D*, rise. *A rise in planting or clearing costs in our basic model implies a longer rotation cycle.* Intuition works well here. Consider the first rotation. A rise in *D* implies that the second rotation and subsequent ones are worth less because these fixed planting and clearing costs have risen. The response should be to delay getting to the second and subsequent rotations. (There is no way to avoid incurring the costs in the first rotation.) This intuition is confirmed by algebraic analysis in the appendix. (The tenfold increase in *D* in our numerical example, graphed in Figure 11.6, lowers the value *W** somewhat, but leads to a small increase in *I**.)

Suppose now that the discount rate changes. Intuitively we associate a higher r with more impatience or a desire to get results sooner. This intuition is correct for our basic discounted socially optimal model: An increase in r implies a shortening of the optimal rotation period, and we establish this formally in Appendix I. A numerical example with r changed from .05 to .25 is reported in Figure 11.7. I^* is reduced only slightly, though W^* drops considerably.

When forest plots differ in their accessibility to markets, we can examine this case as one where gross harvesting costs differ among plots. Plots located farther from markets will have higher total harvesting costs when these costs include transportation. We solve for dI^*/dc in the appendix and find it positive. Thus, *less accessible plots have longer rotation periods in the discounted socially optimal model*. A numerical example, graphed in Figure 11.7, illustrates how increased c lowers the value of the land. The I^* is lengthened only a small amount, however, in this example.

Ledyard and Moses (1977) investigated this question in considerable detail in a slightly different model. They let both the rotation period and the resources devoted

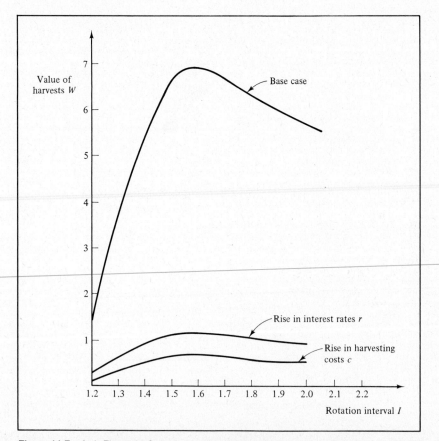

Figure 11.7   As in Figure 11.6, the base case is plotted for the various rotation intervals. As interest rates rise (r increases), the interval declines slightly. As cutting costs (c) rise, the interval increases slightly.

to planting be choice variables for a landowner or planner. In their more complicated model, they discovered that indeed the optimal rotation period would be longer for less accessible regions or plots. They also solved for the differences in site values between regions of differing accessibility and determined that site value per acre would decline with distance and the rent-distance function would have the familiar convex shape — like a sagging electric transmission wire.

Our model also yields a convex rent-distance function. Suppose our cost per unit of wood harvested, c, comprises a cutting and processing cost of $1 per pound plus $1 x, where x is distance to the market for the lumber. The $1 represents the cost of moving the lumber a unit of distance and getting the equipment back to the site for another delivery. Costs then become $1 + $1 x. Solving for W^* for different values of x indicates the price of land used in forestry at different distances from the central market. (rW^* is land rent corresponding to those distances.) We plot aggregate rent (the price of land) against constant harvesting/processing costs plus variable distance costs in Figure 11.8. Our choice of parameters has resulted in only a slight curvature to the land price-distance function.

The issue of how I^* varies with accessibility was reanalyzed by Heaps (1981) in a model that allowed for declining average costs of harvesting. He discovered that there could be cases in which I^* declined with distance from processing plants or that the basic Ledyard-Moses result could be reversed. The upshot of these investigations

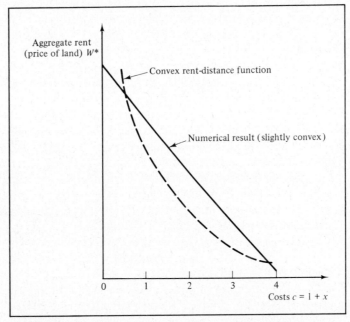

Figure 11.8 As transportation costs increase, the site value of a plot of land dedicated to forestry declines in our basic model. (This is an actual numerical example.) There is a slight convexity in this land value-distance schedule. For different transportation costs, there is a distinct optimal interval for rotating the forest. For our basic model this optimal interval increases with transportation costs.

is that a *general law of rotation periods is not available.* Each specification of the underlying model requires a detailed examination for responses of the rotation period to changes in parameters. These parameters define the natural and economic environment in which the forestry is being pursued.

We summarize our results in the following table:

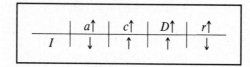

	$a\uparrow$	$c\uparrow$	$D\uparrow$	$r\uparrow$
I	$\downarrow$	$\uparrow$	$\uparrow$	$\downarrow$

where a is a fertility index, c is harvesting cost per ton, D is site clearing and preparation after each harvest, and r is the discount rate.

Optimal Harvests in a Mature Forest

The notion of optimal rotations can seem at odds with actual forestry use, where there may be trees or stands well past the optimal rotation age. We can see using planned rotations in a cultivated or artificial forest, but not somehow in a natural setting. One reason is that the first cut involves trees of different sizes and ages. In later cuts, perhaps, the forest has regenerated itself or been cultivated as a planned forest. But the first cut involves a distinctly unplanned forest. Does this make the analysis of optimal rotations irrelevant? Suppose the forest is to be clear cut.

The first cut in clear cutting a natural forest results in a net revenue of $\$K$, presumably positive, and is independent of rotation time. This $\$K$ is a fixed value at the beginning of the problem and does not affect subsequent marginal decisions. That is, after clear cutting, the forest becomes managed in the same way as our bare land model covering an infinite series of rotations. We can incorporate this initial "messiness" into the framework of optimal rotations without amending our model or general concept of a planned planting and harvesting cycle. However, if the original natural forest is thinned and gradually adjusted to an optimal program with selective cutting, a very complex planning problem emerges.

Selective harvesting of certain trees might be a reasonable strategy, but this type of harvesting can be costly. The issue becomes one of bringing a forest toward some sort of long-run equilibrium from a historically given setting. We might never get to a clear-cutting rotation cycle on the plot; for example, we might obtain an equilibrium with many ages of trees growing simultaneously and selective harvesting of those at the optimal age being the optimal policy. People have inquired into these issues in formal models, and some long-run equilibriums do indeed involve maintaining a plot of land in trees of different ages and harvesting selectively rather than clear cutting—see, for example, Kemp and van Long (1980).

Costs obviously bear heavily on the strategy chosen. Clear cutting may be the least-cost alternative if leaving some trees makes removing others quite costly. In the west of North America, patches on mountainsides are cut bare and logging roads can be seen exposed. It may be cheaper to clear cut and "run" rather than to cut selectively and return in five years for another cut. Alternatively, selective cutting may be optimal because it prevents erosion of the soils and ensures continued productivity of the forest over time. (See Hyde, 1980, for more detailed analyses of harvests in natural forests.)

When may it pay to "mine" the forest? Under an optimal rotation plan, a capital value W^* could be obtained which we indicated could be ascribed to the land as the surplus or price of the plot of land. rW^* was called site value (land rent). It could be that if the plot were cleared and used for agriculture or housing, a surplus W that exceeds W^* could be obtained net of clearing costs. In this case, it makes economic sense to "mine" the existing trees (clear the land) and use the plot for agricultural activity or leave the land idle. Obviously not all treed land has as its best use forestry activity. Anderson (1979) finds, for example, that with certain forests in Ontario, reforestation costs may exceed the benefits. In these cases, mining the forest may be optimal (assuming no adverse environmental effects).

THE FOREST INDUSTRY: PRICE DETERMINATION WITH MANY DIFFERENT FOREST TYPES

Our discussion so far has focused on a plot of land in which someone is maximizing the return from the plot, given a fixed price for output and a known cost structure. The scale of the operation is by assumption small. A lumber industry would involve many plots being worked by many owners. If the plots were controlled by a single owner, a monopoly situation would prevail, and the monopolist would control the price of output as well as the phasing of rotations over all plots. An important industrywide issue is how the smoothing of the delivery of wood over time is arranged. We assume that all plots will not be harvested on the same date. Prices of timber today and into the future (expected prices or contracted futures prices) will govern harvesting decisions.[3] Inventory holdings can also be used to smooth out the quantities for sale relative to deliveries from plots. Middlemen can do this coordination, or for a few large firms, smoothing can be done within coordinated land management. It is not unlike coordinating sales and harvests of agricultural products — an important but not impossible task.

The price at the industrywide level of analysis will then be *endogenous* and its level will depend on: (a) how the coordination of harvests and sales is handled, and (b) how concentrated or monopolistic those controlling supply are. Industry models that examine the coordination of harvests and sales are generally more complex than the optimal rotation model applied to the owner of a small plot of forest land; see Hyde (1980). Now we consider the supply question more generally, in terms of plots of different fertility in different locales.

The Relative Profitability of Forestry Use in Different Locales

The relative accessibility of forests to markets and their soil fertility can make the surpluses accruing to landowners involved in commercial foresting quite different. If we envisage a world market for a particular type of delivered wood, some suppliers can be earning relatively high rent per delivered ton and others conceivably zero. The former would be supplying timber from very accessible and/or relatively fertile areas.

It will be the marginal area that will, roughly speaking, determine the price in the market. That supply point will have zero rent, and intramarginal areas will have positive rent per delivered ton. We illustrate in Figure 11.9.

Figure 11.9 shows three regions in the world with different fertilities of soil but identical accessibility characteristics. The differences in fertility are represented by different harvesting costs per region. In region 1, timber can be harvested at an average cost of e; in region 2 at a cost of f; and in region 3 at a cost of g. The area used for forestry differs among regions, and amounts of delivered marketable wood differ. In Figure 11.9, we assume that the marginal region produces quantity cd and earns zero rent, so that price per ton, p, equals average cost per ton, g. The most profitable and fertile area produces quantity ab and earns rent per ton delivered of price p minus cost e per ton. A region of middle fertility produces quantity bc with positive rent per ton $(p - f)$. Recall that in our analysis of optimal rotation periods, a plot with a fertility coefficient $a = 10$ had a longer rotation period and lower aggregate rent than an otherwise identical region with fertility coefficient 12 (12 indicating superior fertility).[4]

A similar relationship would be observed for regions with differing accessibility to the main world markets.[5] The marginal region will have zero rent, and intramarginal regions will have positive rent per ton delivered. Recall our numerical illustration above for the case in which gross harvest costs (gross of delivery costs) differed between two identical regions. There we observed that the less accessible region had the lower aggregate rent and the longer rotation interval. Some Canadian observers argue that their lumber industry is threatened by producers in regions with more rapid rotation periods. They argue that climatic conditions in Canada are unfavorable for rapid growth. This is, of course, a general argument about the relative fertility of the different regions and is an important example of what is being illustrated in Figure 11.9.

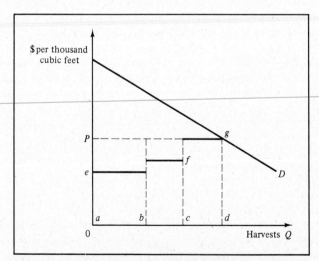

Figure 11.9 The steps indicate different average costs for different plots of timber in different regions. Cost can differ because of soil fertility differences and/or accessibility differences.

Effects of Taxes on Forestry Use

We now consider briefly various types of taxes that have been levied on the forest industry. Our objective is to see the effect of these taxes on the rotation period of a forest plot and resulting harvests. If the value of the forestry activity on the plot of land is positive (that is, W^* is positive), there is a surplus that is potentially taxable. Different types of taxation will have different effects on the activity on the plot. Clearly a sufficiently high rate of taxation will make the operation unprofitable and end commercial forestry on the site. Let us consider some intermediate cases, which we assume do not take the activity from a profitable to a loss position.

A Tax per Ton Harvested This is, in terms of our simple model, equivalent to an increase in harvesting costs. Costs rise from c to $c + t$, where t is the tax per ton. An increase in c leads to a longer interval between planting and harvesting. More heavily taxed regions will have, other things being equal, longer rotation periods for the stand of trees grown. Total tax revenue, in present value, will be $tVe^{-rI}\left(\dfrac{e^{rI}}{e^{rI}-1}\right)$ if the policy is carried on in perpetuity. A smaller quantity of wood will be harvested over all forest tracts per unit of time because of the increase in the interval I. However, the larger I implies that the trees cut will be slightly older and have slightly more volume.

A Site-Use Tax A government might levy a tax per acre each time land is brought into forestry use. This would be equivalent to an increase in our setup costs, D. The effective setup cost would become $D + T$, where T is the total site-use tax. The effect of an increase in D was to increase the profit-maximizing rotation period. Hence the site-use tax causes the interval to increase, and again, per unit of time, less wood would be harvested though more per acre will be cut at each harvest date.

If the tax on site use is levied at harvest time, the total tax revenue will be $Te^{-rI}\left[\dfrac{e^{rI}}{e^{rI}-1}\right]$ rather than $T\left[\dfrac{e^{rI}}{e^{rI}-1}\right]$. The qualitative impact will be the same. The interval between planting and harvesting will be increased, and less wood per unit of time will be harvested in perpetuity.

A Profit Tax If W^* is reduced by a tax of t percent, there will be no change in the optimal rotation interval. Since "profit" here is the residual income ascribable to land in forest production, this "profits" tax can be viewed as a tax on the income accruing to landowners. The tax cannot be shifted by altering the rotation interval.

A License Fee for Foresting on the Land An outright license fee per acre is the same as an increase in our setup costs, D. We saw above that a rise in D for all rotations lengthened the interval between planting and harvesting. If the license fee is levied *per year* rather than per rotation, it can be viewed as F dollars per unit of time, which amounts to a fixed cost of F/r for the perpetual forestry use program. Hence the present value of profits falls from W^* to $W^* - (F/r)$ when the annual license fee is imposed. *The optimal rotation interval is unaffected.* This is because the license fee is related neither to the amount harvested nor indirectly to the planting-harvesting interval.

So far we have focused on the effects of taxes on a single plot of land devoted to forestry. Taxes obviously affect the relative profitability of different types of plots, possibly in different locations, and of forestry activity relative to other types of economic activity. Profits do not have to turn negative in order for commercial forestry activity to cease; they need only fall below a threshold set by the profitability of other lines of economic activity. Tax increases can lead to "flights of capital" from one sector to another or one region to another.

Another way to say this is that the level of taxes will determine the extent of activity in the sector in question. Is there an optimal level of activity? A so-called first best approach would have no taxes and a maximum of net consumer and producer surplus generated. However, if the government must raise X dollars from the forestry sector or must levy charges on timber cut from public lands, different types of taxes will "take" more or less consumer and producer surplus while generating those X dollars of tax revenue. An *optimal tax* generates the X dollars of revenues and reduces consumer and producer surplus least. The corresponding intensity of forestry activity one might refer to as the *optimal extent of forestry use.* It is, however, based on the notion that X dollars of revenue must be raised in the forestry sector. How this level of X dollars is arrived at involves tradeoffs at the level of the economy, not just the forestry sector.

Property Rights and the Incentive to Replant

In Canada, much land in forestry is owned by the provincial and the federal governments and is leased to forestry companies. At the same time, reforestation has, it appears, been poorly developed in Canada. Would a forestry sector owned primarily by private companies rather than governments behave differently? (We deal with this question in part in the next section when we look at management on private and public lands in the United States.) It would be inaccurate, however, to attribute all the problems in reforestation to differences in ownership arrangements.

Taxation arrangements can also change the pace of reforestation. Ownership may induce longer-term planning by foresters than does a regime of leasing, but not if, for example, a threat of expropriation by the public sector is looming. In the 1930s, the threat of expropriation in the United States induced the private sector to engage in better forestry management practices. The issue of the incentive to reforest by users is one of direct incentives on the desired target. Do public policies inhibit or foster reforestation? Ownership rights are one dimension of the issue, but not the only policy instrument leading to the observed outcomes.

FORESTRY PRACTICES AND POLICIES

Commercial forests make up one-quarter of the total land area in the contiguous 48 states of the United States. A commercial forest is one capable of growing annually 20 or more cubic feet per acre of wood from a fully stocked natural stand at an age approximately near the maximum on the growth curve shown as point B in Figure

---

BOX 11.2
Canada's Forestry Industry Could Be Gone in a Century

One man now harvests 130 trees, each almost 300 years old, in a 6.5-hour day in British Columbia. However, almost half of each tree felled is wasted, and replanting is not consistently done. If replanting had occurred in the past, the current anxiety would not be present. Canada's chief forester, F. L. C. Reed, says: "The next crop of trees is going to be smaller than the last one, and it's going to take longer to grow." Forty percent of Canada is covered by trees, which represents one-tenth of the productive forest area of the world. Smaller spruce in the east makes excellent pulp and paper products. Canada leads world in forest exports, with the value of shipments in excess of $12 billion. Forest products are presently one-seventh of all manufactured goods.

However, one-fifth of acreage harvested each year fails to regenerate. Fire and disease takes about 300,000 acres annually. The spruce budworm in the east is a persistent problem. Estimates range from 11.5 to 70 million acres of forest lands lost for the production of timber. Adverse effects of air pollution on forest productivity appear to be increasing.

Canadian provincial and federal governments own 90 percent of Canada's forest land and lease logging rights to companies. By 1985, they will have increased regeneration spending to $650 million from the $250 million five years earlier. There remains the issue of destroying the economically worthless stands of hardwood, mostly aspen, now growing where rich spruce forests were earlier.

Forestry experts agree that more land in forests would be desirable, but they also indicate that proper management could cut in half the time needed to grow a commercial tree. The timber industry has doubled its capital outlays to $15.3 billion in the current five-year period over the earlier one. It is not yet clear how much must be spent to improve forest productivity and whether or not these expenditures are economically warranted.

Source: Adapted from the *New York Times,* August 28, 1983.

11.2 (Clawson, 1977). The wood must be potentially useful for industrial purposes (nonfuel). This is a purely biological definition that does not take into account costs of harvest or silviculture, or nonmarket benefits from the forest, such as recreational uses. In 1977 commercial forests totaled about 482 million acres, of which 134 million were publicly owned (two-thirds in national forests and the remainder in state and other public forests), and 69 million were owned by what is called the forest industry—typically large corporations that are vertically integrated. The remaining 278 million acres were owned by nonindustrial private individuals or firms that generally do not process the wood they harvest.[6] This pattern of ownership has been relatively stable since the early 1950s.

The patterns of timber growth and harvests since 1952 are shown in Tables 11.2 and 11.3. Since 1952, the trend in all ownership classes has been increasing wood growth per acre, and for sawtimber a generally decreasing annual harvest as a percentage of this growth. But there are fairly substantial differences in the figures among the various ownership classes. The reasons for the differences in growth on public versus privately held land is the issue we address here. Note, for example, that the forest industry in particular has consistently obtained higher net annual growth per acre (Table 11.2) than any of the other categories. Clawson (1977) notes that in 1977 industrial firms grew more wood than the national forests and almost as much as in all public forests, which had almost twice the acreage. Even the private nonindustrial owners obtained greater productivity than the national forests. If nonforest uses of this land (notably for recreation) are excluded, the nonindustrial figures approximate those of the industrial firms. Why is this so?

In part, the explanation is that they generally have the most fertile land. But there are also differences in the way the private industrial firms manage their forests compared to the public forests, particularly the National Forests, which are administered by the U.S. Forest Service (USFS) of the Department of the Interior. We will examine some of the practices of the USFS to see why the harvests per acre are lower than that of industrial firms. We will contrast their management with some revealed behavior of the industrial firms. The basic issue we address is why output per acre on public forests is less than on private forests. We will examine the harvests in the two ownership classes—national forest and industrial forest—and compare them to

Table 11.2 NET ANNUAL GROWTH PER ACRE OF ALL SPECIES, GROWING STOCK AND SAWTIMBER, BY MAJOR OWNERSHIP GROUP
(Cubic feet and board feet per acre)

Forest ownership	Actual net growth*				Potential capacity†
	1952	1962	1970	1977	
Growing stock, all species					
National forests	23	26	28	35	72
Other public	26	32	39	54	77
Forest industry	43	50	52	59	88
Other private	27	31	34	45	74
All	28	32	37	46	75
Sawtimber					
National forests	83	98	107	143	
Other public	87	109	130	184	
Forest industry	158	174	185	213	
Other private	81	89	108	140	
All	91	103	120	151	

* Net growth is total or gross wood growth minus mortality from storms (blowdowns), fire, disease, and insects. Timber harvest is not deducted from gross growth to arrive at net growth.

† Potential capacity, or productivity, is the ability of the site to grow potentially usable industrial wood under defined management and at defined age of the stand. It is better understood as an index of capacity to grow wood than as an actual output; the latter may vary greatly, depending upon management of the forest.

Source: Marion Clawson, *The Economics of U.S. Nonindustrial Private Forests,* Research Paper R–14 (Washington, D.C., Resources for the Future, 1979) pp. 86–93 and 153. Source of basic data. Forest Service reports on timber supply. Reprinted by permission.

Table 11.3 ANNUAL REMOVAL OF TIMBER AS A PERCENTAGE OF NET GROWTH, COMMERCIAL FORESTS, BY GENERAL OWNERSHIP CLASS

Forest ownership	Softwood				Hardwood			
	1952	1962	1970	1977	1952	1962	1970	1977
Growing stock								
National forests	61	87	89	86	29	25	28	22
Other public	59	67	77	79	28	23	29	24
Forest industry	146	99	114	126	76	79	66	49
Other private	102	69	65	61	71	66	61	49
Total	100	80	83	82	66	61	56	45
Sawtimber								
National forests	93	133	129	108	43	34	44	33
Other public	79	91	105	109	38	24	36	32
Forest industry	199	138	152	171	94	85	73	65
Other private	126	79	74	69	89	76	76	64
Total	133	104	109	105	83	70	71	60

Source: Marion Clawson, *The Economics of U.S. Nonindustrial Private Forests,* Research Paper R – 14, (Washington, D.C., Resources for the Future, 1979) p. 184. Source of basic data, Forest Service reports on timber supply. Reprinted by permission.

what would be an efficient harvest and rotation period derived from an economic model.

Unlike some areas in Canada and the tropical forests, the question of excessive depletion of the forest does not appear to be an important policy concern in the United States at this time. There is also the issue of whether private firms practice more or less intensive silviculture than the USFS. We will not be able to deal with this question here, but refer the reader to several USFS publications—USFS (1974, 1980).

BOX 11.3
Tropical Forests in Decline?

According to an article by Golden in the *Boston Globe,* April 9, 1984, tropical forests from the Phillipines to Zaire, from Indonesia to Brazil, are being cut down for timber, converted to farmland, and burned for firewood at a rate of about 50 acres per minute. The ecosystems of these unique habitats are being threatened with extinction. By the year 2000, some conservationists expect that half of the world's jungle will be gone, along with a thousand species of plants and animals. These plants and animals have value not only for their role in the forest environment, but commercially as well. A number of our well-known drugs (curare), pesticides (rotenone), and pigments are derived from plants in tropical forests. Tropical forest plants provide genetic diversity for new agricultural products as well.

Adverse environmental consequences may be felt from the loss of tropical forests. The forest is a large sink that converts carbon dioxide into oxygen. Destruction of these forests may exacerbate the worldwide buildup of CO_2 (the

Box 11.1 continued

greenhouse effect) and cause a warming of the earth's temperature. The warming may adversely affect agriculture and threaten coastal cities if polar ice caps begin melting.

One source estimates that Latin America has lost about 37 percent of its original rain forest, Southeast Asia 38 percent, and Africa 52 percent.

Can anything be done? A number of policies could reduce the pressure on these resources. Changes in the leasing arrangements may provide incentives to use the forest more efficiently. For example, in Southeast Asia international forest companies are given rights to harvest trees for periods of only three to five years, with no certainty of renewal. These companies currently harvest the most valuable hardwood, then move on. This mining of the forest severely damages the ecosystem. If companies were given the incentive to manage the land over a longer period of time, some of the destruction would be contained and new sites protected.

In South America, much of the damage comes from peasants and cattle ranchers moving into the forest. The settlers burn the forest for agricultural land. But the soils of the forest are poor and are soon exhausted. This leads to a new cycle of cut and burn, exhausting more trees. Once removed, natural regeneration will take centuries, if it occurs at all. Cattle grazing in the forest kill trees as well. Some of the pressure on these forests could be reduced by using more intensive techniques on the existing agricultural and grazing lands. New crops and animals can be substituted for the more destructive ones. In Panama, for example, iguanas are being raised rather than cattle. Iguanas apparently do not destroy the forest.

In Southeast Asia, where forests are destroyed for agriculture and firewood, plantations of fast-growing trees may deter the destruction of timber on new sites. The Leucaena tree is fast growing, provides firewood and forage, and is also a natural fertilizer. If the cleared forests can be converted to managed plantations, the forests may be saved. (See Sedjo, 1983, for an economic assessment of plantation forestry around the world.)

Some of the forests are being preserved as refuges, which may save some unique species, but the acreage is small. Agencies such as the World Bank are also beginning to incorporate environmental concerns such as the long-term stability of the forest into their funding arrangements.

But the negative side still dominates. Increases in population in tropical regions continues to put pressure on the forest for food, forage, and housing. Peter Ashton, Director of the Arnold Arboretum at Harvard University, fears that in 15 years the accessible rain forest resource will be exhausted.

Mean Annual Increments and Allowed Cuts in National Forests

Forest management practices on public lands are based largely on biological factors, not economic criteria (see Table 11.1 and Figures 11.2 and 11.4). A basic biological decision rule of when to cut a tree (and then replant or allow natural regeneration) is to cut when the tree or stand is at the culmination of the mean annual increment (MAI), as defined above. The rule of maximizing the MAI has been widely adopted for foresters. It is a biological criterion; no consideration of harvesting, replanting, or silviculture costs enter into the calculation. Indeed, it is like the maximum sustainable yield concept in the fishery — harvest the fish when their change in biomass over time (say within a year) is the greatest.

The MAI concept is best applied in what Clawson (1977) calls a "fully regulated forest" — one with a number of forest plantations of equal area containing identical aged trees within a given area, but different age classes among areas. Some legislation recommends cutting a stand when it reaches its maximum MAI, the CMAI. The National Forest Management Act of 1976 states that the secretary of the interior shall establish forest stands so as "to ensure that, prior to harvest, stands of trees throughout the National Forest System shall generally have reached the culmination of the mean annual increment of growth." While this clause is somewhat vague and undoubtedly difficult to implement, it does suggest that the CMAI is or will be an important harvesting rule.

The difficulties with this rule should be apparent: No economic criteria are incorporated. Indeed, the CMAI makes sense only if all harvesting, replanting, and processing costs, the markets for timber products, and the interest rate are of no concern and the only objective is to maximize the volume of annual wood production. There is also a notion among some managers of public forests that the CMAI rule stabilizes employment and incomes in communities dependent on the forest industry. But this belief does not correspond to economic reality. Forestry is a procyclical industry because the uses of forest products increase and decrease with the GNP. Simply producing a constant volume of wood per year will do nothing to protect forest employment in a recession when new construction declines. Indeed, constant production may make the employment and income situation worse.

There are additional problems with implementing the CMAI rule. As noted above, measurement of the growth relationships for the forest is imprecise. There are also many uncertainties associated with forestry practices. A manager never knows when fire, insect pests, or heavy winds will decimate a stand. As a biological resource, forests are subject to hazards that cannot always be counteracted by human intervention. These exogenous factors suggest that for a particular stand, the standardized growth relationships may not be observed year after year.

The second concept that has a prominent position in forest management practices on public lands is the *annual allowed cut*. The allowed cut is important when the forest is inherited in a natural state, with a variety of trees of different ages. The objective of rules that determine the allowed cut is gradually to convert the forest which has many trees that are mature into a standardized forest amenable to MAI rules. Hyde (1980) presents some variants of the formulas used to determine allowed annual cuts under different types of natural forests.[7] Again, in these formulas detailed economic considerations are not taken into account: The formulas are designed to convert a mature forest with old growth into a managed forest of stands of even-aged trees on which sustained rotations can be implemented.

Policies and Practices of the U.S. National Forest Service

The USFS is charged with managing the national forests in a manner that ensures their continued production of wood over many years. They must be concerned with very long time periods generally, because trees such as the Douglas fir do not even reach the CMAI until around the age of 60 years. We will examine some of the constraints the USFS operates under, then look at some of its practices. First, and perhaps most important, the USFS is the largest seller of timber in the United States. It has no processing facilities of its own, and must sell the rights to harvest the timber to private companies. The USFS is required to sell cutting rights by competitive auction, but bids may not represent true values even in the absence of inflation. Much has been written on the auctions of timber rights in the United States (and elsewhere) and the effects of various auctioning schemes and types of cutting rights on timber harvests and rotations. See Box 11.4 on bidding, and the work by Mead (1966), and articles and references in Mead and McKillop (1976). The Forest Service knows that the volume of wood it advertises for sale (and ultimately sells) will have a large impact on timber markets and prices. Our competitive model with a perfectly elastic demand curve may not be appropriate in some situations.

How has the Forest Service behaved under these circumstances? Very cautiously. Substantial volumes of mature and, from an economic point of view, overly mature timber remain on national forest lands. As Clawson (1977) notes, if the USFS were to sell the cutting rights to the slow-growing overmature timber alone, it would amount to some 50 billion board feet of timber, or about three to four times the largest annual sale of timber ever experienced in the United States. The result is that maximum biological yields are not being obtained on much national forest land because of the predominance of the mature and overmature timber.

Other constraints reinforce the retention of timber beyond the CMAI. The USFS must act so as to conserve forest lands and to ensure that continued tree growth can occur. This has meant that no harvests are allowed where the land is too steep and soils are unstable, where regeneration is uncertain, and where the costs of growing new crops may be high. The Forest Service is also charged with preservation of the environmental values of the forest, preventing damage to ecosystems, and managing competing uses for the same land. So, for example, forestry operations are to be prohibited where they may have adverse effects on water quality, fisheries, or wilderness habitats. Where the value of the forest for recreation or wilderness preservation exceeds the value of timber, logging operations are discouraged. All these factors mean that land in the national forests will be withheld from timber operations.

While allowed harvests on national forest lands have increased over time and the sustainable yields possible from these forests have increased, the lands are not being managed in a way that maximizes the present value of the forest or even the maximum volume of timber. Clawson (1977) considers a number of different management techniques for a particular class of forest for the Douglas fir (see Table 11.4). Site class II is land that is relatively fertile (site class I is most fertile, class V the least).

Management schemes A through D all allow for natural regeneration. There is no replanting or silviculture designed to increase the productivity of the stand. The difference among these is in the length of the rotation period. Plan A, for example,

Table 11.4 ALTERNATIVE TIMBER MANAGEMENT POSSIBILITIES OUTPUT, SITE CLASS II, DOUGLAS FIR

Item	Management alternative				Intensive	
	A	B	C	D	High estimate	Low estimate
Stand growing rotation— years	164	50	127	60	50	50
Harvest to harvest rotation —years	171	57	134	67	51	51
Annual volume of merchantable timber						
Final cuts—cu ft per A	123	155	146	165	333	275
Thinnings—cu ft per A	0	0	0	0	265	206
Total	123	155	146	165	598	480
Total volume at each final cut, plus thinnings—cu ft per A	21,000	8,850	19,500	11,050	30,500	24,500

(handwritten annotations above bottom row: 26550 24884 24202 102264 82,147)

Source: M. Clawson (1977), *Decision Making in Timber Production, Harvest, and Marketing,* Washington, D.C.: Resources for the Future, Research Paper R–4. Reprinted by permission.

allows the stand of Douglas fir to grow for 164 years, and harvests occur every 171 years. The difference 171 and 164 is the number of years needed for the stand to be established through natural regeneration. This type of scheme would be applied to a forest that in the first rotation consists of trees of differing ages, with some at ages beyond 164 years. The bottom row shows the total volume at each final cut. The scheme is similar to current practices in U.S. national forests (in combination with the formulas mentioned above for cutting mature and overmature wood).

Plan B, by contrast, has the same natural regeneration period of 7 years, but a much shorter rotation period of 50 years: 57 years between harvests. Thus there will be *three* cycles of harvest, regrowth, and harvest under this scheme compared to A. The annual growth is much higher than in A (155 cubic feet per year versus 123 cubic feet), and over the three cycles about 25 percent more timber will be produced than with plan A (8,850 per rotation times three rotations). Plans C and D are variations of A and B. C illustrates that with a shortening of the rotation period to 127 years, far more wood will be produced per year, with a total volume per cut close to that of plan A. It represents a relatively small change from most existing practices (compared to B), with much higher yields (24 percent more than A over four of its cycles to three of A's). Plan D allows for two cycles compared to C, the maximum annual volume produced of the four plans and the largest total volume over time.

The last two columns of Table 11.4 indicate that annual and total wood volume could be increased further by engaging in intensive management of the forest, which includes replanting rather than allowing for natural regeneration. Replanting (of two-year-old seedlings) means that the stand will be reestablished in one year as opposed to seven for natural regeneration. Seedlings are spaced optimally for growth so that the annual productivity (in terms of tree volume) is 20 to 30 percent more than occurs under natural conditions. The stands can also be fertilized and thinned periodically. Thinning not only allows the remaining trees to grow faster, it also yields some salable wood. Two estimates are provided of the effects of intensive management on yields. With a rotation period of 50 years, annual growth and total volume when cut increase substantially compared to all the previous plans.

This analysis does not consider the costs of the different management schemes. While Table 11.4 clearly indicates the increases in forest productivity under shorter rotation periods and more intensive management, do the gains from intensive management cover the costs? Hyde (1980) has done a detailed analysis of different management schemes for the Douglas fir and finds generally that for the most fertile classes of sites (classes I and II and in some regions III as well), the rate of return on intensive management is high — investment in the forest does pay off. In the poorer site classes (IV and V), it does not. Clawson (1977) refers to other studies that support these findings. There is thus great potential to increase the output from the public forests.

The Social Losses from Public Forest Management

In his paper on timber supply, Berck (1979) asks what the values of nonmarket activities such as recreation, wildlife, watershed, and range use would have to be to warrant the historical harvests and harvests projected into the next century from national forests. He computes the present value of the forest under private management, then contrasts that with the value when the forest is cut at the CMAI. His calculations are for the Douglas fir, a valuable tree found in the Pacific Northwest used in construction and for plywood.

As noted above, timber supply from the national forests is governed by allowable cut rules, with the objective of harvesting when the tree reaches the CMAI. The U.S. Forest Service must also, in accordance with the National Forest Management Act (1976), maintain an even flow of timber that is not declining over time. While these policies are designed to account for nontimber values, Berck shows that they result in large unrealized gains — foregone revenues from timber not harvested at a private optimum.

BOX 11.4
Bidding for Timber Rights

The U.S. Forest Service administers the sale of timber rights on federal lands. Government appraisers "cruise" a tract and set a floor value or reserve bid. Thirty days later, an auction is held and the highest bidder wins the rights to exploit the timber. Five percent of the selling price is the downpayment, and this outlay can be allocated to interim payments after 25 percent of the tract has been exploited. Payment rates can be arranged at the outset on the basis of timber cut. These arrangements are referred to as "scale sales," since payment depends on the scale of the cutting operation. Rates can be adjusted in accord with the specification of a Stumpage Rate Adjustment (SRA) clause. An index of the value of final lumber products is calculated, and rates paid by contractors can rise by 50 percent of any increases in the index or decrease by the full amount of the decline in the index. This procedure removes considerable risk from the bidder.

If cutting is not complete by the termination date of the contract, an extension can be arranged if 75 percent of the tract is already cut. With an extension in effect, monthly payments must be made on the basis of the remaining timber, whether cutting is done or not. In the event of default, the contractor must pay the costs of a resale auction plus a fraction of the decline in value of the tract. It turns out that for contracts signed between 1977 and 1979 in Oregon and Washington, actual prices have been $150 per thousand board feet below expected prices.

In aggregate terms, lumber companies in the Pacific Northwest have contracted to pay more than $5 billion for federal and state-owned uncut timber which they indicate has a current value of $3 billion. In the summer of 1983, President Reagan granted 384 companies with $4.5 billion in timber contracts, an additional five years in which to cut and pay for the trees. Some interest payments were waived. Still, many companies are at risk of bankruptcy, they assert. Twenty-two billion board feet were contracted to be cut between 1980 and 1984.

Source: R. Rucker and K. Leffler, "Federal Timber Policy: An Analysis of Bidding and Cutting Incentives." Discussion Paper #83-12, University of Washington, 1983, and *New York Times,* January 29, 1984.)

Table 11.5 presents the calculations. They are based on a model of private market behavior we discuss below and the historical pattern of harvests of Douglas fir from the national forests. Two site classes are represented. The high class is more productive in growing timber than the low class. The row marked "age" refers to the initial age of the stand when the calculations are made. Thus the first column mea-

Table 11.5 VALUE PER FULLY STOCKED ACRE FOR FORESTLAND WITH TREES ASSUMING OPTIMAL HARVESTING AND CMAI* HARVESTING BY SITE CLASS AND AGE, 1970

Site class	High			Low		
Age	25	50	75	25	50	75
Value with optimal harvesting	3,680	6,117	7,663	719	1,150	1,932
Value if harvested at CMAI†	2,956	4,962	7,663	572	1,018	1,686
Shadow loss per acre	724	1,155	0	147	132	246

* Culmination of the mean annual increment.

† Equals 100 years old on high site and 125 years old on low site. Figures assume normal yield table growth.

Source: P. Berck (1979), "The Economics of Timber: A Renewable Resource in the Long Run" *Bell Journal of Economics* 10, p. 459. Reprinted by permission.

sures the values from a stand of 25-year-old trees when held to the age at which a private firm would cut them versus the CMAI, which is 100 years for high-quality sites or 125 years for low-quality sites. The value under private management is the value per acre of the forest to the private entrepreneur maximizing profits under a 5 percent real rate of return (before tax) and holding rational expectations about future timber prices. The next row is the value of the forest under the CMAI rule, and the last row simply subtracts the value under CMAI from the private solution. In all instances but one, a shadow loss exists. Holding the timber in the ground longer than would the private entrepreneur results in foregone revenues.

But do these losses simply reflect the nonmarket benefits from preserving forests for alternative uses and thus not social losses at all? Berck says "no." He refers to a study by Calish, Fight, and Teeguarden (1978) that calculates the nontimber uses of the forest. Their calculation is that a stand of timber on a 60-year rotation yields an average of $85 per acre per year in nonmarket values. These values do not warrant postponing the harvest to the CMAI. Other measures of nonmarket timber values may exist, but they would have to be significantly higher for older-aged stands of Douglas fir to justify the CMAI rule. A policy implication of this analysis is that low-quality forest land should be chosen for recreational and environmental activities (if suitable), while the high-quality land should be used for timber production (under economic harvesting rules).

The even-flow policies of the USFS imply that the same amount of timber must be cut each decade. When a significant stock of the existing timber contains mature and overmature trees, as does the Douglas fir, this management policy means it will take a very long time for this old timber to be harvested. Berck estimates that the shadow loss of holding old-growth timber for 50 additional years (which is a reasonable estimate of the time it can take to draw down this stock) is about 45 percent of the timber's value, or about $6,000 per acre. It thus appears that the management policies on public lands results in losses due to revenues that could be obtained with more efficient use.

Do Private Firms Harvest Too Quickly?

There has been concern that the manager of a private forest will cut too quickly and threaten the long-term viability of the industry. Berck examines this issue as well for the privately held stands of Douglas fir and finds no support for the belief that the cut is excessive. Rather, he finds the opposite: The harvest on private lands is lower than optimal. First we must see what "excessive" means. A simple interpretation is that private entrepreneurs operate under higher discount rates than are socially optimal. The private firm may discount the future at a higher rate than society as a whole due to distortions caused by taxation, lack of regard for the preservation of environments, future generations, and so on. If the harvests on the private lands are consistent with a before-tax real interest rate of more than 10 percent, we'll call the harvest excessive. Berck solves for the discount rate the private firms must have implicitly been using to obtain the harvests observed on these lands from 1950 to 1970 and the harvests a firm operating with rational expectations would plan over the subsequent 150 years.

The basic assumptions are that entrepreneurs decide for each base year between

1950 and 1970 how much timber will be sold in each of the next seven quarter-centuries, based on their expectation of the price in each of these subsequent periods. Entrepreneurs then maximize the present value from the forest subject to initial endowments of land and timber and the biological relationship for timber growth. A supply function for timber for each of the seven quarter-centuries is derived from the profit function, and it is assumed that expected prices will clear the market in each of these periods. After specifying and estimating a demand curve for timber, Berck then solves for the implicit private discount rate most consistent with the firm's rational expectations of market-clearing prices and the historical supply over the period examined. He finds that the private sector owners have acted as if they faced a real interest rate before tax of about 5 percent. This value is well below the critical value of 10 percent noted above, and thus inconsistent with the belief that private sector producers are discounting the future at too high a rate. In this example, private timber harvests from the Douglas fir cannot be interpreted as excessive.[8]

SUMMARY

1. On a plot of land devoted to commercial forestry, trees are cut and new ones planted or allowed to regenerate on their own. There is a cycle of harvesting, growth, harvesting, growth, and so on. Certain key factors determine the length of a cycle and how these cycles, or rotation periods, are affected.

2. Differences in harvest costs can result in different effects on the length of the rotation period for a forest. In a simple model with linear and multiplicative harvest costs, higher harvest costs imply longer rotation periods. Higher interest or discount rates imply shorter rotation periods, as do higher site-clearing or preparation costs. More fertile sites have shorter rotation periods.

3. Regular rotation periods may not describe all forestry operations; they are associated with forestry farming, rather than use of a "natural" forest. To a limited degree this is true, but "natural" forests can also be managed in the sense that harvest dates are coordinated with average tree maturity and artificial reforestation is often undertaken. Nevertheless, a historically given "natural" forest does impose constraints on future harvesting strategies. It may not be optimal to clear cut trees of diverse ages, and special rotation strategies may be pursued to avoid wasting trees on the verge of highly productive growth.

4. For some forests, "mining" or clearing is most profitable so that the land can be used for more productive activity such as agriculture. The relative fertility and accessibility of different sites makes some more profitable than others. A heavily forested area is not necessarily a commercially attractive area for forest use. Rotation cycles may be relatively long and delivery costs relatively high.

5. Taxes were equivalent to increases in costs in most cases and led to longer intervals between planting and harvesting and less wood per unit of time in perpetuity. Ownership arrangements as well as taxation arrangements can affect the incentive to plant new trees, as well as the length of the rotation period.

6. Actual forestry practices in the United States, in particular the policies of the U.S. Forest Service toward the sale of timber cutting rights and the allowed

harvests, have resulted in a very slow drawing down of mature and overmature timber. This is because the stand is typically harvested no sooner than the culmination of its mean annual increment. This is a biological harvesting rule, which maximizes the growth rate of the stand but does not incorporate economic criteria. In addition, allowable cut regulations are imposed on national forests to ensure an even flow of harvests over time. These allowable cuts further exacerbate the excessively slow harvests on public lands. A shadow loss results—the difference between the net value of the harvest under the economic optimum versus the harvests actually occurring in national forests.

7. The U.S. Forest Service is also charged with preservation of environmental values in the forest, multiple use of forest lands for recreation and other economic activity, and so on. An estimate of the value of these generally nonmarket activities does not cover the shadow losses from noneconomic management of the Douglas fir in national forests.

8. Harvests of Douglas fir on private forest lands in the United States are found to be consistent with a real (before-tax) discount rate of 5 percent. At this discount rate, it appears that harvests of Douglas fir from the private sector are far from excessive.

DISCUSSION QUESTIONS

1. For an infinite-period model in which the optimal rotation period for a forest is determined, explain the economic intuition for:
   a. The condition that determines the year (or time) the trees are cut.
   b. Why each rotation period is the same length of time.
   c. The role of the discount rate.

2. a. How does the optimal rotation period change when:
      (1) Planting costs fall.
      (2) A tax on the volume of wood harvested is imposed.
      (3) A license fee is imposed for using the land.
   b. Suppose there are two plots of land, one more fertile (produces more wood volume per acre) than the other. Explain the optimal rotation period for each plot.

3. Air pollution has been observed to retard the growth of trees in forests in, among other places, the eastern part of the United States. Must we redevelop our model of optimal tree management and cutting, or is this matter of "atmosphere" a part of the existing model? Discuss.

4. "To maximize the volume of wood harvested, a forest should be cut when the mean annual increment reaches a maximum." True, false, or uncertain? Explain your answer.

5. Ontario's Algonquin Park was populated with very large conifers in the nineteenth century, photographs indicate. Now it is thickly forested with smaller conifers. Was a mistake made in harvesting all the very large trees? What characteristics should a forest display for an observer to know that it is being used properly for tree harvests?

6. What is the allowed annual cut in regulatory policies for forest management? Why is it used?

7. Explain why in practice trees harvested by private firms may be cut too soon compared to the socially optimal harvest, while trees on public lands may be cut too slowly.

8. Many observers lament the clearing of forests in Third World countries to make new land for farming. Are the private decisions of these landowners at odds with the social value of the land with forest remaining on it? Was England, for example, stripped of its forests at the wrong pace and date?

NOTES

1. Ledyard and Moses (1977) made planting costs vary with the amount planted, rather than associating these costs simply with clearing the site and planting on it, as we have done. Their model involves two choice variables: how many resources to devote to planting, and how long to work the crop from planting to harvesting. Their analysis is much more complicated than the familiar one-variable models of which ours is a representative.
2. For a similar graphic determination of the optimal rotation period, see Pearse (1967).
3. To see how price expectations affect harvesting decisions in a forestry model, see Berck (1979).
4. Fertility differences may arise from the type of trees planted. For example, selective planting is being vigorously persued in the southern part of the United States. The first generation of the selected trees planted commercially today is expected to grow 10 to 15 percent faster than normal trees. "Enough research has been done that by the year 2010, the plantations will be producing twice as much wood as they are today." Edwin A. Gee, chairman, International Paper (*New York Times,* December 4, 1983).
5. Comolli (1981) has incorporated forestry output into an economywide growth model like those we discussed in Chapter 6.
6. See Clawson (1976, 1977) for more details on the structure of the U.S. forest industry.
7. See Pearse (1976) for a similar discussion of cutting practices in British Columbia.
8. For other discussions of the long-term supply of timber from private forest owners, see Adams et al. (1982) and the references therein.

chapter *12*

An Introduction to Environmental Resources: Externalities and Pollution

INTRODUCTION

Our topic here is how the economy utilizes natural resources that are not exchanged in well-defined markets. The natural resources we examine are air, water, and the general state of the environment. We have already discussed in detail the case of the fishery exploited under open access. The distinct problem with the fishery under open access was the lack of property rights to the fish stock, which led to excessive use of factor inputs to exploit the stock and the possibility that the stock would be extinguished. As we will see, environmental resources also suffer from nonoptimal exploitation due to the lack of property rights.

As we pointed out in Chapter 1, there are few instances in which a property right to a particular environmental resource is assigned explicitly to an individual (or group of individuals). No one "owns" the air surrounding them; and although riparian (water) rights have existed in common law for many years, these rights do not prevent others from using lakes, streams, and oceans as a waste depository. Our discussion will focus on the problems associated with nonoptimal use of these resources.

We first define an *external effect* or *externality* and show why it can arise. We then examine different types of externalities and illustrate the economic problems that emerge when externalities exist. In particular, we look at externalities that arise in the consumption and production of goods and services. Once the economic problems are identified, we examine methods of reaching an optimal allocation of resources. The tools we discuss include taxes, subsidies, and regulations governing outputs. In Chapter 13, we examine some actual environmental problems: what causes them, what can be done to eliminate the problems, and what has been done in practice.

An *externality* can arise when two conditions are present:

Condition 1: For any two (or more) economic agents (consumers or firms) i and j, an externality is present whenever agent's i's utility or production relationship includes variables whose magnitudes are chosen by the other agent(s), j, without regard to i's own preferences.

Condition 2: The ith individual or firm has no control over the variables chosen by j because the variables have no explicit exchange value. No markets (or imperfect markets) exist for the variables entering i's objective function.

What these conditions signify is a technological interdependence among agents which persists because no market mechanism operates to allow for the optimal pricing of the interdependent variables.

Let's consider some examples before examining externalities more completely. I like flowers, but am too lazy to plant them in my garden. My neighbor loves to work in the garden and spends a lot of effort making it colorful. I walk by the garden and enjoy its beauty without spending any of my time and energy to nurture the garden. This is an example of a positive externality, or an *external economy*. My neighbor's garden increases my utility, and I have not spent any of my own resources to obtain this enjoyment. My neighbor's garden is a variable in my utility function that my neighbor controls, but the garden nonetheless affects me. Furthermore, his attractive garden can help me sell my house at a premium. A negative externality or *external diseconomy* arises when another agent's actions affect me adversely. I'm having a nice meal at a restaurant when two obnoxious people come in and start talking loudly. Their actions reduce the enjoyment of my meal.

Both types of externality involve no exchange through a market. In the case of the flower garden, my neighbor is not paid anything for the benefits others receive from the garden. In the restaurant, no one offers me a reduction in the price of my meal simply because I'm now too upset to enjoy it.

What then can be done about the externality? The gardening neighbor could erect a high fence around the garden and charge admission to see the flowers. If some payment or compensation is received for the externality, one is said to be *internalizing* the externality. The agent responsible for the externality now incorporates the effect its actions have on the utility or production function of the recipient. When the fence is built, I will now pay the neighbor the value of my flower enjoyment. The neighbor is thus compensated for the benefits received by passersby and may, in fact, plant more flowers. In the restaurant, some private action could be taken. I could complain to the restaurant and ask that the noisy people be asked to be quiet or to leave. I could leave as well. In these cases, an externality is likely to be internalized by private actions—actions taken by individuals. However, as we will see, most important examples of externalities cannot be internalized solely by private actions; some form of government intervention is required. To see why, let's examine more fully why an externality can persist.

In our study of natural resources, most of the externalities we encounter are the negative kind. Air and water pollution are examples of external diseconomies— cases where individuals and firms discard waste products into the environment without acknowledging the damages these products cause to others. We know these externalities arise when some sort of technological interdependency exists (I am seated next to noisy eaters in the restaurant, toxic wastes are dumped on the land and in streams, adversely affecting people, animals, and plants). Why do the external effects not get appropriately priced and allocated by the operation of market mechanisms? Alternatively, what are the possible causes of market failure? We highlight four.

Cause 1 Markets may be too thin or too costly to operate. A market is *thin* when there are not enough traders to allow it to operate. If there is just me and my neighbor with the garden, then it is unlikely that some formal exchange of money for the benefits of flower viewing will be established. This externality will probably persist because it does not pay the flower grower to erect a fence to get my fee every time I want to look at the garden. There are too few of us to make the establishment of a formal arrangement worthwhile. Another way to say this is that there may be transaction costs in operating a market. If the value of the item to be traded (flower viewing) is much lower than the costs of establishing a mechanism to extract payment for that item (erecting a fence), no formal market will exist.

Cause 2 Agents may lack information about the activities that are affecting them. This makes it very difficult for markets to work to internalize externalities. Information may also be asymmetric. That is, one agent may have more or better information than another. When this is the case, exchange through market mechanisms becomes quite difficult. For example, asbestos is now known to be a potent carcinogen. Asbestos fibers in the lungs can cause emphysema and a virulent form of lung cancer (mesothelioma). But these health problems can take decades to appear after the individual is exposed to the asbestos. Workers in asbestos mines (and others employed in the manufacture of asbestos products) did not know 30 years ago that their exposure to asbestos would result in debilitating disease and premature death. There is considerable debate about what the asbestos companies knew and whether they withheld information about the harmful effects of asbestos from their workers. But the point is that if you don't know what is affecting you, it is very difficult to take remedial action.

Cause 3 Probably the most significant reason why externalities persist is because the natural resource affected are typically common property resources (air, oceans), and the externality generated is *nonappropriable*. The common property nature of the environment means that anyone can use it as a depository of pollutants. Nonappropriability means that any one agent's consumption of the externality (pollution) does not reduce the consumption of that same externality by others. My consumption of polluted air does not affect your consumption of polluted air. I do not in any meaningful way reduce the amount of air you breathe. When a resource or the externality which arises in the use of the resource is nonappropriable, it is very difficult — indeed virtually impossible — for private markets to function efficiently or at all. We will show why in the next section.

Cause 4 Finally, a market failure may persist when nonconvexities exist either in the operation of the market or in the technological interdependence among agents. A nonconvexity is present, for example, when the production possibility schedule (introduced in Chapter 1) fails to be everywhere bowed out; over some of its length, it is "punched" in. A nonconvexity in the market can be caused by setup costs — say a large bureaucracy of some sort is needed to operate the market. We have encountered nonconvexities before (see Chapter 3), so it should come as no surprise that their presence interferes with the efficient operation of markets.

When these market failures are present, external effects are likely to persist in economies where exchange occurs through the operation of markets governed by the private interests of individuals.[1] Are these externalities a social problem? Few are likely to be bothered by the persistence of the flower garden externality. There may be too few flower gardens, but this does not represent a pressing social problem. Similarly, if I cannot resolve the problem with the noisy restaurant patrons, again there may be little social loss. But what about some major externalities — toxic chemical dumps or acid rain? The fact that these external diseconomies persist in all economies *is* a matter of concern to many individuals and a problem warranting government action.

Individuals, animals, and plants are harmed by these pollutants and resources are being allocated inefficiently in the economy when these environmental externalities persist. Factor inputs and the output of certain goods are not priced according to their social value. That is, private valuations of inputs and outputs are different from their social valuations. If toxic chemicals are dumped into the environment, it is generally because the ground (and water sources) onto which the chemicals are dumped are not valued by the firms doing the dumping. If these firms had to pay for the dump sites, far less (legal) dumping would be done. Without the incorporation of social valuations of the prices of these resources, too much toxic waste is spilled into the environment, and too few unpolluted areas remain. This is why many externalities are a serious social problem.

The question is, what do we do about these externalities? Some schools of economic thought argue that what exists is optimal. That is, if we see the persistence of certain environmental problems, that is because it is too costly to internalize the externality. They argue that any externalities we observe do not warrant any social concern. This view is not shared by others; their argument is precisely the opposite. The fact that we observe the persistence of a number of external effects means that the market is simply unable to cope with these problems and that another method of allocating resources is required. The solution advocated by many economists is to use the powers of government to impose a *price* on the external effect, so that agents are forced to include the external effect in their calculations of what goods to produce and consume. Government policies that impose prices include taxes, subsidies, and the use of marketable permits to pollute. Alternatively, the amount of the externality can be regulated through the use of pollution standards.

But we want to emphasize that there is a difference in *belief* about the importance of externalities among economists and politicians. We do not accept the view that all relevant externalities are internalized by private markets and that the ones remaining are not relevant. We will follow the tradition that attempts to find ways through regulatory action to internalize externalities and will show why this may be in the social interest. As a first step, we distinguish between private and public externalities.

A TAXONOMY OF EXTERNALITIES

Our analysis of public externalities illustrates that markets operating without government intervention will be unable to internalize this sort of externality. We present two types of private externality: a consumption externality and a production externality. The presence of the externality leads to an inefficient use of resources. In each case, the externality arises because of a technological interdependency. In the consumption case, one person cannot avoid inhaling smoke released from another. In the production case, one firm's production process is adversely affected by the waste products emitted by another firm. The emergence of an externality is, however, only the first part of the problem. We must also show why an externality persists without government intervention. Our objective is to show that there is no completely general model of why an externality persists. Markets fail for different reasons, and our analysis will highlight the different types of market failure and methods of internalizing the externality that may be appropriate for each case.

Public versus Private Externalities

We focus in this section on external diseconomies that affect natural resources—air and water. A *public* external diseconomy arises when a natural resource is used without payment, and the "consumption" of the externality by one agent does not reduce the consumption of the externality by others. There are many examples of public external diseconomies, notably air and water pollution. Air (and to a lesser degree) water are open access resources. Anyone is free to use the air in the way he or she sees fit. If it is used as a waste depository, no market price exists that reflects this use. Air pollution then emerges as a "public bad"—something consumed by a lot of people simultaneously. As we will see, the "jointness" in the consumption of the externality makes it difficult, if not impossible, to internalize it through private actions.

The nonappropriability in consumption of the externality is often accompanied by a large number of "producers" of the externality. For example, there are many emitters of the gases and particulates that comprise air pollution. These include static sources such as electric generating plants and mobile sources such as automobiles. Thus, the externality is "public" in consumption, and it is also difficult to determine the degree to which a particular source is responsible for particular amounts of pollution. When many people are affected and the consumption is the same (or very similar) for all, government intervention of some form is generally the only way the externality can be internalized.

A *private* external diseconomy is typically bilateral, or involves relatively few agents. One party's actions affect the actions of another party, but there is no spillover of the externality to other agents. We will examine some two-party cases in this section. (It is not strictly necessary to have two parties, but it is necessary that the effects on each agent are unique and do not affect other agents simultaneously.) The key characteristic of a private externality is that the external effect must be fully appropriated by the parties involved. If a chemical company dumps toxic chemicals into a pond in a residential area, those who live around the pond are the only ones affected (assuming the contamination of the pond does not seep into other bodies of water).

Generally, there are more methods of internalizing a private externality than a public one. The role for private action through negotiation by the parties involved or the emergence of a market is much more likely when few agents are involved. Private externalities are a useful model for heuristic purposes, because they enable us to illustrate cases using simple graphic techniques rather than more cumbersome algebra. However, it is more difficult to think of actual cases in which an externality is private. There are typically some spillover effects and some degree of nonappropriability in most externalities. In addition, private externalities tend not to persist; they are more readily internalized than are public externalities.

The line between public and private is often hard to draw in practice. Our objective here is to present public and private externalities as separate cases, so that we can analyze the ability of market and nonmarket mechanisms to internalize externalities. We turn now to an examination of a public external diseconomy.

Suppose we have a *public external diseconomy*—air pollution. There may be many agents who produce the pollution. It can come from automobiles, factories, electrical power plants, and so on. Also, large numbers of individuals "consume" the pollution by breathing air filled with particulates, sulfur dioxide, and oxides of nitrogen. Producers of the externality can also be consumers of air pollution. Anyone who drives a car and lives in an area of low air quality is both a producer and consumer. The reason this public externality arises is simple: Air is an open access resource. Because no property rights to air exist, those who generate air pollution are free to use the air as a waste dump without paying any fees. Once air pollution is generated, large numbers of individuals (animals, vegetation, and property) are affected. Each person affected might be willing to pay something to reduce the pollution, but if he or she did so, others who did not pay would also benefit.

Air pollution is thus quite different from ordinary goods in which consumption is fully appropriated or received by the individual purchasing the good. If I buy a television set and you don't, only I get to enjoy (or suffer) from the programming available on TV. But if I pay to have air pollution reduced and you don't, you also get some benefits from cleaner air without any outlay of funds. Those who would benefit without any payment are called *free riders*. This is the public nature of the air pollution externality and why it is so difficult to internalize through markets and private actions. No decentralized market can handle a situation where those receiving the pollution (the demand side) are individually willing to pay nothing for the pollution or its cleanup because those who pay will benefit those who do not pay. On the supply side, producers of the pollution also face a zero price because they are able in an unregulated situation to use the air free. Thus, air pollution exists because no one is willing to pay for its reduction in an unregulated market.[2]

Let's see why the public externality cannot be internalized without government intervention. There are a number of ways to analyze this problem: We can view it from the perspective of the supply of and demand for "clean" air, which we can think of as a *public good* in that once provided (in this case by nature), all get to consume it equally. Person i may get more satisfaction from a public good such as clean air than person j, but they each get the same amount of clean air. Or we can start with a situation in which the air is already dirty because of the past failure of markets to lead to prices for the right to use the clean air. In either case, the same general principles will emerge. The precise equilibrium will, however, be different. This is a problem of the starting point. If we start with clean air and ask what people would be willing to pay to dirty it, we typically get a different equilibrium than if the starting point is polluted air and we ask what people are willing to pay to clean it up.

Let's start with the case where the air is clean. Suppose we are given a stock of clean air. We want to abstract from any complex meteorology here. Air has both stock and flow characteristics, and there may indeed be a stock that can become polluted. But natural processes such as precipitation and movement of air masses tend to dissipate pollution over time. An appropriate model of air pollution thus requires analysis of the dynamic paths of pollution emission and air recovery. Rather than deal with these issues, we assume there is simply a finite supply of clean air. Clean air is thus like a depletable resource.[3]

Figure 12.1 illustrates the "market" for clean air. In each of the three parts we show the supply of clean air as some fixed amount, Q. Supply is finite because there will always be some natural impurities human activity can do nothing to control (eruptions of volcanos spill tons of particulates into the atmosphere). In (a), we show the demand curve of agent A (an individual or a firm) for clean air. The demand curve slopes down in the normal fashion because we assume that like any other good, clean air yields diminishing marginal utility as consumption increases. At the stock of air shown, Q, agent A would be willing to pay the price P_A for the air. Figure 12.1(b) shows the demand for clean air by agent B. We have drawn agent B's demand curve such that B is willing to pay less for any amount of clean air than A. With the stock Q, B is willing to pay P_B. So far, nothing is different from the case of consumer demand for an ordinary good. The difference between public goods (or bads) and ordinary goods comes in the determination of the *market demand curve.*

Because everyone consumes the same amount of air, we must aggregate individual demand curves by summing them *vertically* rather than horizontally, as in the case of an ordinary good. That is, we pick a quantity of air, say Q'. If that were the supply of air, it would be available to everyone. We then ask what each agent would be willing to pay for that amount. Agent A would be willing to pay P'_A, while agent B would be willing to pay P'_B (where P'_A exceeds P'_B). The sum of these two prices is shown in (c) as P'. A similar exercise for the stock of air at Q and Q'' leads to the determination of other points on the market or aggregate demand curve.

With the *quantity of the good fixed,* the only thing individuals' demand curves reflect is *the price they would be willing to pay* for the good. In the case of an ordinary private good, the individual typically faces a single price and chooses how much to buy. Addition of individual demands is thus done horizontally across quantities they

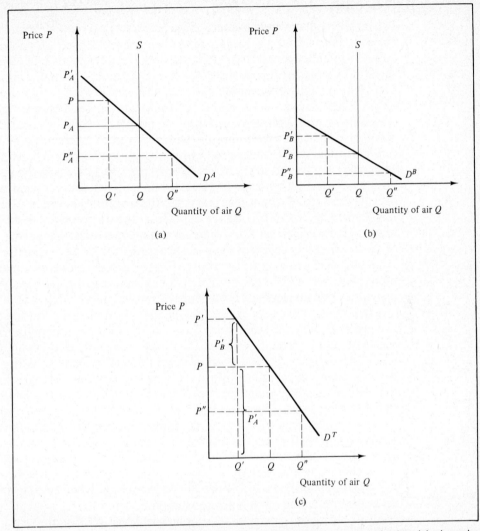

Figure 12.1 For a given stock of clean air, Q, each individual's willingness to pay for that air is shown by their demand curve. If the stock of air is Q, individual A would be willing to pay P_A, while individual B would be willing to pay P_B. The "market" demand curve is obtained by the *vertical* summation of the prices each person is willing to pay for a particular amount of the clean air. If the stock of air is Q', the sum of these demand prices is P'. If the stock of air is Q, total demand sums to P. Finally, if the stock of air is Q'', the total willingness to pay is P''.

are willing to purchase. In the case of the public good, there is no discretion over available quantities, so preferences are summed over prices.

What, then, does an equilibrium mean in a market with a public good? Suppose the stock of air is indeed Q. If air were a normal good, the equilibrium price of air would be P, as shown in Figure 12.1(c). With a private good, each person would then take P as given and decide how much of the good to buy. But with the public good, there is no choice over how much to buy: Q is the amount supplied; all individuals can do is reveal how much they would be willing to pay. But notice that the equilibrium price then has no meaning. Agent A is willing to pay P_A for an amount of air equal to Q, while agent B is willing to pay only P_B for that same quantity. It is difficult to see how a market that charges uniform prices could ever exist in this situation.

Suppose price P was in fact charged. At P, consumer A would be willing to buy Q' units of clean air, but B would buy nothing because P exceeds the maximum price B is willing to pay. Total sales would be Q', not Q. The equilibrium at P and Q is not feasible. This means that the equilibrium price and quantity cannot be decomposed into individual sales that are consistent with aggregate supply. Therefore, either one price must be charged to all, in which case individual demands are not recognized (consumer sovereignty is violated) and total supply does not equal total demand except by change, or a multiplicity of prices must be charged. We have only illustrated the demand curves for two agents. In practice, there are many times this number of agents, which means that many different demand prices would exist for a given stock of air. No perfectly competitive market can exist to deal with all these prices.

But could a private market operate with a number of different prices? Suppose a monopolist was able to discriminate perfectly among all consumers with different demand curves for clean air. Each demander would then be charged a different price, and the monopolist could ensure that demand equals supply. But there are at least two problems with a discriminating monopolist. First, the monopolist receives all the consumer surplus from the market. This may not be desirable socially. Second, and more important, one of the essential requirements for perfect discrimination by a monopolist is that the monopolist must be able to prevent consumers from reselling their allotment of the good to others. When the good in question is clean air, prevention of resale is impossible: All get the same amount of air regardless of what they pay. The monopolist would be unable to charge different prices because it could not prevent one agent from consuming the air received by another agent who paid a lower price. Indeed, it is difficult to imagine that any sort of contract made at different prices could be enforceable.

Can a public body do any better? In principle, governments have the ability to act as discriminating monopolists because they can force everyone to "pay" for the clean air by imposing taxes or some other sort of fee. No discriminating monopolist could operate without the government giving it the right to collect payments for air (who would pay for something they can receive free?). Therefore, it seems more sensible to consider the government as the operator of the clean air "market." But the government will face the same problem a private monopolist would in determining what people are willing to pay for the clean air. Suppose the government plans to levy a fee on each agent equal to what that agent says it is willing to pay for clean air. If agent i thinks that agent j is willing to pay less for clean air than it is, why should agent i tell the government it will pay a higher price, even if i values clean air more than j? Some individuals may be truthful and reveal their actual willingness to pay for clean air, but others will not. There is a strong incentive to cheat. If the government is unable to tell what your true preferences are, the result is that clean air will be underprovided relative to the "true" social optimum.[4]

Figure 12.2 illustrates this case. Suppose there is some "cost" to the government to provide clean air. We then allow the supply curve for air to be upward-sloping. To get more air, more expenses must be incurred per unit. If the government wishes to determine the optimal amount of clean air, it will equate supply with demand, produce that amount of air which is indicated by the equilibrium, and then charge everyone a price that reflects the demand curves the individual has revealed to the government. The problem is then evident. Agents will have a strong incentive to underreport their demand for clean air.

Suppose each individual reveals a demand curve that aggregates (vertically) to the "market" demand curve D in Figure 12.2. Each person would be charged a "tax price" derived from his or her individual demand curve. But some people would be willing to pay more than they reveal and would misrepresent their preferences in the hopes that others will share more of the tax burden. Total demand is less than people really want. The supply of clean air will be Q. If they truthfully revealed their preferences and the market demand curve were D', the supply of clean air would be Q', which exceeds Q. The amount of clean air which then would exist is less than the optimal amount. People will in a sense be cheating themselves, but because of the nonappropriability of the clean air, will do nothing about it.

Suppose alternatively that the government asks people what they would be willing to pay, but does not base the fee or tax they charge agents for clean air on the amount revealed. In this case, just the opposite result is expected. Agents will have an incentive to overreveal their willingness to pay for clean air. There will be a tendency then to have "too much" clean air relative to the social optimum. Such a result would occur if, for example, the government asks people their preferences for clean air and

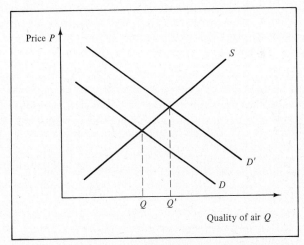

Figure 12.2 If people are charged a "tax price" based on their revealed demand for clean air, they will have an incentive to underreport their true willingness to pay for the air. The demand curve D results. The government will then supply Q units of clean air. If the "true" demand for clean air is represented by D', the desired supply of air is really Q'. Clean air is then undersupplied.

then charges everyone the same price (a flat tax) regardless of the response. Some people will pay more than they are willing to pay, others will pay less. The equilibrium will not be optimal.

A final word on prices and markets for public goods. It is in theory possible to arrive at the right price each person should be assessed for consuming the commodity — so-called personalized prices, since they will vary from one person to another. But there is (a) no natural mechanism causing these correct prices to emerge (part of the free rider problem), and (b) if consumers got together to register their preferences, the transaction costs of getting together and deciding even if the correct preferences were to emerge would be very high. Thus we see that:

1. No private market can supply a public good such as clean air. Some form of government intervention is required.
2. Even if the government does regulate the supply of clean air and charges a tax to individuals for that air, it is quite likely that the supply will be different from the optimum because individuals have an incentive to hide their true preferences.

Note that the same type of result would occur if we viewed the problem from the standpoint of the demand for pollution abatement. The demand for abatement would fall as the price of abatement rose. Those demanding abatement would have an incentive to underreveal their demand if the fee they were charged by the government reflected their stated willingness to pay. The amount of pollution would thus be higher in the equilibrium than is socially optimal because there would be too little abatement.

BOX 12.1
Water: The Large View

The earth has a fixed endowment of water — 97 percent is salt water in the sea, and 3 percent is fresh. Three-quarters of this fresh water is locked in glaciers and ice caps, leaving less than 1 percent in rivers, lakes, groundwater (subsurface), soil, and atmosphere. Most of this 1 percent is groundwater, leaving only a tiny fraction of all water in rivers and lakes. There is a dynamic cycle in any region involving precipitation, evaporation, runoff, and accumulation or decumulation of stocks. Management can influence the amount for use in a region, and infrastructures of varying costs are required.

On a global scale 60 percent of end use is for irrigation in agriculture and less than 20 percent for municipal and industrial uses. Averaging over personal and industrial uses for a city, a New Yorker uses about 276 gallons a day and a resident of Bombay, 32. For making a ton of steel, water use ranges from 65,000 gallons to as little as 1,400 gallons. Water use is expected to triple in the next 25 years. China is expanding irrigated land by 2.5 to 5 million acres per year. Between 1950 and 1970 irrigated land in India grew by 50 percent, much of it watered from wells. New reservoirs can provide new supplies, but evaporation can draw off some of the new stock. In the lower Colorado, evaporation equals accumulation for the reservoirs. New groundwater from wells is another source, but replenishment is slow. In parts of California and the High Plains of Texas, the cost of a new well exceeds the value of the water produced owing to the great depth of the water table. Recycling holds great promise as a new source of water supply; conservation or technical change is also promising. Since 1950, there has been a fivefold reduction in water used to process a ton of coal.

In general, water is not priced efficiently. Water is generally not traded in "markets." Prices for water may reflect some but not all of the costs of supplying the water. For example, in the United States water for irrigation is less than one-quarter the price charged to cities and industry. In *Business Week* ("Should Water Subsidies Go Down the Drain," March 5, 1984, pp. 104–105), it was noted that water in the Imperial Valley of California—a major agricultural area—was selling for $10 an acre-foot, while the Metropolitan Water District of Southern California was paying about $250 per acre-foot for water distributed to consumers and industrial users.

The U.S. government has been subsidizing water projects since 1902 on the grounds that low water prices were essential to encourage economic growth in the West and Southwest. Many thousands of acres of marginal farmland have been brought into cultivation because water was selling far below its "shadow price." Cheap water deters conservation and leads to shortages over time. These shortages then put pressure on the federal government to develop additional supplies of water. In 1984, President Reagan, succumbing to political pressure from agricultural interests, proposed $700 million worth of new water projects. These new projects may supply more water in the short run, but unless the water is priced more efficiently excessive consumption and subsequent shortages will recur.

It might be quite difficult to raise water prices to agricultural users due to legal constraints. Federal laws in the United States base water payments not just on the cost of supplying water, but on the user's ability to pay. Users of water for irrigation pay in the form of taxes. Taxes are based on contracts between the government and irrigation districts, and many of these contracts have been in effect for years. It is difficult to adjust water prices in this setting. One proposed solution to the pricing problem is to establish a market for the transfer of water rights (see Chapter 13 for a detailed discussion of markets for pollution rights). Many legal and institutional difficulties impede the development of a system of water rights, but the recognition of the problems associated with underpricing and overuse of water may stimulate action. Because many observers feel that water may be the crucial "scarce" resource of the 1980s and 1990s, we can expect to see a lot of discussion of water rights and other forms of pricing in the near future.

Sources: M. G. Wolman, "Water." *The Americana Annual 1978,* Danbury, Conn.: Grolier, pp. 52–60.

"Should Water Subsidies Go Down the Drain?" *Business Week,* March 5, 1984, pp. 104–105.

Externalities in Consumption

In this section, we examine in more detail the case where the consumption of one agent is affected by the generation of an external diseconomy by another agent. The agent generating the externality may be another firm, but to keep the case simple, we assume it is another consumer. We examine a private externality. This is because we rely on a two-dimensional graph for the analysis. However, a number of the results we obtain for this case can be carried over to that of a public externality. We will note when the results are generally applicable and when they are specific to this case.

Suppose we have two individuals, Amanda and George. Amanda and George work in the same office. George smokes heavily and Amanda does not. Amanda dislikes secondhand smoke because it irritates her eyes and lungs. As our story begins, George is smoking and Amanda is suffering. There is no antismoking ordinance in effect in the office, so clean air is in effect the unpriced open access natural resource. Let's think of Amanda (A) as the party *afflicted* by smoke pollution, and George (G) as the party *generating* the pollution.[5] Each individual is assumed to have a utility function defined over normal goods, which we will call X and think of as some basket of consumer goods, and smoke Z.[6] George controls the smoke that each of them consumes. We can write their utility functions as:

$$U^A = U^A(X^A, Z)$$
$$U^G = U^G(X^G, Z) \tag{12.1}$$

We assume that Amanda's utility is lowered when Z increases (that is, the derivative of U^A with respect to Z is negative). This reduction in Amanda's utility due to George's smoke is the external diseconomy. George's utility increases whenever X or Z is increased. Both individuals maximize their utility subject to their own budget constraints, which are given by Equation (12.2):

$$Y^A = P_X X^A$$
$$Y^G = P_X X^G + P_Z Z \tag{12.2}$$

where Y is the total income for each person, P_X is the price of other goods, and P_Z is the market price of cigarettes. We also assume that a production possibility frontier, $F(X,Z)$, represents the economy's ability to produce X and Z. For simplicity, we assume the frontier is linear and that the economy is always on the boundary—that is, $F(X,Z) = 0$—producing the maximum amount of each good. Each individual then maximizes his or her utility subject to the budget constraint. George does not take into account initially the effect his cigarette smoke has on Amanda. The solution to the maximization problem yields the following familiar conditions:

$$MU_X/MU_Z = P_X/P_Z = MRT_{XZ} \text{ (George)}$$

$$\frac{MU_X}{MU_Z} \neq \frac{P_X}{P_Z} \neq MRT_{XZ} \text{ (Amanda)} \tag{12.3}$$

For George, we have the usual condition for where a consumer's well-being is maximized—namely, that the ratio of the marginal utilities *(MU)* from each good consumed is equal to the ratio of the prices of the two goods, and also equals the marginal rate of transformation *(MRT)* of X into Z. For Amanda, a quite different result occurs. Her marginal utility from consuming good X is affected by the presence of Z, the smoke. She can do nothing about the smoke while in the office, and the presence of George's smoke therefore lowers her utility. George does not take into account the adverse effect he is having on Amanda. Put differently, the market price of cigarettes, P_Z, does not reflect the external effects smoking has on Amanda (and people like her).

We can show graphically, with the aid of a geometric device, what the equilibrium for the two parties looks like with the externality and how a socially optimal outcome can be obtained.[7] In deriving and explaining this diagram, we can also point out the difference in the equilibrium that will result when Amanda has the right to clean air (smoking is prohibited in the office) versus the situation now, where smoking is allowed and George effectively has the right to smoke. Methods of internalizing the externality that include bargaining, smoking regulations, and taxes are illustrated.

Consider Figure 12.3. In (a), we have the indifference curves for George for goods X and for smoking, Z. They are the normal shape. Each good has a diminishing marginal utility of consumption as the quantity consumed increases. Figure 12.3(b) illustrates Amanda's indifference curves. They are positively sloped because smoke is an external diseconomy to Amanda, an undesirable good. The more smoke she has, the more other goods she requires to maintain the same level of utility. Utility increases as Amanda moves from indifference curve IA_0 to IA_1 to IA_2. In (c), we have the production possibility frontier (PPF) for smoke and goods, X. The frontier is assumed to be linear, as noted. With a finite amount of factor inputs in the economy, more Z can be obtained by producing less X, but the tradeoff occurs at a constant rate.

What we want to do is to combine the indifference maps of George and Amanda to solve for equilibriums under different assignments of property rights. That is, we want to know how much smoke and X goods each will consume when smoking is permitted or prohibited. By assuming that Amanda and George are the

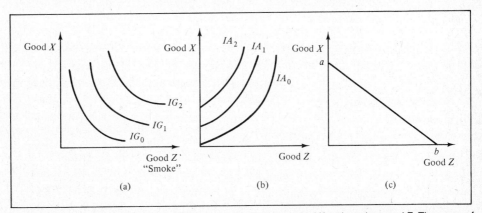

Figure 12.3 (a) shows George's indifference curves between good X and smoke, good Z. These are of the normal shape, indicating that increases in the consumption of either good increase George's utility. In (b), Amanda's indifference curves are shown. They are positively sloped to indicate that an increase in her consumption of smoke (good Z) reduces her utility. Therefore only an increase in the consumption of good X will keep her on the same indifference curve. An increase in Z must be matched by an increase in X to keep Amanda's utility constant along an indifference curve. (c) shows the production possibility frontier for goods X and Z. It is assumed to be linear.

only two consumers of X and Z, we can also show how much is produced of both goods in the different equilibrium solutions.

Figure 12.4 illustrates the possible solutions. We will derive an Edgeworth box for the case of smoke pollution. We start with the indifference map of George. We then want to combine that with the indifference map of Amanda. But smoke is a good consumed jointly by Amanda and George. The amount of smoke is thus like a public bad, except that in this case we have only two individuals. To reflect this, we must transform Amanda's indifference map. We plot on Amanda's indifference map a line that is the absolute value of the slope of the production possibility frontier. This is shown in Figure 12.4(a) as the line ab. We then treat the line ab as the Z origin for Amanda, and add to each of her indifference curves, at each level of smoke, the difference between the origin and the curve ab. Thus indifference curve IA_0 becomes IA_0', IA_1 becomes IA_1', and so on. This is a geometric device which combines the PPF with the indifference curves to allow for the optimal consumption of both goods when one of the goods being consumed is a public (jointly consumed) good.

We now flip Amanda's adjusted indifference map over so that the point a becomes the point a' in Figure 12.4(b). Amanda's origin is a', which means that her consumption of good X increases as she moves down the X axis shown in (b), while George's consumption of good X decreases as he moves down the axis. Any point on the X axis shows the division of the total amount of X produced between Amanda and George. We thus have consistency between production and consumption. Aggregate consumption by the individuals must add up to aggregate production. That is what the PPF does for us.

Now along the Z axis, whatever George picks as his optimal amount of smoke consumption also gets passed along to Amanda. In other words, smoke is determined by George, but jointly consumed by both parties. George will determine the amount of smoke he consumes by maximizing his utility. Given the prices of X and Z, and his income, George finds the highest indifference curve tangent to his budget constraint. Suppose George's budget constraint is given by the line BE. If George is free to maximize his utility without any smoking prohibitions, he will pick point A, where his budget constraint is tangent to indifference curve IG_2. He will consume $0Z_2$ units of smoke and $0X_2$ units of the other goods. What about poor Amanda? She is forced to also consume Z_2 units of smoke. George's smoking habit then becomes a constraint on her choice of the X goods.

We do not put in a budget constraint for Amanda to avoid clutter, but what she must do is find the highest indifference curve that intersects the amount of smoke Z_2 (and satisfies her budget constraint). Suppose this occurs on Amanda's indifference curve IA_1' (recall that these are Amanda's transformed indifference curves). Amanda then consumes Z_2 smoke and X_1X_2 of the X good. The amount of X Amanda consumes is determined by the PPF and George's smoking. At Z_2, $0X_2$ plus X_1X_2 sum to the point C on the PPF.

What are the characteristics of this equilibrium, and is it socially optimal? Notice that at point A, we are at an intersection of George's indifference curve IG_2 and Amanda's indifference curve IA_1'. We know from the analysis of ordinary goods that in a bilateral exchange situation where the parties are at the intersection of two indifference curves, each can be made better off by moving to a point that lies within

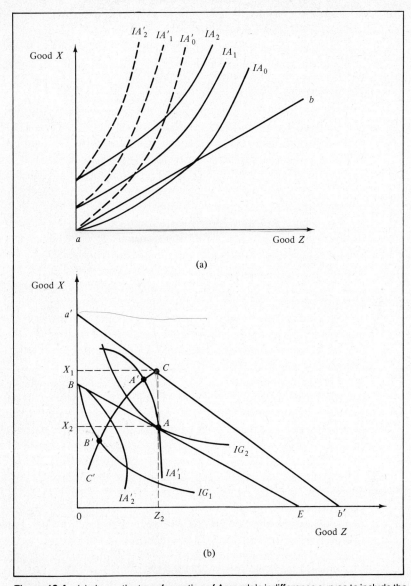

(a)

(b)

Figure 12.4 (a) shows the transformation of Amanda's indifference curves to include the absolute value of the marginal rate of transformation of X into Z. (b) shows two initial equilibriums before the parties bargain to a Pareto optimal equilibrium. If George has the property right to smoke, the initial equilibrium is at point A. Bargaining may then lead to an optimal equilibrium on the contract curve CC' at point A'. If Amanda has the right to clean air, the initial equilibrium will be at point B, while bargaining may take the parties to an optimal equilibrium at point B'. It is unlikely that the final Pareto optimal equilibrium will be the same regardless of who has the right to the air.

the boundary of the two indifference curves. The optimum occurs when the parties' indifference curves are tangent to one another. But because each one of Amanda's indifference curves reflect both her marginal rate of substitution *(MRS)* between X and Z and the marginal rate of transformation of X into Z, the optimality condition for this external diseconomy is that the *sum of the marginal rates of substitution for the parties equals the marginal rate of transformation.*

In the case of an ordinary good, the optimality condition is that each person's MRS is equal to others' MRSs and also equals the MRT. The MRSs must be summed in the case of the externality to incorporate the interdependencies among individuals. Recall also that there may be many such tangencies, the locus of which is the contract curve, which is shown here as CC'. The same sort of argument applies in this case. Could George and Amanda somehow get to a point where their indifference curves are tangent within the shaded area bounded by the indifference curves through point A? Yes. There are many possible methods of increasing at least one of the party's utilities without reducing the utility of the other. We will examine the methods after we note how the initial equilibrium would change if smoking were prohibited (Amanda had the property right to clean air).

If Amanda has the right to clean air, the initial equilibrium will be at a point along the X axis. That is, no smoke will be consumed at all. Amanda will choose the largest amount of X feasible, given her budget constraint. To make the graphic analysis simple, suppose this occurs at point B in Figure 12.4, which is also a point on George's budget constraint and one of his indifference curves (IG_1).[8] Again, the two individuals will not be consuming good X optimally because the equilibrium at point B is not on the contract curve CC'. Amanda is in a sense harming George because he is not allowed to smoke. The area of exchange that will make no one worse off and someone better off is the area between Amanda's indifference curve IA_2' and George's indifference curve IG_1. Notice that this area has no points in common with the area of trade when George had the property rights. We now want to show that it is most unlikely that the equilibrium will be the same regardless of who has the property right to the air. Let us reflect on this for a moment. The allocation of property rights affects what equilibrium results. If the property rights allocation is precise, the final equilibrium will be efficient in any case. So clarifying property rights has been proposed as a method of dealing with externalities. However, bargaining is generally involved in sorting out the final equilibrium once property rights have been assigned, and these bargaining or transactions costs can be relatively high.

Both George and Amanda realize that they could be made better off if they could negotiate to alter their consumption of X or Z and move to higher indifference curves. We cannot tell precisely where they will end up after this bargaining procedure without some very explicit information about their skills in bargaining, the intensity of their feelings about smoke, and so on. We make what are reasonable assumptions that the person with the property right will not agree to change from the initial equilibrium unless she or he is made better off. The party without the property right will not agree to a solution unless he or she is no worse off than in the initial equilibrium. If George has the right to smoke, the initial equilibrium is at point A. The best George can do is bargain to a position such as point A'. Amanda is no worse off than before. There is less smoke in total and George now has a greater amount of good X, while Amanda has less. If Amanda has the right to breathe clean air, the starting point is B, and the best Amanda can do by bargaining with George is to move to point B'. George is now allowed to smoke a little bit, and is no worse off than before. Amanda is better off because she has more of good X to compensate for the smoke she must now breathe. (Question: If Amanda derives infinite displeasure from smoke, is there an internal equilibrium possible from bargaining? What would Amanda's indifference curves look like in this case?)

Points A' and B' are on the contract curve and are thus socially optimal. Let's compare points A' and B'. The relative prices of X to Z are not identical at A' and B', nor is the quantity of the smoke consumed.[9] The property rights thus affect the final equilibrium. If the afflicted party has the right to clean air, we would expect to see less smoke in the final equilibrium and a higher implicit price of smoke pollution. If the party smoking has the right to pollute the air, we would expect to see more smoke and a lower implicit (exchange) price of smoke. It is possible that a common point could be obtained by bargaining under the different property rights and the same amount of smoke and good X observed in either case, but this seems unlikely. The common point under either assignment of rights would have to be where the individual with the property right gained nothing by bargaining. It is hard to imagine that people with an initial advantage would have any reason to accept a bargain that does not make them any better off.[10]

Suppose that instead of just one Amanda and one George, there were lots of Amandas and Georges. What would then happen to the bargaining solutions? The more pervasive the externality—the more people generating it and being afflicted by the smoke, the less likely a bargaining solution becomes. There are costs to bargaining (transaction costs) which make it difficult for this method of internalizing an externality to work. The transaction costs include costs of identifying the afflicted and generating parties (recall that who is afflicted and who is generating the externality differs depending on who has the right to the air). Then some sort of bargain must be worked out and long hours spent negotiating. The more public the externality, the less likely a bargaining solution, because the transaction costs would become quite high. We therefore consider means of internalizing the externality through government action.

Let's make the realistic assumption that the status quo or beginning situation is one in which smokers have been polluting the air. We are thus at a point such as A in Figure 12.4. Is there a tax the government can impose on smoking that internalizes the externality? Yes. The government could simply charge all smokers a unit tax on cigarettes equal to the afflicted parties' marginal disutility from the smoke—the reduction in their utility due to a marginal increase in smoke emitted. As long as smoker's demand for cigarettes was not perfectly inelastic, the tax would pivot the smokers' initial budget constraint down toward the origin. In Figure 12.5, one such tax causes the smoker's budget line to shift from BE to BE'.

George will maximize his utility subject to the new budget constraint (again without any regard for Amanda) and obtain point F. Now if the government has a lot of information—it knows individual's valuations of smoke and clean air—it will

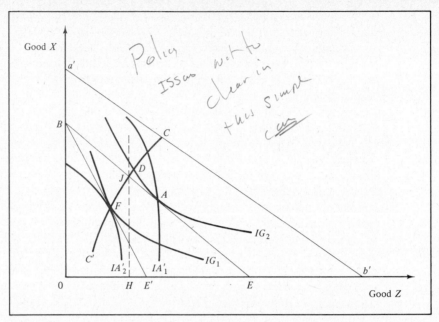

Policy Issues not to clear in this simple case

Figure 12.5 If the initial equilibrium is at point *A* where smokers are polluting the air, a tax that pivots smokers' budget constraints from *BE* to *BE'* will lead to an optimal amount of smoke at point *F*. At *F*, smokers' and nonsmokers' indifference curves are tangent, thus satisfying the condition for an efficient allocation of resources. But smokers are worse off. A lump sum subsidy that moves their budget constraint to a tangency at point *D* makes everyone better off than at point *A*. A standard that restricts smoke might achieve a Pareto optimal equilibrium. A standard at *OH* reduces the utility of smokers and increases that of nonsmokers.

pick a tax such that point *F* is on the contract curve. The tax will then yield an optimal amount of smoke and good *X*. Governments typically do not have such information, so there may have to be some trial and error in finding the optimal tax.

Notice, however, that at point *F*, George is worse off than he was before the tax was imposed. He has been forced on to a lower indifference curve from his starting position. Although the economy is on the contract curve, which means that the conditions for an efficient allocation of resources are met, smokers' real incomes have fallen because of the tax. If the government wishes to keep real incomes constant, it must then find a way to compensate smokers. A lump sum subsidy could be used. This means that smokers will get a fixed payment just equal to the loss of real income resulting from the tax. In terms of Figure 12.5, the government would have to give George a payment equal to the difference between his income at point *F* and his income at point *D*, where *D* is a tangency between George's original indifference curve and one of Amanda's indifference curves. *D* is a point on the contract curve. The subsidy would then give George a new budget constraint parallel to *BE'* and tangent to IG_2 at point *D* (we do not show this in Figure 12.5 to avoid clutter).

What is happening is that the tax changes the relative price of smoke to other goods, and then the subsidy shifts the new budget line of the smoker until a point is reached on the contract curve where the smoker is no worse off than in the starting position. There are many difficulties with this policy. First, there is no unique tax and subsidy solution. The contract curve shows all the Pareto optimal allocations, but does not determine a unique point. There is no practical way the government could ever pick a point on the contract curve that satisfies all individuals. The important point about the tax is that it changes the relative price of smoke to take into account the disutility it causes people. But taxes also affect incomes and may require some form of subsidy to prevent a loss in well-being.

What about a quantity control? Would it be simpler for the government simply to ban smoking or place a limit on the amount of smoke allowed in particular areas? If the government seeks the optimal quantity regulation or standard, it must have as much information as it had to have when trying to determine an optimal tax. A point on the contract curve should be chosen for efficiency, but again, which point is chosen depends on initial conditions and will affect the utilities and incomes of different parties. Unless the government picks a standard consistent with George's initial equilibrium (point A), the utility of the smoker will fall. Consider a standard set at OH in Figure 12.5. If the preregulation equilibrium was at point A and the government restricts smoke to OH, the budget constraint for the smoker becomes BJH. The smoker (George) will then be worse off because he can no longer reach indifference curve IG_2. The nonsmoker (Amanda) will be better off because she will be on a higher indifference curve than IA_1'. If J is a point on the contract curve (as illustrated), there will be little scope for bargaining. Neither person will have an incentive to move from this point.[11]

To reach any standard, the government would have to evaluate the marginal valuations for smoke and clean air by all affected individuals. There is no informational distinction between determining the optimal regulation or tax in the context of this model. However, there may be informational distinctions after the policies are implemented. Regulations must be monitored and enforced. How will the government know if the smoke levels are being kept to the amount OH unless it has machines that sample air quality? How will the regulation be enforced if violations of the standard occur? If the tax is used, smoke must also be monitored (to assess the tax payment), but there is no need to devise an enforcement scheme. Of course, this assumes that the optimal tax has been set initially and that no other exogenous events have appeared which alter the optimal solution. These assumptions are most unlikely. From an economist's viewpoint, then, the tax is typically a lower-cost device than a regulation. We will come back to these issues later and in Chapter 13.

always makes george worse off

Thus we have seen that:

1. When few parties are involved in the externality, bargaining can internalize the externality—that is, it can lead to an optimal solution.
2. The property right to the resource matters. The amount of pollution that exists after the externality is internalized is typically higher if the starting point for bargaining is polluted air than if the starting point is clean air.
3. The imposition of a tax on pollution can internalize the externality and obtain an optimal allocation of resources. But if the government wishes to keep real incomes constant, it must also subsidize those facing the tax.
4. Quantity restrictions on pollution can also optimally internalize an externality, but typically require higher costs of enforcement than the optimal tax.

Externalities in Production

We turn now to a case where the external diseconomy arises from the production processes of firms. Most types of pollution fall into this category. In the process of producing a good, waste products (effluents) are emitted into the atmosphere, waterways, or ground. Without any market valuation placed on these environmental resources, they will be used excessively as depositories of wastes. In the process, other agents—consumers and firms—may find that their activities are adversely affected by the emission of the industrial effluent. In this section, we focus on a two-firm example. One firm discharges its waste products into a lake. Another firm is also located on the lake and uses the water in its production process.

Suppose the Creative Chemical Company discharges the by-products from the production of its chemicals into the lake. The Agrigoods Company is also located on the lake and uses the water to irrigate its major crop—apples. We will abstract from all the problems of who located first on the lake and whether each party was familiar with the production technologies of the other at the time they located there.[12] Suppose, for simplicity, that both firms have been located on the lake for a long time and have coexisted without any external effects until Creative began production of a new chemical which created wastes that adversely affected the quality of the water and reduced the production of apples by Agriproducts.

We illustrate algebraically and graphically the effect of the chemical effluent on apple production, then discuss possible means of internalizing the externality. Let each firm's short-run production function be given by Equation (12.4):

$$Q^A = f(x,z)$$
$$Q^C = g(y) \tag{12.4}$$

where Q^A is the output of apples and Q^C is the output of chemicals, x is Agriproduct's use of its major input water, and y is the chemical company's major factor input, say chemical compounds.

We assume for simplicity that each firm needs only one variable input to produce its product. Both have fixed inputs (such as capital) which we are not concerned with, because this is a short-run model. The results would be fundamentally the same if multiple factor inputs were used, except if one of the inputs is some abatement technique that can reduce the amount of pollution emitted by the chemical company. The term z is the effluent from the chemical company. It enters into the production function of the apple company in the same way as a factor input. The difference between z and the x input is that an increase in z reduces the output of apples rather than increases it. Another way of saying this is that the partial derivative of A's production function with respect to z is negative. This is the external diseconomy. For an ordinary input, the change in output with respect to an increase in the use of an input would be positive. We assume that z is generated by the chemical company's use of input y. That is, z is some function (unspecified) of y, $z = h(y)$. The use and subsequent discharge into the lake of a particular compound in the production of chemicals is what adversely affects apple production.[13] The unpriced factor input in this case is the water. Neither the apple nor the chemical company pays anything for the use of the water.

The effects of the emission of chemical effluent are now shown. We will examine each firm's profits in a static framework and assume no other agents are affected. This means that we are dealing with a partial equilibrium model and a private externality. Each firm's profits are given by Equation (12.5):

$$\pi^A = P^A Q^A - wx$$
$$\pi^C = P^C Q^C - wy \qquad (12.5)$$

where P^A is the market price of apples, P^C the price of chemicals, and w the unit price of the factor inputs x and y. We assume that the inputs x and y are available in infinitely elastic supply, and thus w is a constant. We also assume that apple and chemical input prices are identical. This assumption does not affect the results; it just simplifies notation. We then substitute each firm's production function, given by Equation (12.4), into Equation (12.5). This yields Equation (12.6):

$$\pi_A = P^A[f(x,z)] - wx$$
$$\pi_C = P^C[g(y)] - wy \qquad (12.6)$$

Each firm then maximizes its profits independently of the other firm. For a profit maximum for each firm, we know that[14]

$$P^A f_X - w = 0$$
$$P^C g_Y - w = 0 \qquad (12.7)$$

where f_X is $\partial f/\partial x$ and g_X is $\partial g/\partial y$. In Equation (12.7), the first term is the value of the marginal product of the factor input (x or y). Each factor input must thus be chosen so that the value of its marginal product is equal to the factor's marginal cost, which in this case is w. This is the normal condition for a profit maximum found in any industry. But there is a difference in this case: For the apple company, the marginal product of its input x also depends on the presence of z, the chemical effluent, where z in turn depends on the chemical firm's use of y. This means that the two firms are not independent of one another. When each firm maximizes its profits independent of the other firm, apple profits will not be at the highest level possible.

To see this, we note that in equilibrium, the change in profits with respect to a change in input use must be zero. This is what Equation (12.7) requires. While this will be true for the chemical company, it will not be the case for the apple company. Whenever the chemical company increases its use of factor y even a small amount, apple profits are reduced. Apple profits fall because either more water must be used to compensate for the decline in its quality, or apple production is reduced due to the lower water quality. A marginal change in the use of factor y does have an effect on the apple producer. But for an efficient allocation of resources, a small change in y should not have an effect. The externality arises because the profits of A and C combined fall whenever y is increased (and conversely when y is decreased). An efficient use of inputs requires that there be no change in the profits of *both* companies with a very small change in the use of each factor input. To reach an efficient solution, the companies must *jointly* maximize their profits.

We now compare the equilibrium obtained above to a socially optimal equilibrium where the firms take into account the effect of the effluent, z, on the output of Agrigoods. To determine the efficient use of inputs, we must jointly maximize the profits of the two firms. This is the appropriate means of determining the optimal use of inputs for each firm because it accounts for the interdependence between them. The combined profits of the two firms are then given by Equation (12.8):

$$\pi_{A+C} = P^A f[x, h(y)] + P^C g(y) - w(x + y) \tag{12.8}$$

where we have now substituted for the relationship between chemical effluent, z, and the chemical firm's use of the input y. Equation (12.8) is maximized with respect to both x and y (by differentiating with respect to x and y). The resulting conditions for a profit maximum are given by Equation (12.9):

$$P^A f_X - w = 0$$
$$P^A[(\partial f/\partial h)(\partial h/\partial y)] + P^C g_Y - w = 0 \tag{12.9}$$

We now want to compare Equation (12.9) to (12.7). The first equation in (12.7) and (12.9) is identical. The value of the marginal product of input x is still equated to its marginal cost, as seen in the first equations of 12.7 and 12.9. But the second equations differ due to the presence of the term $P^A[(\partial f/\partial h)(\partial h/\partial y)]$. This is the value of the marginal damage done to the apple company by the chemical company's use of input y. It measures the reduction in output of apples resulting from a marginal increase in the use of y, which of course leads to an increase in pollution, z. The term in the expression, $\partial h/\partial y$, shows how much pollution results from a small increase in y (a positive amount), while $\partial f/\partial h$ shows how the pollution affects apple production (a negative amount). These terms are valued at the market price of apples, and the expression is negative.

Equation (12.9) says that the value of the marginal product of factor y net of the value of the marginal damage done by factor y should be set equal to its marginal cost, w. When the chemical company does not take into account the damage created by its production process, too much y is used. The efficient solution requires that y be reduced. Assuming both firms operate in competitive product and factor markets, and using consumer surplus as a measure of social welfare, we can then say that the socially optimal amount of pollution requires that the marginal damage done by the chemical company be taken into account in its determination of the amount of input y to use in its production process. With the aid of a graph, we will now investigate methods of internalizing this externality.

Figure 12.6 illustrates the private market solution before any interdependencies among the two firms are recognized, and the social optimum. The diagram presented is commonly used in the analysis of externalities, but it must be interpreted with care. The curves drawn have particular meanings that correspond to the algebra we have just presented. Their shapes in actual externality cases might be quite different from the ones shown here. Recall as well that this is a partial equilibrium analysis.

In Figure 12.6, we have drawn the change in each firm's profits as the chemical firm increases the amount of input y it uses in the production of chemicals. The curve MB is the value of the marginal product of input y net of its marginal cost, as presented in Equation (12.9). The curve MD is the value of the marginal damage to the apple company that results from C's use of input y, and it reflects the first term in the second equation of (12.9). We have drawn the MB as negatively sloped. This is a reasonable assumption, because a variable factor input typically has a diminishing

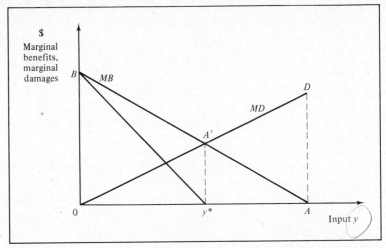

Figure 12.6 The chemical firm maximizes its profits independently of the apple firm where the marginal benefits from the use of input y are equal to zero at point A. The apple firm suffers from damages AD. Internalization of the externality requires that the marginal damages be equated to marginal benefits. This occurs at point A' with y^* of the input. Bargaining, a tax which shifts the MB curve from BA to By^*, or a quota restricting the use of input y to the amount Oy^*, will internalize the externality.

marginal product as its use increases. The MD function is positively sloped, which indicates that marginal damages rise as greater amounts of y are used by the chemical company.

Most empirical studies of the effects of various effluents on production and consumption activities lend some support to the shape shown. Typically, when the use of the factor responsible for the effluent increases, so does the effluent, and as the effluent increases, so does the damage at the margin. Both the MB and the MD curves are drawn as linear functions of y. This is simply for convenience. Later we will look at the effects of different shapes of these functions on the determination of the optimal amount of the externality-causing input.

In Figure 12.6, we examine the choice of input y from the viewpoint of the chemical company, because it is the firm that controls the amount of pollution which will be emitted in a private market setting. If the chemical company does not take into account the effect its production process has on the apple company, it will simply set the net value of the marginal product of y equal to zero. That is, it will satisfy the second equation in (12.7). The equilibrium occurs at point A in Figure 12.6, where the MB equals zero. We can tell by looking at the figure that this is not a social optimum, because at point A the apple firm incurs a marginal damage equal to the amount AD. The total value of the input to the chemical firm is given by the triangle OAB, while the total damages to the apple company are shown by the triangle OAD.

To achieve the optimal use of input y requires that both the benefits to the chemical company and damages to the apple firm be taken into account. The net gain to society will be the greatest where the marginal benefits to C equal the marginal damages to A. This occurs where the MB curve intersects the MD curve at point A'. The optimal amount of input y to use in the chemical company is thus y^*, not A. We can also see in this graph that the net benefits to society from the use of input y are the largest at point y^*. The chemical company loses total benefits (the value of the output) equal to the area y^*AA', but the apple company gains the amount (in terms of increased value of output) y^*ADA'. The gain to A exceeds the loss to C. Thus net benefits are maximized and equal ADA'. Because social welfare is measured by the consumer surplus from the consumption of both apple and chemical products, we are not concerned at this point about the distribution of the gains and losses among the companies. It is clear from our analysis above that if the chemical company is forced somehow to reduce its use of y without compensation, it will be worse off than in an unregulated situation.

There are some important points to note. First, the optimum is reached where *marginal benefits* and *marginal damages* are equated. That means that in designing methods of achieving the optimum, we must know the shape of the MB and MD curves. Second, the *optimal amount of pollution is not equal to zero.* Because the optimal amount of input y is positive, the apple company will still have its production process affected by the chemical company's effluent. The effluent will be reduced, but not to zero. Again this follows from the shape of our MB and MD functions. Both companies have outputs that are valued positively by society. Social welfare would fall if chemical production ceased. Under what conditions would the optimal use of y be zero? In this analysis, that would occur if the MD curve intersected the MB curve at point B. Think about what would happen to the optimal amount of y if the price of apples increased, the price of chemicals increased, or the pollution per unit of input y fell (due, say, to a technological change). Try shifting the curves and determining the new equilibrium (see the problems for this chapter).

Income Distribution Dimensions of Internalizing Externalities

We have focused on replacing inefficient equilibriums involving externalities with efficient outcomes. As we have noted before, improvements in the economy are associated with more goods and services so that all members of society can gain in theory, but some may gain more than others in practice. For example, abating noise pollution along an urban freeway with baffles may cost all residents a small amount, but will benefit those who live near the freeway much more than those who live away from the road. Virtually every outcome from "solving" externalities has these distributions of real income dimensions. Compensation of losers may be in order. If pollution controls make a plant unprofitable and yet the benefits from a reduction in pollution levels outweigh the loss of output from the plant, compensation to the workers and owners of the plant makes sense. We have discussed these matters in Chapter 1 and will return to them in Chapter 14, where we focus on government and natural resource use.

Alternative Pollution Control Mechanisms

We will look at two basic methods of internalizing this externality: market mechanisms and government regulation of some sort. While all are capable of achieving the social optimum in theory, there may be reasons in practice why some types of regulation are more likely to succeed in optimally internalizing the externality than others. We begin with the market mechanisms.

Perhaps the simplest way of internalizing the externality conceptually is for the two companies to *merge*. One company purchases the assets of the other company and then has the power to control the operations of both divisions. This is called *unitization*. The optimum will be reached because the company will now maximize profits jointly, using the objective function presented in Equation (12.8). As long as all markets remain competitive, merger yields the optimal use of both factor inputs, x and y, and the optimal amount of pollution, z. The new company then automatically equates MB to MD to achieve the optimal y^*. It is possible that one operation would be shut down. If, say, the marginal damage done to apple production is so large that it swamps the value of the marginal product of factors producing chemicals, then the company may cease chemical production if no effective means of controlling chemical wastes exists. Recall that we have not introduced methods of *abating* the discharge of effluent. There may be techniques that reduce the amount of effluent discharged (waste treatment plants for chemical effluents or scrubbers which remove particulates and sulfur oxides from power plants, smelters, and other manufacturing processes). If it is cheaper to use the abatement technology than to control inputs causing pollution or shut down operations adversely affected by the pollution, the company will use these techniques.

The advantages of merger are that it is done through market mechanisms. No costly regulatory process is required to impose restrictions on the polluter, no compensation of the afflicted party is necessary, no monitoring of pollution required, and so on. There are, however, numerous difficulties. First, merger may reduce the degree of competition in the economy, which in turn may reduce consumer welfare. Second, if the externality "spills over" and affects other economic agents, merger of the two companies will not result in an optimal internalization of the externality for the bystanders. For example, people who use the lake for recreational purposes are not likely to find the marginal damage function of the apple division of the new company exactly the same as their personal marginal damage function resulting from the chemical division's use of the lake as a waste depository. If the marginal damage functions are not identical for all agents, merger between the generating party (the chemical company) and *one* of the afflicted parties (the apple company) will not lead to the optimal amount of pollution except by accident. Thus the more "public" the externality, the less likely is merger as a means of optimally internalizing the externality. Finally, there may be financial and legal impediments to merger that limit its use in controlling pollution in actual situations.

There is another general "market" solution — a series of negotiations and side payments between the agents involved. The apple company may simply offer the chemical company a payment to reduce the use of input y. If the payment is equal to the value of the lost production from using less of input y, the chemical company will accept. In terms of Figure 12.6, if the apple company offers a payment equal to the area y^*AA', the chemical company will reduce its use of input y from the amount A to the amount y^*, and we again see an optimal outcome. If both companies know their own MB and MD curves, this sort of "bargaining" can lead to the social optimum. The apple company will continue to offer payments as long as the value of the reduction in its marginal damages exceeds the payment. The chemical company will accept payment as long as the payment exceeds the foregone value of the marginal product of factor y not used. The values of the MB and MD curves coincide at point A'.

In theory, the chemical company could also offer the apple firm compensation for the damage inflicted by its effluent. But this is most unlikely in an unregulated environment. If the chemical company has been dumping its waste products into the lake, the company implicitly or explicitly has the property right to use the lake as a disposal site. The existence of the pollution means that the status quo or starting point is that the chemical company has the right to pollute. Why would the chemical company *voluntarily* make a payment to the apple firm to compensate for the value of the apple firm's lost production? We dealt with this issue in the case of the consumption externality and argued there that the original distribution of property rights would affect the equilibrium as long as income effects were included in the calculation. The same sort of argument applies in the case of the two firms. There is no reason to expect that the equilibriums are identical regardless of the initial possession of property rights, because firms' profits will differ depending on who has the rights. Whichever equilibrium is achieved after the externality is internalized by bargaining will be efficient. (This basic insight is called the Coase theorem, named for Professor R. Coase of the University of Chicago.)

These "bargaining" solutions involve no government intervention: Individual agents simply negotiate until a mutually agreeable solution is found. Bargaining thus has advantages similar to those of merger. When few agents are involved, it is a plausible means of internalizing the externality. However, as with merger, when the externality becomes more "public" in nature, bargaining generally will not internalize the externality. If large numbers of agents are affected and the external effects are nonappropriable, bargaining becomes extremely costly and generally unfeasible. If, say, we are talking about air pollution that comes from many different sources and affects many different people, it is hard to imagine them getting together and coming to some agreement. Could all the emitters and consumers of air pollution in Los Angeles County (millions of people) even find the means of negotiating, let alone agree on some form of payment? In the two-firm case above, it is quite likely that some sort of agreement would be reached. But cases like this one are rare. Indeed, one would not expect to observe them because the externality would already be internalized. This is the situation in which those who claim that "all meaningful externalities that can be internalized" are accurate. If all externalities were private, we'd expect some form of market mechanism to emerge that internalizes them. But the more pervasive and public the externality, the less able markets are to deal with them.

We turn now to methods governments can use to internalize the two-firm externality in production. As is usually the case, the government has two basic policies at its disposal—taxes and quantity controls (and combinations of these policies). While taxes, if set correctly, guarantee that the optimum will be reached, they are rarely used.[15] Quantity controls can also reach the optimum, but may lead to some inefficiencies. A tax can be levied on the polluting firm in two ways. In the case of the apple and chemical firms, we assumed that the pollution flows from the use of input y through some sort of technological relationship between input y and pollution z (the h function). Either pollution itself or input y could be taxed. From the conditions for a social optimum given by Equation (12.9), this means that the optimal tax on pollution would be equal to $P^A(\partial f/\partial h)$ while the optimal tax on input y would be $P^A[(\partial f/\partial h)(\partial h/\partial y)]$. In Figure 12.6, an optimal tax on y pivots the MB curve from BA to By^*.[16] The chemical firm maximizes its profits subject to the tax and sets the value of the marginal product of input y net of the tax equal to zero. This occurs at y^*, the optimal amount of the input. It is important to note that these taxes must be evaluated at the optimum. Not just any measure of marginal damage works, only that measured at point y^*. What this means is that the government must know the precise equation for *both* the marginal damage and marginal benefit functions.

A quantity control that yields the optimal amount of pollution is also easily shown in Figure 12.6. Again, the government must know the equations for the marginal damage and marginal benefit functions. The optimal amount of the input causing the pollution is then calculated, and a restriction on the use of this input is imposed. In the example above, chemical firms would be prevented from using more than the amount y^* of input y. Alternatively, the government could restrict emissions of the effluent generated by input y. To do this, it must then also know the functional relationship between input y and pollution z [the function we called $z = h(y)$]. In practice, regulations that restrict the use of pollution-causing inputs and the pollution itself are the most common forms of government control of externalities. But as we will see in the next chapter, these forms of regulation are difficult and very costly to impose and enforce. There is no guarantee that the quantity restrictions imposed are in any way related to the socially optimal amount of pollution.

We postpone a discussion of the practical problems associated with quantity restrictions to Chapter 13 and turn now to some additional topics in pollution control: when it is best to use taxes, subsidies, and standards to internalize the externality pollution.

BOX 12.2
Productivity Slowdown: A Cost of Environmental Regulations?

The costs of controlling pollution include the direct outlays firms must make to abate pollution, the expenses involved in operating government environmental departments and monitoring emissions, and the impact of regulations on the economy's ability to produce goods and services over time. The research and development (R&D) activity of firms directed toward meeting environmental regulations may reduce the growth of measured productivity of labor and factor inputs taken as a whole.

In a 1982 study that examines the relationship between R&D expenditures and productivity growth in the United States, Link found that R&D expenditures for environmental control reduced the total productivity of factor inputs in a survey of 97 manufacturing firms in industries active in environmentally related R&D. Link estimated an equation derived from a Cobb-Douglas production function relating total factor productivity *(TFP)* to R&D ex-

Box 12.2 continued

penditures on pollution abatement per unit output (RD_E/Y) and other "traditional" R&D expenditures per unit of output $(RD_T Y)$, and an index of industry unionization *(U)*. For the 97 firms taken as a whole, the estimated equation was (*t*-statistics shown in parentheses):

$$TFP = .062 \quad - 1.22 \, (RD_E/Y) + .538 \, (RD_T/Y) - .092 \, U$$
$$(3.01) \, (-1.72) \qquad\qquad (2.87) \qquad\qquad (-1.90)$$
$$R^2 = .389$$

The intercept in the equation is interpreted as the marginal product of technical capital. The coefficient on traditional R&D expenditures is positive, as was the expected sign in R&D studies done in the 1960s, before environmental regulations were a significant cost to firms. The coefficient is significant at the 1 percent level. Pollution R&D has a negative effect on productivity, but is only weakly significant (at the 10 percent level of a two-tailed test). The inclusion of environmental R&D expenses that negatively affect productivity growth appear to be offsetting the positive effect obtained from traditional R&D expenses.

These results are important. Previous studies that attempted to examine the slowdown in productivity that has occurred in the United States in the 1970s suggested that R&D expenditures were no longer having a significant effect on economic growth. Link's results suggest that what constitutes R&D has changed. Environmental expenses were very small in the 1960s, but not in the 1970s. A study by the Industrial Research Institute cited by Link estimated that R&D expenses for environmental improvements grew at an average annual rate of 15.4 percent between 1974 and 1977, while total R&D expenditures grew at 9.4 percent over the same period. It is the change in the composition of R&D rather than the total amount of R&D expenses that could be an important cause of the productivity slowdown. One cost of environmental regulation may thus be less economic growth. This cost must be added to other costs of pollution control when determining the optimal amount of pollution.

Source: A. Link, "Productivity Growth, Environmental Regulations and the Composition of R&D." *Bell Journal of Economics* 13, (1982), pp. 548–554.

TOPICS IN THE THEORY OF ENVIRONMENTAL CONTROLS

In this section, we cover two additional topics. First, we consider whether subsidies to polluters to reduce their emissions will yield the socially optimal amount of pollution compared to an equivalent tax. Second, we examine what happens when the government cannot determine the optimal tax because it lacks information about the nature of the marginal benefit or marginal damages from pollution. We see when quantity restrictions (standards) would be the preferred policy and when some combination of taxes and standards is indicated. This topic is of practical appeal, because until very recently most regulations were in the form of standards—limitations on the emissions of pollution.

Taxes versus Subsidies

To internalize an externality, a tax on pollution (or the factor responsible for the pollution) must be set equal to the marginal damage caused by the pollution at the point where marginal damages equal marginal benefits. However, suppose those responsible for the pollution were simply offered a subsidy for each unit of effluent removed from the environment? Wouldn't this sort of subsidy also internalize the externality? No. Subsidies, even if equivalent to taxes on the margin, will not yield the socially optimal amount of pollution. We can show why with a simple model.

To show the difference between taxes and subsidies, we must be careful to distinguish between their effects on the firm versus their effects on the industry as a whole. This is the key to the difference between the two forms of pollution control. We will continue to assume that the pollution affects only two particular sectors of the economy—say the chemical industry and apple growers. We maintain our partial equilibrium model. We begin with the firm: Suppose each firm in the chemical industry produces z units of pollution for each unit of chemical output produced. We now drop the relationship between a particular input and pollution output for simplicity, and assume there is always a fixed proportion between output q and pollution z. The pollution adversely affects apple firms, as in the previous section. We assume that a large number of chemical and apple firms are involved and that they are dispersed throughout the country. Merger and bargaining solutions to the pollution problem are thus not feasible by assumption.

The federal government seeks the socially optimal amount of pollution. The government first evaluates the effect on each chemical firm and the chemical industry of a tax set at rate t on each unit of pollution (where the tax rate is determined by the marginal damages to apple growers from the pollution). For simplicity, we assume that the chemical industry is perfectly competitive and faces a constant price p for each unit of output produced. We also assume that the total costs of producing the chemical product are given by the function $c(q)$. Then $\partial c / \partial q$ is marginal cost, which is denoted by c'. For now, we assume that the only way the firm can reduce the amount of pollution it emits is by producing fewer units of output. We later consider the possibility that the firm can invest in abatement technologies.

Each chemical company will maximize its profits subject to the tax. The after-tax profits, $\hat{\pi}$, for each chemical firm are given by Equation (12.10):

$$\hat{\pi} = pq - c(q) - tzq \tag{12.10}$$

Maximization of Equation (12.10) yields the following condition for a profit maximum: $p - c' - tz = 0$. This condition says that the firm will equate price of each unit of chemicals *net of* the *marginal* tax payments on each unit of output to marginal cost c'. This is precisely the result we obtained above.

Alternatively, suppose the government considers a subsidy to polluters who abate. The subsidy would work in the following way. The government must first pick a benchmark amount of pollution, call it Z. This is the level of emissions of each firm where no subsidy is paid—a maximum level. The government then offers to pay each firm amount s for *each unit* of pollution it emits below the benchmark. That is, the subsidy takes the form $s(Z - z)$. If the firm emits Z or more units of pollution, it receives no subsidy. If it emits less than Z, it receives a subsidy of s dollars times the difference between Z and z. Thus we see already one small initial difference between the tax and the subsidy—the government must set both the rate of subsidy and the benchmark level, whereas only the tax rate need be determined in the other case.

When faced with the subsidy, the chemical firm will maximize its profits taking the subsidy into account. If the firm does not reduce its pollution emissions, the subsidy becomes an opportunity cost—what the firm foregoes by not reducing its pollution. The profits for the firm are given by Equation (12.12):

$$\tilde{\pi} = pq - c(q) + s(Z - z)q \tag{12.12}$$

Profits are maximized where $p - c' + s(Z - z) = 0$—that is where price *plus* the subsidy payment for each marginal unit of pollution reduced is equal to marginal cost. Now if the tax rate t is equal to the subsidy rate s, the two government policies have *exactly the same effect on the margin.* Each firm is indifferent on the margin between the tax and the subsidy because the opportunity cost to the firm is the same. If pollution increases by 1 unit, the firm either pays the tax or does not receive the subsidy—the revenue foregone is exactly the same. What is the difference between the two policies? The tax and the subsidy have quite different effects on the incentives for firms to enter and exit from the industry, as we will see.

In Figure 12.7 we illustrate the effects of the tax versus the subsidy. In (a), the

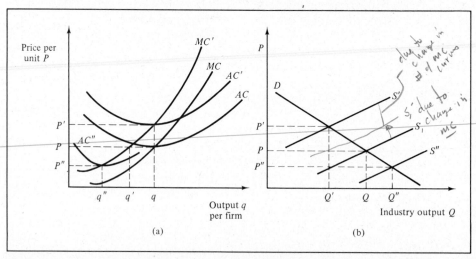

Figure 12.7   Both a tax and subsidy set at the same rate will reduce the output of a firm in the short run, because both policies shift the marginal cost curve from MC to MC'. A reduction in output from q to q' results in a reduction in pollution. In the long run, the tax will lead to exit from the industry because at price P, firms cannot cover their average costs AC', which have risen due to the tax. The supply curve in (b) for the industry shifts from S to S'. The subsidy lowers average costs to AC''. In the long run, firms will then enter the industry. The industry supply curve would shift to S''. Industry output and aggregate pollution thus falls with the tax and rises with the subsidy.

effects are shown for each firm in the industry, while in (b), the effects on the industry supply curve are represented. Suppose each firm is initially in a long-run equilibrium with price equal to marginal cost at the minimum of the average cost curve AC. Initial output of the firm is q and price is P in Figure 12.7(a). In (b), we show the market equilibrium where aggregate supply equals aggregate demand for the good in question at price P. Total industry output is Q. The government then imposes a tax on pollution at rate t per unit of pollution emitted. The tax will shift up *both* the average and the marginal cost curves of each firm to, say, AC' and MC'. The output of each firm will fall *in the short run* to q', where MC' is equal to the market clearing price of P.

What are the *long-run* effects of the tax? Note that in (a), average costs, AC', exceed the price, P. Firms thus incur a loss for each unit of the good sold. Over time, then, some of the firms must exit from the industry as their capital is depreciated.[17] Exit is shown in (b) by the leftward shift of the industry supply curve from S to S'. A new long-run market equilibrium will be established at price P' with an aggregate output of Q'. At P', firms remaining in the industry are again in a long-run equilibrium. Thus, the effect of the tax in the long run is *to reduce the aggregate amount of pollution from the industry because the number of firms has fallen.* We don't know if in the long run pollution per firm falls unless we specify the precise position of the AC' and MC' curves. As illustrated, pollution per firm remains the same. But it is possible for pollution per firm to rise or fall, depending on the shape and location of the AC curve.

Suppose now that a subsidy is granted to firms that reduce their pollution emissions below the established benchmark. The unit subsidy rate s is assumed equal to the tax rate t. Each firm will again see its *marginal cost* curve shift up to MC'. The marginal cost curve shifts by the same amount as with the tax because for each unit of additional output produced, the firm foregoes a subsidy identical to the tax payment under the alternative scheme. But the *average cost* curve of each firm shifts down to AC'' because the firm will receive compensation if output and hence pollution is lowered. Thus costs, on average, fall. The *short-run* equilibrium will again be where price is equal to marginal cost. This again occurs at an output level of q' for the firm. The effect of the subsidy on the output of the firm is *exactly the same* as that of the tax in the short run. But notice that the firm will now earn an *excess profit* with the subsidy; average costs are less than the price. This is a signal for *entry* into a competitive industry. The effect of the entry is shown in Figure 12.7(b).

Over time, as new firms enter the industry (and receive their subsidies for polluting less than the benchmark), the industry supply curve shifts to the right to S''. If the demand curve does not shift, the new industry equilibrium will occur at a price P'' and aggregate output Q''. The price falls from its initial level at P to P'', where zero profits are obtained for each firm and the long-run equilibrium is established. At this long-run equilibrium, the effect of the subsidy is to increase the amount of pollution. This occurs because although pollution per firm may fall to q'', as shown in (a), the total number of firms in the industry has risen.

The effect of the subsidy is thus counterproductive to the policy seeking a reduction in emissions of pollutants. Note as well that the subsidy may allow firms that are unprofitable to remain in the industry. Suppose a firm had average costs slightly above that given by *AC*. The subsidy may then reduce these average costs so that the firm can stay in business. Eventually these inefficient firms will be driven out by efficient (lower cost) firms, but the process may take some time. No such incentive for inefficient firms to remain in the industry exists with the tax.

There are some qualifications that must be made. First, the model is in partial equilibrium. If we allow for effects to spill over into other markets (factor and goods markets), the strong distinction between the effect of the tax versus the subsidy on aggregate pollution weakens.[18] Almost anything can happen in a general equilibrium model under particular assumptions about factor proportions and elasticities.

It is also unlikely that the government would introduce a subsidy in the precise form we assumed above. In our model, any firm that reduces pollution below the benchmark receives the subsidy, whether it is an existing firm or a new entrant. In practice, it is doubtful that the government would allow the new entrant to receive the subsidy. Actual subsidies are generally tied to the use of particular equipment that reduces pollution emissions.

We have also ignored the possibility that firms can reduce emissions of pollutants by introducing abatement technologies. Will the tax and subsidy be equivalent if they are based on abatement equipment rather than pollution emissions? We cannot say for sure without more careful analysis. Subsidies will generally allow more firms to remain in the industry than would a tax. If the relationship between pollution emitted and abatement capital installed is the same for each firm, then again we would expect more pollution under the subsidy. Thus the tax remains the preferred policy to achieve both a reduction in pollution and an efficient use of resources.

But it is unlikely that the government could ever implement an optimal tax, simply because the information requirements to determine such a tax are quite high. We do not know the shape of the marginal damage function with any degree of confidence. Nor do we know the shape of the marginal benefit function. If the government must guess at the appropriate tax rate, it may indeed reduce rather than increase social welfare and end up with quite undesirable amounts of pollution. We turn now to a brief discussion of taxes versus quantity controls or standards under conditions of uncertainty.

Taxes versus Standards

Let's return to the case of a single firm that emits a pollutant as a result of the use of a particular input. We drew in Figure 12.6 a marginal benefit *(MB)* curve which measured the value to the firm of using the input that generated the pollution. The curve was downward-sloping because it represented the value of the marginal product of the input. In this section, we assume that for each unit of the input used, one unit of pollution is emitted. We will therefore talk about the firm's emission of pollutants rather than its use of the factor input. We do this because pollution regulations often refer to individual pollutants rather than the inputs responsible for the pollutants. We continue to assume that the *MB* function is linear, as is the marginal damage function *(MD)*, which measures the damages done by each additional unit of pollution emitted.[19]

Suppose now that the government agency responsible for pollution control is trying to estimate this *MB* curve so that an optimal tax or standard can be calculated. Although the firm knows its own *MB* curve, the government does not. The government is uncertain about the location of the *MB* curve for the firm. The government makes an estimate of the expected marginal benefit curve, which in general will not be the actual curve, except by chance. For simplicity, we assume that the government is able accurately to measure the marginal damages *(MD)* from pollution. While this assumption is not realistic, it will not alter the fundamental results.

Figure 12.8 illustrates a case in which the government *underestimates* the marginal benefits of pollution to the firm, and what will happen in this case with the imposition of a tax or a standard set at the wrong level. Suppose the government's estimate of the marginal benefit of pollution to the firm is *MB*. Marginal damages are given by *MD*. The government then equates *MB* to *MD* to determine what it thinks is the optimal amount of pollution. The *MB* curve intersects the *MD* curve at an emission level of *Z* pollution. To obtain *Z* units of pollution, the government can impose a tax equal to 0*t* per unit of pollution emitted, or it can simply implement a standard that restricts emissions to *Z*. If the actual marginal benefit curve were *MB*, the two policies would be equivalent.

Suppose, however, that the actual marginal benefit curve were *MB'*, which lies everywhere above *MB*. That is, the government's estimate of the value of pollution to the firm is less than the actual value. Both the tax and the standard will then lead to nonoptimal amounts of pollution, but the amount of pollution will no longer be the same for each policy. The optimal amount of pollution is *Z**. With the standard set at *Z*, there will, of course, be no more than 0*Z* units of pollution emitted regardless of

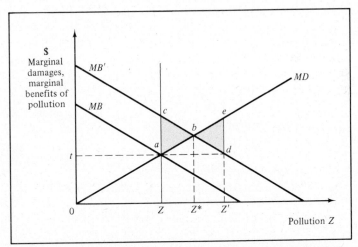

Figure 12.8 If the government estimates the marginal benefit of pollution (*MB*) to be *MB* but the true curve is *MB'*, both a standard and a tax will lead to an inefficient amount of pollution. A standard based on *MB* and set at *Z* leads to too little pollution and an efficiency loss equal to the area *abc*. A tax set at 0*t* leads to too much pollution (*Z'* rather than the optimal *Z**) and an efficiency loss of *bde*.

where the actual *MB* curve is. However, there will be a social or efficiency loss equal to the foregone benefits to the firm (the producer surplus) because *too little* pollution is emitted compared to the optimum. The cost to society of these foregone benefits is the triangle labeled *abc.* These net costs are the difference between the foregone value of production from the firm emitting pollution net of the reduction in damages due to the lower amount of pollution.

What then is the effect of the tax, which is still set at 0*t*? The firm will equate the tax to its actual marginal benefit curve and emit 0*Z'* units of pollution. *Too much* pollution is now emitted: Those who are harmed by pollution now lose, because pollution exceeds the optimal level. The value of the additional damage done by the pollution (foregone benefits of pollution abatement or loss in consumer surplus) is equal to the triangle *bde.* (Note that similar results would occur if the government were uncertain about the location and shape of the *MD* function.)

What is the government to do when faced with uncertainty in its measurement of the *MB* function? Is it better to use a tax or a standard? In general, the government should choose the policy that minimizes the expected efficiency loss — the policy that minimizes the sum of the triangles over all possible realizations of the *MB* (or *MD*) curves. We will look at particular examples where one policy is preferred over the other.

Consider Figure 12.9. In Figure 12.9(a), we have an *MB* function that is *flatter* (in absolute value) than the *MD* function. Let's compare the effects of the tax and standard when they are set at a nonoptimal level. Suppose the actual marginal benefits of pollution are *MB'*, but the government has calculated them as *MB*. The

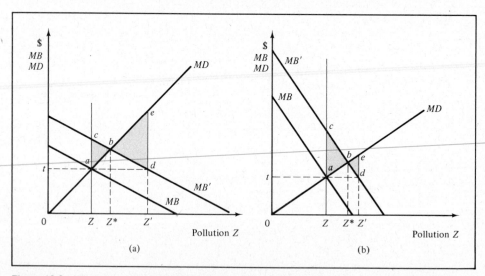

Figure 12.9   When the government does not know the location of the marginal benefit of pollution curve (*MB*) but it does know the slope of the *MB* curve relative to the marginal damage curve (*MD*), it can find the policy that minimizes the expected efficiency losses due to uncertainty about the *MB* curve. If the *MB* curve is flatter (in absolute value) than the *MD* curve as in (a), the standard minimizes the expected losses. The pollution emissions are closer to the optimum and the efficiency losses are smaller than if a tax is used. If the absolute value of the slope of the *MB* function exceeds that of the *MD* function, the tax policy will minimize the expected losses from miscalculating marginal benefits.

tax is then set at $0t$ or the standard at Z. Under the standard, the firm will emit slightly less pollution than is optimal (Z versus Z^*), and the efficiency loss will be the small triangle abc. With the tax, the firm will emit far more pollution than is optimal (Z' versus Z^*), which results in a large efficiency loss of bde. Thus, if the MB function is flatter than the MD function, a standard is the preferred second-best policy because it minimizes the efficiency loss resulting from the nonoptimal policy. Note that the government's uncertainty about the MB function must be in its location rather than its slope. If the government knows neither the location nor the slope of the MB function relative to the MD function, even these second-best policies become extremely tenuous.

The second-best policy is reversed when the slope of the MB function is steeper than that of the MD function. Figure 12.9(b) illustrates this case. Again, suppose the optimal amount of pollution is Z^*, where the actual marginal benefit curve MB' equals the MD curve. The government has estimated the marginal benefit curve as MB and thus implements either a tax of $0t$ or a standard of Z. Under the standard, the actual level of pollution will be far below the optimum, and the efficiency loss will now be quite high (triangle abc). Under the tax, pollution will be slightly above the optimum, and the efficiency loss will be relatively small (triangle bde). A tax would then be the preferred second-best policy because it minimizes the expected efficiency loss.

Obviously, actual pollution cases will not be as simple as the examples presented here. Our model contains linear and continuous functions, models uncertainty very simply, has pollution damages well defined, and examines the behavior of one firm. If the firm is operating in a competitive market, increasing the number of firms presents no difficulty; the basic results are the same. Noncompetitive markets would require the use of game theoretic models—a topic beyond the scope of this chapter. We will not go into more complex models of uncertainty at this point, but will examine what happens to the results when the functions are no longer continuous because threshold effects are present.

Figure 12.10 illustrates a case where a threshold exists in the damages inflicted by pollution. In (a), we present the total damages from pollution as its level rises, while in (b) we show the marginal damage function. As pollution increases from zero to Z^+, total pollution damages increase monotonically and marginal damages are constant. At Z^+, however, the total damage function takes a large discontinuous jump upward and then again increases at a constant rate. Z^+ is the *threshold* where the impact of the pollution changes dramatically.

Many actual pollutants may have such thresholds. The existence of a threshold again means that the policy which minimizes expected efficiency losses under uncertainty depends on the shape and location of the MB and MD curves. Suppose the government knows the shape of the MD function. In particular, it knows where the threshold is, but it does not know where the MB function lies. If the government underestimates the MB function by assuming that the function intersects the MD function anywhere in the region from 0 to Z^+, it will set a tax equal to $0t$. If the actual MB function lies within this region, the optimal amount of pollution is emitted. The tax policy thus works well if the government knows that the MB function intersects MD to the left of Z^+. If, however, the government imposes a tax equal to $0t$ but the

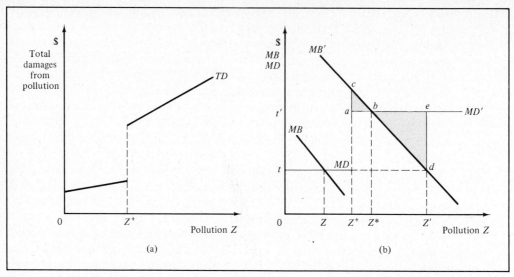

Figure 12.10   If the marginal damage function (*MD*) is discontinuous due to the presence of a threshold effect in pollution damages, a combined policy using both a standard set at the threshold and a tax set equal to *Ot* will minimize the expected losses from miscalculating the *MB* function. If only a tax is used and marginal benefits are *MB'* rather than the estimated *MB*, the efficiency loss is *bde* and excessive amounts of pollution are emitted. If the standard is used alone, too little pollution is emitted and the efficiency loss is equal to *abc*.

MB function intersects the *MD* function to the right of Z^+, the tax can lead to excessive amounts of pollution.

Suppose the actual *MB* function is *MB'*. A tax of $0t$ will then yield Z' pollution rather than the optimal amount Z^*. Z' greatly exceeds Z^*, leading to large efficiency losses (and of course large pollution damages). The loss-minimizing policy in this situation is then to impose a standard at the threshold level or a high tax, t which is equal to *MD* above the threshold. The standard ensures that pollution does not exceed the threshold, but may result in efficiency losses (due to too little pollution) if the *MB* curve is actually *MB'*. The tax at t' will prevent excessive amounts of pollution emissions. If, however, the marginal benefit curve is *MB*, the high taxes will be punitive and lead to much too little pollution.

Perhaps the best policy when the location of the *MB* curve is uncertain is to combine the tax and the standard. Suppose the standard is set at the threshold level of pollution and a tax is imposed equal to the lower portion of the *MD* function ($0t$). If the marginal benefit curve turns out to be *MB*, the tax is the binding constraint for the firm, and the optimal amount of pollution results. If the actual marginal benefit curve is *MB'*, the standard is the binding constraint. Pollution will be less than is optimal (Z^+ rather than Z^*), but the efficiency loss is much lower than would be the case if only the tax at rate t were operative. If the government does not know the shape of the *MD* function, again it would be prudent to set both a tax and a standard. An optimal policy will be impossible to find, but the risks of having far too much or far too little pollution compared to the optimum will be minimized with a combined policy.

The combination of taxes with standards will also tend to minimize the direct costs of controlling pollution in the case where the government does not have good information about the *MB* or *MD* functions. That is, in addition to minimizing the expected efficiency losses when there is uncertainty about the *MB* or *MD* function, a combined policy can lead to lower *abatement costs* in controlling pollution.[20]

Suppose the government has established a target level of reduction in pollution. The total amount of pollution has been estimated, and the government seeks to cut this amount by 50 percent. We assume that the government does not know either the *MD* or the *MB* curve and does not know if a 50 percent reduction is reasonable or not, but is going to use this reduction as a standard. How should the standard be implemented to minimize the costs to firms of meeting the standard?

Suppose that there are two types of firms in the economy — firms that face high costs of reducing the pollution emissions and firms that face low costs. One can think of metal smelters where old smelters have technologies that cannot reduce emissions of sulfur dioxide without the addition of expensive stack scrubbers. The scrubbers not only add to capital costs (which we ignore), but greatly increase operating costs because they reduce efficiency of operation. New smelters already have the abatement equipment incorporated, and their operating costs are much lower. Figure 12.11 shows the marginal costs of abating pollution for the two types of firms. Pollution emissions are measured on the horizontal axis. The *MCA* curves show the marginal costs of reducing pollution from its maximum uncontrolled level (100 percent) to 0. We have drawn the curves without positive intercept to indicate that it is probably technically impossible to remove 100 percent of the emissions. The old

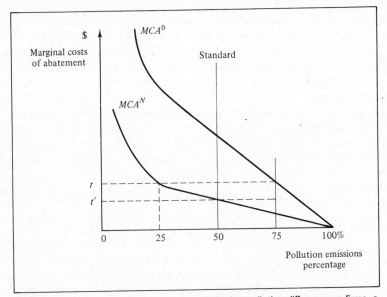

Figure 12.11 When the marginal costs of abating pollution differ among firms, a standard will maximize the costs of abatement. A tax minimizes the costs of abatement. A combination of a standard and a tax will ensure that abatement costs are minimized while the desired reduction in emissions is achieved.

smelter faces higher marginal costs of abatement, shown by MCA^0, than the new smelter with MCA^N.

If the government tries to achieve a reduction in the emissions of pollution by 50 percent by imposing a *uniform standard* on each firm, total abatement costs will be maximized. If each firm must reduce its emissions by 50 percent, the old smelter will incur total costs equal to the area under its MCA^0 curve from 50 to 100 percent emissions. The new smelter total costs will be the area under its MCA^N curve between 50 and 100 percent. Notice that at 50 percent the old smelter faces a much higher marginal abatement cost. This is not efficient; the old smelter will be using far too many resources to reduce its pollution, while the new smelter will not use enough compared to the optimum. In addition, if this is a competitive industry, the old smelter may be forced out of business over time if the metal price is less than the average costs of production inclusive of the abatement costs. *The optimal amount of abatement is where the marginal costs of abatement are equal for all firms.* This would result if the government levied a uniform tax on all firms.

Suppose a tax equal to $0t$ were imposed. Then the old smelter would reduce its pollution by 25 percent, while the new smelter would reduce its pollution by 75 percent. Each firm sets the tax equal to its marginal costs of abatement. Both firms can continue to operate efficiently. The problem is to ensure that the standard is met. There is no guarantee that a 25 percent reduction in pollution from one firm combined with a 75 percent reduction from the other firm will achieve the overall standard. The government can then do a number of things. If it is suspected that there is a threshold effect in the marginal damage function, the government can impose an overall standard on the industry at the suspected threshold — say pollution must not exceed 75 percent of the previous level. A tax is then imposed, and either the tax or the standard is the binding constraint on each firm. In Figure 12.11, if the tax is equal to say $0t'$, the new smelter will reduce its emissions by 50 percent (where the tax equals its marginal abatement costs), while the old smelter will reduce its pollution to 75 percent of its previous level. The government can then change the tax rate until the desired objective is met.

The advantages of this policy are that the tax minimizes the cost of meeting the standard. Firms with high abatement costs reduce their emissions by less than firms with low abatement costs. The information costs of the policy are relatively low. The government does not have to calculate individual firm's marginal benefits of pollution (or abatement costs); it simply measures the aggregate amount of pollution emitted after the imposition of its standard plus fees. Individual quotas per firm could be used, but these are costly to impose and monitor. The disadvantages of the policy are that it may not be administratively feasible to implement the tax scheme and change the tax rates frequently enough to obtain the desired reduction in pollution. There may also be a problem with nonconvexities and discontinuities in the MD or MB functions. If so, it is possible that the scheme can lead the economy away from the optimum. (We will not consider these cases here, but simply note the problem.)

We have yet to see a real example of this type of policy, which suggests that it may be administratively or politically unfeasible. However, in the next chapter we will examine a policy that is very similar in its potential economic impact to the standards plus tax scheme — marketable permits to emit pollution.

SUMMARY

1. External effects or externalities arise because of technological interdependencies among economic agents that persist because of the failure of markets to price these external effects.
2. An external economy exists when the actions of one agent benefit another party; an external diseconomy exists when the agent's actions harm the other party. In each case, the affected party has no control over the actions of the agent generating the externality.
3. An externality is internalized when the external effect is incorporated into the objective function of both agents and a "price" is imputed for the external effect.
4. Markets may fail and externalities persist when transactions costs are high or markets are thin; information is imperfect and/or asymmetric; nonappropriability exists; nonconvexities exist.
5. Private externalities are bilateral or involve relatively few agents. One party's actions affect another party, but there is no spillover to other agents. Private externalities can generally be internalized by bargaining.
6. Public externalities typically involve natural resources that have open access and affect large numbers of individuals. "Consumption" of the externality by one agent does not reduce the consumption of the externality by others. Private negotiations are generally incapable of internalizing a public externality, and some form of government intervention is required.
7. When an externality is public, individuals' demand curves, which reflect their willingness to pay for the internalization of the externality, must be summed vertically to obtain the aggregate demand curve. This is because the quantity supplied is consumed by all. Individuals cannot determine how much they consume, but only the value they place on the amount supplied.
8. A government trying to internalize an externality and achieve the optimal amount of pollution through the use of taxes or fees that reflect individuals' willingness to pay for reduction in pollution will have difficulty determining the optimal tax. Individuals have an incentive to reveal valuations less than their true preferences if they think others are being honest. This is the "free rider" problem, and it can result in too much pollution compared to the social optimum.
9. In a consumption externality involving air pollution, property rights and the initial position for bargaining over the amount of pollution to emit will affect the final equilibrium. The amount of air pollution that exists after the externality is internalized is typically higher if the starting point is polluted air and the polluters have the right to use the air as a waste depository than if clean air is the starting point and pollution is not permitted.
10. The imposition of a tax on pollution can internalize an externality and obtain an optimal allocation of resources. But if the government wants to keep real incomes at their pretax levels, it must also subsidize those facing the tax.
11. Quantity restrictions on pollution can also internalize the externality, but typically entail higher enforcement costs than the optimal tax.
12. A production externality that leads to pollution is internalized where the marginal benefits *(MB)* from pollution equal the marginal damages *(MD)*

from pollution. The optimal amount of pollution is generally not equal to zero. If the externality is private, merger and bargaining can internalize it. If the externality is public, taxes and/or standards are required.

13. A subsidy to polluters for reducing pollution emissions will encourage entry into an industry and lead to an increase in pollution over time, while an equivalent tax will lead to exit from the industry and reduce aggregate emissions.

14. When the government has imperfect information about the marginal benefit or marginal damage curves for pollution, it should use a quantity policy (a standard) if the *MB* curve is flatter than the *MD* curve and a tax if the reverse is true, if it wishes to minimize the expected efficiency losses from using a nonoptimal policy.

15. When the government is uncertain about the shape and location of both the *MD* and the *MB* curves, a policy that combines a standard with a tax will generally minimize both the expected efficiency losses from a nonoptimal policy and the pollution control costs.

DISCUSSION QUESTIONS

1. Distinguish between private and public externalities and give an example of each kind. Why are public externalities difficult to internalize by private actions? Explain graphically and verbally.

2. Suppose the rock band High Noise practices in a garage adjacent to the home of Mr. T, the movie star. The band likes to blast its songs out over very large amplifiers—the more noise the better. The average reading near the garage is 120 decibels (well above the pain threshold for people with "normal" hearing). Derive graphically and explain verbally what the level of noise will be in each of the following circumstances:
   a. Mr. T and High Noise bargain to a mutually agreeable outcome.
   b. Mr. T calls the police, who tell the band that their noise cannot exceed 90 decibels. High Noise and Mr. T bargain after the noise limit has been imposed.
   c. The city council imposes a "tax" on noise equal to a tax rate of *t* per decibel. Noise monitors are installed on the outside of each house or apartment.
   d. High Noise moves out of Mr. T's neighborhood and locates on the fifteenth floor of a 25-story apartment building. Everyone in the building now gets to hear the band practice. Would bargaining among the affected parties now lead to an optimal outcome? Explain.

3. The chemical dioxin, which is very toxic to plants, animals, and people, is occasionally released into Lake Ontario by accidental discharges from chemical companies located around the lake. Suppose you work for an environmental control agency of a state government that borders Lake Ontario. What policy or policies would you adopt to deal with this pollutant? Use graphic (or mathematical) analysis to support your prescriptions, and discuss the practical problems of implementing the policy.

4. Consider the case of the town beach downstream from the pulp and paper mill emitting pollutants into the stream. If the factory were deemed the owner of the river, how much swimming and pollution would develop? What system of user fees would be likely to arise? If the town's beach users were deemed the owner, how much swimming and pollution would develop? What system of user fees would be likely to arise?

5. "Taxes on pollution are equivalent to subsidies paid to reduce pollution." Is this statement true, false, or uncertain? Explain your answer.

6. With a positive externality, such as occurs when the fruit grower's trees provide pollen for the honey farmer's bees, a market failure can arise. In what sense can the economy be said to be inefficient when the externality is positive rather than negative, such as water pollution?

7. Suppose you are designing policies to reduce water pollution for a government environmental agency. You have consulted industry experts who tell you the shape and location of the marginal benefit of pollution function (the function that shows the value to firms of using inputs that create pollution, or of using the waterways as a waste depository). Assume this *MB* function is linear and all polluters are identical. However, you do not know for certain the shape or the location of the marginal damage function to those affected by pollution.

   a. Assume first that the *MD* function is linear. What policy would you advocate, and why?

   b. Suppose now that the *MD* function could be discontinuous. Does this change your policy recommendation derived in (a)? Explain.

8. "A standard always maximizes the cost of abating pollution." True, false, or uncertain? Explain your answer.

NOTES

1. We do not mean by this statement that externalities can arise only in market economies. Pollution, for example, is a problem in centrally planned economies as well. Whether decision-making is done on a decentralized basis, as in a market economy, or by a central planner, an externality will arise whenever the interdependencies among agents are not taken into account in making decisions.

2. In Chapter 13, we examine in some detail government-organized markets that issue permits to pollute.

3. The alternative is to look at a steady-state where pollution and recovery of the air are in some sort of balance.

4. There is a large literature on mechanisms the government can use to extract the true preferences of individuals for a public good. These include methods of determining from voting behavior what people want. See, for example, R. Boadway, *Public Sector Economics* (1979). The practical relevance of these preference-revelation techniques has not yet been fully ascertained.

5. If the property rights to clean air were reversed, say by an ordinance that banned smoking in offices, George would be the afflicted party, since he would suffer from the prohibition of smoking.

6. We could be more precise and have smoke, Z, be a function of George's cigarettes, for example, $Z = h(Y)$, where Y is cigarettes smoked. We do not add this functional relationship in this section, but do consider something like it in our discussion of externalities in production. The assumption that smoke is in itself a good illustrates the concepts without adding more complexity.

7. The graphic technique originated with Dolbear (1967) and Shibata (1971).

8. Amanda's budget constraint will be virtually horizontal, given the transformation of her indifference curves. She can therefore obtain a tangency of one of her indifference curves at a zero amount of smoke.

9. If the production possibility frontier were not linear, we could trace through the effects of the different relative prices on factor and output markets.

10. There is one situation in which the same equilibrium is reached regardless of who has the property rights: when the contract curve is vertical. The contract curve will be vertical when each party has zero income elasticity for smoke, which means that each person's

marginal utility for good Z is constant and independent of the amount of good X consumed. A utility function consistent with a vertical contract curve would be one that has strong (additive) separability between X and Z. In the model presented in this section, additive separability implies that, say, Amanda will suffer from a *fixed* amount of smoke pollution regardless of the amount of other goods she consumes. So, for example, even if she wears a gas mask, her marginal disutility from smoke is the same as if she did not. This seems unlikely. It is therefore difficult to imagine cases in practice where additive separability will hold.

11. The government could compensate the smoker for his loss in real income resulting from the standard.

12. These are complex issues of property rights and information. See, for example, Coase (1960), Demsetz (1967), Starrett (1972), Furubotn and Pejovitch (1972), Scott (1983), and the references cited therein.

13. We could have the output of chemicals themselves as the variable that adversely affects the apple firm analogous to our previous consumption externality example. The results will be similar. But the assumption that it is a particular factor input that is responsible is typically more realistic and allows us to examine a richer set of corrective devices.

14. These results can be derived by differentiating each equation with respect to its factor input, x or y.

15. The same thing occurred in the fishery.

16. A horizontal line at height $A'y^*$ would also illustrate an optimal unit tax on input y. The firm then uses input y up to the point where the tax line intersects its MB function at y^*.

17. Alternatively, if abatement is possible new techniques may be installed that reduce pollution emissions per unit of output. Firms may then not have to exit.

18. See Mestelman (1981, 1982) for some discussion of qualifications to the results presented above.

19. We could alternatively label the MD function the marginal cost of pollution control or removal. The MC of abatement would typically be a positive function of the amount of pollution, but need not be linear. Weitzman (1974) was one of the first to discuss the asymmetry of taxes versus standards in the context of uncertainty. His model is more complex than ours, but the basic results are similar. Morgan (1983) has a similar model with an MC of abatement or pollution removal curve. He is concerned with the problem of emission of heavy metals into sewage treatment systems. The linearity of the MD function is relaxed below in an example similar to that of Morgan.

20. See Baumol and Oates (1975) for a fuller discussion of these concepts.

chapter *13*

Pollution Policy in Practice

INTRODUCTION

In this chapter, we examine the methods of obtaining the optimal amount of environmental quality or pollution emissions. In Chapter 12 we determined the optimal level of pollution where the marginal benefits from pollution—the gain to emitters from using the environment as a waste depository—equal the marginal damages. Alternatively, we can define the optimal amount of pollution in terms of environmental quality. In this case, the marginal costs of abating pollution would be set equal to the marginal benefits of greater levels of environmental quality. If properly measured, the approaches yield equivalent emissions of pollutants at the optimum. In the first part of this chapter, we discuss the links between pollution, environmental quality, and the marginal benefits from an improvement in quality. We look at a particular example—the benefits from an increase in water quality at recreational sites.

Our emphasis in the second part of the chapter is on the actual practices used to internalize externalities. We explain and evaluate different approaches not just with regard to their connection to economic principles in achieving the optimal amount of pollution/environmental quality, but to see which are administratively feasible, and to note the practical difficulties in carrying out environmental regulation. We keep the optimality conditions—equating marginal costs and benefits—as a basis for evaluation.

Then we examine a *positive* externality, the bees and the blossoms, that is internalized by private actions. No government intervention is required, because a set of contracts has emerged through bilateral bargaining between affected parties to reach a mutually agreeable solution. Next, we examine types of government regulations dealing with a public externality—water pollution. We evaluate the effects of the policies on pollution emissions, the costs of abating pollution, and administrative feasibility.

The final section examines a new and promising approach in the regulation of pollution — the permit to pollute. While economists have long advocated the use of a pollution permit that can be exchanged among polluters to minimize the costs of reducing emissions, it has not been until fairly recently in the United States that regulatory authorities have begun to change the law so that these permits might be used. A standard is still imposed, but the means of obtaining the standard is quite different under the marketable permit than with the restrictions imposed under the standard-only scheme. We focus on air pollution and examine the theoretical basis for marketable permits, the different types of permit markets under consideration, and how they might be implemented, along with the results of several studies evaluating different permit schemes with respect to their effect on emissions of air pollutants, costs of abatement, and the structure of the permit market.

ENVIRONMENTAL QUALITY AND THE VALUATION OF THE MARGINAL BENEFITS FROM POLLUTION ABATEMENT
General Issues

Suppose a policy-maker wishes to determine the optimal amount of pollution abatement and to evaluate alternative methods of obtaining an abatement target. The technique of *cost benefit analysis* (CBA) is used. The fundamental role of CBA is to establish principles by which the costs and benefits of any public program are measured. Many of the components of costs and benefits are not exchanged in markets and thus have no well-defined prices. In addition, many markets contain distortions — taxes, subsidies, quotas, monopoly, monopsony — that make the prices misrepresentative of the resource-scarcity or shadow price of the commodities exchanged.

Our focus will be on the use of CBA to determine the marginal benefits from reducing pollution emissions. We do not deal with the marginal costs of abating pollution because typically, these are easier to determine. We will also have much more to say about the abatement costs of alternative regulatory policies in subsequent sections. There are many excellent studies on the problems of measuring abatement costs.[1] Measuring benefits from improving environmental quality is difficult because most of these benefits must be *imputed* by cost-benefit techniques. Some benefits routinely evaluated for cost benefit studies of pollution are the value of life (mortality and morbidity), the value of intangibles such as the quality of life, the value of the natural environment (air and water quality), and property values. We will look at a specific example — valuing the benefits from improving water quality at recreational sites. Our discussion is based on the work of Freeman (1979) and Greenley et al. (1981).

Three relationships link any change in the emissions of a particular pollutant to the ultimate measurement of the benefits of reducing the emissions. Technical models that link the change in emissions to a change in ambient quality are first required. These models predict the path of the effluent from particular sources to zones surrounding the source. Meteorological factors and chemical processes are incorporated, and environmental quality is defined. Below, we note the parameters that have been used to measure water quality. These include the oxygen demand of organic wastes as they are decomposed (BOD), suspended solids (SS), toxic chemicals, and heat.

It is not enough merely to define water quality; the change over time must also be noted. Can the elements be diluted or altered by complex chemical and biological processes? These analyses require extensive scientific expertise, and they are an area where much has been learned in the past 10 to 20 years. Prior to the mid-1970s, for example, many toxic chemicals that were present in waterways could not even be detected. We now have a much better idea of not only *what* pollutants are showing up in the environment, but in what *concentration.*

After the models that link changes in effluents to changes in environmental quality are determined, the next step is to see how the change in quality affects the flow of environmental services to individuals. Biological effects incorporate the impact on human health, effects on the economic productivity of natural resource sectors, and recreational uses of the ecosystem. One may also want to examine the overall stability of the ecosystem as the level of pollutants changes. Will plant and animal species become less able to deal with ordinary stress when their systems are also affected by pollutants such as toxic chemicals and noise pollution? Many different nonliving systems can incur economic loss from decreased environmental quality. Materials are damaged by air pollutants. Soiling, odors, reduced visibility, effects on production costs, climate, and weather (the greenhouse effect and the melting of the polar ice caps) are other effects.

Not only are there synergies or interdependencies between the effects of variations in environmental quality on living and nonliving systems, but what is beneficial to one component may be disasterous to another. Swimmers may not mind the effects of acid rain or thermal pollution on lakes because the water quality to them is enhanced—the lake is "cleaner" and warmer. But to the fish and those fishing, acid rain represents a substantial decline in benefits. The link between a change in environmental quality and its impact on environmental services thus combines science and social science.

The final relationship is that between the change in environmental services and the change in *economic welfare,* or the benefits of abatement. This is where the major focus of economic evaluation occurs (although economics plays a role in the previous two relationships as well). How are economic benefits measured? Economists typically use some type of quantitative technique—econometric analysis (regressions) and risk analysis (see, for example, Crandall and Lave, 1981; Peskin and Seskin, 1975; Halvorsen and Ruby, 1981; and Freeman, 1979, and the references within each). What we want to do here is look at the principles involved in the measurement of the recreational benefits derived from changes in water quality.

Water Quality and Recreation Benefits

Recreational use of water has significant economic value. Freeman cites two statistics. A study for the U.S. Environmental Protection Agency estimated that the loss of recreational benefits due to water pollution was some $10.1 billion per year, or 60 percent of the total water pollution damages estimated.[2] In another report, the recreational benefits of implementing the best available technology for reducing water pollution were estimated at \$3.2 to 4.2 billion per year. What economists attempt to do is calculate individual's *marginal willingness to pay* for a change in water quality. What this means in practice is that the demand curve for recreational services must be determined, as well as changes in the demand curve due to changes in water quality. Let's see how this is done.

The benefits from a change in water quality depend on an individual's utility function. The utility function can, as usual, include all sorts of things; but we must assume it includes some measure of water quality, and option and preservation values. *Option* and *preservation* values arise when an environmental asset, say a particular wilderness area, has alternative uses. Suppose one use is to leave the wilderness area in its existing state, and the alternative use is to open the area for coal mining. Open pit coal mining generates waste products that may irreversibly damage the environmental quality of the site. If the decision is to allow mining to proceed, the decision later to use the site for recreation is precluded. If preservation of the site is the choice in the present, then the option of later choosing between mining and wilderness still exists. In these cases, there is uncertainty about the decision.

People may be uncertain about their demand for recreational services or unsure about the outcome of the development choice. The point is that a value is placed today on the ability to make choices in the future.[3] Preservation values include bequest and existence values. *Bequest* values are the willingness to pay for the satisfaction derived from having one's heirs and future generations in general enjoy environmental services. *Existence* values are what people are willing to pay just to know that the environmental asset is preserved, even if they do not intend ever to directly consume those services.

Now let us consider how water quality affects demand. Assume that along with income, and private goods and services including recreational services, there is a variable in the utility function called water quality. Figure 13.1 illustrates the aggregate demand for recreation at a particular site measured in recreation days—days at the beach, tubing down the river, and hiking in the wilderness. We assume that the demand for recreational days is derived from individuals' utility functions, holding everything in those utility functions constant except for the price of the recreational services. This price can be thought of as an entry fee for now.

Figure 13.1 shows what happens to the demand curve at a recreational site when the water quality of that site changes. If individuals value improvements in water quality, the demand curve for recreation at that site will shift to the right as water quality increases. The curve D_P is the demand curve for recreation with polluted water (but not so polluted that people can't use the water), while D_C represents their demand when water quality increases. Holding all else constant, the benefits of the increase in water quality can be measured by the area between the two demand curves above the entry price, P, (which can of course be zero). The area $ABCDE$ is the measure of the total benefits from an improvement in water quality.

This area can be broken into two components. There is an increase in consumer surplus associated with the original level of consumption $0Q_1$. This is the area $ABDE$. There is also an increase in the total use of the recreational site equal to Q_1Q_2. The site is now more desirable, so people stay more days than when the beach was full of slime.

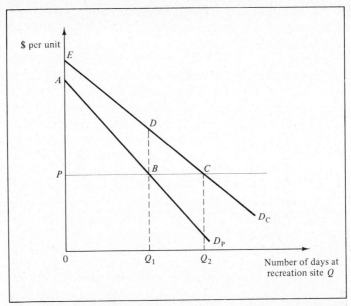

Figure 13.1   An increase in water quality shifts the demand curve for recreation to the right. The value of the higher water quality is the total consumer surplus *ABCDE*. The consumer surplus consists of the value of the increased benefits at the original level of consumption Q_1 — the area *ABDE* plus the consumer surplus from the increase in recreation use Q_1Q_2 — the area *BCD*.

The additional quantity demanded could also come from other recreational sites that have not had improvements in water quality. The consumer surplus then from the increased use of the site is the area *BCD*. If the recreation site also involves a decision where option and preservation values exist, these values will shift the vertical intercept of the demand curve upward. When measuring environmental benefits, both the option value and value of increased water quality are added together.

While these benefit measures are straightforward to explain in theory, they are difficult to obtain in practice. The bad news is that not only must the demand curve for recreation at the site be estimated, we must also know how it shifts whenever quality changes occur or option and preservation values are present. This is where cost benefit techniques enter. We first focus on the measurement of the demand curve for recreation, then see how the shifts due to changes in water quality or the existence of option values can be measured.

The problem with trying to estimate a demand curve for recreation is that there is not enough variation in the "price" of recreation. Many recreational sites have no entry fee, or one that is nominal and rarely fluctuates. The technique commonly used is to substitute in the *travel costs* to the site. The approach obviously must be applied to specific sites; we cannot aggregate travel to different sites to get an aggregate demand curve for total recreational uses. There is an extensive literature on estimating the demand for recreation using travel data; see Freeman and the references cited therein, Smith et al. (1983), and the *Journal of Environmental Economics and Management* for many recent examples.

Consider a very simple travel cost model. For any recreation site, let's say a lake, the area surrounding it is divided into concentric circular zones. This is done to measure the return-trip costs from the zone to the site. Visitors to the lake are sampled to find out what zone they come from. A calculation is made of the visitor days per capita to the lake for each zone. Travel costs are then calculated. These costs include not only the estimated actual money outlay (gas, food, etc.), but the opportunity cost of one's time in getting to the site. Visitor days per capita are then regressed on travel costs and socioeconomic variables such as average income and education. The hypothesis is that visits per capita depend negatively on travel costs (so that the demand curve slopes down). The total visits from all zones then represent one point on the demand curve for that site. That is, the point is the intersection of the entry fee (which is assumed constant) with the true underlying demand curve for recreation.[4] The other points on the demand curve are found by assuming the visitors respond to a marginal increase in the entry fee in the same way they respond to a marginal increase in travel costs. The coefficient on travel costs in the estimated equation is used to predict the change in trips taken when travel costs from each zone are changed. Visits from all zones are again summed to obtain a point on the demand curve for each different travel cost.

Ideally, one would like to have actual data on the variation in trips with changes in travel costs, rather than the estimated equation. This is especially true when the econometric properties of the equation are not strong (low goodness of fit, low t-statistics, and other problems). But despite problems, such as defining large travel zones, coping with sites that are imperfect substitutes, and getting biased samples, the technique remains a valuable tool in determining recreational demand.

But the travel cost approach determines only the location of the demand curve; the shifts in demand must also be incorporated. We examine first water quality, then option demand. In principle, it is simple to incorporate water quality or option demand into the regression. Variables measuring environmental quality and option demand are simply estimated, along with the other explanatory variables of the recreational demand function. In theory, both variables should have a positive coefficient. Holding all else constant, increases in option demand or water quality shift the demand curve up. The estimated value of each coefficient is then used to predict shifts in the demand curve. The problem here is how to measure water quality and option value. Let's first consider water quality.

Should technical measures such as BOD, SS, and toxic chemicals be used in the analysis of water use? It is unlikely that most recreational users will be able to evaluate these measures. But does this matter? People may not know the precise pollution components of the water but their perceptions of whatever it is that determines water quality may correspond to the technical measures. David (1971) surveyed individuals in Wisconsin to find their perception of water quality. People tended to look at characteristics such as algae content (green scum), murkiness, odor, and debris in the water. But when people's perceptions of what constituted "polluted water" (and variations in polluted water) were matched with scientific determination of degrees of polluted water using objective criteria, a close correlation resulted.

Other studies have not had such positive results. Surveys taken of people traveling to the beaches found that water quality was a determinant of their visiting pattern, but not a significant one. Other factors such as the nearness of the beach to one's home, the congestion at the beach, and who "hung out" at the beach were more important. Water quality perceptions may be subject to threshold effects. It is only when the water looks and smells terrible or when we read about the presence of unpleasant critters or chemicals that we react. Water quality will also be more important at some sites than others. If you've come thousands of miles to see a coral reef in the Caribbean and an oil spill has just wiped out all the aquatic life, water quality is more important to you than it is when water skiing on a lake whose living things have been destroyed by acid rain.

Let's now see how water quality has been estimated. The study by Greenley et al. (1981) contains measures of people's willingness to pay for improvements in water quality *and* the option and preservation values associated with a choice of use of a particular recreation site. The site is the South Platte River Basin in Colorado. In this case, a hypothetical decision was to be made about whether to continue to use the basin for recreation or to allow mineral and energy development to occur. Mineral development would irreversibly degrade the water quality of the river. We will not examine their theoretical model, but their empirical results.

The authors first measure the implicit benefits of water quality improvements along the basin and then measure option and preservation values. The technique used in each case is sampling of people's willingness to pay. A random sample of 202 households in two cities in Colorado were interviewed in the summer of 1976. There was little evidence of sample bias or any strategic behavior of the part of the individuals questioned. People were asked what they would be willing to pay for incremental improvements in water quality and for the option of maintaining the river at the highest quality attainable, rather than allowing mineral development to proceed immediately. They were told that the decision to start mining could be made in the future. Two types of payment were proposed—incremental increases in sales taxes for the state, or an increase in the water and sewer fees paid by all residences. The funds collected were to go to improving water quality. These fees were chosen because they were familiar to individuals and seen as a practical means of financing improvements.

To determine different levels of water quality, people were shown color photographs of three sites that represented the range of quality. They were also given technical information about the pollutants (heavy metals) present in the three sites. The photos allowed people subjectively to evaluate certain aspects of water quality (algae, debris), but not others (odor). They were asked what they would be willing to pay to increase quality to the highest level shown in the photographs by 1983. Eighty percent of those sampled were willing to pay to increase water quality. On average, these people were willing to incur an additional $57 per year through an increase in the rate of the state sales tax to have water quality at the highest attainable level. The amount they were willing to pay through an increase in water and sewer fees was much smaller.

The authors feel the divergence between the two forms of payment may be due to considerations of equity (or spreading the payments over a broader group of people). The sales tax would be paid by residents of the state and by out-of-state tourists who visited the site. Only residents pay the water and sewer fees. There had also been a recent increase in the water and sewer fees, and people were perhaps more sensitive to that form of financing. What is important to note is that the method of financing changes in water quality will influence willingness to pay for the improvements.

To determine option values, people were asked if they preferred preserving the river basin at the highest quality or permitting mineral development. They were told that if mineral development occurred, recreational use of the basin would end. If they chose to preserve the site, they were asked how many additional cents per dollar of sales tax they would be willing to pay to postpone any development decision to the future.

Eighty percent of the sample expected to use the site for recreation; 60 percent of the total sample had a positive option value. Twenty percent had a zero option value because, although they intended to use the site for recreation, they did not believe that the pollution would affect their use. The remaining 20 percent also had a zero option value because they did not intend to visit the site for recreation. The average option value for the 80 percent who intended to use the site came to $23 per year. Preservation values were calculated at an average of $42 per year per household increase in sales taxes when the 20 percent who did not intend to use the site for recreation were included. These people were willing to pay for the option of having the site preserved for future generations and simply to have the site there. When the preservation values for only those using the site are averaged, the increase in the sales tax comes to $67 per year per household.

When these values are applied to all households near the river basin, the total benefits of an improvement in water quality came to $61 million per year, of which $26.4 million represented direct improvements in water quality, $10.5 million the option values, $14.4 million existence value, and $9.8 million bequest value. The present value of these benefits over an infinite period at a discount rate of 6 and 3/8 percent is approximately $1 billion. This is a substantial number and suggests a strong willingness to pay for improvements. One can criticize the techniques used to obtain the numbers, but the numbers provide a basis with which to compare the actual costs of abatement.

Cost benefit analysis has been maligned by those who say that it is useless because the numbers are so bad. This criticism misses the point of the exercise. If we have no numbers, no intelligent environmental policy can be designed. What is important is to provide as much information as possible about how the numbers are obtained, what assumptions are made, and how the results would be altered if slightly different assumptions were made. The estimate of the benefits of environmental control is crucial if we are to evaluate the tremendous costs of reducing pollution and make informed judgments about the social value of improving environmental quality.

BEES AND BLOSSOMS

Picture a lovely cabbage patch. The cabbage plants are flowering and bees are flying around gathering nectar from the cabbage and pollinating the plant. Here we have what was thought to be a classic example of an external economy that was reciprocal in nature. The bees benefit the cabbage grower by pollinating the crop. The cabbage grower benefits the beekeeper by providing nectar for the production of honey. Economists such as Meade (1952) suggested this was an externality that would persist because it would be difficult to organize markets and write contracts for the pollination services of the bees and the nectar provision of the farmers. However, contrary to Meade's notions, this is precisely the type of situation in which an externality is readily internalized through private actions. There is little need for government involvement because the externality is *private* in nature.

Our information comes from papers by Cheung (1973) and Johnson (1973). According to Cheung, there are actually three types of technological interdependence among beekeepers and farmers that depend on whether pollination is needed to set the fruit (or produce seed) which is commercially harvested and whether the crop in question provides sufficient nectar for honey production. The three are shown in Table 13.1. Apples for example, require bees for pollination, but yield virtually no honey. Mint, on the other hand, does not require pollination but does yield honey. The first two examples are cases of a unilateral externality—one party benefits because of the actions of the other. The final case is that of the reciprocal externality. Cabbages and blueberries need pollination and provide honey, as do alfalfa and red clover when they are harvested for seed. The questions are these: Do any "markets" for the exchange of pollination services and nectar exist? Do the prices generated by these markets incorporate the external effects? The answers are "yes" in both cases.

Beekeeping is a very old activity. Bees are not public goods, but private goods once they have been "hived." Property rights to bees go back to about 500 B.C. in common law. Even if a beekeeper's bees fly all over the place, they are still considered the keeper's property, and the keeper is entitled by common law to the proceeds of the foraging bees. Farmers have long paid for the pollination services of the bees, and beekeepers have paid for the nectar services of the crops. As Cheung notes, all one has to do is consult the Yellow Pages of the phone book in agricultural areas to see that a market for this activity exists and that prices indeed are levied. But are the prices efficient?

Cheung attempts to test the proposition that the externality is internalized optimally. He cannot do this directly, but presents evidence from data on bee contracts in the state of Washington in the early 1970s. Although there may be reciprocal externalities involved, the market operates sequentially. In the early to late spring, it is the farmers who need the bees for pollination. Very little harvestable honey is

Table 13.1 POLLINATION AND NECTAR PROPERTIES OF SELECTED PLANTS

	Apples, cherries almonds	Mint	Blueberries cabbage, alfalfa
Pollination needed to set fruit	Yes	No	Yes
Surplus honey produced	No	Yes	Yes

Note: Alfalfa requires pollination when the seeds are to be harvested, not when the crop is used for hay.

Source: Cheung (1973).

produced in this period. In the summer and late fall, the opposite is true. Few crops require pollination, but the bees are busy making surplus honey. One would expect, then, that fees for pollination would be higher in the spring than in the summer and fees for nectar provision would be higher in the summer.

This is exactly what Cheung finds. There is a strong negative correlation between the pollination fees and the expected honey yield. Pollination fees in the late spring average around $8 to $9 per hive, while the payment for nectar services is zero. By summer and early fall, beekeepers are paying an implicit price of 15 to 65 cents per hive for nectar services. (This is an implicit price because the unit of exchange in most nectar contracts was honey.)

Unfortunately, Cheung cannot test directly for efficiency, but examines the two types of externalities and then draws inferences from the number of hives used and the price of hives. Figure 13.2 illustrates the argument. In (a), the marginal product curves for bee hives is shown for the unilateral externality cases. The *MPP* curve shows the value of the marginal product of the hive when used to pollinate crops, while the *MPH* curve reflects marginal product in producing honey. Figure 13.2(b) illustrates the reciprocal externality case where the two marginal product curves are reproduced and then summed vertically for the aggregate *MP* curve (remember hives provide a joint product). Figure 13.2(c) illustrates the market for hives with an aggregate demand and supply curve of the usual shapes. Beehives apparently satisfy all the normal conditions for factor inputs.

Johnson notes that the beekeeping industry is competitive, and characterized by constant average and hence marginal costs of production. Cheung finds that the rental price of hives is fairly uniform across beekeepers and suggests that these prices are approximately equal to the average costs of beekeeping. Pricing of hives therefore appears to be efficient. Cheung cannot tell directly whether the rental price of the

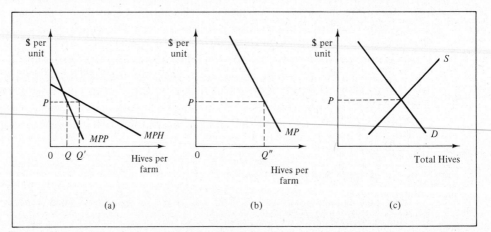

Figure 13.2   With a competitive market for hives, the value of the marginal product of the hive will be set equal to its rental price in an efficient market. When hives are needed only for pollination services, the price *P* is set equal to *MPP,* and *OQ* hives are used per farm. If hives only yield honey, *MPH* is set equal to *P* and *OQ′* hives are employed. When the hives yield both pollination and honey, the *MPP* and *MPH* curves are summed vertically to obtain *MP* in (b). Joint services then lead to a larger number of hives used than in (a)—*OQ″*.

hives is being set equal to the marginal product of the hives (either for nectar production, pollination, or both), as is necessary for efficiency, but finds that the use of hives is greatest in crops where the externality is reciprocal. This result is consistent with equating hive price to the value of the marginal product of the hive. That is, Figure 13.2(b) shows a greater use of hives than either of the unilateral cases in (a).

What the pictures and facts suggest, then, is that hives are being valued and used like any other good. The externality has been internalized. This result is reinforced when we examine the contracts for pollination and nectar production. Pollination contracts cover the number and strength of the bee colonies, the rental fee per hive, time of delivery and removal, and provisions to protect bees from pesticides. While there are fewer formal contracts for nectar gathering, they too specify a rent the beekeeper pays the farmer. The reason for the wider variation in the nectar prices is that honey production is very sensitive to exogenous factors such as weather. Beekeepers typically have escape clauses in their contracts to allow for lower than average yields of honey.

There are, however, two possible externalities one may think are not internalized by contractual arrangements. Bees cannot read and are not stopped by fences; they don't know when they have crossed over one farmer's property and on to another's. Do the contracts take into account this possible spillover of bee benefits? Johnson notes that extensive arrangements have been made over time to internalize this externality. First, there are cooperative arrangements among farmers. For example, all agree to employ bees at the same time. Then, if bees spill over, no one is riding free. There have also been extensive unilateral actions. Crops have been bred to entice bees, bees have been bred to like certain crops, and farmers plant crops in sequence so that pollination services are required at different times than those for the neighbors' crops.

The second possible problem comes from pesticides. As noted above, those hiring the bees guarantee that they will do no spraying while the bees are foraging. But a neighbor may spray and have the toxins reach the bees. Again, there is evidence of substantial cooperation among farmers and beekeepers to internalize this externality. Spraying schedules are coordinated and/or bees are removed from all properties in a region when spraying begins. When these measures do not work because of the nature of the crop, beekeepers require a risk premium to insure against damage.

Thus, none of the factors we listed in Chapter 12 that contribute to the persistence of an externality prevails in this case. There is a technological interdependence, but the externality is internalized.

STANDARDS VERSUS FEES IN PRACTICE

In this section, we wish to contrast the use of a standard to achieve a given environmental quality target with the use of fees or charges. There is no system we know of that employs fees without also maintaining a standard. And we know of no system that levies a fee which represents the marginal damages from pollution. Our discussion will not correspond to the clean theoretical distinction between fees and standards in Chapter 12. Rather, we will point out the differences between policies that tend to omit economic considerations when implementing and administering pollution standards and policies that have some taxlike component. Our examples pertain to water pollution control in the United States, the Netherlands, and France. In the United States until quite recently, the primary form of regulation of water quality has been the standard, whereas in the European countries examined a standard has been combined with fees for water treatment. Neither system results in an efficient amount of abatement, but the European system comes closer to providing the appropriate incentives to abate water pollution at minimum cost.

France and The Netherlands: Fees for Emissions

For the cases of France and the Netherlands, we will evaluate the pollution fees in four areas: (1) The purpose of the charge—is it to raise revenue or provide some incentive to abate emissions. (2) How the charges are calculated. (3) The administration of the charges—how they are implemented and how the system operates. (4) The economic incentive effects—do the charges induce any emitters to seek the cost-minimizing mix of discharge of pollutants plus fee and abatement, and are the water quality standards met? Our information comes from the OECD (1980) and Bower et al. (1981).

In the case of France and the Netherlands, the charges consist of two components—a *user fee* that reflects the cost of treating emissions in the sewage systems and an *effluent fee*—a charge for the use of the environment as a waste depository. The effluent fee until quite recently has been quite small and does not reflect marginal damages from each source. It is used to provide a pool of funds the water authorities can use to compensate firms for installing abatement equipment. The funds are to go to the firms with the most cost-efficient abatement. So the fee is a rather roundabout method of providing some incentive to minimize the costs of meeting the standards.

In both countries, charges are defined for dozens of different pollutants for different types of emissions sources. Not every characteristic of the effluent that can affect water quality is measured, but the water authorities attempt to cover the most common factors and ones easiest to monitor and measure by both the firms and the regulators. The most common factors incorporated into the charges are biochemical oxygen demand (BOD), chemical oxygen demand (COD), organic matter (N), suspended matter (SN), salinity, toxicity, and temperature. In France, the charges are based on the flow discharged in kilograms (kg) per day. This is an absolute value, not a relative value. The absolute measure prevents avoidance of fees by diluting the effluent.

The pollutants are measured as follows: For suspended solids, the fee is based on grams or kilograms emitted per day. France has no fee for nitrogen compounds, bacteria, viral pollution, or thermal pollution. These omissions are a problem because they affect water quality, and methods of incorporating them are being studied by the regulatory authorities. Different rates are then applied to each category. For each source of emissions, a linear function summing the charges per category is imposed. For example, an industrial firm would pay a fee equal to:

$$\text{fee} = t_{SS}SS + t_{OM}OM + t_{\text{salt}}\text{salt} + t_{IS}IS$$

Rates for 1978 (in U.S. dollars) were \$9.65 per kg per day for suspended solids, t_{SS}, \$19.30 per kg per day for oxidisable matter, t_{OM}, \$201.20 per equitox per kg for inhibiting and toxic substances, t_{IS}, and \$271.60 per year for soluble salts, t_{salts}. The fees were scheduled to increase from 1979 into the 1980s. Fees in The Netherlands are based on a single charge rather than a rate for each pollutant.

An advantage of the French system is that discharges are measured or estimated at the source, rather than at some point downstream. It is expensive to monitor each source of effluent, so in France only major sources are actually measured (and even then not regularly). Other sources have their emissions estimated from the production characteristics of the source. In the Seine Normandy Basin, for example, the 200 largest polluters, which account for 80 percent of the pollution, are the ones that have emissions measured. The next 1,400 sources, which account for the remaining pollution, have estimated flows. Residences must also pay a fee based on the number of individuals residing in the house. Appeal is possible for sources who feel their fees are not representative of their emissions, and all rates are determined after consultation with the sources.

Rates also incorporate seasonal peaks in emissions. In France, the charge is based on an average day in the month with the worst pollution for each industry. Rates may vary across regions in both The Netherlands and France, although the treatment is not consistent. In France, for example, some downstream polluters who emit large amounts of effluent pay a higher rate than upstream users with lower emissions per source. In other places the upstream users that discharge less than those downstream pay a higher rate, because there are economies of scale in treating the large amounts of emissions occurring downstream and because the rivers have more assimilative capacity downstream.

In France, six river basins are regulated by a Comité de Bassin. An Agence Financiére collects the fees. In The Netherlands, a water board or the province has the responsibility for both regulation and fee collection. What is important is that the regulatory agency is defined on the basis of the waterways, not simply by the political jurisdiction. In both The Netherlands and France, there has been some opposition to the system. In The Netherlands, some polluters refused to pay when the charges were introduced. In France, municipalities were the big opponents because they saw the system as an additional tax that would deter industry from locating within their boundaries. These difficulties have been reduced over time.

What are the effects of these systems on economic efficiency? First, in both countries the fees have been too low to reflect any sort of damages resulting from pollution. They were designed primarily to pay for a portion of the treatment costs. But the fees in France cover only about one-third to one-half the capital costs of the treatment system (Bower et al, 1981). Two factors modify this result. First, the fees are scheduled to rise substantially in the 1980s. The regulatory authorities recognize the gap between estimated damages and fees, and have been raising the fees. What is important is that the system for levying fees is in place. Even though the fees have been low, the potential to incorporate marginal damages exists and is administratively feasible. It would not take a major reorganization of the regulatory authorities or their legal powers to implement a scheme where fees more closely corresponded to the effects of the effluent on the environment. Second, even though the fees have been modest, they have still induced some firms to reduce their emissions rather than pay the charge.

In France, the fees have also been used to compensate certain polluters for the installation of abatement equipment. Again, economic incentives are present. The water authorities know which dischargers are more efficient in abating and have tried to allocate the funds to them. Exactly how well this system has worked is not known. It seems to us that there is a danger in the redistribution of funds that the regulatory authorities could be influenced by factors other than the polluter's abatement performance (such as bribes). Nonetheless, what is important about the systems in place in the two countries is that a quantity control — the standard — is not the only means used to reduce pollution.

The United States: Water Pollution Standards

Our focus in this section is the Water Pollution Control Act of 1972. This is the major legislation governing emissions into U.S. waterways (see Marcus, 1980, for further discussion of the drafting and enactment of this legislation). The act was passed by Congress in October 1972. It required the Environmental Protection Agency of the United States (EPA) to meet six deadlines. These were:

1. By 1973, to issue effluent guidelines for major industrial categories of water pollution.
2. By 1974, to grant permits to all water pollution sources.
3. By 1977, all sources were to install the "best practicable technology" (BPT) for abatement of pollutants emitted.
4. By 1981, all major U.S. waterways were to be fishable and swimmable.
5. By 1983, all sources were to install the "best available technology" (BAT) to abate pollution.
6. By 1985, all discharges to waterways were to be eliminated.

This is an ambitious program, to say the least, and none of the deadlines have been met.

The initial deadline was the basis on which the remaining five depended. The guidelines were to be the standards for every major pollutant and the basis on which the permits were to be distributed. Each firm was to be given a permit (by 1974) that specified exactly how much it was entitled to emit. Permits were obviously intended to be consistent with the guidelines in that the sum of the emissions allowed under the permits was to equal the guideline for each pollutant. For each pollutant, the BPT was the average of the best *existing* technology for abatement for the "good" plants — those removing pollutants effectively. If no plants were in this category, the EPA was to establish its own BPTs based on technical information (engineering cost data).

The BAT was to be the best control measure available. It meant each source of a particular pollutant would have to use a uniform technology. The BAT was the means by which the 1985 requirement was to be met.

There was no way the EPA could meet the first two deadlines. It was faced with an enormous task and had insufficient human resources to carry out the agenda. Over 200,000 industrial polluters emitting 30 major categories of pollution (and 250 subcategories) had to be examined. Information on the manufacturing process of each polluter, its discharges, technological options for abatement, and so on had to be determined and converted into guidelines within one year. EPA simply did not have the time to gather and evaluate the data, nor sufficient research experience and personnel to complete the task. EPA employees visited the polluters, hired outside consultants (often very closely linked to the firms they were evaluating), and made an attempt to obtain the information necessary to set the guidelines. They did not meet the 1973 deadline.

By May 1973, when the official guidelines were due, there existed only interim guidelines for 22 industrial categories. EPA decided at that time to begin issuing permits on the basis of the interim guidelines. This created a legal battle. As a result of its failure to establish final guidelines for all categories, the EPA was sued by the National Resources Defense Council for delay in establishing guidelines. By January 1974, 38 guidelines for 30 different major categories and 100 subcategories were in place. Virtually no engineering or economic analyses were undertaken in setting these guidelines.

While it was wrestling with the guideline deadline, work on establishing permits for each source was underway. As noted above, permits were being issued by mid-1973. The EPA had a bit more expertise in this area, because prior to 1972 it had tried to regulate emissions through the use of permits. The permits specified abatement requirements, described surveillance procedures, and specified the legal action that would be taken for noncompliance. The legal basis of the pre-1972 permits was an act passed in 1899 governing disposal of refuse (the Refuse Act). EPA's permit scheme was thwarted by Congress, state water pollution authorities, and the companies receiving the permits.

Congress was unhappy because EPA did not consult it prior to launching its scheme. The states thought EPA would supersede their own standards, passed in 1965. The polluters didn't want to reveal any information and did not submit the required applications for a permit. And even the environmentalists were skeptical that the scheme would reduce emissions. EPA's actions were ended when a district court in Ohio found that each permit issued had to be supported by an environmental impact statement—a detailed evaluation of the costs and benefits of the action. Environmental impact statements are time-consuming and very costly. There was no way the EPA could evaluate each of the 50,000 operations for which it had permits. The program ended, but it did provide the EPA with information useful in establishing permits under the 1972 act.

Unfortunately, because the guidelines were not in place when many of the permits were issued (94 percent of the major sources of water pollutants had received a permit before the guidelines were released), there was much inconsistency between the permits and the guidelines. Permits and guidelines were established simultaneously by different offices within EPA using different information bases. The interim guidelines were also typically more restrictive than the guidelines ultimately issued. As a result, a slew of legal challenges to the permits occurred. Companies contested the permits because of inconsistency with the interim guidelines (in over 2,000 adjudicary proceedings), then challenged the final guidelines themselves (in over 150 lawsuits). In these proceedings and suits companies argued that the EPA did not have the authority to set an exact number in its guideline, but only a range of numbers; that it had not obtained sufficient cost information on which to base the permit; that it failed to incorporate differences in discharges seasonally; that not enough subcategories were included, and so on.

What resulted from all this was extensive delay in establishing every component of the act. A court would find against the EPA, the ruling would be appealed in a higher court, and meanwhile the guideline and permit, and the BPT and BAT, were all delayed. Clearly, the regulatory procedures established by the Water Pollution Control Act were not working very well throughout the 1970s and into the 1980s.

Even without the legal challenges and the difficulties the EPA had in establishing guidelines and permits, there are problems with the law. First, and very important, there are *no economic incentives.* Firms were given a permit that cannot be traded and required to abate all emissions by 1985. (This deadline has since been extended.) No calculation, however rough, was made of the marginal damages from water pollution versus the marginal benefits of pollution (or the marginal costs of abatement). It is most unlikely that it is in society's interest to remove *all* pollutants from waterways unless there is no intersection of marginal damage and marginal benefit functions at a positive amount of pollution. The requirement that all emissions be terminated has a detrimental effect on meeting even more modest reductions in emissions. Legal battles can tie up the regulatory procedure so completely that even the more moderate guidelines cannot be imposed. Note as well that legal battles are costly to both the private and public sector.

It is instructive to contrast the U.S. experience with that of France and The Netherlands. The European method of standards plus charges may have initially led to greater than optimal discharges, but the policies were implemented and emissions were being reduced throughout the 1970s. Charges were established so that far fewer legal and procedural difficulties occurred than in the United States. The European countries are now able to further reduce emissions through higher fees, while the United States is still trying to figure out how to deal with water pollution.

Other features of the U.S. Water Pollution Control Act of 1972 also serve to increase the costs of pollution control and delay reductions in emissions. The notion of a uniform "best technology" is unreasonable. Within the same industry, there are large differences among plants. Imposing a uniform abatement technique is bound to increase greatly the total costs of pollution control. Firms have a great incentive to challenge these technologies on the grounds that they are unfairly treated or that the technologies are not feasible to implement or so costly that the firm cannot stay in business. BATs do not allow for a tradeoff between pollution and economic activity. The effect of the abatement requirements may be to alter market structure as some firms are forced out of business, and/or foreign firms facing much less severe pollution controls increase their exports to U.S. markets. These economic effects may make the standard a very costly means of reducing pollution. These are some of the income distribution dimensions of policy we noted in Chapter 12. Losers in these income redistribution situations who are not compensated can often exert great political pressure and discredit an otherwise good approach.

Some form of pollution control is very much in the public interest, but the methods required by the Water Pollution Control Act lead to a high-cost form of control which does not guarantee improved water quality. We turn now to an alternative method of reducing pollution that deviates substantially from the dependence on the standard and lack of economic incentives—the marketable permit for pollution.

BOX 13.1
Preserving Illusions—The Clean Water Act after
Ten Years

If the inconclusive deliberations of the Ninety-seventh Congress are even a partial guide to the future, the Ninety-eighth Congress is likely to vote to extend the 1972 Clean Water Act with only minor changes. In contrast to the Clean Air Act, controversy surrounding the Water Act is almost nonexistent. Republicans and Democrats, industrialists and environmentalists, federal and local officials all seem quite satisfied with efforts to clean up the nation's waters.

Lukewarm opposition

The lack of strong opposition on the part of business is not hard to fathom. Despite occasional protests to the contrary, the act has not been much of a burden on industry, mainly because it emphasizes uniform application of "best" pollution-control strategies. Typically, *best* is defined by the Environmental Protection Agency (EPA) as that approach already used by the largest, most progressive firms in an industry. For those firms—which usually account for most of their industry's production—the additional cost of the EPA regulations over and above what they already spend is very small. As a result, for most of the industry the annualized costs of the act average well under 2 percent of each firm's sales. Even when additional costs are more substantial, the fact that the regulations apply uniformly to all firms in an industry means that most of these costs can be passed on in higher prices.

The sanguine attitude of local officials is even easier to understand. The 75-percent federal subsidy provided goes a long way to lessen the pain of the act's requirement to upgrade municipal treatment systems.

The approval of environmentalists is more difficult to explain. It is true that noteworthy improvements have been made in a few waterbodies, such as Lake Erie and the Potomac River, but overall the act has not done much to improve the nation's waters. According to monitoring data and theoretical water modeling, the biggest improvements appear to be in dissolved oxygen content. Yet this is a questionable achievement: in 1972—before the act—only about 30 percent of the nation's waters failed to meet acceptable dissolved oxygen standards.

More important, ten years of effort have produced very little improvement with respect to nutrients, sediment, and toxic substances. The 1977 amendments to the act may improve matters, but serious problems with these pollutants are likely to remain indefinitely, chiefly because of the act's relative

Box 13.1 continued

neglect of the main "nonpoint" sources of pollution—agricultural and urban runoff. Urban runoff often is the major source of certain toxics, even in such highly industrialized cities as Houston and New Orleans.

Intentions and illusions

Measured objectively, the act's performance has been weak in precisely those areas where improvements were most needed. Why, then, does it receive so much support from the environmental movement? One possibility, suggested by Allen V. Kneese, is that environmentalists place a high ethical value on doing one's "best." Since most dischargers to the nation's waters have permits that supposedly guarantee the use of *best* technologies, the act from this ethical point of view has been a success.

Another possibility is that environmentalists—along with the rest of us—are forced to rely too much on monitoring data to determine how well or poorly the act has done. However, our monitoring is so sketchy that it would not be surprising if environmentalists are suspicious of this source of information. Uncertain of the effect on water quality, the environmentalists turn more confidently to the effects on polluters. Since these polluters—at least the industrial ones—have permits that restrict their polluting activities, the act offers the illusion of working.

The implication of either possibility is that it does not matter much how well the act does in cleaning up the water as long as tough action *appears* to be directed against polluters. Thus, without having to look at water quality, Sen. John Chafee (R-R.I.) can confidently assert that a "water quality-based approach to pollution control failed before 1972 and could clearly fail again." In a world where form has priority over substance, it is apparently easier than one thinks to make an environmentalist happy.

Source: Henry M. Peskin, "Preserving Illusions." *Resources* 72 (February 1983), p. 12, Washington, D.C.: Resources for the Future.

MARKETABLE PERMITS: THE NEW WAVE IN POLLUTION CONTROL?

Economists have long argued that a government-organized market which trades in permits to pollute can be organized to internalize an externality. The government establishes a desired level of environmental quality or quantity of pollution emissions, then distributes permits which sum to that level. Government involvement is necessary to administer the market and ensure that emissions do not exceed permitted levels. As long as the market is competitive, the optimal amount of pollution should result from this scheme, with firms minimizing their costs of compliance.

Dales (1968) was one of the earliest proponents of the use of markets to deal with pollution problems. Montgomery (1972) proved that the market would lead to a set of efficient prices for pollution. And recently, some states and the Environmental

Protection Agency in the United States have begun to investigate the possibility of using permits that are traded in markets to deal with some significant pollution problems. The change in the legal and regulatory environment that has emerged in the past few years has given rise to a number of interesting economic analyses of marketable pollution permits. Our focus here will be on air pollution.

Institutional Background

The primary regulatory apparatus for controlling air pollution is the Clean Air Act and its amendments in 1970, 1977, and 1979. Prior to 1970, state and local governments had primary responsibility for air pollution control other than automobile exhaust. In 1970, the Clean Air Act was amended to give federal jurisdiction over new sources of industrial pollution. The Environmental Protection Agency (EPA) was established in that year to determine and administer the new federal policies. The EPA was responsible for setting standards for new sources of pollution (the new-source standards), developing other standards, overseeing the states' plans to implement the new standards, and enforcing standards and monitoring air quality. The primary form of control was regulation, as in the case of water pollution. The EPA established ambient standards—targets for concentrations of air pollutants. Each state had to file with the EPA a plan showing how these ambient standards would be obtained for pollutants not classified as "new sources." The new-source pollutants were directly controlled by EPA through standards.

One of the EPA's major tasks was to determine how to prevent deterioration of air quality in areas that are not heavily polluted. In the early 1970s, there was considerable concern over the degradation of areas of high air quality. Prodded by litigation that reached the Supreme Court of the United States (*The Sierra Club* v. *Ruckelshaus,* 1972), the EPA responded with an amendment to the Clean Air Act in 1977 to prevent clean areas from becoming dirty. The country was divided into three types of regions with allowable increments in emissions designated for each type. Pollution increments were allocated to firms desiring to locate in any region on a first-come, first served basis.

The difficulty with a nondegradation policy is that it becomes a deterrent to economic growth in regions with good air quality. This may lead to a loss in social welfare if the value of the output from these potential entrants exceeds the damages due to air pollutants. This is a basic problem with standards—marginal damages and marginal benefits of pollution are not equated at each point in time. Because pollution regulations act as a barrier to entry to firms in particular locations, they may give firms already existing in those regions some monopoly power and create economic rents. Consumers may be worse off because markets are less competitive.

However, the allocation of pollution increments may have been the first step in the move toward a system of marketable permits for controlling air pollution. In 1979, additional amendments to the Clean Air Act furthered the possibility that a market mechanism could be used. Two reforms in the transferability of implicit rights to pollute were made. The first was the introduction of an emission reduction scheme that has become known as the *bubble policy.* For a particular pollutant, the bubble allows an increase in emissions from one plant or firm (in a given area) *if* another source of the same pollutant in the same area reduces its emissions by the same amount. When first introduced in 1979, these tradeoffs were allowed only within a given plant; the bubble has since been extended to different plants and even different firms. All trades must be approved by the EPA.

The bubble represents a move toward a system of permits that are transferable, although in a very restricted sense. The transferability is crucial, though, as rights to pollute must be exchangeable if firms are to meet a given standard at minimum cost. The other significant feature of the bubble is that it moves the EPA away from its policies of imposing specific standards on each emitter. The advantage of the trading permit is that no information on abatement costs from individual firms is required, and no firm is restricted to a rigid individual standard.

The second component of the 1979 amendments was the *emissions offset policy.* Prior to 1979, if an area was not meeting its ambient standard, no new firms that contributed to air pollution were allowed to enter. Problems similar to those associated with nondegradation emerged. To allow for new entry into these areas, the EPA now allows new firms to enter if they succeed in getting existing firms to reduce their emissions by exactly the same amount as the expected emissions that will come from the new firm. Existing firms thus have a valuable property right for which they can extract payment. EPA must again sanction these exchanges and ensure that there is no net change in total emissions. The EPA also requires new sources to meet the technical standards established for the region. Exchanges do not occur through an organized market, but as a result of bargaining among firms. However, it is not a big step from the offset policy to one of a pollution market with a fixed number of pollution permits per area.

BOX 13.2
Environmental Regulations, Costly Abatement, and
Regional Growth

Could the Clean Air Act be causing an increase in pollution? Does it affect the location of industries in the United States? These are questions addressed by an economist, Robert Crandall, in a study done for the Brookings Institute. The nondegradation policies of the Clean Air Act require all new industrial and electrical utilities to install stack gas scrubbers to prevent sulfur oxide emissions from being discharged into the atmosphere. No new plant is allowed to enter an area if it decreases the air quality there. These regulations add to the capital and operating costs of new concerns and may influence their locational decisions. Other regulations in the act require all fossil-fuel burning facilities to reduce the *percentage* of their emissions to the maximum amount possible. Each plant must remove the same percentage of emissions regardless of the initial level of discharge. These regulations may make air pollution worse over much of the country. Let's see why.

The major sources of sulfur oxide emissions in the United States are coal- and oil-burning plants, especially electric power plants. The United States produces two types of coal — coal with a high sulfur content in the East (from Appalachia), and low-sulfur coal from the West (Colorado, Montana, Wyoming). Power plants and other facilities located in the East burn eastern coal for the obvious reason that it is cheaper than western coal (largely due to transportation costs). Plants located in the East are typically old and are therefore exempt from the requirement that they must install scrubbers.

Crandall argues that firms attempting to locate in the West and air quality are the losers from the Clean Air Act. First, requiring scrubbers of all new facilities means that fewer will be built than if these concerns were able to seek a cost-minimizing method of meeting air pollution standards. Scrubbers are very expensive to construct and to operate. They are prone to malfunction unless maintained in top condition. Fewer new plants will be built because of these high costs, and old plants will be discouraged from installing scrubbers. Because old plants emit a lot of sulfur oxides, aggregate emissions can rise. But even if the new plants are built, the overall air quality will decline unless the old plants increase their abatement or shut down. The plants are still operating. Then there is the high-sulfur coal problem. New plants will have an incentive to use high-sulfur coal because it is cheaper than low-sulfur coal. They are required to install scrubbers and effectively prevented from using low-sulfur coal to meet the standards without having to use scrubbers. However, if an absolute standard were in effect — so many tons per day of emissions must be reduced — plants would have an incentive to shift to the low-sulfur coal to meet the standard.

Crandall argues that the Clean Air Act represents more than just a desire on the part of Congress to reduce pollution. It may be a means of protecting eastern coal producers at the expense of the western producers. The representatives who strongly support environmental regulations come from high-income, low-growth states in the northern part of the country. The votes these politicians cast for environmental measures are also frequently unrelated to the local air and water quality in the representatives' state or district. Could their votes be designed to inhibit development in the West and protect jobs in the East? Whatever the answer, the economic incentives provided by the regulations are clear — requiring firms to install scrubbers increases the fixed costs to new or relocating firms. Fixed costs can be a barrier to entry. Requiring equal percentage abatement and the installation of scrubbers regardless of the amount of emissions that would be generated inhibits firms from seeking cost-minimizing methods of abating pollution. If existing firms face less restrictive environmental regulations than new entrants, markets can become less competitive and pollution emissions can rise. Is the consumer, who values cheap goods but isn't worried about pollution, or the environmentalist, who worries about pollution but not the prices of goods, better off as a result of these policies? You be the judge.

Source: Robert W. Crandall, "Clean Air and Regional Protectionism." *The Brookings Review,* Fall 1983, pp. 17–20.

Characteristics of Marketable Permits

Our analysis of the characteristics of permits follows that of Hahn and Noll (1981), Krupnick et al. (1983), and Montgomery (1972). Suppose there are m point sources of pollution and n different receptor points. A receptor point can be a location where air quality is monitored or a region identified by an air diffusion model of roughly homogeneous air quality. We can then define a vector of air quality $Q(q_1, \ldots, q_n)$ where q_j is the concentration of a particular pollutant, say sulfur dioxide, at point j. An air diffusion model incorporating meteorological information and the analysis of air flows can then determine the contribution of, say, one unit of sulfur dioxide emissions from any of the m sources to pollution concentrations at any of the n receptor points.

The objective of the air pollution control authority is to achieve a set of standards—one for each receptor point—that specifies the maximum concentration of pollution at that point. The problem is to obtain the standard at minimum aggregate costs of abatement. The regulator thus seeks a pattern of emissions from each source of pollution that minimizes abatement costs while satisfying the constraint that the standard be met. There will be a set of emission levels that solves the problem and if polluters are cost minimizers, the shadow prices (on the regulatory constraint) that emerge are the same prices that would result from the operation of a competitive market in pollution permits.

What are the practical implications of the model? Let's first see what the government must do to implement the system. Let's first consider questions which must be addressed in designing a system of marketable permits (see Tietenberg, 1980, for a more detailed discussion of these points.) The government regulators must initially establish environmental goals. The existing system is based on ambient standards. However, the government does have a choice as to whether the standards will be defined in terms of the ambient standards that specify concentration levels of each pollutant measured at a specific location for a specific period of time (tons per day), or actual emissions of pollutants (as was the case with water).

The advantage of the ambient standard is its relatively close relationship to damage from pollution. The more locations defined, the more precisely the relationship between emissions and damages. The disadvantage with an ambient standard simply enforced as a quantity constraint on firms is that pollution flows from one source may range over a number of locations. To meet the standard in the locations closest to the source of the pollution, large reductions in emissions may be required. This may mean that pollution concentrations in locations far from the source may be too low. Marketable permits can solve this problem, as we will see below.

The alternative standard is one based on *aggregate emissions*. No attempt is made to measure concentrations at particular locations; emissions are simply restricted in the entire region. This sort of regulation would be easier to implement, monitor, and enforce, but can lead to excessive amounts of pollution in particular locations within the region. It is an emissions-based system (EBS). A scheme based on local or ambient standards is an ambient-based system (ABS).

The next question the regulator must address is the geographic extent of the market. In many cases this is predetermined by political boundaries. Air pollution control authorities may exist in some states to regulate a particular air basin. This may be a reasonable jurisdiction in some areas such as the Los Angeles basin, where the authority roughly corresponds to the area affected by the pollution. In other areas, the jurisdiction may be far too small. In heavily polluted areas of the eastern United States, pollution spills over state lines (and the U.S. border). State and local authorities may thus have little control over significant portions of the pollution that passes over their boundaries. Even within the jurisdiction, the regulators must determine the number of locales or receptor areas that will have separate standards if an ABS is to be implemented. Ideally, this should be done if the pollutant has significant variation in concentration within the jurisdiction.

Once the market is defined, the coverage of the permits must be determined. Do all polluters need permits, or just the major polluters? Should there be separate markets for firms and individuals (cars versus power plants)? How will the permits be distributed? If the market for permits is and stays competitive, it doesn't matter from an economic point of view how the permits are distributed—the efficient allocation will result. But it is unlikely for all locales and types of pollution that the structure of the market will be competitive. If the rights are given away (as is being done right now), the initial holders of rights may be able to extract rent from the rights or may use them as entry barriers to new firms without rights. This problem will be more severe the fewer the number of large polluters in a given locale. Not surprisingly however, polluters would tend to favor free distribution as opposed to some form of auction. They then receive the rents from the permits, not the government. Politically, it may be much easier to give away the permits than sell them. Some locales are also prohibited from "taxing" polluters by auctioning rights. If an auction were used, the money would have to be refunded or redistributed in some way. All these factors make it likely that the rights will be given away.

Finally, the regulators must determine how to enforce the scheme. They must be able to detect violations, which means that emissions and/or air quality must be measured. The regulators, of course, also need the legal authority to deal with violations. Monitoring of emissions can be technically difficult and costly. One approach is to follow the European example of actually measuring effluent for major polluters, then estimating it statistically for others. But any scheme that does not entail continuous monitoring runs the risk that it will miss accidental spills of large amounts of pollution. If the regulator is unable to determine who is responsible, these occurrences will be difficult to prevent. Once a violation is detected, the question of how to penalize the perpetrator arises. The current array of penalties includes cease and desist orders, financial penalties, and shutdown orders. The first is typically an insufficient deterrent, because there is no penalty for noncompliance in the past. If a firm continually exceeds its permit, the cease and desist order simply attempts to prevent future emissions from exceeding the permit.

Financial penalties certainly have the ability to deter violations, but in the past they have been far too low to matter.[5] Firms violating the standards have found it cheaper to pay the penalties than to abate. If a financial penalty were imposed, it could be done in a number of ways. One proposal is to set a predetermined fee based on, say, marginal damages incurred for each unit of pollution emitted beyond the permitted level. This type of scheme is designed to get the optimal amount of compliance with the permit. If the cost of compliance does exceed the penalty for noncompliance, then it is optimal not to meet the permit. This type of scheme may be easy to administer (if pollution per permit holder can be measured), but it might run into legal difficulties.

An alternative is the so-called Connecticut plan because of its use in Connecticut for enforcing standards. This scheme relates the penalty to the costs of pollution control that are avoided by the emitter who violates the standard (or the permit once in place). The plan removes the incentive to emit more than the standard (or permit) because the polluter knows it will face the same costs no matter what it does. This scheme may not yield the optimal amount of compliance, but it should prevent noncompliance.

We now turn to a more specific examination of different types of marketable permit schemes. We examine three variations: an ABS, an EBS, and a system that combines some features of both.

The Ambient-Based System

To establish an ABS system of marketable permits, the government must first determine the receptor areas. This task requires the use of models predicting air diffusion from sources of pollution. Fairly sophisticated and reliable models exist. Then the total emissions permitted in each receptor area consistent with the ambient air quality standards must be determined. The setting of air quality standards ideally should be done with some computation of expected benefits net of costs of controlling pollution to particular levels. One would hope for some notion of establishing the "optimal" amount of pollution. But if this task is impossible, a reasonable standard can be set and altered over time.

Once the standard is determined for each area, the government issues the number of permits consistent with this total. The government can give the permits to existing polluters, or auction them off. If the permits are given away, the government lets the market determine the final allocation of the permits and hence emissions among the pollution sources. No further regulation of the method of allocating permits among polluters is required, except to ensure that the market operates efficiently. Finally, the government must enforce emission standards by determining if the source emitting the pollutant is in compliance with the number of permits it holds and penalize noncompliers. These monitoring and enforcement tasks are roughly comparable for all the permit schemes, so we will not comment further on this aspect of the scheme.

What are the advantages of the ABS marketable permits over other policies? First, an ambient-based system would be relatively simple and less costly to operate from the viewpoint of the regulator than any other type of pollution policy. The information requirements for establishing and operating the permit system are lower than what is necessary to impose taxes (fees) or have pollution standards imposed on individual polluters. The government need not gather information about the abatement costs for each polluter. Nor must it attempt to compute marginal damages and marginal benefits of pollution, as was necessary in determining the optimal tax on pollution. When one compares the marketable permits to the extensive fee-setting activities we investigated in the case of water pollution charges in Europe or the untradable water pollution permits found in the United States, the information requirements of the marketable permits seem quite modest. Second, as we have noted before, the permit scheme does achieve the target at minimum cost. It also allows firms to pursue cost-reducing innovations in abatement technology (as would a tax).

There is one serious flaw with the ABS system that makes it unlikely that it will be implemented: Polluters would find it extremely burdensome. Each polluter would have to have permits for every receptor area into which its pollution flowed. There would be as many markets as there were receptor areas, and firms might find it very costly to make transactions in a large number of markets. How costly these markets would be to firms is an empirical question.

The Emissions-Based System

The EBS has been proposed as one alternative that eliminates the problem of multiple markets and permit prices per polluter. Permits are defined in terms of the level (or rate) of emissions from the source, rather than in terms of the effect of the emissions on the ambient air quality in all the receptor areas. Any emissions within a particular zone are treated as equivalent regardless of where they drift. The advantage of the system is that each firm would have to operate only in one market where its permit is tradable one for one within the zone. No trades across zones would be permitted.

There are, however, a number of problems with this approach. First, pollution can be concentrated within an area and yield "hot spots," locales within the zone that have pollution levels which exceed the standard. The hot spot problem can be reduced by defining the zones more narrowly, but then the system drifts closer to the ABS, with its problem of multiple markets for firms. Second, within the region polluters with very different dispersion characteristics may be combined. Then the one-for-one trades will not reflect differences in the pollution concentrations of the emitters. The implicit price of emissions established by the market will not be the shadow price of the binding standard.

If pollution spills over a zone, there is no market to handle those transactions. Recall with the ABS that firms must have permits for wherever their pollution flows. The EBS works if the pollutant in question is either very local in impact or is quickly dispersed into the environment and affects large areas of the country equivalently. For example, chlorofluorocarbons (CFCs) are a global pollutant that comes from aerosol sprays. No matter where the source of the pollution, the CFCs are rapidly dispersed into the upper atmosphere, where they break down the ozone layer surrounding the earth (and can lead to increased penetration of ultraviolet rays leading to increased incidence of cancers). An EBS system could work well in this case because the market truly *is* global; there are no spillovers or hot spots.

Another case where the EBS may work is where the dispersion characteristics for emissions within a zone are relatively similar. If the zones where these characteristics are roughly the same can be defined, the hot spots and cost inefficiencies can be reduced. But even if there are no differences in the dispersion characteristics within a zone, the regulatory authority must still determine how many permits to issue per zone. This calculation requires far more data than the computation of the number of permits required in the ABS. The authority must solve the cost minimization problem defined above. This means that it needs to have an air quality model and inventory of emissions, as before, also but it must know as well the source-specific

---

BOX 13.3
CO_2 Emissions and the Greenhouse Warming of the Earth

A $2°C$ increase in global temperature by the year 2040 is predicted in a recent monograph of the U.S. Environmental Protection Agency. The burning of fossil fuels is the principal source of the carbon dioxide (CO_2) which is responsible for the increase in global temperature. The additional CO_2 increases the greenhouse effect of the earth's atmosphere—the trapping of the sun's rays inside the atmosphere. The predictions are derived using three models: an energy-use model, a carbon-cycle model used to translate CO_2 emissions into increases in atmospheric CO_2 concentrations, and an atmosphere temperature model used to estimate changes in temperature based on increases in atmospheric CO_2 and other greenhouse gases. Over the past 100 years, the temperature rise has been about $0.04°C$ per decade, and the projection is for a $0.3°C$ rise per decade. The implications are, of course, profound. For example, a major eruption from a single volcano has been documented to affect *world* climate for many months subsequently (Tambura in Indonesia in 1816 resulted in 6 inches of snow in New England in June.) Temperature increases from an increase in CO_2 will change precipitation and storm patterns and cause the global sea level to rise. With less assurance, temperatures are predicted to increase by $5°C$ by the year 2100. These are predictions with apocalyptic implications—the polar ice caps could melt. How seriously should the predictions be taken?

Seidel and Keyes considered responses such as the banning of coal by the year 2000 and suggested that the $2°C$ rise would be delayed until 2055. Other severe measures of restraint in using fossil fuels were examined, and no avenue appeared to prevent the global warming from increasing CO_2 in the atmosphere.

On a more optimistic note, in March 1985, an international agreement was signed in Vienna by many nations to take action to prevent the destruction of the ozone layer surrounding the earth. Ozone is being depleted by chlorofluorocarbons (CFCs). CFCs are a global pollutant like CO_2 that are released into the atmosphere primarily from aerosol sprays and refrigerants. Depletion of the ozone layer may contribute to the greenhouse effect, increase the incidence of skin cancers, and reduce agricultural yields. The international agreement may thus be a significant step toward control of a global pollutant.

Source: S. Seidel and D. K. Keyes, *Can We Delay a Greenhouse Warming?* Washington D.C.: U.S. Environmental Protection Agency, September 1983.

monopsonist will try to minimize the price it pays for the permits, recognizing that the greater its purchases, the higher the price. It will therefore tend to *overabate* compared to the efficient market. The sellers of the permits will have to abate less and thus will tend to face lower marginal costs of abatement. How much of a social loss this represents depends on the nature of the abatement cost functions for all the sources. If marginal abatement costs are relatively flat over a wide range of reductions in emissions, the loss in efficiency could be relatively small. If the marginal costs were sharply increasing, efficiency loss could be great.

Generally, it was found that when the possibility of noncompetitive behavior exists, the process by which the market is started and operates will have to be carefully evaluated prior to launching a marketable permit system, since private actions alone will not lead to the efficient allocation. This type of analysis is extremely valuable in determining the appropriate type of system to implement.

Acid Rain: Can Marketable Permits Help?

Our final topic on marketable permits considers whether there is any possibility that acid rain — a pollution problem that is international in scope — can be internalized through the implementation of some sort of marketable permit system. We take as our example the acid rain problem facing the United States and Canada.

Acid rain is what is called a case of *transfrontier pollution.* The sulfates do not stop at the border, but flow on wherever the air masses take them. Acid rain is a problem for many European countries as well. It is a difficult situation both in terms of the complexity of the transmission of the pollutants and, of course, the political factors. In the case of Canada and the United States, acid rain is a symmetrical externality. Each country emits sulfur oxides that harm themselves and the other country. Ironically, acid rain is largely the result of past regulatory policies of both countries. The increase in the deposition of acid precipitation is not primarily due to increased sulfur dioxide emissions from major polluters. Rather, it is because of regulations designed to reduce the *local* emissions of SO_2.

To meet state and provincial standards, major sources of sulfur oxides were allowed to increase the height of the stacks discharging the pollutant into the atmosphere in lieu of installing scrubbers (typically very expensive abatement equipment to install on older plants). Scrubbers remove sulfur from the flue gases. Air quality in the regions near the polluters may have increased, but more acidic precipitation was the result as the SO_2 was converted to SO_4 and carried over much farther distances than in the past. Finally, there are very complex political and economic issues surrounding the substitution of high-sulfur coal for oil in the generation of electricity.

Acid rain may turn out to be a very significant pollution problem in North America and elsewhere because of its adverse impact on recreation, forests, agriculture, and water supplies. Today, acid rain is an important news item. In March 1984, five New England states (excluding New Hampshire) filed suit against the Environmental Protection Agency for failure to proceed with regulations required under the terms of the Clean Air Act. In March 1985, the leaders of Canada and the United States agreed to examine the problem of acid rain. To date, no definitive regulatory policy exists in North America for acid rain.

We want to ignore the political issues in this section not because they are not important or *the most important* problem, but because we want to see if there is any reason to believe that marketable permits could alleviate the pollution. We know of two papers that address the question of acid rain and marketable permits—one by Atkinson (1983) and another by Scott (1984). Neither paper addresses all the complex issues about acid rain, but each makes a simple point.

Atkinson, investigating the use of an EBS, employs a programming model similar to that used by Atkinson and Tietenberg to determine the effect of an emissions permit system for the Cleveland region of the Ohio River Basin. This region is presumed to be a significant contributer to acid rain because it contains many industrial operations, and coal- and oil-fired electric utilities. It is also unlikely to meet the ambient standard for sulfur dioxide. The programming model indicates that the emissions permit is far more costly than either the ABS or the local SIP strategy to meet the ambient standard. An ambient permit system would be far less costly, but would reduce the amount of abatement from the plants with tall stacks and increase the emissions of sulfur dioxide in the region relative to the local SIP and EBS, unless global restrictions on the transmission of the sulfur dioxide out of the region are imposed.

The EBS reduces emissions the most, but is costly ($158.2 million per year versus $144.3 million for the SIP and $112.9 for the ABS, where the numbers are based on abatement costs under a constraint on the long-range transmission of the emissions). Whether these cost differentials are significant politically is an open question. There is also a problem of potential lack of competitiveness in the market under either permit scheme. Only eight of the 25 point sources that emit 95 percent of the sulfur dioxide from the region are owned independently. The electric utility plants generate 95 percent of the emissions from the group, and problems similar to those discussed by Hahn and Noll would be expected.

These results should not be surprising. Acid rain is not the kind of pollutant that would be well suited to an ABS. Given the administrative difficulties, the ABS is an unlikely candidate for a marketable permit system for acid rain. But are the cost effects of the EBS sufficient to deter its use?

The paper by Scott suggests the use of an EBS with a new twist—the introduction of predetermined reductions in the allowable emissions per permit per year. Scott's proposal is as follows: An international (Canada–U.S.) commission in conjunction with the EPA and Ministry of Environment in Canada issues permits to all major sources of sulfur dioxide emissions in both countries. These permits allow the source to emit *its current level of pollution.* A schedule of reductions in emissions per year is also stipulated on the permit. The reductions would be designed to meet an ambient standard after so many years. Holders of the permit would then know what reductions in emissions are required each year, and they can reduce their emissions or buy more permits. Permits would be tradable, but as usual with an EBS, the cost-minimizing solution need not occur.

What is crucial in the plan is the geographic scope. If polluters that contribute very little to acid rain are aggregated with major sources of sulfur oxide emissions, hot spots and increases in aggregate emissions could occur. Scott notes this and says that one solution is to try to establish zones for polluters with similar SO_2 emissions. But the more finely the zones are determined, the higher the costs of abatement, because firms might then need to buy permits in many zones. Scott makes the interesting suggestion of trades across zones with "emission discounts" if the dispersion characteristics between the zones are quite different.

The advantages of Scott's proposal are that it would start the process of dealing with acid rain. Continued studies on the problem could occur simultaneously, but meanwhile something would be being done. The reductions in emissions stipulated on the permits could be small initially while the two countries continued to work on the problem. Another advantage is that those downstream from the sources could help finance the reduction in emissions by purchasing permits and retiring them. The firms would sell only if the price exceeded their abatement costs. Thus some of the heated discussion about the distribution of the burden of abating sulfur oxide emissions could be dampened. If Canada and New England want a faster reduction than that stipulated by the permits, they can buy them up. Finally, the system allows more data to be collected to help in the analysis of this type of pollution.

The proposal by Scott is in a preliminary stage of discussion and evaluation. Certainly, many unanswered questions need to be addressed, such as just how costly this kind of EBS would be, how viable it would be in the international context, what type of market equilibriums would obtain in the different regions defined, how the reductions stipulated on the permit would be determined, and what would happen if they were later found to be too high or low. Scott has sketched a concept that requires more empirical evaluation. But it is a hopeful proposal — one that may be possible to implement before the problem worsens while we wait for the results of more studies.

SUMMARY

1. Cost benefit analysis is the technique used by economists to evaluate the marginal benefits and marginal costs of abating pollution. The basic cost-benefit principle is to measure all values in terms of their shadow prices — prices that reflect resource scarcity. Shadow prices are required whenever market prices do not exist and when market-determined prices include distortions such as taxes, quotas, subsidies, and forms of imperfect competition.

2. The marginal benefits from pollution abatement are typically difficult to determine because they are often intangible (the value of preserving the environment) and are not market-determined. Frequently, marginal benefits must be imputed from other related economic activities (such as inferring recreational demand from travel data).

3. To measure marginal benefits from pollution abatement or improved environmental quality, three sets of relationships must be formulated and evaluated: (1) The relationship between changes in emissions to changes in the ambient quality of the environment. (2) How changes in environmental quality affect the flow of environmental services to individuals. (3) How the changes in environmental services affect economic welfare.

4. In measuring the benefits of improved water quality for recreational services, economists attempt to calculate individuals' willingness to pay for small changes in quality. Willingness to pay may include demand for the

recreational services at a site and/or option and preservation demand—willingness to pay to prevent an irreversible development from occurring on the site (regardless of whether the individual plans to visit the site). All these values require the estimation of a demand curve for recreational services today and into the future. From the demand curve, estimates are needed of the price elasticity of demand and the size of the shift parameters—water quality, and option and preservation values. The data for these values are typically obtained from travel cost models and surveys of recreational use. Econometric techniques are used to derive the estimates needed.

5. The story of the bees and the blossoms illustrates how private externalities can be internalized without explicit government controls. When well-defined property rights exist to the activities that are technologically interdependent, the parties involved can bargain to a mutually agreeable result. Contractual arrangements and markets emerge to internalize the externality when relatively few parties are involved and the externality does not spill over to affect other parties.

6. Standards combined with fees have been used in several European countries to help finance water treatment facilities and to provide economic incentives to abate emissions to waterways. Until recently, fees have been too low to provide much incentive for emitters to abate at the source. However, with the fee structure in place, recent increases in charges may provide greater incentive for cost-reducing abatement in the future.

7. In the United States, water pollution has been controlled by standards alone. Regulations imposed deadlines for the establishment by the Environmental Protection Agency (EPA) of standards for all important categories of emissions to waterways. Each major emitter of pollution was then to receive a permit by 1974 to discharge specified levels of the pollutants. By 1983, all sources were to install the best feasible technology. No choice over abatement techniques was to be allowed. By 1985, all discharges to waterways were to be eliminated. None of these deadlines have been met due to EPA's lack of personnel in the early 1970s, and to legal and political difficulties. The standards provide no economic incentives to abate pollution and can lead to very high costs of pollution control.

8. Marketable permits, which are now under consideration by the EPA, are a means of achieving pollution standards at potentially lower cost than standards imposed on each emitter. The policies now used by the EPA do not allow free trading of permits to pollute. The existing policies are: (1) The *bubble,* which allows an increase in emissions from one plant or firm in a given locale if another source of the same pollutant in the same region reduces its emissions; (2) the *offset,* which allows new firms to enter a region if existing firms in the region decrease emissions by the same amount as the expected emissions of the new firm. The new source of pollution must also meet the technical standards established for the region.

9. Some proposed systems of marketable permits are: (1) The ambient-based system (ABS), which is the cost-minimizing method of meeting a given standard. An ABS requires polluters to hold permits for all regions into which their emissions flow. The government regulatory authority determines the aggregate number of permits consistent with the standard (or level of environmental quality) for each region, distributes the permits to existing polluters (or auctions them), and allows firms to trade. The market

"price" of the permits is then the marginal cost of abatement for the marginal firm in each region. (2) The emissions-based system (EBS) defines the number of permits for a given region consistent with a desired standard in that region. Polluters can trade only within the region. Emissions within the region are treated as equivalent, regardless of their effect on environmental quality at different points within the region. (3) The offset system combines features of the ABS and EBS. Permits are defined in terms of emissions as in the EBS and are tradable within a zone as long as the air quality is maintained at any receptor point within the zone. The standard must be satisfied at all points within the zone. One market then operates for each zone (like the EBS), but hot spots would be prevented. Cost-minimizing trades may result if the market contains a sufficient number of participants.

10. Simulation exercises for St. Louis covering various types of marketable permits have led to mixed results. The ABS is the most cost-efficient system, as expected, and guarantees that the ambient standard is always met, but it may not yield stable market prices under different pollution standards and at different receptor points in the system. The EBS results in very high compliance costs and may not achieve a given standard. A modified ABS with trades limited to one zone achieves most air quality targets at a cost second to the pure ABS.

11. In Los Angeles, an EBS was found to perform very similarly to an ABS. The study examined the effect of the EBS on the structure of a permits market and found that noncompetitive (monopsonistic) behavior could result. This would result in too few permits being purchased and overabatement. The efficiency loss from monopsony depends on the shape of the abatement cost function and the demand curve for permits.

12. No formal marketable permit system has been proposed for acid rain, an international pollution problem. One simulation study of an EBS for acid rain found that this type of marketable permit would lead to costly abatement. An ABS may worsen long-range transmission of sulfur dioxide — the cause of acid rain — unless global restrictions on emissions are imposed. If these restrictions are imposed, the cost of the ABS rises substantially but is still less than the EBS and the current state implementation plan for the region studied. An alternative scheme is to implement a modified EBS with the permits set at existing emission levels. Over a specified time period, allowed emissions per permit are to be reduced at a rate indicated at the time the permit is issued. To minimize hot spots, zones would be established for polluters with similar dispersion characteristics.

DISCUSSION QUESTIONS

1. The Province of Ontario wants to know whether it should open up a particular wilderness site for recreational use or allow forestry firms to harvest trees there. The province will choose the activity that maximizes net benefits to the province (benefits minus costs), where benefits and costs include any nonmarket values such as pollution from forestry operations or the value of recreational benefits. What would comprise the costs and benefits for each use of the land? Briefly explain how you would measure these costs and benefits.

2. How would a "price" be set for a factor input that is used jointly by two firms, where once either firm uses the factor, the other also receives the factor's services without paying for them?

3. Suppose there are two lakes in a municipality. The municipal government enacts a water pollution standard that improves water quality at one lake (lake A), but doesn't change water quality at lake B. Demand for recreational services at lake A rises, while demand for recreation at lake B falls. Suppose the inverse demand curve for recreation at both sites before the change in water quality is given by $P = 100 - .5Q$. After the standard is imposed, demand at site A shifts to $P = 120 - .4Q$, while demand at site B changes to $P = 60 - .2Q$. There is no charge for using the lakes. How would you measure the benefits of improved water quality for the municipality?

4. Explain graphically and verbally under what circumstances a market for the trading of pollution permits will minimize the costs of meeting a given pollution standard.

5. *a.* Explain the differences between the ABS, EBS, and offset systems of marketable permits for pollution in theory.

   b. What are the advantages and disadvantages of implementing each type of system?

   c. Which system would you advise using, and why, for each of the following pollution problems: toxic chemicals dumped into rivers and lakes; chlorofluorocarbons.

   d. Could a marketable permit system be used when emissions of a pollutant are the result of "accidents" such as oil spills from supertankers or radioactivity "spills" from nuclear power plants? Explain why or why not.

NOTES

1. See, for example, Peskin and Seskin (1975), Halvorsen and Ruby (1981), Dewees in Friedlaender (1978), and the studies by Arthur D. Little on air pollution.

2. One should not take these numbers too seriously, as all are fraught with measurement problems.

3. Formally, there is a distinction between option value and quasi-option value (see Crabbe, 1984, for more details). *Option value* is the amount a risk-averse individual would be willing to pay to prevent an irreversible investment from being made when the person cannot fully insure against this risk. It is an amount above the expected consumer surplus from the site. People may wish to visit the wilderness site in the future, but are uncertain if they will or not. Option value is their willingness to pay to reserve that choice rather than have mining proceed today. Option values are subjective and depend on individual's utility functions. *Quasi-option* value is the willingness to pay for information about choices when a given investment decision is irreversible. It is an objective value determined by investors who place a value on delaying an irreversible decision until the information they seek can be revealed. An environmental site may thus have both option and quasi-option value. We will deal with the subjective evaluations associated with option values in this section.

4. There may be problems of identification of this demand curve when other complicating factors such as travel congestion arise. These are ignored here.

5. A recent ruling by the Justice Department may indicate a change in the size of fines for failure to comply with environmental regulations. One company was fined $4 million for violations of the Clean Air Act in March 1984.

6. The authors contrast their approach with that of Montgomery (1972), who required that no trades were permitted if they resulted in a decrease in air quality at the initial distribution of rights. If the distribution was Q_2, the firms were constrained to be on the line parallel to AB that intersects point Q_2. This constraint prevented the attainment of the optimal emissions at point Q^*. Krupnick et al. suggest that the way around this is to use their broader constraint or, what in effect comes to the same thing, allow firms to obtain permits freely from the government as long as no decrease in air quality occurs.

chapter *14*

Government Regulation and Policy in Natural Resource Use

INTRODUCTION

Why do we regulate natural resource use? In previous chapters, we have examined a variety of regulations in our discussions of minerals, fisheries, forests, and environmental resources. In this chapter, we present economic rationales for regulation in general. We see when in theory regulation is indicated and what types of regulations governments can use. However, because theory and practice often do not coincide, we examine some of the regulatory practices and agencies in the United States and Canada and present a detailed case study: regulation of natural gas prices at the wellhead in the United States.

There is no single or simple theory of regulation. Many economists have long argued that government intervention in the operation of markets is required to promote economic efficiency whenever there is a failure of competitive markets to exist or operate efficiently, such as when monopoly exists, to correct externalities, or provide public goods. In addition, government policies may be required to achieve an equitable distribution of income. There are many examples of regulations that affect natural resources which are based on promoting economic efficiency or equity. Environmental pollution, as argued in Chapters 12 and 13, is often a public bad that will not be rectified by private markets. Imperfect competition in mineral markets (such as cartels) will lead to inefficient extraction paths and prices that can be too high or too low. The common property problem in many fisheries requires controls of some sort on fishing effort and/or harvests. These are all cases when there exists some clear inefficiency in the operation of private markets. The rise in oil prices and other mineral commodities in the 1970s generated large rents and led to a redistribution of income from oil consumers to oil producers. Many governments have sought to redress this change in income distribution with taxes, price ceilings on petroleum, and other policies.

Efficiency and equity will explain why some regulation exists, but not all. There are cases where no regulatory actions are taken when an economic model predicts there should be, and many cases where regulation exists without compelling economic justification. Why is this so? First of all, not all regulation is the result of concerns for economic efficiency and equity. Much regulation of an economic nature results from individuals and groups acting to promote a particular belief or cause in the public interest or their own self-interest, and politicians responding to these pressures. Even if market failure is present, this fact may not lead to regulation. For example, environmental regulations were enacted in the United States primarily in the 1970s, long after economists identified and analyzed pollution as a market failure that required government intervention. Factors other than the promotion of efficiency explain much of this environmental legislation.

A number of theories of regulation encompass these notions. They fall generally into regulations motivated by *public interest* or *private interest.* Among the public interest theories that focus only tangentially on efficiency and equity are notions that individuals and political decision-makers act so as to promote social concerns and national security that benefit the public. The problem with these theories is that it is quite difficult to specify an objective function which captures the notion of the public interest people are trying to maximize. The private or self-interest theories are based on the notion that every group attempts to promote its own special causes, and generally to obtain as large a share of the economic pie as possible. These notions have been more recently called "rent seeking." Economic analyses of regulation based on self-interest theories attempt to see why some groups succeed in getting regulation that benefits them, to identify the gainers and losers from regulatory actions, and to quantify the gains and losses.

The private interest theories encompass notions of producer protection and regulatory capture. Under *producer protection,* it is argued that firms agree only to regulations that benefit them. *Regulatory capture* means that regardless of the initial intent of a particular regulation or mandate of a regulatory agency, the regulatory agency will soon be the pawn of particular interest groups and do their bidding. It is usually argued that particular industries capture regulatory agencies.

Finally, there are analyses of bureaucratic behavior and political process models. These theories focus on the behavior of regulatory agencies, legislative bodies such as Congress or Parliament, the executive branches of government, and the courts. While there are some general theories developed in these models, most studies examine a particular regulatory action and its causes.

Unfortunately, testing any of these theories is extremely difficult. It is often impossible to distinguish empirically between competing hypotheses. Some of the approaches that have been taken include historical (nonstatistical) case studies of particular regulatory actions. These studies focus on the origins of the regulation, using documents such as newspapers, speeches, and legislation at the time of the action to evaluate the policy. Statistical economic histories cover the same ground, but are structured around economic notions such as rent seeking and use statistical techniques to evaluate the policies. There are also studies which attempt to predict when and what type of regulation occurs across different political jurisdictions or industries or professional groups; studies which attempt to explain patterns of voting behavior in Congress and other political bodies by the economic interests of the politicians and/or their constituents, and models of legislative control. The latter models look at the relationship between legislatures and regulatory agencies to see how special interests in, for example, the U.S. Congress affect the behavior of particular bureaucracies. Does, for example, Congress control the actions of a regulatory agency, or does the agency operate under its own objectives and rules? When do bureaucracies become uncontrollable and carry out activities unrelated to their mandate?

We will not examine any of these public and private interest theories. Unless one is testing competing theories over, say, a data set of regulatory actions, it is our view that studies of regulatory processes and actions are best done on a case-by-case basis with some guiding principles of public policy analysis.

We have already looked in detail at some regulatory practices in the case of fisheries in Chapter 9, forests in Chapter 11, and environmental resources in Chapter 13. In the remainder of this chapter, we first review and pull together the rationales for government intervention mentioned in previous chapters. We discuss not only static efficiency concepts, but emphasize the intertemporal aspect of natural resource use and the need to design regulations that incorporate intertemporal tradeoffs. Regulatory instruments are then linked to various types of market failure. We look at equity issues, problems of correcting one distortion when other uncorrected distortions exist, and financing government actions. Then we look at some actual regulatory policies: What are the rationales for regulation? Are they consistent with economic criteria or other motives for regulation? Were the policies enacted compatible with the regulator's objectives? What can go wrong? We look in detail at the regulation of the wellhead price of natural gas in the United States. This case study illustrates many of the general points made throughout the chapter and is an example of an economic analysis of regulatory actions. We conclude with a brief discussion of some political concerns in regulation.

BOX 14.1
Regulating Resource Use of the Oceans

The United Nations Convention on the Law of the Sea (UNCLOS) was completed in December 1982 with at least 129 nations pledged to accept its provisions. (The United States is not in the signing group.) The agreement is a comprehensive framework for regulating the use of the world's oceans. The 320 articles, 9 annexes, and 5 resolutions regulate fishing, research, exploration, navigation above and below the surface, and mineral exploitation of the world's oceans. A 200-mile exclusive economic zone (EEZs) around the shores of nations is agreed to. Each nation can regulate activity in these zones. Continental shelf rights are to be allowed up to 350 miles or to a line 100 miles beyond the

Box 14.1 continued

2,500 meter depth line if the shelf extends beyond 200 miles. Disputes are to be settled at a new International Tribunal for the Law of the Sea in Hamburg, West Germany.

UNCLOS establishes an international organization for the mining of the seabed beyond the jurisdiction of the coastal states. The principle invoked is that the resources of the seabed beyond national jurisdiction, called "the Area," are the "common heritage of mankind." These resources comprise the manganese nodules, rich in nickel, copper, manganese, and cobalt. The International Seabed Authority will regulate all resource-related activities in the Area, and an "enterprise," the operating arm of the authority, will exploit these resources in tandem with suitably qualified or nationally owned seabed mining consortiums. Under this "parallel system," a consortium must identify *two* mine sites when applying for a production license, one of which will be allotted to the enterprise. To ensure the viability of the enterprise, parties to the convention will have to jointly fund one enterprise mine site, and those engaged in seabed mining will have to transfer any necessary mining technology if this technology is not available on the open market.

Although exploratory and development work has been going on in seabed mining, commercial exploitation is not expected until the late 1990s or early 2000s. The richest nodule deposits are in the North and Central Pacific. Mineral content (dry-weight) is 18 to 24 percent manganese, 0.75 to 1.25 percent nickel, 0.50 to 1.15 percent copper, and 0.25 to 0.35 percent cobalt. (The deposits in Sudbury, Ontario, are of 1.4 percent nickel and 1.2 percent copper.)

Estimates in 1980 suggest that an extraction unit would require a capacity of 3 million tons per year to be profitable. Such a rate would satisfy approximately 5 percent of current total world nickel demands, 22 percent of current demand for cobalt, about 3 percent of current demand for manganese, and approximately 0.3 percent of annual world demand for copper.

Source: Geological data from Ministry of Natural Resources, Government of Ontario, "The Future of Nickel and the Law of the Sea," Mineral Policy Background Paper No. 10, Mineral Resources Branch, February 1980.

PROMOTING EFFICIENCY AND EQUITY IN NATURAL RESOURCE USE

In this section, we will summarize the conditions for an efficient allocation of resources, then give examples of situations in which failure to satisfy these conditions suggests the need for regulation. We discuss first the conditions for efficiency in a static environment, and when these conditions are not met; then we turn to the thornier issue of intertemporal efficiency. Government policy instruments available to correct market failures and promote efficiency are examined as well.

Efficiency and Market Failure in a Static Economy

We will not go into detail about the derivation of the efficiency conditions, because they should be familiar from an intermediate microeconomic theory course.[1] An efficient allocation of productive resources and goods in an economy is achieved when the conditions given in Equation (14.1) are satisfied. For all consumers i and j, all producers a and b, and all goods x and y, it must be the case that:

$$MRS_{xy}^{i} = MRS_{xy}^{j} = \frac{P_x}{P_y} = \frac{MC_x}{MC_y} = MRT_{xy}^{a} = MRT_{xy}^{b} \qquad (14.1)$$

Equation (14.1) shows the requirements for overall efficiency in production and exchange. For efficiency in exchange, each consumer's marginal rate of substitution (MRS) between any two goods must be identical to the MRS between the same two goods for another individual, and in turn equal to the relative price of the two goods. This will occur when each individual is maximizing utility subject to a budget constraint, given the market-determined relative prices of the two goods (P_x/P_y). If the markets are operating perfectly, then the relative price of the goods will in turn equal the relative marginal cost of producing the goods (MC_x/MC_y). For efficiency in production, the marginal rate of transformation (MRT, or rate of technical substitution) of turning inputs into outputs for both goods for each producer must be identical and equal to the relative marginal costs.

It is well known that if markets exist for all goods and services exchanged, all such markets are perfectly competitive, everyone has perfect information, property rights are fully assigned, and no externalities exist, Equation (14.1) will be satisfied when individuals maximize utility and firms maximize profits. Our intent now is to identify situations in natural resource industries when these conditions for efficiency are not satisfied.

In modern economies in the West, the division is made between activities successfully carried out by "the market" and activities displaying a generic market failure. Market failures are associated with externalities, common property, imperfect competition, natural monopolies, public goods provision, and certain kinds of uncertainty. These might be labeled *natural market failures.* Artificial market failure or welfare costs are created by particular government regulatory and tax policies. Different types of taxes lead to levels of output being produced in various sectors, which result in some consumers being left worse off than they would be in the absence of taxes. Regulations may often prevent markets from operating efficiently. These are the sort of *artificial market failure* we have in mind. Let us now review the natural market failures in light of our analysis in previous chapters.

Externalities   This is a situation in which the profit-maximizing activity of firm or consumer i affects the activities of consumer or producer j without financial compensation. If externalities in consumption exist, then in Equation (14.1) the MRS_{xy}^{i} will not equal MRS_{xy}^{j} if, say, person i's consumption of good x benefits i but harms j. If production externalities exist between firms, MRTs will not be equated and/or prices will diverge from marginal costs. Thus the smoke from factories can damage nearby homes and harm individuals. Or acid rain resulting from sulphur dioxide emissions from coal-burning furnaces can affect crop yields in agriculture and forestry and catch sizes in fishing.

Common property resources are another type of externality. Without the exclusive assignment of property rights over the natural resource, be it a fishery, pool of oil, forest, or environmental resource, the resource will be exploited inefficiently. The pumping of oil by firm i from a common pool will affect the overall "take" of firm j, also extracting from the pool. The catch of boat i in a fishing ground can affect the cost of boat j, since a slightly thinner array of fish stock will be available to boat j after i has harvested his catch.

Congestion is also an externality. The presence of person i on, say, a crowded road (or in a fishery) slows all other people down slightly (or affects the catch). Naturally the effect is reciprocal. Person j slows all others down also, including person i. In general, congestion increases costs for all users. One might say that these "external" effects are present when my purchase of, say, oranges deprives other persons of those oranges. Is this not an externality? No, because my purchase is fully covered by my expenditure for my oranges. In a sense, any deprivation I inflict by purchasing oranges I fully pay for, whereas in the congestion case, my implicit outlay for a trip covers only part of the cost of my trip, not the cost I inflict on others by slowing them down slightly by my being on the crowded road at the same time, or by affecting their fish harvest.

Externalities such as pollution can also interfere with obtaining an efficient use of factor inputs. We observed in Chapter 2 that a piece of land would not be generating the largest value of output when the price per acre at the margin between competing uses differed. Congestion and pollution will cause divergencies in prices of land — a factor input — and lead to suboptimal amounts of land being used in competing uses. Efficiency is not obtained because units of land which are identical except for whether or not they are polluted are not valued identically. Generally land receiving pollution will be undervalued, and competing activities will expand onto the undervalued land. There will be too many smoky factories and not enough agriculture. An appropriate policy would stop or curtail pollution and have a reallocation of land uses. This holds for any input affected by an externality (or other distortion).

Monopoly Another generic inefficiency is monopoly, which puts a wedge between prices and marginal costs of producing a product (price exceeds MC) as we showed in Chapter 4. Other forms of imperfect competition (oligopoly, monopsony) also interfere with Equation (14.1). In the absence of strong increasing returns to scale, policies should be designed to prevent the price of a product diverging from its marginal cost in a static context. For a monopoly or oligopoly, this means regulating the sellers so that an outcome occurs with price equal to marginal cost.

Estimates of gains for the United States of eliminating all monopolies range from .5 to 10 percent of GNP. In the United States, the Federal Trade Commission acts as a watchdog, alerting legal officers to the presence of noncompetitive practices by firms.[2]

Natural monopolies exist in an industry when average costs of production continuously decline as output is increased. This is also called persistently increasing returns to scale. Consider an entrepreneur planning to enter the automobile industry.

Suppose this competitor decides to compete with the Chevrolet line of General Motors. If he produces to start 10,000 units, his cost per car will be higher than GM's cost per car of producing 100,000 of the same units. An entrant cannot compete if he operates on a small scale. If the competitor *starts* with 100,000 units, the market will be flooded and either the entrant will be left with unsold cars if he sells at cost per unit or GM will be left with unsold cars. Entry is not rational in such an industry, because the incumbent can sell at lower unit cost because of his scale of production.

Telephone companies had these characteristics of a natural monopoly. It did not pay to start a rival network for at least the local part of telephone service. It is often a specialized technology such as a telephone *network* that makes a natural monopoly. Utilities such as gas and electric companies also have some characteristics of natural monopolies. In order to prevent such monopolists from restricting output and maintaining unduly "high" prices, such companies are regulated. But note that regulation of natural monopolies cannot require that price be equated to marginal cost. Figure 14.1 illustrates the problem.

With average costs declining continuously, marginal costs will also decline and lie below AC. Given a market demand curve D, if price is set equal to MC, the firm will incur persistent losses at output Q_C and must eventually shut down. If the firm is allowed to operate as a monopolist, output Q_M will be produced at a price P_M, which is well above marginal and average costs. There is effectively no decentralized approach to achieve efficiency in declining average cost industries. Most regulatory

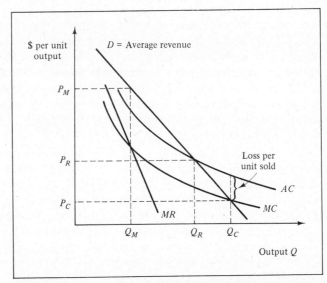

Figure 14.1 In a natural monopoly, average and marginal costs decline continuously. If governments attempt to regulate price in this industry by setting it equal to *MC* (the efficiency condition), the firm will incur losses on each unit sold. If the firm is allowed to operate as a monopoly, the price will rise and output will fall. The regulated pricing of output from natural monopoly generally involves setting price equal to average cost, with an allowed return on investment.

agencies impose some sort of average cost pricing on the firm. That is, price is to be set equal to average cost, where average costs include an allowed rate of return on investment. Output Q_R and price P_R result. We look at one example of these types of regulations in our discussion of natural gas.

Public Goods   National defense is the classic example of a public good — one everyone consumes equally (but does not in general get the same utility from). When public goods exist, our efficiency condition (14.1) changes to the requirement that the *sum* of the MRSs among individuals be equated to the relative prices. No private producer can supply a public good in the optimal amount as we saw in Chapter 12.

Navigation guidance systems are public goods. Though shippers are the principal beneficiaries, no single company would establish a complete system of buoys and lighthouses, so it is done collectively and government is the coordinator, finding the optimal level of service provision and a means of collecting revenues to pay for the service. Clearly the matter could be handled by shippers forming a consortium to provide navigation services, and they could levy fees on one another to pay for the system. However, with many independent shippers, the difficulty (costs) of organizing the group and reaching a binding agreement would be great. There remains the issue of charging outsiders for use of the navigation system. The matter gets solved by having government arrange for the provision of services and for the paying for the service, or devising a means of charging for the service either directly (through fees) or indirectly (through general taxes).

The provision of information on weather, pest control, the geology of areas, and the location and size of fish stocks resembles the provision of services for safe navigation. These information services are public goods that benefit a large group in society. It is difficult for private suppliers to make the services available because it is expensive to exclude consumers who do not pay for the services. People who consume and do not pay are referred to as *free riders*. Public goods are often defined as those for which it is impossible or prohibitively expensive to exclude free riders. Certainly with national defense it seems impossible to exclude those who do not pay, and thus the government steps in and coercively extracts payment in the form of taxes.

Particular Kinds of Uncertainty   People organize their lives in purposeful ways in the presence of much uncertainty. So uncertainty per se does not destroy the relatively smooth functioning of the economy. However, the presence of uncertainty contributes to many shortfalls of full efficiency. For example, one expects a bidding system for mineral leases to transfer rent to the government. We observed in Chapter 5 that this is typically not the case. The combined uncertainties to bidder i of deciding what the mineral tract might be worth and then whether his bid will win over other bids leads to bidding systematically less than the full expected rent from the lease.

As long as uncertainty is viewed as a cost to individuals, there is a dollar payoff from getting information that will reduce the uncertainty. Uncertainty about sizes of natural resource stock underground is reduced by carrying out surveys of various sorts before an extracting plan is initiated. If governments can provide geological information relatively cheaply, then private resources in exploration can be used more efficiently and known deposits of uncertain size can be more efficiently exploited. Knowledge of stock sizes permits more efficient extraction paths to be followed. This is the rationale for government publication of maps of the geology and topography of various regions.

Why should the public sector be involved at all in this sector? This is a subtle point turning on some scale factors and the appropriability (public-good nature) of information. A single private organization could do the surveying the government does and sell the information — that is, sell the maps and related surveys. Once sold to one customer, however, reproduction by the buyer could follow, and the original surveyor would get very little revenue to cover the substantial costs of information acquisition. This is a defect in the market associated with appropriating the benefits from producing information. Once one user sees the information, it becomes almost impossible for the producer to get revenue from subsequent users. This difficulty lies at the basis of the government's role in information acquisition and dissemination. In recent years, the government in the United States has provided fishermen with reports, via satellite, of likely locations of fish stocks. Weather reports are of great value to farmers as well as fishermen.

Efficiency over Time

Our discussion of market failure has been in the context of a *static* economy. But an economy will change over time as capital goods such as factories, roads and dams are accumulated, stocks of nonrenewable resources are run down, and stocks of reproducible resources rise and fall. How is efficiency characterized in these situations? What characterizes intertemporal efficiency as opposed to static efficiency? There is really no body of doctrine that might be labeled "intertemporal welfare economics" which is nearly as fully developed as its counterpart, welfare economics in a static context. Any current use of nonrenewable resources results in an irreversible change in the economy. Potential irreversibilities also result from the use of other natural resources such as changes in water tables, ambient air and water quality, forestation, soils, and topography. Is there a role for government intervention in these cases, and if so, what? The admonition to avoid irreversibilities is not helpful, since that would imply using no coal, oil, copper, and so on. Government decision-makers must determine the degree of irreversibility that is sensible to plan for, and here we have a body of doctrine that is quite sparse. However, we do have some guidance from our previous analysis of resource use over time in Chapter 6.

We referred to Hotelling's rule for using up nonrenewable resources in Chapters 3 and 6 as an efficiency condition, and so it is in an economywide intertemporal framework. This is easy to see in a simple example. Suppose producible capital K and exhaustible resource flows R are the two inputs in a world that produces one output. A schedule of consumption levels has been worked out up to period $t - 1$ and beyond period t. We are given $\overline{K}(t - 1)$, $\overline{K}(t + 1)$, and a given amount of resource stock $\overline{S} = R(t - 1) + R(t)$ to be allocated to make $C(t)$ as large as possible. (A bar over a variable signifies that it has been predetermined.) Now consumption is output minus product used for investment, or

$$C(t) = f[K(t), R(t)] - [\bar{K}(t+1) - K(t)] \qquad (14.2)$$

and

$$K(t) = f[\bar{K}(t-1), R(t-1)] - \bar{C}(t-1) + \bar{K}(t-1) \qquad (14.3)$$

Using the fact that $\bar{S} = R(t-1) + R(t)$, we find that $C(t)$ is a maximum when

$$\frac{f_R(t) - f_R(t-1)}{f_R(t-1)} = f_K(t) \qquad (14.4)$$

where the subscripts mean that a derivative is taken with respect to the relevant variable. This is our generalized Hotelling rule, derived in Chapter 6. We illustrate this problem in Figure 14.2. The level of consumption in period t is highest when a tangency occurs between the exhaustible resource constraint $\bar{S} = R(t-1) + R(t)$ and the iso-consumption schedules for different values of $C(t)$ expressed in terms of $R(t-1)$ and $R(t)$. Inefficient exhaustible resource utilization would result in a value of $C(t)$, less than maximal, and the efficiency condition above would not be in effect.

Many forms of mineral taxation or profits taxation in general (for sectors other than the resource sectors) prevent the efficiency condition being satisfied and thus prevent the realization of the highest consumption levels attainable with known technologies and resource endowments.

Intertemporal efficiency conditions must hold for any variable, including re-producible capital goods, which is subject to choice over time. Optimal consumption programs are selected from those satisfying the intertemporal efficiency conditions. Different taxes, such as profit taxes, can lead to inefficiency for a variety of time paths of input utilization. Heritage Funds (funds formed from revenues from the sale of nonrenewable resources) represent an intervention to correct some perceived inter-

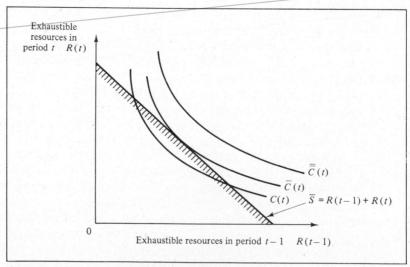

Figure 14.2 Intertemporal efficiency is satisfied when $\bar{S}$ is used to get the consumption level $C(t)$ as high as possible. $\bar{S}$ must be used in adjacent time periods efficiently. This occurs when Hotelling's rule is satisfied.

temporal market failure. The point here is that in the absence of such centrally organized funds, society is consuming too much of current income and not providing enough capital goods for future generations.

Mitigating the Effects of Market Failures

What policies can the government use to achieve an efficient allocation of resources? We will comment on six policies used both individually and together. First, the government might *buy out a firm* or industry and become the new management. One sees this in the telecommunications sector in many European countries, in mining industries, and in railways in many countries of the world. Or, it may break up a monopoly into different firms. Second, government can *regulate a sector with special rules.* Since virtually all sectors are regulated, if only by tax rules, we should emphasize that the rules we have in mind here will be sector-specific. For example, fisheries in Canada and the United States has been subject to rules governing use of equipment, duration of fishing seasons, and at times, entry. The presumption is that the common property characteristics of fishing dictate outside intervention to mitigate the inefficiencies associated with common property problems.

A third approach is to *impose taxes and subsidies* to restructure the quantities produced in a sector to bring about a more favourable composition of output. Taxing the quantities of a pollutant emitted is intended to lead to a reduction in the amount of pollution produced. Most frequently, as we have seen, pollution is controlled by means of legislated standards or quantity constraints. Subsidies are employed in the research and development sector because in part the private sector will not undertake highly risky ventures that are in the public interest. The development of solar and fusion power and synthetic hydrocarbons are examples of subsidized R&D activity. The riskiness of such research is associated with the uncertain profitability of a successful invention.

A fourth approach to controlling market failures is *unitization.* For example, if one firm undertakes all drilling in a single oil pool, this will avoid the problem of competing firms drilling close to one another in order to preempt a rival and ending up with excessive drilling and overly rapid depletion of the pool. Unitization means bringing activity under a single decision-maker. When there are relatively rapid speeds of oil drilling due to "competitive" extraction by many firms from one pool, the total amount of oil extracted will be smaller (due to physical properties relating natural pressure in the deposit to speed of oil removal) than under a regime of slower extraction rates. In these situations, there are social gains to be made from slowing the extraction rate and lengthening the period over which the pool is exhausted.

Unitization can also be applied to fisheries operating under common property conditions. If one company owned all the boats, interdependencies among fishing vessels could be anticipated and built into the calculation of profit-maximizing harvesting for all boats taken together. Unitization thus effectively reassigns property rights to the resource.

Governments also assign property rights through leasing arrangements (forests, offshore mineral rights), and operating "markets" (pollution rights). The development of a large piece of land by one decision-maker is a form of unitization, since the externalities associated with "nonconforming uses" can be balanced off by the single developer in such a way that it maximizes profit.

Zoning per se is a means of dealing with the adverse external effects of neighboring but generically distinct land uses—factories adjacent to residential areas, for example. Suppose there is a noisy factory in the middle of a residential area. These activities "conflict" in the sense that the factory makes life less pleasant for the nearby residents and in fact will push down the value of the residences. Zoning boards that dictate uses for sites can mitigate land use clashes to some extent. Zoning can preassign activities to locations. Since one or both parties in a conflict concerning adjacent sites can be made better off by a reassignment of activities, one might speculate as to why the conflicts are not sorted out in the absence of zoning to everyone's advantage. To some degree, this happens. Houston, Texas, is a city with no traditional zoning authority. The zoning board, however, can (a) forestall conflict by preassigning activities to sites, and (b) act as an informed arbitrator in ironing out disagreements. In the absence of zoning, lawyers and judges become the arbitrators.

The fifth approach the public sector takes to correcting for market failures is *information production and dissemination.* We noted that topographic and geological surveys can improve the efficiency of exploration by the private sector. Once a mineral deposit has been located, there are also gains to be reaped from knowing how much mineral is available and what quality. We noted that optimal paths might not be followed if mining companies had to determine the size of their uncertain deposit simply by digging through it. This is a striking case for providing information about deposit sizes. A case can be made for government to subsidize the surveying of a deposit once it has been located. Of course, the process of acquiring information involves costs, and there has to be a balance between the payoff to further research or plain search and the cost of conducting the research.

A sixth approach used by government for correcting market failures is with the *tax and savings rules.* Profits taxes, inheritance taxes, capital gains taxes, and personal income taxes affect the decisions of people to consume relatively more today rather than to save. The level of savings affects the pace of growth in an economy. Government expenditure decisions also affect the growth rate of an economy. The provision of roads, ports, and so on provides new infrastructure and makes for growth, whereas expenditures on military personnel and equipment have a major consumption as distinct from an investment component. Thus the government can affect the time path of the economy's development—whether relatively more savings or consumption takes place at the margin, period by period.

Tax regimes also affect the time paths of nonrenewable resource use. Use can be tilted toward the current generation or toward the future. Heritage Funds or special resource revenue savings funds represent an instrument for increasing savings currently to provide for future generations. Implicit here is the notion that in the absence of such special funds, the tax and financial environment favours current consumption of income relative to saving. National forests or permanently natural public lands are in part like nonrenewable resource revenue funds: They represent an endowment of the natural environment to future generations, as well as providing a place for recreation for the current generation.

Table 14.1 MAJOR PROBLEMS REQUIRING PUBLIC INTERVENTION AND TRADITIONAL GOVERNMENT APPROACHES TO DEALING WITH THEM

Problems/ instruments		I Buy out	II Regulate with rules	III Regulate with taxes and subsidies	IV Unitize	V Provide free information	VI Special savings and income taxes
A	Monopoly Oligopoly	X	X				
B	Pollution Water		X	Some			
	Air		X	Some			
C	Strip mining		X				
D	Road congestion			X Subsidize public transit			
E	Common property — Oil pools		X		X		
	Fish		X		X		
F	Pest control		X	X Subsidize prevention		X	
G	Underexploring for minerals & alternative energy sources	X		X		X	
H	Insufficient forestry replanting		X	X Subsidize replanting			
J	Future generations Minerals recreation areas	X Public parks					X

Note: X indicates that an instrument and problem have often been found together in the recent past.

Table 14.1 provides a summary of key market failures in the natural resource area and policies which have been directed to "solving" the market failures. The links indicated are those observed in practice. Many other approaches have been written about by observers, and there may be better ways of solving the problems than those implemented to date.

BOX 14.2
The Value of Publicly Supplied Information

If producers and consumers knew what price wheat was going to be six months or a year hence, they could plan their activities better. They would not have to make arrangements to hedge against the possibility of high prices, for example. Accurate wheat crop forecasts could result in predictable prices for wheat and wheat products in the future. The U.S. Department of Agriculture makes crop forecasts, and Bradford and Kelejian (1978) have estimated the payoff in 1975 dollars of having (a) more frequent and (b) more accurate forecasts. Making good-quality wheat crop forecasts monthly instead of bimonthly results in benefits of $33 million, and making better-quality forecasts alone results in benefits of $64 million. They do not estimate the cost of making these improvements in forecasting, nor do they estimate the cost of providing the existing forecasts or the benefits from existing forecasts.

Weather forecasts must be beneficial, because many organizations pay to receive them from private companies. In the United States there has been discussion about making the government-run meteorological service into a private profit-seeking agency.

Recently, information via satellite has started to be produced on the location of fish off the west coast of the United States. Albacore fishermen report their search times have been reduced by 25 percent. The information is provided free by the National Oceanic and Atmospheric Administration, the Jet Propulsion Laboratory, and the Scripps Institution of Oceanography. The satellites detect areas of warm and cold water and sharp changes in the ocean's color. Tuna like warmer water and cruise along the color breaks. The pictures are posted once a week in port offices. Since many color breaks persist for up to a week, the fishermen can use one map for several days. The Jet Propulsion Laboratory receives $100,000 per year from NASA to support the service.

Source: D. F. Bradford and H. H. Kelejian, "The Value of Information for Crop Forecasting with Bayesian Speculators: Theory and Empirical Results." *Bell Journal of Economics* 9, 1 (Spring 1978), pp. 123–144.

Second-Best Policies

We now arrive at one of the thorniest aspects of welfare economics and policy. If the primary energy sector is operating inefficiently—say there are common pool problems—and the retailing of gasoline (another sector) is subject to inefficiency—say it is an oligopoly—then we cannot be sure that using any of the policies mentioned above to promote efficiency in just one sector will improve matters. This is known as the *difficulty of the second best.* Simply put, if you have two wrongs (inefficiencies), clearing up one may not improve matters. If there is *one* wrong in the economy, clearing it up will in general improve matters. This is a fundamental stumbling block to piecemeal policy-making—policy-making on a sector-by-sector or problem-by-problem basis. How do economists as policy advisors react to this monumental stumbling block? They generally try to design policies that incorporate difficulties in related sectors in one complete prescription. Thus if a sector is relatively large but relatively autonomous from other sectors in the economy, improving many inefficiencies at once within the large sector may improve welfare. Whether this does indeed work out as hoped depends on the links between sectors. Links of any kind can lead to counterproductive changes overall if one of two wrongs in separate sectors is righted piecemeal.

Another posture for the policy advisor is to abandon existing welfare theory in economics as providing an appropriate philosophical foundation for policy and to proceed on an ad hoc basis. The advisor might then appeal to rules of thumb, such as prevent concentrations of market power and wealth, and avoid impediments to the free flow of goods and services among sectors and regions. This is not an attractive approach, but it may be the best we have.

A third approach which is receiving considerable attention given the development of large computers is to model an entire economy in detail and then to simulate a prospective policy. If the consequences are desirable, the policy can be implemented. The difficulty here, of course, is that accurate and detailed models of an economy are not available. Compromises must be made, and predictions can be inaccurate.

A fourth approach involves analyzing in the presence of many distortions what might improve matters in the abstract. This represents a pencil-and-paper detour around the large-scale computer-based approach. The fact remains that we have no simple answer to the second-best problem.

Equity Concerns

Efficient allocation of resources is compatible with a wide range of distributions of personal income. Pitifully low incomes or even huge variations in personal incomes are not viewed as acceptable in many modern societies, and redistribution programs have long been in place. The goal of equity is complex because (a) different individuals hold different views on the appropriate degree of equity or relative dispersion in incomes of persons, and (b) equality of incomes can lead to negative efficiency effects when people curtail their labor supply because they are not being appropriately rewarded for their contributions.

Despite these problems, many policies exist to redistribute income. Transfers are made to the handicapped, the unemployed, the elderly, and so on. Relatively high incomes are taxed to finance the transfers, thus inducing a tendency to equalize relative personal incomes. Rents from natural resource exploitation in part are redistributed in Canada through equilization formulas that differ across provinces. Other redistributive policies include subsidized energy pricing. What about transfers in kind, such as free medical care? These are indirect forms of income equalization, but they can lead to inefficient levels of production and consumption. There is no rationing by price—demanders can consume as much as they like. An argument can be made using a type of indifference curve analysis to show that recipients can be made better off by transferring them the same income in dollars rather than in kind. But many government regulations and welfare programs are designed to redistribute income indirectly and not to improve efficiency. For example, in Canada a major goal of fisheries policy is the maintenance of reasonable incomes for workers in the industry, not the removal of inefficiencies.

However, increased equality no doubt creates a disincentive for people to work hard on average, and thus the potential maximum size of the pie is not reached. People curtail effort because they are not rewarded at the margin and substitute leisure for effort, since the reward for extra effort is blunted. This is the tradeoff between increasing income equality and maintaining efficiency. There is no simple solution to this tradeoff.

REGULATORY AGENCIES AND THE EFFICACY OF REGULATION
Regulatory Agencies in the United States and Canada

Below we list agencies of the U.S. federal government primarily involved in regulating natural resource use. The federal level has primary responsibility for most natural resources. We use the numerals and letters from Table 14.1 above to classify the agency, given its description in the government organization guide. We then describe the agency and note the analogous agency in the Canadian federal government. In Canada, the provincial governments have primary jurisdiction over the commercial use of minerals, forests, and fish south of the Yukon and Northwest Territories. The provincial governments are also responsible for pollution control. Offshore mineral rights have been bargained for by the two levels of government. An exception is the area in the north of Canada, the Yukon and Northwest Territories. In this region, the federal government exercises control over mineral rights.

Forest Service (H,I,V,VI), Department of Agriculture (USFS): Administers 191 million acres of national forests, grasslands, and land utilization projects in 44 states. The USFS carries on basic forestry research, often in cooperation with State agricultural colleges. The Canadian Forestry Service in Environment Canada is a research and data gathering agency.

Soil Conservation Service (C,G,I,II,VI), Department of Agriculture: Carries out joint water and soil conservation, often through local conservation districts; 2 billion acres are covered by about 3,000 conservation districts. This service provides subsidies for reclaiming abandoned coalmined lands and water. The Canadian Lands Directorate in Environment Canada implements federal policy, publishes maps, and performs land use research and planning.

Environmental Protection Agency (B,II,III,V): Supervises control and abatement of pollution of air, water, and land, including noise, radiation, and toxic material pollution. Coordination with state and local governments is pursued. The Ministry of the Environment deals in part with these issues in Canada, though primary responsibility rests with the provincial governments.

National Oceanic and Atmospheric Administration (B,G,V), Department of Commerce: Maps the global oceans and its living resources; issues nautical, aeronautical, and geodetic charts; provides weather forecasts and tide schedules. The Canadian Hydrographic Service (in the Department of Fisheries and Oceans) provides charts for navigation purposes. Other oceanographic data is also collected. Climate research and meteorological services are located in Environment Canada.

Energy Research (G,V), Department of Energy: Manages basic energy sciences, high-energy physics, fusion research, administers university energy researchers and other projects not covered by other DOE agencies. The Atomic Energy of Canada crown corporation conducts nuclear energy research. Other energy research is carried out in the Ministry of Energy, Mines and Resources.

Fossil Energy (G,V), Department of Energy: Administers research and development programs involving coal, petroleum, and gas. The Ministry of Energy, Mines, and Resources in Canada has an Energy Division doing research in and monitoring the coal, petroleum, and gas sectors.

Conservation and Renewable Energy (G,III,V), Department of Energy: Directs programs designed to increase production and utilization of solar, biomass, wind, geothermal, and alcohol fuels and improve energy efficiency of transportation, buildings, and industrial systems through support of long-term, high-risk research and development activities. The office provides financial assistance for weatherization of housing owned by the poor, and energy conservation by schools, hospitals, local units of government, and public care institutions. Canada's Ministry of Energy, Mines and Resources deals with these issues.

Environmental Protection, Safety and Emergency Preparedness (B,G,I,II), Department of Energy: Ensures department programs comply with environmental safety and health regulations and administers the Strategic Petroleum Reserve and the Naval Petroleum and Oil Shale Reserves. Canada's Ministry of Energy, Mines and Resources has an Emergency Oil Stocks/Inventory branch. No stockpiling is done.

Nuclear Energy (G,V), Department of Energy: Administers the department's fission energy program, including nuclear reactor development, nuclear fuel cycle, space nuclear applications, and uranium enrichment and assessment. In Canada, the Crown Corporation, Atomic Energy of Canada Limited, is the center for nuclear research and reactor sales.

Civilian Radioactive Waste Management (B,II,II,VI), Department of Energy: Administers interim storage of spent nuclear fuel and repositories for disposal of high-level radioactive waste and spent nuclear fuel. In Canada, the Whiteshell Nuclear Research Establishment in Manitoba supervises nuclear waste disposal.

Energy Informational Administration (G,V), Department of Energy: Collects and publishes data in areas of energy resource reserves, energy production, demand, consumption, distribution, and technology. The Department of Energy, Mines and Resources collects such information in Canada.

Federal Energy Regulatory Commission (A,II,III), Department of Energy: Sets rates and charges for the transportation and sale of natural gas and for the transmission and sale of electricity and the licensing of hydroelectric projects. Canada's National Energy Board regulates these activities.

Power Administrations (A,I), Department of Energy: Administers and sells power from five regional systems in which some electric power is produced by agencies controlled by the federal government. Provincial governments in Canada administer electrical power systems.

Fish and Wildlife and Parks (J,V,VI), Department of the Interior: Administers the development, conservation, and utilization of fish, wildlife, recreation, and historical resources of the nation and the national park system. The National Park Service is the bureau in charge of the 330 units in the park system. The United States Fish and Wildlife Service administers 413 National Wildlife Refuges and 149 Waterfowl Production Areas, 13 fish and wildlife laboratories, and 77 National Fish Hatcheries. Parks Canada is in the Environment Canada Ministry. The Department of Fisheries and Oceans is the principal government group involved in commercial fishing in Canada. It deals in licensing vessels and ports, sets quotas, and coordinates chartmaking for coastal and interior waters.

Energy and Minerals (B,G,J,II,V), Department of the Interior: Stimulates the private sector in producing fuel and nonfuel minerals, administers the national mineral policy, regulates operations for minerals on the outer continental shelf, manages federal mineral leases, and evaluates water resources. The Office of Surface Mining Reclamation and Enforcement assists the states in developing programs that protect society and the environment from the adverse effects of coal mining. The Bureau of Mines is primarily a research agency. It publishes information on mineral exploration, production, shipments, demand, stocks, prices, imports, and exports. The Geological Survey conducts the National Mapping Program, classifies federally owned lands for minerals, energy resources, and water power potential, and investigates natural hazards such as earthquakes, volcanoes, and landslides. Canada's Geological Survey and related data-gathering activities are located in the Ministry of Energy, Mines and Resources. The Minerals Division provides information on mining and minerals.

Land and Water Resources (B,G,J,I,VI), Department of the Interior: Administers programs dealing with public land management, mineral leasing, and water resource management. The Office of Water Policy (OWP) is the central water policy analysis and state liaison office. The Bureau of Land Management is responsible for administering 341 million acres of public lands, mostly in the Far West and Alaska. The BLM is also responsible for subsurface resource management of an additional 169 million acres where mineral rights have been reserved to the federal government. The Bureau of Reclamation administers grants for land reclamation projects and operates 50 hydroelectric power plants on federal lands. Canada's Inland Waters Directorate and Lands Directorate are in the Environment Canada Ministry.

The Efficiency of Regulation

We have outlined the rationale for intervention in resource allocation by public authorities. People can attain higher indifference curves or more output can be produced with given inputs and/or more equitable income distributions can be achieved. The public sector is also a producer of many goods and services, ranging from improved land, water, and mineral surveys to national defense. The benefits of government intervention can be substantial. One estimate cited in Litan and Nordhaus (1983, pp. 14–16) for benefits of air pollution control in the United States is of $6 to $58 billion per year. This represents a saving of up to 15,000 fatalities and 15 million days of illness prevented. For water pollution control, the estimate is of about $10 billion per year.

However, much can go wrong between the cup and the lip with regulatory policies. In practice, because of insufficient information, political interference, or bureaucratic inertia, this function of government may not be carried out effectively. Agencies are not costless to operate ($2 billion in 1981 of direct outlays measured in 1972 dollars; Litan and Nordhaus, 1983, p. 130), and the net benefits they yield — net of the costs of administration — may be negative. Litan and Nordhaus (1983, pp. 15–21) present estimates of the costs of those complying with regulations in the United States for 1977. For controlling air and water pollution, the estimate is from $13 to $38 billion. For federal health and safety regulations, the estimated cost of complying is between $7 and $17 billion. About half was spent to improve the safety of automobiles. Elsewhere Denison (1978) estimated the total cost of social regulation to be about 1.39 percent of GNP, or $26 billion in 1977. Many regulatory activities require much information before decisions can be made properly, and the accumulation of the required data can be costly. For example mapmaking, mineral surveying, pest monitoring, and weather forecasting are information-gathering and disseminating services that require many personnel and resources.

Most activities of the government are financed not by fees levied on the beneficiaries, but from general revenues. The raising of revenue via taxation inevitably drives a wedge between the price of a product and its marginal cost, or the payment to an input and its marginal value in supply. These wedges or gaps represent inefficiencies and cause the "artificial" market failures we noted above. The income tax, for example, distorts the worker's decision on how much time to work for pay and how much time to consume as leisure. Thus the need to raise revenue from taxation leads to inevitable inefficiencies. The task becomes one of raising the required X and imposing the least welfare loss from induced inefficiencies. This is often a Catch-22, since the government should be reducing inefficiencies but in order to do so must introduce some itself and put the economy into the domain of the second best.

Recall that given an inefficiency in sector i, it may not improve matters to eliminate the inefficiency in sector j, and the need to raise revenue may be the cause of the inefficiency in sector i. A new task for policy is arriving at taxes that induce relatively small inefficiencies. The search for neutral taxes is a statement of this principle. Taxation of nonrenewable resources has been particularly complex because the notion of neutrality over time is more difficult to conceive when the stock is continually changing in size.

Another example of regulatory policy that creates distortions is government-imposed rationing. Suppose a particular input is rationed to one sector of the economy by government decree; the other input used by the sector is not rationed. It will then be the case that the ratio of the marginal products of two inputs will not equal their market prices and less aggregate output will be produced than is potentially producible. We illustrate in Figure 14.3. The slope of the line ab is the ratio of input

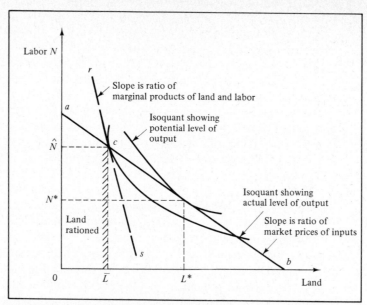

Figure 14.3 When land is rationed, actual output on land used is less than is potentially producible. The ratio of the marginal products of inputs do not equal the ratio of input prices. An inefficiency exists.

prices for land and labor and the area $0ab$ represents the maximum (unconstrained) input set given the input prices. The slope of the isoquant along tangent rs is the ratio of the marginal products. Suppose land is rationed—fixed at $\bar{L}$. The maximum level of output obtainable is determined where an isoquant is tangent to $0ac\bar{L}$ (the constrained input set).

$\hat{N}$ and $\bar{L}$ are inputs used in production. The ratio of the two inputs' marginal products at point c is given by the tangent to the isoquant at c, rs. In the absence of rationing of land, N^* and L^* would be used, resulting in the same dollar outlay for inputs as before but yielding more output—permitting a "higher" isoquant to be attainable. At this higher level of output, the ratio of input prices (slope of line ab) equals the slope of the isoquant (the ratio of marginal products of inputs). When land is rationed, the ratio of the marginal products does not equal the ratio of input prices, as Figure 14.3 shows. Thus government policies in agriculture, for example, which ration acreage for certain activities are generally inefficient. They may lead to higher prices for certain outputs and help farmers at the expense of consumers of certain agricultural products.

Policies designed to improve efficiency also have consequences for the distribution of income. For example, deregulating airline activities may have lowered prices for consumers, but it also drove many operators and shareowners into a relatively low profit position. The introduction of new technology generally favors consumers and many producers, but often leads to unemployment and the forcing of certain sectors to adjust to new market conditions. Even temporary work interruption can be a great hardship for a person settled in a job and locality for many years. Forestry has changed from a primarily labor-intensive sector to an extremely capital-intensive one. The fishery has experienced a technological revolution also. The welfare economist recognizes the distributional implications of policies designed to improve efficiency. The doctrine which has been developed is: If the gainers from a new policy can compensate the losers and still be better off after compensation, a policy is desirable.

This is called the *compensation test*. The test has technical difficulties associated with measuring gains and losses. However, the most severe difficulty with the compensation test is that compensation is not necessarily made — it need only be potentially payable. As a practical matter, it is too complicated to make specific compensation for every policy change, though in some cases, of course, actual compensation is provided. For example, in British Columbia the government bought trawlers at a fair market price when it sought to reduce the size of the commercial fishing fleet off Canada's West Coast. One justification for not providing compensation is that since so many policy changes occur weekly, it is presumed that a particular individual will benefit from some and be harmed by others but that on balance he or she will not be severely harmed. This may be unduly optimistic.

For any policy, the gainers and those harmed will lobby in some form to alter the policy to favor their position. Often the losers are the consumers, a widely dispersed, difficult-to-organize constituency. The gainers are often producers of a particular product — a group often well organized and united in its lobbying efforts. So, on average, we expect policies that favor smaller, well-organized and well-financed groups to be implemented and those that favor large, dispersed constituencies not to be implemented. Certainly agricultural programs in Canada and the United States favor producers at the expense of consumers in the short run. But we should also not overlook the fact that the agricultural sectors in both countries are extremely productive and competitive in an international context. It may well be that capital in agriculture ends up being subsidized by consumers in Canada and the United States and that this makes productivity relatively high.

Another aspect of this problem is the issue of *regulatory capture*. Regulatory agencies are designed with a goal or mission. However, once established, the agencies frequently pursue different goals. The most conspicuous of these diversions of mission would be the often-cited case of "capture" of a regulatory agency by the parties the agency was intended to regulate or control. Continued contact of agency personnel from board members down to staff officers with the personnel in the sector supposedly being regulated often leads to a deflection of purpose on the part of the agency. The 1983 crisis at the Environmental Protection Agency in Washington, centering on Chairman Burford, revealed a posture of compliance between the regulatory agency and those who were to be regulated (Tolchin and Tolchin, 1983, pp. 74–79).

Another form of diversion of purpose involves the regulatory agency superimposing a noncompetitive environment on the sector being regulated. The agency becomes the implicit protector of the firms it is supposed to regulate. Capture is not the issue here. Regulation of commercial airline companies in the United States had some of these characteristics before deregulation. Pricing and route determination were regulated, and firms had a predictable competitive environment. Regulators presumably made profitability of ongoing firms a consideration. But consumers lost out from a lack of price competition among carriers and many firms had excess capacity, indicating excessively high-cost operations for the prevailing level of service. But carriers were not opposed to the regulated environment, since once a carrier was established, it was protected from unfettered competition. Under deregulation, seat prices have fallen and bankruptcies of carriers have occurred. Competition among carriers has been intense, and survival is a persistent issue for each carrier.

A final general issue in regulation is the design of the agency itself. The budget may be inadequate for the task involved. The agency may then be obliged to rely excessively on information granted by the firms it is supposed to regulate. Or its budget may be too large, and it becomes an unproductive "blanket" over the sector it was supposed to regulate. Staff members may meddle for no useful purpose in the activities of the firms under scrutiny. More subtle is the design of policy instruments. For example, the regulation of automobile emissions by dictating standards to be met seems less efficient than the taxing of owners of automobiles for driving polluting vehicles. Taxation provides a monetary incentive to the owner to drive a vehicle with low emissions. Vehicles with poor pollution records will be more expensive to operate. Monitoring may be a problem, however. The existing standard-setting policies have led to confrontation between regulators, the automobile companies, and consumer groups over the standards and scheduling of implementation. Legal challenges to the regulations and the efforts of lobbyists have succeeded in delaying implementation of most of these regulations. A tax on vehicle owners would leave the automobile producers to innovate at a schedule they found most profitable, given consumer demands, which would be affected by the tax. Less regulatory detail would be subject to dispute between the agency and companies involved. Of course, how the tax schedule is designed would affect the product mix manufactured by the automobile producers.[3]

The Regulation and Deregulation of Natural Gas Prices in the United States: A Case Study[4]

Natural gas comprises about 25 percent of the energy consumed in the United States. About one-half of this total is used to heat homes and buildings. Other uses include the generation of electricity and use in manufacturing processes. Natural gas use has grown both absolutely and relative to other energy sources, such as oil and coal, since the 1960s. In 1960, for example, the share of natural gas was 38.3 percent of the residential/commercial market for energy and 37.4 percent of the industrial market. By 1972, these shares had grown to 50.1 and 45.6 percent, respectively, and they have continued to grow into the 1980s. Part of the reason for the increased use of natural gas is its desirable properties as a fuel. It is clean and relatively easy to use. But the other factor responsible for the growth in the consumption of natural gas is its price. In both Canada and the United States, the price of natural gas has been regulated from the time it leaves the ground to the point of final consumption. Until quite recently, the price has been below that of comparable fuels (in terms of BTU equivalents).

Regulations affect virtually all aspects of natural gas production and distribution. We wish to focus on the regulations affecting wellhead prices, but we will briefly explain the process of getting natural gas from the wellhead to consumers and note the ways in which natural gas is regulated.

Natural gas is found in gas fields located primarily in Texas, Oklahoma, Louisiana, California, and West Virginia in the continental United States. It is also found offshore and in Alaska. In Canada, substantial deposits exist in Alberta and the Northern Territories, and also in British Columbia and Saskatchewan. Mexico has considerable supplies as well. Gas from the field must be transported through pipelines. Pipeline companies then sell their gas either to gas companies in municipalities or other political jurisdictions or directly to large industrial consumers. The local gas companies are generally natural monopolies which sell gas to residential, commercial, and industrial consumers.

Gas was not an important energy resource until after World War II. Natural gas is often found as a joint product with oil, and it was simply flared (burned off) as a waste product during the 1920s and 1930s. The reason is that there were generally no means of transmitting the gas to market. The areas where gas was found were not at that time industrial centers, and there was no demand for the gas at the wellhead. Before the gas could be used, pipelines had to be constructed. In the 1930s, technological changes in pipeline construction occurred and a system of pipelines was developed to bring gas supplies to major markets. The pipeline system grew along with the demand for natural gas.

In the postwar period, there was more exploration for gas. However, until the 1970s, most significant discoveries of natural gas fields were found by accident—while explorers were looking for oil. At present, there are thousands of producers of natural gas in the United States and Canada. The primary extractive industry can thus be characterized as relatively competitive. However, few pipeline companies buy the gas from the primary producers. While most pipeline companies in the United States operate across many state lines (the *interstate* pipelines), there are some which have operated solely within one of the producing states (the *intrastate* companies). The intrastate pipelines sell gas directly to industries and utilities.

Regulation of the natural gas industry began in 1938 with the regulation of the interstate pipeline companies by the Federal Power Commission (FPC), changed to the Federal Energy Regulatory Commission, FERC in 1977. Interstate pipelines were considered public utilities and seen as natural monopolies in the late 1930s. It was felt by the U.S. Congress that the pipelines acted as monopolists which conspired to prevent new entry from competing pipelines and could thus charge any price the market would bear. Although no careful work supported these arguments for regulation, it does seem plausible that natural gas pipelines possess the characteristics of a natural monopoly as distributors and of a monopsony as buyers from producers.

No explicit regulations were imposed on the field prices of natural gas at this time, but in the 1930s and 1940s, many gas fields were owned by the pipelines, so the field price was in effect regulated. However, once gas markets grew in the postwar period, pipelines were forced to purchase supplies from independent producers, and the field prices were no longer under effective regulation. Regulations on pipelines were analogous to those imposed on other public utilities—on a *cost of service* basis. A price for gas was set based on operating and capital costs and including a fair return on investment. For example, the wholesale price of gas at some terminal point t in the pipeline system, P_{wt}, would be determined by the formula:

$$P_{wt} = \sum_i P^i / \sum_i q^i + P_{Tt}(d)$$

where P^i is the price of gas from each field i

q^i is the quantity of gas purchased from each field i

$P_{Tl}(d)$ are the allowable transmission charges—the capital, labor, pumping
costs, and so on that depend on distance d

The wholesale price of gas is thus based on the *average costs* of gas purchased by
pipelines, plus the allowable expenses incurred in moving the gas to consumers.

The local gas companies which purchased supplies from the pipeline companies were regulated in essentially the same way. The gas utilities were allowed to
charge a price that reflected the average costs of their purchases from pipelines plus a
transmission charge. The transmission charge reflected primarily the utilities' overall
capital and operating expenses. Final consumers typically paid the same rate per unit
consumed (generally with declining block rates—the first 1,000 cubic feet cost one
price, then next 1,000 cubic feet a lower price, and so on) regardless of their location
within the gas company's region, as with postage stamps.

This system of regulation of pipelines and gas utilities continued until the
mid-1950s, when public pressure succeeded in getting the field price of natural gas
regulated directly. What we wish to focus on are the factors leading up the regulation
of field or wellhead prices and the economic effects of the policies. Several factors led
to the regulation of the wellhead price of natural gas. As noted previously, demand for
natural gas began rising after World War II. A large excess supply of gas was eliminated, and companies began exploring for new fields. The monopsony power of the
pipelines was greatly reduced. Gas prices began to rise and the major gas consumers
—the gas companies and final consumers—petitioned the Federal Power Commission (FPC) to regulate the field prices of natural gas. The FPC responded that it had
no authority to regulate field prices. Some states then sued the government, and the
Supreme Court of the United States ruled that the FPC had to regulate the contracts
entered into by the *interstate* pipeline companies in *Phillips Petroleum Co.* v. *Wisconsin,* 347 U.S. 672 (1954). A maximum price was set for the gas purchased by the
interstate pipeline companies. Purchases of gas by intrastate companies were not
regulated.

One rationale for the Supreme Court decision was that monopoly elements
existed at the field level and that consumers were being forced to pay unreasonably
high prices as a result. However, there was no evidence of imperfect competition
among field producers at that time. On the contrary, the primary industry was fairly
competitive by the mid 1950s. The main argument for regulating field prices was to
redistribute rents from natural gas producers to consumers. Consumers argued successfully that it was "unfair" that producers of "old" (inframarginal fields) received
all the rents arising from the use of higher-cost gas from newly discovered and
developed wells.[5] The Supreme Court ruled that some of these rents had to be passed
back to consumers in the form of controlled prices set lower than the marginal price
of a new discovery. No account was taken of the adverse effects this ruling would have
on resource allocation over time, as we will see.

It is one thing, however, to require the FPC to regulate field prices and quite
another to implement the ruling. Regulating wellhead prices has been a problem
since the 1954 ruling. The reason is obvious—there are *thousands* of natural gas
wells. The FPC's expertise was with limited numbers of public utilities, and it tried

initially to set gas prices for each field producer on a case-by-case basis, as it did with utilities.[6] Between 1955 and 1960, over 3,500 producers of natural gas applied to the FPC for price increases above the maximum allowed level. In this interval, 10 applications were processed: It became clear to the FPC that gas prices could not be set for each producer. Individual price controls for each well were abandoned in 1960, to be replaced by control of prices by region — or *area ratemaking,* as it was known. The country was divided into 23 areas. Ceiling prices were set for natural gas contracts between field suppliers and interstate pipelines for each area. A two-price system for "old" and "new" gas was also imposed for each area. Old gas was gas extracted from wells producing prior to 1960. The "price" of old gas was set at its historical average cost of extraction. New gas was that discovered after 1960, and its price was based on the average costs of discovery and extraction over the period 1958–1961. (See MacAvoy, 1983, for details on the precise method of computing the allowed prices for each category.)

　　Let's see what the short-run effects of this sort of two-price system could be if gas markets clear. Figure 14.4 illustrates the simple allocative effects of the policy. Into any interstate pipeline will flow old and new gas, which of course are physically identical. We assume pipelines will buy the cheaper old gas at price P_0 until its supply is exhausted at, say, q_0. Suppose new gas is available in perfectly elastic supply at P_N. The price of gas to consumers (gas companies and ultimately final consumers) is thus the weighted price of old and new gas where the weights are the relative quantities of the two types of gas. If P_0 is the price of old gas and P_N the price of new gas, then P_A

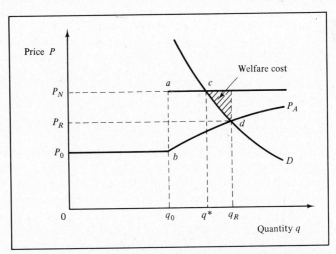

Figure 14.4　The welfare effects of regulating wellhead prices of natural gas. Let P_0 represent the price pipelines are allowed to pay for old gas which has a total stock Oq_0. P_N is the price of new gas which, say, is available in perfectly elastic supply. The average price of gas to consumers is given by $P_0 bd P_A$. If demand is D and the market clears, the equilibrium price is P_R with q_R consumed. This results in a *transfer of rent* from producers of old gas to consumers. These producers lose $P_0 P_N ab$; consumer surplus gains are $P_R P_N cd$. An *efficiency loss* is due to overconsumption of gas. The efficient (unregulated) equilibrium is P_N, q^*. But here consumers pay P_R for gas costing P_N to extract, and consume q_R. The welfare cost is the shaded area.

illustrates an average price schedule to consumers. If D is the demand curve for gas from the pipeline *and* the market clears (we see below that it often did not), the regulated market-clearing price will be P_R, with q_R consumed. The welfare effects of the policy are as follows: Producers of old gas will lose rents equal to the area $P_0 P_N ab$. Consumers of gas will gain consumer surplus equal to $P_R P_N cd$. Thus a major effect of the policy is to redistribute rents from gas producers to gas consumers. But *overconsumption* of gas relative to its real resource cost — the cost of supplying additional units of new gas at price P_N — also occurs. In an unregulated market facing demand curve D, price would be P_N and quantity consumed q^*. The regulatory policy lowers the price to P_R, inducing greater consumption than is efficient. The welfare cost of this policy in the short run is the shaded area shown in Figure 14.4.

The allocative effects over time of the two-price policy are even more adverse than illustrated by Figure 14.4. Regulation of gas prices can lead to disequilibrium in natural gas markets and adversely affect the long-run supply of natural gas. Let us see why.

Primary natural resource supply is quite different from public utilities in many respects. Public utilities (telephone companies, electric companies) have an obligation to provide service to all paying customers; primary gas producers have no such obligation. As we know from the theoretical analysis in Chapter 3, they will supply gas in accordance with its price, their costs, and any contractual arrangements made. There are many complications as a result. First, only gas supplied to interstate pipelines is regulated. Whenever the price intrastate pipelines are willing to pay exceeds the regulated interstate price, there will tend to be a shortage of gas to interstate consumers. Second, we must look at not only the market for existing gas supplies, a relatively short-term market that was illustrated in Figure 14.4, but also at long-term gas markets, which depend on additions to reserves made by exploratory drilling, discoveries, and expansion of existing capacity. If gas prices are held below the expected price of developing new reserves, as is likely to be the case when prices are determined by the historical average costs of production (as is the case with cost-of-service pricing), shortages of gas will appear over time. This can be shown easily in Figure 14.5.

If S represents the supply curve of new gas reserves as measured by the marginal costs of bringing in these reserves, but the price of gas to the producers is based on historical average costs of exploration and extraction (the AC curve), it is likely that S will lie above AC. Given demand D, the regulated price in a market equilibrium will be P_R, with consumption equal to q_R. At P_R, however, supply of new gas will be only q_S, leading to an excess demand of $q_S q_R$. Pipelines will have to fill this excess demand from other sources, or curtail gas consumption to some or all consumers. The efficient equilibrium is at P^* and q^*. There will still be some gas available from producers with extraction costs less than or equal to P_R, so there may be no apparent shortage in the short run. But because these supplies are finite, shortages must occur eventually. Unless the regulators are calculating the expected costs of developing new reserves into their average cost prices, they may be surprised to find shortages of gas developing.

Finally, recall that oil and gas are often found jointly. Any regulation of natural gas prices must find some method of allocating costs between oil and gas. There is no

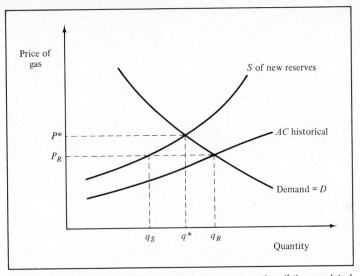

Price of gas

P^*

P_R

S of new reserves

AC historical

Demand $= D$

q_S q^* q_R

Quantity

Figure 14.5 Shortages of natural gas will occur over time if the regulated price is held below that needed to bring new supply on stream. Regulations that limit the wellhead price of gas to its historical average cost of discovery (AC historical) will lead to an equilibrium with q_R demanded at price P_R given demand equals D. At price P_R, producers of "new" gas will only be willing to supply q_S. A shortfall in reserves will then occur as the distance $q_S q_R$. Over time this shortfall will lead to actual shortages of gas and curtailments in service as "old" gas reserves are exhausted.

clear way to do this. Any arbitrary formula (such as cost of service) is bound to influence exploration and extraction decisions as a result. As we will now see, a number of serious problems have in fact resulted from the regulation of field prices of natural gas.

By the late 1960s and early 1970s, shortages of natural gas were occurring in the United States, especially in the upper Midwest and Atlantic seaboard regions. The shortages took a variety of forms, some of which were not obvious until later in the 1970s. First, gas was being added to the reserves of the intrastate market only. From 1970 to 1973, reserves available to intrastate consumers rose by 20 percent, while there were no additions to reserves available to interstate pipelines. Indeed, over the longer period 1965–1978, gas reserves available to interstate pipelines fell by 98 trillion cubic feet, while those available to intrastate pipelines rose by 12 trillion cubic feet (MacAvoy, 1983). The shortages were thus solely in the interstate markets. The reserve additions in the respective markets reflected the growing price differential between intra and interstate gas. Because it was costing more to develop new supplies of natural gas, prices were rising in the intrastate markets, but were held to the lower historical average costs in interstate markets. By 1973, when the intrastate price of gas was twice that of the interstate prices, it is not difficult to see why there were shortages in interstate markets. Table 14.2 shows the growing difference between acquisition prices for inter and intrastate pipeline companies over the period 1963 to 1979.

In the early 1970s, interstate pipelines found themselves unable to sign new contracts to ensure continued supplies of gas. The effect of these shortages was felt

Table 14.2 AVERAGE ACQUISITION PRICES IN GAS PIPELINE PURCHASES, 1963–1979

Year	Interstate price*	Intrastate price*
1963	35.7	49.7
1964	35.0	44.8
1965	34.5	42.2
1966	33.5	39.3
1967	33.0	39.6
1968	32.3	37.7
1969	31.3	38.3
1970	30.5	36.5
1971	30.8	36.5
1972	31.9	32.7
1973	32.9	39.5
1974	35.7	64.0
1975	42.1	96.3
1976	55.8	112.0
1977	76.5	131.2
1978	86.2	133.8
1979	114.9	142.4

* 1979 cents per million BTUs.

Source: U.S. Department of Energy, *Intrastate and Interstate Supply Markets under the Natural Gas Policy Act,* October 1981, p. 40, as cited in MacAvoy (1983).

differentially by gas consumers, because of the way in which the pipeline companies and local gas utilities handled the shortages. Residential and most commercial consumers continued to get all the gas they wanted. But the pipeline companies refused to sign any new contracts with large industrial consumers. Recall that the first oil price shock hit in 1973–74, and many industries were attempting to diversify their energy supplies at this time. A number of these industries were prevented from making the substitution to gas because of the shortages. In addition, pipelines could not guarantee supplies to gas utilities, which in turn refused to service some potential new industrial and other nonresidential consumers.

In general, throughout the early 1970s a sort of "invisible" shortage of natural gas was occurring. Residential and commercial buyers did not have any curtailment in service, but some potential buyers (industries) could not obtain gas at the prevailing price. This means that the demand curves shown in Figures 14.4 and 14.5 do not capture all the potential demand for gas. The equilibriums shown in these figures thus understate the welfare costs of the regulatory policies, which include the unfulfilled demands of industrial consumers.

By the mid-1970s, gas supplies to existing consumers were curtailed. All the curtailments occurred in interstate markets. The worst period was between 1976 and 1979. Gas was cut off during periods of peak demand (winter), and some industries and schools in northern states were forced to close down. Public outcries for changes in the regulatory policies began, and a number were made. Rationing was a first response. A priority of "needs" was established by the FPC (later FERC), with residential consumers given first priority because they were assumed to have a perfectly inelastic demand curve (they could not switch fuels for heating and cooking readily). Industrial users with fuel-switching capability were given low priority. While rationing schemes of this sort may have been necessary to ensure that individuals did not freeze, they exacerbated the inefficiencies of the regulatory system.

Because the price of gas was kept artificially low, consumers receiving gas had little incentive to reduce consumption. Some companies whose most efficient fuel input was gas (even at higher prices) could not receive any supply, while residential customers were still able to heat their swimming pools. Industrial firms were also induced to locate their operations in areas where gas was available from intrastate pipelines (such as Texas). Some of the adverse effects of this relocation (such as plant closings and layoffs in the North and East) would have been prevented by allowing field prices of gas to reflect the cost of new reserves.

The FPC also raised prices for new contracts signed between gas suppliers and pipelines, eliminated the two-price area rates, and went to three price categories applied nationally. The distinction between old and new gas remained, but another category was added—"new new" gas. The price of gas discovered after 1975–76 was to be pegged to the price of gas in intrastate markets. It was thus allowed to respond to market conditions. This is a reasonable move, but it does not eliminate the problem of charging consumers an *average price* that is less than the marginal costs of additional supplies, and it retains the distinction between vintages of gas.

The worst gas shortages occurred in 1977 as a result of a cold winter and the cumulative effects of gas regulation and oil price shocks. People were demanding a change in public policy because they were no longer benefitting from artificially low prices of natural gas. The response of the Carter administration and Congress was the Natural Gas Policy Act (NGPA) of 1978. The act had the joint objective of gradually deregulating some field prices of natural gas without adverse distribution consequences. Such an objective was hard to meet in principle and in practice; any change in policy was bound to affect some groups adversely. And compromises to satisfy all interests may result in policies that create even more economic distortions.

The 1978 act is a case in point. It is very complex and reflects the competing interests of consumers and producers; it is also a merger of quite different bills from the House and the Senate. The House bill sought to make regulation more comprehensive, while the Senate bill wanted prices on interstate contracts deregulated. In the final bill price controls were gradually eliminated for some classes of gas, but not for others. The price of new gas was to be deregulated by 1985, but the low prices for various categories of old gas remained. However, the distinction between intra and interstate pipelines was eliminated: All gas was now to be regulated.

The NGPA also increased the number of categories of gas to 30: Gas wells were distinguished not only by date of discovery, but by where they were found and physical characteristics such as depth, the size of the producer, and so on. Only three of these categories involved production that would ultimately be deregulated over the period 1978 to 1985. (See MacAvoy, 1983, for details on how the price of the gas to be deregulated was increased over this period.) The supplies of gas from these categories was limited. All gas under old contracts, all Alaskan, and all old offshore gas, for example, were still to be regulated even after 1985, although the prices in these categories were also to rise somewhat. Thus Congress was aware in 1978 that the act would most likely not eliminate gas shortages. Forecasts by government agencies, by industrial analysts in the private sector, and by academics all warned that the price increases allowed by the act would be insufficient to eliminate the shortages.

The short-term effects of the NGPA from 1978 to 1980 were largely positive. There was lots of exploration for gas in the categories to be deregulated, and aggregate reserves grew. Pipeline companies were signing new contracts, and most consumers received gas. But the regulated price was still less than the efficient market-clearing price. Some pipeline companies, desperate for supplies, agreed to terms very desirable to gas producers, such as take-or-pay contracts. The gas shortages disappeared.

But in 1979, oil prices doubled with the second oil shock. People worried that oil prices would continue to climb, so that by 1985, a large "spike" in the price of natural gas to be deregulated would occur. A debate ensured over what to do about this potential price spike. Then the recession began in 1981, and oil prices came down (in real and later nominal terms). Gas demand began falling, and pipelines found they could not sell all the gas they had agreed to buy from producers. A gas "glut" emerged—but *gas prices did not fall.*

Because of the contractual agreements made in the late 1970s, pipelines were forced to buy more expensive "new" gas and leave the cheaper old gas in the ground. Regulatory policies had again led to a perverse situation—high prices and excess supply (compared to the previous low prices and excess demand in the 1970s). Since 1982, pipeline companies have been breaking their contracts. There was no demand for gas at the contracted price, so these contracts have effectively been abrogated. The average price of gas is now closer to a market-clearing price because ceiling prices no longer effectively regulate most types of gas.

This gas glut may be only temporary. If the economic recovery in the United States of the mid-1980s is sustained, a gas shortage could again occur if the NGPA is not changed. The policy encourages the use of high-cost new gas (gas to be deregulated) and discourages the use of older, low-cost supplies. Exploration will be for gas in the categories to be deregulated. Production from old wells may even be abandoned prematurely because of the rigid price schedules applied to these categories. Methods of recovering additional supplies from these wells will not be used if the price does not correspond to the costs of recovery. MacAvoy cites some empirical support for the substitution of high-cost for low-cost gas. In 1977 there were fewer than 50 wells that qualified for deep-well status—a high-cost category to be deregulated in 1985. In 1980, the number of these wells rose to 350. From 1979–80, the price of high-cost wells rose to over 2.5 times that of low-cost regulated wells. It is not clear that there will be sufficient supplies of gas from these high-cost deposits to meet demand over time. In addition, the price of gas to many consumers is still relatively low; in many cases, it is less than the price of equivalent fuels (in BTU terms). Consumers will continue to substitute gas for other fuels and be less inclined to conserve gas supplies than if the price were market-determined.[7] This too may contribute to a future shortage.

What will happen over time? It seems certain that another gas policy will have to be developed. Many observers suggest that all gas prices will have to be deregulated and the distinction between different vintages eliminated. Proposals to deregulate all field prices were put forth by the Reagan administration in 1983–84 and by others in

Congress, but no definitive action has been taken up to now. The difficulty government decision-makers face is how to deregulate an industry without adversely affecting certain groups. Deregulation of the price of natural gas at the wellhead would lead to more efficient development of reserves, and better extraction and consumption decisions. But deregulation can raise the price. Consumers with low incomes and no alternative source of fuel for heating and cooking will be hit hard. The effects of the NGPA have already been felt by those with lower incomes; many have been unable to pay their gas bills since the price of gas began to rise in the late 1970s. Their real incomes have simply not kept up with the increase in all fuel prices.

There are many policy implications to be drawn from the natural gas story. It is difficult to deregulate a regulated industry, because it is impossible to design a deregulation policy that does not entail allocative and redistributive costs. Once a policy is in place, economic interests constrain decision-makers and may prevent the passage of a policy that contributes to economic efficiency. Finally, in the case of natural gas, there was no compelling reason to control wellhead prices in the first place. The original issue was the distribution of resource rents, not some inefficiency in gas extraction. Regulating prices is not the appropriate tool to redistribute income because of the inefficiencies such regulation promotes. Interfering with the price mechanism in as complex an industry as natural gas production was bound to have significant allocative effects (not to mention very high costs of operating the regulatory bureaucracy).

CONCLUDING COMMENTS: POLICY FORMATION AND THE POLITICAL PROCESS

We have treated "the government," for the most part, as another agent whose primary role is to intervene when decentralized activity fails to bring about socially desirable outcomes. This assumes that the government acts single-mindedly and arrives at the best action to pursue. However, there are many branches of government. And although in theory these branches were designed to coordinate their activities, actual practice is another story.

Economists have been analyzing the political process fairly intensively since 1951, when Kenneth Arrow published his monograph *Social Choice and Individual Values*. From one perspective, the most important political problem to an economist is how to take the views of individual citizens and arrive at a collective and single social view on the many matters that affect the functioning of a society. This is the aggregation problem. Lobbying, campaigning, vote-trading, and voting itself are processes for transforming the views of individuals into collective views or social prescriptions for action, but they are not without problems. Majority voting has been known for at least two hundred years to yield cycles of group rankings. For example, for three issues to be ranked for action, the group can end up with x over y, y over z, and z over x. In an individual, such a cycle would be said to indicate irrationality. Many see such a cycle in group choice as the fundamental defect of social choice based on individual choices. The group does not arrive at the best action when a cycle is present.

Should we in exasperation believe that "the government" cannot act optimally in reality? This seems unreasonable. Governments do not produce a stream of strange laws and random administrative judgments. We may not observe precisely tailored products from the legislative and administrative processes, but much law gets a passing grade when evaluated from the point of view of the college classroom. Thus, in spite of the extensively analyzed shortcomings of the political process as generator of good social decisions, social decisions do get made. A recent view of government as a Leviathan preying on the incomes of the citizens of a country for its own aggrandizement seems fantastic, certainly in Western countries. Is a neutral position defensible? Some government policies do benefit large numbers of people, such as Medicare; and other decisions, such as local public works projects, benefit relatively few. Government decisions are affected by voting patterns that can represent the views of the majority (at least those interested enough to vote), but they can also be influenced by powerful and often wealthy pressure groups that represent the interests of a few individuals or organizations. If governments did not intervene to mitigate market failures, many people living today and certainly future generations would be worse off.

Because of the intertemporal nature of natural resource extraction, we want to emphasize here the possible relationships between present and future generations. There are, at best, indirect guarantees for the rights of future generations, for they have no vote. It is the accumulation of capital in the form of natural resources, buildings, roads, factories, and knowledge by past generations that makes future generations well off, and all this accumulation occurs without central direction and in the absence of pressure from those future generations. The desire of an adult to leave a respectable amount of wealth upon his or her death is pervasive and is explained by ascribing utility to person i for the well-being of his or her offspring. Self-interest and altruism are often viewed as opposite motives, and yet the bequest motive combines the two.

To the resource economist, there are four special types of capital the current generation passes on to future generations: unused mineral stocks; forests; the environment, including the air and water; recreation lands; and fish and wild animal stocks. The latter three have distinct shared consumption or public goods characteristics, and we might expect them to be passed on through different social channels compared with, say, a factory or farm. Discovered mineral stocks and some forests are often privately controlled items of wealth, like claims on factories and the like. Undiscovered mineral stocks share a public goods quality like that of fish in the oceans, and so we might expect the individualistic bequest motive not to operate in the same way in this area as it does with private holdings of wealth.

The door is open for collective responsibility by the current generation for future generations. Recreation lands and natural environments must be set aside by government, since groups of individuals will generally not band together to provide such amenities for future generations. Similarly, government must protect animal and plant stocks from extinction, because once again individuals cannot be expected to plan for such bequests. And the stocks should be passed on at some just level, not in a severely depleted state. The best guarantee for future generations to be well-endowed is to have the actions of the current generation correspond to the desires of those future generations. If the current generation, for example, is very keen about having wilderness areas or clean air, lakes, rivers, and oceans, then future generations are protected against inheriting a polluted environment and few wilderness areas.

But there is an inevitable conflict in the areas of mineral exploitation, forestry, and commercial fishing. The current generation wants to consume products, and minerals, timber, and fish get used up in the process. Indirectly, however, if minerals get embodied in capital goods such as roads, buildings, and schools, future generations will not necessarily be impoverished by the actions of their predecessors. We noted one approach to formalizing this notion of bequeathing minerals in produced capital goods in Chapter 6, when we discussed economic growth and intergenerational equity.

We have surveyed the welfare theory of a market economy and guides for regulation. We have seen that regulation in practice is complicated and frequently at odds with the goals legislators have in mind when they initiate regulatory activity in a sector. Should we then abandon regulation on both theoretical and practical grounds? We would not endorse such a move. Pollution, for example, is too large a problem to be ignored, and the unregulated market will not clean up the environment or prevent further deterioration. New drugs must be tested by independent review agencies. The public cannot be cast in the role of guinea pigs by manufacturers anxious to earn extra profits by not adequately testing a product. And if free entry to a fishery makes consumers worse off than restricted entry and threatens fish populations with extinction, some form of control should be undertaken.

There are two basic lessons to be learned from this chapter. First, there are many instances of natural resource use in which government intervention is essential not just to promote efficiency and equity today, but to ensure continued production of goods and services over time. Second, government intervention is not costless, either in direct outlays of money or in the potential (and actual) inefficiencies government actions may create. We are left with a tradeoff. We know there are benefits from regulation of natural resource use, but regulatory policies are far from perfect.

SUMMARY

1. Natural resource use can often be improved by sensible government intervention. Areas for intervention in natural resource use include regulation of pollution; zoning of land use; improved collection and dissemination of information concerning geology, topography, and fish stocks; effective regulation of entry to fishing grounds; and replanting of forests. In addition, we expect monopolistic practices in any resource sector to be controlled.
2. Market failures fall into classes, and different types are usually assigned specific regulatory mechanisms. Federal government agencies in Canada and the United States are charged with particular regulatory functions.
3. Government intervention requires detailed design of policy in the form of regulations and an administrative unit to supervise the intervention. It is clearly difficult to get a perfect fit between an abstract ideal plan for regulation and the practice of intervention. Laws are enacted after compromises among legislators and reflect the idiosyncrasies of many individuals. We discussed a major bias of regulation — the tendency for regulators to fall into step with those they are charged with regulating.
4. Regulation is costly. Ideally, regulatory policies should be undertaken when the net benefits are positive. In practice, this may not occur; for example,

there may be inefficiencies generated by the regulations or simply faulty information.

5. No compelling economic rationale supported regulating natural gas prices at the wellhead. The methods of regulation have also given rise to substantial inefficiencies and transfers of income. However, once a sector is regulated, it is very difficult to deregulate it without affecting incomes (creating gainers and losers).

6. Certain market failures have repercussions for future generations. Severe depletion of an aquafer can leave an area without irrigation or forced to rely on distant water. There are degrees of irreversibility associated with these types of market failures, and successors may suffer while matters right themselves by natural renewal. Acid rain and depletion of ozone in the atmosphere are current "market failures" with significant irreversibilities. Future generations are best served when the current generation takes remedial action and in so doing protects future generations.

DISCUSSION QUESTIONS

1. Describe briefly some of the theories that attempt to explain the regulation of natural resource sectors of the economy. What type of regulations would one expect to see in the fishing industry if the regulations are based on self-interest theories such as "rent seeking"? Would the regulations be different from those based on market failure recognition? Explain.

2. Explain and derive the conditions that must be met to have an efficient allocation of resources and goods in an economy. Show how various types of market failure violate these conditions. Give three examples. For each market failure identified, show how a particular government policy can be used to obtain an efficient allocation of resources and goods.

3. List three reasons why the actual rate of mineral extraction may be too rapid or too slow. Are there government actions involved in each of the three situations you describe that are "tilting" the pace of mineral extraction in an unfavorable direction? in a favorable direction?

4. Give three examples of types of government policies that decrease economic efficiency, and explain why the inefficiency is created.

5. A few observers suggest that the damage caused by most traditional market failures is minor and that remedial action by public authorities is not worthwhile (see, for example, Milton and Rose Friedman, *Free to Choose*). Make a balance sheet of costs and benefits of government regulation in air pollution, water pollution, land use, fishing activity, and mineral exploration. If government withdrew from regulation, would groups form to carry out some of the activities formerly carried out by government?

6. Explain graphically and verbally the short-run and long-run allocative and distributive effects of keeping the wellhead price of natural gas regulated at a level below the cost of finding new gas deposits.

NOTES

1. See, for a review, Mansfield (1979), Hirshleifer (1984), Nicholson (1979).

2. Posner (1975) has argued that the potential gains to consumers from regulating monopoly are dissipated by (a) the cost of conducting the regulation by government, (b) the costs

incurred by those being regulated in keeping out potential entrants, and (c) the costs incurred by potential entrants in trying to enter the monopolized industry.

3. This is one of six examples Litan and Nordhaus (1983, pp. 94–96) discuss in order to illustrate the point in the text: If a goal or target is set, there remains the issue of designing the most efficient mechanism for attaining the goal. Other examples dealt with oil prices, air pollution from factories and electricity-generating plants, coal miners' safety, and toxicity of food additives.

4. This discussion is based on lectures by Paul Joskow at MIT in April and May 1984, and on MacAvoy (1983).

5. We should also point out that most gas consumers came from the industrialized northern states. The conflict was a rent-seeking action between northern consumers and southern and western producers.

6. These regulatory problems are similar to those encountered by the Environmental Protection Agency when it attempted to set individual emission permits for major polluters of waterways, as we saw in Chapter 13.

7. This is not to say that consumers have been unresponsive to increases in gas prices. Consumption has generally fallen since the rise in gas prices in 1978. Russell (1983) notes that in 1981, 5.8 percent more consumers used 8.8 percent less gas than in 1978. The point remains that gas consumption will be encouraged over time by the differential between gas prices and those of comparable fuels.

Appendixes

APPENDIX A: Intermediate Goods and Mixing Activities on Land

We have two goods. Good 1 is a final good and is sold at the central location at price p per unit. Good 2 is an intermediate good and is needed to produce good 1. Each unit of good 1 requires one unit of good 2. Good 1 requires one unit of land per unit of output and good 2 requires $1/a$ units of land per unit of output. The unit distance transportation costs for goods 1 and 2 are t_1 and t_2.

We will solve the land use problem for two cases. In case I there is integrated land use: Good 2 shares the site with good 1 and no transportation costs for the intermediate good are incurred. In case S, we have segregated land use: Good 2 is produced in a separate subarea and is shipped to the edge of the subarea occupied by good 1 (we work with circular subareas). Good 1 must be shipped to the center.

Case I

We maximize rent to get the efficient land use. Aggregate rent R^I is

$$R^I = pQ_1^I - T_1^I$$

where $Q_1^I = \dfrac{a}{1+a} \int_0^{x_1^I} 2\pi x\,dx$

$$T_1^I = \frac{a}{1+a} \int_0^{x_1^I} t_1 x 2\pi x\,dx$$

R^I is maximized when rent falls to zero at the boundary, or

$$p_1 - t_1 x_1^I = 0$$

or

$$x_1^I = p_1/t_1$$

This results in an aggregate rent

$$R^I = \frac{1}{3} \left(\frac{pa}{1+a} \right) \left(\frac{p}{t_1} \right)^2$$

Case S

The intermediate good must be shipped to the area in which the final good is produced. Aggregate rent R^S is

$$R^S = pQ_1^S - T_1^S - T_2^S$$

and must be maximized subject to $Q_1^S = Q_2^S$.

where $Q_1^S = \displaystyle\int_0^{x_1^S} 2\pi x dx$

$Q_2^S = \displaystyle\int_{X_1}^{x_2} a2\pi x dx$

$T_1^S = \displaystyle\int_0^{x_1^S} t_1 x 2\pi x dx$

$T_2^S = \displaystyle\int_{x_1^S}^{x_2^S} t_2(x - x_1^S) a2\pi x dx$

We form the Lagrangian (suppress the superscript S for the moment):

$$L = pQ_1^S - T_1^S - T_2^S + \lambda[Q_2^S - Q_1^S]$$

$$= 2\pi \left\{ \frac{px_1^2}{2} - \frac{t_1 x_1^3}{3} - at_2 \left[\frac{x_2^3 - x_1^3}{3} \right] + at_2 x_1 \left[\frac{x_2^2 - x_1^2}{2} \right] \right.$$

$$\left. + \lambda \left[\frac{ax_2^2}{2} - (1+a)\frac{x_1^2}{2} \right] \right\}$$

Let $L^x = L/2\pi$. Then the first order conditions are

$$\frac{\partial L^x}{\partial x_1} = px_1 - t_1 x_1^2 + at_2 \frac{x_2^2}{2} - at_2 \frac{x_1^2}{2} - \lambda(1+a)x_1 = 0 \qquad (1)$$

$$\frac{\partial L^x}{\partial x_2} = -at_2 u_2^2 + at_2 x_1 x_2 + \lambda ax_2 = 0 \qquad (2)$$

$$\frac{\partial L^x}{\partial \lambda} = a\frac{x_2^2}{2} - (1+a)\frac{x_1^2}{2} = 0 \qquad (3)$$

From (3) we get $x_2 = kx_1$, where $k = \left(\frac{1+a}{a} \right)^{1/2} > 1$. Using this result in (1) and (2) yields:

$$\bar{x}_1 = p \left/ \left[t_1 + at_2(k-1) + t_2 \left(k - \frac{3}{2} \right) \right] \right.$$

$$\bar{x}_2 = kp \left/ \left[t_1 + at_2(k-1) + t_2 \left(k - \frac{3}{2} \right) \right] \right.$$

We sketch the equilibrium in Figure A.1.

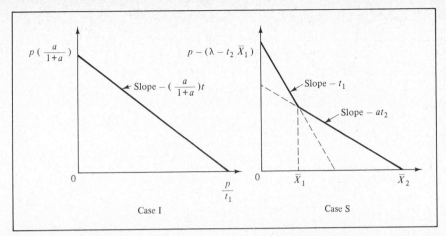

Figure A.1   Case I has land use integrated or the intermediate good shares the site with its final good. Case S has the final good produced closest to the central point and the intermediate good shipped in from its outlying subarea—hence, segregated land use. The efficient pattern, S or I, depends on transportation costs and the technology of production. The efficient pattern maximizes aggregate land rent.

The main result is that aggregate rent $R^S \gtrless R^I$ as $\bar{x}_2 \gtrless p/t_1$ or the efficient land use is the one which yields the highest rent and uses the largest total area of land. (One proves this by showing that if $\bar{x}_2 = p/t_1$, then $R^S = R^I$ first of all.) Since land area is proportional to output of the final good because of fixed coefficients, the efficient solution is the one that results in the most final good produced.

Now $\qquad\qquad\qquad\qquad\qquad x_2 \gtrless p/t_1$

as $\qquad\qquad\qquad\qquad\qquad t_1 \gtrless (a + v)t_2$

where $v = \left(k - \dfrac{3}{2}\right) \bigg/ (k - 1) - k$

in fact must exceed 3/2 for a sensible economic solution. Hence, the efficient solution depends on relative transportation costs weighted by production coefficients.

APPENDIX B: Mathematical Derivations of the Mine and Industry Problems in Continuous Time

The Problem of the Mine in Continuous Time with a Homogeneous Stock

For periods transformed to smooth collections of infinitesimal units of time, the mine owner's problem is to maximize the present value of profit by choice of a path of quantities in:

$$\int_0^T e^{-rt}[p \cdot q(t) - C(q(t))]dt$$

subject to the stock constraint on production

$$\int_0^T q(t)dt \leq S_0$$

where r is the rate of interest or discount
             p is price per unit output of ore and is fixed over time
             $q(t)$ is quantity of ore produced at instant t
             $C[q(t)]$ is the total cost of hoisting $q(t)$ tons

$\dfrac{dC[q(t)]}{dq(t)}$ is the marginal cost and is assumed to be positive for $q(t) > 0$. We can write $dC[q(t)]/dq(t)$ as $C'q(t)$

S_0 is the total stock of ore in the mine

For the constraint binding (all ore used up), we have $S_0 = \int_0^T q(t)dt$.

The change in the stock size per unit of time is dS/dt (often written as $\dot{S}$) and is $-q(t)$ or $\dot{S} = -q(t)$. This is a dynamic optimization problem, and control theory is the branch of mathematics developed for such problems. We will follow the rules of control theory. First, we use the specification of the problem presented earlier to define a function labeled the Hamiltonian (not unlike a Lagrangian in static optimization).

$$H(t) = e^{-rt}[p \cdot q(t) - C(q(t)] - \varphi(t)q(t)$$

where $\varphi(t)$ is called the *co-state variable* and is like a "shadow price" on stock S. In general, $\varphi(t)$ will have different values over the path of $q(t)$. A pair of time paths, $q(t)$ and $\varphi(t)$, and a value of T constitute a solution to the original maximization problem. These paths satisfy via the Hamiltonian, $H(t)$

(A1) $$\frac{\partial H}{\partial q(t)} = e^{rt}[p - C'q(t)] - \varphi(t) = 0$$

or the Hamiltonian assumes a maximum at each point in time with respect to $q(t)$.

Also the paths satisfy

(A2) $$\dot{S} = \frac{\partial H}{\partial \varphi} \quad \text{or} \quad \dot{S} = -q(t)$$

and S is given initially as $S(t_0) = S_0$. And optimal paths also satisfy

(A3) $$\dot{\varphi} = -\frac{\partial H}{\partial S} \text{ or}$$

$$\dot{\varphi} = 0$$

plus some condition on $\varphi(t)$ at the end of the path at T. The condition depends on the type of problem in hand. For our problem, we have at T

$$[p - C'(q(t))]q(T) = pq(T) - C[q(T)]$$

(A3) indicates that $\varphi(t)$ is constant over time ($\dot{\varphi}(t) = 0$). Differentiating (A1) with respect to time yields

$$\dot{\varphi}(t) = -re^{rt}[p - C'(q(t))] + e^{-rt}\frac{d[p - C'(q(t))]}{dt} = 0$$

or $$\frac{\dfrac{d[p - C'(q(t))]}{dt}}{p - C'(q(t))} = r$$

which indicates that along an optimal path of $q(t)$, rent $p - C'(t)$ must increase at a rate equal to the rate of interest. Of the family of paths that satisfy this flow condition, one will satisfy the stock constraint:

$$S_0 = \int_0^T q(t)dt$$

and at the end $[p - C'(q(T))]q(T) = pq(T) - C[q(T)]$ or marginal rent equals average rent equals zero at T.

The Industry in the Hotelling Model: A Planning Problem in Continuous Time

The planner chooses a path of quantities of mineral to extract in order to maximize the present value of social welfare. Using a consumer surplus measure of welfare we maximize

$$\int_0^T e^{-rt}[B(q(t)) - cq(t)]dt$$

Subject to the stock constraint

$$\int_0^T q(t)dt \le S_0$$

where $B[q(t)]$ is the area under the demand curve up to $q(t)$
c is cost of extraction per ton
$q(t)$ is quantity extracted at t
r is the interest or discount rate
S_0 is the amount of stock to be mined

Again we get $\dot{S} = -q(t)$ or how the stock changes over time. We form the Hamiltonian

$$H(t) = e^{-rt}[B(q(t)) - cq(t)] - \psi(t)q(t)$$

where $\psi(t)$ is the co-state variable. If we follow the steps from previous analysis, we get the flow condition:

$$\frac{\dfrac{d(p(t) - c)}{dt}}{p(t) - c} = r$$

which says that the percentage increase in rent per ton at each instant of time equals the rate of interest, r. The terminal condition derives from the mathematical end-point condition, namely:

$$[p(T) - c]q(T) = B(q(T)) - cq(T)$$

or marginal rent on the quantity extracted at T (namely, $p(T) - c$) equals average rent— namely,

$$\frac{B[q(T)] - cq(T)}{q(T)}.$$

APPENDIX C: Declining Quality of Stock

One approach to introducing declining quality of stock is to have the cost of getting $q(t)$ tons extracted rise as one works deeper into the mine. Deeper here means stock size $S(t)$ getting smaller. Formally, we index the cost of extracting $q(t)$ tons by $S(t)$. The smaller $S(t)$ is, the higher the cost of extracting $q(t)$ tons. The total cost function is $C[q(t), S(t)]$, with

$$\frac{\partial C(q(t), S(t))}{\partial q(t)} > 0 \quad \text{and} \quad \frac{\partial C(q(t), S(t))}{\partial S(T)} < 0$$

Marginal costs are positive given the "index" $S(t)$ and are also presumably increasing in $q(t)$, while the cost of extracting $q(t)$ decreases as $S(t)$ gets larger.

In the text we used a different approach. Each ton is labelled with its extraction cost. If $\hat{c}$ is the cost for some tons in question then $(\hat{c} \cdot q(\hat{c}))$ is the cost of extracting those $q(\hat{c})$ tons. For a smooth distribution of grades (costs of extraction per ton), we can have a batch of different but similar qualities:

$$Q = \int_{\underline{c}}^{\bar{c}} q(z)dz$$

is a batch of ore of grades (costs of extraction per ton) between $\underline{c}$ and $\bar{c}$. The total cost of extracting this batch is

$$C(Q) = \int_{\underline{c}}^{\bar{c}} c(z)q(z)dz.$$

Let us consider an example. For a two-period problem of the mine described in the text, the owner chooses a cutoff grade (marginal grade) in period 1 to maximize the present value of profit over the two periods: Maximize by choice of c^*

$$P_1 \cdot \int_{\underline{c}}^{c^*} q(z)dz - \int_{\underline{c}}^{c^*} c(z)q(z)dz + \frac{1}{1+r}\left[P_2 \cdot \int_{c^*}^{P_2} q(z)dz - \int_{c^*}^{P_2} c(z)q(z)dz \right]$$

Maximization yields

$$P_1 q(c^*) - c(c^*)q(c^*) - \frac{1}{1+r}[P_2 q(c^*) - c(c^*)q(c^*)] = 0$$

or
$$P_1 - c(c^*) = \frac{1}{1+r}[P_2 q(c^*) - c(c^*)q(c^*)] = 0$$

which is our flow condition, illustrated in Figure 3.2. We assume $P_2 > P_1$ as illustrated in the figure. If $c(z)$ increases in z, we have cost per ton rising as z, an index increases. This can capture declining quality.

APPENDIX D: Constant Elasticity of Demand Example

The demand schedule is

$$p = f(q) = q^{-a} \quad 0 < a < 1$$

Marginal revenue,

$$v = (1 - a)q^{-a}$$

and for the backstop with constant c,

$$\bar{v} = (1 - a)c$$

Monopoly Extraction—No Backstop (Asymptotic Depletion)

Since marginal revenue must rise at the rate of interest (we have zero extraction costs), we have

$$v(t) = v(0)e^{rt} \qquad T_0 \leq t \leq T$$

and

$$T \int_0^T q(t)dt = S_0$$

T will be infinite with asymptotic depletion. We get

$$q(t) = q(0)e^{-(r/a)t}$$

upon substituting the expression for marginal revenue in $v(t)$. Upon integrating all quantities to sum to S_0, we have

$$q(t) = \frac{r}{a} S_0 e^{-(r/a)t}$$

Monopoly Extraction to a Ceiling Marginal Revenue, $\bar{v}$

Now exhaustion occurs as $\bar{v}$ is reached, so the summing of quantities extracted changes from that above to

$$\hat{T} \int_0^T q(t)dt = S_0$$

where T is the date that the ceiling $\bar{v}$ is reached. Marginal revenue at T will be $\bar{v} = (1 - a)c$. Given $v(t)$ rising at the rate of interest, we have

$$q(t) = \left(\frac{1-a}{c}\right)^{1/a} e(r/a)(T - t)$$

Now integrating for stock size S_0 yields

$$\left(\frac{1-a}{c}\right)^{1/a} e(r/a)T = \frac{r}{a} S_0 + \left(\frac{1-a}{c}\right)^{1/a}$$

which can be written

$$q(t) = \left[\frac{r}{a} S_0 + \left(\frac{1-a}{c}\right)^{1/a}\right] e^{-(r/a)t} \quad \text{for} \quad t < T$$

Note as $c \to \infty$, our quantity path reduces to the one in the case when the backstop did not exist. Instant by instant $q(t)$ above lies above that schedule for the case above given comparable dates, t.

Monopoly Extraction to a Competitive Backstop Supply

In this case, marginal revenue rises at the rate of interest between $T_0 = 0$ and T. Then marginal revenue is constant beyond T to date τ at value $c(1 - a)$. The complete marginal revenue schedule can be expressed as

$$v(t) = \min[ce^{-r(T-t)}, c(1 - a)]$$

The corresponding extraction schedule is

$$q(t) = \max[c^{-(1/a)}(1 - a)^{1/a}e^{(r/a)(T-t)}, c^{-(1/a)}]$$

Recall that marginal revenue jumps up beyond T and declines. It in fact declines, in present value terms, to the value it jumped from at T. From our $v(t)$ schedule, we have

$$e^{-r(\tau-T)}c = (1 - a)c$$

or

$$(\tau - T) = -\frac{1}{r} \ln(1 - a)$$

which gives us the length of time of the second phase (of constant current marginal cost and price). The length of this phase does not depend on stock size S_0. In fact, S_0 must be "large" in order for a first phase of rising marginal revenue to be viable. Over the two phases, total extraction must sum to S_0 or

$$[(1 - a)^{(1/a)}e^{(r/a)t}] \int_0^T e^{-(r/a)t}dt + (\tau - T) = c^{(1/a)}S_0$$

Using our result on the length $\tau - T$ of phase 2 and integrating, yields

$$(1 - a)^{1/a}e^{(r/a)} = \frac{r}{\alpha} S_0 c^{(1/a)} + \frac{a + \ln(1 - a)}{a}$$

Substituting in our $q(t)$ definition above yields

$$q(t) = \max \left\{ \left[\frac{r}{a} S_0 + \frac{a + \ln(1 - a)}{a} c^{-(1/a)} \right] e^{-(r/a)t}, c^{-(1/a)} \right\}$$

and

$$q(0) = \frac{r}{a} S_0 + \frac{a + \ln(1 - a)}{a} c^{-(1/a)}$$

which for $0 < a < 1$ has $a + \ln(1 - a) < 0$ and results in $p(0)$ for $q(0)$ above, greater than the initial price when no backstop is in effect. This is the Gilbert-Goldman paradox: Competition from the backstop suppliers increases the monopolist's initial price.

APPENDIX E: Arbitrage Rule When the Date of Arrival of the Backstop Is Uncertain

Suppose the backstop comes on stream at a known cost of producing the substitute but at an unknown date in the future.

a. If the substitute has not arrived during the interval $(t, t + \theta)$, the price $p_{t+\theta}$ must satisfy the Hotelling Rule (we assume zero costs of extraction of the known stock)

$$(p_{t+\theta} - p_t)/p_t = r_t\theta$$

Upon taking the limit $\theta \to 0$, we get the familiar $\dot{p}_t/p_t = r$.

b. During the interval $(t, t + \theta)$, there is probability $\lambda_t\theta$ that the invention of the substitute occurs. Once it occurs, the resource stock owner sets a new price $\hat{p}_t$ in order to deplete his remaining stock S_t for maximum profit. (He will undercut the price at which the substitute would be sold.) So we get $\hat{p}_t$ depending on the remaining stock S_t, or we write $\hat{p}_t = \hat{p}(S_t)$. $\hat{p}_t$ will generally be lower than p_t.

Thus in the interval a ton of ore will suffer the capital loss $p_t - \hat{p}(S_t)$ with probability $\lambda_t\theta$ and capital gain dp_t with probability $(1 - \lambda_t\theta)$. This is for the ton left in the ground. Hence expected profit is $-\lambda_t\theta[p_t - \hat{p}(S_t)] + (1 - \lambda_t\theta)dp_t$. Alternatively, if the ton were extracted and sold at t, profit from interest accumulation would be $r_t\theta p_t$. For risk-neutral speculators to be indifferent between waiting or extracting, we must have

$$-\lambda_t\theta[p_t - \hat{p}(S_t)] + (1 - \lambda_t\theta)dp_t = r_t\theta p_t$$

Taking limits as the interval tends to zero (i.e., $\theta \to 0$) yields

$$\dot{p}_t/p_t = r_t + \lambda_t(1 - \hat{p}(S_t)/p_t)$$

which is the basic arbitrage rule for the case of an uncertain date of the arrival of the backstop technology for producing the perfect substitute.

c. For the special case $\lambda_t = 0$, (i.e., there is no chance of the invention occurring in the next instant), we get

$$\dot{p}_t/p_t = r$$

Similarly if $\hat{p}(S_t) = p_t$ (i.e., the invention has no influence on the value of the resource), we get $\dot{p}_t/p_t = r$. Generally, we will have $\hat{p}(S_t) < p_t$ or as the invention occurs, one must speed up extraction of the remaining stock. Thus our basic arbitrage rule can be written as

$$r_t \le \dot{p}_t/p_t \le r_t + \lambda_t$$

For the special case $\hat{p}(S_t) = 0$ or the invention renders the ore of no value, we have $\dot{p}_t/p_t = r + \lambda_t$. This case has the invention of the substitute showing up as a risk premium for being in the extraction business.

Source: P. Dasgupta and J. E. Stiglitz (1981).

APPENDIX F: Mathematical Analysis of the Model with Nonrenewable Resources and Reproducible Capital

In the text we had a single output, fiber, produced with flows $R(t)$ from a nonrenewable resource stock $S(t)$ and reproducible capital, $K(t)$. For $Q(t)$ as fiber, we had $Q(t) = f[K(t),R(t)]$. Part of the output was consumed at $C(t)$ and part invested in more reproducible capital, $\dfrac{dK}{dt} [= \dot{K}(t)]$. The planning problem was to (1) run down the nonrenewable resource stock $S(t)$, and (2) add to the reproducible capital stock from output each period in order to maximize the discounted utility from consuming fiber period by period into the future. We have formally

$$\text{maximize } W = \int_0^\infty e^{-rt} U(C(t)) dt$$

$$\text{subject to } \dot{K} = f[K(t), R(t)] - C(t)$$
$$\text{and } R(t) = -\dot{S}(t)$$

where

$$\int_0^\infty R(t) dt \leq S(0)$$

$U[C(t)]$ is the utility of consumption at time t
r is the discount rate

The Hamiltonian function defined at each instant of time t for this dynamic optimization problem is

$$H(t) = e^{-rt} U[C(t)] + \psi[f(K,R) - C] - \lambda R$$

At each date $H(t)$ is maximized by choice of C and R, yielding

$$e^{-rt} U_c - \psi = 0 \tag{A.1}$$
$$\psi f_R - \lambda = 0 \tag{A.2}$$

and the differential equations, $\dfrac{\partial H}{\partial \psi} = \dot{K}$ and $-\dfrac{\partial H}{\partial K} = \dot{\psi}$ must be satisfied as well as transversality and boundary conditions [transversality conditions on $K(t)$ and $S(t)$ at $t \to \infty$ and boundary conditions on initial stocks of $K(t)$ and $S(t)$]. Thus we have

$$\dot{K} = f(K,R) - C \tag{A.3}$$
$$\dot{\psi} = -\psi f_K \tag{A.4}$$

Equations (A.1) to (A.4) characterize the family of optimal paths for our dynamic system. *The optimal path is the member of the family that satisfies initial conditions and transversality conditions.* From (A.1) and (A.2), we get, respectively:

$$\dot{\psi} = -re^{-rt} U_C + e^{-rt} U_{CC} \dot{C}$$
$$\dot{\lambda} = \dot{\psi} f_R + \dot{f}_R \psi = 0$$

Substituting in (A.4) yields

$$\frac{U_{CC} \dot{C}}{U_C} - r = -f_K \tag{A.5}$$

which is called the Ramsey optimal savings relation, and substituting in (A.4) using the second expression above yields

$$\frac{\dot{f}_R}{f_R} = f_K \tag{A.6}$$

which is the efficiency condition for using up the nonrenewable resource (a variant of the Hotelling rule). Since $\dot{f}_R = f_{RR} \dot{R}$, Equation (A.6) is a dynamic equation in R. The revised equations for the family of optimal paths are (A.3), (A.5), and (A.6), three dynamic equations in $C(t)$, $R(t)$, and $K(t)$. These could be analyzed using standard methods. (When a dynamic system involves only two variables, time paths can be plotted in two dimensions as the phase plane and a full analysis performed. With three equations, such methods can be applied only if the system can somehow be reduced to two equations in a precise fashion.)

For the case of the particular utility function

$$U(C) = \frac{1}{v^2} C^v$$

and Cobb-Douglas production function, $Q = K^\alpha R^{1-\alpha}$, our three dynamic equations in (A.3), (A.5), and (A.6) can be written, respectively, as

$$g_K = \frac{Q}{K} - \frac{C}{K} \tag{A.7}$$

$$(v - 1)g_c = r - \alpha \left(\frac{Q}{K}\right) \tag{A.8}$$

$$g_R = -\frac{Q}{K} \tag{A.9}$$

where $g_x \equiv \frac{\dot{x}}{x}$ is a growth rate for variable x. Since g_c and g_R are linked by a simple equation, we can analyze g_c separately and g_R will follow.

It is convenient to put things in ratios of $C/K = \gamma$ and $Q/K = \eta$. Now

$$g_Q = \alpha g_K + (1 - \alpha)g_R \tag{A.10}$$

Substitute (A.9) in (A.10), and we have $g_Q = \alpha g_K - (1 - \alpha)\frac{Q}{K}$, giving us g_K, g_C, and g_Q in terms of $C/K = \gamma$ and $Q/K = \eta$. Since $g_\gamma = g_C - g_K$ and $g_\eta = g_Q - g_K$, we can obtain

$$g_\gamma = \left(\frac{r}{v - 1}\right) - \left(\frac{\alpha + v - 1}{v - 1}\right)\eta + \gamma \tag{A.11}$$

$$g_\eta = (\alpha - 1)\gamma \tag{A.12}$$

For $g_\gamma = g_\eta = 0$, Equations (A.11) and (A.12) become, respectively:

$$\gamma = \left(\frac{r}{1 - v}\right) + \left(\frac{\alpha + v - 1}{v - 1}\right)\eta \tag{A.13}$$

$$(\alpha - 1)\gamma = 0 \tag{A.14}$$

We plot these schedules in the $\gamma - \eta$ plane in Figure F.1. $g_K = 0$ divides the space in half. Points above $g_K = 0$ have $\dot{K} < 0$, which we rule out. Paths originating in region A rise and hit the $g_K = 0$ boundary with C/K rising and Q/K falling. This would presumably never be optimal, since collapse seems inevitable unless the path moved down along the $g_K = 0$ boundary with no accumulation taking place. In region B, paths move toward the origin, with C/K and Q/K declining continually. Such behavior seems potentially optimal, since C and Q would presumably decline but not necessarily go to zero in infinite time. This might be called asymptotic decline in the economy. (Recall $g_R = -\eta$, so the growth rate in R declines as $\eta \to 0$ in the figure.)

From region G, a path could rise to the northwest and then bend down to decline toward the origin. A initial rise in $C(t)$ is possible, as Dasgupta and Heal (1974) point out for large initial endowments of resource stock $S(0)$ and capital stock $K(0)$. Paths originating in region D behave the same as those originating in region B. Optimal paths must end in regions B and D with asymptotic decline as $C(t)$ approaches zero, since $\eta \to \gamma$ as time passes.

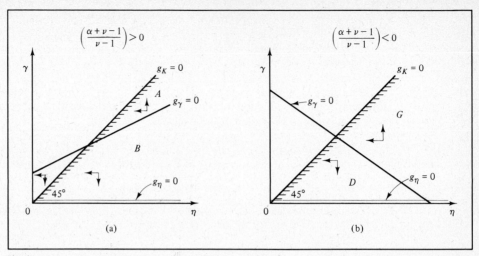

Figure F.1 Phase diagrams for the model of growth with an exhaustible resource whose computer runs were reported on in the text of Chapter 5. Both $\gamma = C/K$ and $\eta = Q/K$ collapse as K grows and resource stocks are depleted.

APPENDIX G: Fishery Equilibriums

The common property equilibrium (CPE) and private property equilibrium (PPE) in a static model can be derived algebraically in two ways—in terms of effort and in terms of harvests. We now illustrate both approaches using the simple model presented in this chapter.

Suppose the biological mechanics are given by

$$F(X) = aX - bX^2 \tag{A.1}$$

where a and b are parameters and X is the biomass. Equation (A.1) is thus a parabola. Let the harvest or catch be given by the teady-state harvest function

$$H = qEX \tag{A.2}$$

where q is a catchability coefficient and E is the index of effort inputs to the fishery. For simplicity, let $q = 1$.

A steady-state bionomic equilibrium requires $F(X) = H$. We can therefore determine the steady-state level of effort, biomass, and harvest as:

$$E = a - bX$$
$$X = \frac{a}{b} - \frac{E}{b} \tag{A.3}$$
$$H = E\left(\frac{a}{b} - \frac{E}{b}\right)$$

Let $\alpha = a/b$ and $\beta = 1/b$. Then the steady state harvest is

$$H = \alpha E - \beta E^2 \tag{A.4}$$

which is again a parabola. Using Equation (A.4), we can now solve for the CPE and PPE, first in terms of costs and revenues as a function of effort, then as functions of the harvest.

In the CPE, the industry will be in equilibrium where total revenues as a function of effort equal the total costs of effort. Assume the price of fish is constant. Then $TR = PH$, and if $P = 1$, $TR = H$. Total costs are given by cE, assuming constant unit costs of effort $= c$. Substituting Equation (A.4) for H, the CPE is where

$$\alpha E - \beta E^2 = cE$$

or
$$E = \frac{\alpha - c}{\beta} = a - bc \qquad (A.5)$$

Equating $TR = TC$ is the same as setting average revenue per unit effort equal to the marginal cost of effort. With the assumption that $P = 1$, the common property harvest is

$$H = cE = c(\alpha - c)/\beta = ac - bc^2 \qquad (A.6)$$

We can also solve for the common property harvest where the price of fish equals the average cost of the harvest, cE/H. This follows from:

$$TR = TC$$
$$PH = cE$$
$$P = cE/H$$

From equation (A.4), we can determine the cost of the harvest. Solving (A.4) for effort, we find

$$E = \pm \sqrt{-\frac{H}{\beta} + \left(\frac{\alpha}{2\beta}\right)^2} + \frac{\alpha}{2\beta} \qquad (A.7)$$

Then
$$AC = \frac{2c}{\alpha \pm \sqrt{-4\beta H + \alpha^2}} \qquad (A.8)$$

The AC curve is the backward-bending "supply" curve of the open access fishery derived graphically in the chapter. Equating AC to the price of fish yields the CP harvest.

What about the private property equilibrium (PPE) for the competitive firm? The PPE in terms of effort is determined where the marginal revenue of effort (MR_E) equals the marginal cost of effort (MC_E). MR_E is the change in total revenue due to a change in effort, dTR/dE, which if $P = 1$, $MR_E = \alpha - 2\beta E$. Marginal cost of effort equals the change in total cost due to a change in effort, dTC/dE, which equals c. The PPE level of effort is then where

$$E^* = \frac{\alpha - c}{2\beta} \qquad (A.9)$$

Comparing (A.9) to (A.5), we find that for this model, the PPE uses one-half the CPE level of effort. The PPE harvest is then $H = \frac{1}{4\beta}(\alpha^2 - c^2) = \frac{1}{4}\left(\frac{a^2}{b} - bc\right)$.

Solving the PPE in terms of harvests requires setting the price of fish equal to the marginal cost of the harvest, MC_H. The MC_H is found by differentiating the TC of the harvest with respect to H. Using the chain rule, $dTC/dH = dTC/dE \cdot dE/dH$. We know that $dTC/dE = C$. Then dE/dH can be found by differentiating Equation (A.7) with respect to H (recall that A.7 shows effort in terms of sustainable harvests). We obtain

$$MC_H = \frac{C}{\sqrt{-4\beta H + \alpha^2}} \qquad (A.10)$$

This marginal cost curve is a monotonically increasing function of the sustainable harvest where marginal costs approach infinity as the sustainable harvest approaches the MSY biomass. Thus setting the price of fish equal to Equation (A.10) yields the private property harvest.

Given the complex nature of the AC and MC of harvest curves, it is generally easier to derive equilibriums in the fishery in terms of effort. The cost curves in terms of the harvest are used in empirical work.

APPENDIX H: Two Countries Competing for Harvests of Fish

Under the Cournot assumption that each country assumes the other country's harvests are fixed and constant indefinitely, we have the steady equations for each country.

$$p^I - C_H^I I = C_X^I/(g_X - r)$$
$$p_B - C_H^B B = C_X^B/(g_X - r)$$

where p^I is price in country I derived from the demand schedule in country I

     $C_H^I I$ is the marginal cost of harvest in country I and total cost is $C^I(X^I, H^B, X)$

     C_X^I is the impact on harvest costs in country I of marginal increase in stock size X

     g_X is the impact on births over deaths of the stock of a marginal increase in stock size X

     r is the interest rate

Terms for country B are similarly defined.

Under a cooperative arrangement between countries, total discounted welfare is maximized and the steady-state equation for the combined units is

$$p^I + p^B - C_H = C_X/(g_X - r)$$

where C_H is marginal cost of harvesting the total catch to be divided equally between our identical countries

     C_X is the impact on total harvesting costs of the combined harvest of a marginal increase in stock size X. The total cost function has the same form as the separate cost functions for each nation, but now $H^I + H^B = H$ is harvested in a centralized administration.

     g_X and r are as defined above.

We make

$$C^I(H^I, H^B, X) \equiv \frac{w(H^I + H^B)}{mX}, \; C^B(H^B, H^I, X) \equiv \frac{w(H^I + H^B)}{mX}, \; C(H, X) \equiv \frac{wH}{mX},$$
$$p^I = A - BH^I, \; p^B = A - BH^B, \text{ and } g(X) = X(a - bX)$$

Our equations above then become

$$\left[A - BH^I - \frac{w}{mX} \right] = \frac{w(H^I + H^B)}{mX^2[r - (a - 2bX)]}$$
$$\left[A - BH^B - \frac{w}{mX} \right] = \frac{w(H^I + H^B)}{mX^2[r - (a - 2bX)]}$$
$$\left[2A - BH - \frac{w}{mX} \right] = \frac{wH}{mX^2[r - (a - 2bX)]}$$

This latter is for the cooperative solution. In a steady-state,

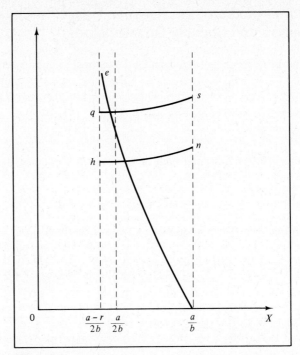

Figure H.1

$$H = X(a - bX) = H^I + H^B \quad \text{or} \quad H^I = \frac{X(a - bX)}{X} = H^B$$

Substituting above yields

$$A - \frac{B}{2}[X(a - bX)] - \frac{w}{mX} = \frac{w(a - bX)}{mX[r - (a - 2bX)]}$$

for each of the first two equations and

$$2A - B[X(a - bX)] - \frac{w}{mX} = \frac{w(a - bX)}{mX[r - (a - 2bX)]}$$

for the third equation representing the cooperative solution.

The left-hand side is price minus marginal cost and must be positive. For the right-hand side to be positive, $\frac{a - r}{2b} < X < \frac{a}{b}$. We sketch the right-hand side as in Figure H.1. We plot $A - \frac{B}{2}[X(a - bX)] - \frac{w}{mX}$ as hn, and $2A - B[X(a - bX)] - \frac{w}{mX}$ as qs. The result is the X in the cooperative solution always is less than X in the individualistic or Cournot competitive solution. For $r \cong a$, both steady-state stocks will be to the right of the stock corresponding to the maximum sustainable yield. For solution values of the Xs to the left of $X = a/2b$, "impatience" is dominant. Otherwise cost reductions for "high" stocks dominate. Rent, $p - mc$, is always positive and is always larger for the cooperative solution.

APPENDIX I: Response of the Rotation Period to Changes in Parameters in the Basic Discounted Socially Optimal Model

Our first-order condition defining the optimal rotation interval was

$$
\left[\frac{dV(I)}{dI} - rV(I) \right] = \left[\frac{r}{p-c} \right] [e^{-rI}(p-c)V(I) - D] \left[\frac{e^{rI}}{e^{rI} - 1} \right]
$$

$$
= \left(\frac{r}{p-c} \right) W^*
$$

where W^* is the optimal value of the program of planting and harvesting in the optimal cycle in perpetuity. An envelope result is that $dW^*/dI = 0$.

Change in $p - c$

Define $t \equiv p - c$ for a moment. Totally differentiating our first order condition yields

$$
\frac{\partial \left[\dfrac{dV(I)}{dI} - rV(I) \right]}{\partial I} dI = \frac{-rW^*}{t^2} dt + \frac{r}{t} \frac{\partial W^*}{\partial t} dt
$$

$$
= \frac{r}{t} \left\{ \frac{-tV(I) + e^{rI}D}{(e^{rI} - 1)t} + \frac{V(I)}{e^{rI} - 1} \right\} dt
$$

$$
= \frac{rD}{t^2} \left[\frac{e^{rI}}{e^{rI} - 1} \right] dt
$$

The left-hand side is negative and the right-hand side is positive, so we have

$$
\frac{dI}{dt} < 0
$$

or

$$
\frac{dI}{dp} < 0 \quad \text{and} \quad \frac{dI}{dc} > 0
$$

A rise in the price shortens the optimal rotation period, while a rise in costs of harvest lengthens the optimal rotation period.

Increase in D

Total differentiating yields

$$
\frac{\partial \left[\dfrac{dV(I)}{dI} - rV(I) \right]}{\partial I} dI = \left[\frac{r}{p-c} \right] \frac{\partial W^*}{\partial D} dD
$$

$$
= \left[\frac{r}{p-c} \right] \left[\frac{-e^{rI}}{e^{rI} - 1} \right] dD
$$

Both sides are negative, so

$$
\frac{dI}{dD} > 0
$$

as we argued in the text.

An Increase in the Interest Rate *r*

Totally differentiating our first-order condition yields

$$\frac{\partial\left[\frac{dV(I)}{dI} - rV(I)\right]}{\partial I} dI - V(I)dr = \frac{W^*}{t} dr + \frac{r}{t} \frac{\partial W^*}{\partial r} dr$$

$$\frac{\partial\left[\frac{dV(I)}{dI} - rV(I)\right]}{\partial I} dI = \frac{W^*}{t}\left[1 - \frac{rI}{e^{rI} - 1}\right] dr + V(I)\left[1 - \frac{rI}{e^{rI} - 1}\right] dr$$

The left-hand side is negative and the right-hand side is positive, so we have

$$\frac{dI}{dr} < 0$$

as we argued in the text.

An Increase in Fertility — Parameter a

We need the expression for $V(I)$ (the integral of our basic growth equation).

$$V(I) = \left[\frac{a}{b + \left(\frac{a - bV_0}{V_0}\right) e^{-aI}}\right]$$

where V_0 is the value of $V(I)$ when $I = 0$. We need derivatives of $V(I)$ also.

$$\frac{dV}{dI} = \frac{V(I)^2 e^{-aI}}{V_0} [a - bV_0]$$

$$\frac{d^2V}{dI^2} = V(I)^2 e^{-aI}\left[\frac{a - bV_0}{V_0}\right]\left\{2\frac{dV}{dI} \Big/ V(I) - a\right\}$$

$$\frac{d\left(\frac{dV}{dI}\right)}{da} = \frac{V(I)e^{-aI}}{V_0}\left[2\left(\frac{dV}{da}\right)(a - bV_0) - V(I)I(a - bV_0) + V(I)\right]$$

$$\frac{dV}{da} = \frac{V}{a} - \frac{V}{\left[b + \frac{a - bV_0}{V_0} e^{-aI}\right]} \frac{e^{-aI}}{V_0} [1 - I(a - bV_0)]$$

We use these derivatives in our basic equilibrium condition. Recall that the equilibrium condition is

$$\left[\frac{dV}{dI} - rV(I)\right] = \frac{r}{p - c} [e^{-rI}(p - c)V(I) - D]$$

The total derivative is

$$d\left[\frac{dV}{dI} - rV(I)\right] dI + d\left[\frac{dV}{dI} - rV(I)\right] da = \frac{r}{p - c} d[e^{-rI}(p - c)V(I)]da$$

which becomes

$$V(I)\left(\frac{a-bV_0}{V_0}\right)e^{-aI}[(2-a-r)V(I)]dI$$

$$+\left\{\frac{V(I)e^{-aI}}{V_0}\left[2\frac{dV}{da}-(a-bV_0)-V(I)I(a-bV_0)\right]-r\frac{dV}{da}\right\}da$$

$$=\left[re^{-rI}\frac{dV}{da}\right]da$$

Our numerical investigation indicated that $\frac{dI}{da}<0$, or the more fertile land has a shorter optimal planting-harvesting interval. We have not derived the sign for the general case, only for the numerical example examined in the text.

References

Adams, D. M., R. W. Haynes, et al. (1982). "Private Investment in Forest Management and the Long-Term Supply of Timber." *American Journal of Agricultural Economics* 64, pp. 232–241.

Agnello, R. J., and L. P. Donnelley (1975). "Prices and Property Rights in the Fisheries." *Southern Economic Journal* 42, pp. 253–262.

——— and ——— (1976). "Externalities and Property Rights in the Fisheries." *Land Economics* 52, pp. 519–529.

Anderson, F. J. (1979). "Ontario Reforestation Policy: Benefits and Costs." *Canadian Public Policy* 3, pp. 336–347.

Anderson, L. G. (1975). "Analysis of Commercial Exploitation and Maximum Economic Yield in Biologically and Technically Interdependent Fisheries." *Journal of the Fisheries Research Board of Canada* 32, pp. 1825–1942.

——— (1977). *The Economics of Fisheries Management.* Baltimore: Johns Hopkins Press.

———, ed. (1981). *Economic Analysis for Fisheries Management Plans.* Ann Arbor, MI: Ann Arbor Science Publishers.

——— (1982). "Marine Fisheries." In P. R. Portney, ed., *Current Issues in Natural Resource Policy.* Washington, DC: Resources for the Future.

Arnott, R., and J. Stiglitz (1979). "Aggregate Land Rents, Expenditure on Public Goods, and Optimal City Size." *Quarterly Journal of Economics* 93, 4 (November), pp. 471–500.

Arrow, K. J. (1951). *Social Choice and Individual Values.* New Haven CT: Yale University Press.

Atkinson, S. E. (1983). "Marketable Permits and Acid Rain Externalities." *Canadian Journal of Economics* 16, pp. 704–722.

——— and T. H. Tietenberg (1982). "The Empirical Properties of Two Classes of Designs for Transferable Discharge Permit Markets." *Journal of Environmental Economics and Management* 9, pp. 101–121.

Barnett, H. (1979). "Scarcity and Growth Revisited." In V. Kerry Smith, ed., *Scarcity and Growth Reconsidered.* Baltimore: Johns Hopkins Press.

—— and C. Morse (1963). *Scarcity and Growth: The Economics of Natural Resource Availability.* Baltimore: Johns Hopkins Press.

Baumol, W., and W. Oates (1975). *The Theory of Environmental Policy.* Englewood Cliffs, NJ: Prentice-Hall.

Beckmann, M. (1975). "The Limits to Growth in a Neoclassical World." *American Economic Review* 65, pp. 695–699.

Bell, F. W. (1972). "Technological Externalities and Common Property Resources: An Empirical Study of the U.S. Northern Lobster Fishery," *Journal of Political Economy* 81, pp. 148–158.

Berck, P. (1979). "The Economics of Timber: A Renewable Resource in the Long Run." *Bell Journal of Economics* 10, pp. 447–462.

—— (1979). "Open Access and Extinction." *Econometrica* 47, 4 (July), pp. 877–882.

Bergstrom, T. C. (1982). "On Capturing Oil Rents with a National Excise Tax." *American Economic Review* 72, pp. 194–201.

Berndt, E. R., C. Morrison, and G. D. Watkins (1981) "Dynamic Models of Energy Demand: An Assessment and Comparison." In E. Berndt and B. Field, eds., *Measuring and Modeling Natural Substitution.* Cambridge, MA: MIT Press.

—— and D. O. Wood (1975). "Technology, Prices, and Derived Demand for Energy." *Review of Economics and Statistics* 57, pp. 259–268.

—— and—— (1979). "Engineering and Econometric Approaches to Industrial Energy Demand: A Reconciliation." *American Economic Review* 69, pp. 342–354.

Beverton, R. J. H., and S. J. Holt (1957). "On the Dynamics of Exploited Fish Populations." *Fishery Investigations,* series III, vol. 19. London: Her Majesty's Stationery Office.

Blumo, V. J., J. P. Nichols, W. P. Griffin, and W. E. Grant (1982). "Dynamic Modeling of the Eastern Gulf of Mexico Shrimp Fishery." *American Journal of Agricultural Economics* 64, pp. 475–482.

Boadway, R. W. (1979). *Public Sector Economics.* Cambridge, MA: Winthrop Publishers.

—— and N. Bruce (1984). *Welfare Economics.* Oxford: Basil Blackwell.

Bohi, D. R. (1981). *Analyzing Demand Behavior: A Study of Energy Elasticity.* Baltimore: Johns Hopkins Press.

Bower, B. T., R. Barre, J. Kuher, C. Russell, with A. Price (1981). *Incentives in Water Quality Management: France and the Ruhr Area.* Baltimore: Johns Hopkins Press.

Brooks, D. B. (1976). "Mineral Supply as a Stock." In W. A. Vogley, *Economics of the Mineral Industries.* New York: A.I.M.E.

Brown, G., and B. Field (1978). "Implications of Alternative Measures of Natural Resource Scarcity." *Journal of Political Economy* 86, pp. 229–244.

—— and —— (1979). "The Adequacy of Measures for Signaling the Scarcity of Natural Resources." In V. Kerry Smith, ed. *Scarcity and Growth Reconsidered.* Baltimore: Johns Hopkins Press.

Cairns, R. (1981). "An Application of Depletion Theory to a Base Metal: Canadian Nickel." *Canadian Journal of Economics* 14, pp. 635–648.

Calish, S., P. D. Fight, and D. E. Teeguarden (1978). "How Do Nontimber Values Affect Douglas Fir Rotations?" *Journal of Forestry* 76, pp. 217–221.

Campbell, H. F. (1980). "The Effect of Capital Intensity on the Optimal Rate of Extraction of a Mineral Deposit." *Canadian Journal of Economics* 13, pp. 349–356.

Cheung, S. (1973). "The Fable of the Bees: An Economic Investigation." *Journal of Law and Economics* 16, pp. 11–33.

Clark, C. W. (1973a). "The Economics of Over Exploitation." *Science* 181, pp. 630–634.

—— (1973b). "When Should Whaling Resume?" Vancouver: Department of Mathematics, University of British Columbia, mimeo.

—— (1976). *Mathematical Bioeconomics.* New York: Wiley.

Clawson, M. (1976). *Economics of National Forest Management.* Baltimore: Johns Hopkins Press.

—— (1977). *Decision Making in Timber Production, Harvest, and Marketing.* Washington, DC: Resources for the Future, Research Paper R-4.

—— (1979). "Forests in the Long Sweep of American History." *Science* 204, pp. 1168–1174.

—— (1982). "Private Forests." In P. R. Portney, ed., *Current Issues in National Resource Policy.* Washington, DC: Resources for the Future.

Coase, R. (1960). "The Problem of Social Cost." *Journal of Law and Economics* 3, pp. 1–44.

Cohen, Jon S., and M. L. Weitzman (1975). "A Marxian Model of Enclosures." *Journal of Developmental Economics* 1, pp. 287–336.

Comolli, P. M. (1981). "Principles and Policy in Forestry Economics." *Bell Journal of Economics* 12, pp. 300–309.

Crabbe, P. J. (1984). "Option Values of Natural Resources." Department of Economics, University of Ottawa, Mimeo.

Crandall, R. W. (1983). "Clean Air and Regional Protectionism." *Brookings Review* (Fall), pp. 17–20.

—— and L. B. Lave, eds. (1981). *The Scientific Basis of Health and Safety Regulations.* Washington, DC: The Brookings Institution.

Crommelin, M., P. Pearse, and A. Scott (1978). "Management of Oil and Gas Resources in Alberta: An Economic Evaluation of Public Policy." *Natural Resources Journal* 18, 2 (April), pp. 337–389.

Crutchfield, J. A. (1981). "The Pacific Halibut Fishery." Technical Report No. 17, in *The Public Regulation of Commercial Fisheries in Canada,* Case Study No. 2. Ottawa: Economic Council of Canada.

—— and G. Pontecorvo (1969). *The Pacific Salmon Fisheries: A Study in Irrational Conservation.* Baltimore: Johns Hopkins Press.

Dajoz, Roger (1977). *Introduction to Ecology,* trans. A. South. London: Hodder and Stoughton.

Dales, J. H. (1968). *Pollution, Property and Prices.* Toronto: University of Toronto Press.

Dasgupta, P. S. (1982). *The Control of Resources.* Cambridge, MA: Harvard University Press.

——, R. J. Gilbert, and J. E. Stiglitz (1982). "Invention and Innovation Under Alternative Market Structures: The Case of Natural Resources." *Review of Economic Studies* 49, pp. 567–582.

——, ——, and —— (1983). "Strategic Considerations in Invention and Innovation: The Case of Natural Resources." *Econometrica* 51, 5 (September), pp. 1439–1448.

—— and G. Heal (1974). "Optimal Depletion of Exhaustible Resources." *Review of Economic Studies,* symposium, pp. 3–28.

—— and —— (1979) *Economic Theory and Exhaustible Resources.* Cambridge, England: Cambridge University Press.

——, ——, and J. E. Stiglitz (1980). "The Taxation of Exhaustible Resources." National Bureau of Economic Research, Cambridge, MA, Working Paper No. 436.

—— and J. E. Stiglitz (1981). "Resource Depletion under Technological Uncertainty." *Econometrica* 49, 1 (January), pp. 85–104.

David, E. L. (1971). "Public Perceptions of Water Quality." *Water Resources Research* 7, pp. 453–457.

Demsetz, H. (1967). "Toward a Theory of Property Rights." *American Economic Review* 57, pp. 347–359.

Denison, E. (1978). "Effects of Selected Changes in Institutional and Human Environment upon Output per Unit Input." *Survey of Current Business,* January, cited in Litan and Nordhaus (1983).

Denton, H. R. (1983). "Nuclear Power, Epilogue and Prologue." *The Energy Journal* 4, pp. 125–141.

Devarajan, S., and A. C. Fisher (1982). "Exploration and Scarcity." *Journal of Political Economy* 90, pp. 1279–1290.

Dixit, A., P. Hammond, and M. Hoel (1980). "On Hartwick's Rule for Constant Utility and Regular Maximin Paths of Capital Accumulation and Resource Depletion." *Review of Economic Studies* 47(3), 148 (April), pp. 347–354.

Dolbear, F. T. (1967). "On the Theory of Optimum Externality." *American Economic Review* 57, pp. 90–103.

Ellet, Charles (1839). *An Essay on the Laws of Trade in Reference to the Works of Internal Improvement in the United States.* Reprinted by A. M. Kelley, New York, 1966.

Energy Modeling Forum (1982). *World Oil.* Stanford, CA: Energy Modeling Forum.

Eswaran, M., T. R. Lewis, and T. Heaps (1983). "On the Nonexistence of Market Equilibria in Exhaustible Resources Markets with Decreasing Costs." *Journal of Political Economy* 91, pp. 145–167.

Feick, J. E. (1983). "Prospects for the Development of Mineable Oil Sands." *Canadian Public Policy* 9, pp. 297–302.

Fisher, A. C. (1979). "Measurements of Natural Resource Scarcity." In V. Kerry Smith, ed. *Scarcity and Growth Reconsidered.* Baltimore: Johns Hopkins Press.

—— (1981). *Resource and Environmental Economics.* Cambridge, England: Cambridge University Press.

Flaaten, O. (1983). "The Optimal Harvesting of a Natural Resource with Seasonal Growth." *Canadian Journal of Economics* 16, pp. 447–462.

Flatters, F., and N. Olewiler (1984). "Dominant Government Firms in an Oligopolistic Industry: The Case of Saskatchewan Potash." Queen's University, Kingston, Ontario: Centre for Research Studies, Working Paper No. 29.

Forrester, Jay W. (1971). *World Dynamics.* Cambridge, MA: Wright-Allen Press.

Freeman, A. M. (1979). *The Benefits of Environmental Improvement: Theory and Practice.* Baltimore: Johns Hopkins Press.

Friedlander, A. F., ed. (1978). *Approaches to Controlling Air Pollution.* Cambridge, MA: MIT Press.

Friedman, M., and R. Friedman (1980). *Free to Choose.* New York: Harcourt Brace Jovanovich.

Furubotn, E., and S. Pejovich (1972). "Property Rights and Economic Theory: A Survey of Recent Literature." *Journal of Economic Literature* 10, pp. 1137–1162.

Gallastegui, C. (1983). "An Economic Analysis of Sardine Fishing in the Gulf of Valencia (Spain)." *Journal of Environmental Economics and Management* 10, pp. 138–150.

Gallini, N. (1982). "The Dynamic Production of an Exhaustible Resource Substitute." In J. R. Moroney, ed., *Advances in the Economics of Energy and Resources,* 4. Greenwich, CT: JAI Press.

—— T. Lewis, and Roger Ware (1983). "Strategic Timing and Pricing of a Substitute in a Cartelized Resource Market." *Canadian Journal of Economics* 16, 3 (August), pp. 429–446.

Gateley, D. (1984). "A Ten-Year Retrospective on OPEC and the World Oil Market." *Journal of Economic Literature* 22, pp. 1100–1114.

Gilbert, R. J. (1978). "Dominant Firm Pricing Policy in a Market for an Exhaustible Resource." *Bell Journal of Economics* (Autumn), pp. 385–395.

—— and S. M. Goldman (1978). "Potential Competition and the Monopoly Price of an Exhaustible Resource." *Journal of Economic Theory* 17, pp. 319–331.

Golden, D. (1984). "Complex Tropical Forests are Losing Ground." *The Boston Globe,* April 9, 1984, pp. 37–38.

Government of Canada (1983). *Index to Federal Programs and Services.* Hull, Quebec: Ministry of Supply and Services, Canadian Government Publishing Centre.

Gray, L. C. (1914). "Rent under the Assumption of Exhaustibility." *Quarterly Journal of Economics* 28, pp. 466–489.

Greenley, D. A., R. G. Walsh, and R. A. Young (1981). "Option Value: Empirical Evidence from a Case Study of Recreation and Water Quality." *Quarterly Journal of Economics* 96, pp. 657–673.

Griffin, J. M., and P. R. Gregory (1976). "An Intercountry Translog Model of Energy Substitution Responses." *American Economic Review* 66, pp. 845–857.

—— and H. B. Steele (1980). *Energy Economics and Policy.* New York: Academic Press.

—— and D. J. Teece, eds. (1982). *OPEC Behavior and World Oil Prices.* London: Allen & Unwin.

Gulland, J. A. (1974). *The Management of Marine Fisheries.* Bristol: Scientechnica Publishing.

Hagel, J. (1976). *Alternative Energy Strategies, Constraints and Opportunities.* New York: Praeger.

Hahn, R. W., and R. G. Noll (1981). "Designing a Market for Tradable Permits." California Institute of Technology, Social Science Working Paper 398.

Halvorsen, R., and M. G. Ruby (1981). *Benefit-Cost Analysis of Air Pollution Control.* Lexington, MA: Lexington Books.

Hanneson, R. (1978). *Economics of Fisheries.* Bergen: Universitetsforlaget.

Hartwick, J. M. (1977). "Interregional Equity and the Investing of Rents from Exhaustible Resources." *American Economic Review* 67, 5 (December), pp. 972–974.

—— (1978). "Investing Returns from Depleting Renewable Resource Stocks and Intergenerational Equity." *Economics Letters* 1, pp. 85–88.

—— (1980). "The Henry George Rule, Optimal Population, and Interregional Equity." *Canadian Journal of Economics* 13, 4 (November), pp. 695–700.

—— (1982). "Free Access and the Dynamics of the Fishery." In L. J. Mirman and D. F. Spulber, *Essays in the Economics of Renewable Resources.* Amsterdam: North Holland.

—— (1983). "Learning about and Exploiting Exhaustible Resource Deposits of Uncertain Size." *Canadian Journal of Economics* 16, 3 (August), pp. 391–410.

——, M. C. Kemp, and N. van Long (1982). "Set-Up Costs and the Theory of Exhaustible Resources." Queen's University, Institute for Economic Research, Discussion Paper No. 412.

—— and David Young (1985). "Preference for Output Price Uncertainty by the Nonrenewable Resource Extracting Firm." *Economics Letters.*

Heaps, T. (1981). "The Qualitative Theory of Optimal Rotations." *Canadian Journal of Economics* 14, pp. 686–699.

Hirschleifer, J. (1984). *Price Theory and Applications,* 3rd ed. Englewood Cliffs, NJ: Prentice-Hall.

Hoel, M. (1978). "Resource Extraction, Substitute Production, and Monopoly." *Journal of Economic Theory* 19, pp. 28–37.

Hogan, W. W. (1983). "Patterns of Energy Use." Draft mimeo. Cambridge, MA: Energy and

Environmental Policy Center, John F. Kennedy School of Government, Harvard University.

———— (1984). "Energy Policy and the Reagan Experiment, 1981–1982." In P. Portney, ed., *Natural Resources and the Environment: The Reagan Approach.* Washington, DC: The Urban Institute.

———— and A. S. Manne (1979). "Energy-Economy Interactions: The Fable of the Elephant and the Rabbit." In R. S. Pindyck, ed., *Advances in the Economics of Energy and Resources* 1. Greenwich, CT: JAI Press.

Hotelling, H. (1931). "The Economics of Exhaustible Resources." *Journal of Political Economy* 39, pp. 137–175.

Hyde, W. F. (1980). *Timber Supply, Land Allocation, and Economic Efficiency.* Baltimore: Johns Hopkins Press.

Idyll, C. P. (1973). "The Anchovy Crisis." *Scientific American* 228, pp. 23–29.

International Pacific Halibut Commission (1976). Technical Report No. 14.

————. Annual Report, 1977–1980.

Johnson, D. B. (1973). "Meade, Bees, and Externalities." *Journal of Law and Economics* 16, pp. 35–52.

Jorgenson, D., and Z. Griliches (1967). "The Explanation of Productivity Change." *Review of Economics and Statistics* 34, pp. 250–282.

Joskow, P. L. (1982). "Prospects and Problems for Nuclear Power in the United States." In A. Danske, ed., *Energy, Economics, and the Environment.* Lexington, MA: Lexington Books.

Just, R. E., D. L. Hueth, and A. Schnitz (1982). *Applied Welfare Economics and Public Policy,* Englewood Cliffs, NJ: Prentice-Hall.

Kay, J., and J. Mirrlees (1975). "The Desirability of Natural Resource Depletion." In D. W. Pearce and J. Rose, eds., *The Economics of Natural Resource Depletion.* London: Macmillan.

Kemp, M. C., and N. van Long (1980). *Exhaustible Resources, Optimality, and Trade.* Amsterdam: North Holland.

———— and ———— (1980). "On the Economics of Forests." Sydney: Department of Economics, University of New South Wales. Mimeo.

Krupnick, A., W. Oates, and E. Van De Verg (1983). "On Marketable Air Pollution Permits: The Case for a System of Pollution Offsets." *Journal of Environmental Economics and Management* 10, pp. 233–247.

Larkin, P. (1966). "Exploitation in a Type of Predator-Prey Relationship." *Journal of the Fisheries Research Board of Canada* 23, pp. 349–356.

Ledyard, J., and L. N. Moses (1977). "Dynamics and Land Use: The Case of Forestry." In R. E. Grieson, ed., *Public and Urban Economics.* Lexington, MA: D. C. Heath.

Levhari, D., and L. J. Mirman (1980). "The Great Fish War: An Example Using a Dynamic Cournot-Nash Solution." *Bell Journal of Economics* 11, pp. 322–334.

Lewis, T. R. (1976). "Monopoly Exploitation of an Exhaustible Resource." *Journal of Environmental Economics and Management* 3, pp. 198–201.

———— (1981). "Exploitation of a Renewable Resource under Uncertainty." *Canadian Journal of Economics* 14, pp. 422–439.

———— and J. Cowans (1982) "The Great Fish War: A Cooperative Solution." Social Science Working Paper 448. California Institute of Technology.

————, S. A. Matthews, and H. S. Burness (1979). "Monopoly and the Rate of Extraction of Exhaustible Resources: Comment." *American Economic Review* 69 (March), pp. 227–230.

Libecap, G. D., and S. N. Wiggins (1984). "Contractual Responses to the Common Pool:

Prorationing of Crude Oil Production." *American Economic Review* 74, 1 (March), p. 97.

Lipsey, R., D. Purvis, G. Sparks, and P. Steiner (1983). *Economics,* 3rd ed. New York: Harper & Row.

———, ———, and P. Steiner (1984). *Economics,* 4th ed. New York: Harper & Row.

Litan, R. E., and W. Nordhaus (1983). *Reforming Federal Regulations.* New Haven and London: Yale University Press.

Loury, G. C. (1978). "The Optimal Exploitation of an Unknown Reserve." *Review of Economic Studies* 45, pp. 621–636.

——— (1979). "Market Structure and Innovation." *Quarterly Journal of Economics* 93 (August), pp. 395–410.

Lovins, A., and L. H. Lovins (1983). "The Fragility of Domestic Energy." *The Atlantic Monthly* 252, pp. 118–126.

MacAvoy, P. W. (1983). *Energy Policy: An Economic Analysis.* New York: Norton.

McKillop, W., and W. J. Mead, eds. (1976). *Timber Policy Issues in British Columbia.* Vancouver: University of British Columbia Press.

McRae, R., and A. Webster (1982). "The Robustness of a Translog Model to Describe Regional Energy Demand by Canadian Manufacturing Industries." *Resources and Energy* 4, pp. 1–26.

Malthus, T. R. (1815). *On the Nature and Progress of Rent,* ed. J. H. Hollander. Baltimore: Lord Baltimore Press, 1903.

——— (1959 edition). *Population: The First Essay.* Ann Arbor: University of Michigan Press.

Mansfield, E. (1979). *Microeconomics, Theory and Application,* 3rd ed. New York: Norton.

Marcus, A. A. (1980). *Promise and Performance: Choosing and Implementing an Environmental Policy.* Westwood, CT: Greenwood Press.

Mead, W. J. (1966). *Competition and Oligopsony in the Douglas-Fir Lumber Industry.* Berkeley: University of California Press.

Meade, J. E. (1952). "External Economies and Diseconomies in a Competitive Situation." *Economic Journal,* 62, pp. 54–67.

Meadows, D. H., D. L. Meadows, J. Randers, and W. W. Behrens III (1972). *The Limits to Growth: A Report for the Club of Rome's Project on the Predicament of Mankind.* New York: Universe Books.

Mestelman, S. (1981). "Corrective Production Subsidies in an Increasing Cost Industry: A Note on a Baumol-Oates Proposition." *Canadian Journal of Economics* 14, pp. 124–130.

——— (1982). "Production Externalities and Corrective Subsidies: A General Equilibrium Analysis." *Journal of Environmental Economics and Management* 9, pp. 186–193.

Mohring, H. (1961). "Land Values and the Measurement of Highway Benefits." *Journal of Political Economy* 69 (June), pp. 236–249.

Montgomery, W. (1972). "Markets in Licenses and Efficient Pollution Control Programs." *Journal of Economic Theory* 5, pp. 395–418.

Moran, T. (1982). "Modeling OPEC Behavior: Economic and Political Alternatives." In J. M. Griffin and D. J. Teece, eds., *OPEC Behavior and World Oil Prices.* London: Allen & Unwin.

Morey, E. R. (1984). "Confuser Surplus." *American Economic Review* 74, pp. 163–173.

Morgan, P. (1983). "Alternative Policy Instruments under Uncertainty: A Programming Model of Toxic Pollution Control." *Journal of Environmental Economics and Management* 10, pp. 248–269.

Newberry, D. (1980). "Oil Prices, Cartels, and the Problem of Dynamic Inconsistency." *Economic Journal* 91 (September), pp. 617–646.

Nichols, A. L., and R. J. Zeckhauser (1977). "Stockpiling Strategies and Cartel Prices." *Bell Journal of Economics* 8, pp. 66–96.

Nicholson, W. (1979). *Intermediate Microeconomics and Its Applications,* 2nd ed. Hinsdale, IL: Dryden Press.

Nordhaus, W. D. (1973). "World Dynamics: Measurement Without Data." *Economic Journal* (December), pp. 1156–1183.

——— (1973). "The Allocation of Energy Resources." *Brookings Papers on Economic Activity* 3, pp. 529–570.

Norgaard, R. B. (1975). "Resource Scarcity and New Technology in U.S. Petroleum Development." *Natural Resources Journal* 15, pp. 265–295.

Office of the Federal Registrar. *The United States Government Manual 1983/84.* Washington, DC: General Services Administration, U.S. Government Printing Office.

Olewiler, N. D. (1980). "Capacity Constraints and Destructive Competition in the Extraction of Non-Renewable Natural Resources." Queen's University, Institute for Economic Research, Discussion Paper No. 421.

Organization for Economic Cooperation and Development (1980). *Pollution Charges in Practice.* Paris, OECD.

Orth, F. L., J. A. Richardson, and S. H. Piddle (1981). *Market Structure of the Alaska Seafood Processing Industry,* vol. II. Anchorage: University of Alaska: Sea Grant Report, 78–14.

Page, W. (1973). "The Non-Renewable Resources Subsystem." In H. S. D. Cole, C. Freeman, M. Jahoda, and K. L. R. Pavitt, eds., *Thinking about the Future: A Critique of the Limits to Growth.* London: Sussex University Press.

Panayotou, T. (1982). "Management Concepts for Small-Scale Fisheries: Economic and Social Aspects." FAO Fisheries Technical Paper No. 228. Rome: Food and Agricultural Organization of the United Nations.

Pearce, I. (1975). "Resource Conservation and the Market Mechanism." In D. W. Pearce and J. Rose, eds., *The Economics of Natural Resource Depletion.* London: Macmillan.

Pearse, P. (1967). "The Optimum Forest Rotation." *The Forestry Chronicle* 43, pp. 178–195.

——— (1976). *Timber Rights and Forest Policy in British Columbia.* Report of the Royal Commission on Forest Resources. Victoria, British Columbia.

——— (1982). *Turning the Tide: A New Policy for Canada's Pacific Fisheries.* The Commission on Pacific Fisheries Policy, Final Report, Vancouver, September.

Peskin, H. M., and E. Seskin (1975). *Cost Benefit Analysis and Water Pollution Policy.* Washington, DC: The Urban Institute.

Pindyck, R. S. (1978). "The Optimal Exploration and Production of Nonrenewable Resources." *Journal of Political Economy* 86, 5 (October), pp. 841–861.

——— (1978). "Gains to Producers from the Cartelization of Exhaustible Resources." *Review of Economics and Statistics* 60, pp. 238–251.

——— (1980). "Uncertainty and Exhaustible Resource Markets." *Journal of Political Economy* 88, 6 (December), pp. 1201–1225.

——— and J. J. Rotemberg (1983). "Dynamic Factor Demands and the Effects of Energy Price Shocks." *American Economic Review* 73, pp. 1066–1079.

Posner, R. A. (1975). "The Social Costs of Monopoly and Regulation." *Journal of Political Economy* 83 (August), pp. 807–827.

Reed, W. J. (1979). "Optimal Escapement Levels in Stochastic and Deterministic Harvesting Models." *Journal of Environmental Economics and Management* 6, pp. 350–366.

Robson, A. (1979). "Sequential Exploitation of Uncertain Deposits of a Depletable Natural Resource." *Journal of Economic Theory* 21, pp. 88–110.

——— (1980). "Costly Innovation and Natural Resources." *International Economic Review* 21, 1 (February), pp. 17–30.

Rosenbluth, G. (1976). "Economists and the Growth Controversy." *Canadian Public Policy* 2, 2 (Spring), pp. 225–239.

Rothschild, M., and J. E. Stiglitz (1970). "Increasing Risk I: A Definition." *Journal of Economic Theory* 2, pp. 225–243.

Russell, M. (1983). "The Natural Gas Price Puzzle." *Resources* 72, (February), pp. 22–24.

Sachs, J. (1981). "The Current Account and Macroeconomic Adjustment in the 1970s." *Brookings Papers on Economic Activity* 1, pp. 201–268.

Salant, S. (1976). "Exhaustible Resources and Industrial Structure: A Nash–Cournot Approach to the World Oil Market." *Journal of Political Economy* 84, 5, pp. 1079–1093.

Samuelson, P. A. (1939). "Interaction Between the Multiplier Analysis and the Principle of Acceleration." *Review of Economics and Statistics* 21, pp. 75–78.

Schaefer, M. B. (1957). "Some Considerations of Population Dynamics and Economics in Relation to the Management of Marine Fisheries. " *Journal of the Fisheries Research Board of Canada* 14, pp. 669–681.

Scott, A. D. (1983). "Property Rights and Property Wrongs." *Canadian Journal of Economics* 16, pp. 555–573.

——— (1984). "Money and Our Environment." Vancouver: Department of Economics, University of British Columbia. Mimeo.

——— (1984). "Does Government Create Real Property Rights? Private Interests in Natural Resources." Vancouver: Department of Economics, University of British Columbia. Mimeo.

——— and P. A. Neher (1981). *The Public Regulation of Commercial Fisheries in Canada.* Ottawa: Economic Council of Canada.

Sedjo, R. A. (1983). *The Comparative Economics of Plantation Forestry: A Global Assessment.* Washington, DC: Resources for the Future.

Sen, A. K. (1981). *Poverty and Famines: An Essay on Entitlement and Deprivation.* Oxford: Clarendon Press.

Shibata, H. (1971). "A Bargaining Model of the Pure Theory of Public Expenditure." *Journal of Political Economy* 79, pp. 1–29.

Sinn, H. W. (1984). "Common Property Resources, Storage Facilities and Ownership Structures: A Cournot Model of the Oil Market." *Economica* 51, pp. 235–252.

Slade, M. E. (1982). "Trends in Natural-Resource Commodity Prices: An Analysis of the Time Domain." *Journal of Environmental Economics and Management* 9, pp. 122–137.

——— (1982). "Empirical Tests of Economic Rent in the U.S. Copper Industry." In J. R. Moroney, ed., *Advances in the Economics of Energy and Resources,* Vol 4. Greenwich, CT: JAI Press.

Smith, J. B. (1980). "Replenishable Resource Management under Uncertainty." *Journal of Environmental Economics and Management* 7, pp. 209–219.

Smith, V. K., ed. (1979). *Scarcity and Growth Reconsidered.* Baltimore: Johns Hopkins Press.

———, W. H. Desvousges, and M. P. McGivney (1983). "The Opportunity Cost of Travel Time in Recreational Demand Models." *Land Economics* 59, pp. 259–278.

——— and J. Krutilla (1979). "The Economics of Natural Resource Scarcity: An Interpretative Introduction." In V. Kerry Smith, ed., *Scarcity and Growth Reconsidered.* Baltimore: Johns Hopkins Press.

Smith, V. L. (1977). "Control Theory Applied to Natural and Environmental Resources: An Exposition." *Journal of Environmental Economics and Management* 4, pp. 1–24.

Solow, R. M. (1974). "Interregional Equity and Exhaustible Resources." *Review of Economic Studies,* symposium, pp. 29–45.

———— (1977). "Optimal Fishing with a Natural Predator." In R. E. Grieson, ed., *Public and Urban Economics: Essays in Honor of William S. Vickery.* Lexington, MA: Lexington Books.

Spence, A. M. (1974). "Blue Whales and Applied Control Theory." In H. W. Gottinger, ed., *Systems Approaches and Environmental Problems.* Gottingen: Vandenhoeck and Ruprecht.

Starrett, D. (1972). "Fundamental Nonconvexities in the Theory of Externalities." *Journal of Economic Theory* 4, pp. 180–199.

Stiglitz, J. E. (1974). "Growth with Exhaustible Natural Resources: Efficient and Optimal Growth Paths." *Review of Economic Studies,* symposium, pp. 123–137.

———— (1976). "Monopoly and the Rate of Extraction of Exhaustible Resources." *American Economic Review* 66, (September) pp. 655–661.

———— (1977). "The Theory of Local Public Goods." In M. Feldstein and R. Inman, eds., *Economics of Public Services.* Toronto: Macmillan.

Stokes, R. L. (1983). *Limited Entry in the Pacific Halibut Fishery: The Individual Quota Option.* Council Document No. 20. Anchorage: North Pacific Fishery Management Council.

Teece, D. J. (1982). "OPEC Behavior: An Alternative View." In J. M. Griffin and D. J. Teece, eds., *OPEC Behavior and World Oil Prices.* London: Allen & Unwin.

Thunen, J. H. von (1826–63). *Der Isolierte Staat in Beziehung auf Landwirtschaft und Nationalokonomie,* 3 vols., Hamburg and Rostock. See also *Isolated State,* ed. Peter Hall and trans. Carla M. Waterberg. Oxford: Pergamon Press, 1966.

Tietenberg, T. (1980). "Transferable Discharge Permits and the Control of Stationary Source Air Pollution: A Survey and Synthesis." *Land Economics* 56, pp. 391–416.

Tolchin, S. J., and M. Tolchin (1983). *Dismantling America: The Rush to Deregulate.* Boston: Houghton-Mifflin.

Uhler, R. (1979). *Oil and Gas Finding Costs.* Calgary: Canadian Energy Research Institute, Study No. 7.

———— (1983). "The Potential Supply of Crude Oil and Natural Gas Reserves in the Alberta Basin." Report for the Economic Council of Canada, Ottawa.

United States Forest Service (1974). *The Outlook for Timber in the United States.* Forest Service Report 20, Washington, DC.

———— (1980). *An Assessment of the Forest and Range Land Situation in the United States.* Washington, DC.

Weinstein, M. C., and R. J. Zeckhauser (1975). "The Optimum Consumption of Depletable Natural Resources." *Quarterly Journal of Economics* 89 (August), pp. 371–392.

Weitzman, M. (1974). "Free Access vs. Private Ownership as Alternative Systems for Managing Common Property." *Journal of Economic Theory* 8, pp. 225–234.

———— (1974). "Prices vs. Quantities." *Review of Economic Studies* 41, pp. 477–491.

Wilen, J. E. (1976). "Common Property Resources and the Dynamics of Overexploitation: The Case of the North Pacific Fur Seal." University of British Columbia, Resources Paper No. 3.

Willig, R. D. (1976). "Consumer's Surplus Without Apology." *American Economic Review* 66, pp. 589–597.

Wright, B. D., and J. C. Williams (1982). "The Roles of Public and Private Storage in Managing Oil Import Disruptions." *Bell Journal of Economics* 13, pp. 341–353.

Zimmerman, M. (1977). "Modeling Depletion in a Mineral Industry: The Case of Coal." *Bell Journal of Economics* 8, pp. 41–65.

Zwartendyk, J. (1972). "What Is 'Mineral Endowment' and How Should We Measure It?" Mineral Bulletin M. R. 126, Ottawa, Department of Energy, Mines and Resources.

Author Index

Subject Index